DANCE LIKE EVERYBODY'S WATCHING!

A ZITS® Treasury by Jerry Scott and Jim Borgman

Andrews McMeel
PUBLISHING®

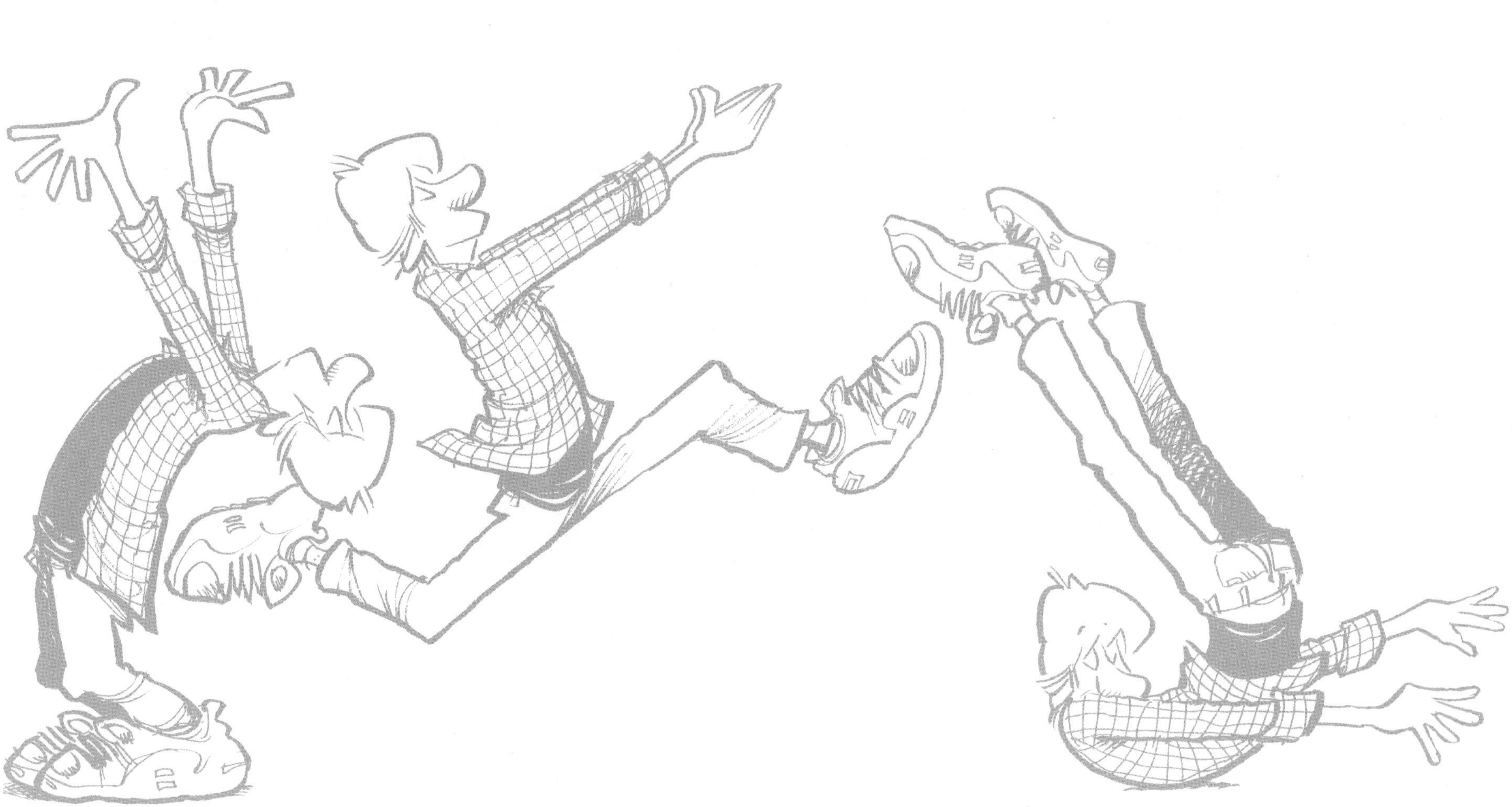

DANCE LIKE EVERYBODY'S WATCHING!

ALSO BY JERRY SCOTT AND JIM BORGMAN

Zits: Sketchbook 1
Growth Spurt: Zits Sketchbook 2
Don't Roll Your Eyes at Me, Young Man!: Zits Sketchbook 3
Are We an "Us"?: Zits Sketchbook 4
Zits Unzipped: Zits Sketchbook 5
Busted!: Zits Sketchbook 6
Road Trip: Zits Sketchbook 7
Teenage Tales: Zits Sketchbook No. 8
Thrashed: Zits Sketchbook No. 9
Pimp My Lunch: Zits Sketchbook No. 10
Are We Out of the Driveway Yet?: Zits Sketchbook No. 11
Rude, Crude, and Tattooed: Zits Sketchbook No. 12
Jeremy and Mom
Pierced
Lust and Other Uses for Spare Hormones
Jeremy & Dad
You're Making That Face Again
Drive!
Triple Shot, Double Pump, No Whip Zits
Zits en Concert
Peace, Love, and Wi-Fi
Zits Apocalypse
Extra Cheesy Zits

TREASURIES

Humongous Zits
Big Honkin' Zits
Zits: Supersized
Random Zits
Crack of Noon
Alternative Zits
My Bad
Sunday Brunch
What Was That All About?: 20 Years of Strips and Stories

GIFT BOOK

A Zits Guide to Living with Your Teenager

For Dorothy

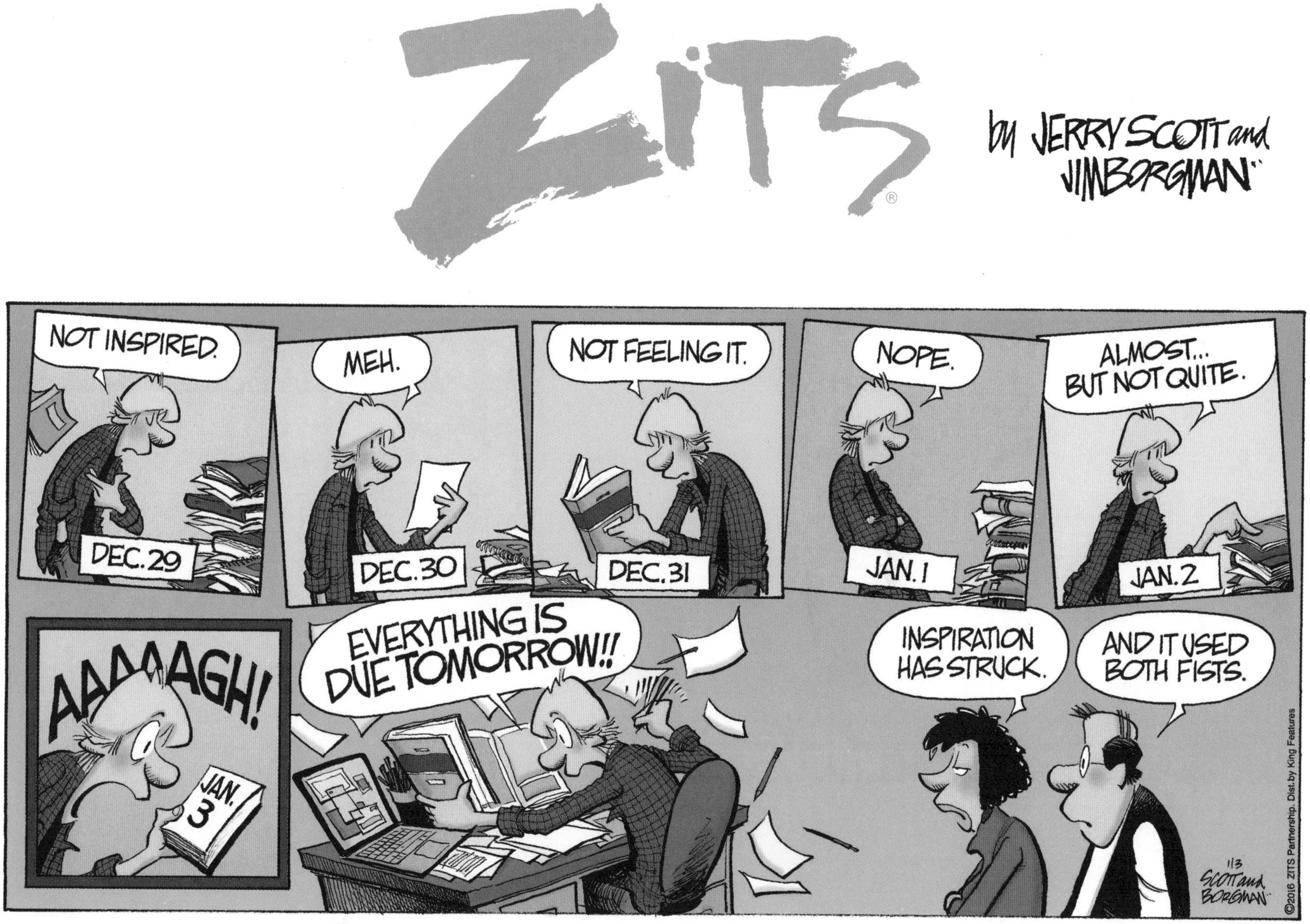
ZITS®
by JERRY SCOTT and JIM BORGMAN
NOT INSPIRED.
DEC. 29
MEH.
DEC. 30
NOT FEELING IT.
DEC. 31
NOPE.
JAN. 1
ALMOST... BUT NOT QUITE.
JAN. 2
AAAAAGH!
JAN. 3
EVERYTHING IS DUE TOMORROW!!
INSPIRATION HAS STRUCK.
AND IT USED BOTH FISTS.
1/3 SCOTT and BORGMAN
©2016 ZITS Partnership. Dist. by King Features

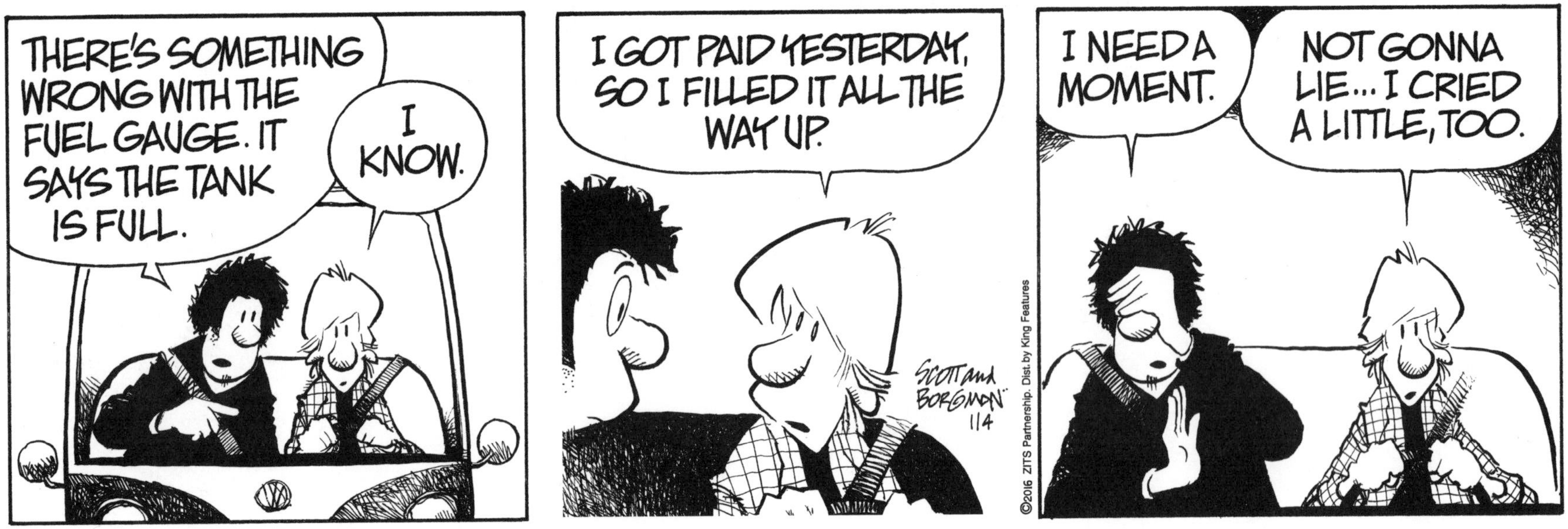
THERE'S SOMETHING WRONG WITH THE FUEL GAUGE. IT SAYS THE TANK IS FULL.
I KNOW.
I GOT PAID YESTERDAY, SO I FILLED IT ALL THE WAY UP.
SCOTT and BORGMAN 1/4
I NEED A MOMENT.
NOT GONNA LIE... I CRIED A LITTLE, TOO.
©2016 ZITS Partnership. Dist. by King Features

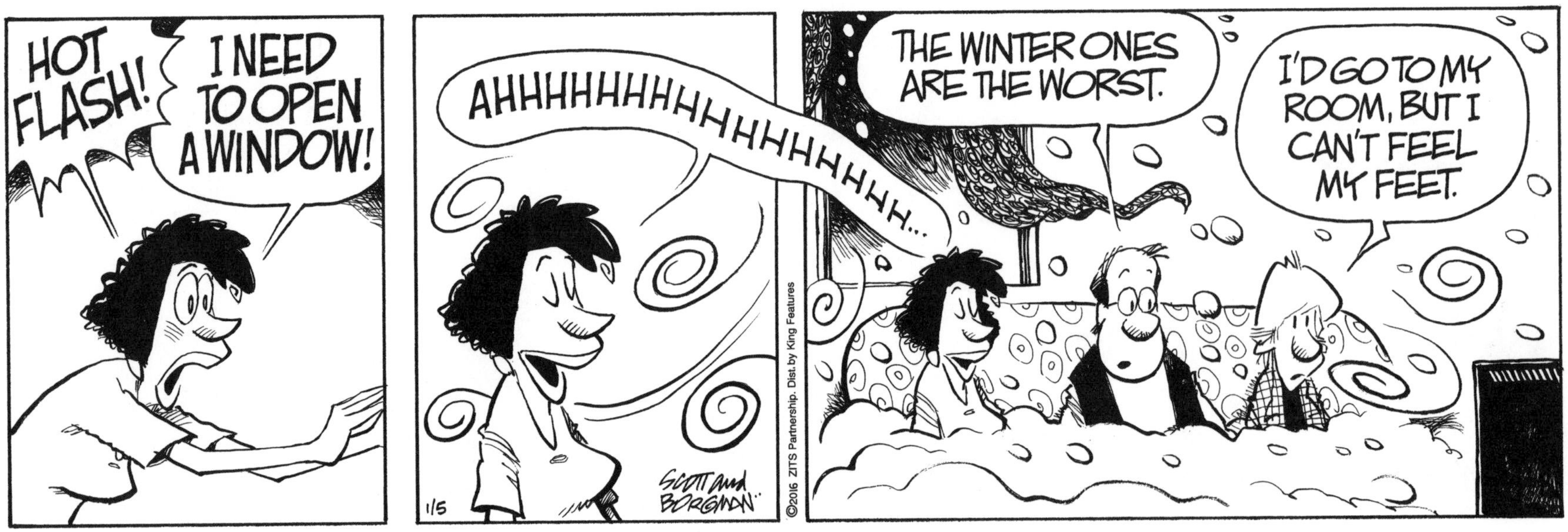
HOT FLASH!
I NEED TO OPEN A WINDOW!
AHHHHHHHHHHHHHHHHHHHH...
1/5
SCOTT and BORGMAN
©2016 ZITS Partnership. Dist. by King Features
THE WINTER ONES ARE THE WORST.
I'D GO TO MY ROOM, BUT I CAN'T FEEL MY FEET.

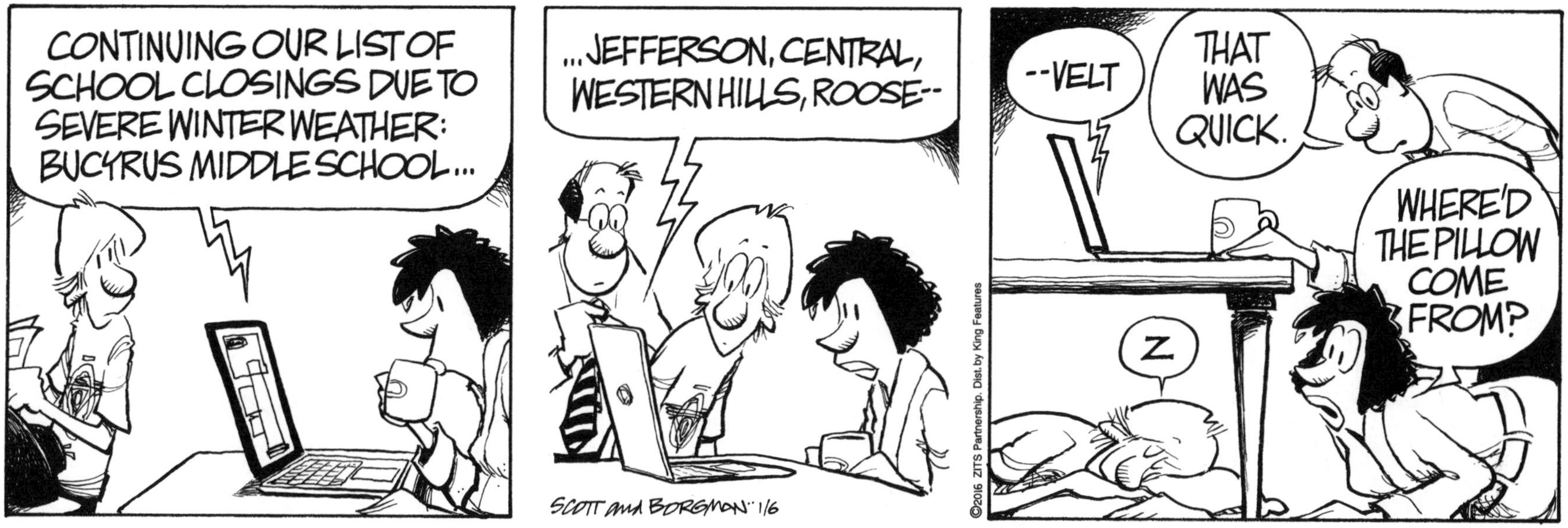
CONTINUING OUR LIST OF SCHOOL CLOSINGS DUE TO SEVERE WINTER WEATHER: BUCYRUS MIDDLE SCHOOL...
...JEFFERSON, CENTRAL, WESTERN HILLS, ROOSE--
SCOTT and BORGMAN 1/6
©2016 ZITS Partnership. Dist. by King Features
--VELT
THAT WAS QUICK.
Z
WHERE'D THE PILLOW COME FROM?

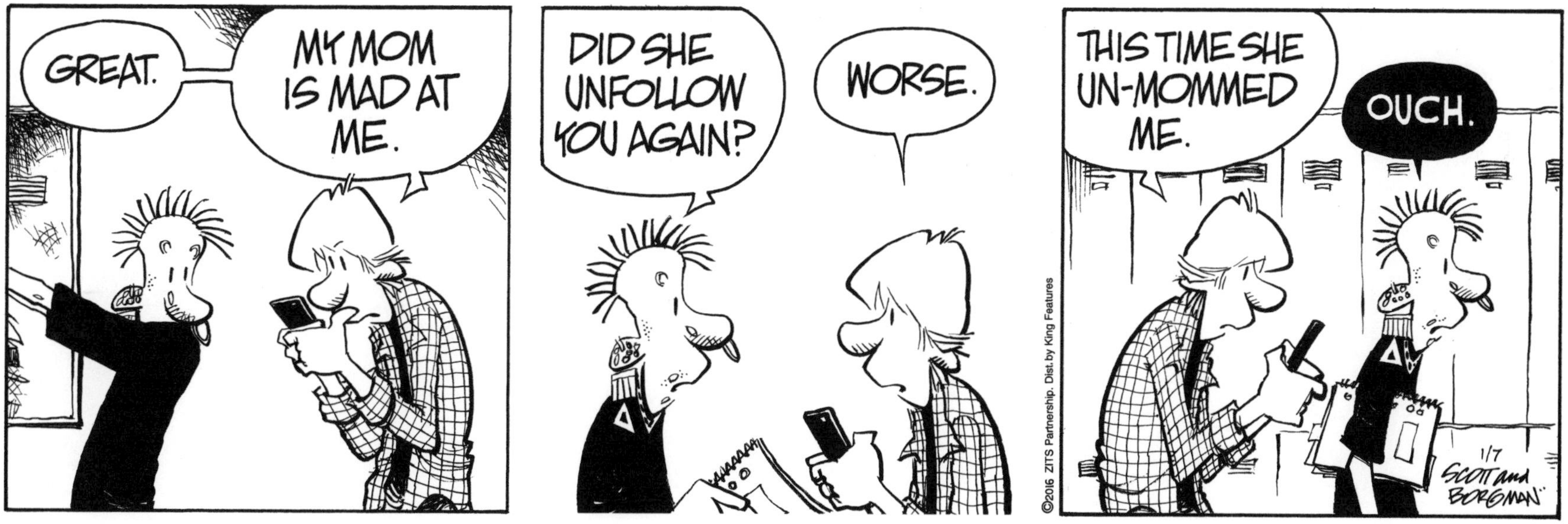
GREAT.
MY MOM IS MAD AT ME.
DID SHE UNFOLLOW YOU AGAIN?
WORSE.
©2016 ZITS Partnership. Dist. by King Features
THIS TIME SHE UN-MOMMED ME.
OUCH.
1/7
SCOTT and BORGMAN

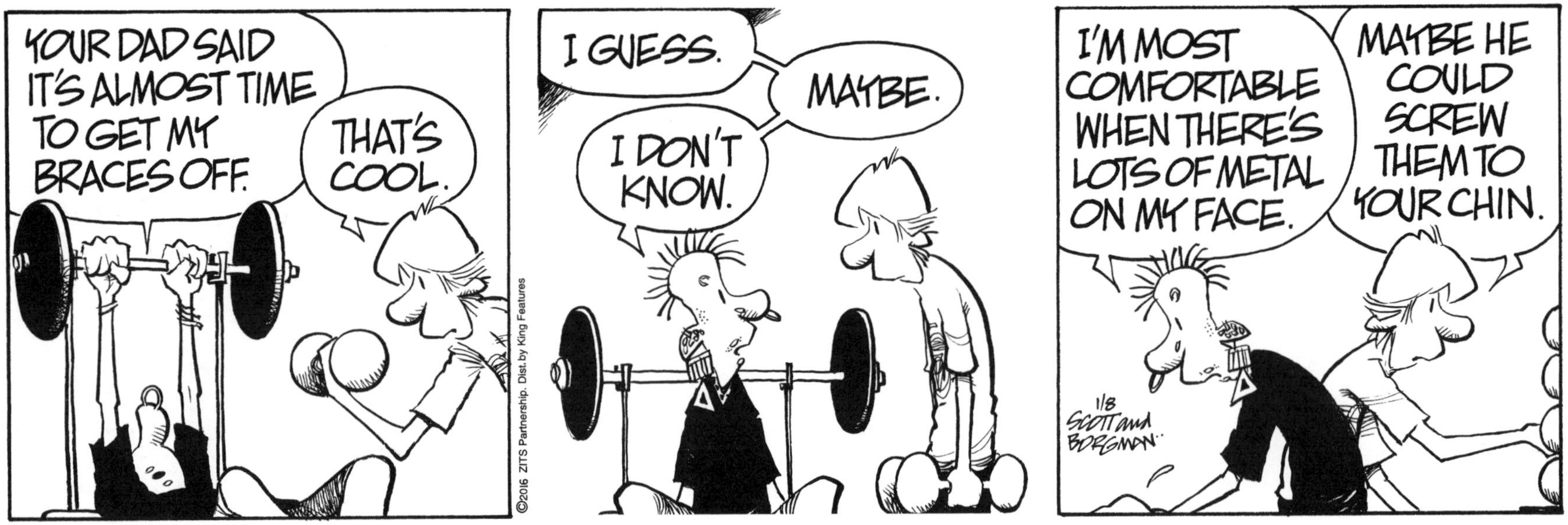
YOUR DAD SAID IT'S ALMOST TIME TO GET MY BRACES OFF.
THAT'S COOL.
I GUESS.
MAYBE.
I DON'T KNOW.
I'M MOST COMFORTABLE WHEN THERE'S LOTS OF METAL ON MY FACE.
MAYBE HE COULD SCREW THEM TO YOUR CHIN.
©2016 ZITS Partnership. Dist. by King Features
1/8 SCOTT and BORGMAN

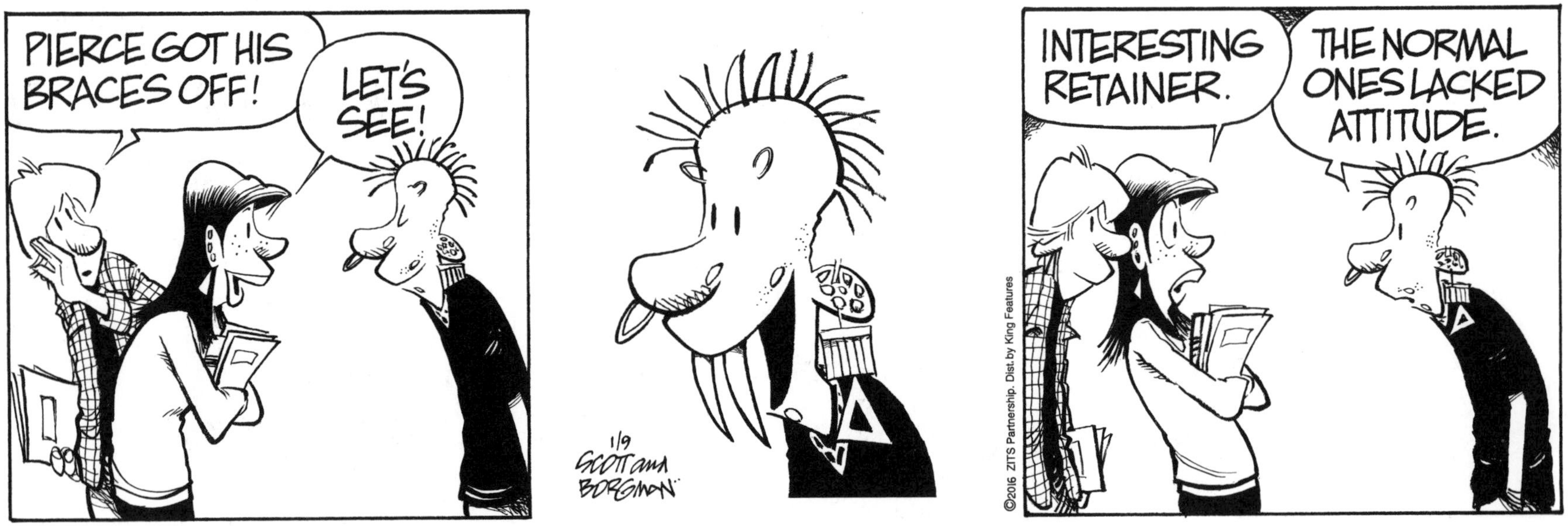
PIERCE GOT HIS BRACES OFF!
LET'S SEE!
1/9 SCOTT and BORGMAN
INTERESTING RETAINER.
THE NORMAL ONES LACKED ATTITUDE.
©2016 ZITS Partnership. Dist. by King Features

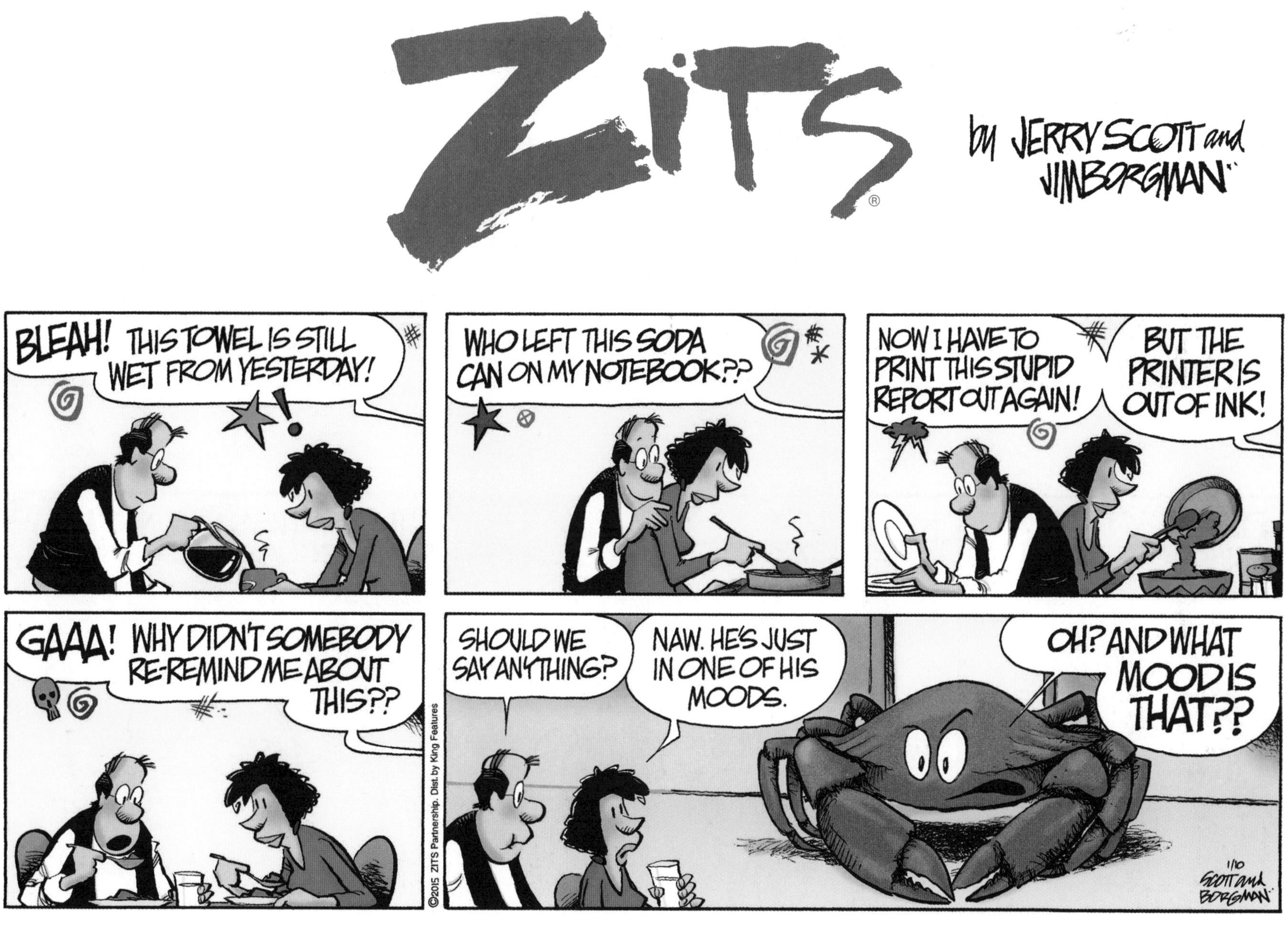
ZITS®
by JERRY SCOTT and JIM BORGMAN
BLEAH! THIS TOWEL IS STILL WET FROM YESTERDAY!
WHO LEFT THIS SODA CAN ON MY NOTEBOOK??
NOW I HAVE TO PRINT THIS STUPID REPORT OUT AGAIN!
BUT THE PRINTER IS OUT OF INK!
GAAA! WHY DIDN'T SOMEBODY RE-REMIND ME ABOUT THIS??
©2015 ZITS Partnership. Dist. by King Features
SHOULD WE SAY ANYTHING?
NAW. HE'S JUST IN ONE OF HIS MOODS.
OH? AND WHAT MOOD IS THAT??
1/10 SCOTT and BORGMAN

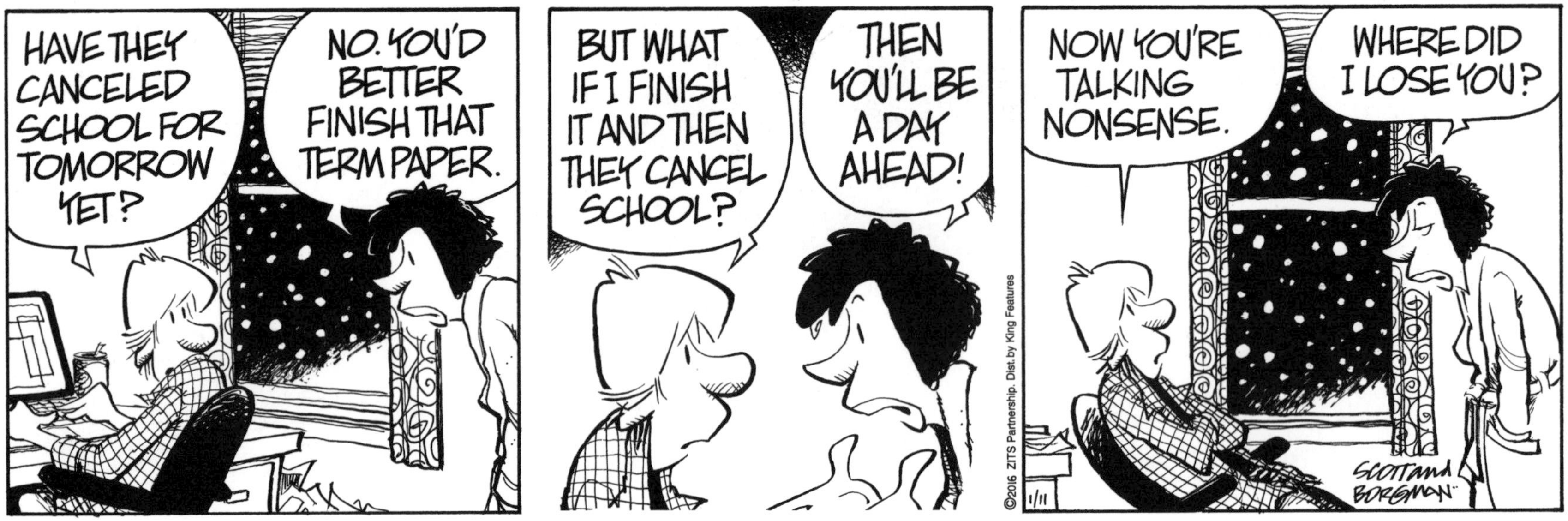
HAVE THEY CANCELED SCHOOL FOR TOMORROW YET?
NO. YOU'D BETTER FINISH THAT TERM PAPER.
BUT WHAT IF I FINISH IT AND THEN THEY CANCEL SCHOOL?
THEN YOU'LL BE A DAY AHEAD!
NOW YOU'RE TALKING NONSENSE.
WHERE DID I LOSE YOU?
©2016 ZITS Partnership. Dist. by King Features
1/11
SCOTT and BORGMAN

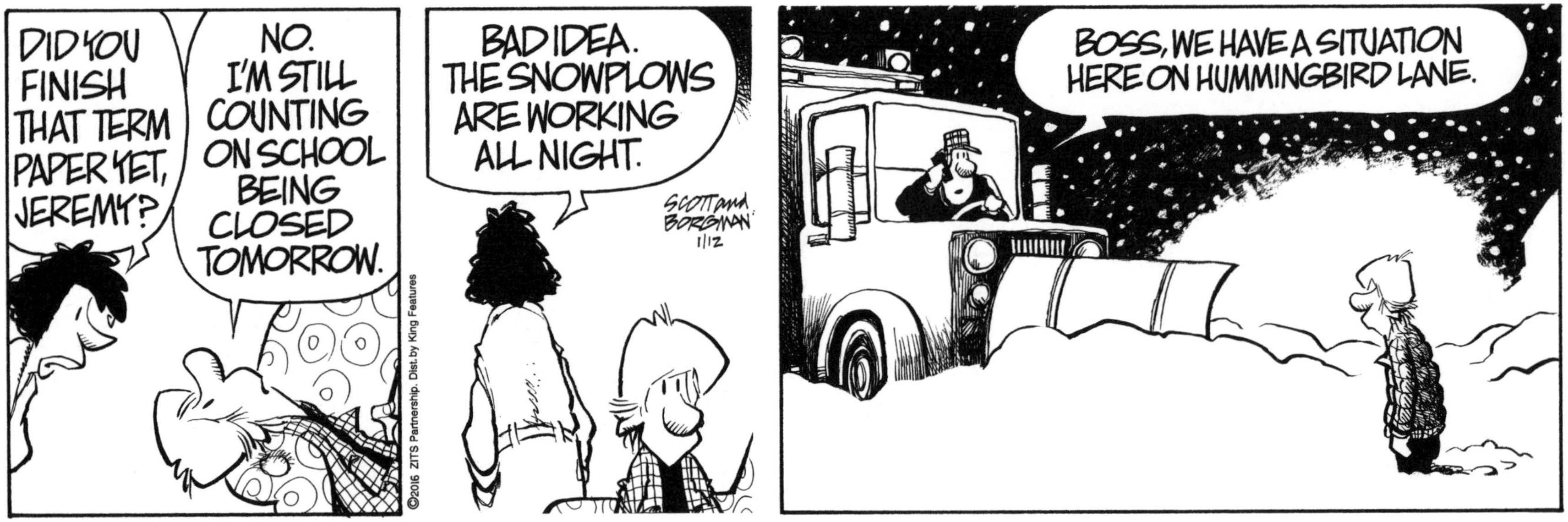
DID YOU FINISH THAT TERM PAPER YET, JEREMY?
NO. I'M STILL COUNTING ON SCHOOL BEING CLOSED TOMORROW.
©2016 ZITS Partnership. Dist. by King Features
BAD IDEA. THE SNOWPLOWS ARE WORKING ALL NIGHT.
SCOTT and BORGMAN 1/12
BOSS, WE HAVE A SITUATION HERE ON HUMMINGBIRD LANE.

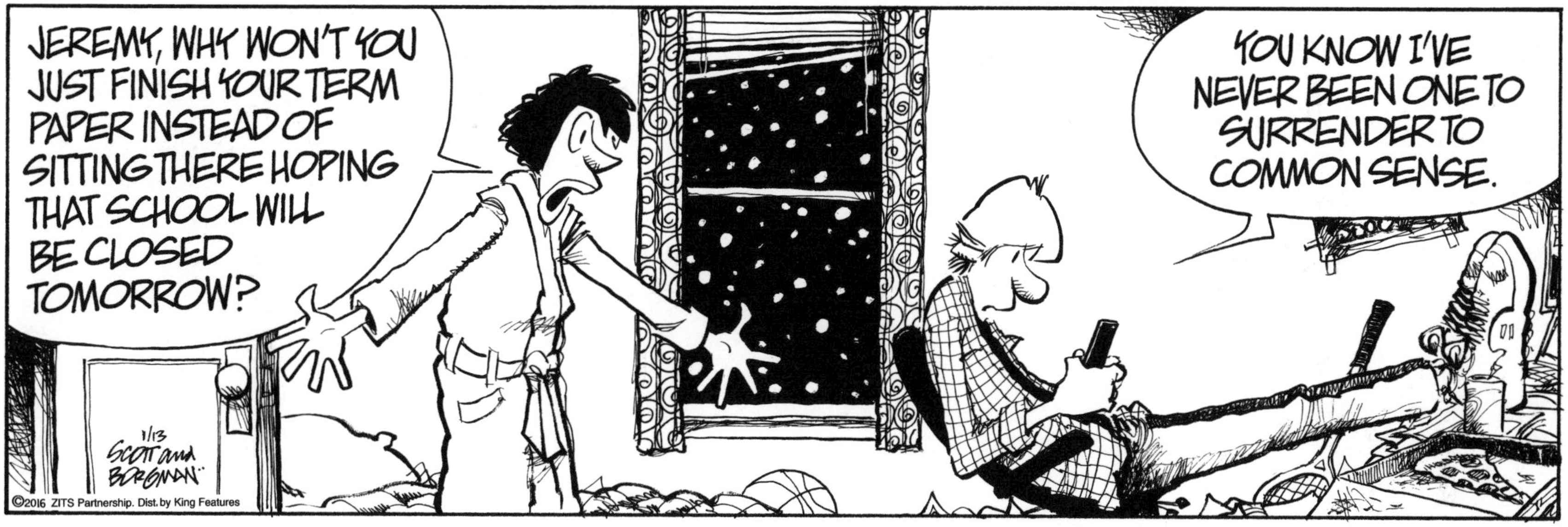
JEREMY, WHY WON'T YOU JUST FINISH YOUR TERM PAPER INSTEAD OF SITTING THERE HOPING THAT SCHOOL WILL BE CLOSED TOMORROW?
YOU KNOW I'VE NEVER BEEN ONE TO SURRENDER TO COMMON SENSE.
1/13 SCOTT and BORGMAN
©2016 ZITS Partnership. Dist. by King Features

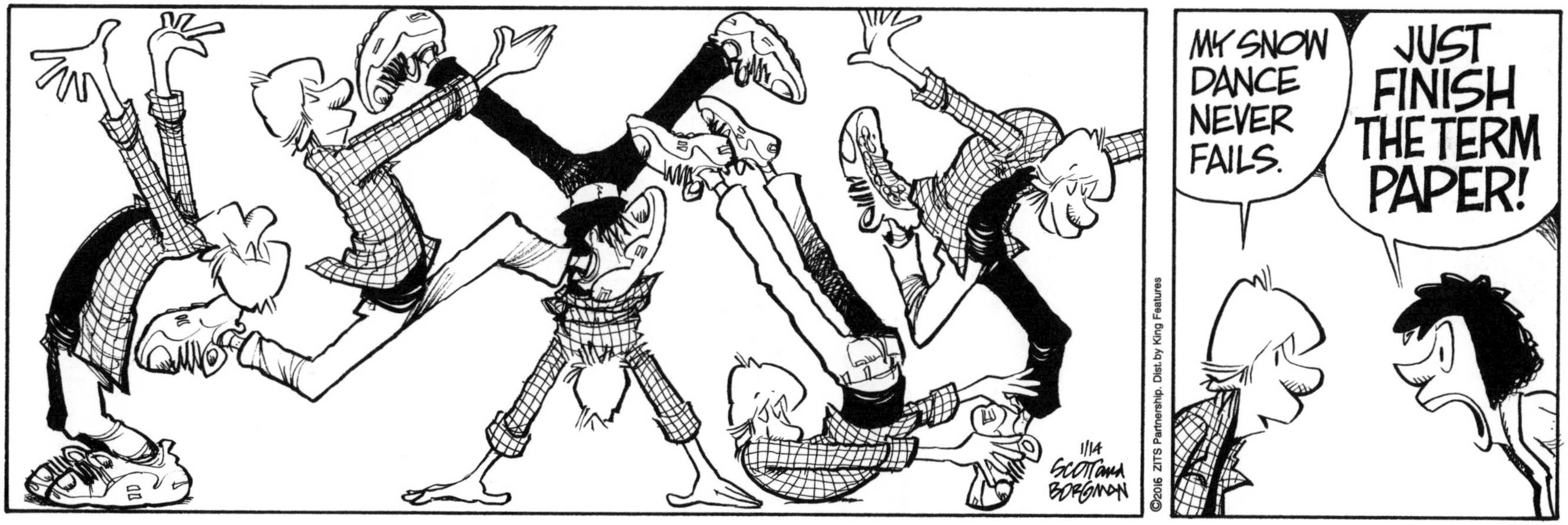
1/14 SCOTT and BORGMAN
©2016 ZITS Partnership. Dist. by King Features
MY SNOW DANCE NEVER FAILS.
JUST FINISH THE TERM PAPER!

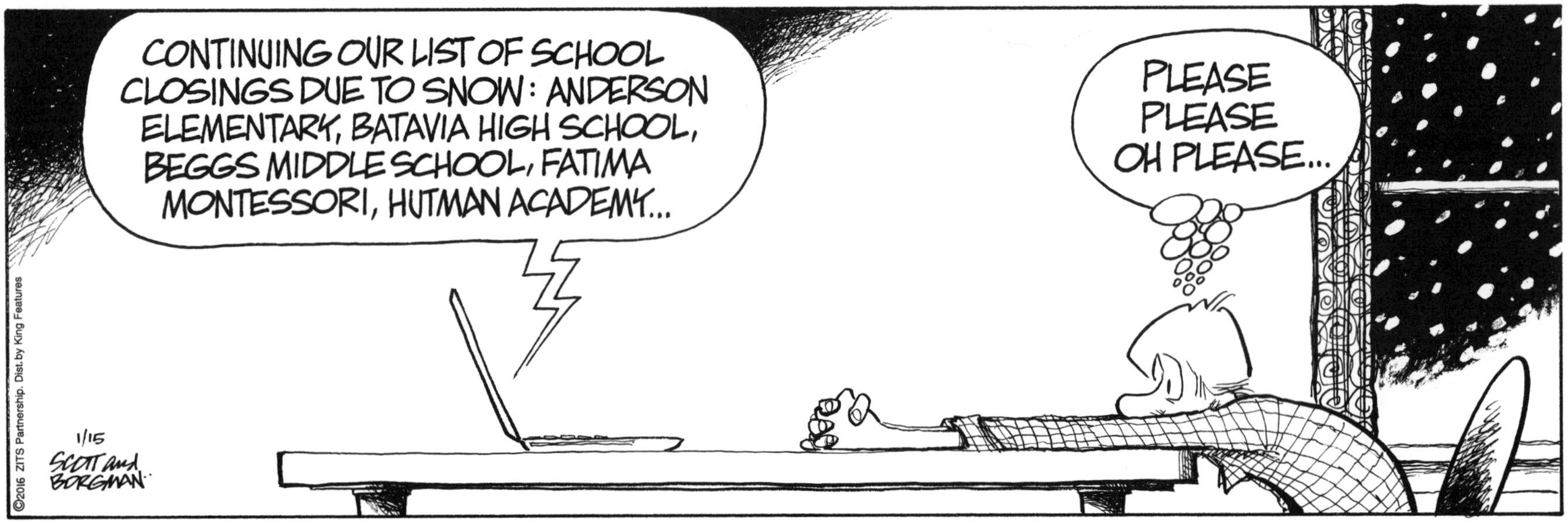
CONTINUING OUR LIST OF SCHOOL CLOSINGS DUE TO SNOW: ANDERSON ELEMENTARY, BATAVIA HIGH SCHOOL, BEGGS MIDDLE SCHOOL, FATIMA MONTESSORI, HUTMAN ACADEMY...
PLEASE PLEASE OH PLEASE...
1/15
SCOTT and BORGMAN
©2016 ZITS Partnership. Dist. by King Features

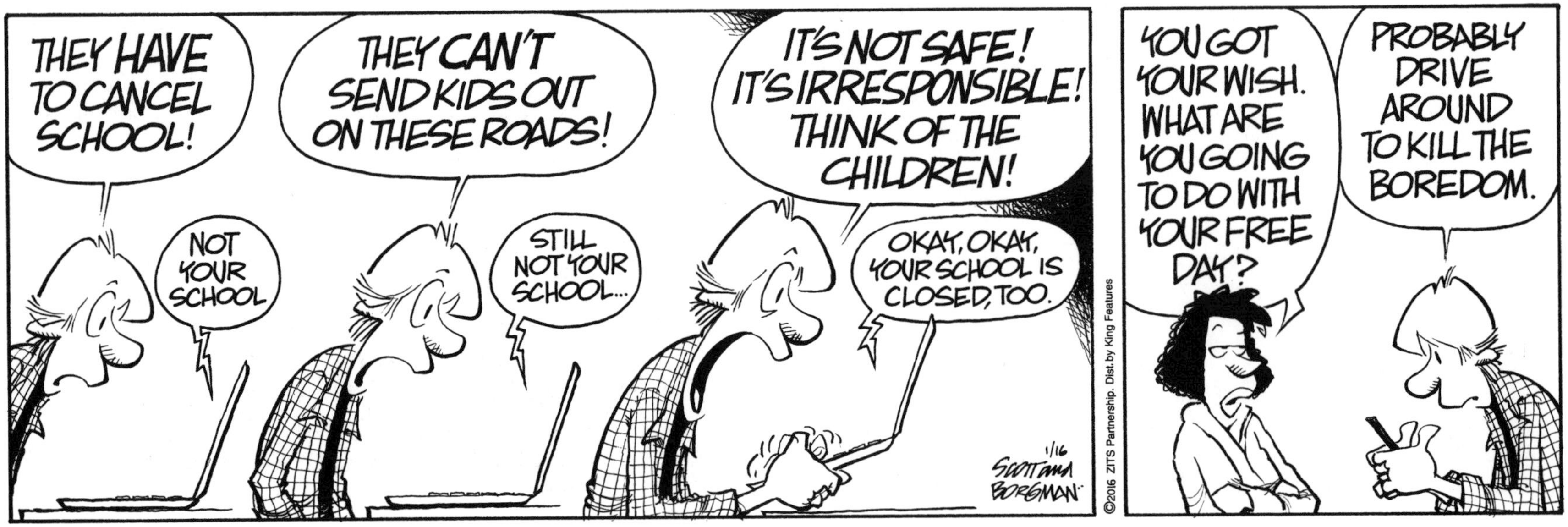
THEY HAVE TO CANCEL SCHOOL!
NOT YOUR SCHOOL
THEY CAN'T SEND KIDS OUT ON THESE ROADS!
STILL NOT YOUR SCHOOL...
IT'S NOT SAFE! IT'S IRRESPONSIBLE! THINK OF THE CHILDREN!
OKAY, OKAY, YOUR SCHOOL IS CLOSED, TOO.
1/16
SCOTT and BORGMAN
©2016 ZITS Partnership. Dist. by King Features
YOU GOT YOUR WISH. WHAT ARE YOU GOING TO DO WITH YOUR FREE DAY?
PROBABLY DRIVE AROUND TO KILL THE BOREDOM.

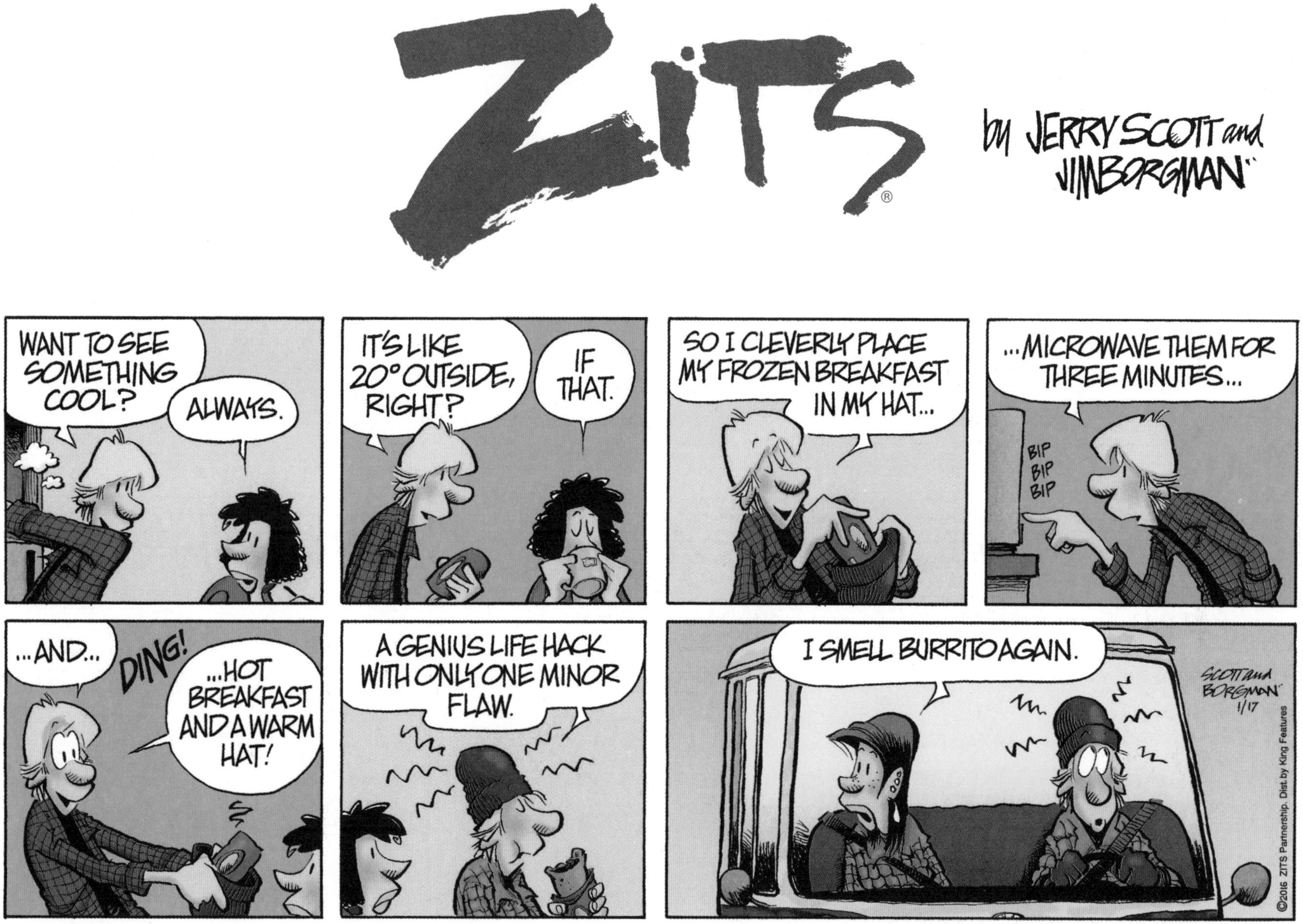
ZITS®
by JERRY SCOTT and JIM BORGMAN
WANT TO SEE SOMETHING COOL?
ALWAYS.
IT'S LIKE 20° OUTSIDE, RIGHT?
IF THAT.
SO I CLEVERLY PLACE MY FROZEN BREAKFAST IN MY HAT...
...MICROWAVE THEM FOR THREE MINUTES...
BIP BIP BIP
...AND...
DING!
...HOT BREAKFAST AND A WARM HAT!
A GENIUS LIFE HACK WITH ONLY ONE MINOR FLAW.
I SMELL BURRITO AGAIN.
SCOTT and BORGMAN 1/17
©2016 ZITS Partnership. Dist. by King Features

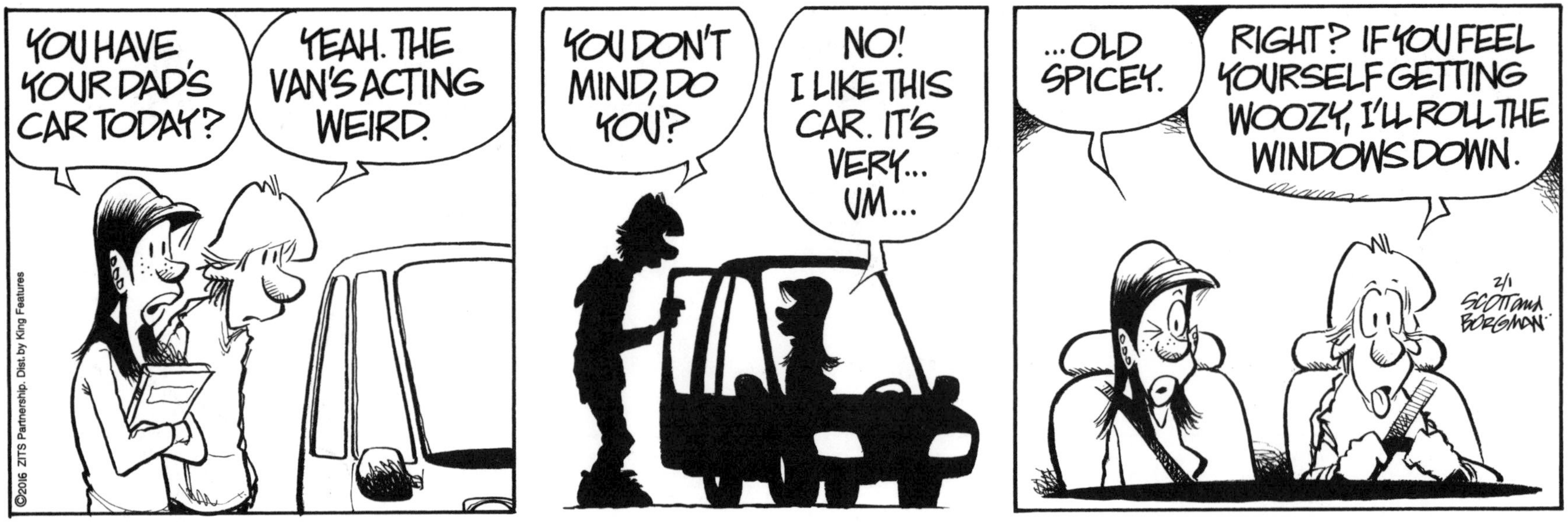
YOU HAVE YOUR DAD'S CAR TODAY?
YEAH. THE VAN'S ACTING WEIRD.
©2016 ZITS Partnership. Dist. by King Features
YOU DON'T MIND, DO YOU?
NO! I LIKE THIS CAR. IT'S VERY... UM...
...OLD SPICEY.
RIGHT? IF YOU FEEL YOURSELF GETTING WOOZY, I'LL ROLL THE WINDOWS DOWN.
2/1 SCOTT and BORGMAN

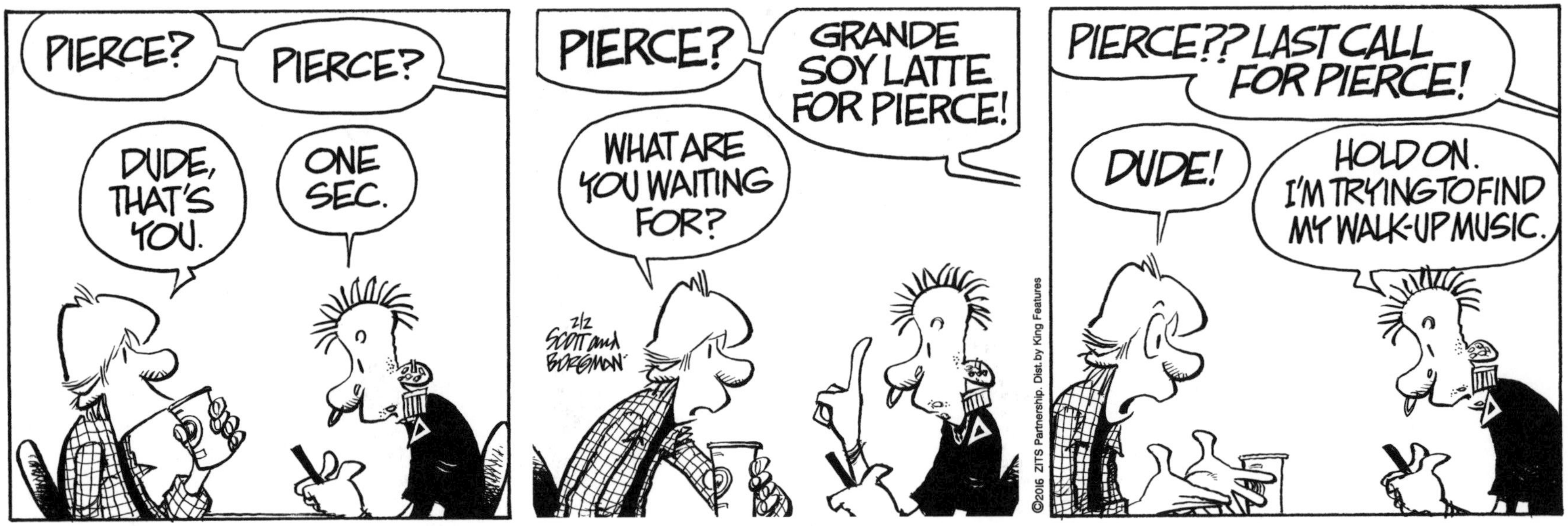
PIERCE?
PIERCE?
DUDE, THAT'S YOU.
ONE SEC.
PIERCE?
GRANDE SOY LATTE FOR PIERCE!
WHAT ARE YOU WAITING FOR?
2/2 SCOTT and BORGMAN
©2016 ZITS Partnership. Dist. by King Features
PIERCE?? LAST CALL FOR PIERCE!
DUDE!
HOLD ON. I'M TRYING TO FIND MY WALK-UP MUSIC.

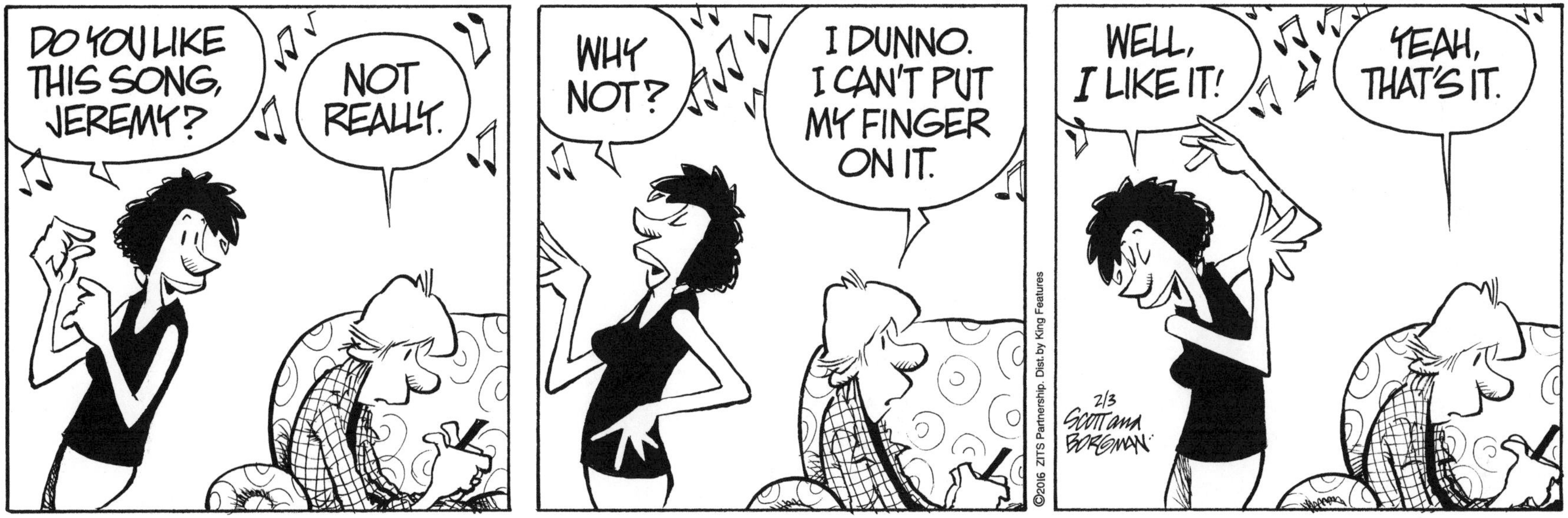
DO YOU LIKE THIS SONG, JEREMY?
NOT REALLY.
WHY NOT?
I DUNNO. I CAN'T PUT MY FINGER ON IT.
©2016 ZITS Partnership. Dist. by King Features
WELL, *I* LIKE IT!
YEAH, THAT'S IT.
2/3 SCOTT and BORGMAN

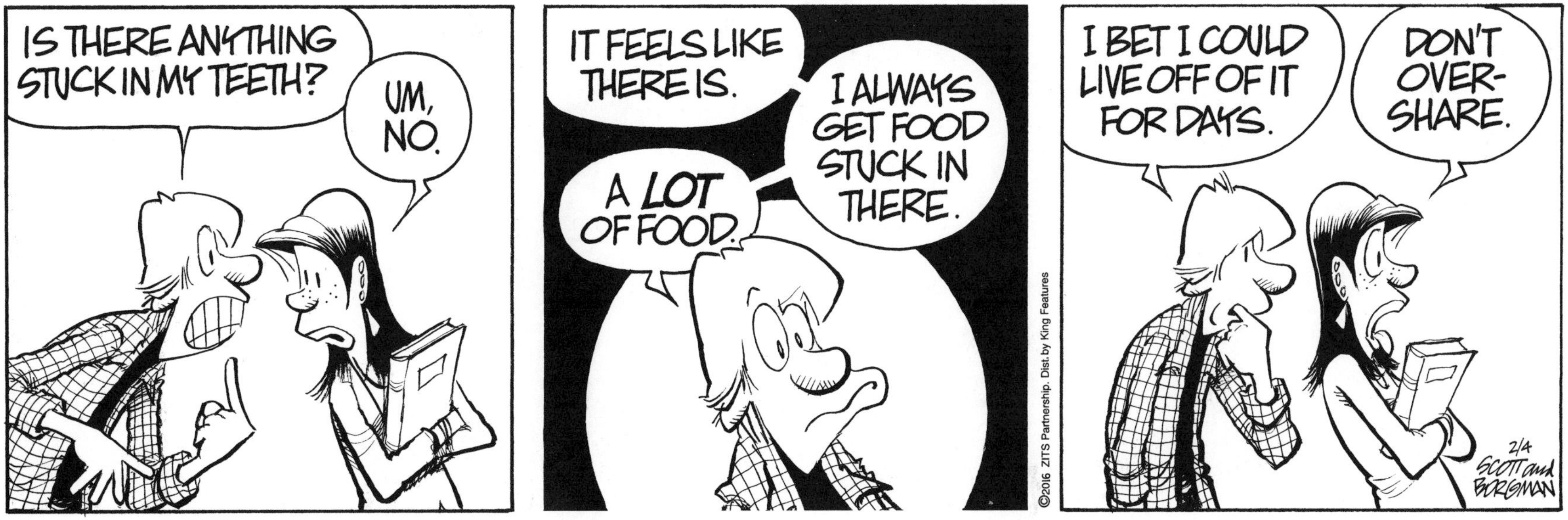
IS THERE ANYTHING STUCK IN MY TEETH?
UM, NO.
IT FEELS LIKE THERE IS.
I ALWAYS GET FOOD STUCK IN THERE.
A *LOT* OF FOOD.
©2016 ZITS Partnership. Dist. by King Features
I BET I COULD LIVE OFF OF IT FOR DAYS.
DON'T OVER-SHARE.
2/4 SCOTT and BORGMAN

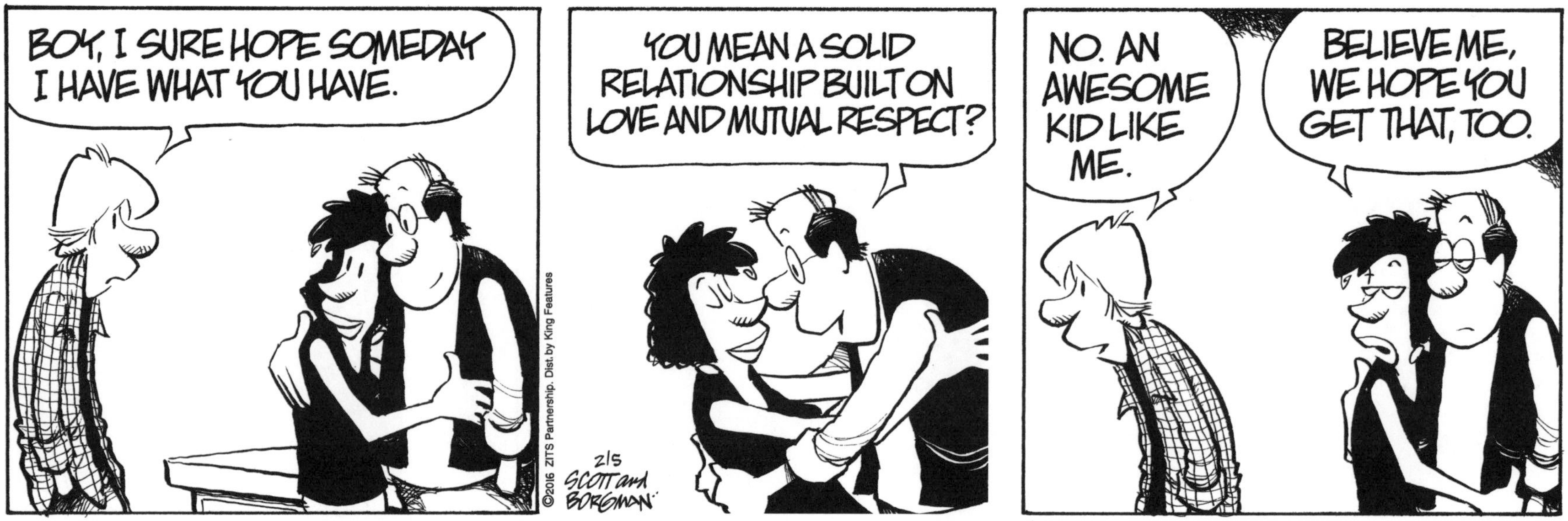
BOY, I SURE HOPE SOMEDAY I HAVE WHAT YOU HAVE.
YOU MEAN A SOLID RELATIONSHIP BUILT ON LOVE AND MUTUAL RESPECT?
NO. AN AWESOME KID LIKE ME.
BELIEVE ME, WE HOPE YOU GET THAT, TOO.
2/5
SCOTT and BORGMAN
©2016 ZITS Partnership. Dist. by King Features

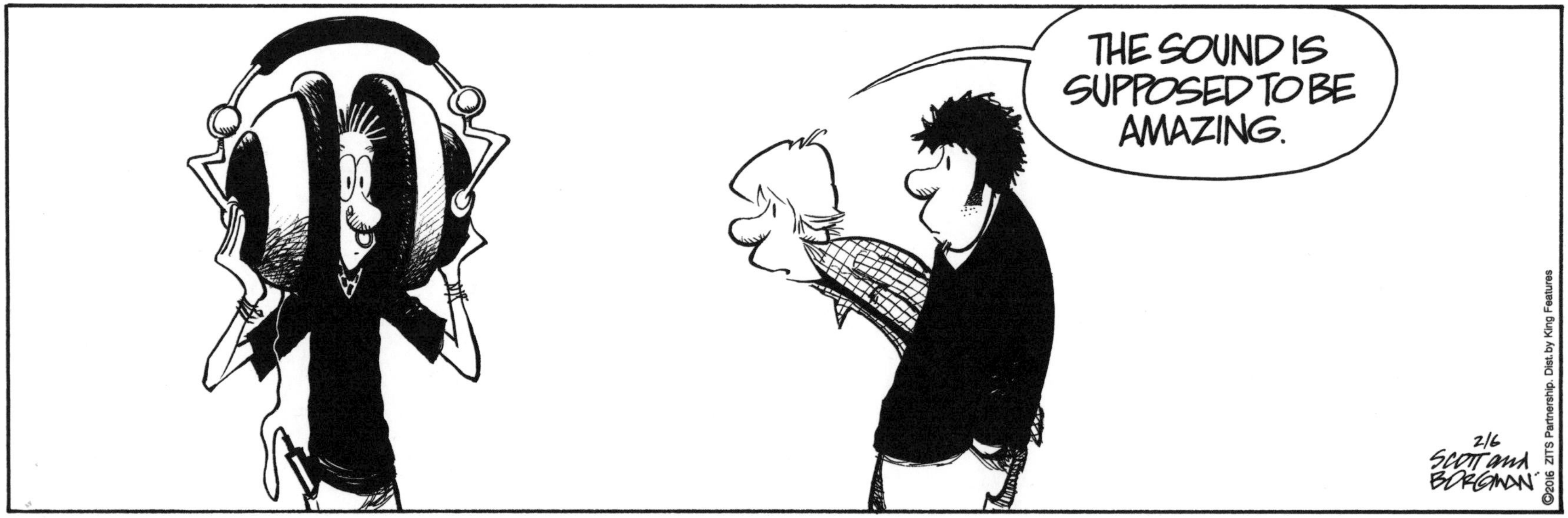
THE SOUND IS SUPPOSED TO BE AMAZING.
2/6
SCOTT and BORGMAN
©2016 ZITS Partnership. Dist. by King Features

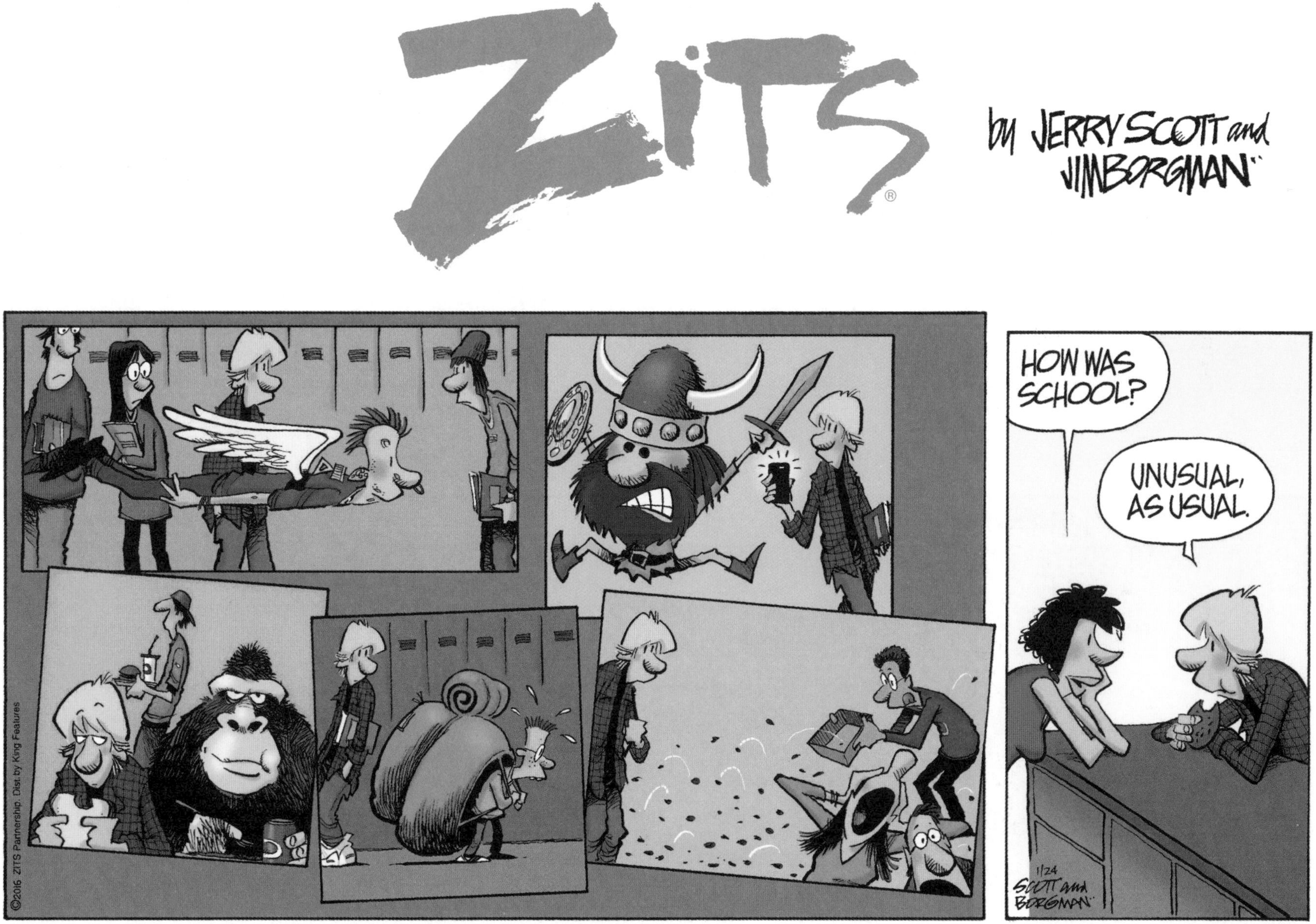
ZITS®
by JERRY SCOTT and JIM BORGMAN
©2016 ZITS Partnership. Dist. by King Features
HOW WAS SCHOOL?
UNUSUAL, AS USUAL.
1/24 SCOTT and BORGMAN

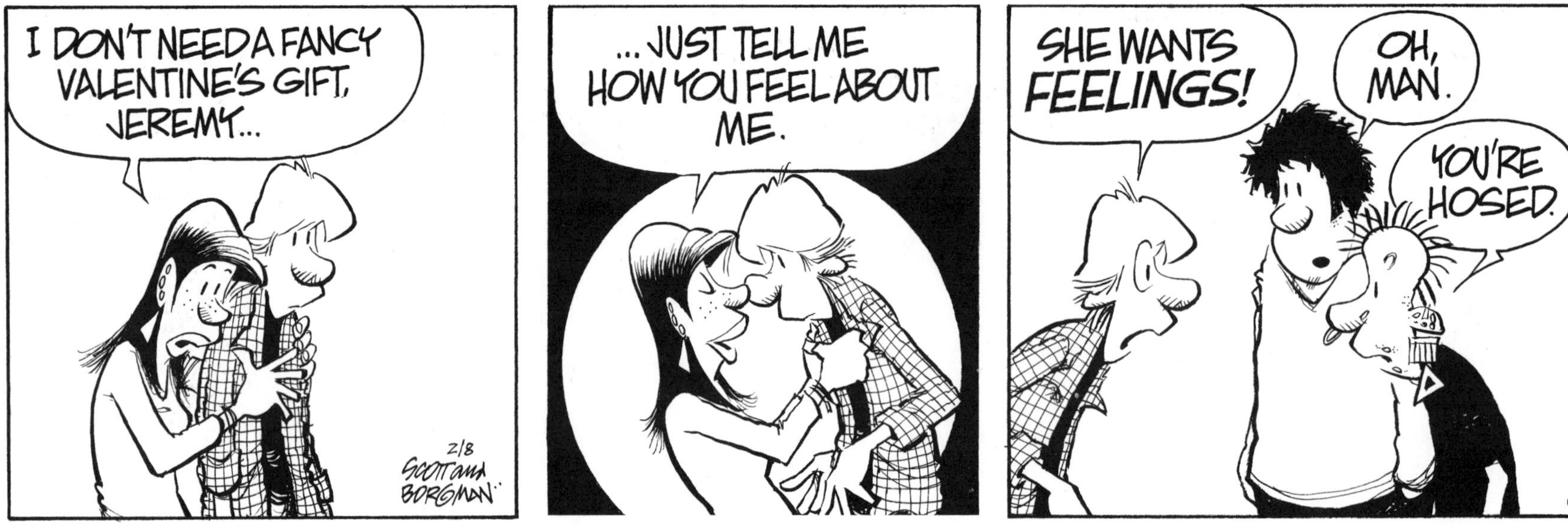
I DON'T NEED A FANCY VALENTINE'S GIFT, JEREMY...
2/8 SCOTT and BORGMAN
... JUST TELL ME HOW YOU FEEL ABOUT ME.
SHE WANTS **FEELINGS!**
OH, MAN.
YOU'RE HOSED.
©2016 ZITS Partnership. Dist. by King Features

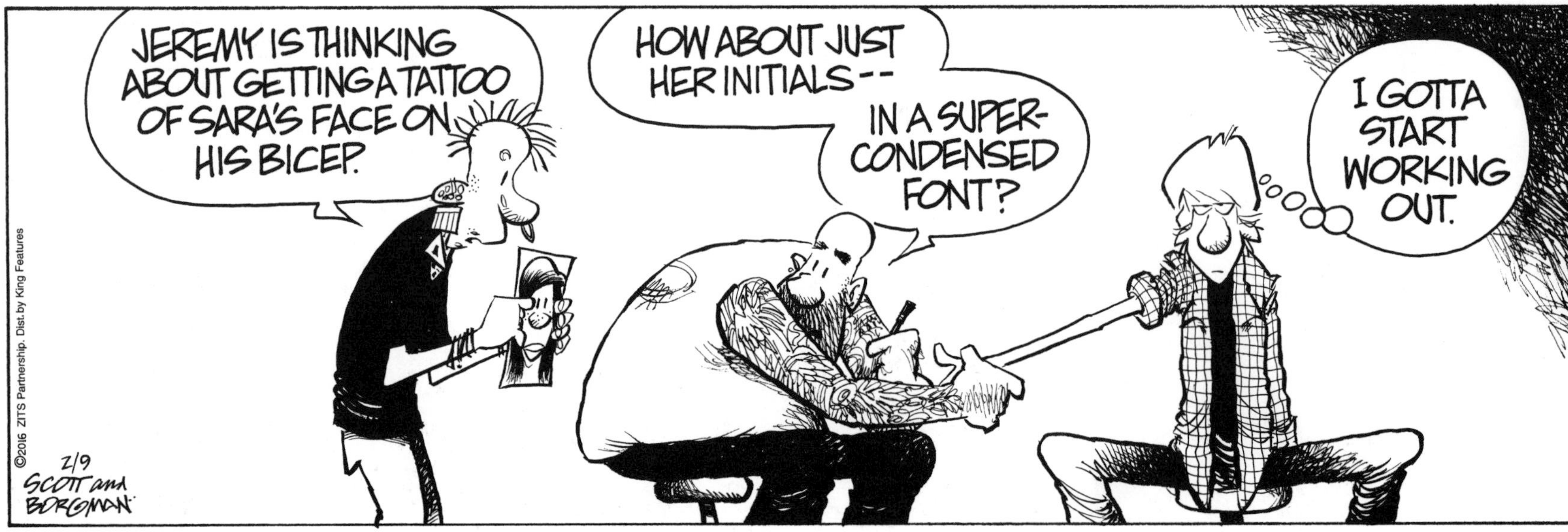
JEREMY IS THINKING ABOUT GETTING A TATTOO OF SARA'S FACE ON HIS BICEP.
HOW ABOUT JUST HER INITIALS--
IN A SUPER-CONDENSED FONT?
I GOTTA START WORKING OUT.
©2016 ZITS Partnership. Dist. by King Features
2/9 SCOTT and BORGMAN

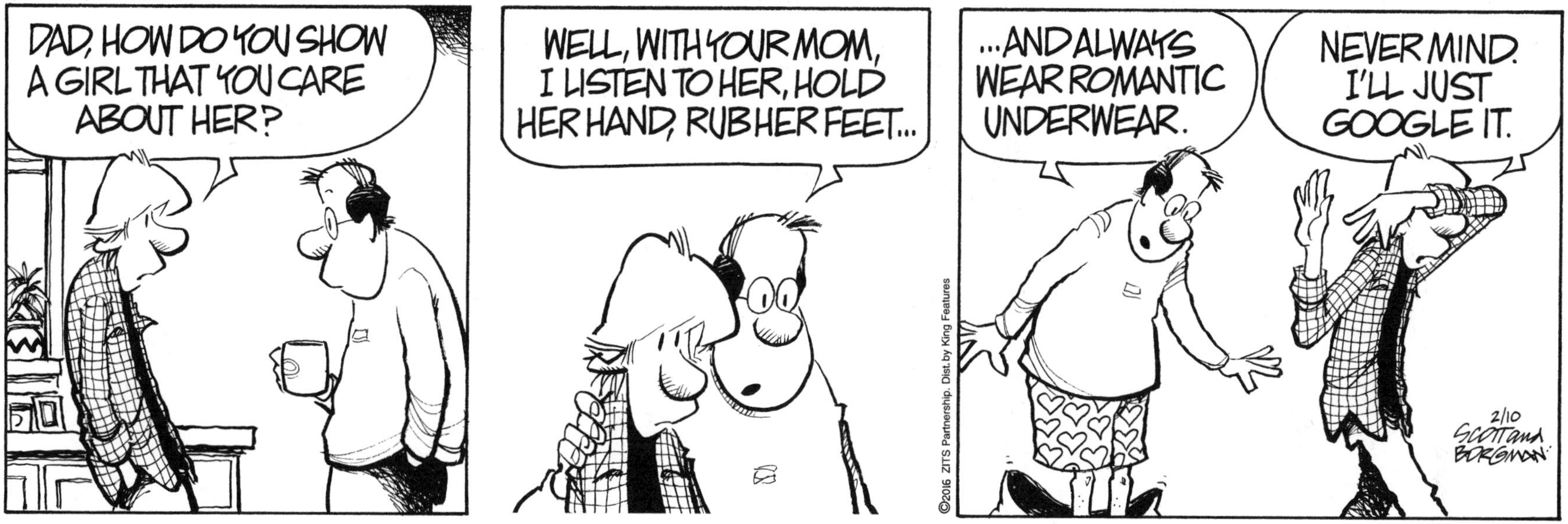
DAD, HOW DO YOU SHOW A GIRL THAT YOU CARE ABOUT HER?
WELL, WITH YOUR MOM, I LISTEN TO HER, HOLD HER HAND, RUB HER FEET...
...AND ALWAYS WEAR ROMANTIC UNDERWEAR.
NEVER MIND. I'LL JUST GOOGLE IT.
©2016 ZITS Partnership. Dist. by King Features
2/10 SCOTT and BORGMAN

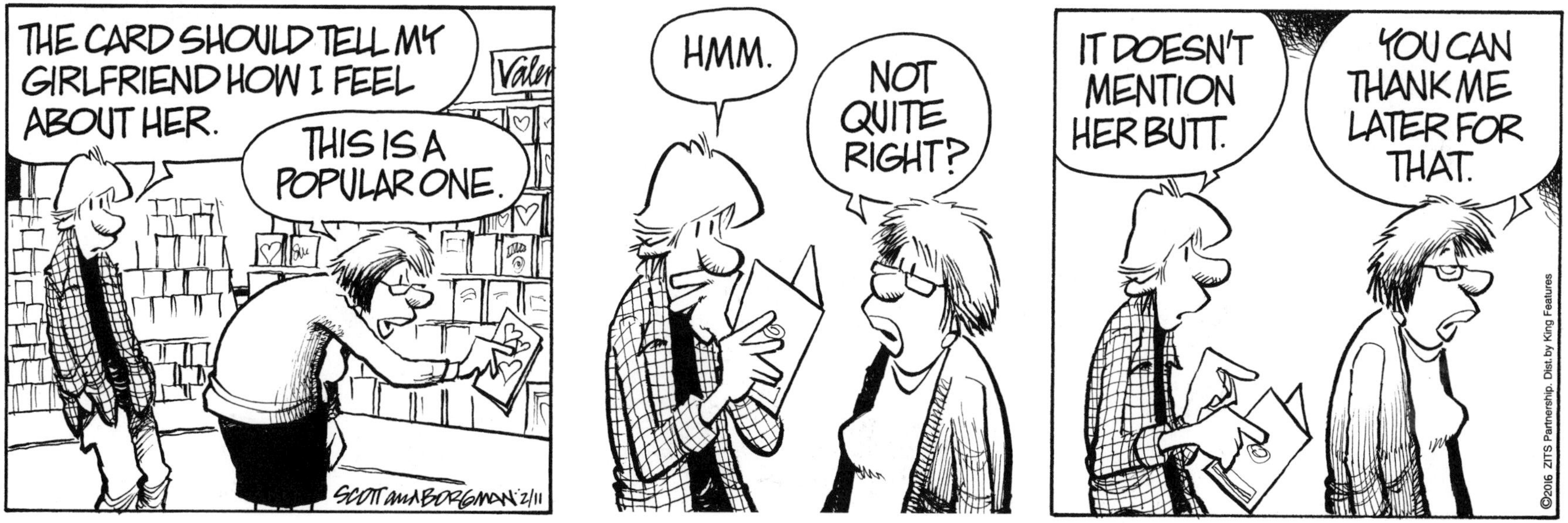
THE CARD SHOULD TELL MY GIRLFRIEND HOW I FEEL ABOUT HER.
THIS IS A POPULAR ONE.
SCOTT and BORGMAN 2/11
HMM.
NOT QUITE RIGHT?
IT DOESN'T MENTION HER BUTT.
YOU CAN THANK ME LATER FOR THAT.
©2016 ZITS Partnership. Dist. by King Features

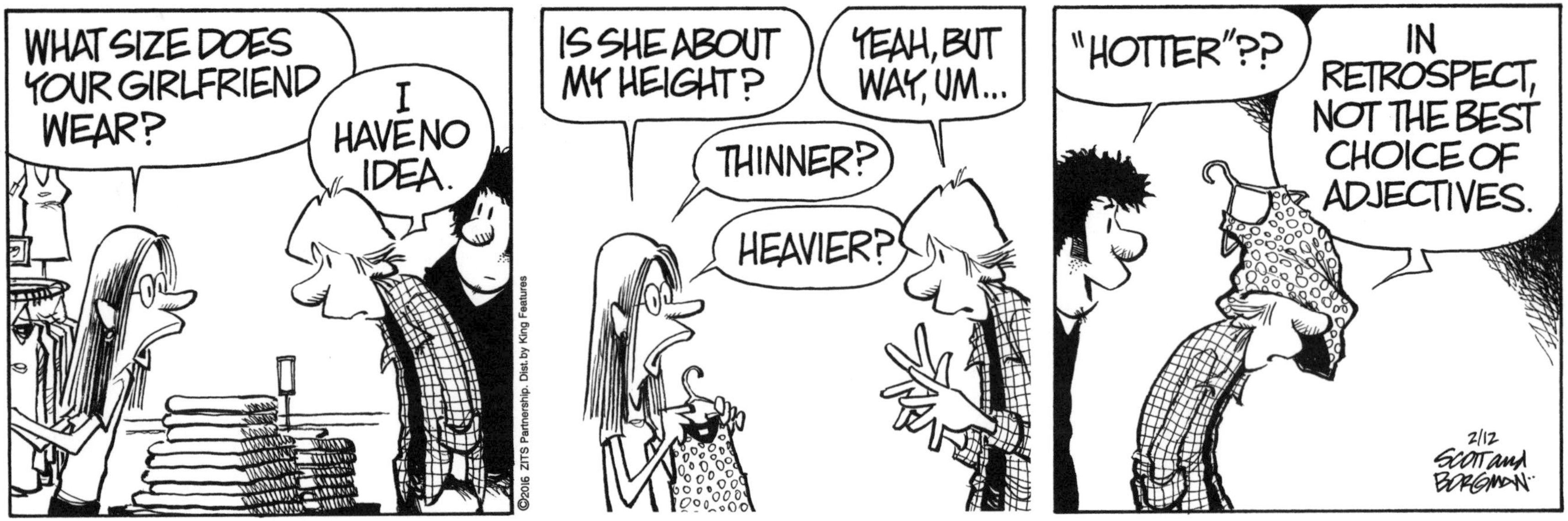
WHAT SIZE DOES YOUR GIRLFRIEND WEAR?
I HAVE NO IDEA.
IS SHE ABOUT MY HEIGHT?
THINNER?
HEAVIER?
YEAH, BUT WAY, UM...
"HOTTER"??
IN RETROSPECT, NOT THE BEST CHOICE OF ADJECTIVES.
2/12 SCOTT and BORGMAN
©2016 ZITS Partnership. Dist. by King Features

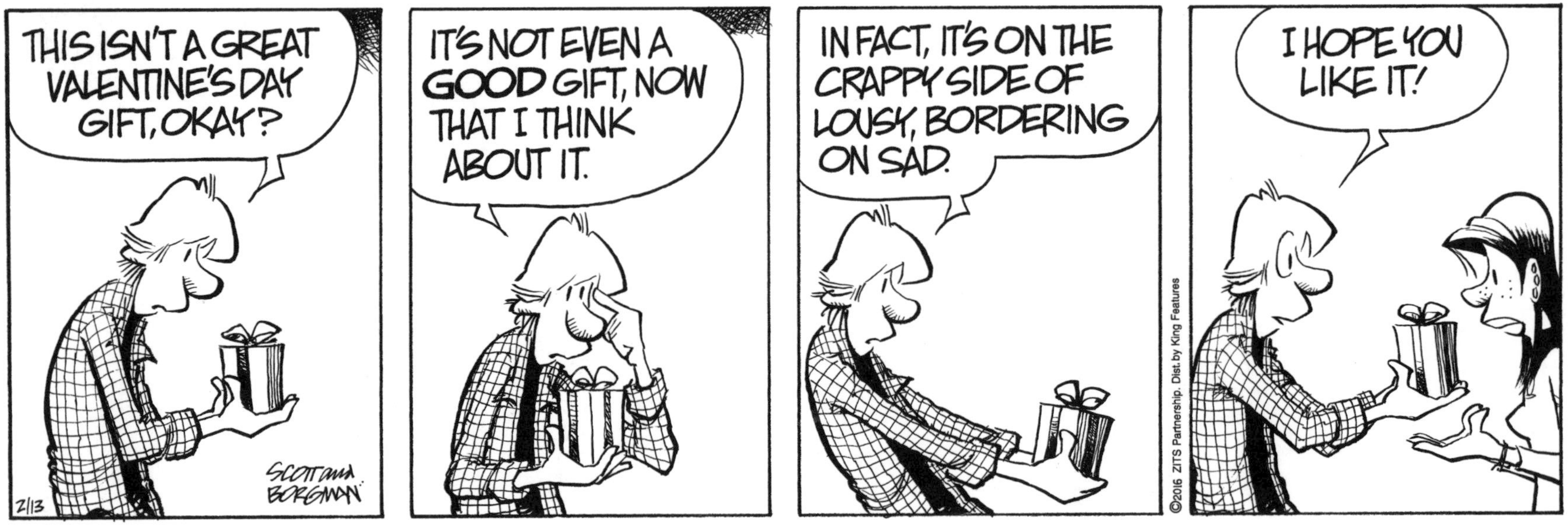
THIS ISN'T A GREAT VALENTINE'S DAY GIFT, OKAY?
2/13
SCOTT and BORGMAN
IT'S NOT EVEN A **GOOD** GIFT, NOW THAT I THINK ABOUT IT.
IN FACT, IT'S ON THE CRAPPY SIDE OF LOUSY, BORDERING ON SAD.
I HOPE YOU LIKE IT!
©2016 ZITS Partnership. Dist. by King Features

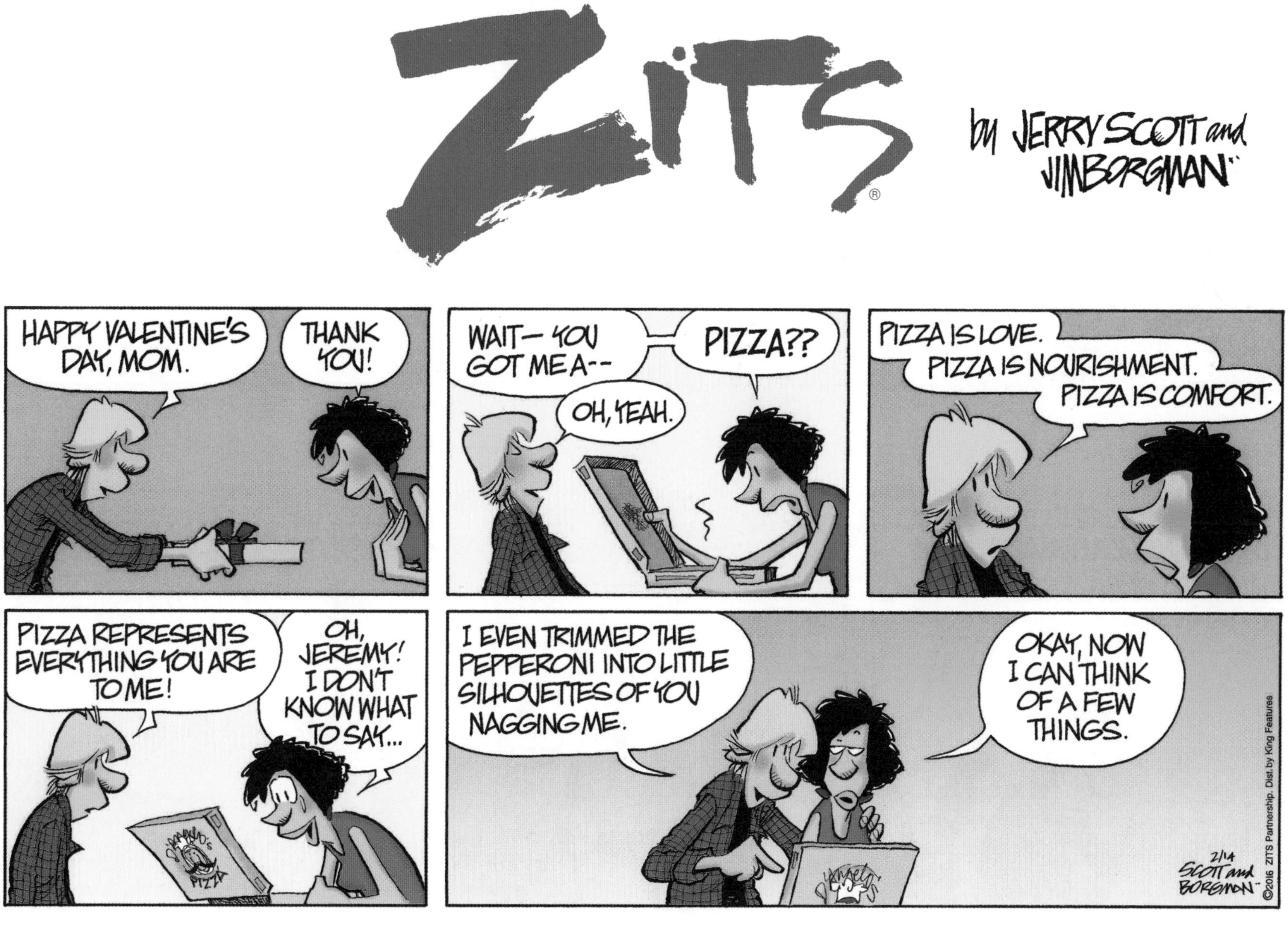
ZITS
by JERRY SCOTT and JIM BORGMAN
HAPPY VALENTINE'S DAY, MOM.
THANK YOU!
WAIT— YOU GOT ME A--
PIZZA??
OH, YEAH.
PIZZA IS LOVE.
PIZZA IS NOURISHMENT.
PIZZA IS COMFORT.
PIZZA REPRESENTS EVERYTHING YOU ARE TO ME!
OH, JEREMY! I DON'T KNOW WHAT TO SAY...
I EVEN TRIMMED THE PEPPERONI INTO LITTLE SILHOUETTES OF YOU NAGGING ME.
OKAY, NOW I CAN THINK OF A FEW THINGS.
2/14 SCOTT and BORGMAN
©2016 ZITS Partnership. Dist. by King Features

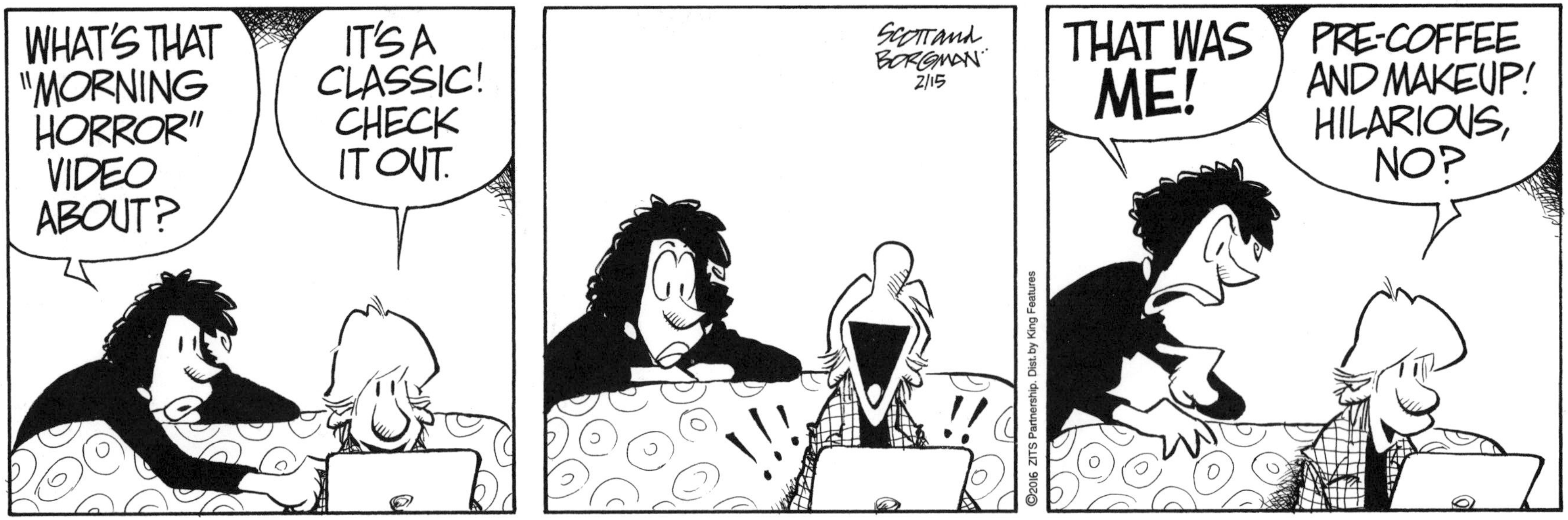
WHAT'S THAT "MORNING HORROR" VIDEO ABOUT?
IT'S A CLASSIC! CHECK IT OUT.
SCOTT and BORGMAN 2/15
!!!
!!
THAT WAS ME!
PRE-COFFEE AND MAKEUP! HILARIOUS, NO?
©2016 ZITS Partnership. Dist. by King Features

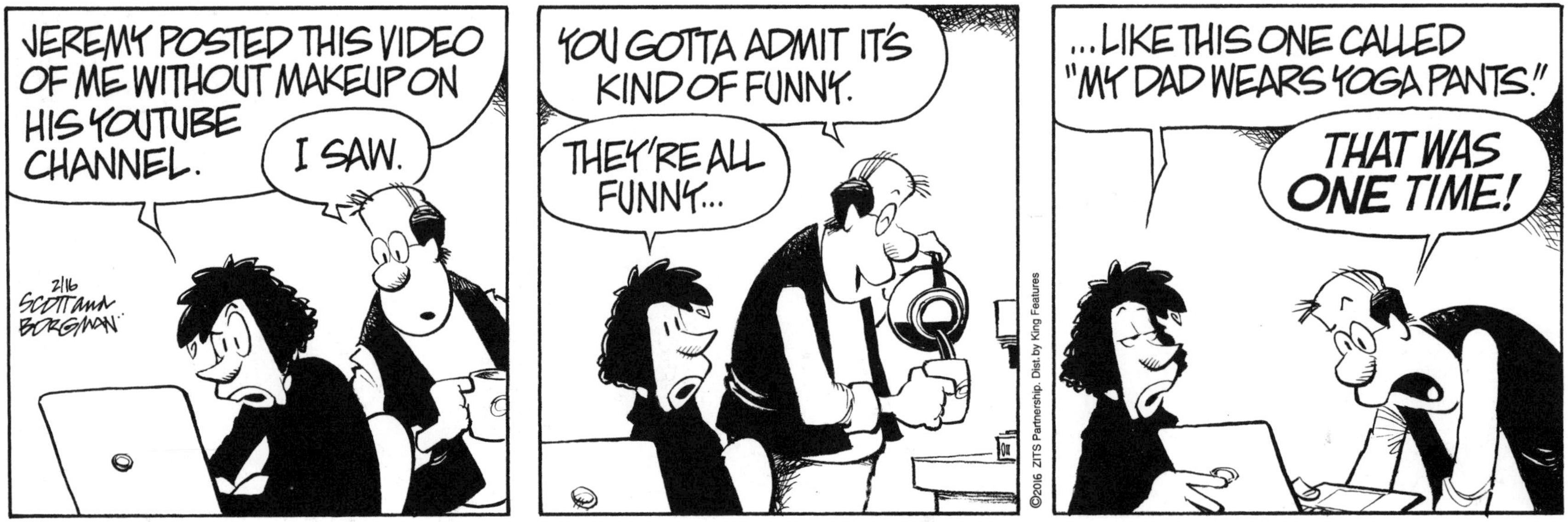
JEREMY POSTED THIS VIDEO OF ME WITHOUT MAKEUP ON HIS YOUTUBE CHANNEL.
I SAW.
2/16 SCOTT and BORGMAN
YOU GOTTA ADMIT IT'S KIND OF FUNNY.
THEY'RE ALL FUNNY...
...LIKE THIS ONE CALLED "MY DAD WEARS YOGA PANTS."
THAT WAS ONE TIME!
©2016 ZITS Partnership. Dist. by King Features

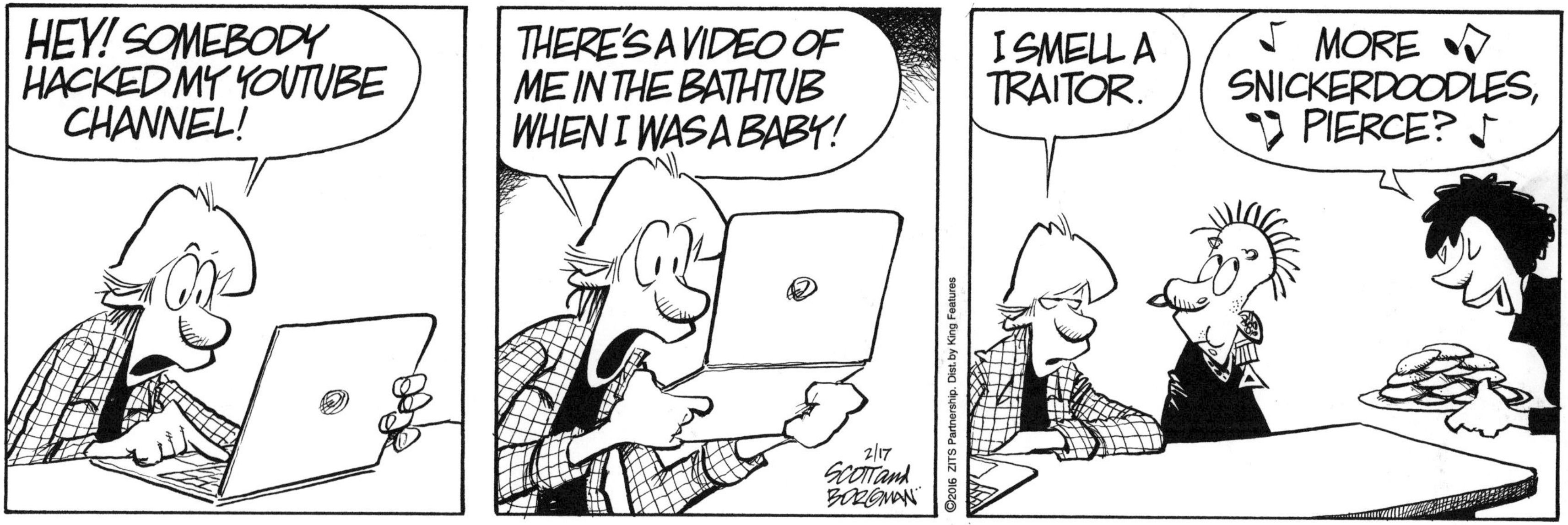
HEY! SOMEBODY HACKED MY YOUTUBE CHANNEL!
THERE'S A VIDEO OF ME IN THE BATHTUB WHEN I WAS A BABY!
2/17
SCOTT and BORGMAN
©2016 ZITS Partnership. Dist. by King Features
I SMELL A TRAITOR.
MORE SNICKERDOODLES, PIERCE?

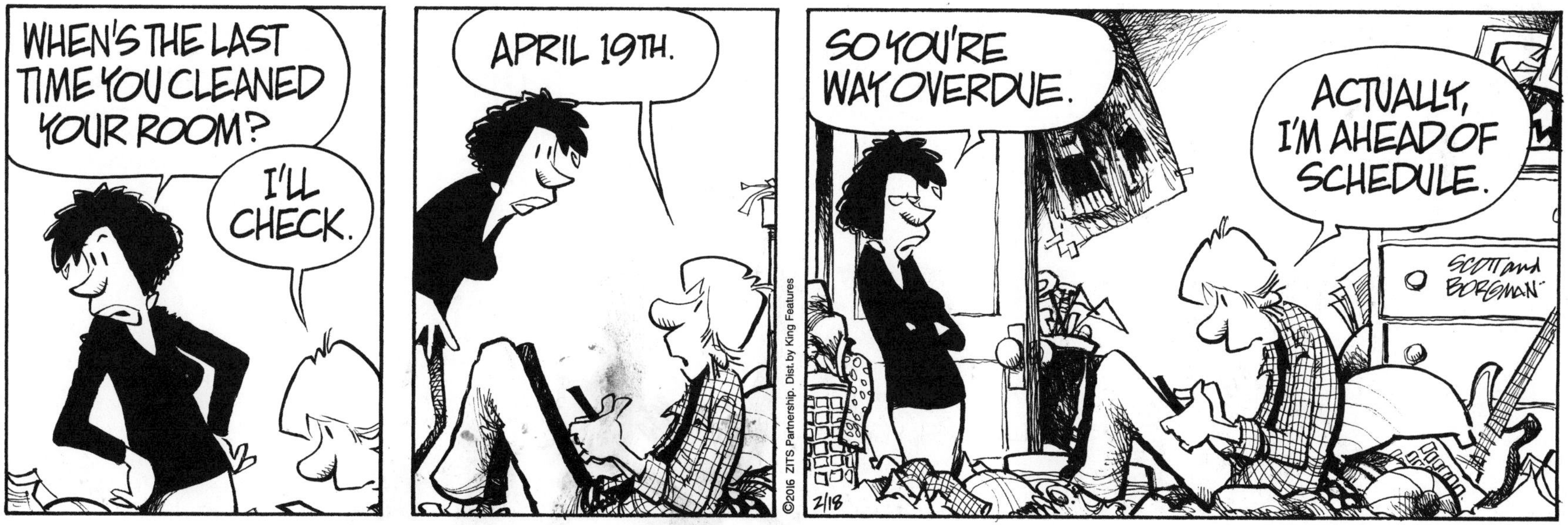
WHEN'S THE LAST TIME YOU CLEANED YOUR ROOM?
I'LL CHECK.
APRIL 19TH.
©2016 ZITS Partnership. Dist. by King Features
2/18
SO YOU'RE WAY OVERDUE.
ACTUALLY, I'M AHEAD OF SCHEDULE.
SCOTT and BORGMAN

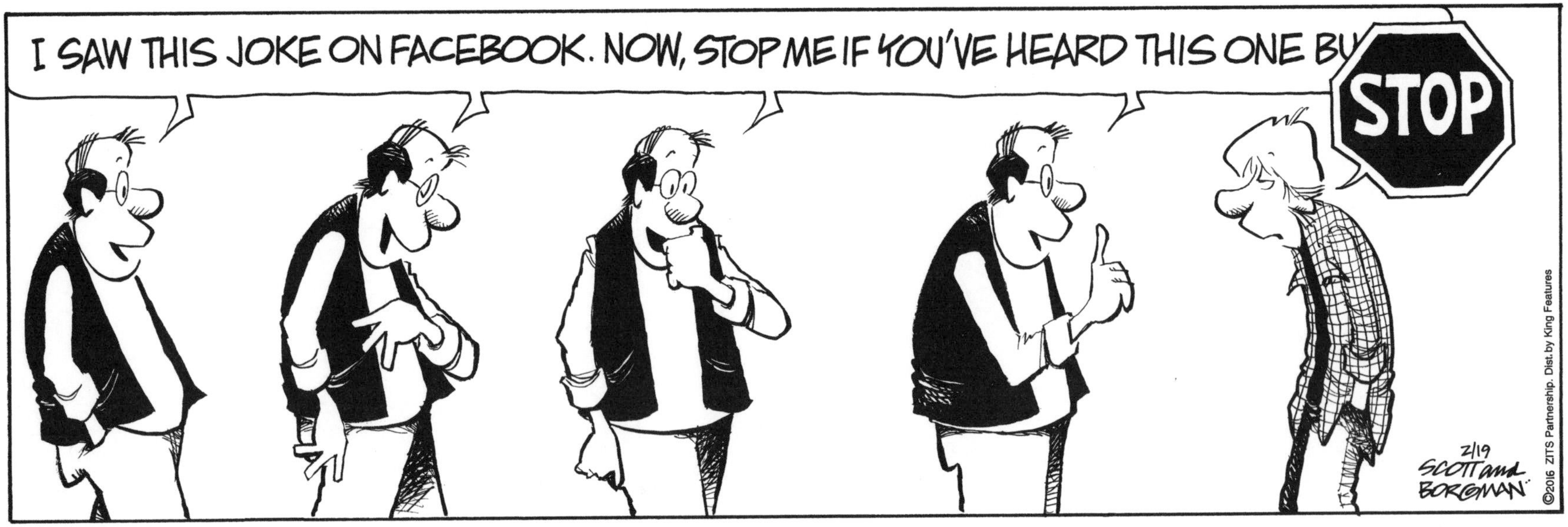
I SAW THIS JOKE ON FACEBOOK. NOW, STOP ME IF YOU'VE HEARD THIS ONE BY
STOP
2/19
SCOTT and BORGMAN
©2016 ZITS Partnership. Dist. by King Features

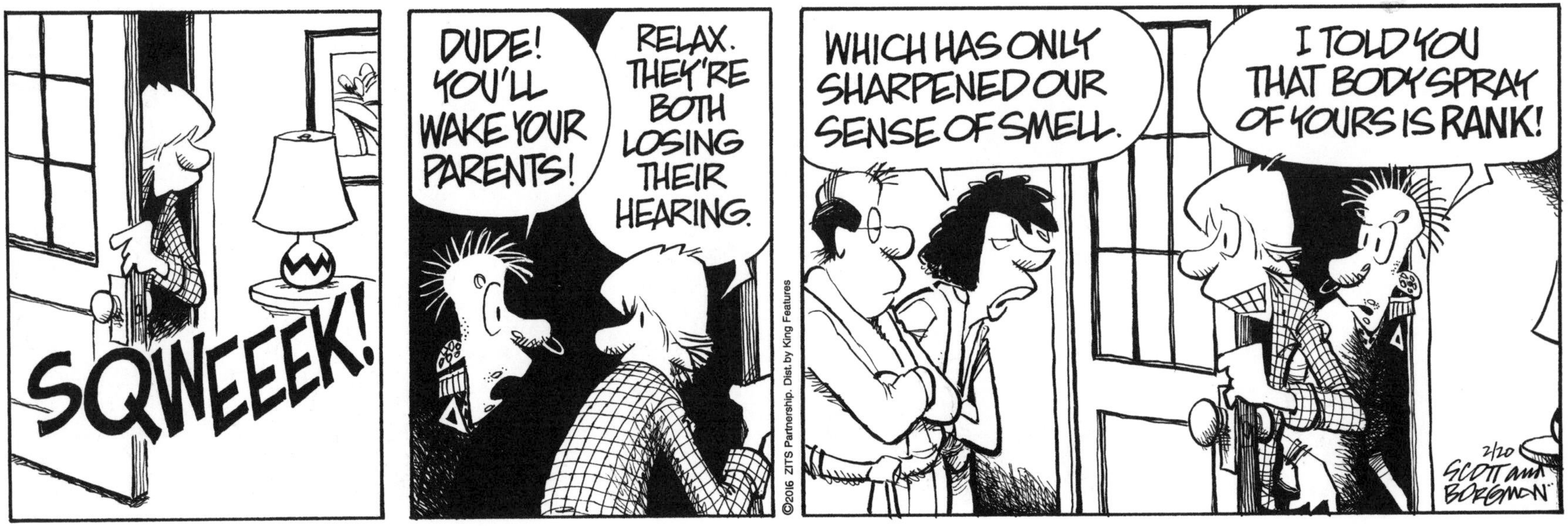
SQWEEEK!
DUDE! YOU'LL WAKE YOUR PARENTS!
RELAX. THEY'RE BOTH LOSING THEIR HEARING.
©2016 ZITS Partnership. Dist. by King Features
WHICH HAS ONLY SHARPENED OUR SENSE OF SMELL.
I TOLD YOU THAT BODY SPRAY OF YOURS IS RANK!
2/20
SCOTT and BORGMAN

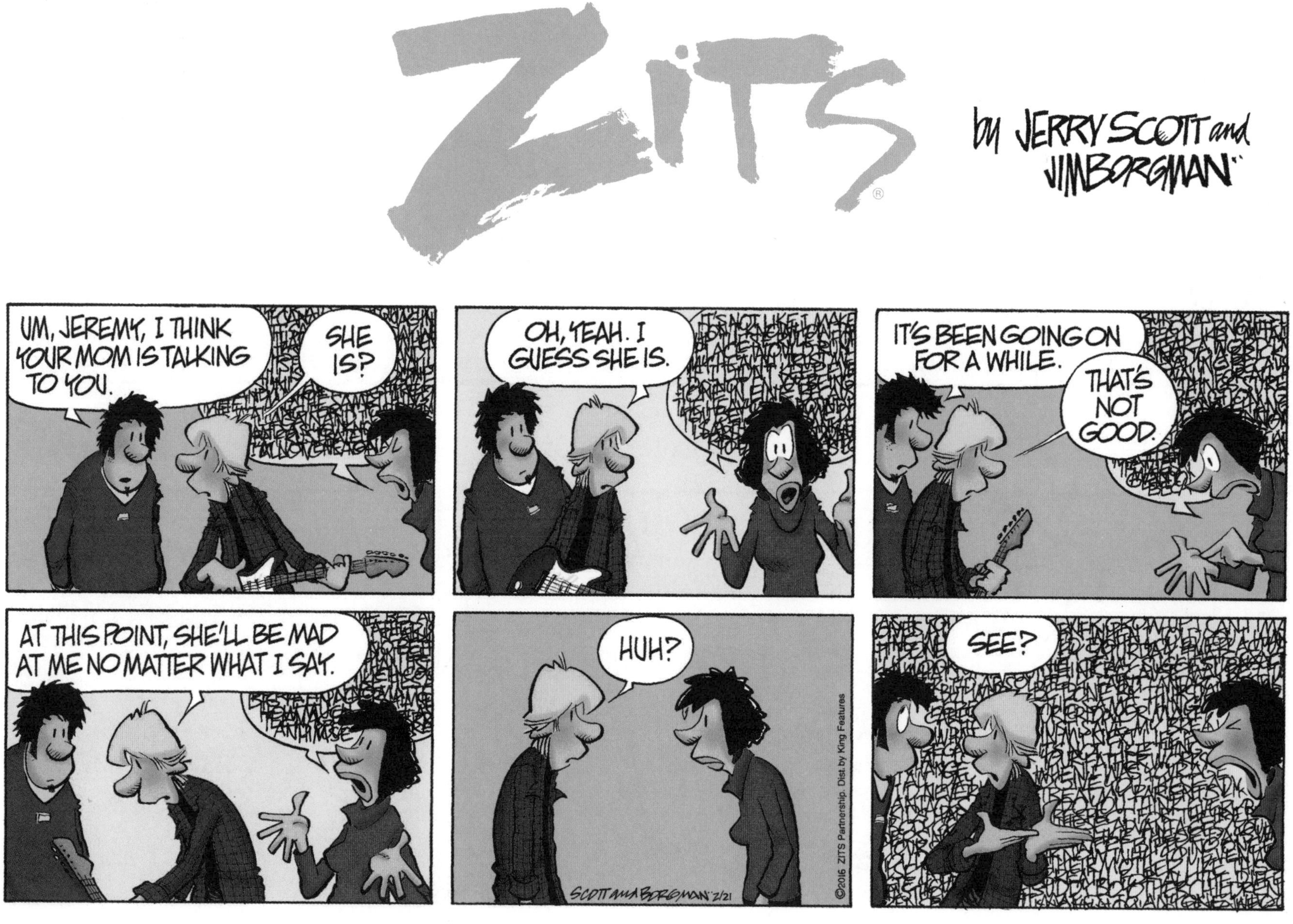
ZITS
by JERRY SCOTT and JIM BORGMAN
UM, JEREMY, I THINK YOUR MOM IS TALKING TO YOU.
SHE IS?
OH, YEAH. I GUESS SHE IS.
IT'S BEEN GOING ON FOR A WHILE.
THAT'S NOT GOOD.
AT THIS POINT, SHE'LL BE MAD AT ME NO MATTER WHAT I SAY.
HUH?
SEE?
SCOTT and BORGMAN 2/21
©2016 ZITS Partnership. Dist. by King Features

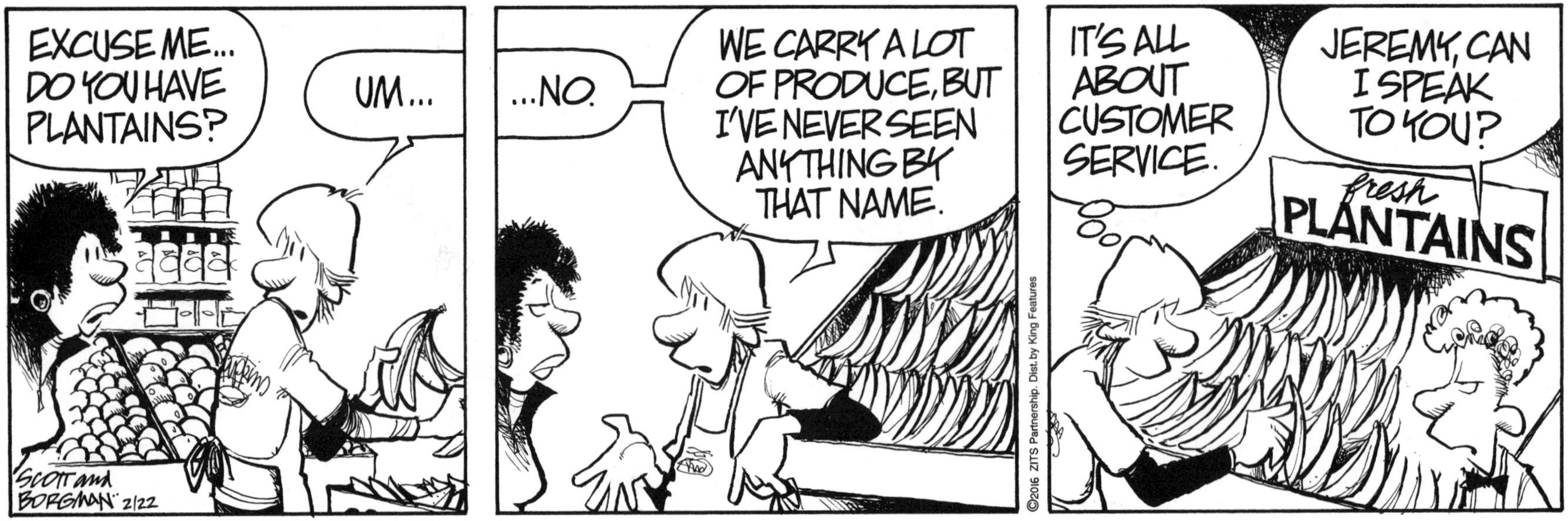
EXCUSE ME... DO YOU HAVE PLANTAINS?
UM...
...NO.
WE CARRY A LOT OF PRODUCE, BUT I'VE NEVER SEEN ANYTHING BY THAT NAME.
IT'S ALL ABOUT CUSTOMER SERVICE.
JEREMY, CAN I SPEAK TO YOU?
fresh PLANTAINS
SCOTT and BORGMAN 2/22
©2016 ZITS Partnership. Dist. by King Features

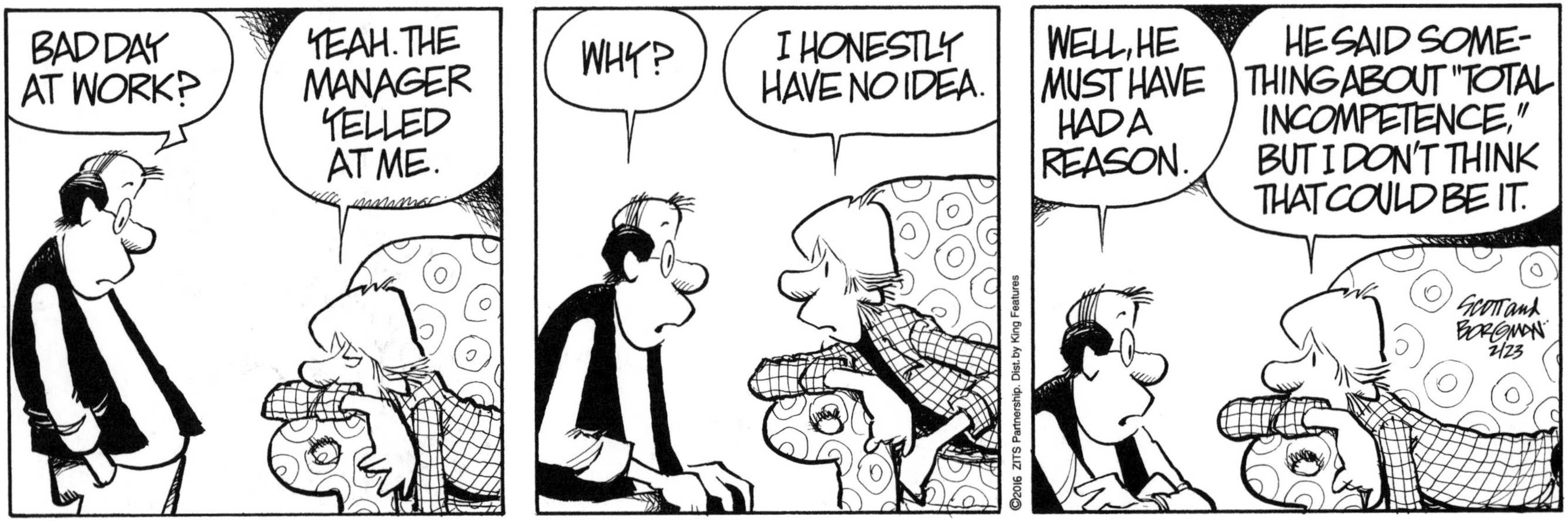
BAD DAY AT WORK?
YEAH. THE MANAGER YELLED AT ME.
WHY?
I HONESTLY HAVE NO IDEA.
WELL, HE MUST HAVE HAD A REASON.
HE SAID SOMETHING ABOUT "TOTAL INCOMPETENCE," BUT I DON'T THINK THAT COULD BE IT.
SCOTT and BORGMAN 2/23
©2016 ZITS Partnership. Dist. by King Features

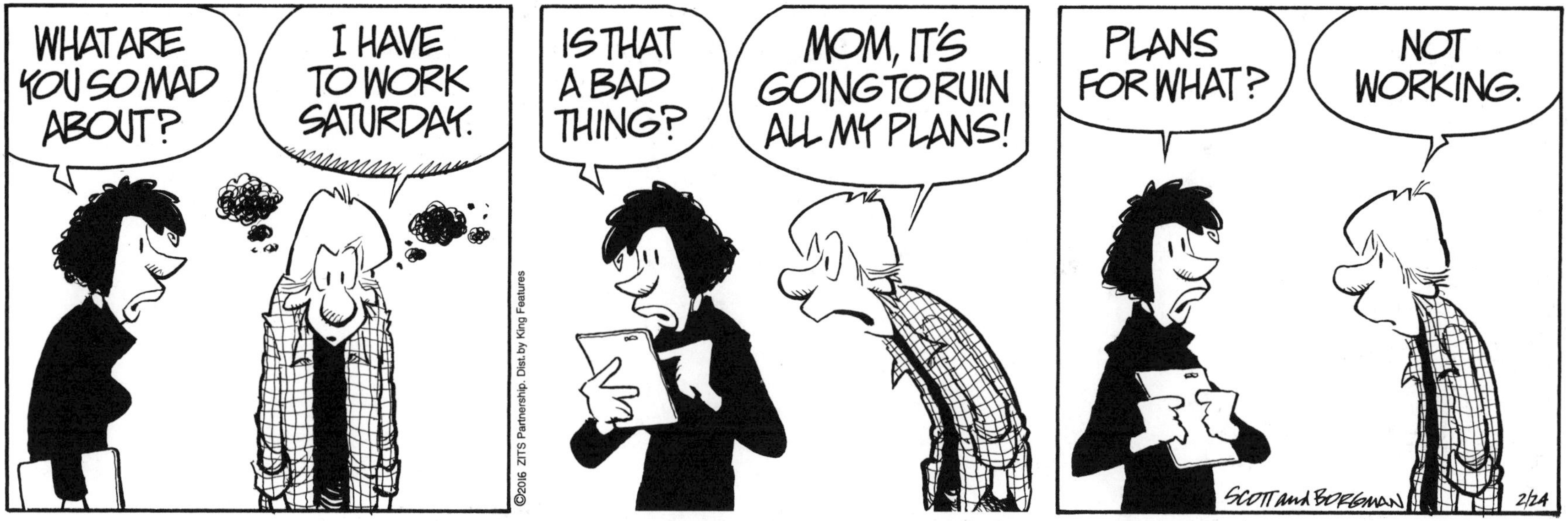
WHAT ARE YOU SO MAD ABOUT?
I HAVE TO WORK SATURDAY.
©2016 ZITS Partnership. Dist. by King Features
IS THAT A BAD THING?
MOM, IT'S GOING TO RUIN ALL MY PLANS!
PLANS FOR WHAT?
NOT WORKING.
SCOTT and BORGMAN
2/24

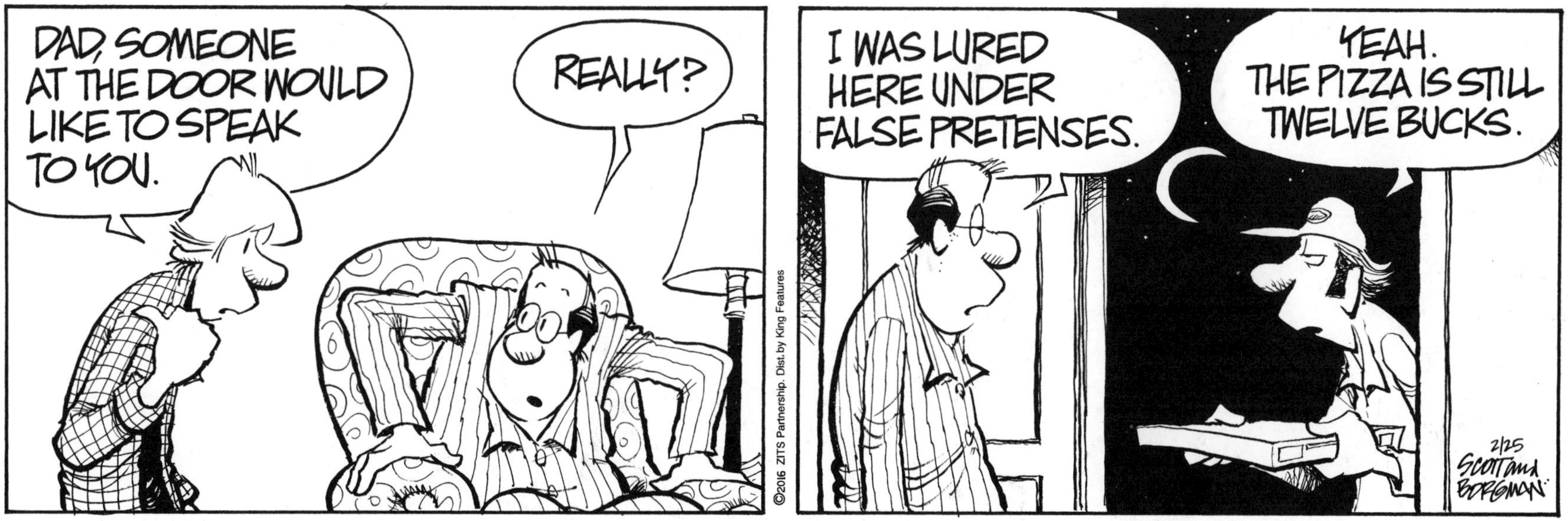
DAD, SOMEONE AT THE DOOR WOULD LIKE TO SPEAK TO YOU.
REALLY?
©2016 ZITS Partnership. Dist. by King Features
I WAS LURED HERE UNDER FALSE PRETENSES.
YEAH. THE PIZZA IS STILL TWELVE BUCKS.
2/25
SCOTT and BORGMAN

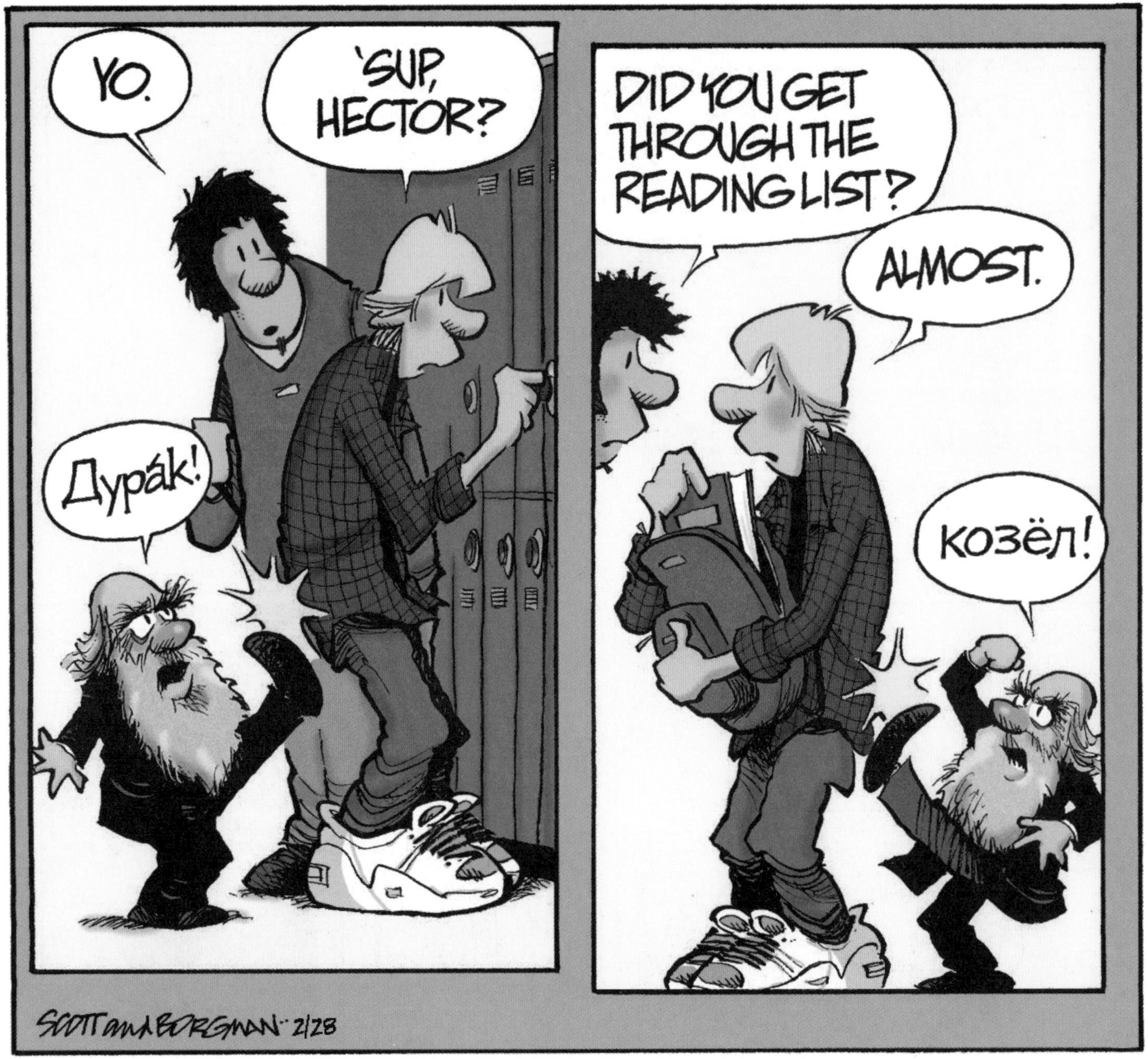

YO.
'SUP, HECTOR?
Дурák!
DID YOU GET THROUGH THE READING LIST?
ALMOST.
КОЗЁЛ!
SCOTT and BORGMAN 2/28

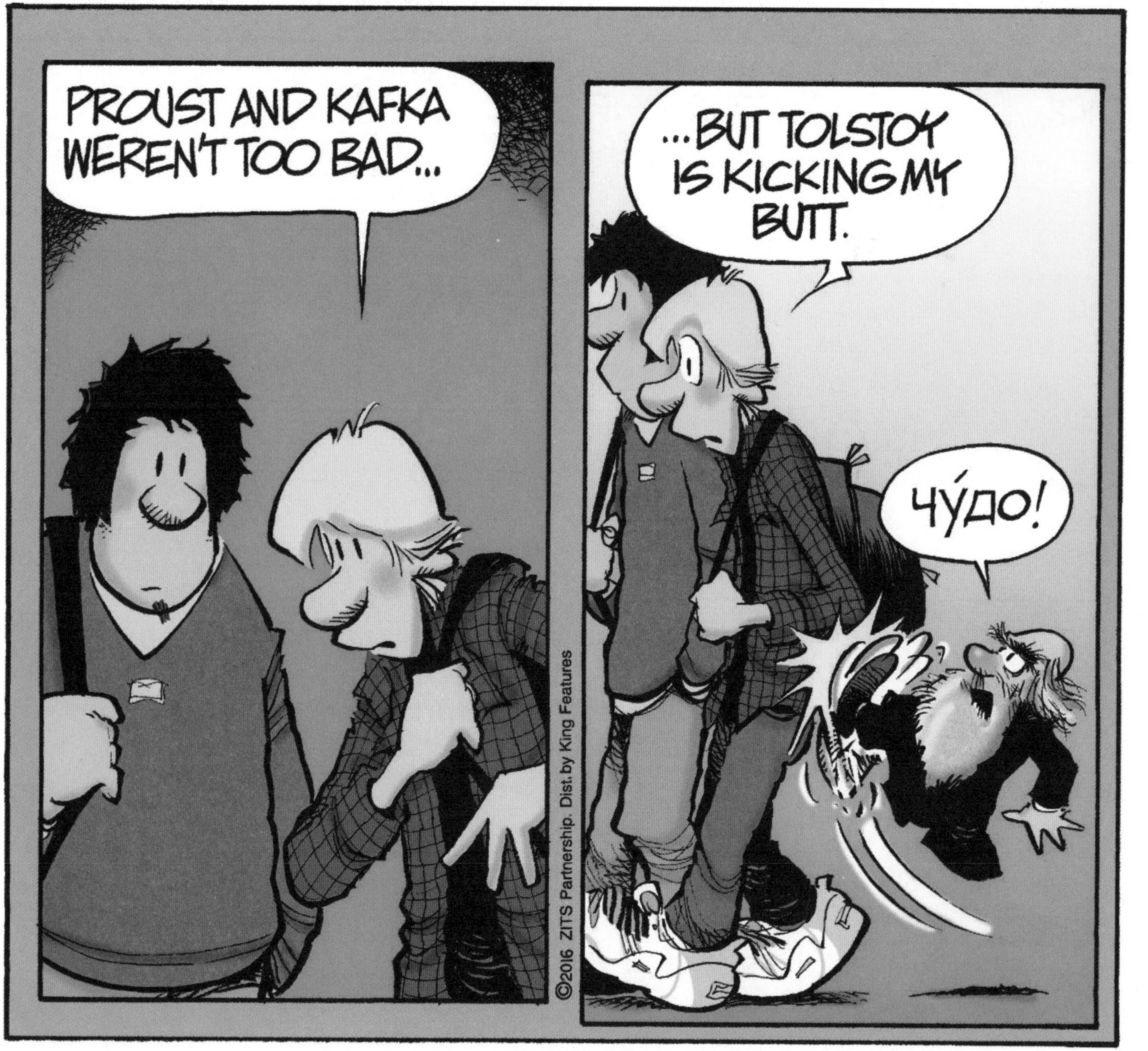
PROUST AND KAFKA WEREN'T TOO BAD...
©2016 ZITS Partnership. Dist. by King Features
...BUT TOLSTOY IS KICKING MY BUTT.
ЧУ́ДО!

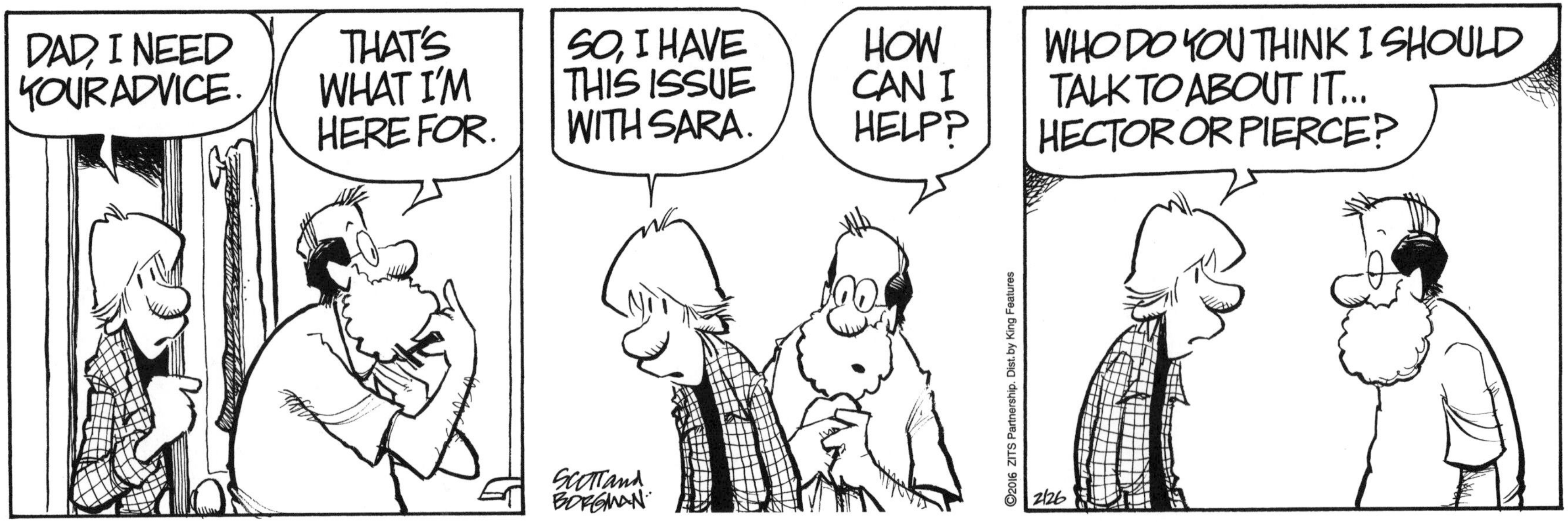
DAD, I NEED YOUR ADVICE.
THAT'S WHAT I'M HERE FOR.
SO, I HAVE THIS ISSUE WITH SARA.
HOW CAN I HELP?
WHO DO YOU THINK I SHOULD TALK TO ABOUT IT... HECTOR OR PIERCE?
SCOTT and BORGMAN
©2016 ZITS Partnership. Dist. by King Features
2/26

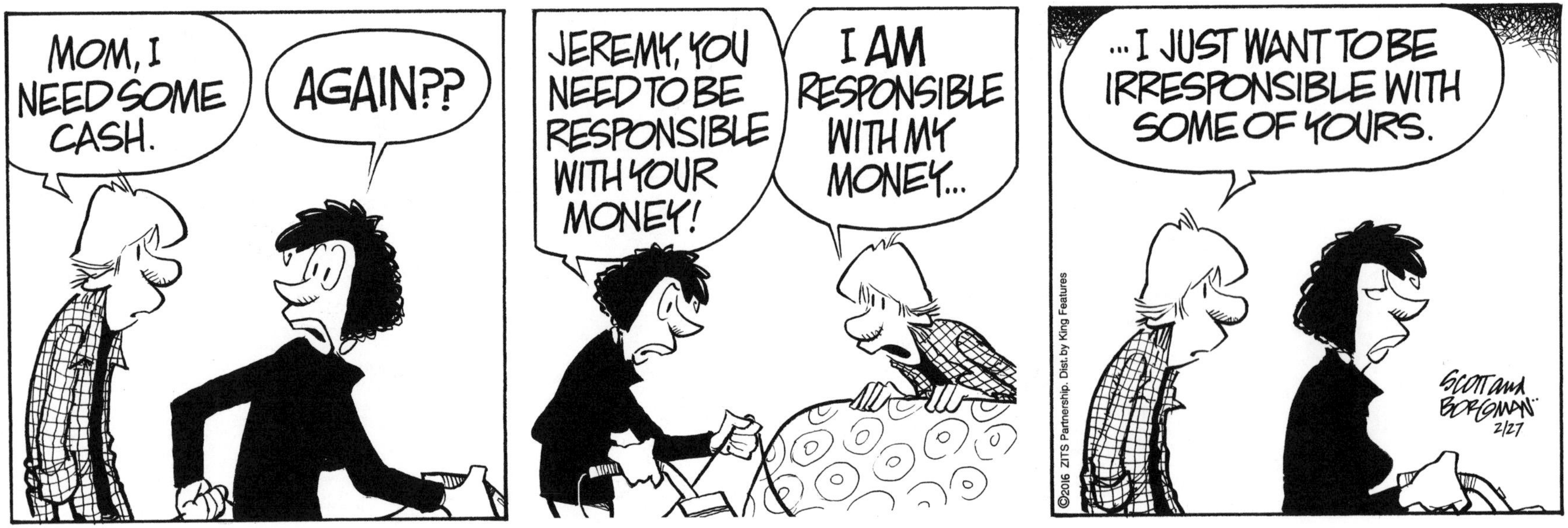
MOM, I NEED SOME CASH.
AGAIN??
JEREMY, YOU NEED TO BE RESPONSIBLE WITH YOUR MONEY!
I AM RESPONSIBLE WITH MY MONEY...
...I JUST WANT TO BE IRRESPONSIBLE WITH SOME OF YOURS.
©2016 ZITS Partnership. Dist. by King Features
SCOTT and BORGMAN
2/27

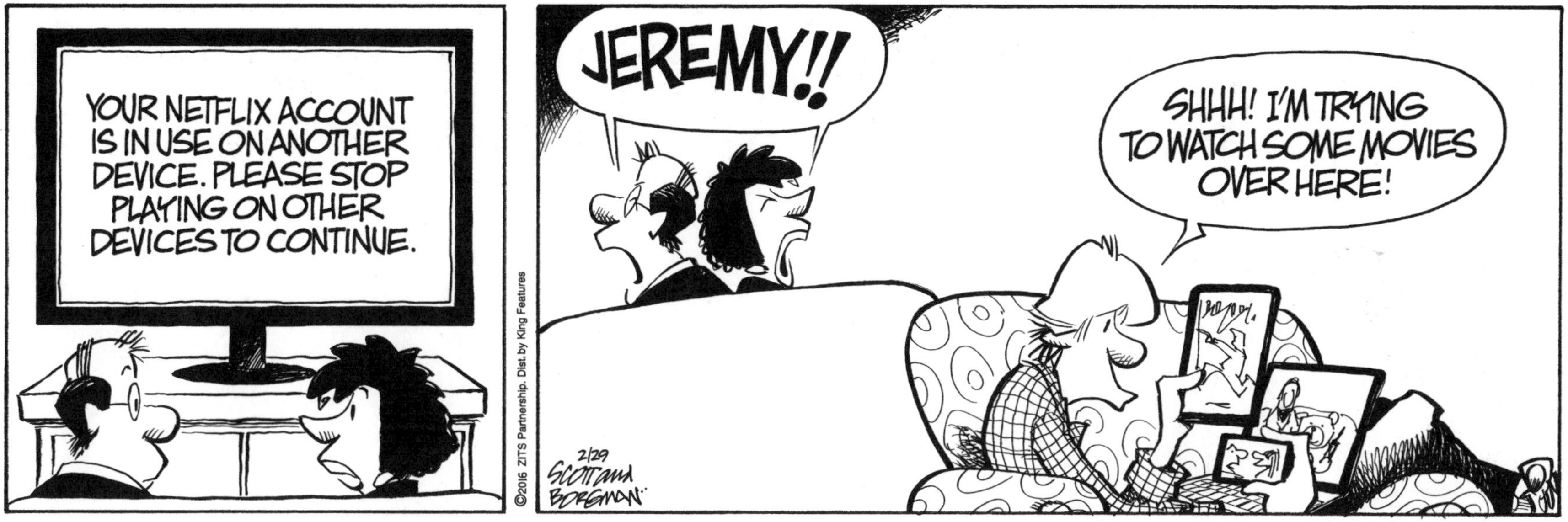
YOUR NETFLIX ACCOUNT IS IN USE ON ANOTHER DEVICE. PLEASE STOP PLAYING ON OTHER DEVICES TO CONTINUE.
JEREMY!!
SHHH! I'M TRYING TO WATCH SOME MOVIES OVER HERE!
2/29 SCOTT and BORGMAN
©2016 ZITS Partnership. Dist. by King Features

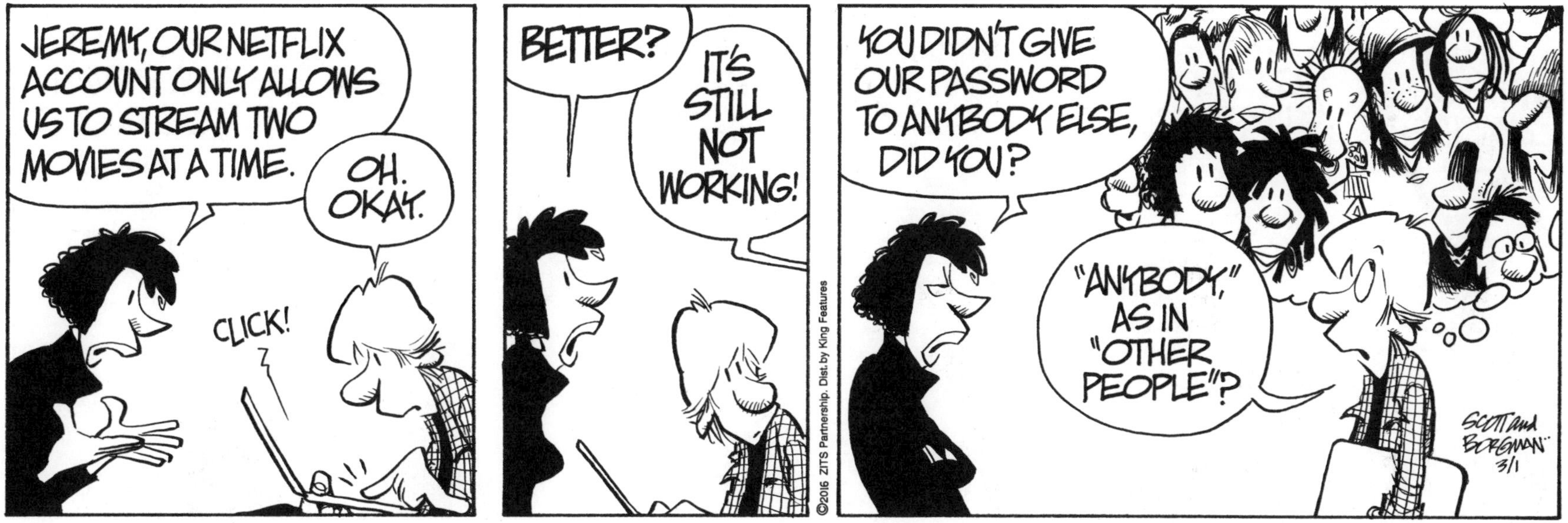
JEREMY, OUR NETFLIX ACCOUNT ONLY ALLOWS US TO STREAM TWO MOVIES AT A TIME.
OH. OKAY.
CLICK!
BETTER?
IT'S STILL NOT WORKING!
©2016 ZITS Partnership. Dist. by King Features
YOU DIDN'T GIVE OUR PASSWORD TO ANYBODY ELSE, DID YOU?
"ANYBODY," AS IN "OTHER PEOPLE"?
SCOTT and BORGMAN 3/1

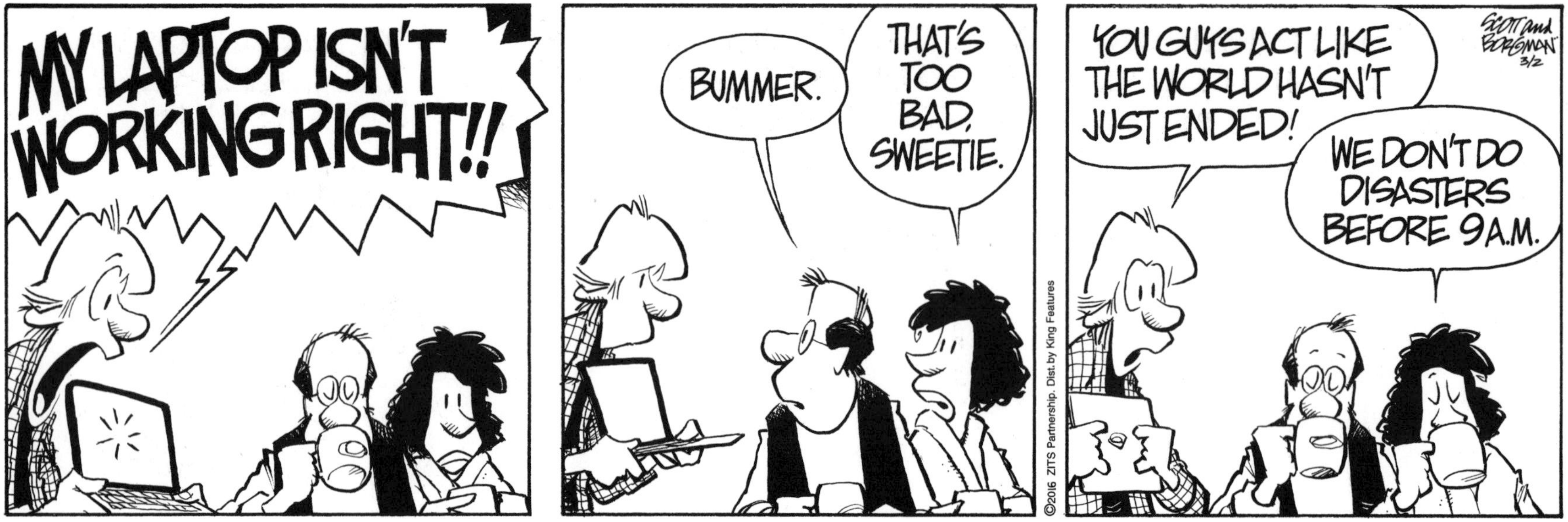
MY LAPTOP ISN'T WORKING RIGHT!!
BUMMER.
THAT'S TOO BAD, SWEETIE.
YOU GUYS ACT LIKE THE WORLD HASN'T JUST ENDED!
WE DON'T DO DISASTERS BEFORE 9 A.M.
SCOTT and BORGMAN 3/2
©2016 ZITS Partnership. Dist. by King Features

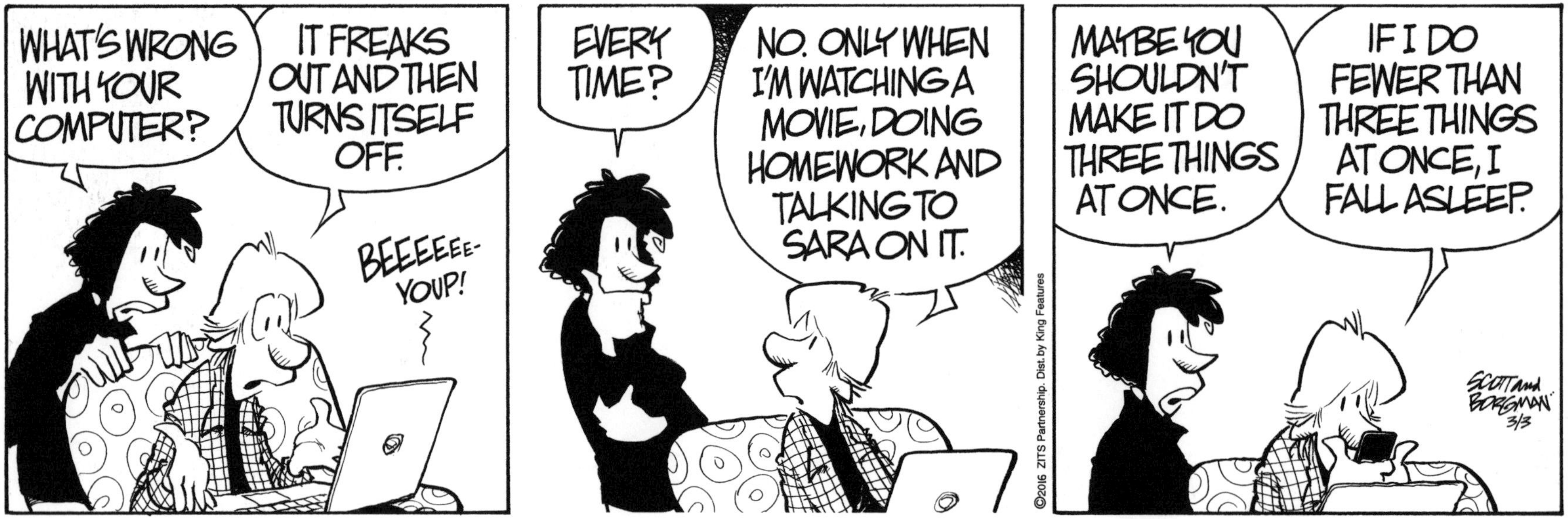
WHAT'S WRONG WITH YOUR COMPUTER?
IT FREAKS OUT AND THEN TURNS ITSELF OFF.
BEEEEEEE-YOUP!
EVERY TIME?
NO. ONLY WHEN I'M WATCHING A MOVIE, DOING HOMEWORK AND TALKING TO SARA ON IT.
MAYBE YOU SHOULDN'T MAKE IT DO THREE THINGS AT ONCE.
IF I DO FEWER THAN THREE THINGS AT ONCE, I FALL ASLEEP.
SCOTT and BORGMAN 3/3
©2016 ZITS Partnership. Dist. by King Features

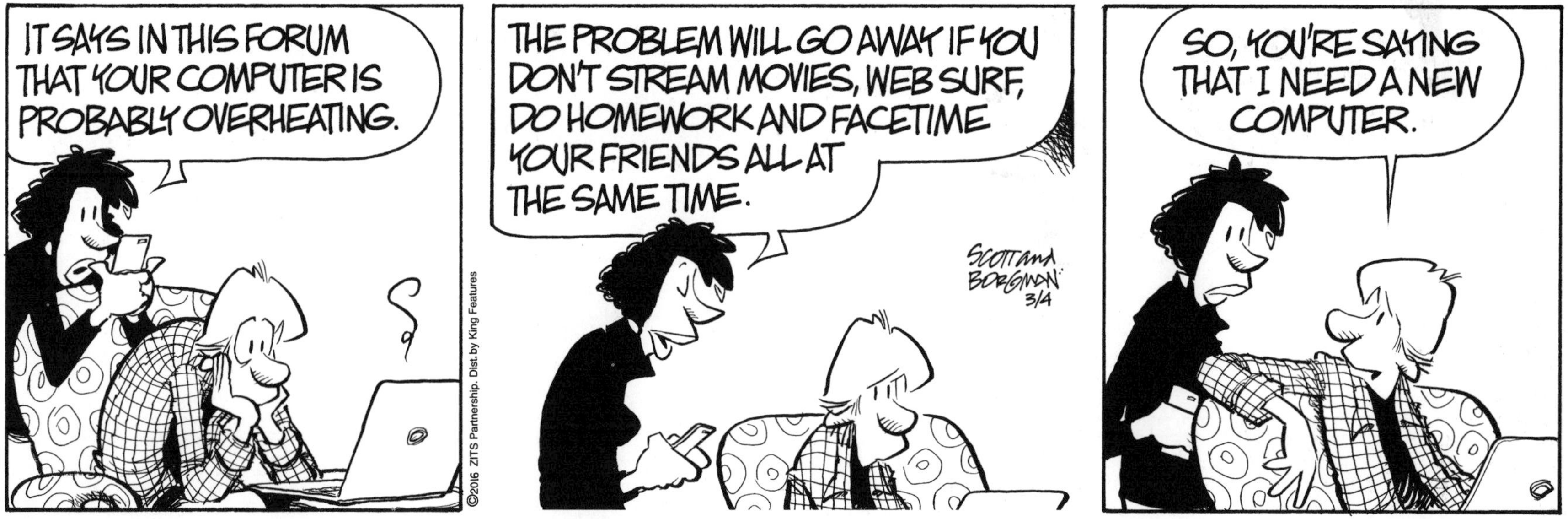
IT SAYS IN THIS FORUM THAT YOUR COMPUTER IS PROBABLY OVERHEATING.
THE PROBLEM WILL GO AWAY IF YOU DON'T STREAM MOVIES, WEB SURF, DO HOMEWORK AND FACETIME YOUR FRIENDS ALL AT THE SAME TIME.
SO, YOU'RE SAYING THAT I NEED A NEW COMPUTER.
©2016 ZITS Partnership. Dist. by King Features
SCOTT and BORGMAN 3/4

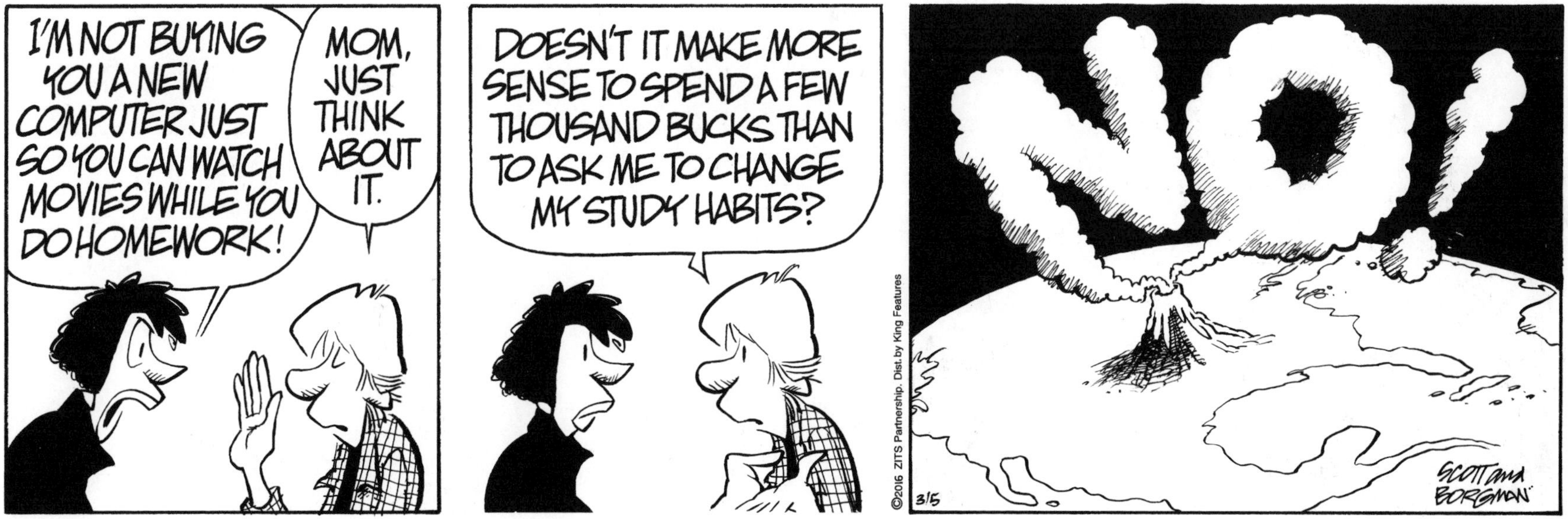
I'M NOT BUYING YOU A NEW COMPUTER JUST SO YOU CAN WATCH MOVIES WHILE YOU DO HOMEWORK!
MOM, JUST THINK ABOUT IT.
DOESN'T IT MAKE MORE SENSE TO SPEND A FEW THOUSAND BUCKS THAN TO ASK ME TO CHANGE MY STUDY HABITS?
NO!
©2016 ZITS Partnership. Dist. by King Features
3/5
SCOTT and BORGMAN

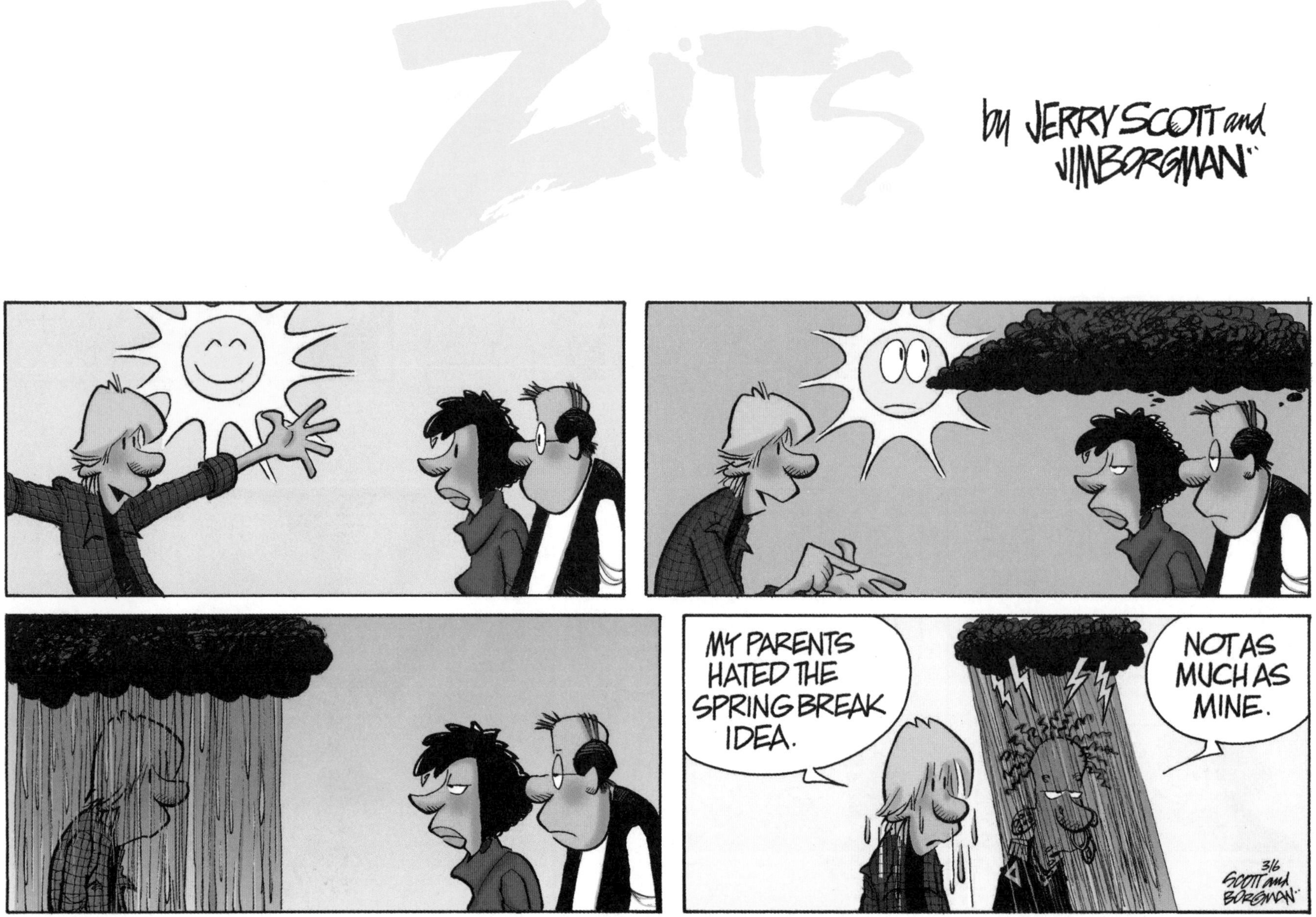
ZITS
by JERRY SCOTT and JIM BORGMAN
MY PARENTS HATED THE SPRING BREAK IDEA.
NOT AS MUCH AS MINE.
3/6 SCOTT and BORGMAN

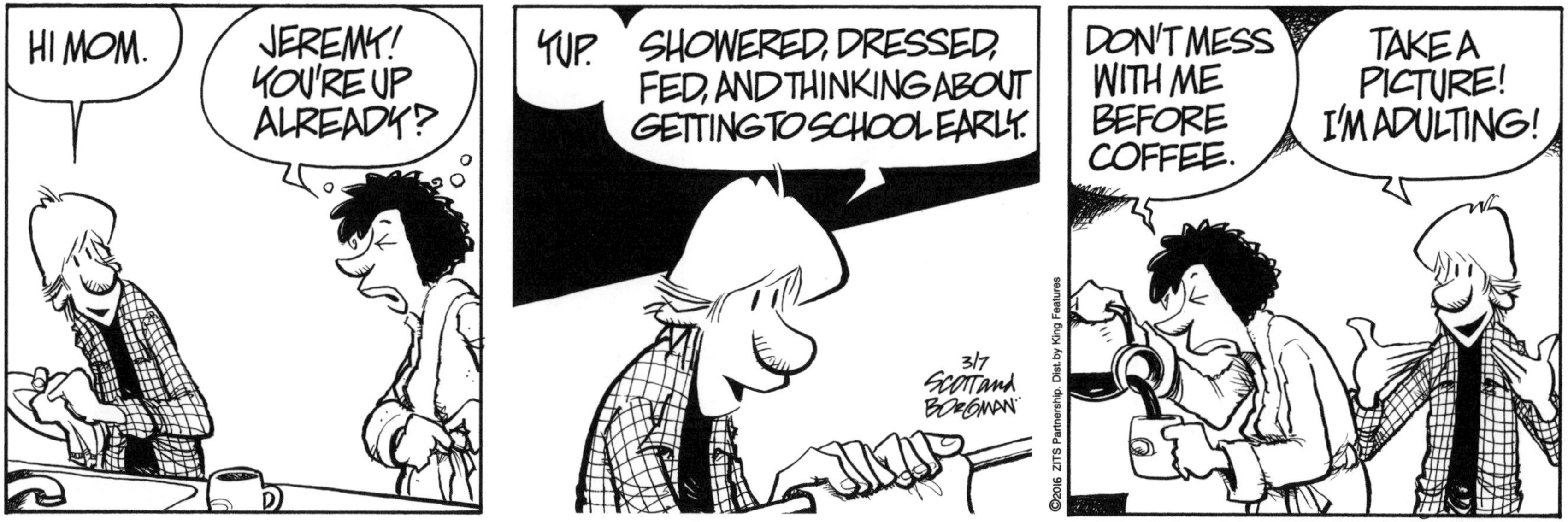
HI MOM.
JEREMY! YOU'RE UP ALREADY?
YUP.
SHOWERED, DRESSED, FED, AND THINKING ABOUT GETTING TO SCHOOL EARLY.
3/7 SCOTT and BORGMAN
©2016 ZITS Partnership. Dist. by King Features
DON'T MESS WITH ME BEFORE COFFEE.
TAKE A PICTURE! I'M ADULTING!

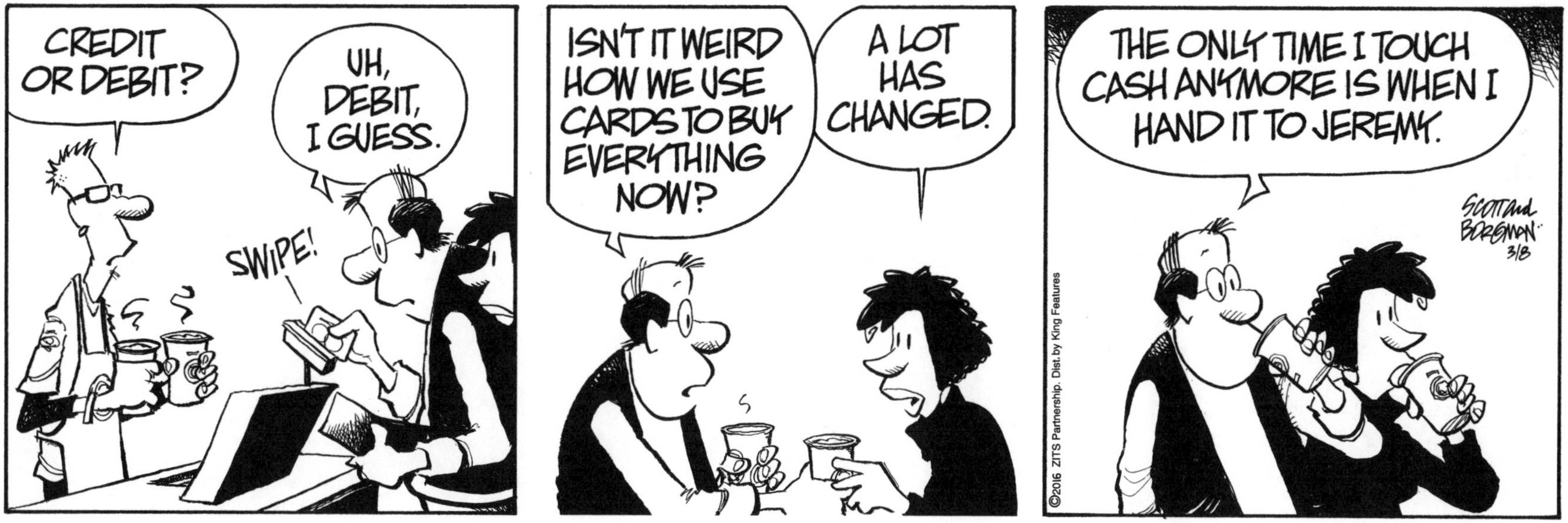
CREDIT OR DEBIT?
UH, DEBIT, I GUESS.
SWIPE!
ISN'T IT WEIRD HOW WE USE CARDS TO BUY EVERYTHING NOW?
A LOT HAS CHANGED.
©2016 ZITS Partnership. Dist. by King Features
THE ONLY TIME I TOUCH CASH ANYMORE IS WHEN I HAND IT TO JEREMY.
SCOTT and BORGMAN 3/8

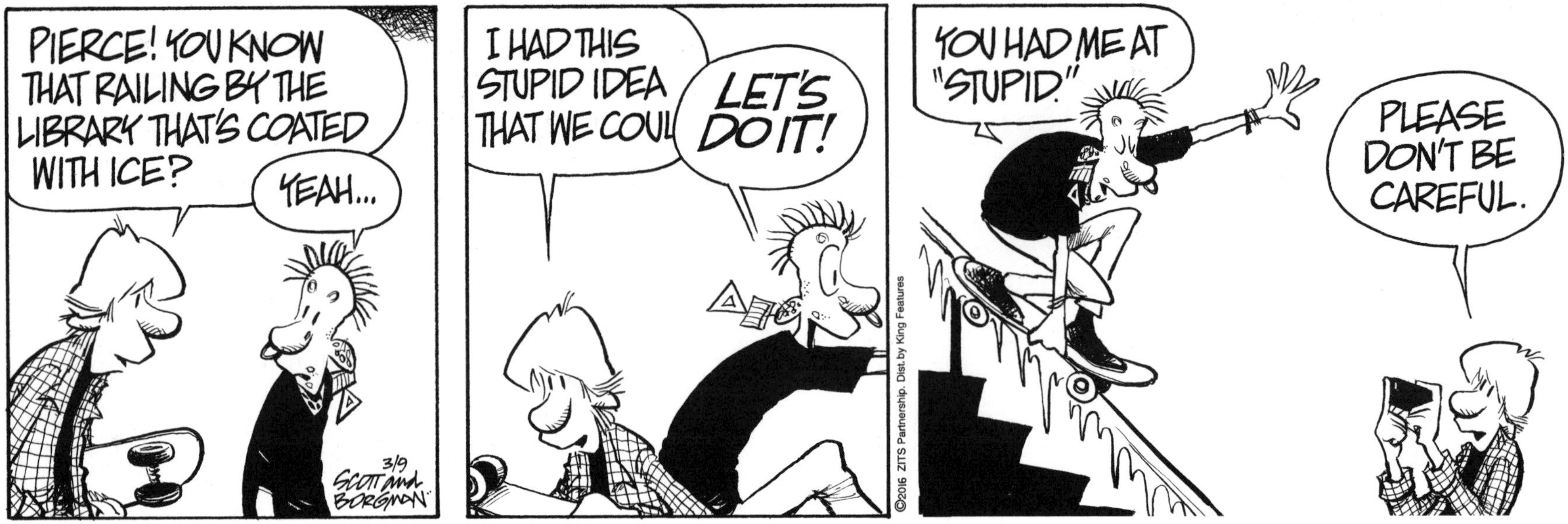
PIERCE! YOU KNOW THAT RAILING BY THE LIBRARY THAT'S COATED WITH ICE?
YEAH...
3/9 SCOTT and BORGMAN
I HAD THIS STUPID IDEA THAT WE COUL
LET'S DO IT!
©2016 ZITS Partnership. Dist. by King Features
YOU HAD ME AT "STUPID."
PLEASE DON'T BE CAREFUL.

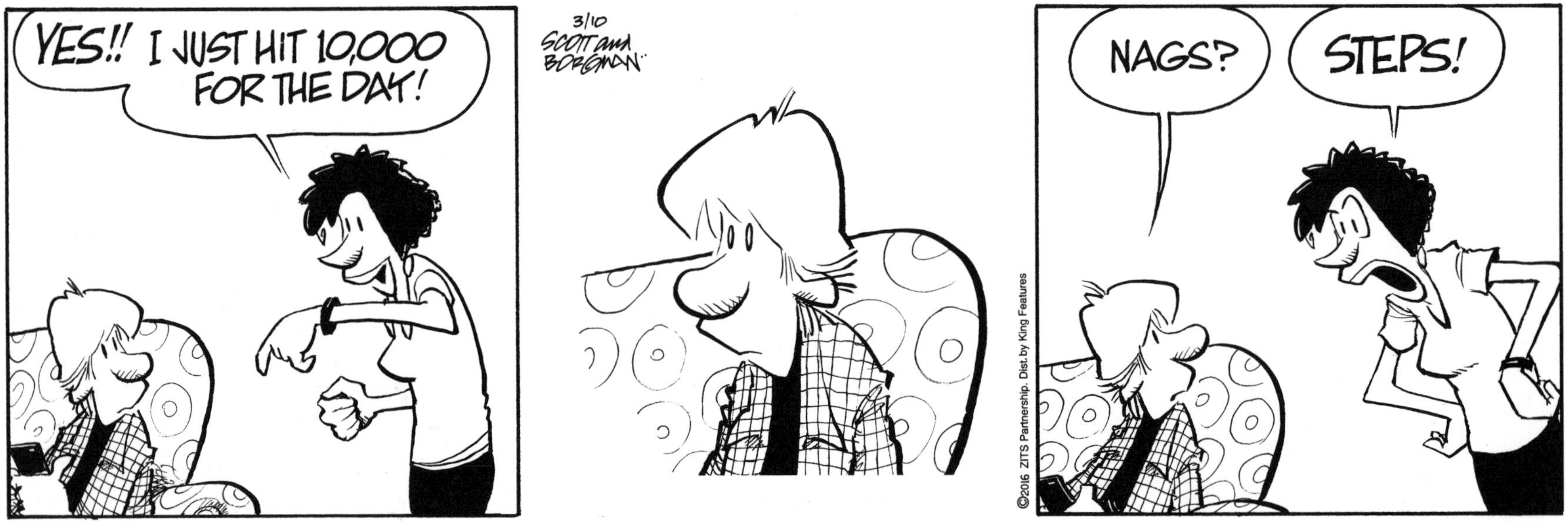
YES!! I JUST HIT 10,000 FOR THE DAY!
3/10 SCOTT and BORGMAN
NAGS?
STEPS!
©2016 ZITS Partnership. Dist. by King Features

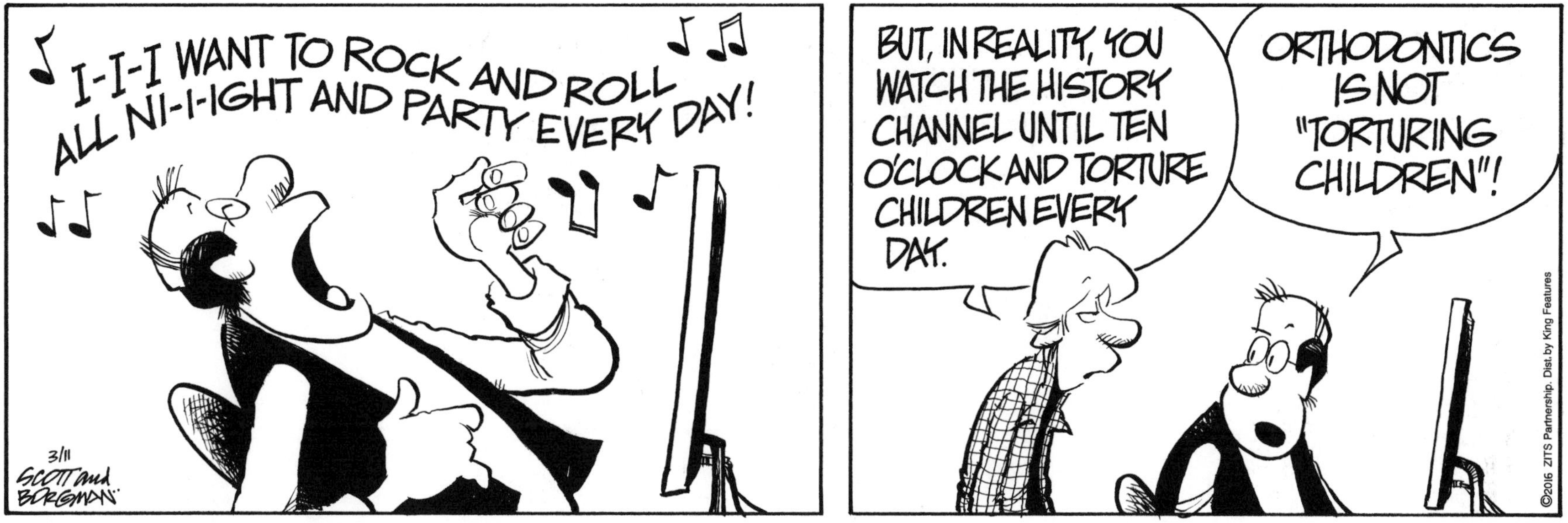
I-I-I WANT TO ROCK AND ROLL ALL NI-I-IGHT AND PARTY EVERY DAY!
3/11 SCOTT and BORGMAN
BUT, IN REALITY, YOU WATCH THE HISTORY CHANNEL UNTIL TEN O'CLOCK AND TORTURE CHILDREN EVERY DAY.
ORTHODONTICS IS NOT "TORTURING CHILDREN"!
©2016 ZITS Partnership. Dist. by King Features

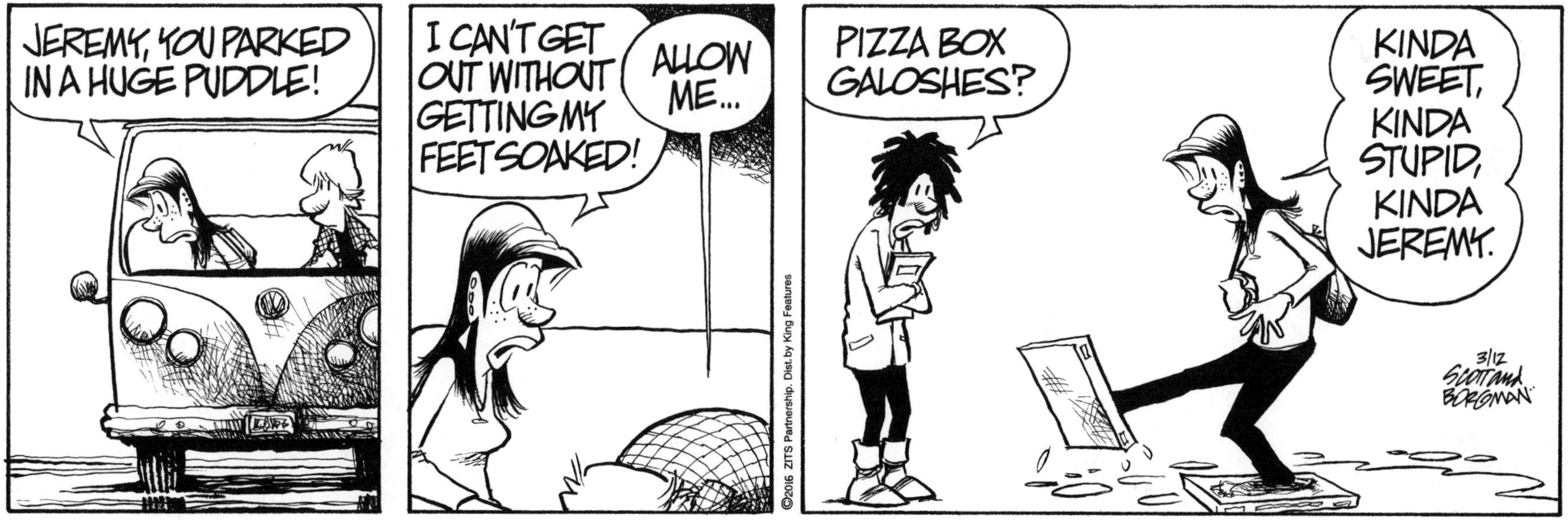
JEREMY, YOU PARKED IN A HUGE PUDDLE!
I CAN'T GET OUT WITHOUT GETTING MY FEET SOAKED!
ALLOW ME...
©2016 ZITS Partnership. Dist. by King Features
PIZZA BOX GALOSHES?
KINDA SWEET, KINDA STUPID, KINDA JEREMY.
3/12 SCOTT and BORGMAN

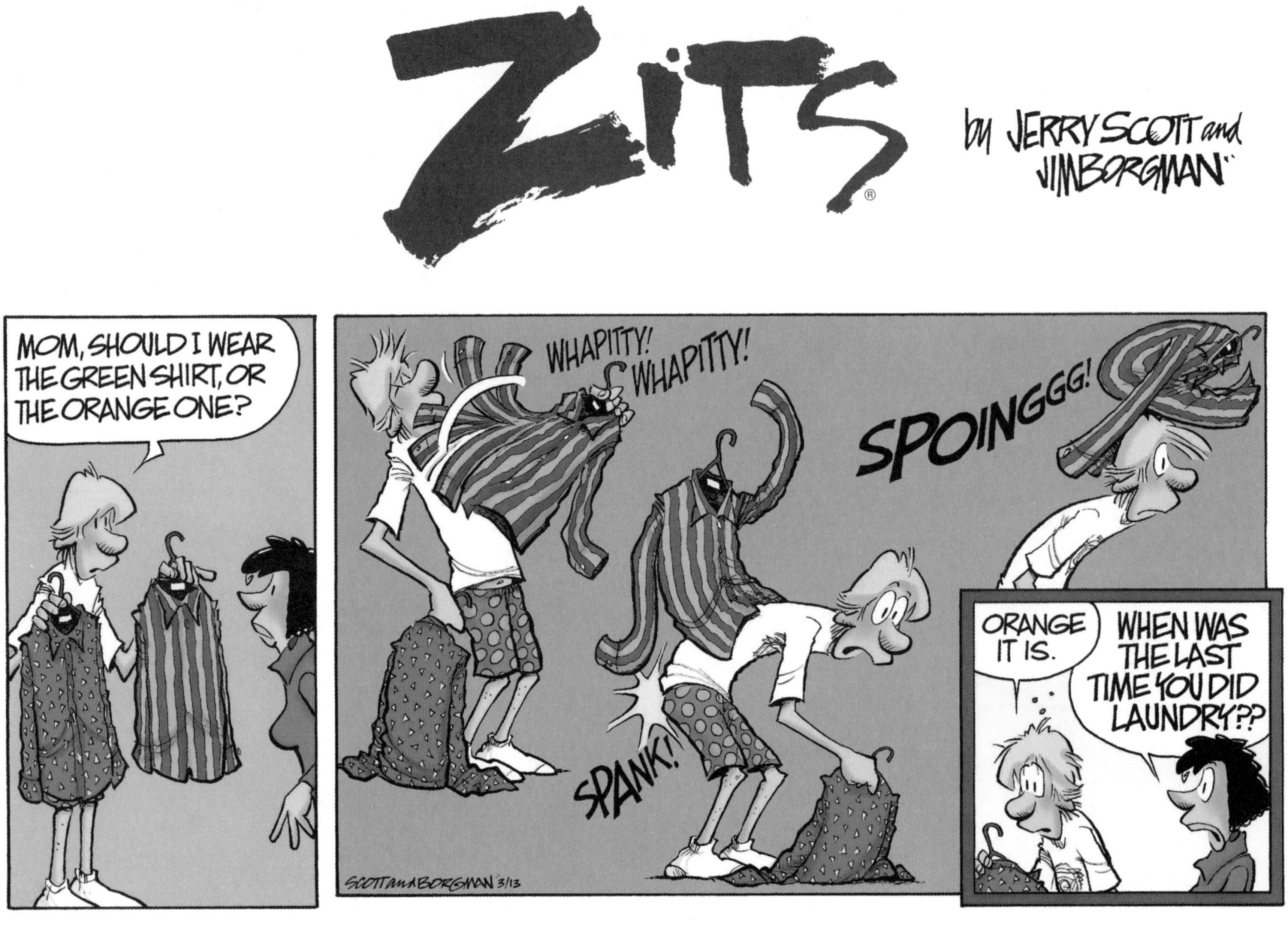
ZITS
by JERRY SCOTT and JIM BORGMAN
MOM, SHOULD I WEAR THE GREEN SHIRT, OR THE ORANGE ONE?
WHAPITTY! WHAPITTY!
SPANK!
SPOINGGG!
SCOTT and BORGMAN 3/13
ORANGE IT IS.
WHEN WAS THE LAST TIME YOU DID LAUNDRY??

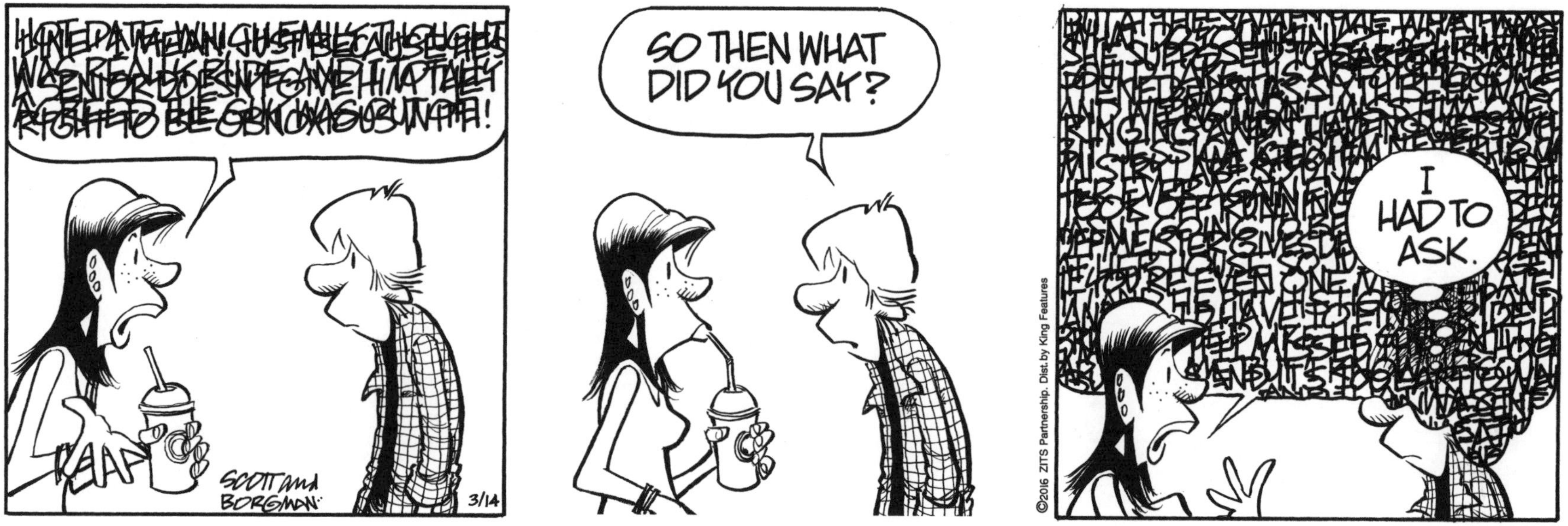
SO THEN WHAT DID YOU SAY?
I HAD TO ASK.
SCOTT and BORGMAN
3/14
©2016 ZITS Partnership. Dist. by King Features

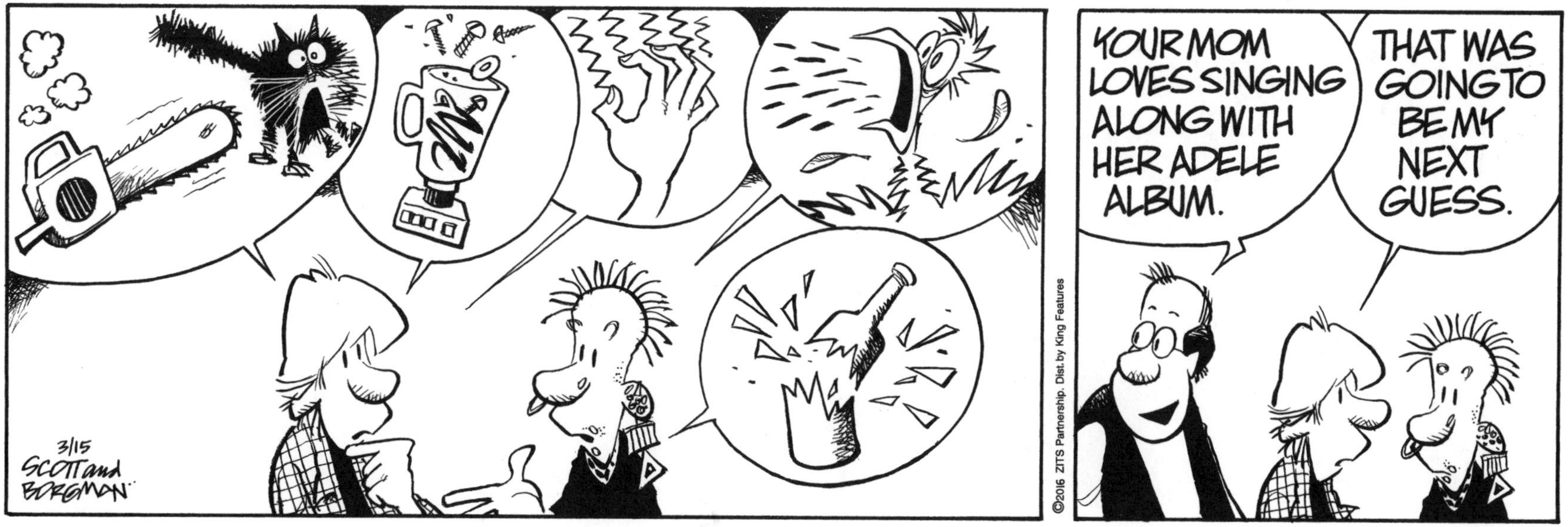
3/15
SCOTT and BORGMAN
©2016 ZITS Partnership. Dist. by King Features
YOUR MOM LOVES SINGING ALONG WITH HER ADELE ALBUM.
THAT WAS GOING TO BE MY NEXT GUESS.

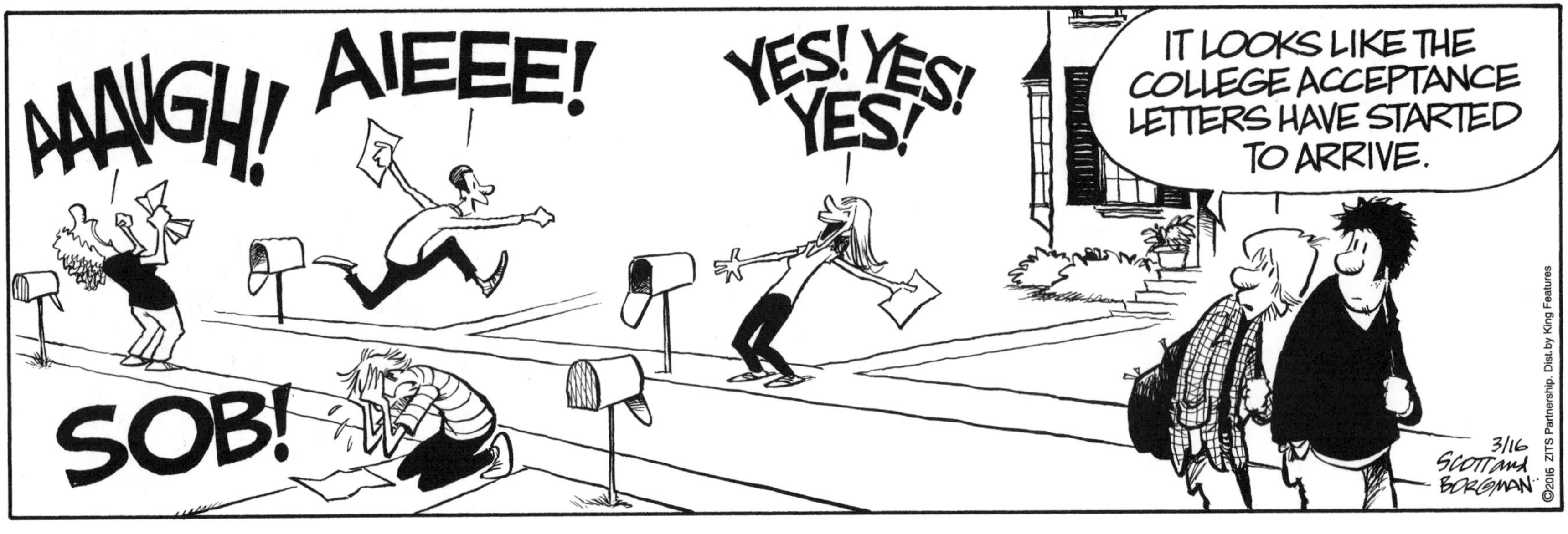
AAAUGH!
AIEEE!
SOB!
YES! YES! YES!
IT LOOKS LIKE THE COLLEGE ACCEPTANCE LETTERS HAVE STARTED TO ARRIVE.
3/16 SCOTT and BORGMAN
©2016 ZITS Partnership. Dist. by King Features

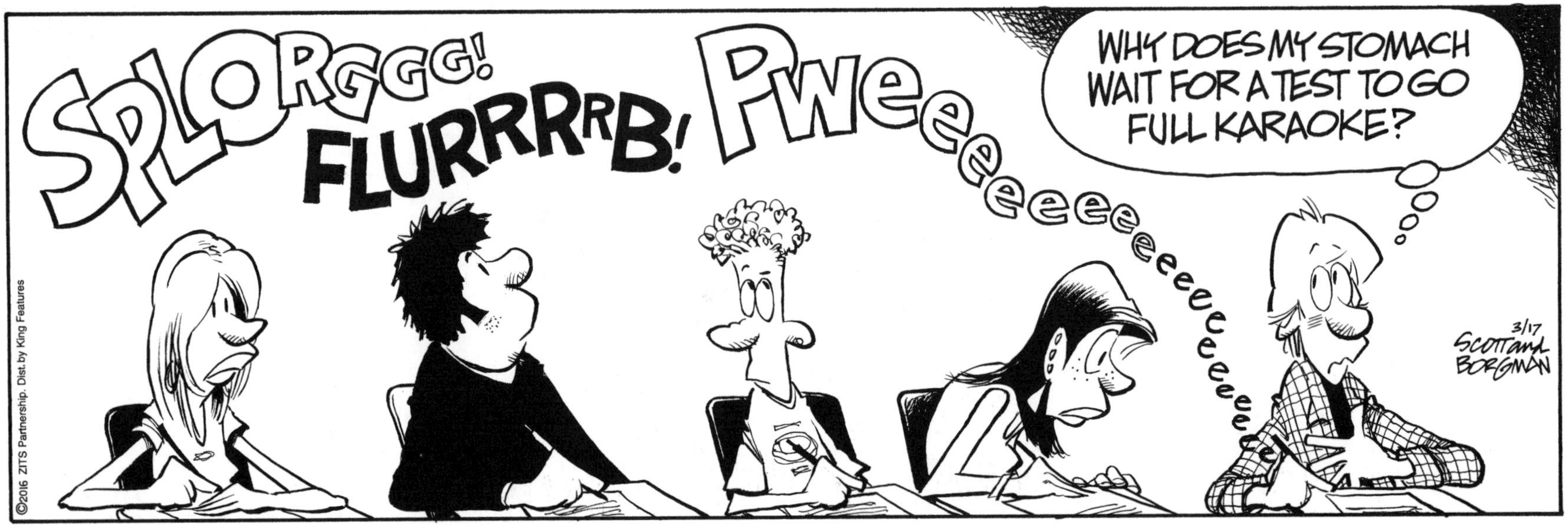
SPLORGGG!
FLURRRRRB!
PWeeeeeeeeeeeeeeeeeee
WHY DOES MY STOMACH WAIT FOR A TEST TO GO FULL KARAOKE?
3/17 SCOTT and BORGMAN
©2016 ZITS Partnership. Dist. by King Features

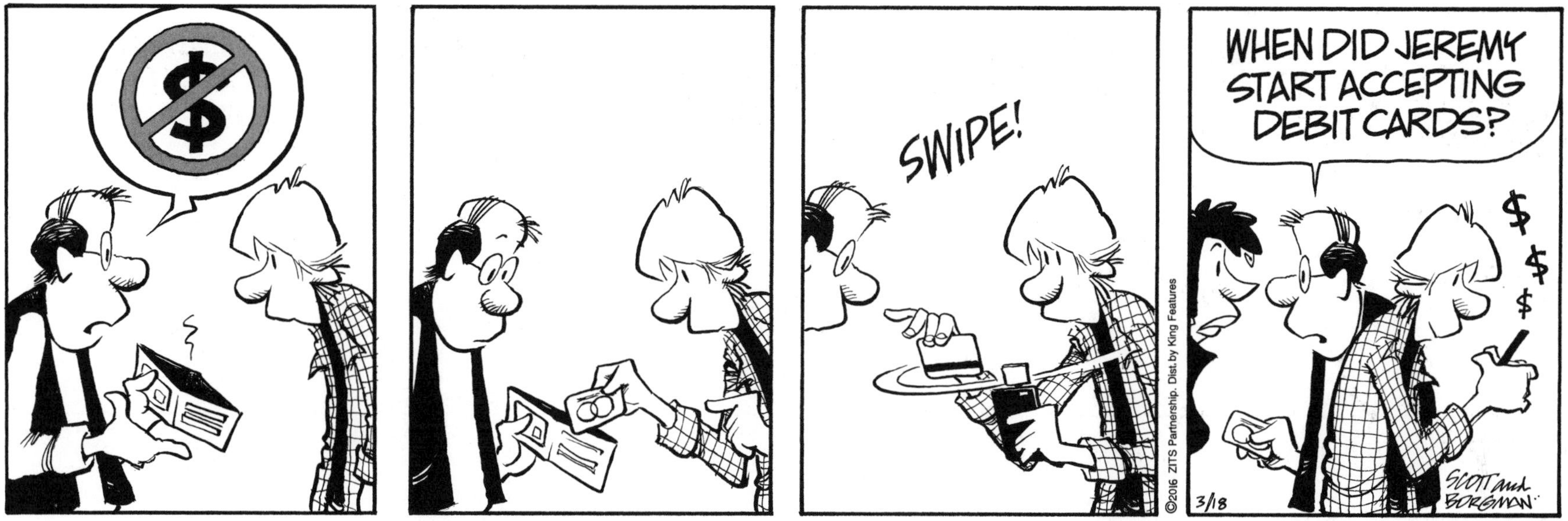
SWIPE!
WHEN DID JEREMY START ACCEPTING DEBIT CARDS?
©2016 ZITS Partnership. Dist. by King Features
3/18
SCOTT and BORGMAN

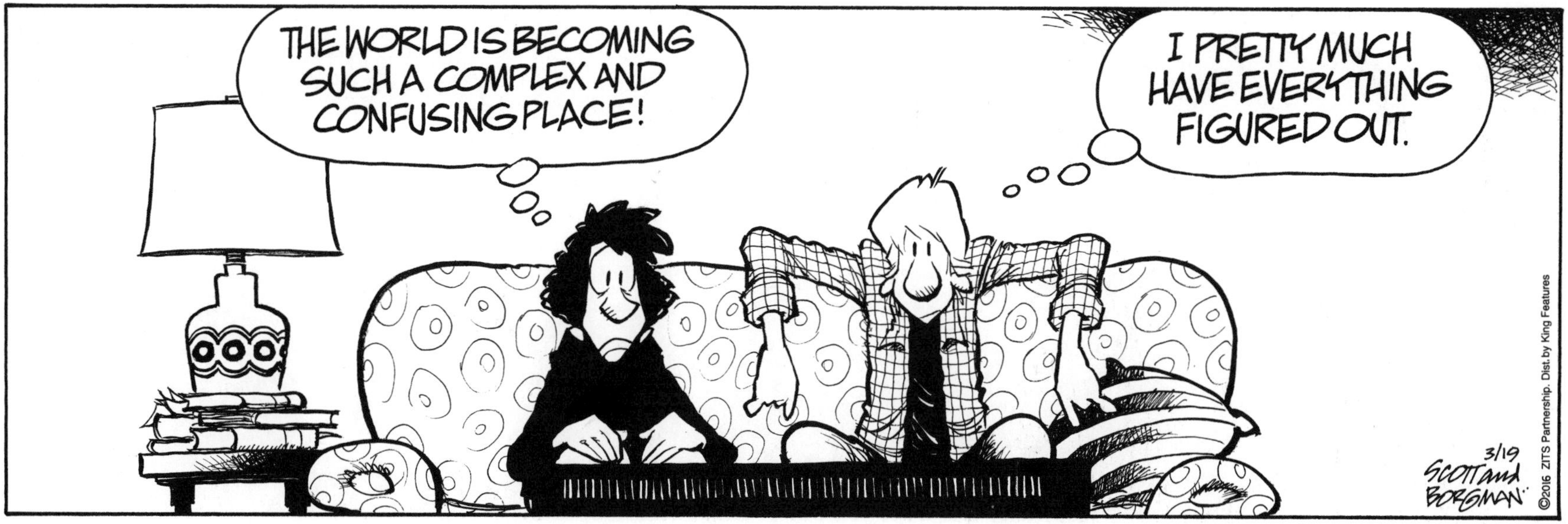
THE WORLD IS BECOMING SUCH A COMPLEX AND CONFUSING PLACE!
I PRETTY MUCH HAVE EVERYTHING FIGURED OUT.
3/19
SCOTT and BORGMAN
©2016 ZITS Partnership. Dist. by King Features

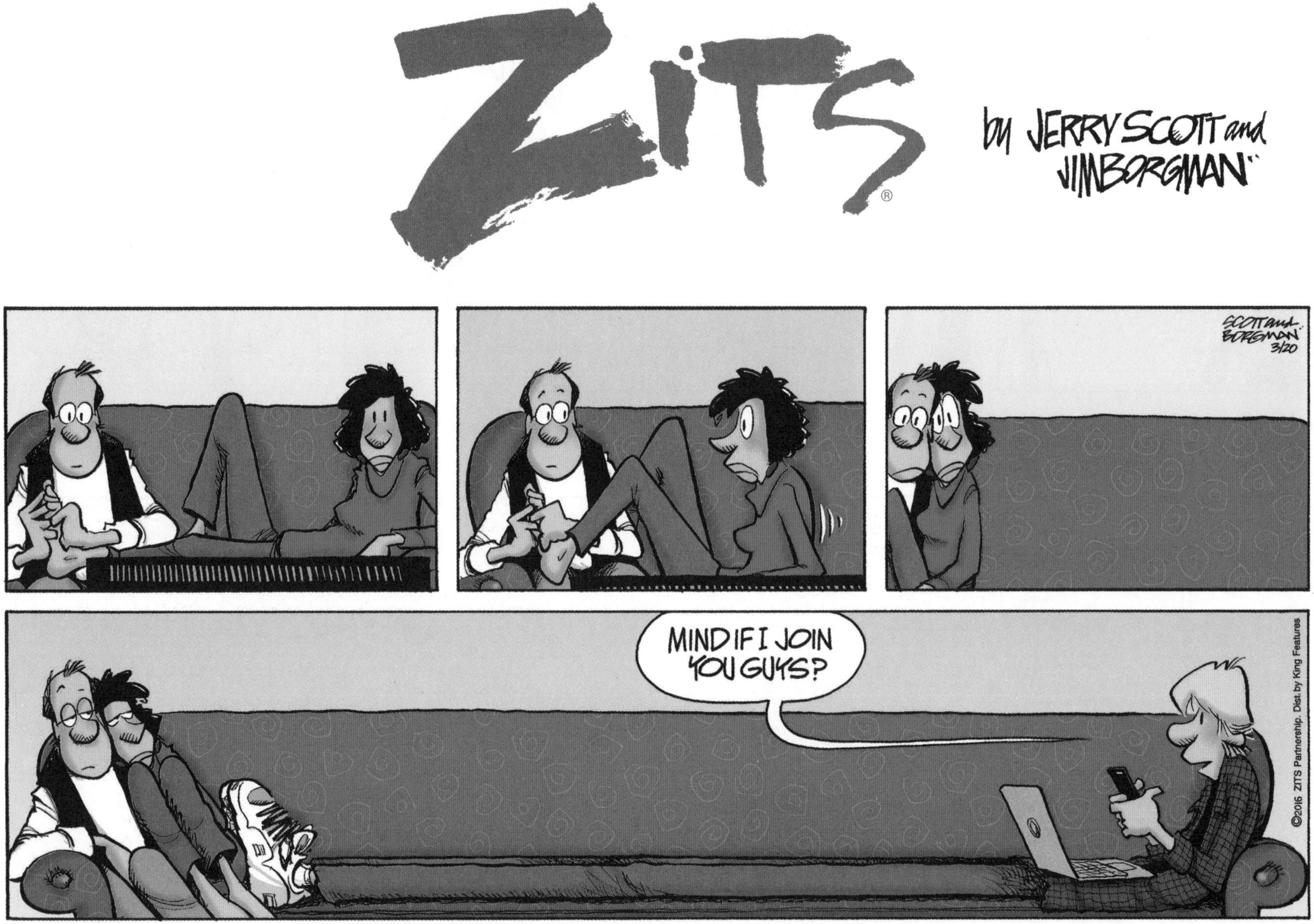
ZITS®
by JERRY SCOTT and JIM BORGMAN
SCOTT and BORGMAN 3/20
MIND IF I JOIN YOU GUYS?
©2016 ZITS Partnership. Dist. by King Features

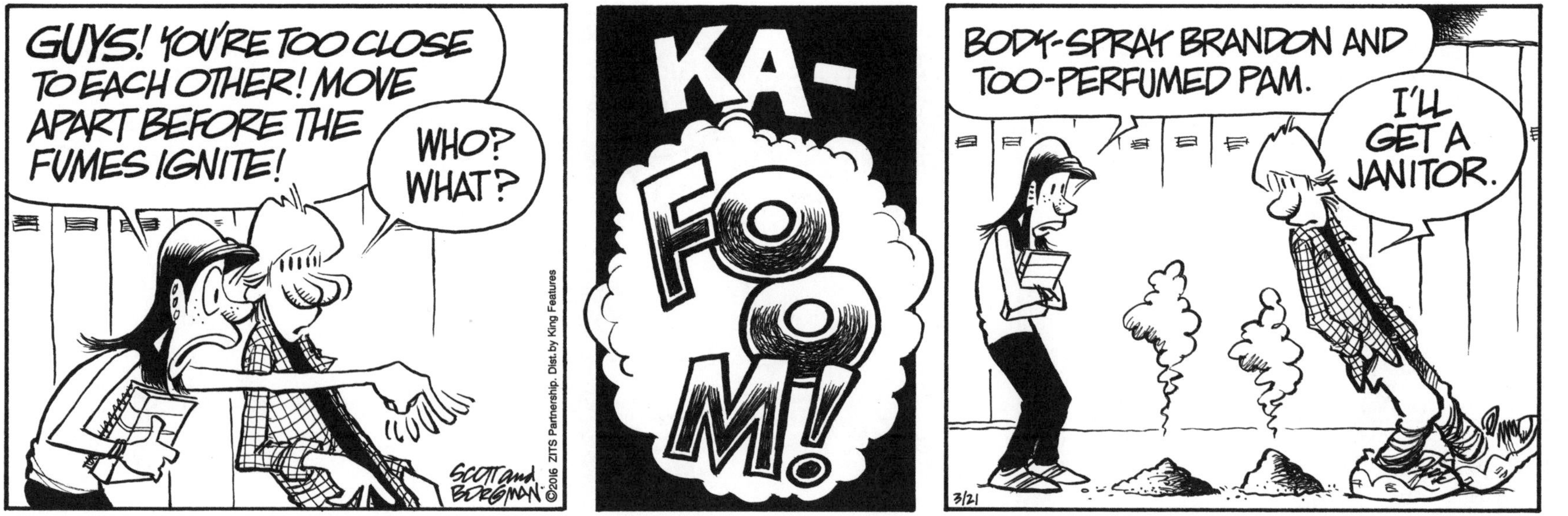
GUYS! YOU'RE TOO CLOSE TO EACH OTHER! MOVE APART BEFORE THE FUMES IGNITE!
WHO? WHAT?
SCOTT and BORGMAN
©2016 ZITS Partnership. Dist. by King Features
KA-FOOOM!
BODY-SPRAY BRANDON AND TOO-PERFUMED PAM.
I'LL GET A JANITOR.
3/21

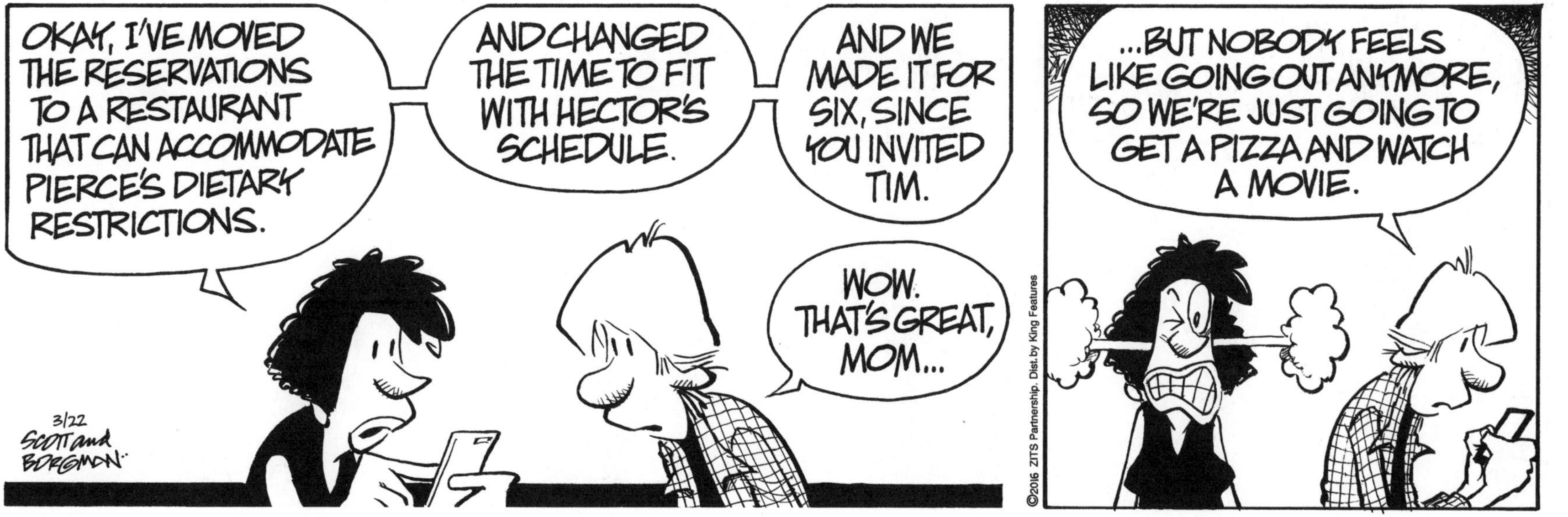
OKAY, I'VE MOVED THE RESERVATIONS TO A RESTAURANT THAT CAN ACCOMMODATE PIERCE'S DIETARY RESTRICTIONS.
AND CHANGED THE TIME TO FIT WITH HECTOR'S SCHEDULE.
AND WE MADE IT FOR SIX, SINCE YOU INVITED TIM.
WOW. THAT'S GREAT, MOM...
3/22 SCOTT and BORGMAN
©2016 ZITS Partnership. Dist. by King Features
...BUT NOBODY FEELS LIKE GOING OUT ANYMORE, SO WE'RE JUST GOING TO GET A PIZZA AND WATCH A MOVIE.

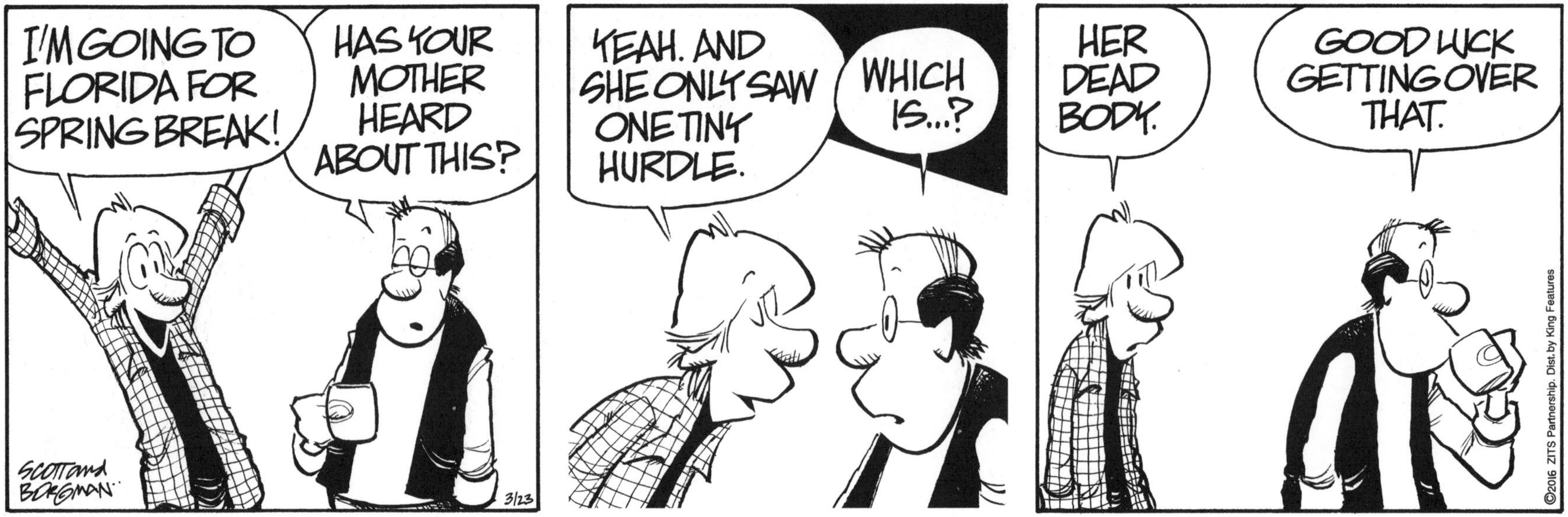
I'M GOING TO FLORIDA FOR SPRING BREAK!
HAS YOUR MOTHER HEARD ABOUT THIS?
SCOTT and BORGMAN
3/23
YEAH. AND SHE ONLY SAW ONE TINY HURDLE.
WHICH IS...?
HER DEAD BODY.
GOOD LUCK GETTING OVER THAT.
©2016 ZITS Partnership. Dist. by King Features

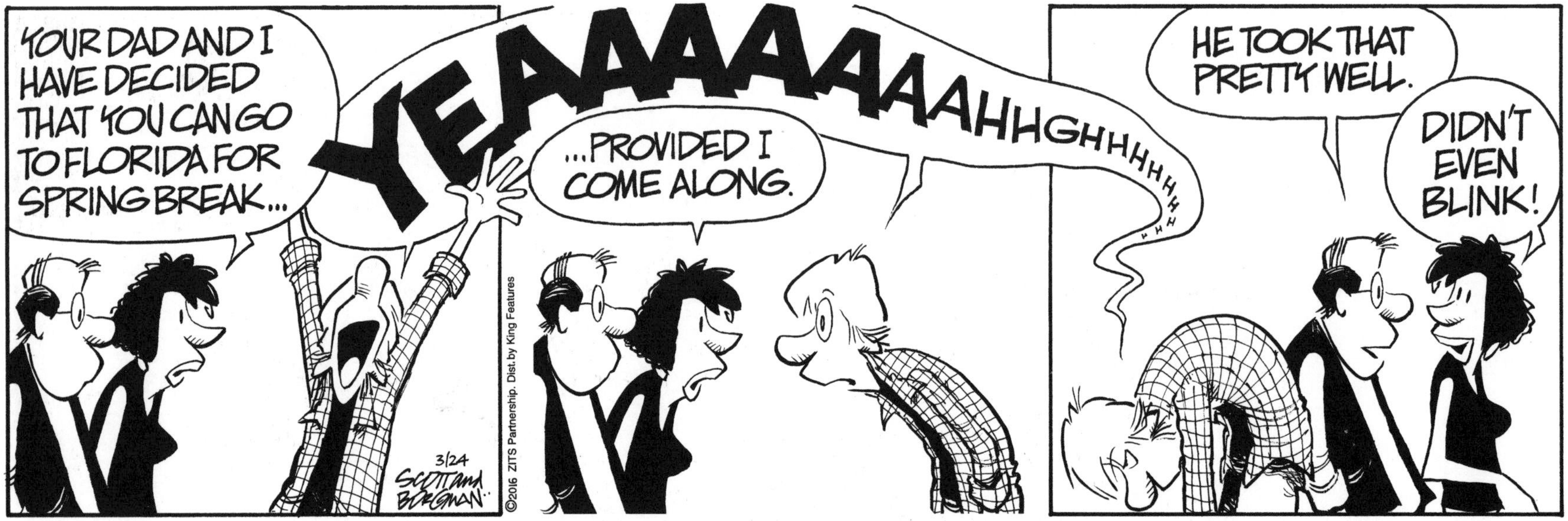
YOUR DAD AND I HAVE DECIDED THAT YOU CAN GO TO FLORIDA FOR SPRING BREAK...
YEAAAAAAAAHHGHHHHHHHH
3/24
SCOTT and BORGMAN
©2016 ZITS Partnership. Dist. by King Features
...PROVIDED I COME ALONG.
HE TOOK THAT PRETTY WELL.
DIDN'T EVEN BLINK!

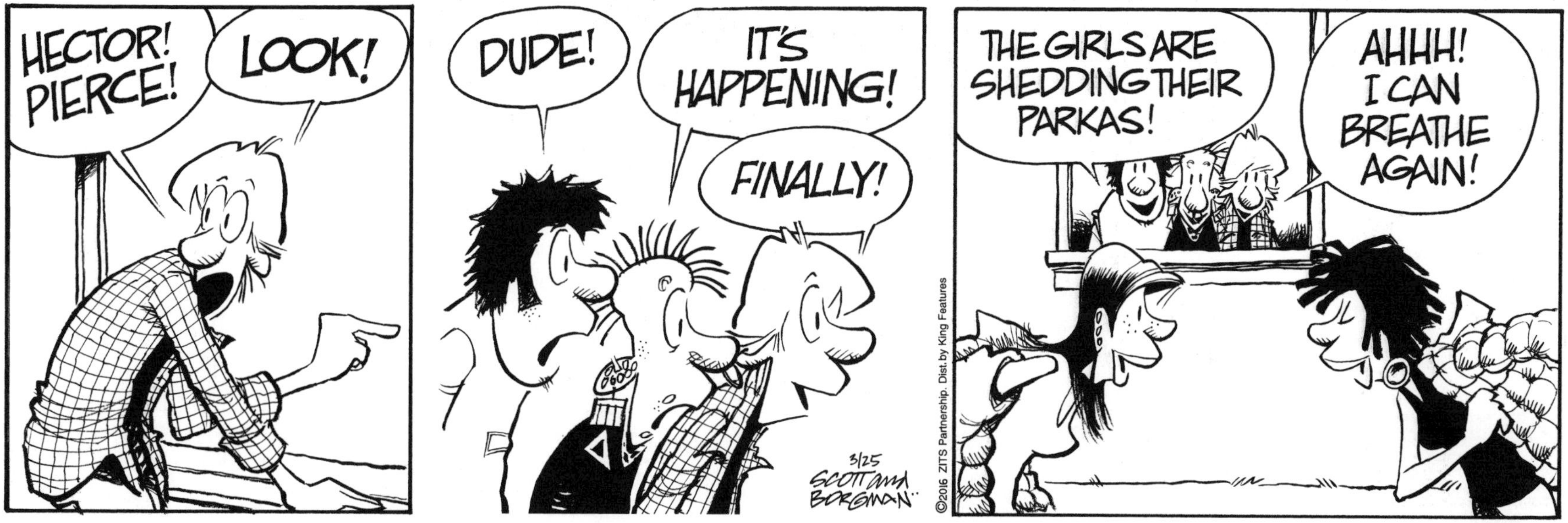
HECTOR! PIERCE!
LOOK!
DUDE!
IT'S HAPPENING!
FINALLY!
THE GIRLS ARE SHEDDING THEIR PARKAS!
AHHH! I CAN BREATHE AGAIN!
3/25
SCOTT and BORGMAN
©2016 ZITS Partnership. Dist. by King Features

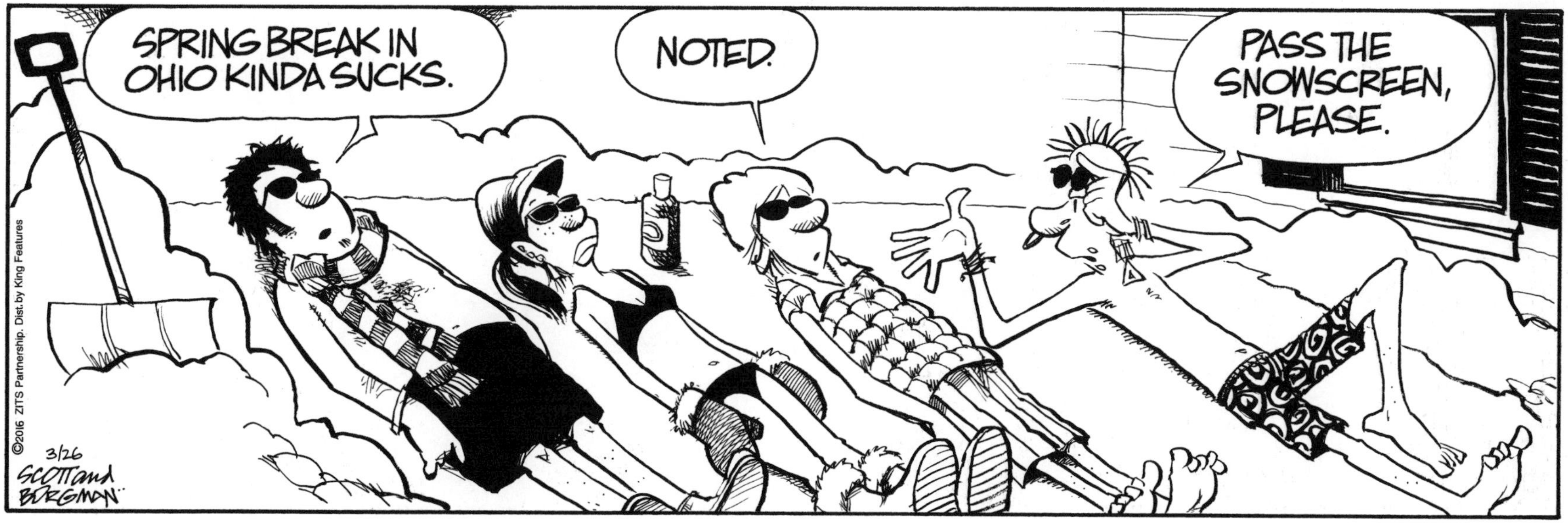
SPRING BREAK IN OHIO KINDA SUCKS.
NOTED.
PASS THE SNOWSCREEN, PLEASE.
©2016 ZITS Partnership. Dist. by King Features
3/26
SCOTT and BORGMAN

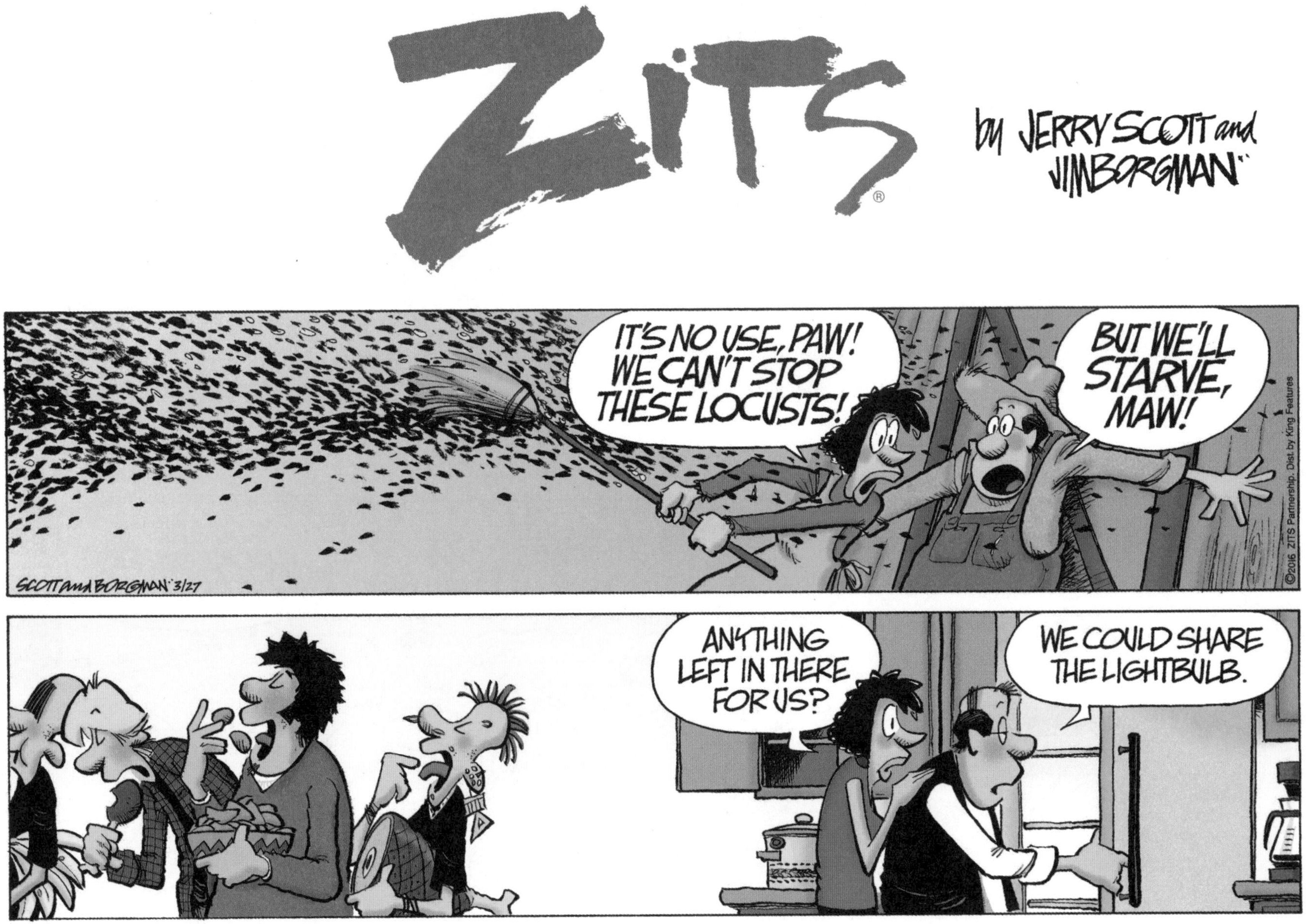
ZITS
by JERRY SCOTT and JIM BORGMAN
IT'S NO USE, PAW! WE CAN'T STOP THESE LOCUSTS!
BUT WE'LL STARVE, MAW!
SCOTT and BORGMAN 3/27
©2016 ZITS Partnership. Dist. by King Features
ANYTHING LEFT IN THERE FOR US?
WE COULD SHARE THE LIGHTBULB.

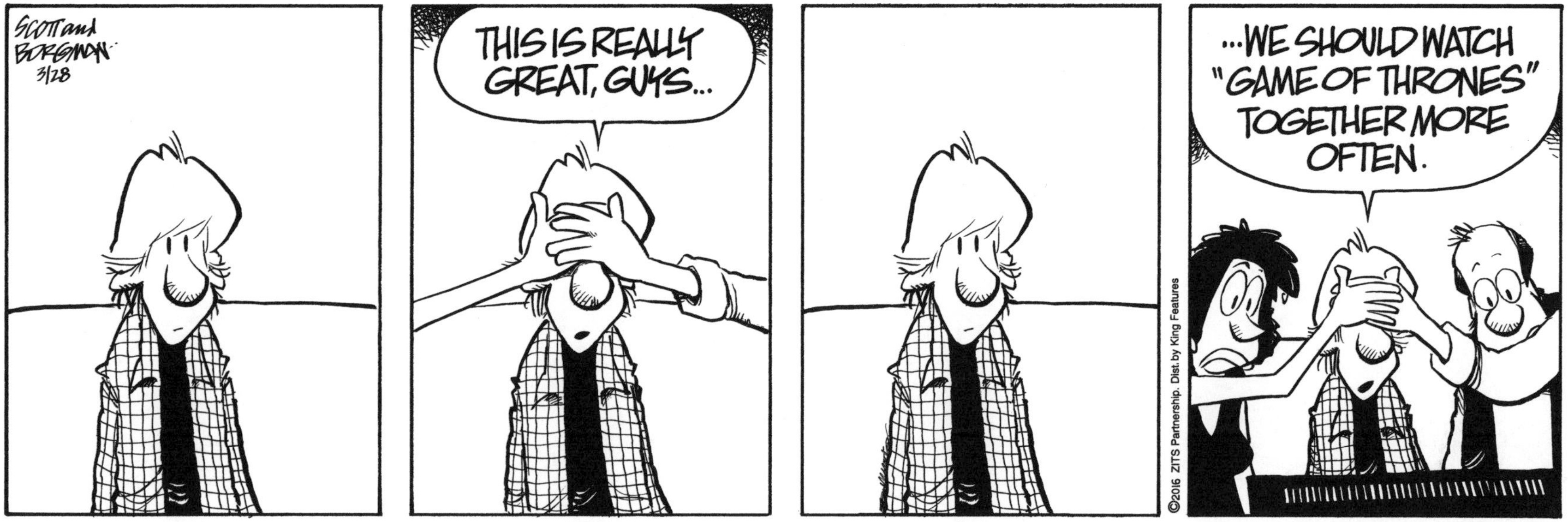
SCOTT and BORGMAN 3/28
THIS IS REALLY GREAT, GUYS...
...WE SHOULD WATCH "GAME OF THRONES" TOGETHER MORE OFTEN.
©2016 ZITS Partnership. Dist. by King Features

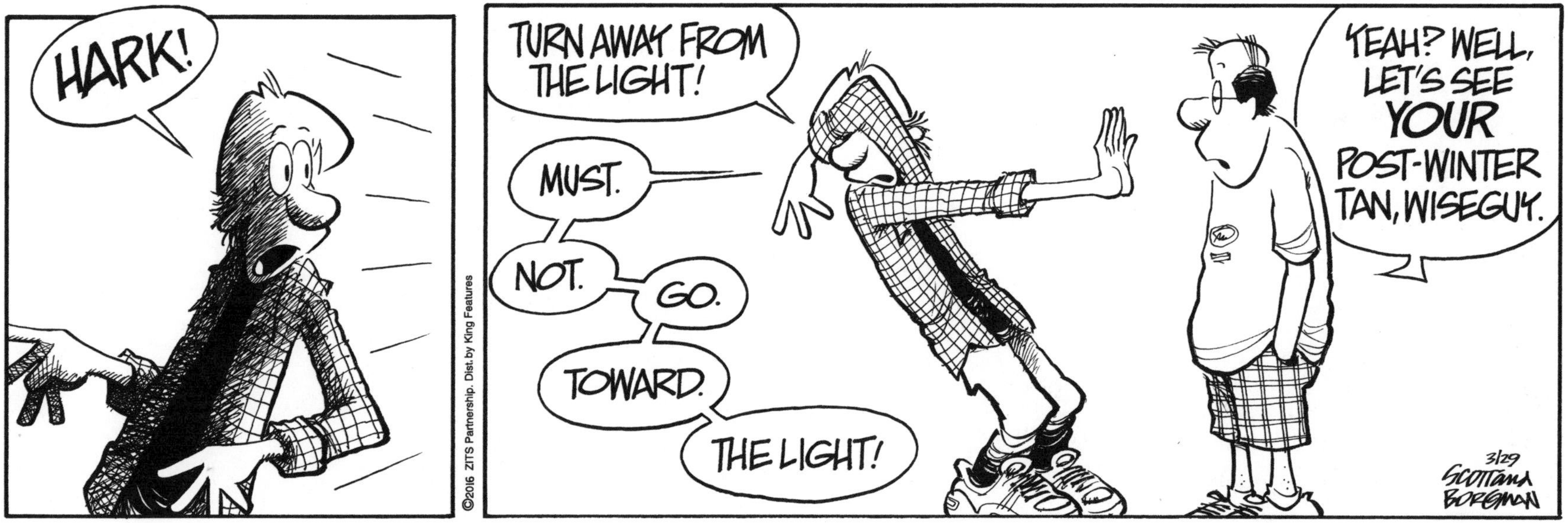
HARK!
©2016 ZITS Partnership. Dist. by King Features
TURN AWAY FROM THE LIGHT!
MUST.
NOT.
GO.
TOWARD.
THE LIGHT!
YEAH? WELL, LET'S SEE YOUR POST-WINTER TAN, WISEGUY.
3/29 SCOTT and BORGMAN

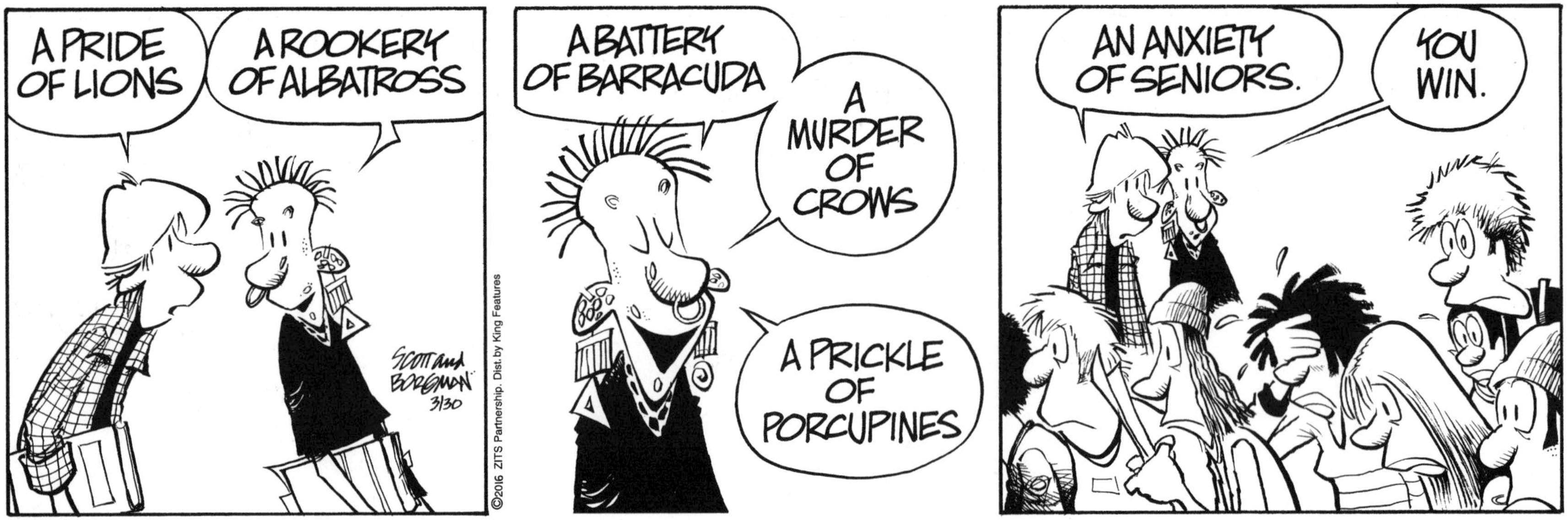
A PRIDE OF LIONS
A ROOKERY OF ALBATROSS
SCOTT and BORGMAN 3/30
©2016 ZITS Partnership. Dist. by King Features
A BATTERY OF BARRACUDA
A MURDER OF CROWS
A PRICKLE OF PORCUPINES
AN ANXIETY OF SENIORS.
YOU WIN.

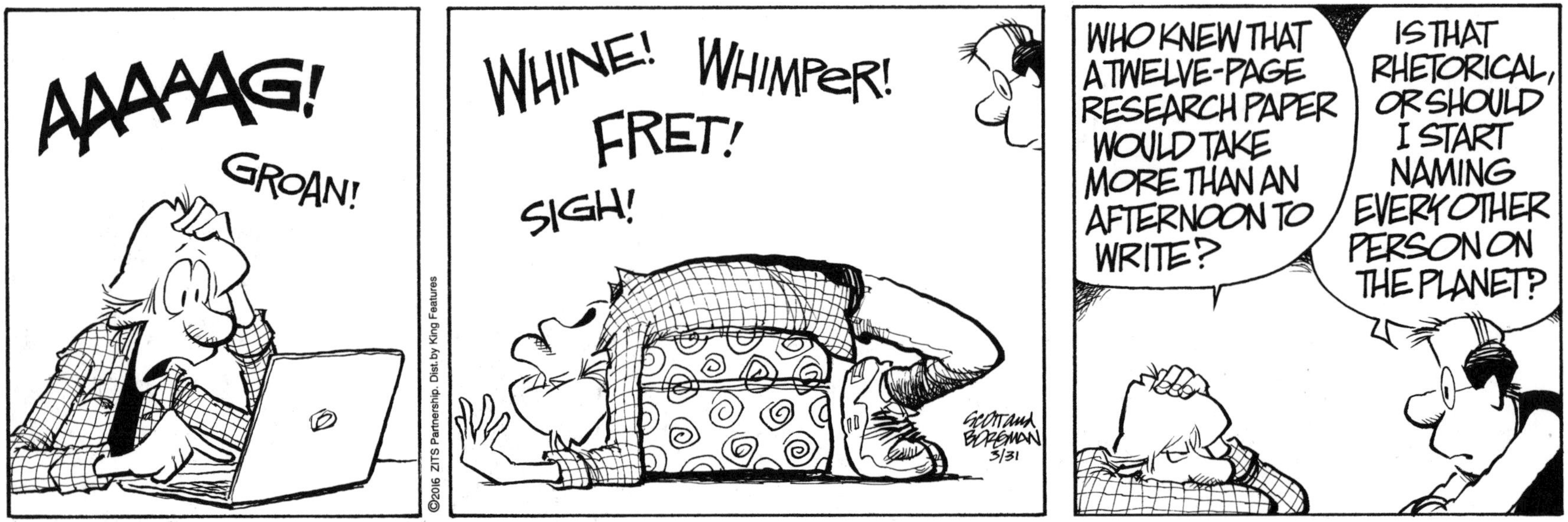
AAAAAG!
GROAN!
©2016 ZITS Partnership. Dist. by King Features
WHINE!
WHIMPER!
FRET!
SIGH!
SCOTT and BORGMAN 3/31
WHO KNEW THAT A TWELVE-PAGE RESEARCH PAPER WOULD TAKE MORE THAN AN AFTERNOON TO WRITE?
IS THAT RHETORICAL, OR SHOULD I START NAMING EVERY OTHER PERSON ON THE PLANET?

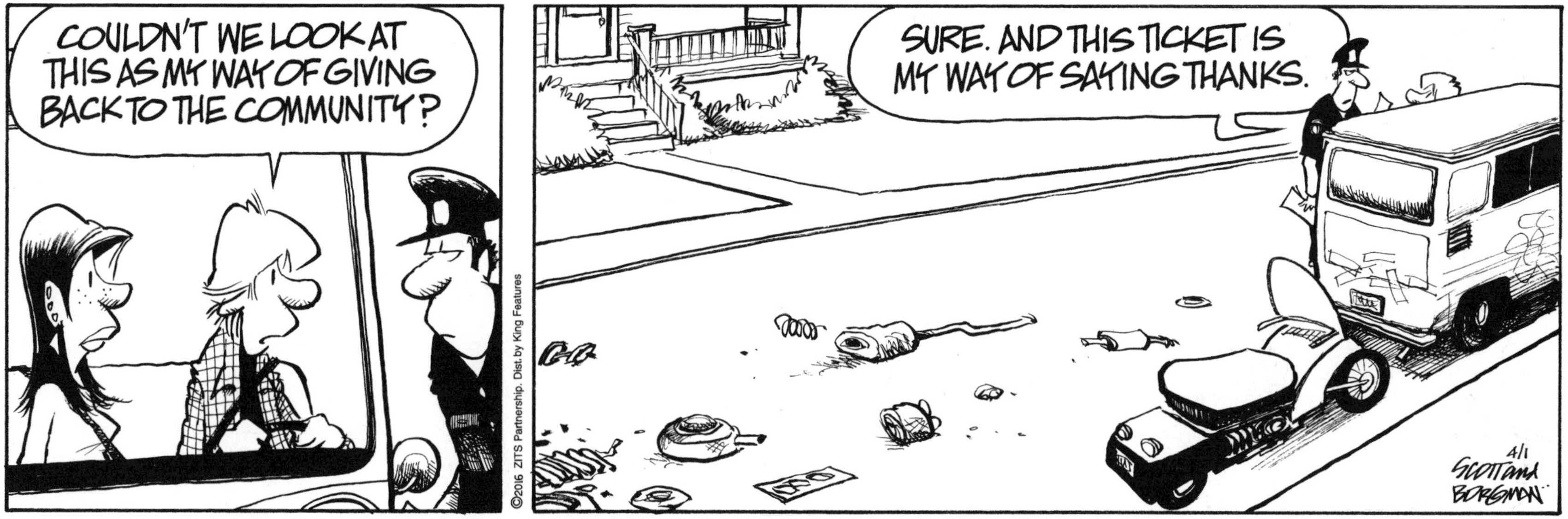
COULDN'T WE LOOK AT THIS AS MY WAY OF GIVING BACK TO THE COMMUNITY?
©2016 ZITS Partnership. Dist. by King Features
SURE. AND THIS TICKET IS MY WAY OF SAYING THANKS.
4/1
SCOTT and BORGMAN

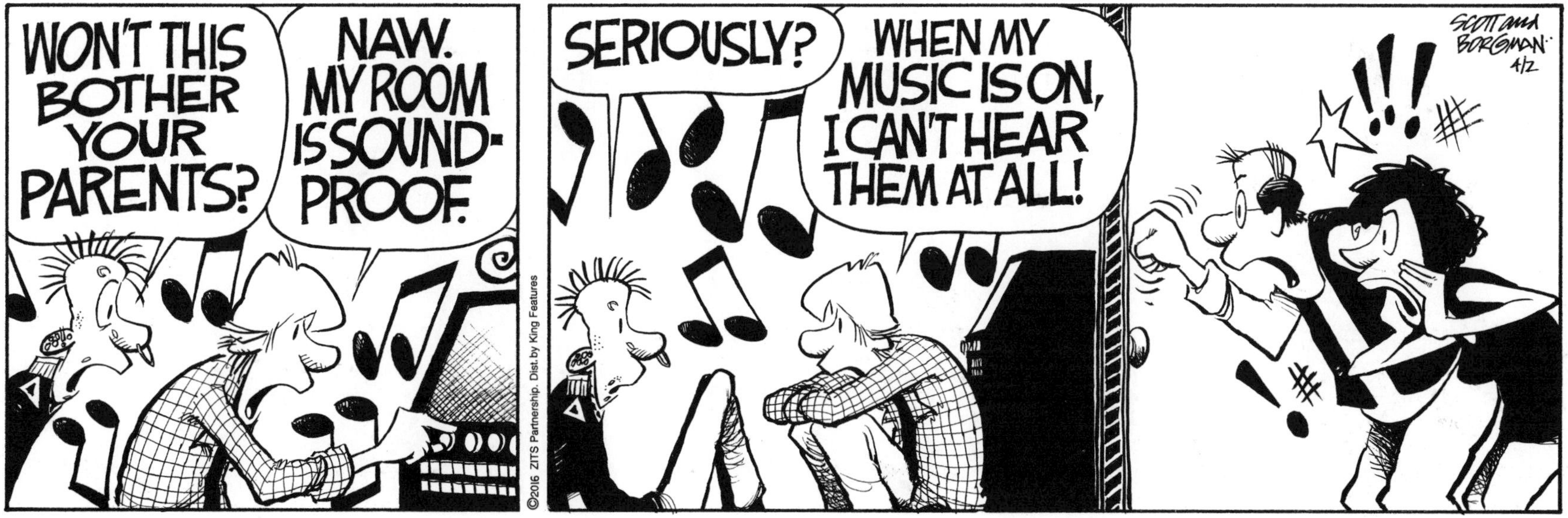
WON'T THIS BOTHER YOUR PARENTS?
NAW. MY ROOM IS SOUNDPROOF.
©2016 ZITS Partnership. Dist. by King Features
SERIOUSLY?
WHEN MY MUSIC IS ON, I CAN'T HEAR THEM AT ALL!
SCOTT and BORGMAN
4/2

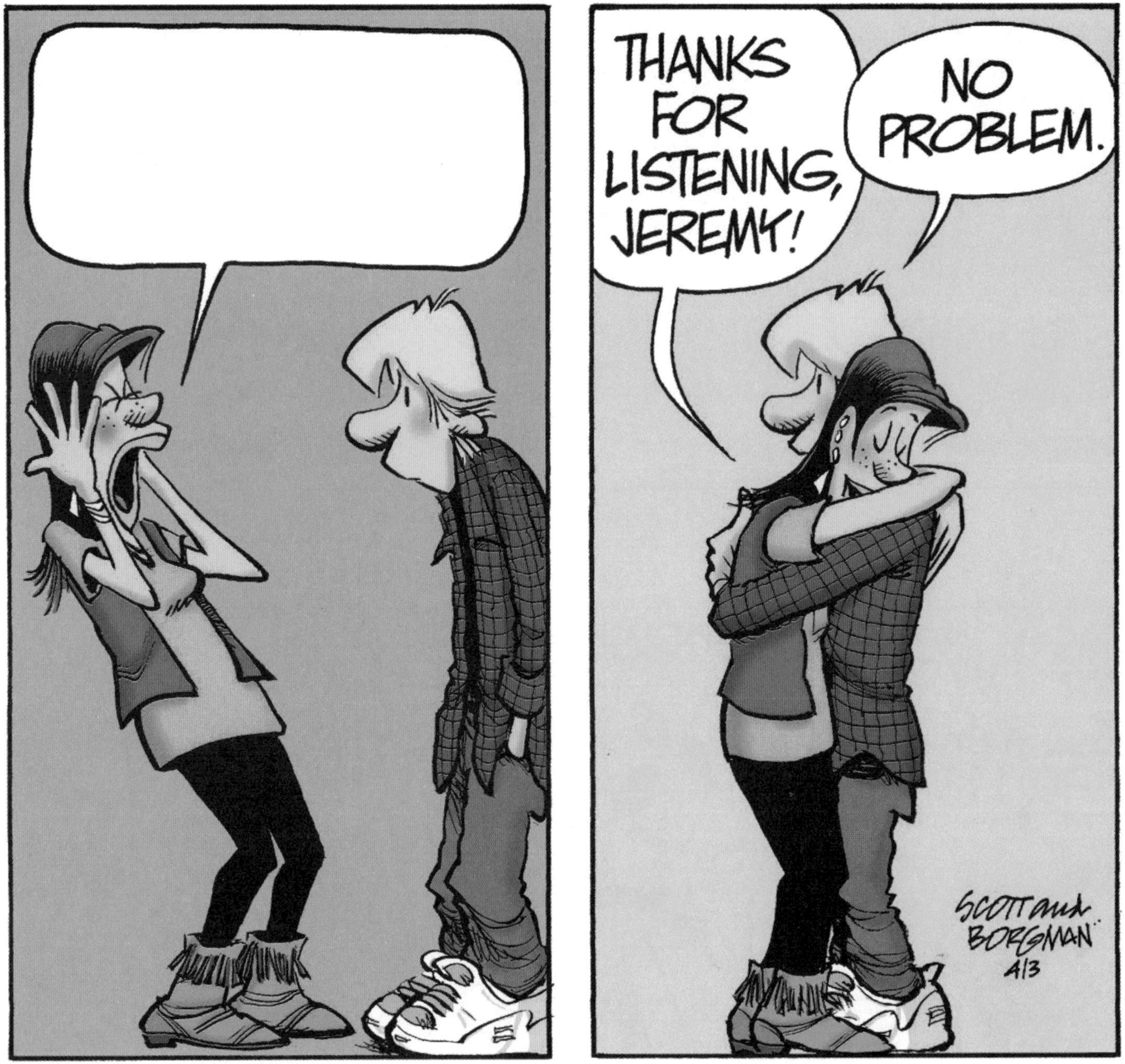
THANKS FOR LISTENING, JEREMY!
NO PROBLEM.
SCOTT and BORGMAN 4/3

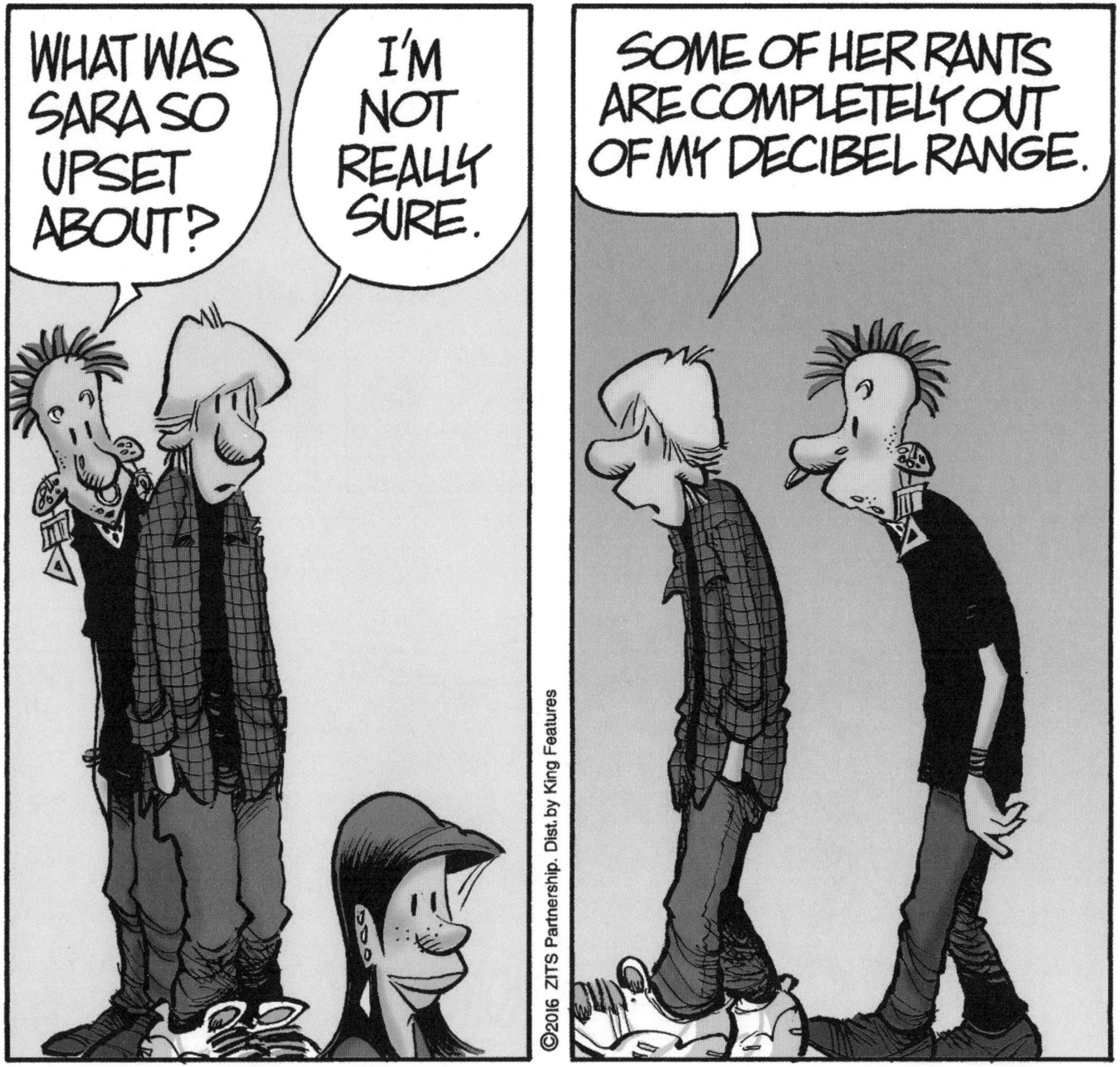
WHAT WAS SARA SO UPSET ABOUT?
I'M NOT REALLY SURE.
SOME OF HER RANTS ARE COMPLETELY OUT OF MY DECIBEL RANGE.
©2016 ZITS Partnership. Dist. by King Features

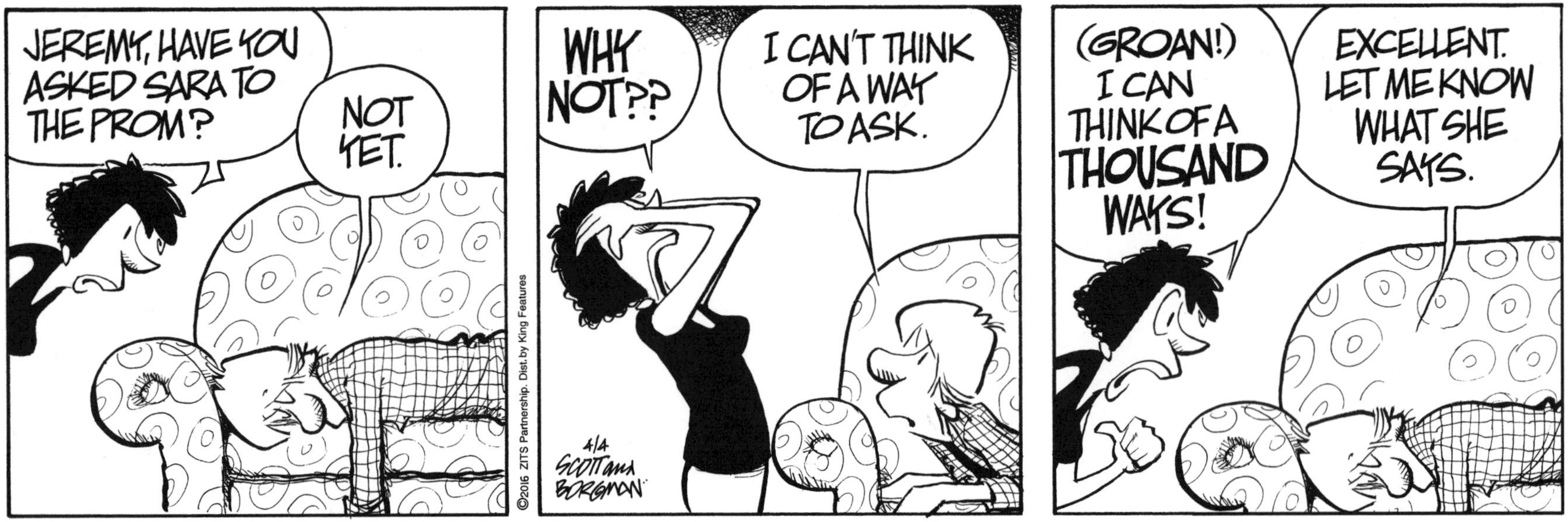
JEREMY, HAVE YOU ASKED SARA TO THE PROM?
NOT YET.
WHY NOT??
I CAN'T THINK OF A WAY TO ASK.
(GROAN!) I CAN THINK OF A THOUSAND WAYS!
EXCELLENT. LET ME KNOW WHAT SHE SAYS.
©2016 ZITS Partnership. Dist. by King Features
4/4 SCOTT and BORGMAN

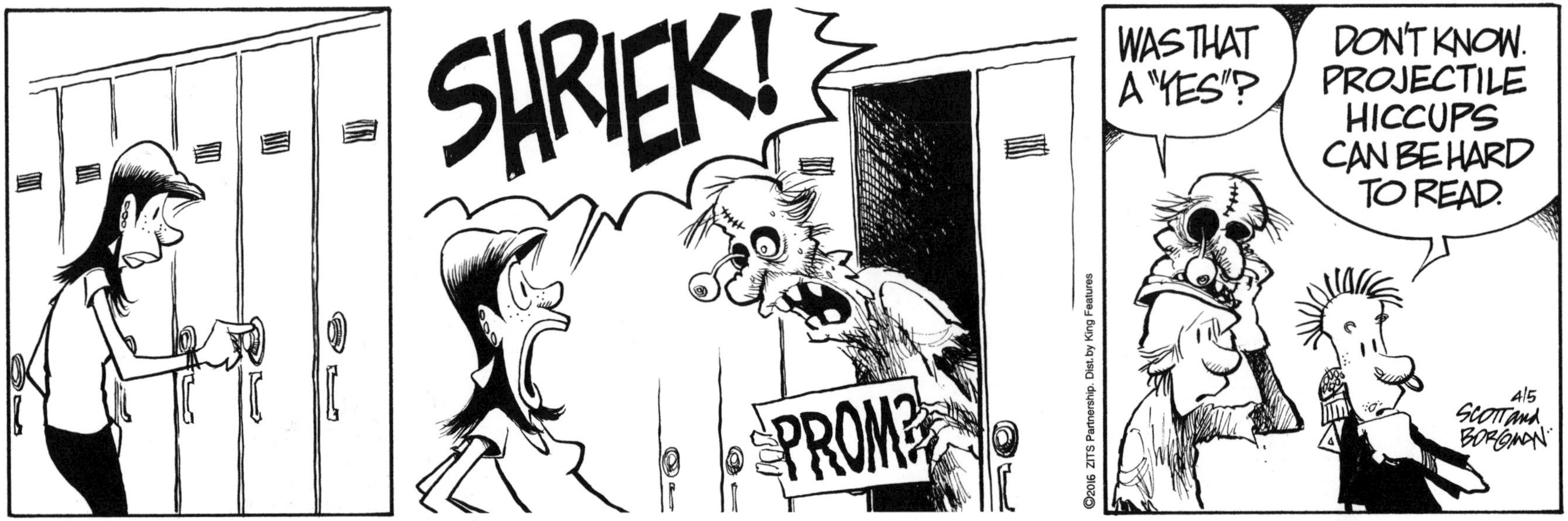
SHRIEK!
PROM?
WAS THAT A "YES"?
DON'T KNOW. PROJECTILE HICCUPS CAN BE HARD TO READ.
©2016 ZITS Partnership. Dist. by King Features
4/5 SCOTT and BORGMAN

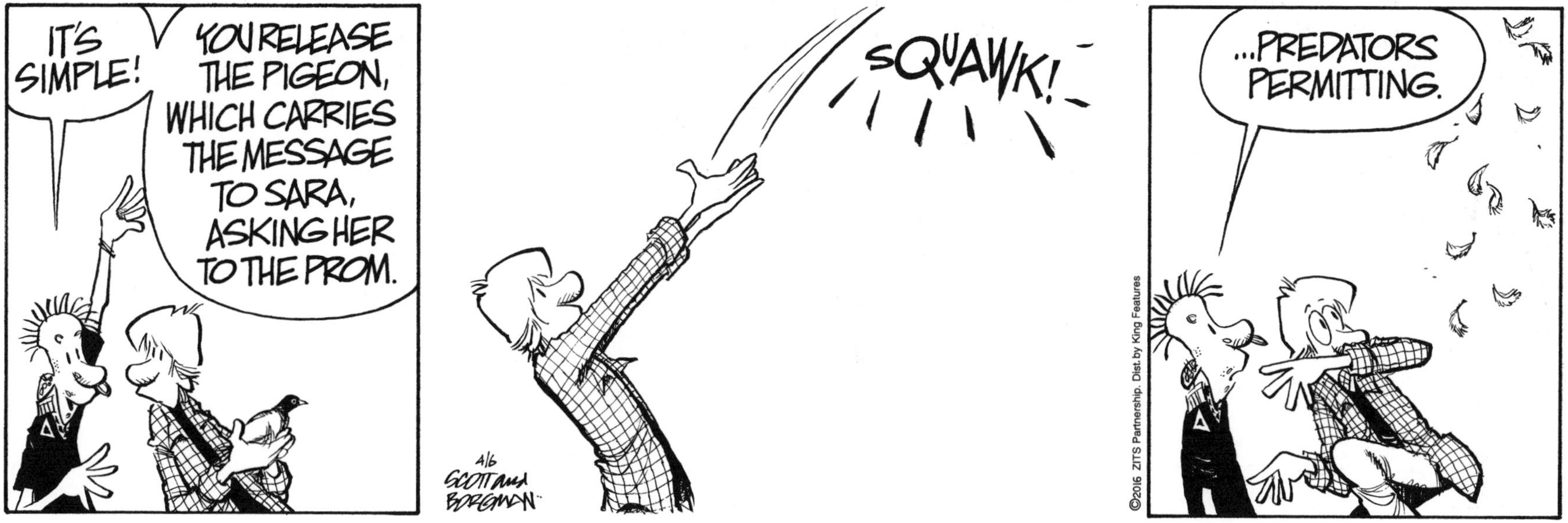
IT'S SIMPLE!
YOU RELEASE THE PIGEON, WHICH CARRIES THE MESSAGE TO SARA, ASKING HER TO THE PROM.
4/6 SCOTT AND BORGMAN
SQUAWK!
©2016 ZITS Partnership. Dist. by King Features
...PREDATORS PERMITTING.

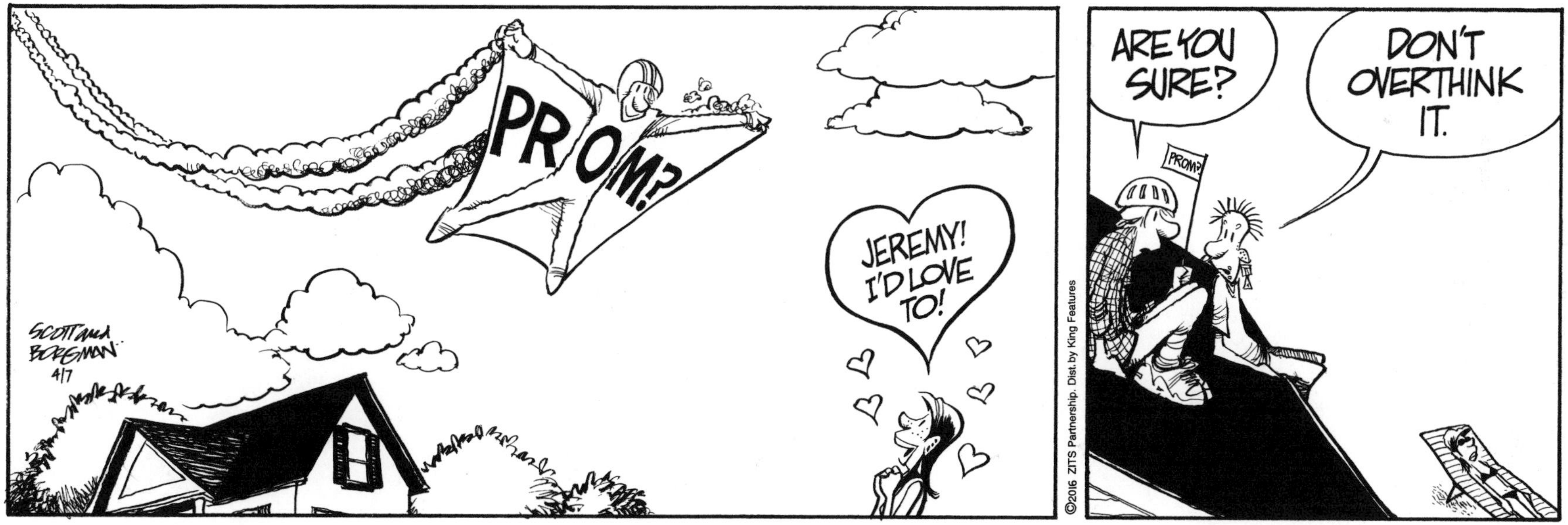
SCOTT AND BORGMAN 4/7
PROM?
JEREMY! I'D LOVE TO!
©2016 ZITS Partnership. Dist. by King Features
ARE YOU SURE?
DON'T OVERTHINK IT.
PROM?

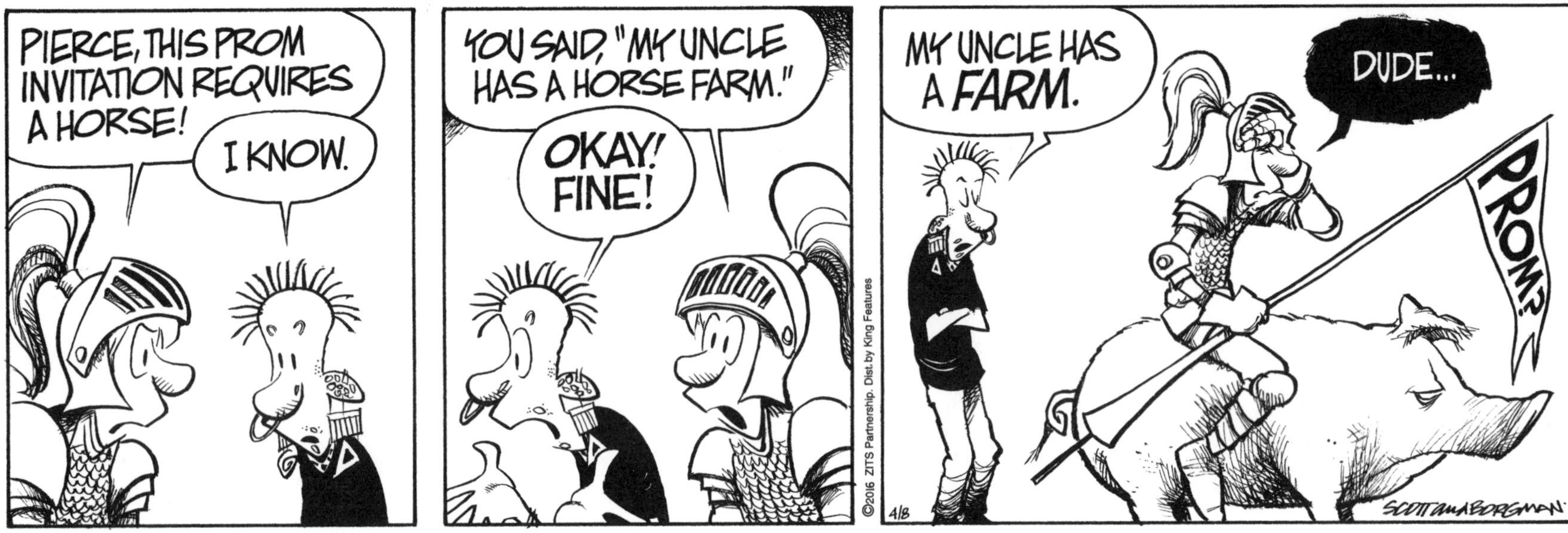
PIERCE, THIS PROM INVITATION REQUIRES A HORSE!
I KNOW.
YOU SAID, "MY UNCLE HAS A HORSE FARM."
OKAY! FINE!
MY UNCLE HAS A *FARM*.
DUDE...
PROM?
©2016 ZITS Partnership. Dist. by King Features
4/8
SCOTT and BORGMAN

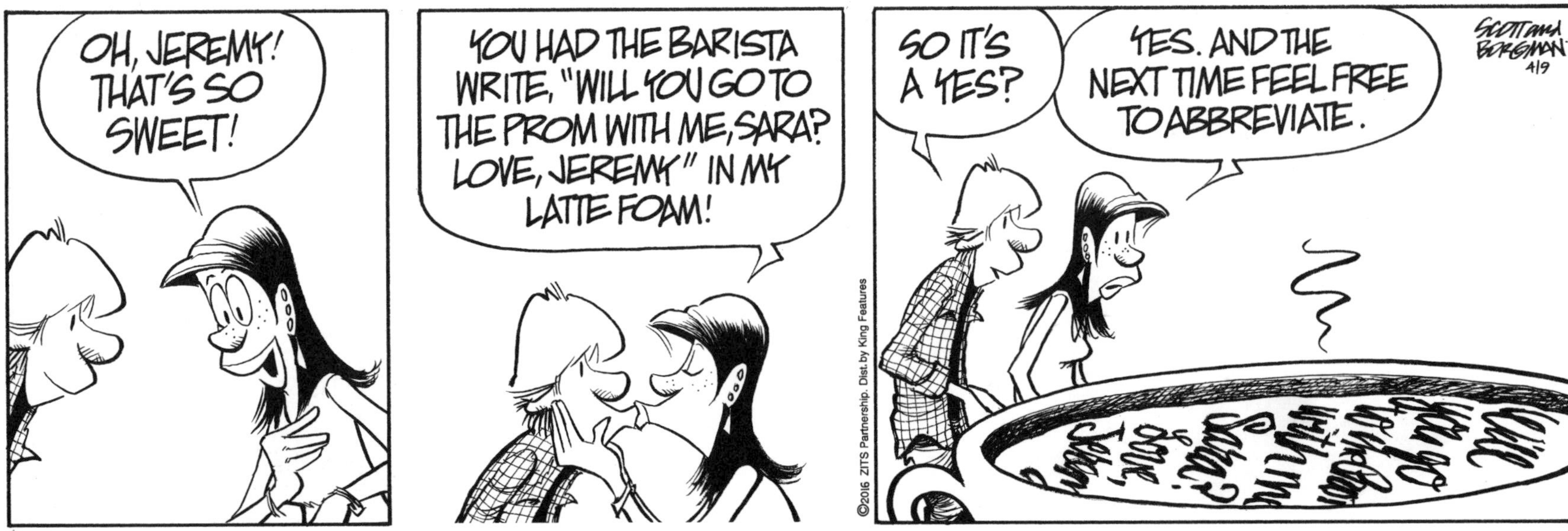
OH, JEREMY! THAT'S SO SWEET!
YOU HAD THE BARISTA WRITE, "WILL YOU GO TO THE PROM WITH ME, SARA? LOVE, JEREMY" IN MY LATTE FOAM!
SO IT'S A YES?
YES. AND THE NEXT TIME FEEL FREE TO ABBREVIATE.
SCOTT and BORGMAN 4/9
©2016 ZITS Partnership. Dist. by King Features

ZITS®

by JERRY SCOTT and JIM BORGMAN

SCOTT and BORGMAN 4/10
©2016 ZITS Partnership. Dist. by King Features
GLUB
SPUTTER
WHEEZE
INTERESTING THEORY... BUT KEEP MOWING ANYWAY.
I'M NOT KIDDING! LAWNWORK IS BAD FOR THE SPECIES!

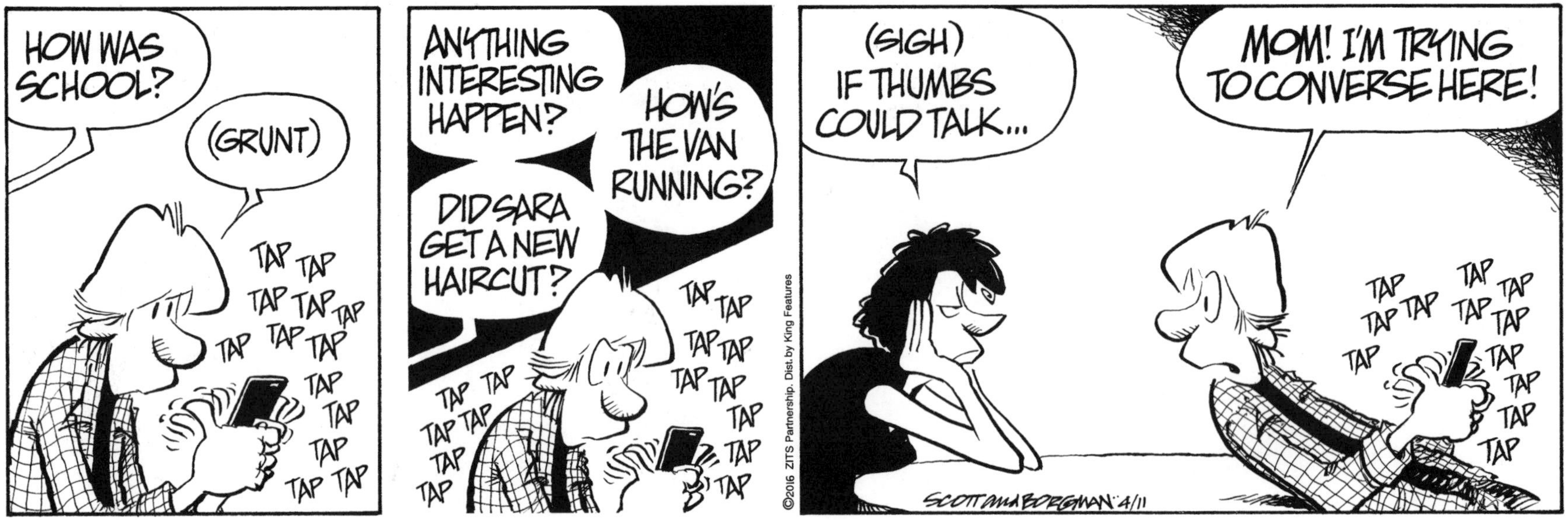
HOW WAS SCHOOL?
(GRUNT)
TAP TAP TAP TAP TAP TAP TAP TAP TAP TAP TAP TAP TAP TAP
ANYTHING INTERESTING HAPPEN?
HOW'S THE VAN RUNNING?
DID SARA GET A NEW HAIRCUT?
TAP TAP TAP TAP TAP TAP TAP TAP TAP TAP TAP TAP TAP TAP TAP
©2016 ZITS Partnership. Dist.by King Features
(SIGH) IF THUMBS COULD TALK...
MOM! I'M TRYING TO CONVERSE HERE!
TAP TAP TAP TAP TAP TAP TAP TAP TAP TAP TAP TAP TAP
SCOTT and BORGMAN 4/11

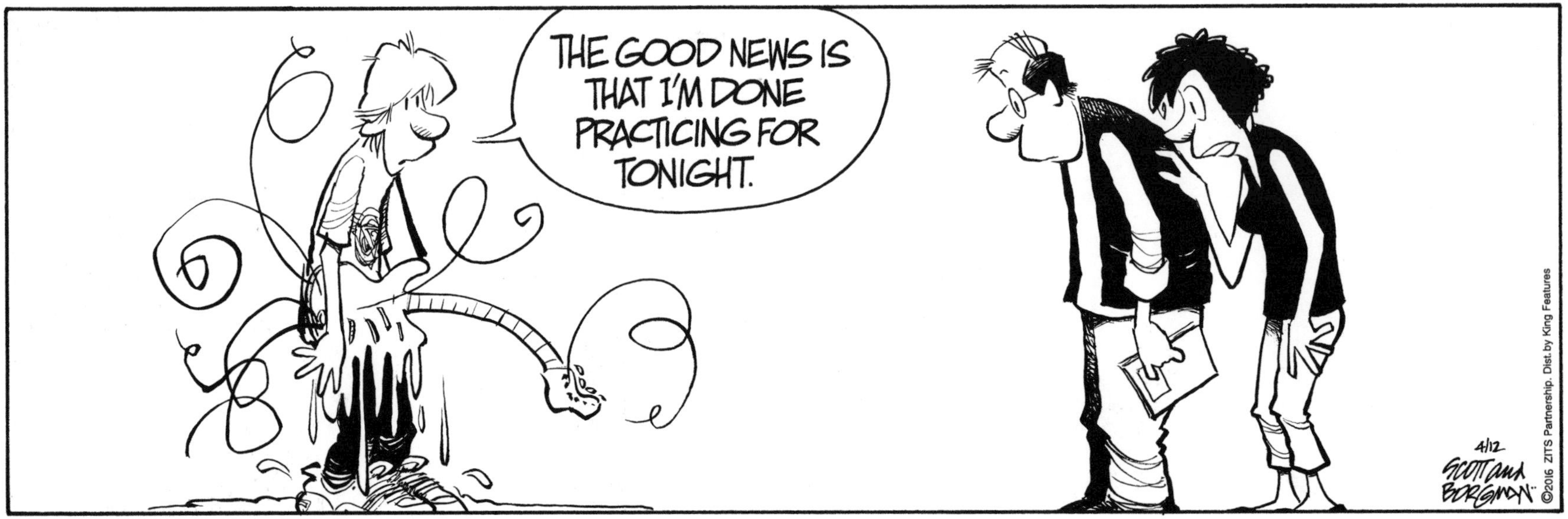
THE GOOD NEWS IS THAT I'M DONE PRACTICING FOR TONIGHT.
4/12 SCOTT and BORGMAN
©2016 ZITS Partnership. Dist.by King Features

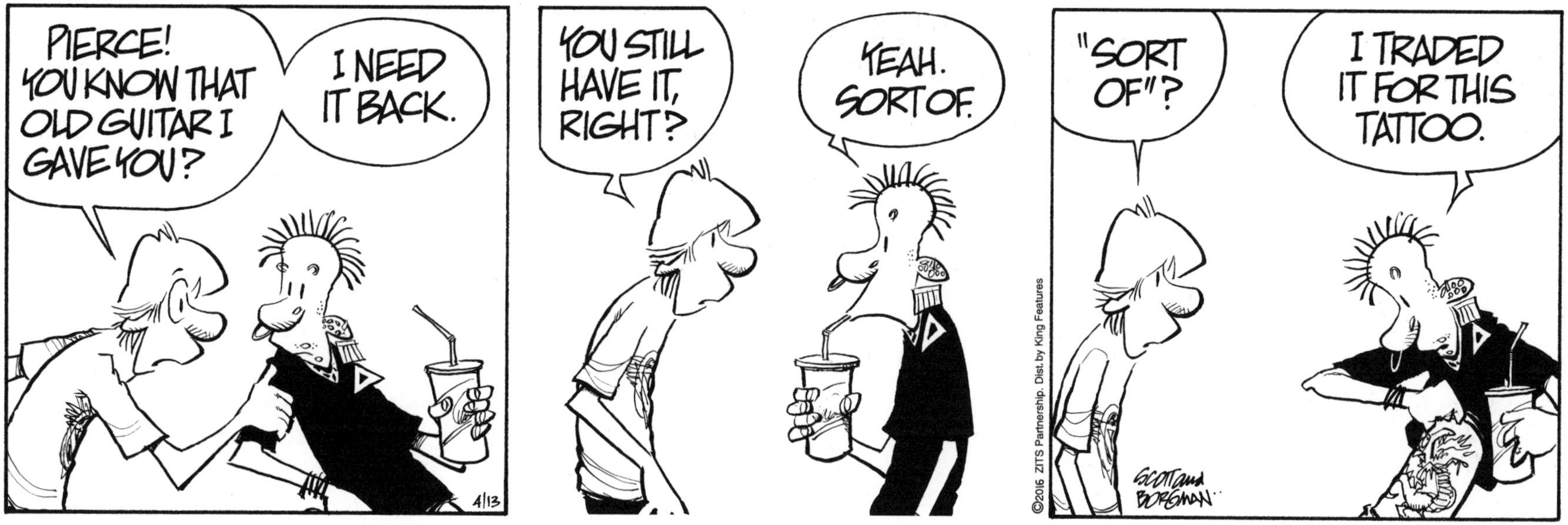
PIERCE! YOU KNOW THAT OLD GUITAR I GAVE YOU?
I NEED IT BACK.
YOU STILL HAVE IT, RIGHT?
YEAH. SORT OF.
"SORT OF"?
I TRADED IT FOR THIS TATTOO.
©2016 ZITS Partnership. Dist. by King Features
SCOTT and BORGMAN
4/13

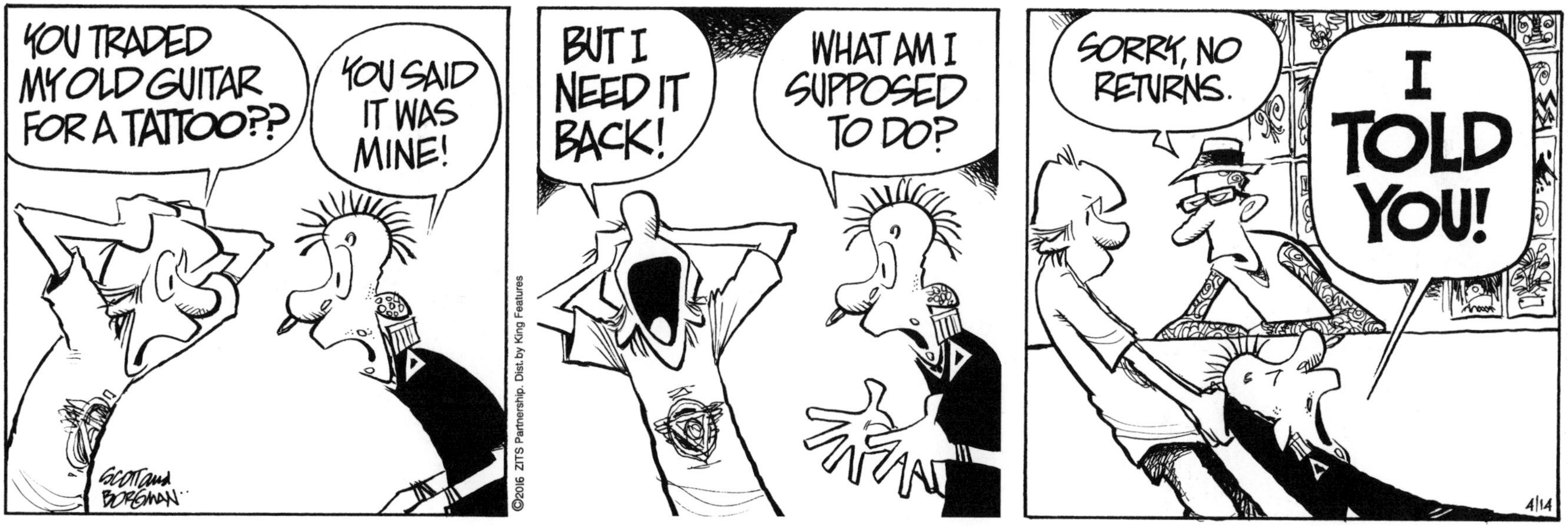
YOU TRADED MY OLD GUITAR FOR A TATTOO??
YOU SAID IT WAS MINE!
SCOTT and BORGMAN
©2016 ZITS Partnership. Dist. by King Features
BUT I NEED IT BACK!
WHAT AM I SUPPOSED TO DO?
SORRY, NO RETURNS.
I TOLD YOU!
4/14

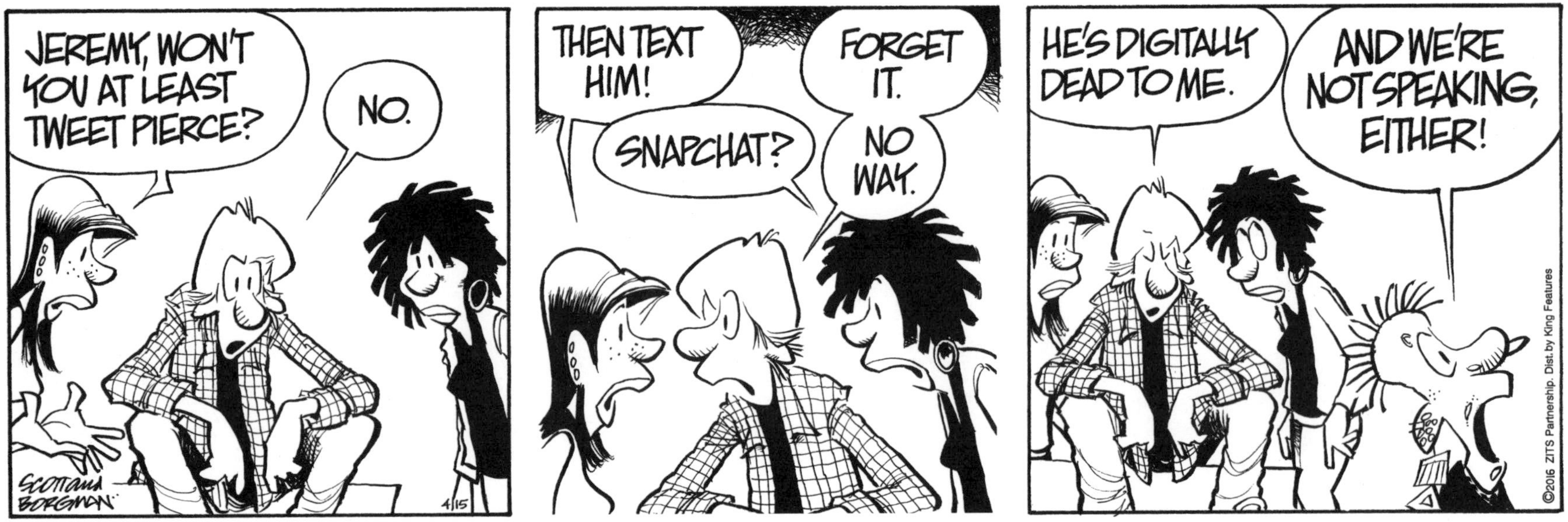
JEREMY, WON'T YOU AT LEAST TWEET PIERCE?
NO.
THEN TEXT HIM!
SNAPCHAT?
FORGET IT.
NO WAY.
HE'S DIGITALLY DEAD TO ME.
AND WE'RE NOT SPEAKING, EITHER!
SCOTT and BORGMAN
4/15
©2016 ZITS Partnership. Dist. by King Features

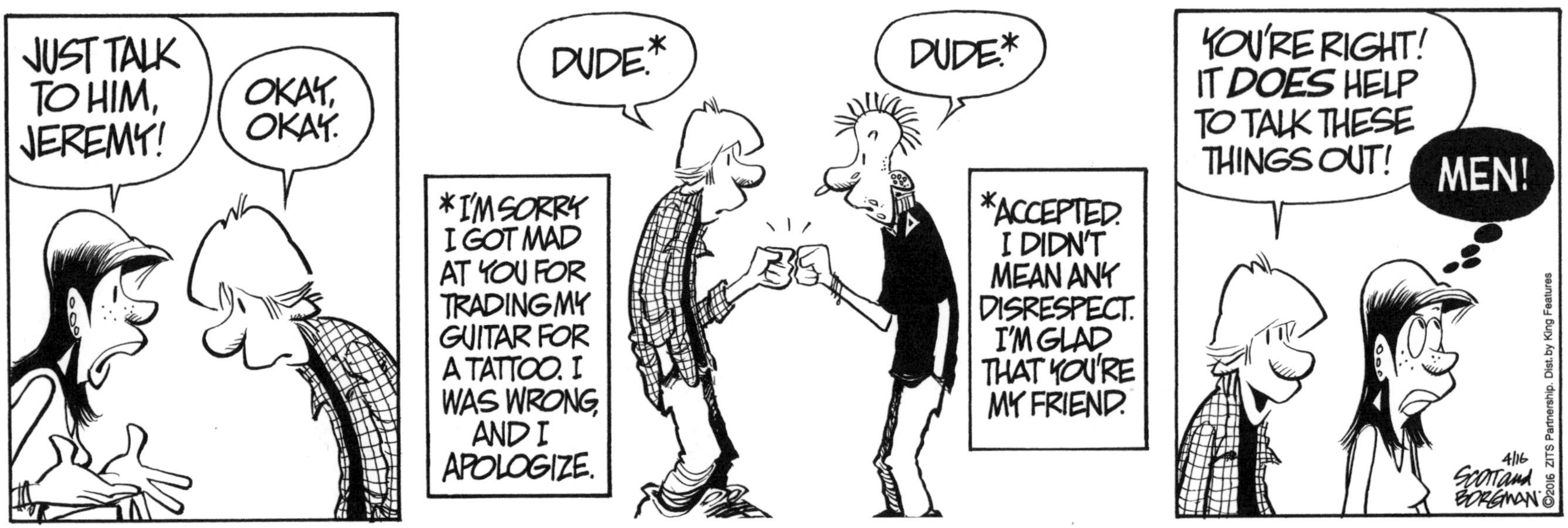
JUST TALK TO HIM, JEREMY!
OKAY, OKAY.
*I'M SORRY I GOT MAD AT YOU FOR TRADING MY GUITAR FOR A TATTOO. I WAS WRONG, AND I APOLOGIZE.
DUDE.*
DUDE.*
*ACCEPTED. I DIDN'T MEAN ANY DISRESPECT. I'M GLAD THAT YOU'RE MY FRIEND.
YOU'RE RIGHT! IT DOES HELP TO TALK THESE THINGS OUT!
MEN!
4/16
SCOTT and BORGMAN
©2016 ZITS Partnership. Dist. by King Features

ZITS

by JERRY SCOTT and JIM BORGMAN

HEY JEREMY, YOU BUSY?
I THOUGHT WE COULD HAVE A CHAT WHILE WE SHARE A PIZZA.
WHAT KIND OF CHAT?
OH, YOU KNOW... GIRLS... POLITICS... STUDENT LOANS...
SORRY! I HAVE TO STUDY.
SCOTT and BORGMAN 4/17
HE GOT AWAY AGAIN.
AND HE STOLE YOUR BAIT.
©2016 ZITS Partnership. Dist. by King Features

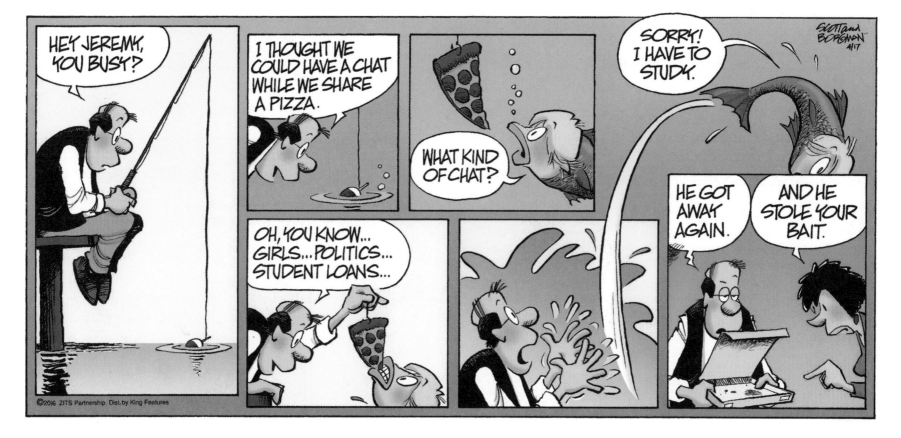

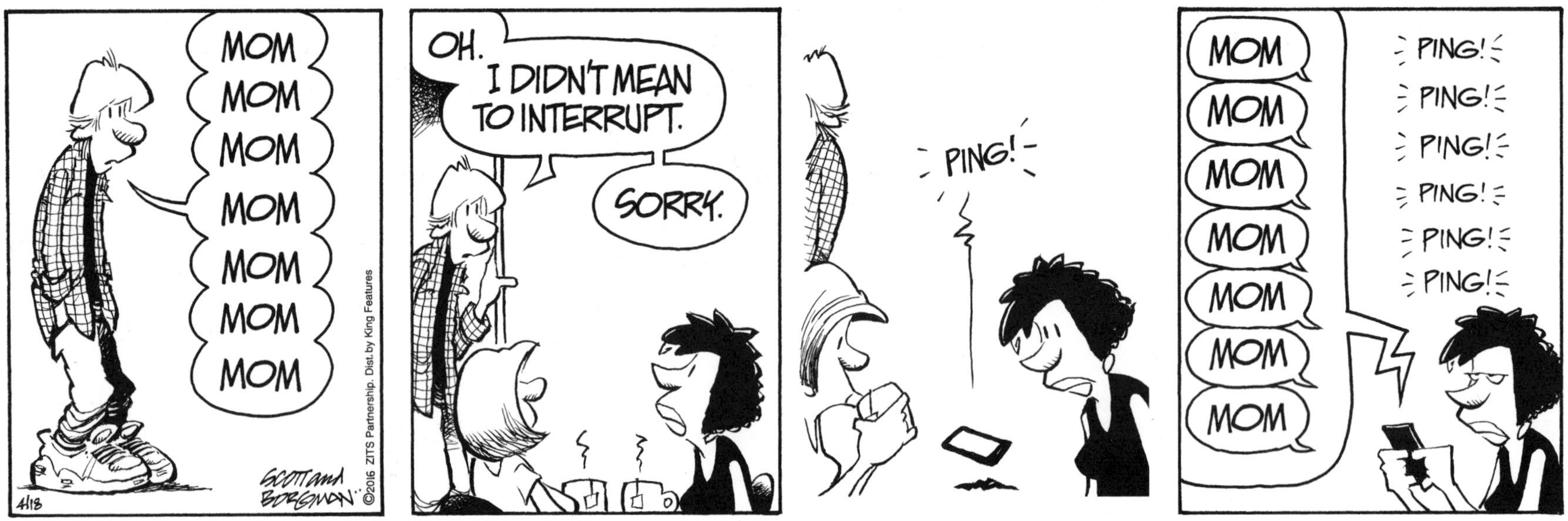
MOM MOM MOM MOM MOM MOM MOM
OH.
I DIDN'T MEAN TO INTERRUPT.
SORRY.
PING!
MOM
MOM
MOM
MOM
MOM
MOM
MOM
PING! PING! PING! PING! PING! PING!
4/18
SCOTT and BORGMAN
©2016 ZITS Partnership. Dist. by King Features

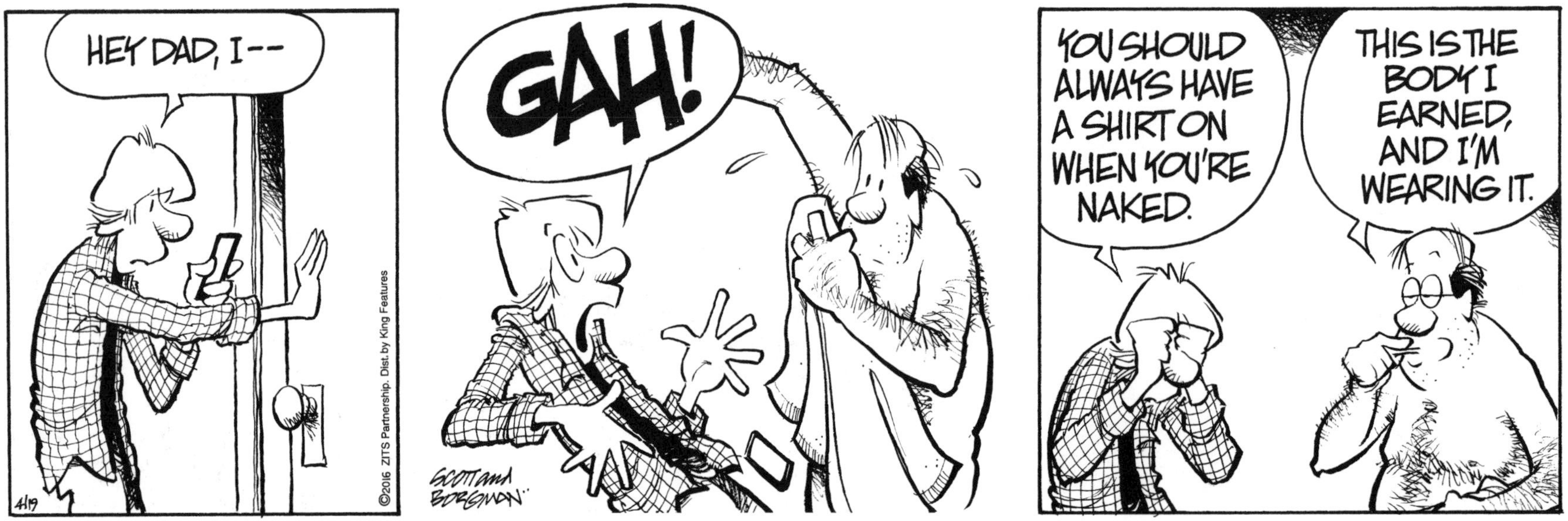
HEY DAD, I--
GAH!
YOU SHOULD ALWAYS HAVE A SHIRT ON WHEN YOU'RE NAKED.
THIS IS THE BODY I EARNED, AND I'M WEARING IT.
4/19
SCOTT and BORGMAN
©2016 ZITS Partnership. Dist. by King Features

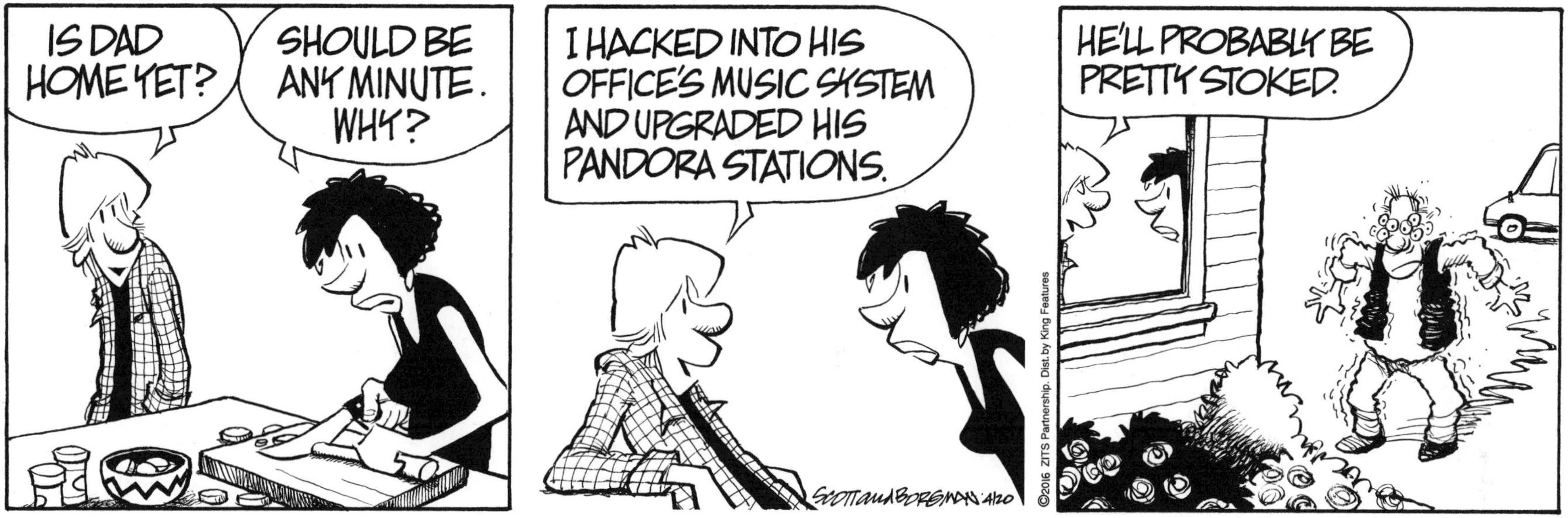
IS DAD HOME YET?
SHOULD BE ANY MINUTE. WHY?
I HACKED INTO HIS OFFICE'S MUSIC SYSTEM AND UPGRADED HIS PANDORA STATIONS.
SCOTT and BORGMAN 4/20
©2016 ZITS Partnership. Dist. by King Features
HE'LL PROBABLY BE PRETTY STOKED.

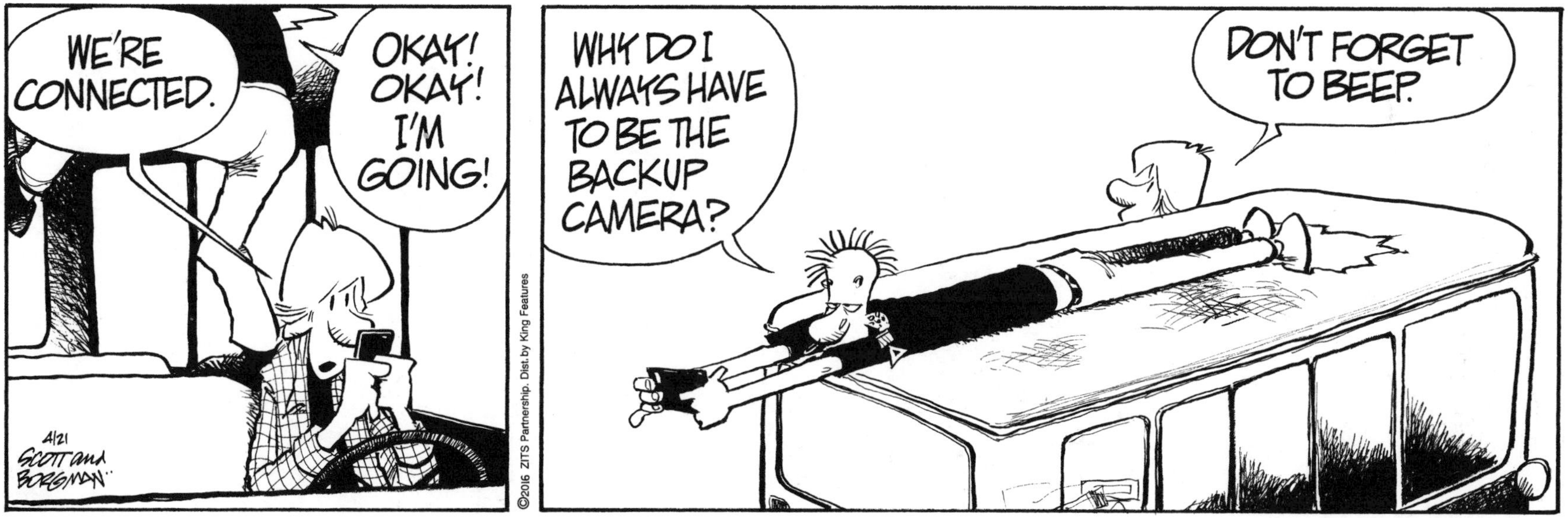
WE'RE CONNECTED.
OKAY! OKAY! I'M GOING!
4/21 SCOTT and BORGMAN
©2016 ZITS Partnership. Dist. by King Features
WHY DO I ALWAYS HAVE TO BE THE BACKUP CAMERA?
DON'T FORGET TO BEEP.

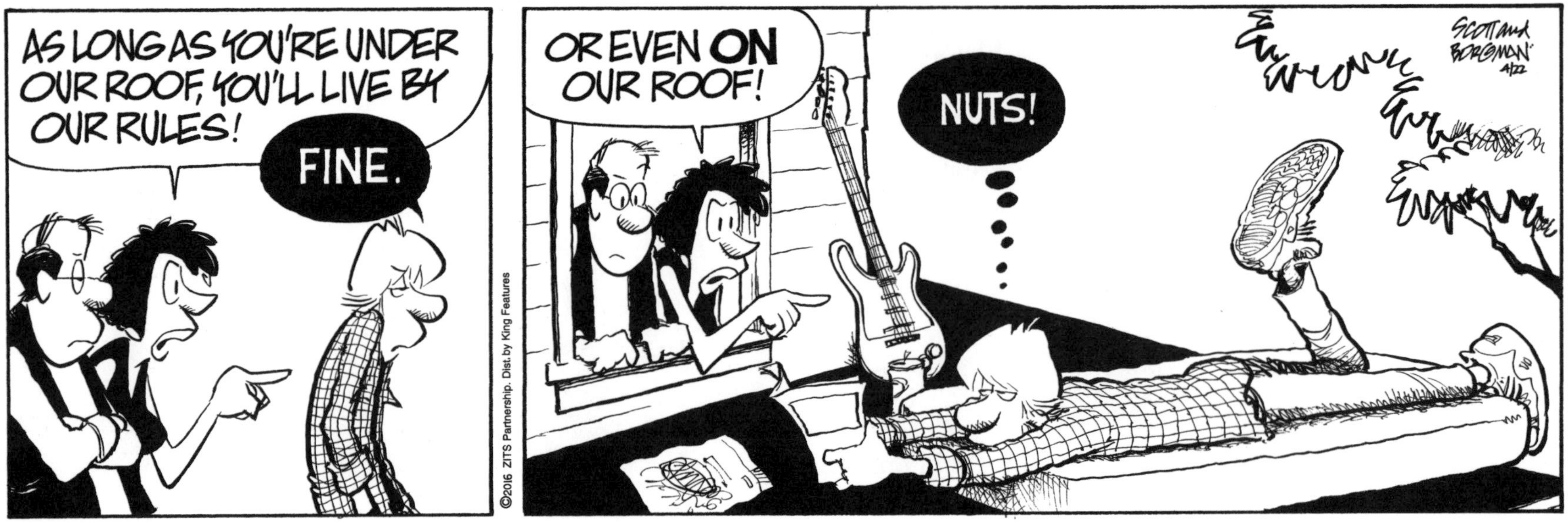
AS LONG AS YOU'RE UNDER OUR ROOF, YOU'LL LIVE BY OUR RULES!
FINE.
©2016 ZITS Partnership. Dist. by King Features
OR EVEN **ON** OUR ROOF!
NUTS!

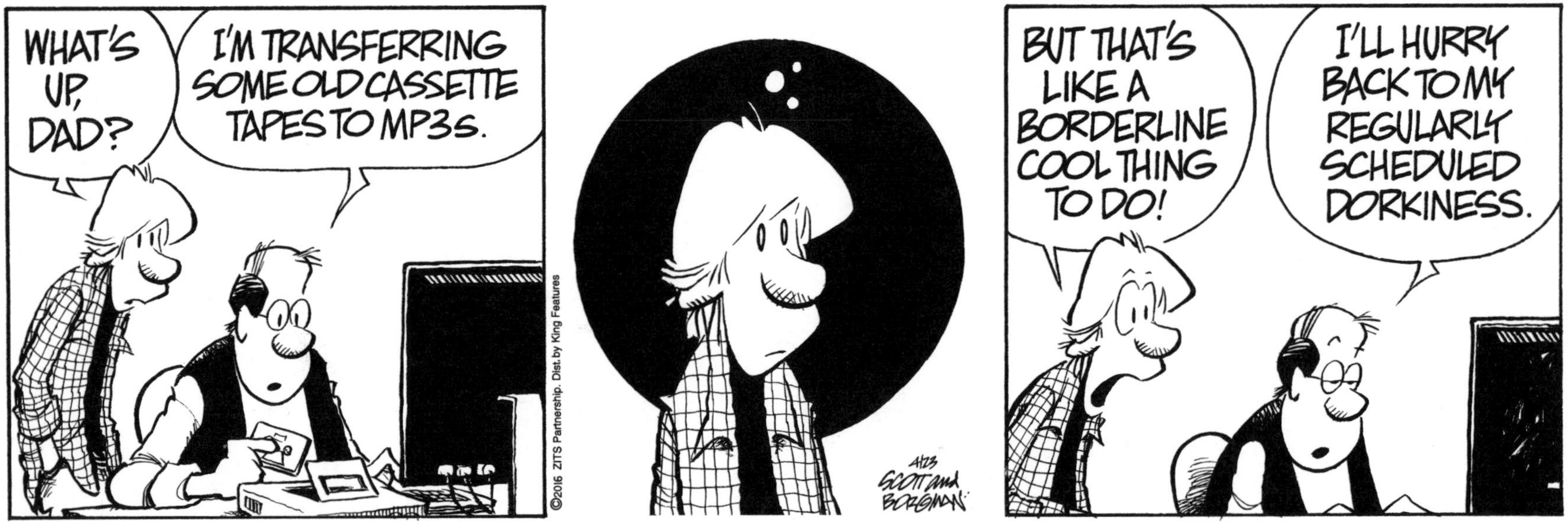
WHAT'S UP, DAD?
I'M TRANSFERRING SOME OLD CASSETTE TAPES TO MP3s.
©2016 ZITS Partnership. Dist. by King Features
BUT THAT'S LIKE A BORDERLINE COOL THING TO DO!
I'LL HURRY BACK TO MY REGULARLY SCHEDULED DORKINESS.

ZITS®

by JERRY SCOTT and JIM BORGMAN

G'NIGHT, JEREMY.
I'Mmm
SCOTT and BORGMAN 4/24
©2016 ZITS Partnership. Dist. by King Features
NEXT TIME TELL ME THAT YOU'RE VIDEO CHATTING!
WILL DO, DAD. SAY GOODNIGHT TO SARA.
AWESOME LEAP, MR. D!

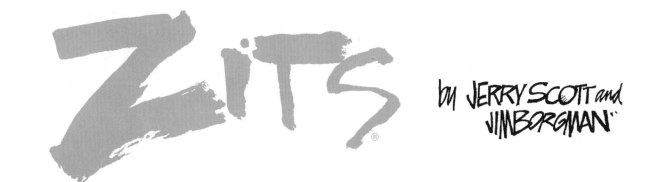

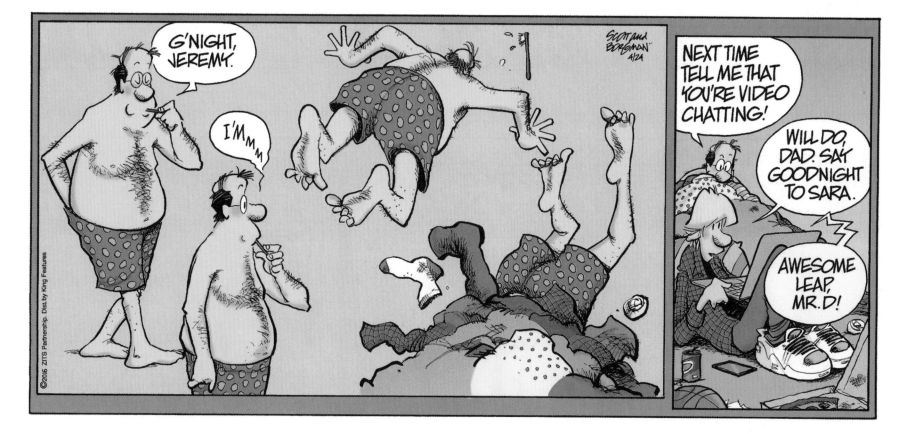

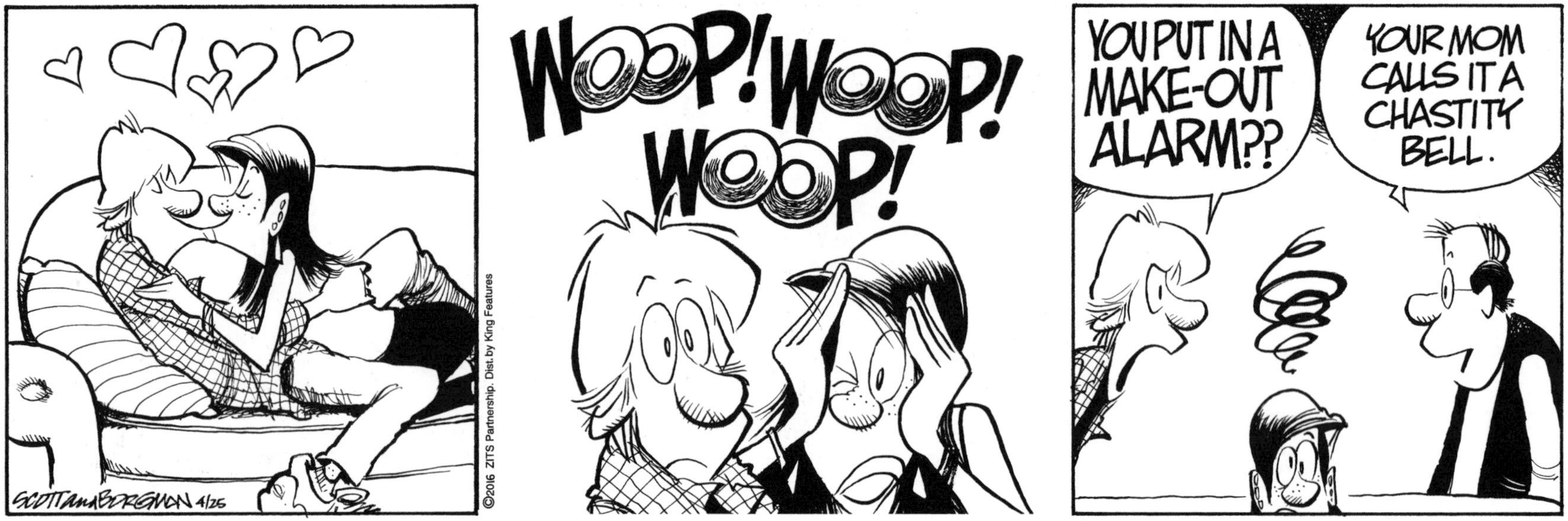
WOOP! WOOP! WOOP!
YOU PUT IN A MAKE-OUT ALARM??
YOUR MOM CALLS IT A CHASTITY BELL.
SCOTT and BORGMAN 4/25
©2016 ZITS Partnership. Dist. by King Features

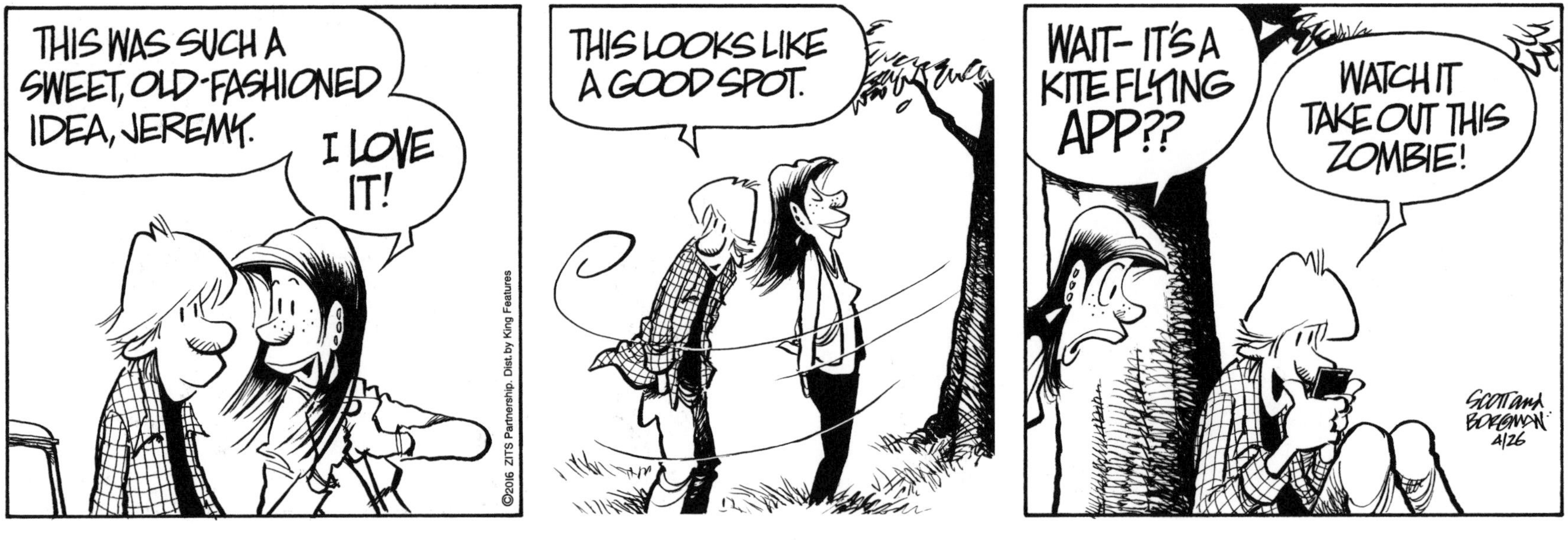
THIS WAS SUCH A SWEET, OLD-FASHIONED IDEA, JEREMY.
I LOVE IT!
THIS LOOKS LIKE A GOOD SPOT.
WAIT- IT'S A KITE FLYING APP??
WATCH IT TAKE OUT THIS ZOMBIE!
SCOTT and BORGMAN 4/26
©2016 ZITS Partnership. Dist. by King Features

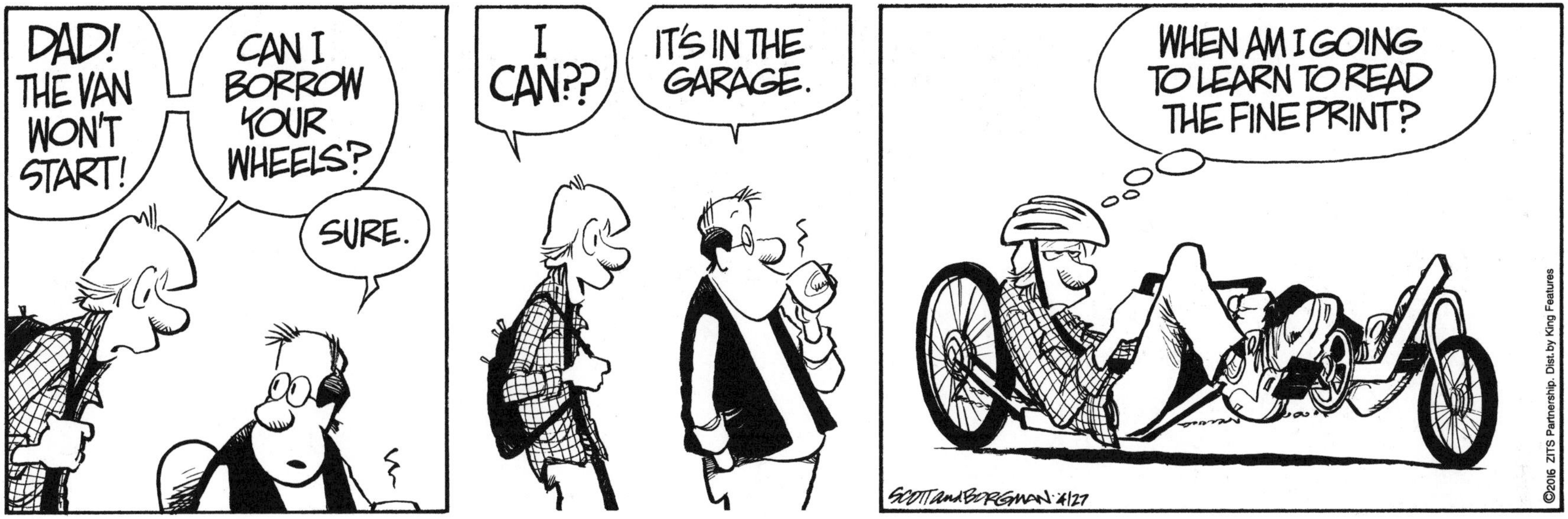
DAD! THE VAN WON'T START!
CAN I BORROW YOUR WHEELS?
SURE.
I CAN??
IT'S IN THE GARAGE.
WHEN AM I GOING TO LEARN TO READ THE FINE PRINT?
SCOTT AND BORGMAN 4/27
©2016 ZITS Partnership. Dist. by King Features

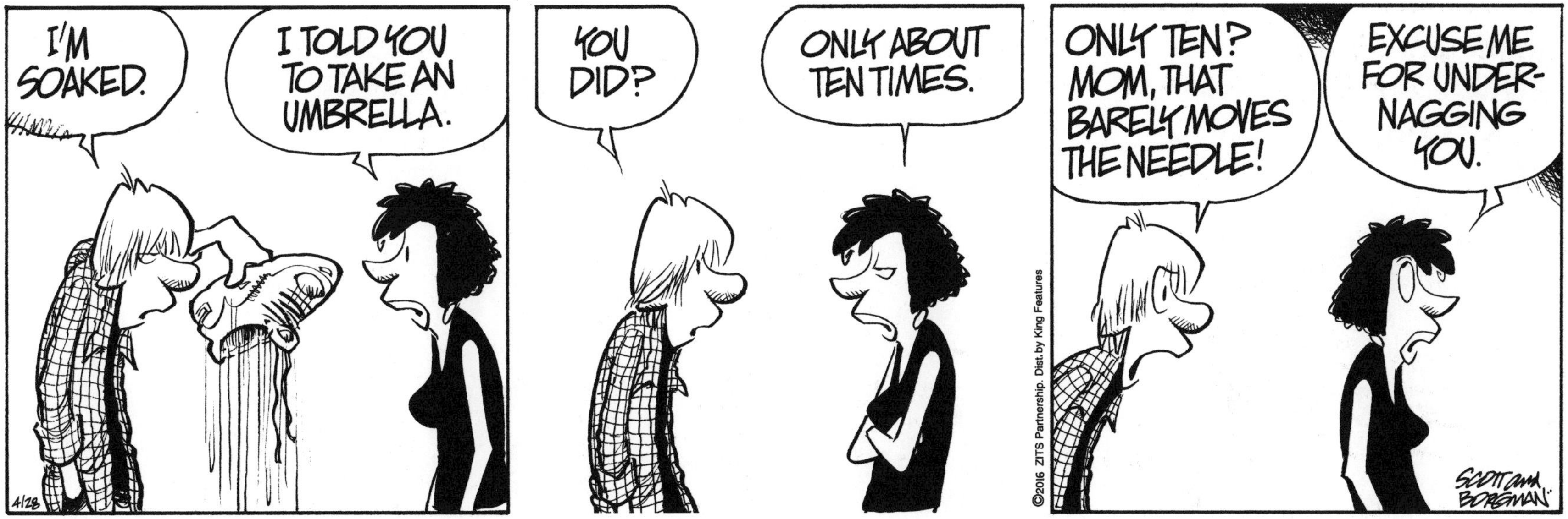
I'M SOAKED.
I TOLD YOU TO TAKE AN UMBRELLA.
YOU DID?
ONLY ABOUT TEN TIMES.
ONLY TEN? MOM, THAT BARELY MOVES THE NEEDLE!
EXCUSE ME FOR UNDER-NAGGING YOU.
4/28
©2016 ZITS Partnership. Dist. by King Features
SCOTT AND BORGMAN

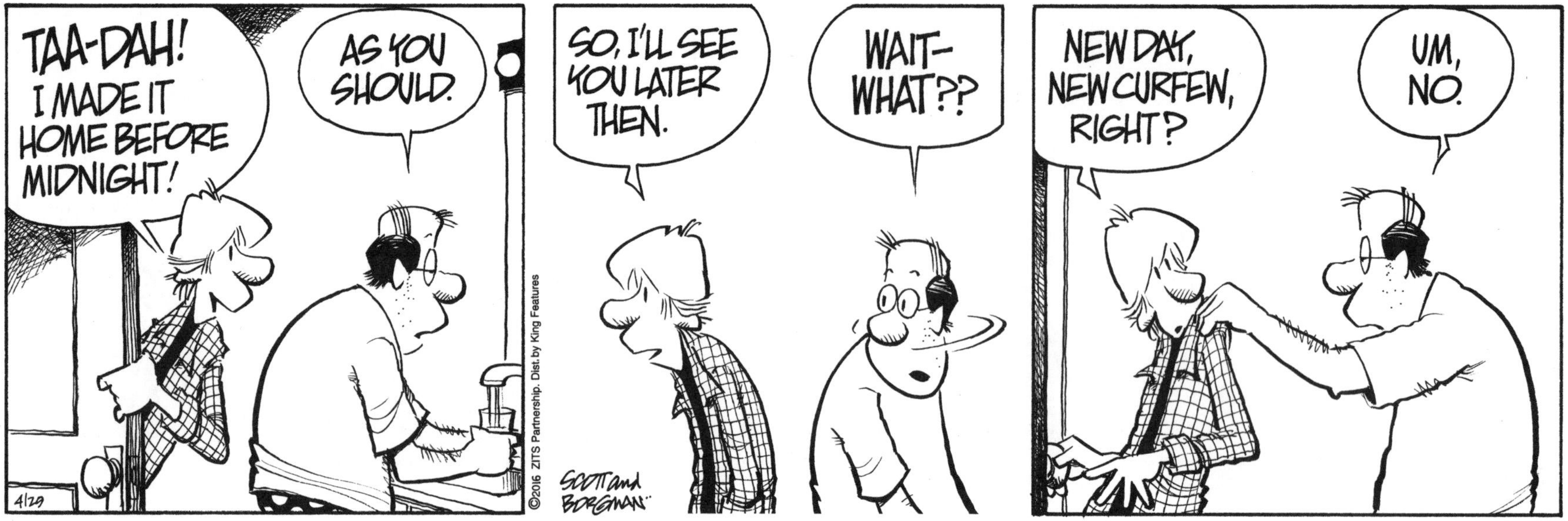
TAA-DAH! I MADE IT HOME BEFORE MIDNIGHT!
AS YOU SHOULD.
SO, I'LL SEE YOU LATER THEN.
WAIT- WHAT??
NEW DAY, NEW CURFEW, RIGHT?
UM, NO.
4/29
©2016 ZITS Partnership. Dist. by King Features
SCOTT and BORGMAN

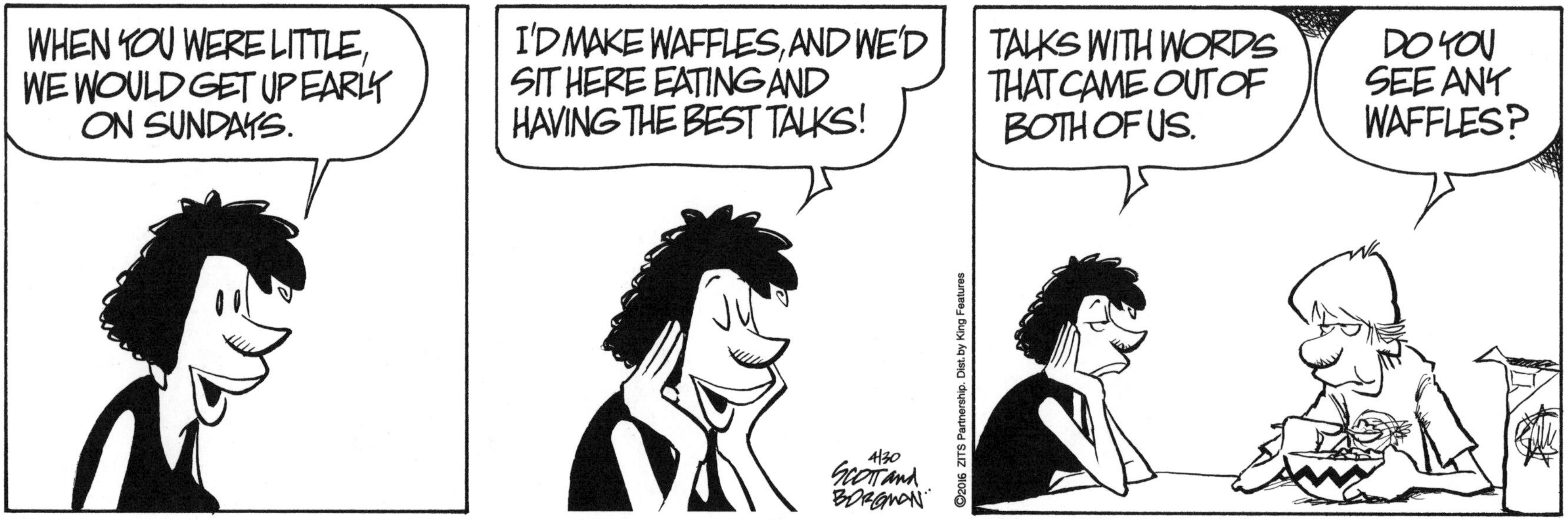
WHEN YOU WERE LITTLE, WE WOULD GET UP EARLY ON SUNDAYS.
I'D MAKE WAFFLES, AND WE'D SIT HERE EATING AND HAVING THE BEST TALKS!
TALKS WITH WORDS THAT CAME OUT OF BOTH OF US.
DO YOU SEE ANY WAFFLES?
4/30
SCOTT and BORGMAN
©2016 ZITS Partnership. Dist. by King Features

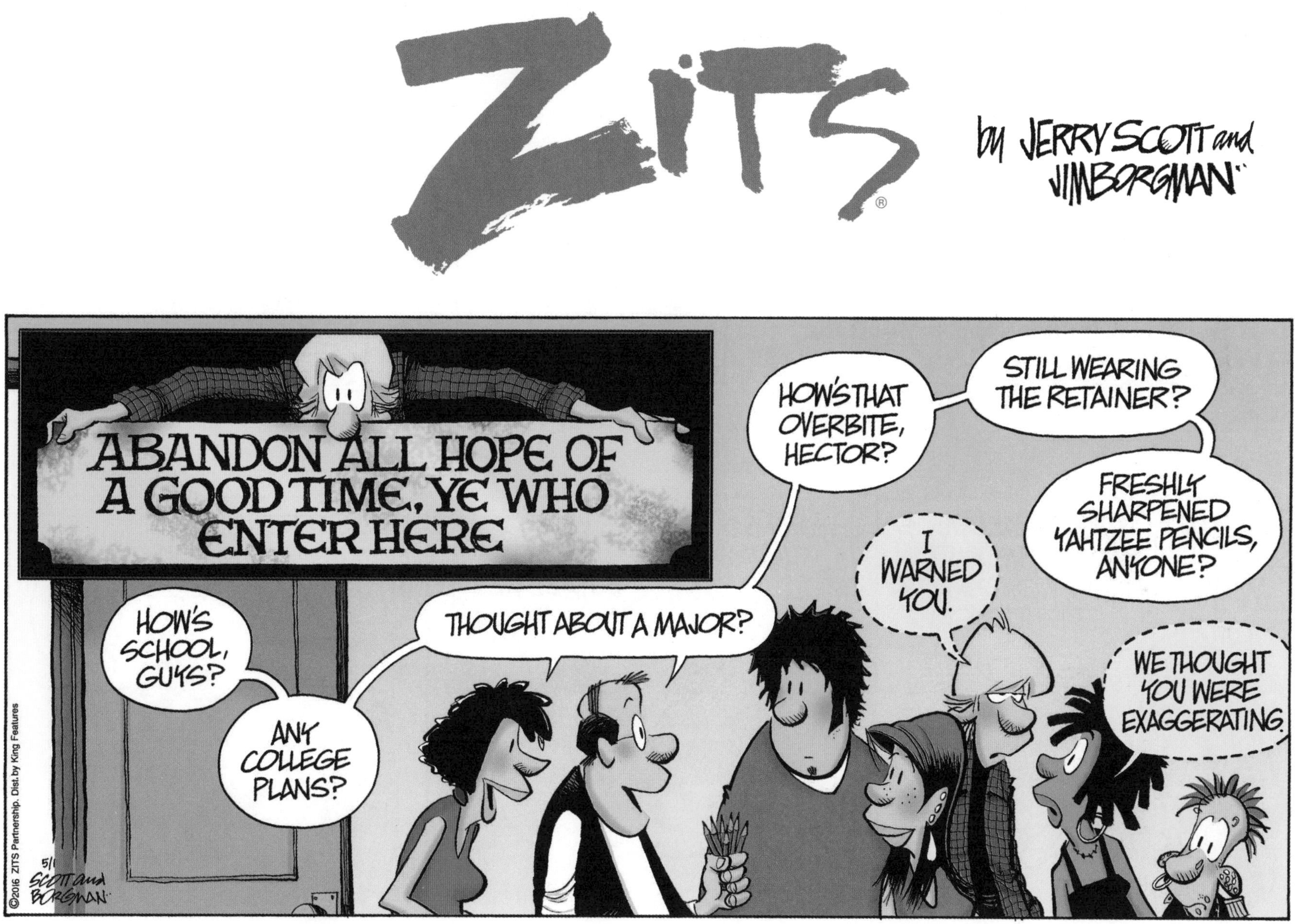
ZITS
by JERRY SCOTT and JIM BORGMAN
ABANDON ALL HOPE OF A GOOD TIME, YE WHO ENTER HERE
HOW'S SCHOOL, GUYS?
ANY COLLEGE PLANS?
THOUGHT ABOUT A MAJOR?
HOW'S THAT OVERBITE, HECTOR?
STILL WEARING THE RETAINER?
FRESHLY SHARPENED YAHTZEE PENCILS, ANYONE?
I WARNED YOU.
WE THOUGHT YOU WERE EXAGGERATING.
©2016 ZITS Partnership. Dist. by King Features
SCOTT and BORGMAN

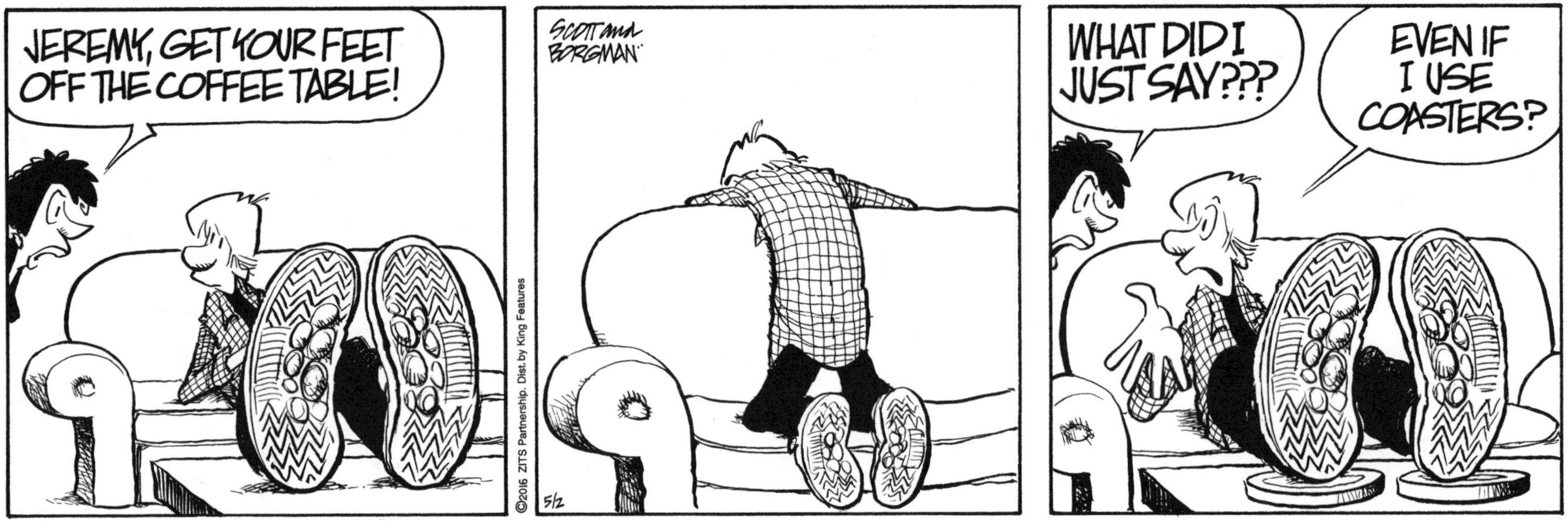
JEREMY, GET YOUR FEET OFF THE COFFEE TABLE!
SCOTT and BORGMAN
©2016 ZITS Partnership. Dist. by King Features
5/2
WHAT DID I JUST SAY???
EVEN IF I USE COASTERS?

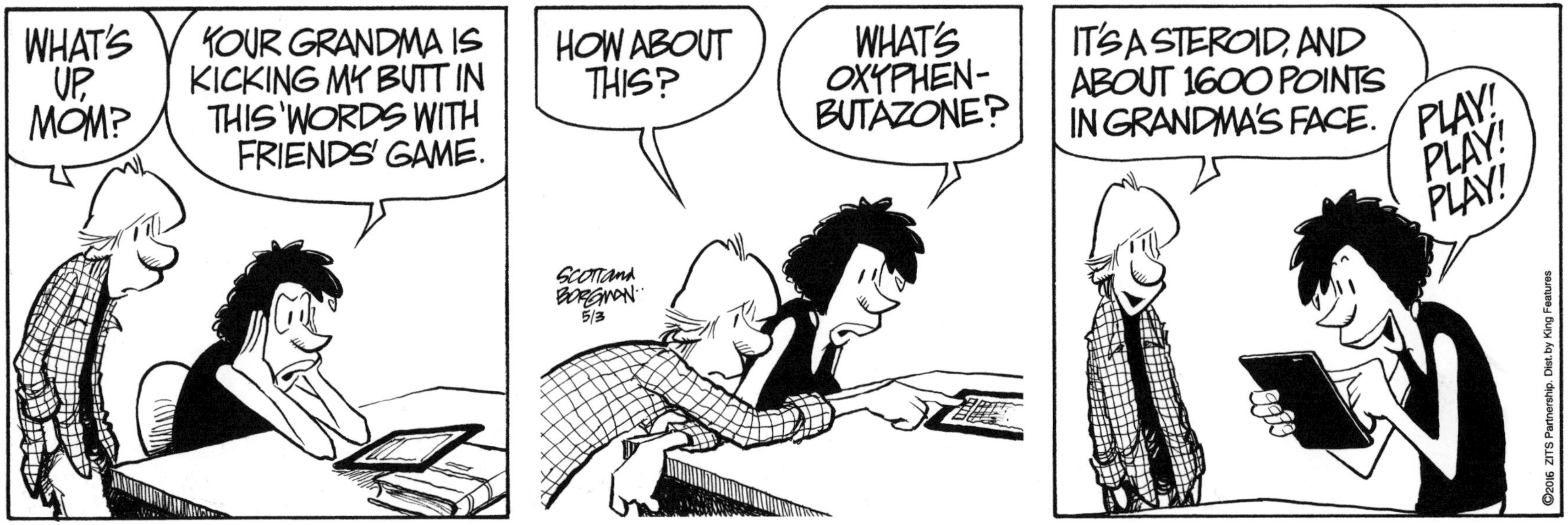
WHAT'S UP, MOM?
YOUR GRANDMA IS KICKING MY BUTT IN THIS 'WORDS WITH FRIENDS' GAME.
HOW ABOUT THIS?
WHAT'S OXYPHEN-BUTAZONE?
SCOTT and BORGMAN
5/3
IT'S A STEROID, AND ABOUT 1600 POINTS IN GRANDMA'S FACE.
PLAY! PLAY! PLAY!
©2016 ZITS Partnership. Dist. by King Features

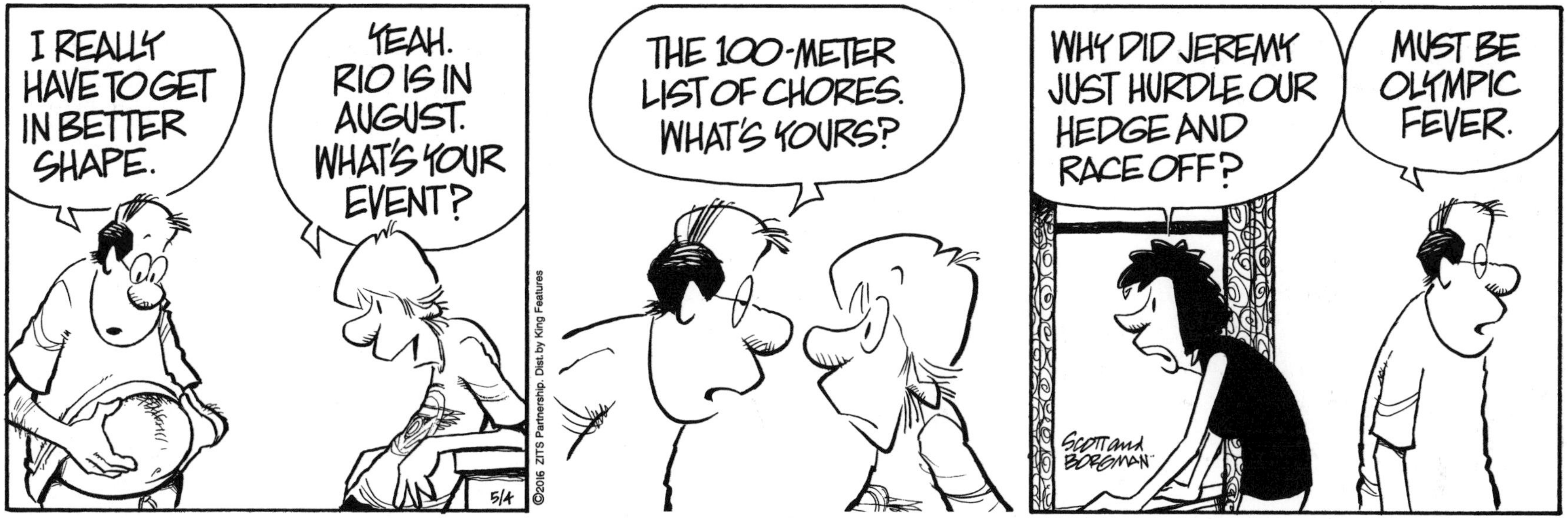
I REALLY HAVE TO GET IN BETTER SHAPE.
YEAH. RIO IS IN AUGUST. WHAT'S YOUR EVENT?
THE 100-METER LIST OF CHORES. WHAT'S YOURS?
WHY DID JEREMY JUST HURDLE OUR HEDGE AND RACE OFF?
MUST BE OLYMPIC FEVER.
5/4
©2016 ZITS Partnership. Dist. by King Features
SCOTT and BORGMAN

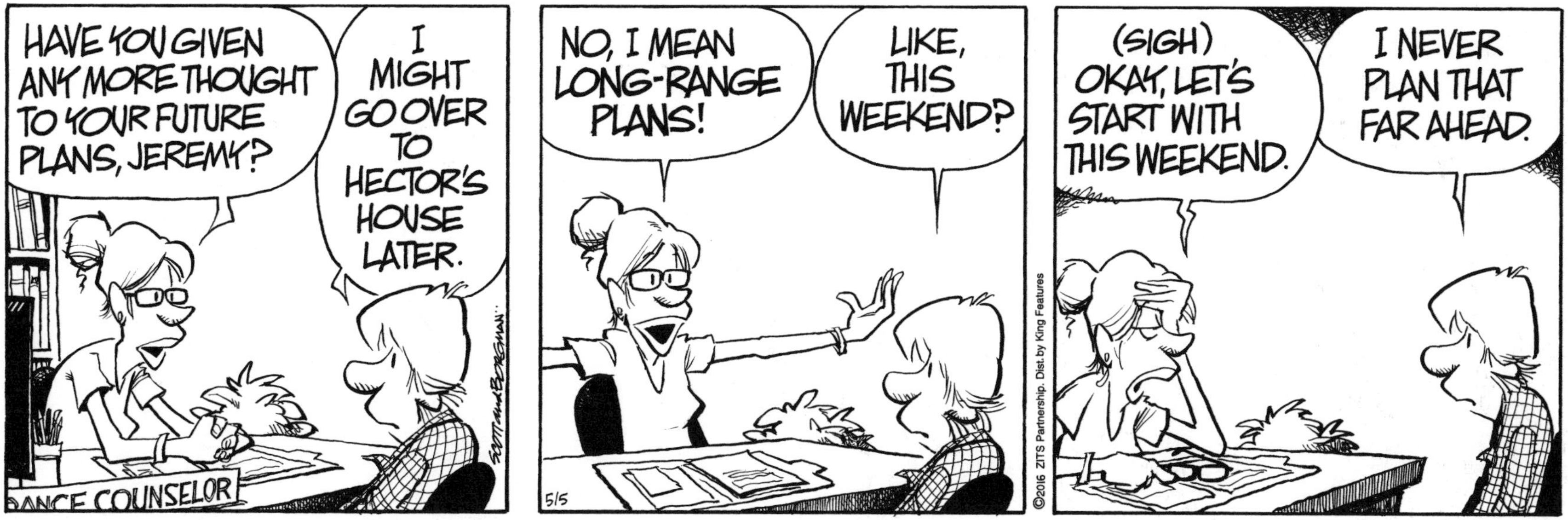
HAVE YOU GIVEN ANY MORE THOUGHT TO YOUR FUTURE PLANS, JEREMY?
I MIGHT GO OVER TO HECTOR'S HOUSE LATER.
ANCE COUNSELOR
SCOTT and BORGMAN
NO, I MEAN LONG-RANGE PLANS!
LIKE, THIS WEEKEND?
5/5
©2016 ZITS Partnership. Dist. by King Features
(SIGH) OKAY, LET'S START WITH THIS WEEKEND.
I NEVER PLAN THAT FAR AHEAD.

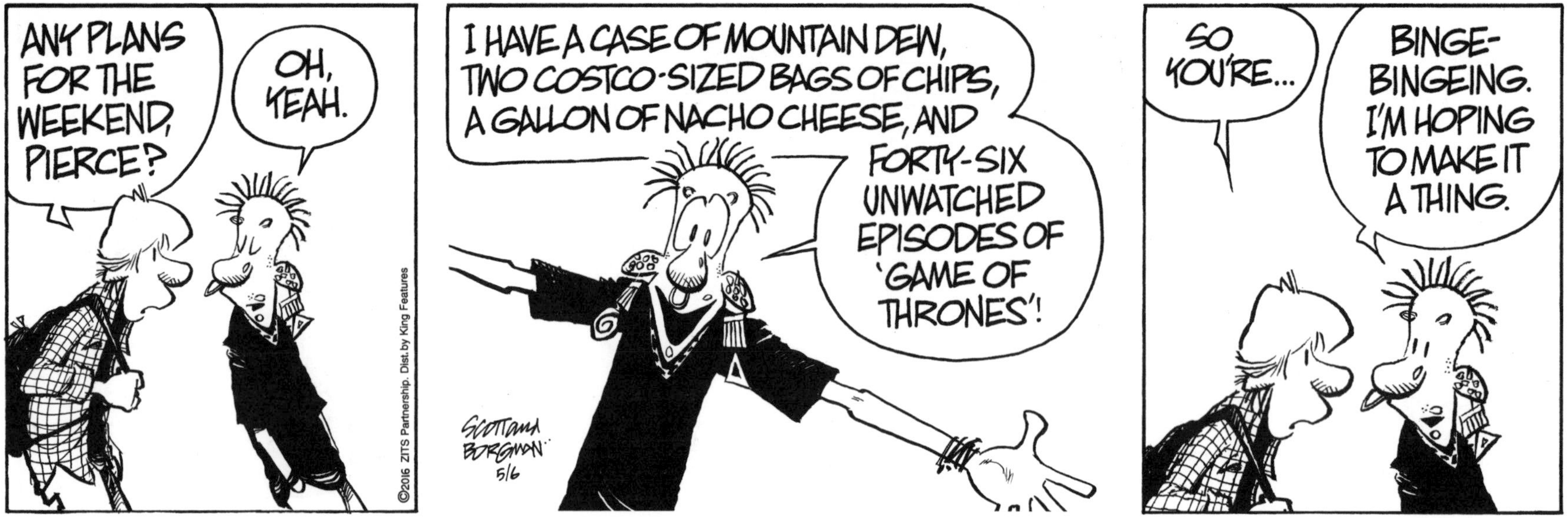
ANY PLANS FOR THE WEEKEND, PIERCE?
OH, YEAH.
I HAVE A CASE OF MOUNTAIN DEW, TWO COSTCO-SIZED BAGS OF CHIPS, A GALLON OF NACHO CHEESE, AND
FORTY-SIX UNWATCHED EPISODES OF 'GAME OF THRONES'!
SO YOU'RE...
BINGE-BINGEING. I'M HOPING TO MAKE IT A THING.
©2016 ZITS Partnership. Dist. by King Features
SCOTT and BORGMAN 5/6

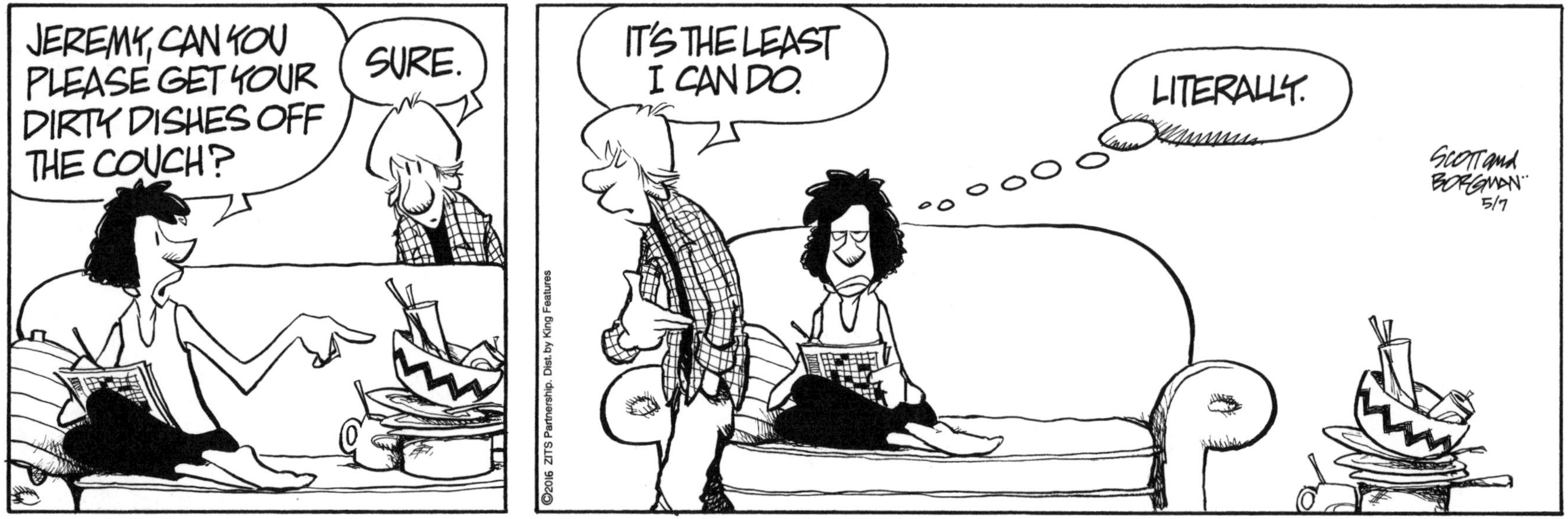
JEREMY, CAN YOU PLEASE GET YOUR DIRTY DISHES OFF THE COUCH?
SURE.
IT'S THE LEAST I CAN DO.
LITERALLY.
©2016 ZITS Partnership. Dist. by King Features
SCOTT and BORGMAN 5/7

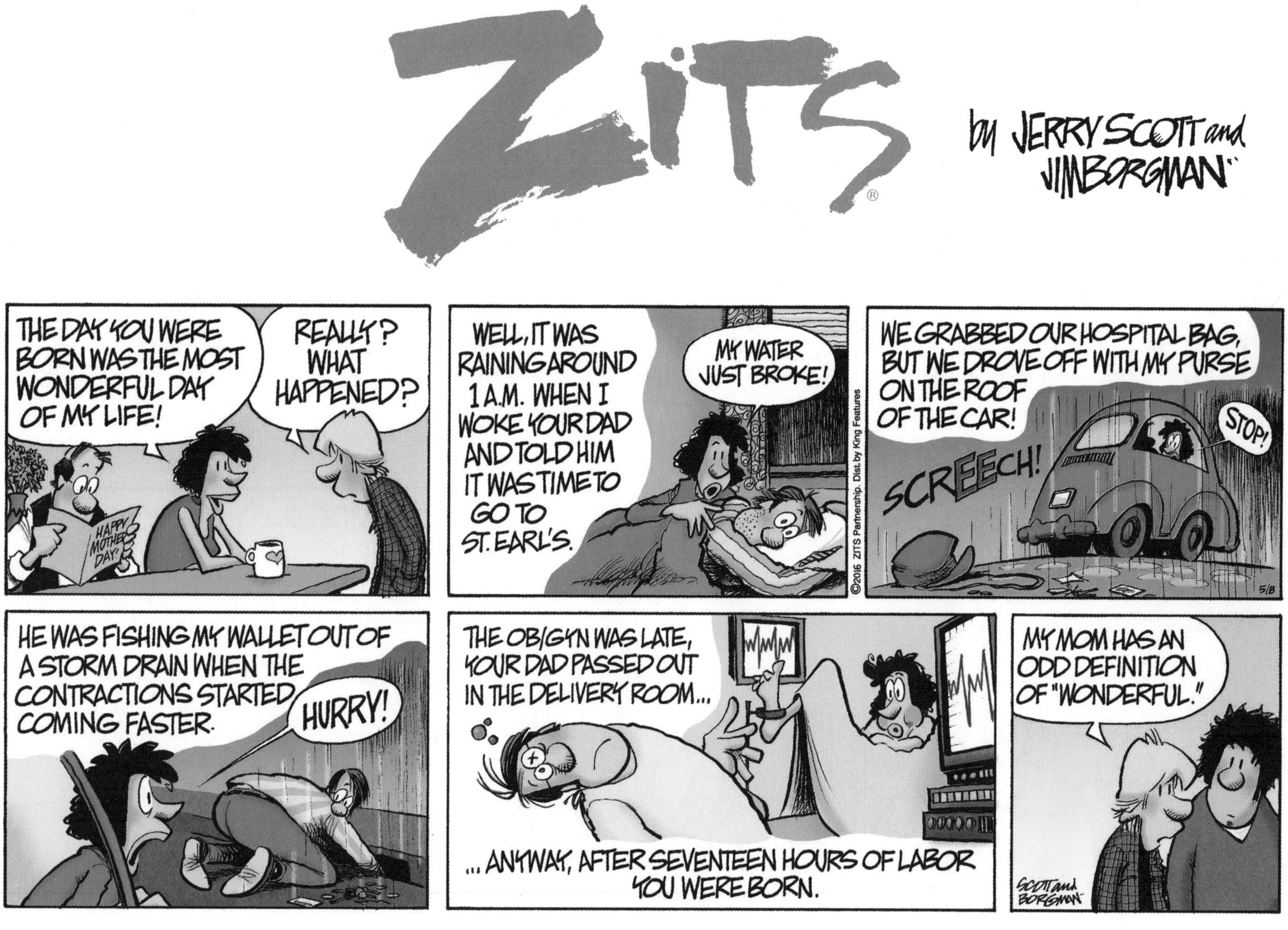
ZITS
by JERRY SCOTT and JIM BORGMAN
THE DAY YOU WERE BORN WAS THE MOST WONDERFUL DAY OF MY LIFE!
REALLY? WHAT HAPPENED?
HAPPY MOTHER'S DAY!
WELL, IT WAS RAINING AROUND 1 A.M. WHEN I WOKE YOUR DAD AND TOLD HIM IT WAS TIME TO GO TO ST. EARL'S.
MY WATER JUST BROKE!
©2016 ZITS Partnership. Dist. by King Features
WE GRABBED OUR HOSPITAL BAG, BUT WE DROVE OFF WITH MY PURSE ON THE ROOF OF THE CAR!
STOP!
SCREEECH!
5/8
HE WAS FISHING MY WALLET OUT OF A STORM DRAIN WHEN THE CONTRACTIONS STARTED COMING FASTER.
HURRY!
THE OB/GYN WAS LATE, YOUR DAD PASSED OUT IN THE DELIVERY ROOM...
...ANYWAY, AFTER SEVENTEEN HOURS OF LABOR YOU WERE BORN.
MY MOM HAS AN ODD DEFINITION OF "WONDERFUL."
SCOTT and BORGMAN

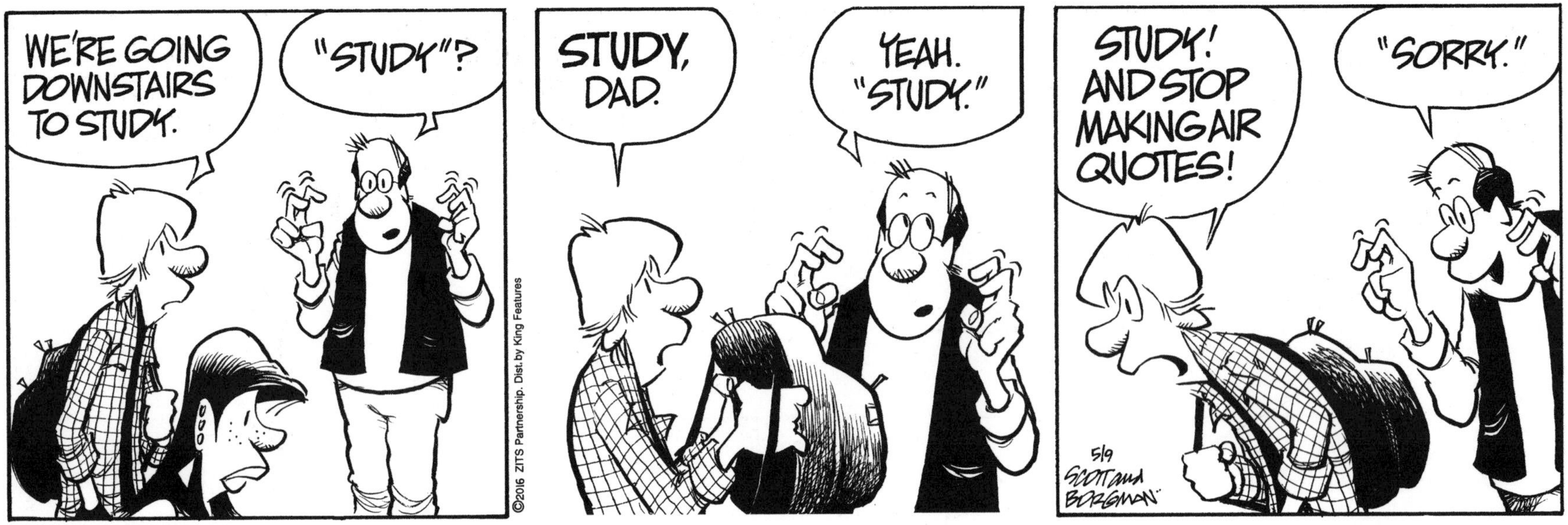

WE'RE GOING DOWNSTAIRS TO STUDY.
"STUDY"?
©2016 ZITS Partnership. Dist. by King Features
STUDY, DAD.
YEAH. "STUDY."
STUDY! AND STOP MAKING AIR QUOTES!
"SORRY."
5/9
SCOTT and BORGMAN

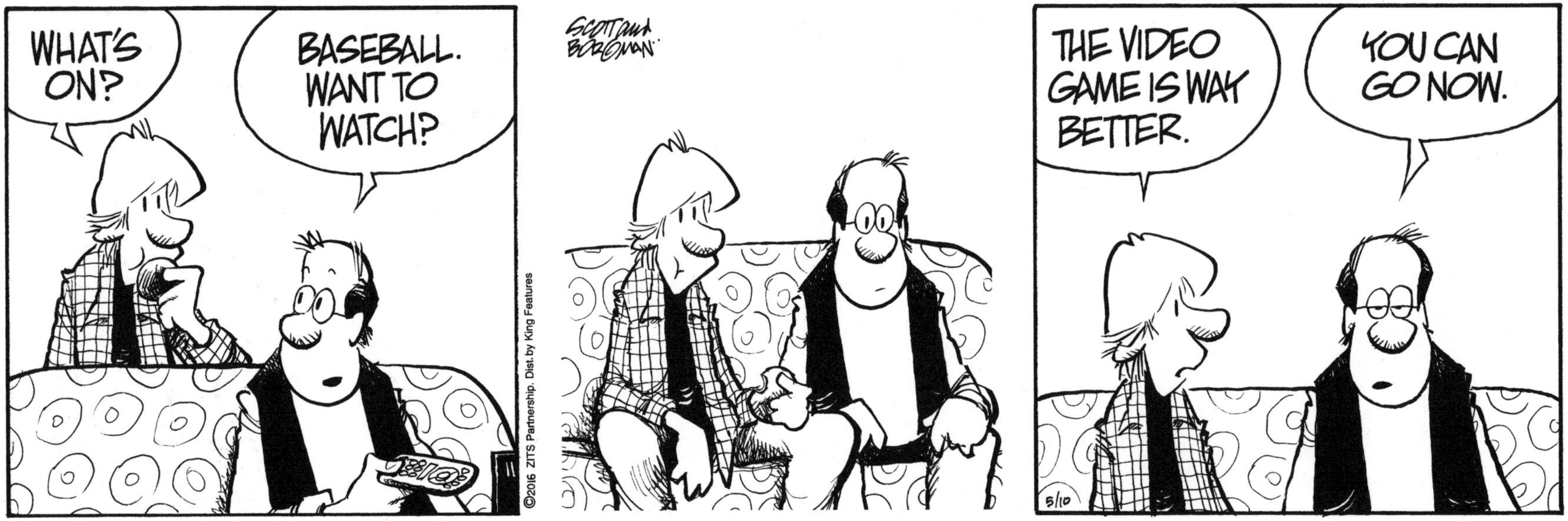

WHAT'S ON?
BASEBALL. WANT TO WATCH?
©2016 ZITS Partnership. Dist. by King Features
SCOTT and BORGMAN
THE VIDEO GAME IS WAY BETTER.
YOU CAN GO NOW.
5/10

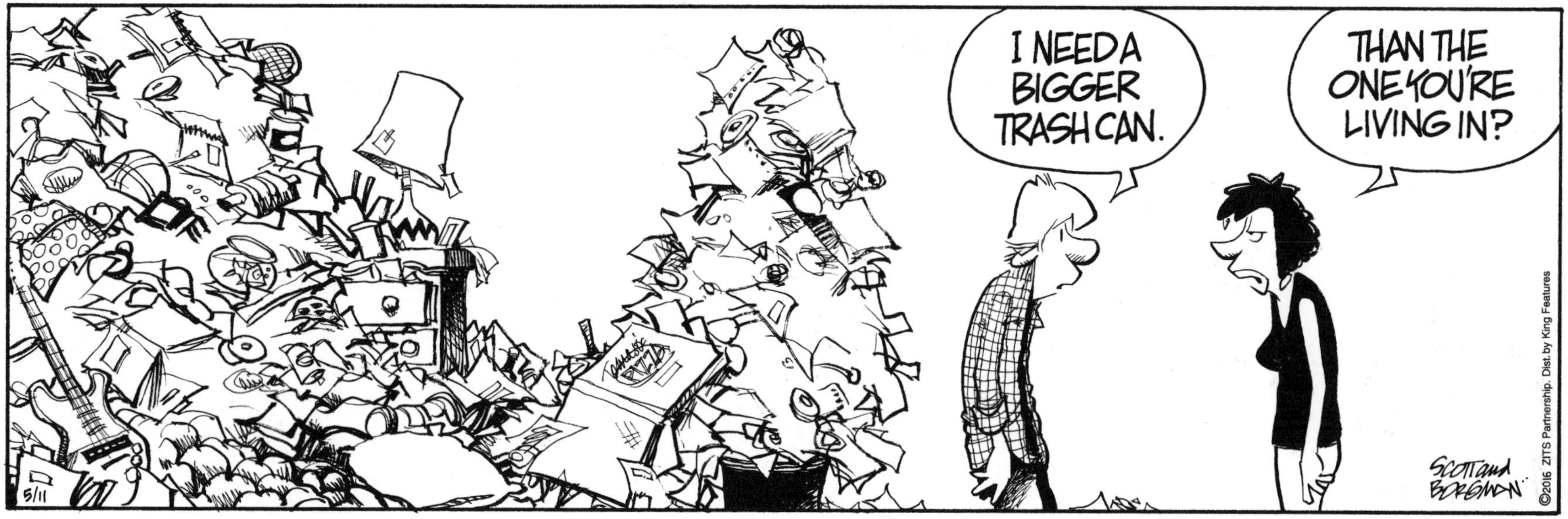
5/11
I NEED A BIGGER TRASH CAN.
THAN THE ONE YOU'RE LIVING IN?
SCOTT and BORGMAN
©2016 ZITS Partnership. Dist. by King Features

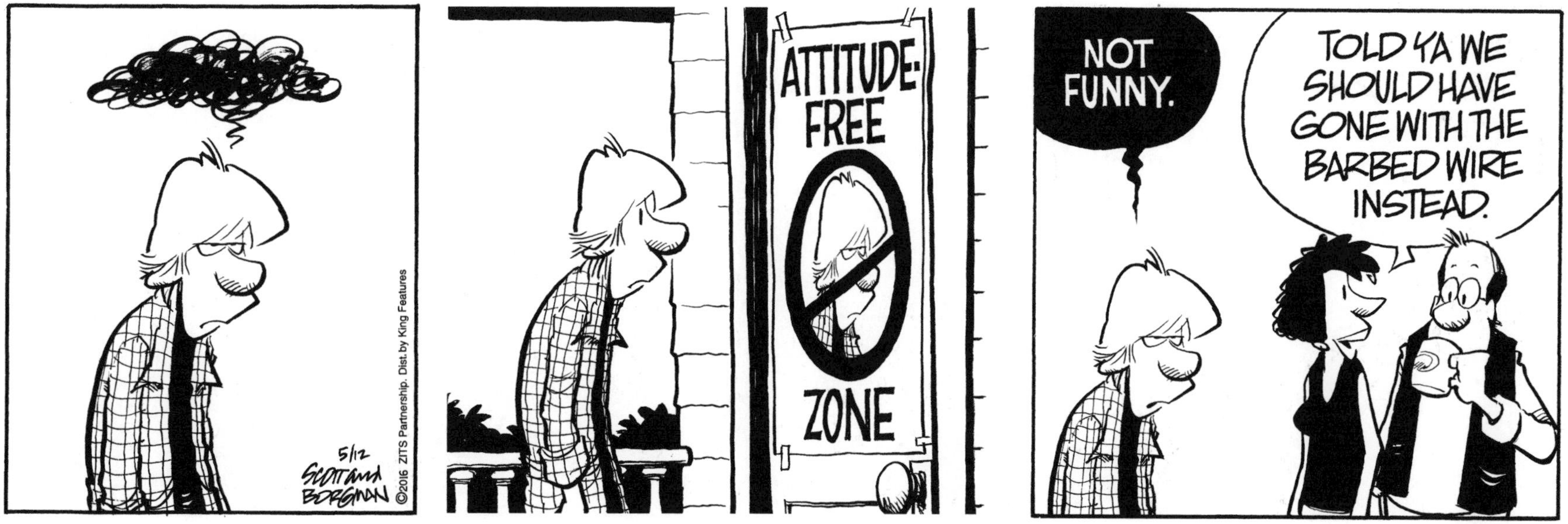
5/12
SCOTT and BORGMAN
©2016 ZITS Partnership. Dist. by King Features
ATTITUDE-FREE ZONE
NOT FUNNY.
TOLD YA WE SHOULD HAVE GONE WITH THE BARBED WIRE INSTEAD.

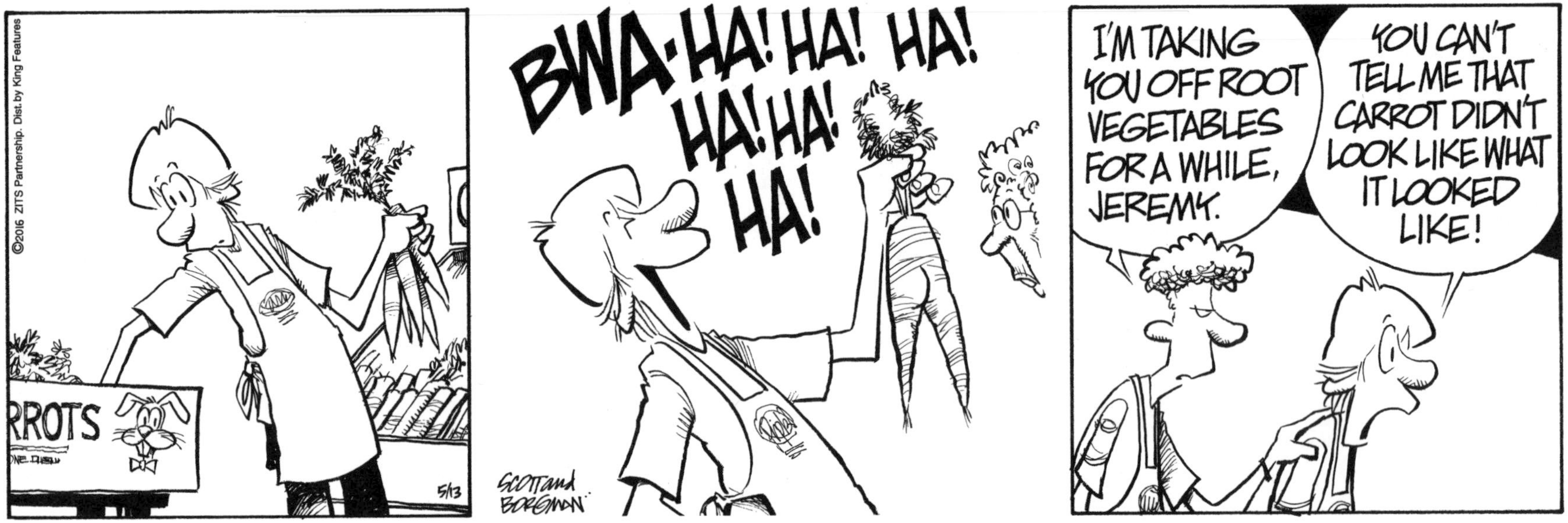
©2016 ZITS Partnership. Dist. by King Features
RROTS
5/13
BWA-HA! HA! HA! HA! HA! HA!
SCOTT and BORGMAN
I'M TAKING YOU OFF ROOT VEGETABLES FOR A WHILE, JEREMY.
YOU CAN'T TELL ME THAT CARROT DIDN'T LOOK LIKE WHAT IT LOOKED LIKE!

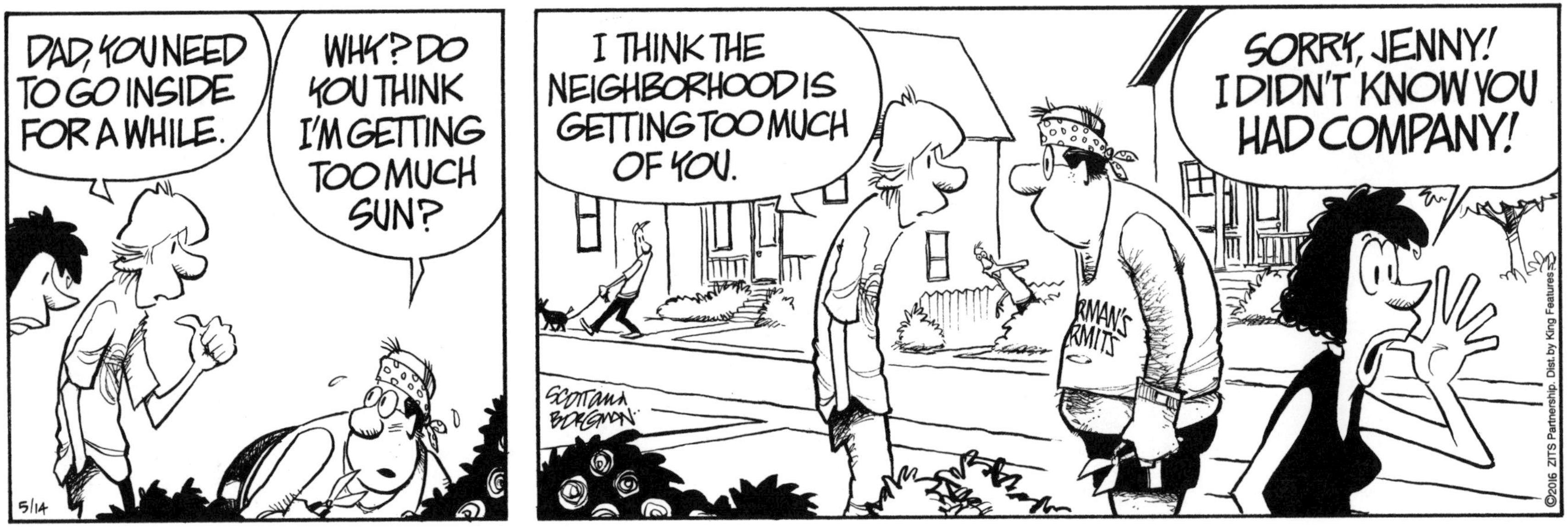
DAD, YOU NEED TO GO INSIDE FOR A WHILE.
WHY? DO YOU THINK I'M GETTING TOO MUCH SUN?
5/14
I THINK THE NEIGHBORHOOD IS GETTING TOO MUCH OF YOU.
SCOTT and BORGMAN
SORRY, JENNY! I DIDN'T KNOW YOU HAD COMPANY!
©2016 ZITS Partnership. Dist. by King Features

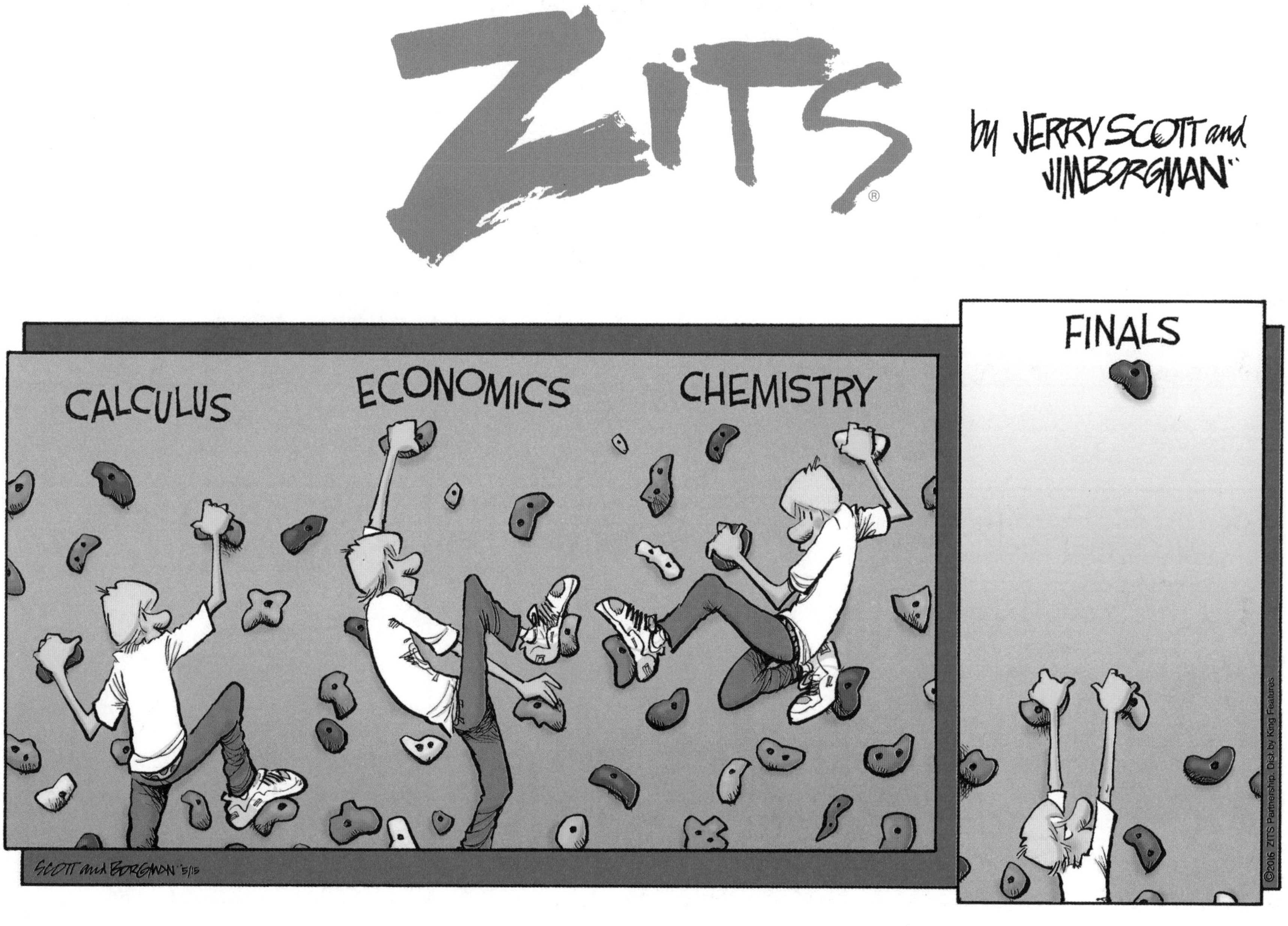
ZITS
by JERRY SCOTT and JIM BORGMAN
CALCULUS
ECONOMICS
CHEMISTRY
FINALS
SCOTT and BORGMAN 5/15
©2016 ZITS Partnership. Dist. by King Features

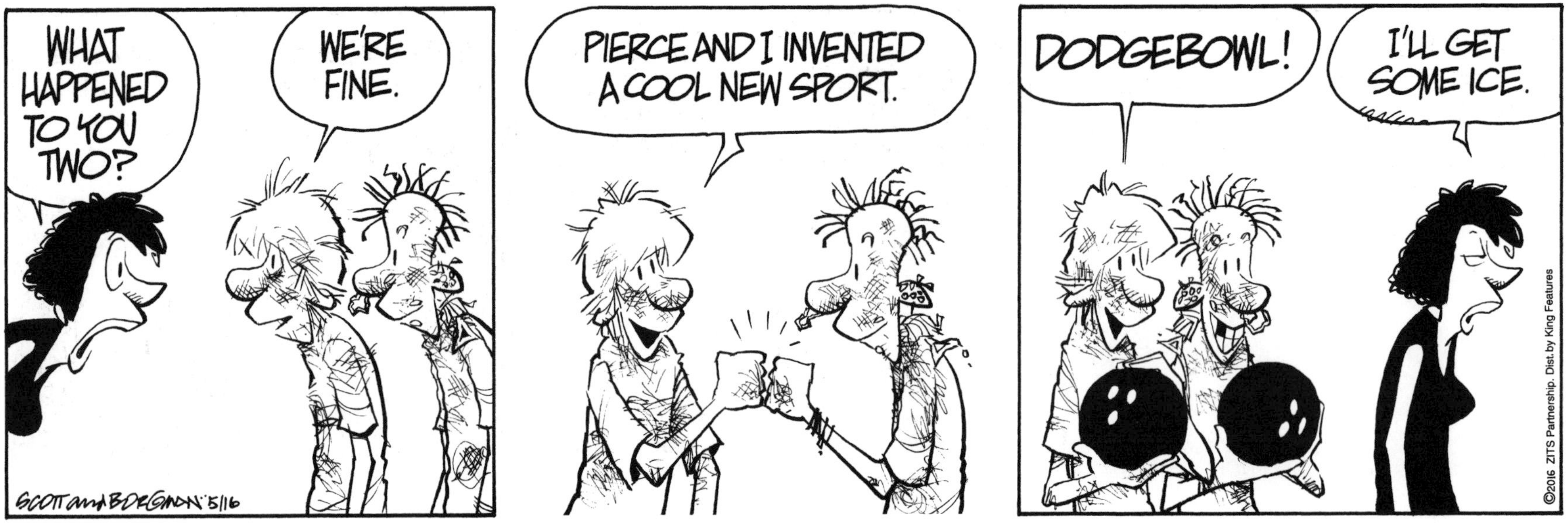
WHAT HAPPENED TO YOU TWO?
WE'RE FINE.
PIERCE AND I INVENTED A COOL NEW SPORT.
DODGEBOWL!
I'LL GET SOME ICE.
SCOTT and BORGMAN 5/16
©2016 ZITS Partnership. Dist. by King Features

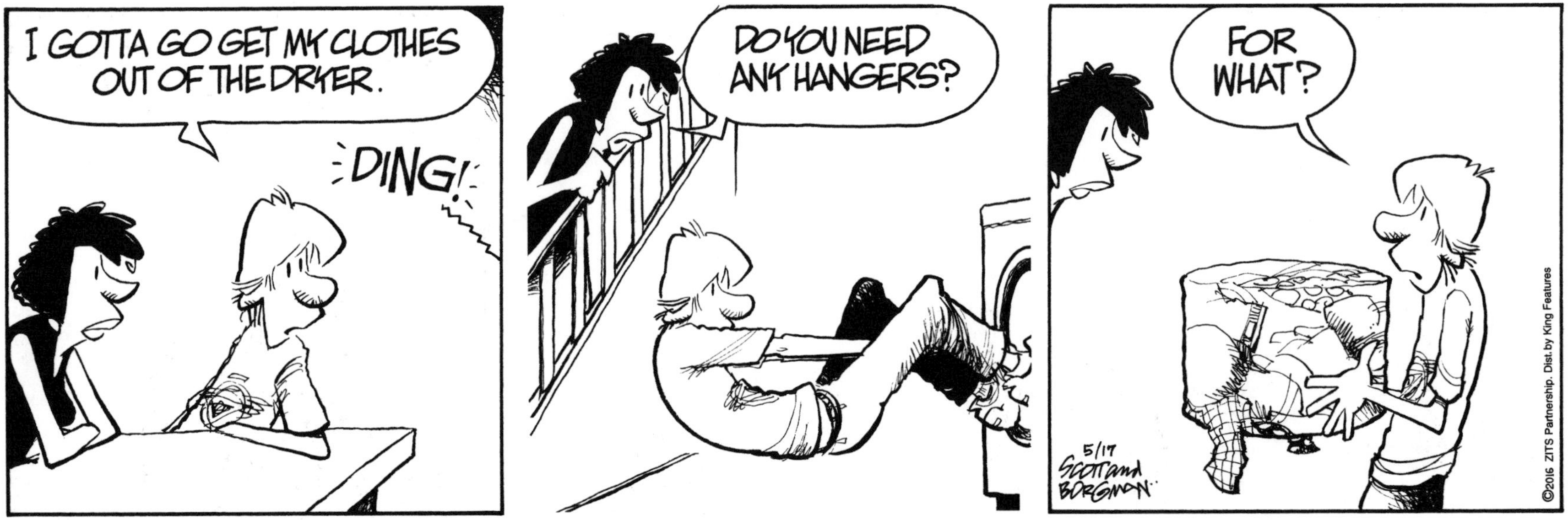
I GOTTA GO GET MY CLOTHES OUT OF THE DRYER.
DING!
DO YOU NEED ANY HANGERS?
FOR WHAT?
5/17 SCOTT and BORGMAN
©2016 ZITS Partnership. Dist. by King Features

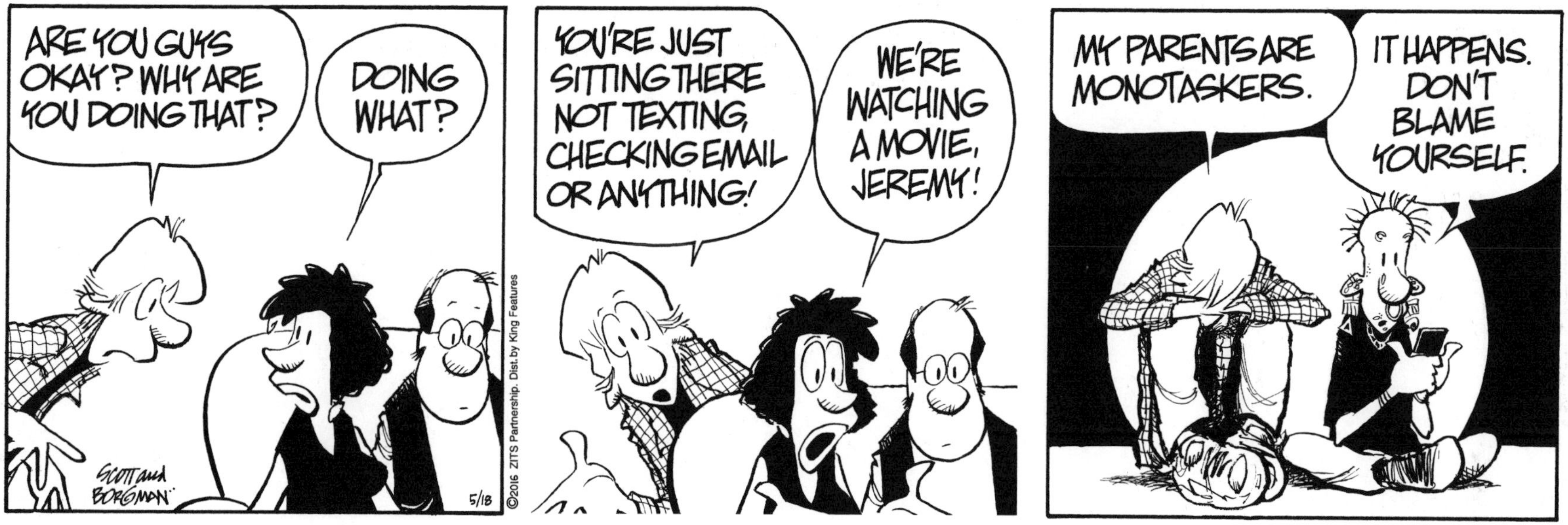
ARE YOU GUYS OKAY? WHY ARE YOU DOING THAT?
DOING WHAT?
SCOTT and BORGMAN
5/18
©2016 ZITS Partnership. Dist. by King Features
YOU'RE JUST SITTING THERE NOT TEXTING, CHECKING EMAIL OR ANYTHING!
WE'RE WATCHING A MOVIE, JEREMY!
MY PARENTS ARE MONOTASKERS.
IT HAPPENS. DON'T BLAME YOURSELF.

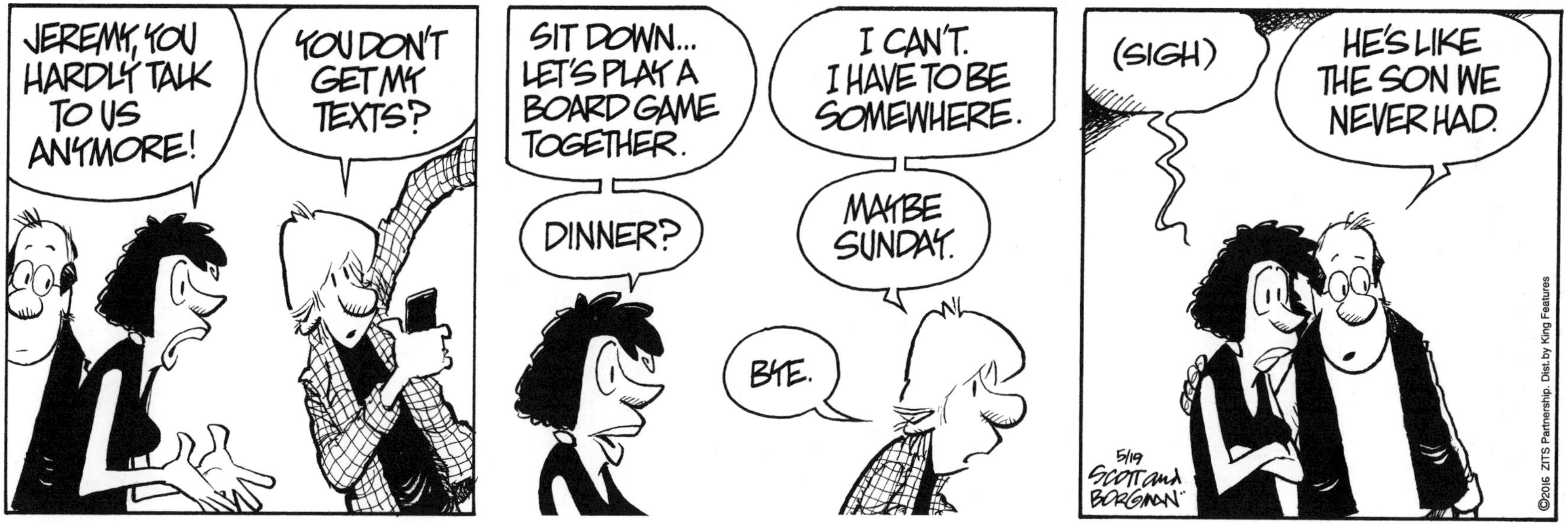
JEREMY, YOU HARDLY TALK TO US ANYMORE!
YOU DON'T GET MY TEXTS?
SIT DOWN... LET'S PLAY A BOARD GAME TOGETHER.
DINNER?
I CAN'T. I HAVE TO BE SOMEWHERE.
MAYBE SUNDAY.
BYE.
(SIGH)
HE'S LIKE THE SON WE NEVER HAD.
5/19
SCOTT and BORGMAN
©2016 ZITS Partnership. Dist. by King Features

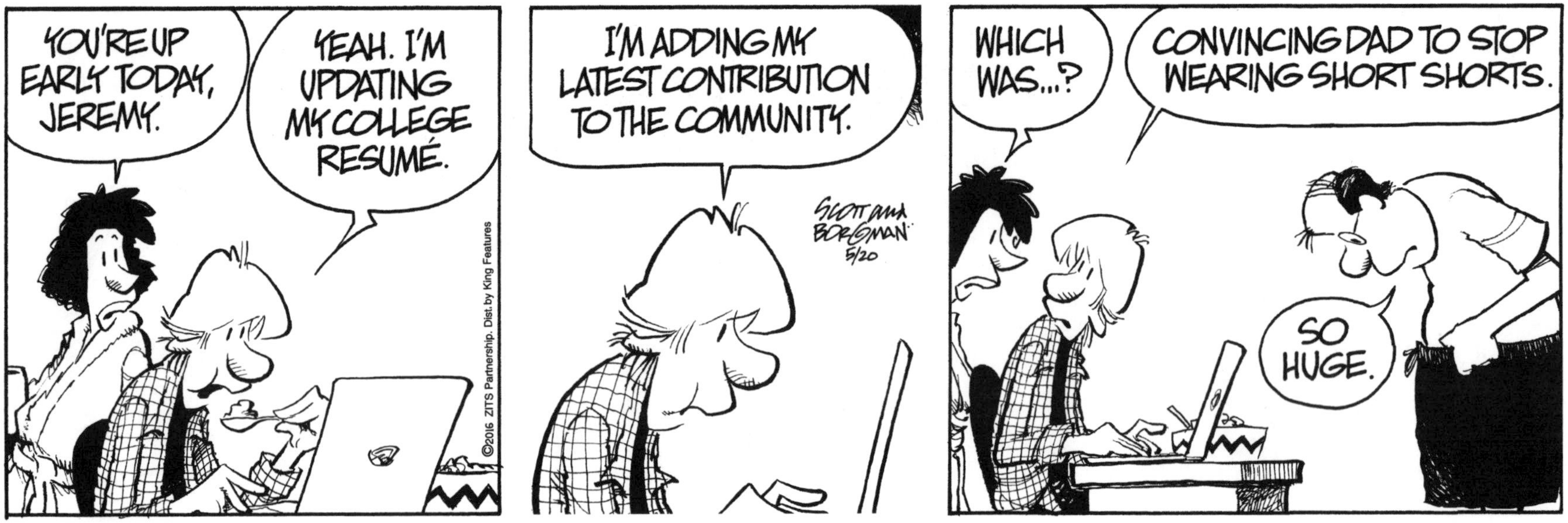
YOU'RE UP EARLY TODAY, JEREMY.
YEAH. I'M UPDATING MY COLLEGE RESUMÉ.
©2016 ZITS Partnership. Dist. by King Features
I'M ADDING MY LATEST CONTRIBUTION TO THE COMMUNITY.
SCOTT and BORGMAN 5/20
WHICH WAS...?
CONVINCING DAD TO STOP WEARING SHORT SHORTS.
SO HUGE.

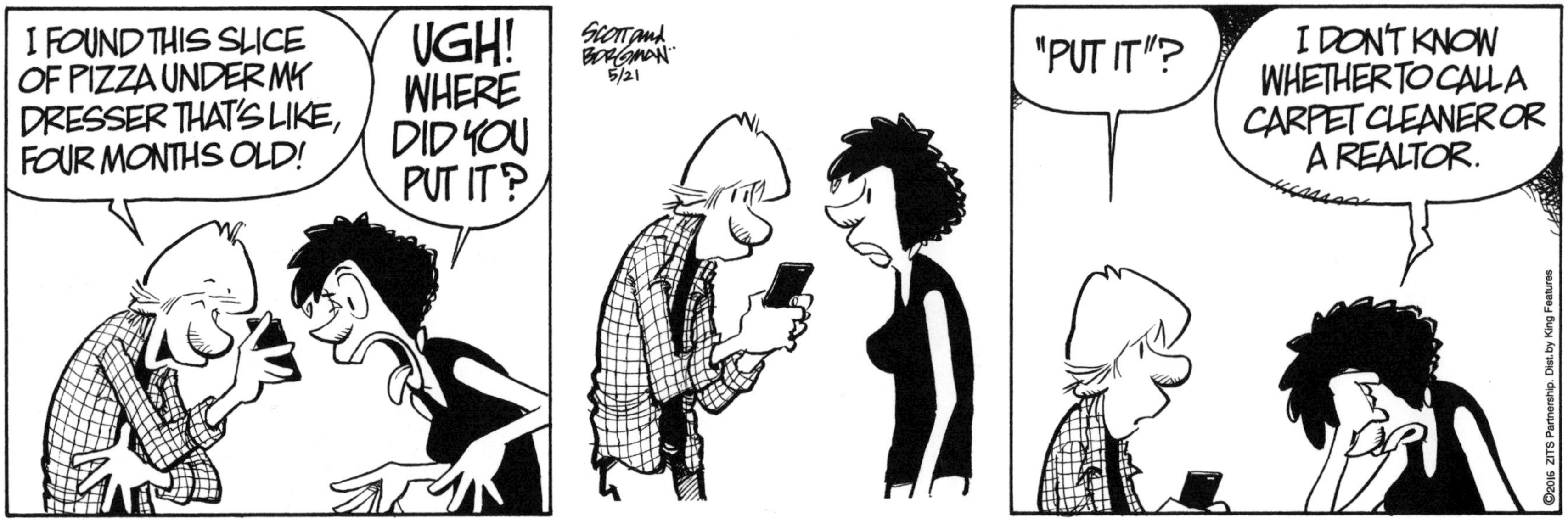
I FOUND THIS SLICE OF PIZZA UNDER MY DRESSER THAT'S LIKE, FOUR MONTHS OLD!
UGH! WHERE DID YOU PUT IT?
SCOTT and BORGMAN 5/21
"PUT IT"?
I DON'T KNOW WHETHER TO CALL A CARPET CLEANER OR A REALTOR.
©2016 ZITS Partnership. Dist. by King Features

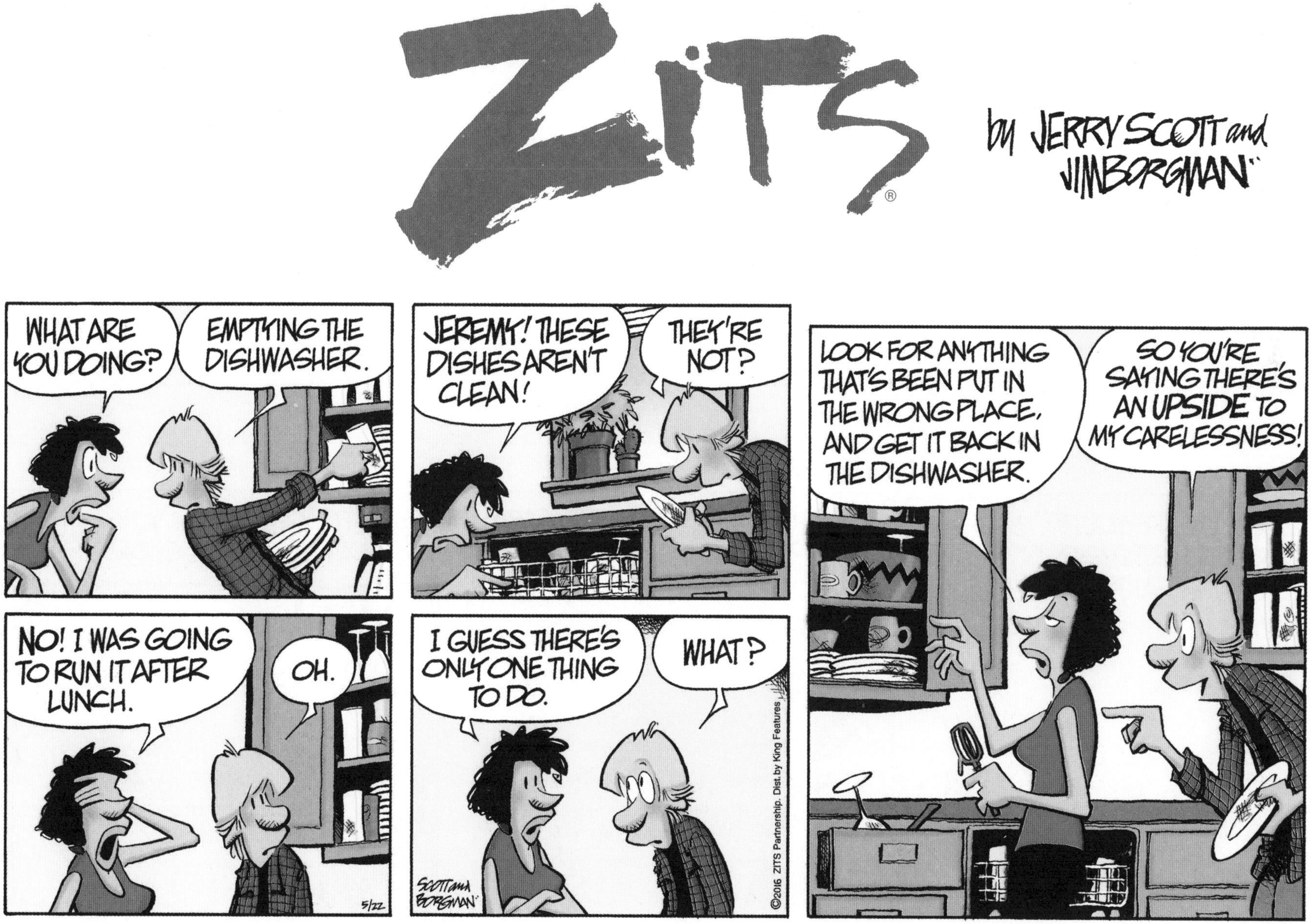
ZITS®
by JERRY SCOTT and JIM BORGMAN
WHAT ARE YOU DOING?
EMPTYING THE DISHWASHER.
JEREMY! THESE DISHES AREN'T CLEAN!
THEY'RE NOT?
NO! I WAS GOING TO RUN IT AFTER LUNCH.
OH.
I GUESS THERE'S ONLY ONE THING TO DO.
WHAT?
©2016 ZITS Partnership. Dist. by King Features
LOOK FOR ANYTHING THAT'S BEEN PUT IN THE WRONG PLACE, AND GET IT BACK IN THE DISHWASHER.
SO YOU'RE SAYING THERE'S AN UPSIDE TO MY CARELESSNESS!

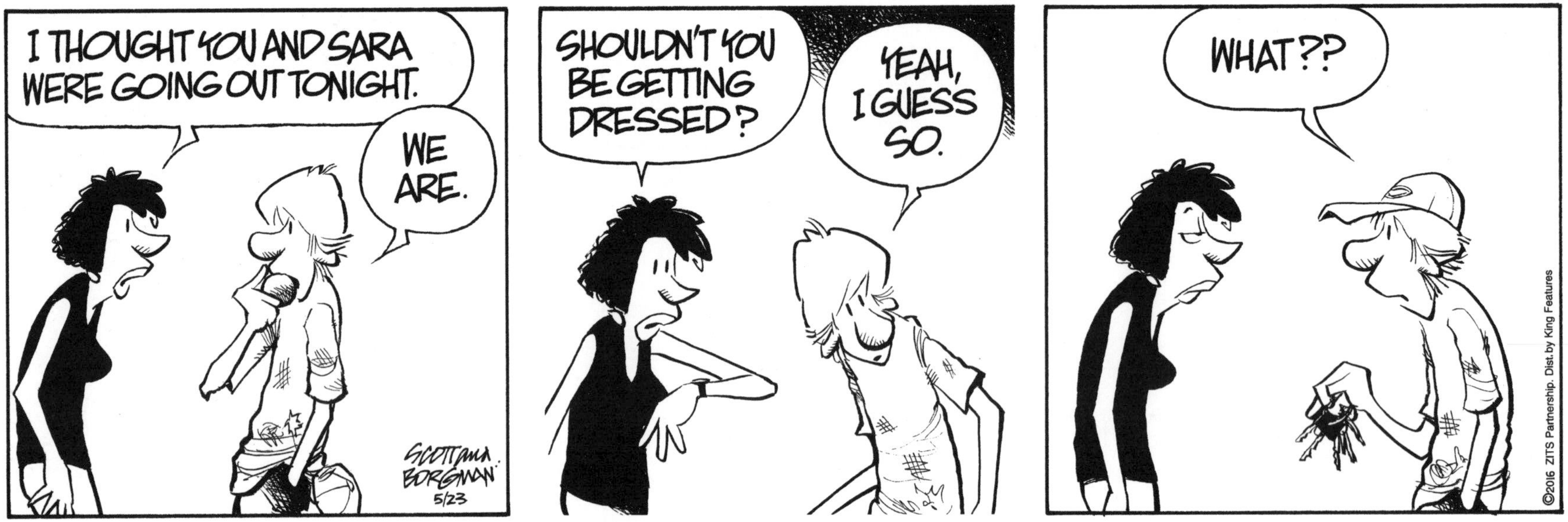
I THOUGHT YOU AND SARA WERE GOING OUT TONIGHT.
WE ARE.
SHOULDN'T YOU BE GETTING DRESSED?
YEAH, I GUESS SO.
WHAT??

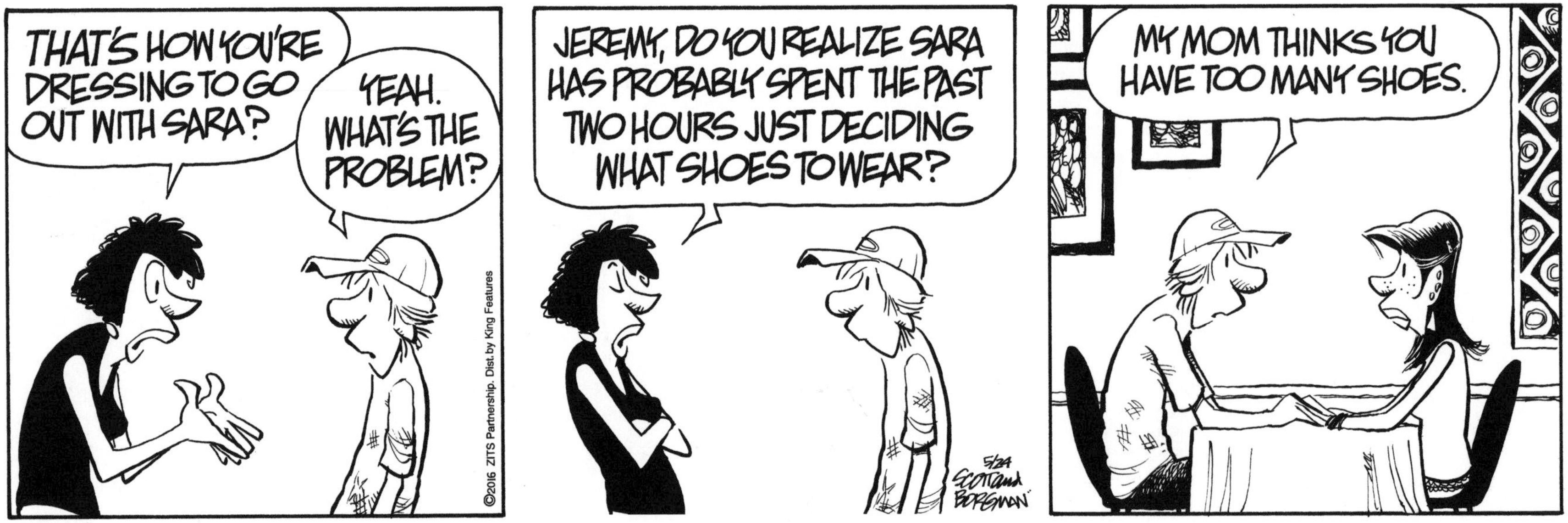
THAT'S HOW YOU'RE DRESSING TO GO OUT WITH SARA?
YEAH. WHAT'S THE PROBLEM?
JEREMY, DO YOU REALIZE SARA HAS PROBABLY SPENT THE PAST TWO HOURS JUST DECIDING WHAT SHOES TO WEAR?
MY MOM THINKS YOU HAVE TOO MANY SHOES.

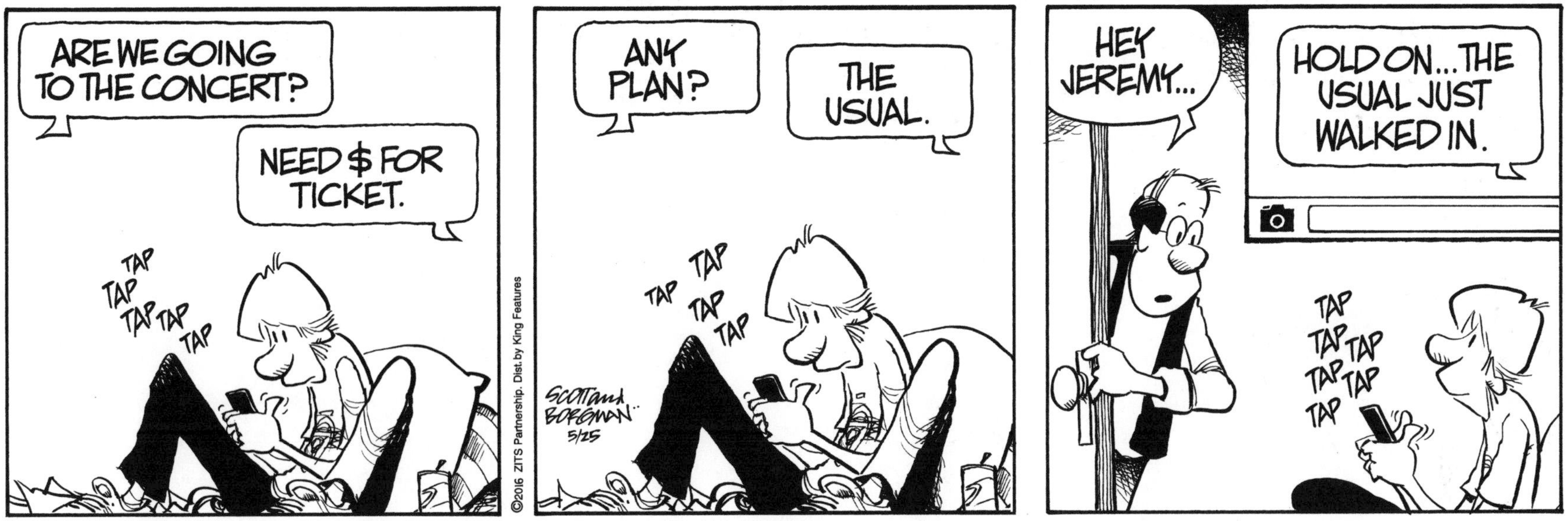
ARE WE GOING TO THE CONCERT?
NEED $ FOR TICKET.
TAP TAP TAP TAP TAP
ANY PLAN?
THE USUAL.
TAP TAP TAP TAP
SCOTT and BORGMAN 5/25
©2016 ZITS Partnership. Dist. by King Features
HEY JEREMY...
HOLD ON... THE USUAL JUST WALKED IN.
TAP TAP TAP TAP TAP TAP

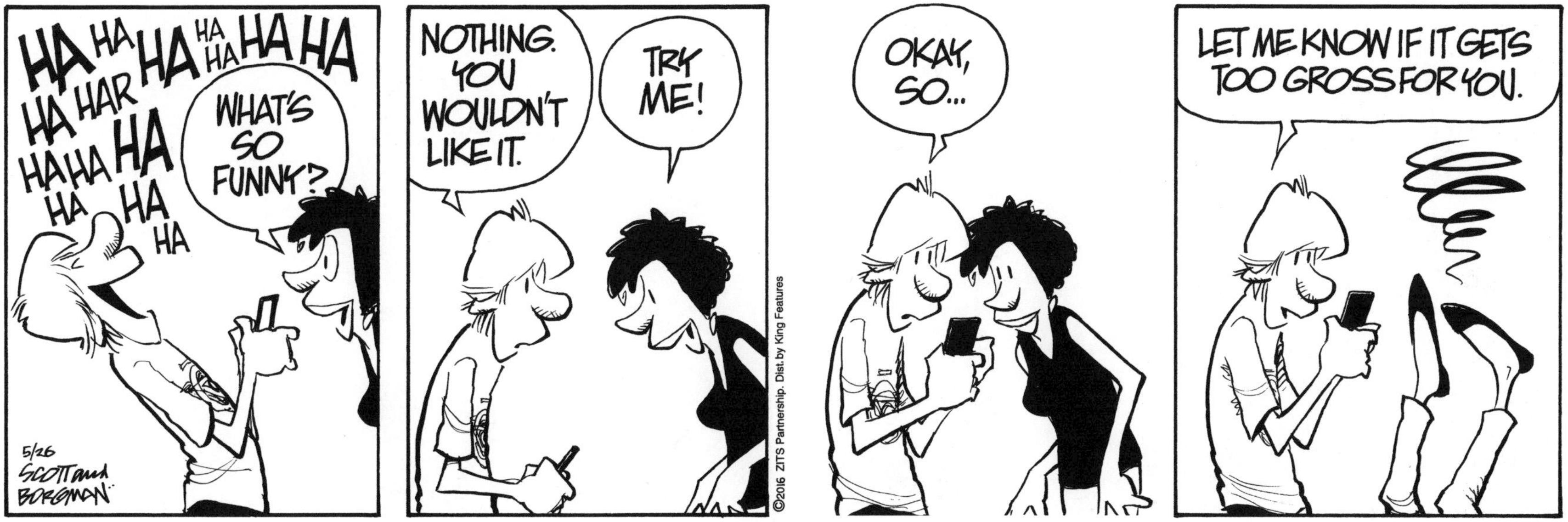
HA HA HA HA HA HA HA HA HAR HA HA HA HA HA HA HA
WHAT'S SO FUNNY?
5/26 SCOTT and BORGMAN
NOTHING. YOU WOULDN'T LIKE IT.
TRY ME!
©2016 ZITS Partnership. Dist. by King Features
OKAY, SO...
LET ME KNOW IF IT GETS TOO GROSS FOR YOU.

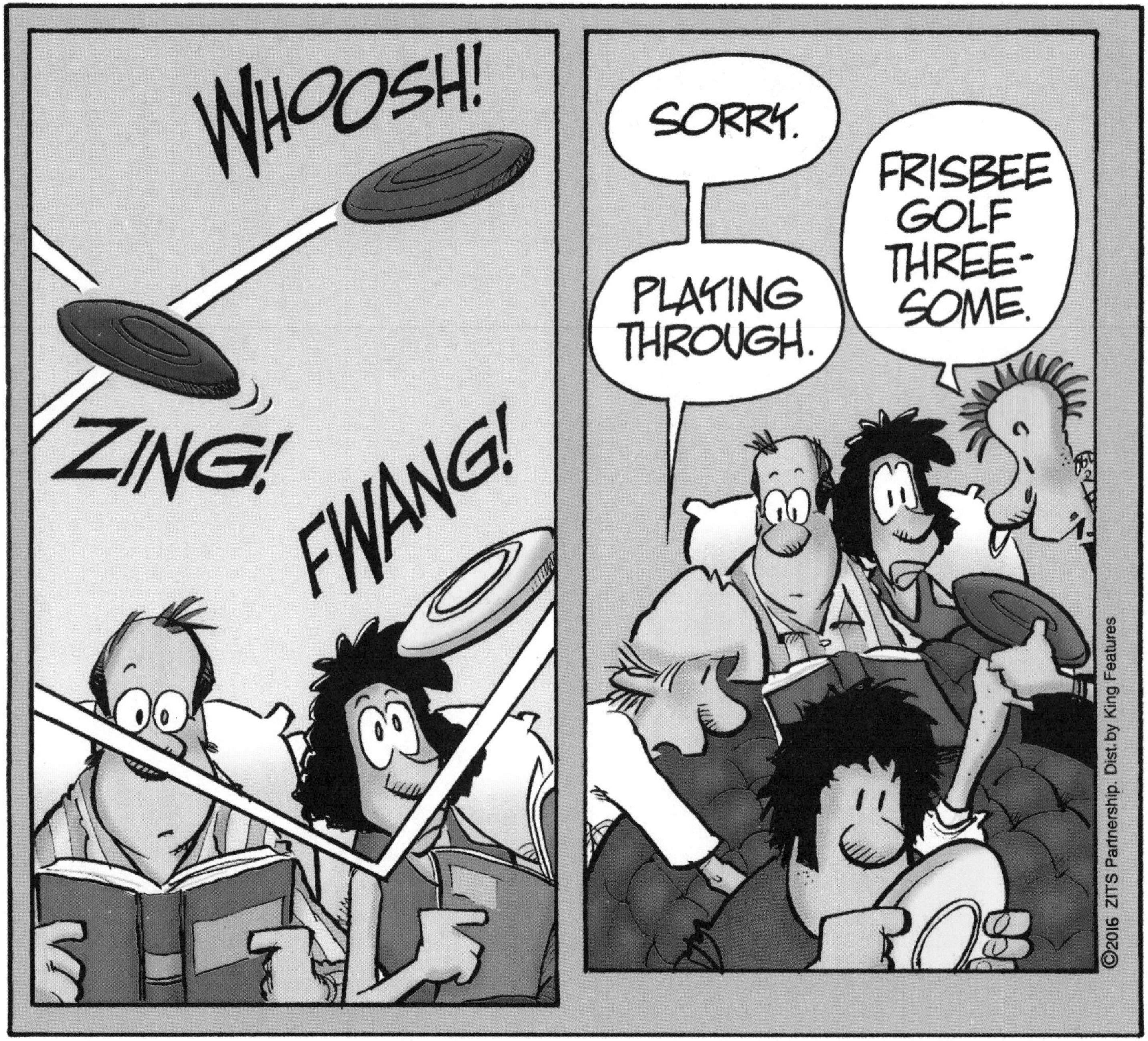
WHOOSH!
ZING!
FWANG!
SORRY.
PLAYING THROUGH.
FRISBEE GOLF THREESOME.
©2016 ZITS Partnership. Dist.by King Features

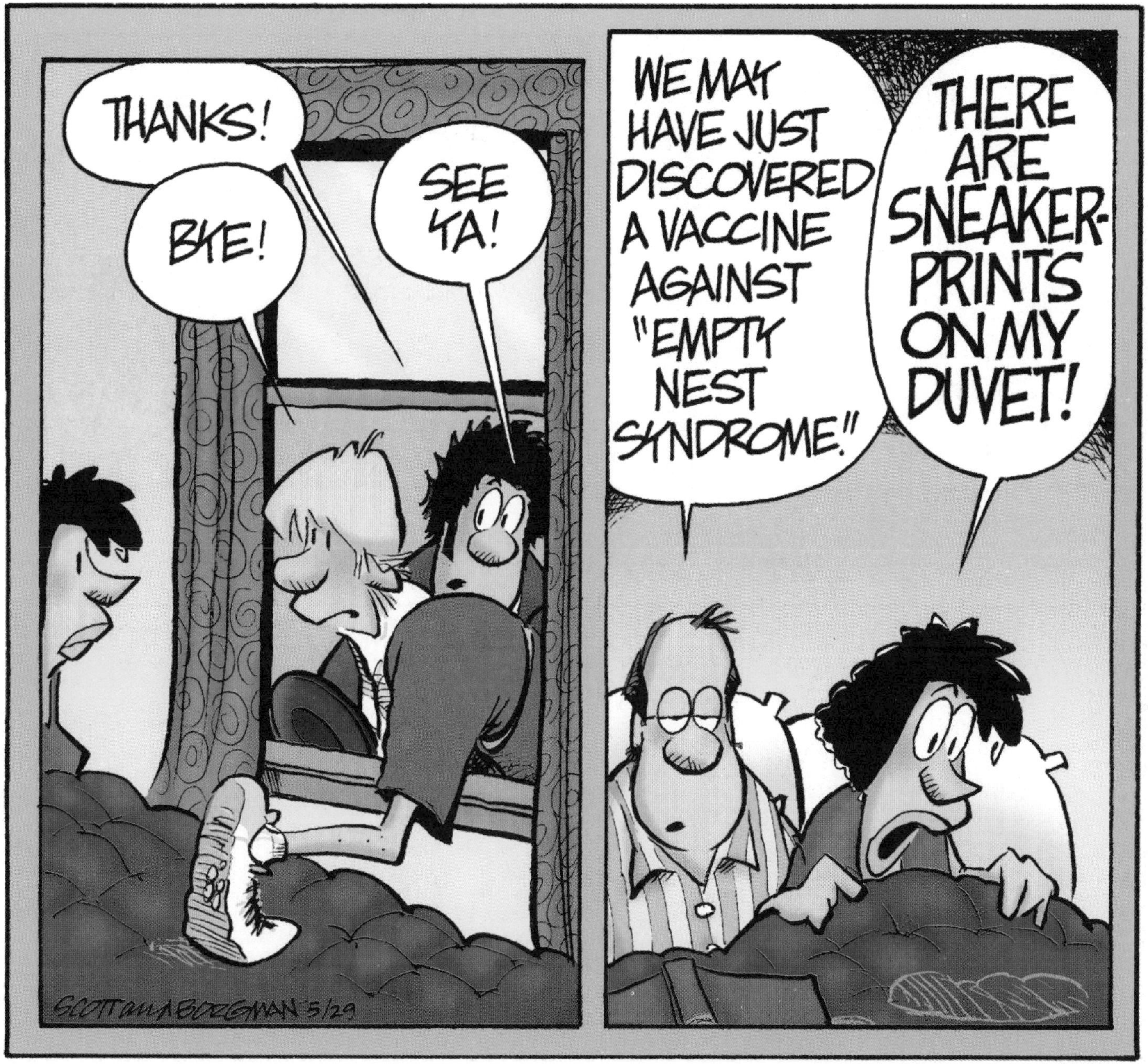
THANKS!
BYE!
SEE YA!
SCOTT and BORGMAN 5/29
WE MAY HAVE JUST DISCOVERED A VACCINE AGAINST "EMPTY NEST SYNDROME!"
THERE ARE SNEAKER-PRINTS ON MY DUVET!

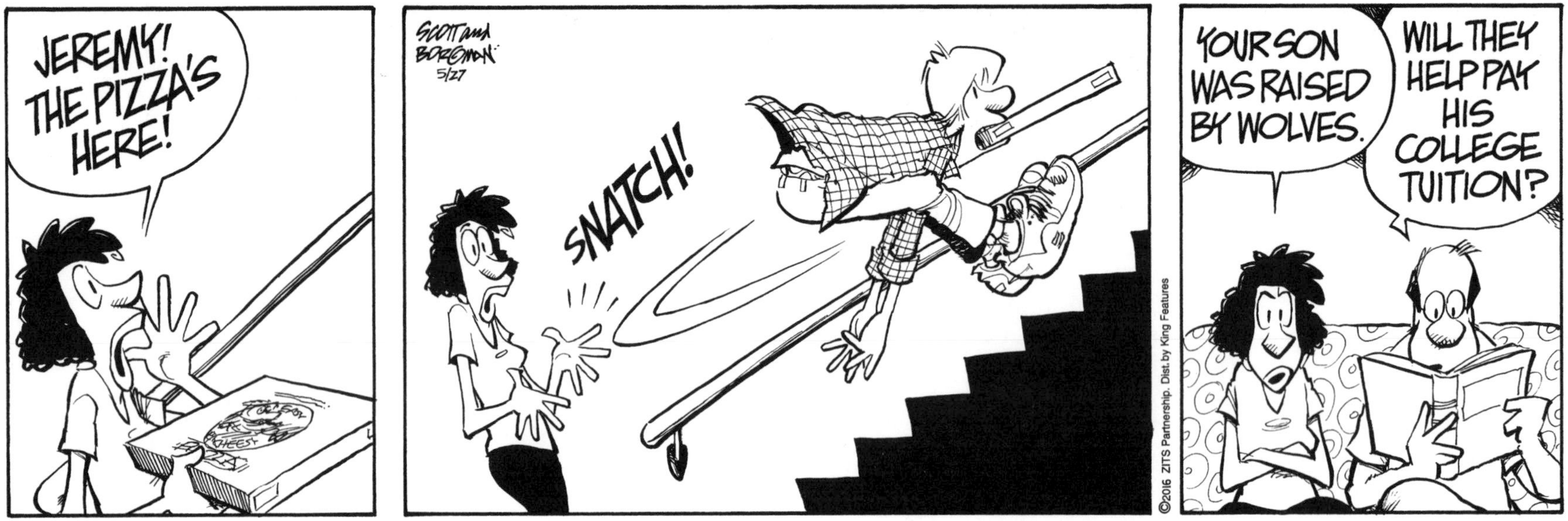
JEREMY! THE PIZZA'S HERE!
SCOTT and BORGMAN 5/27
SNATCH!
YOUR SON WAS RAISED BY WOLVES.
WILL THEY HELP PAY HIS COLLEGE TUITION?
©2016 ZITS Partnership. Dist. by King Features

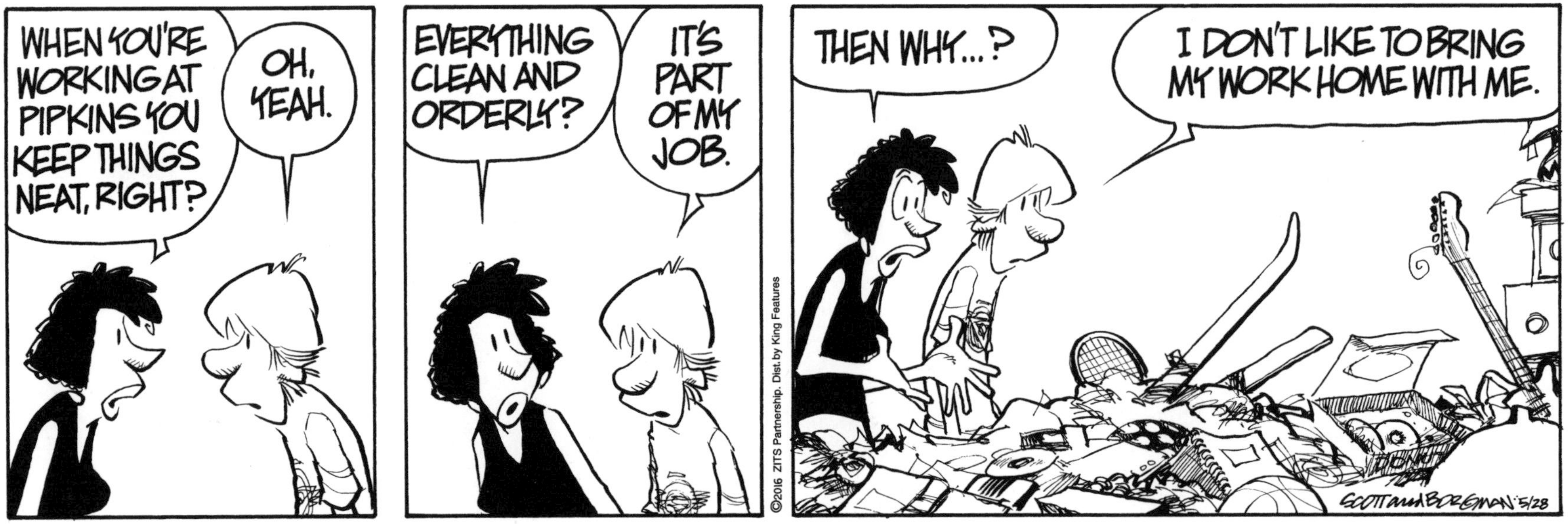
WHEN YOU'RE WORKING AT PIPKINS YOU KEEP THINGS NEAT, RIGHT?
OH, YEAH.
EVERYTHING CLEAN AND ORDERLY?
IT'S PART OF MY JOB.
©2016 ZITS Partnership. Dist. by King Features
THEN WHY...?
I DON'T LIKE TO BRING MY WORK HOME WITH ME.
SCOTT and BORGMAN 5/28

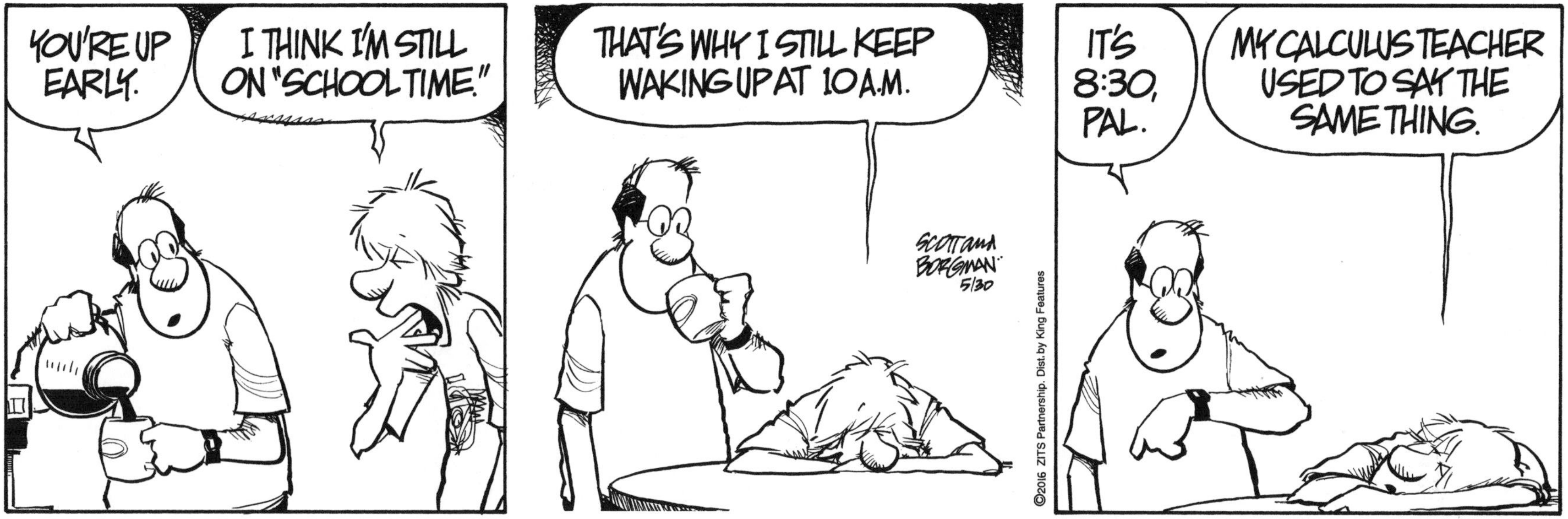
YOU'RE UP EARLY.
I THINK I'M STILL ON "SCHOOL TIME."
THAT'S WHY I STILL KEEP WAKING UP AT 10 A.M.
SCOTT AND BORGMAN 5/30
IT'S 8:30, PAL.
MY CALCULUS TEACHER USED TO SAY THE SAME THING.
©2016 ZITS Partnership. Dist. by King Features

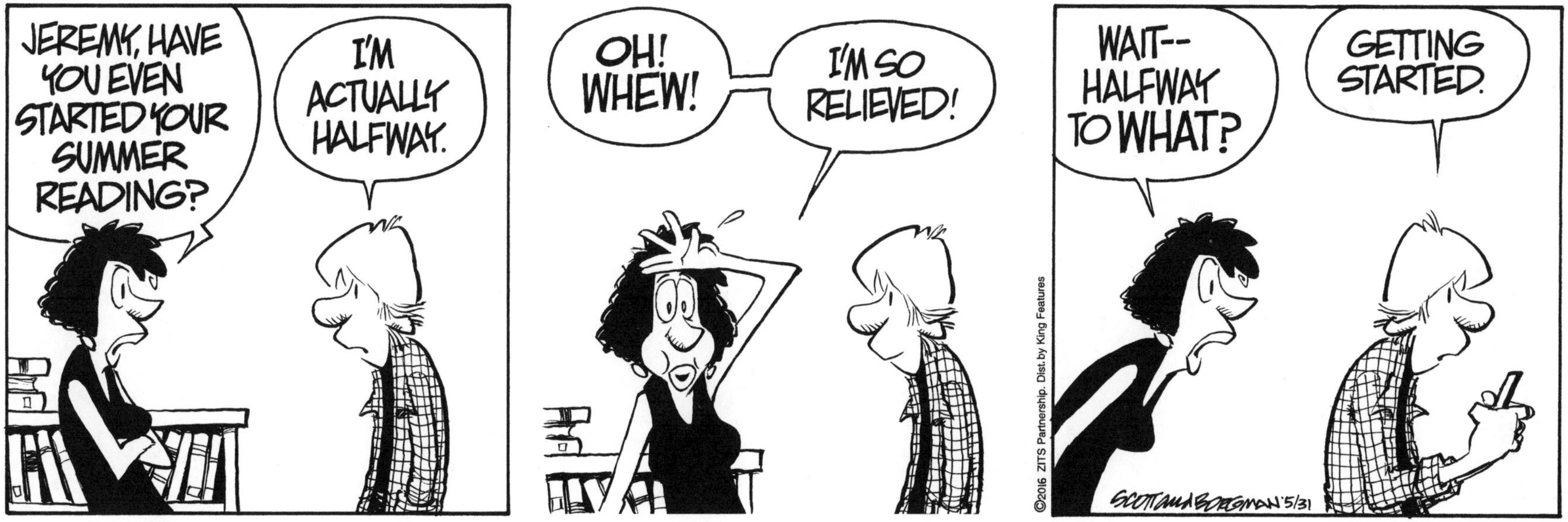
JEREMY, HAVE YOU EVEN STARTED YOUR SUMMER READING?
I'M ACTUALLY HALFWAY.
OH! WHEW!
I'M SO RELIEVED!
WAIT-- HALFWAY TO WHAT?
GETTING STARTED.
SCOTT AND BORGMAN 5/31
©2016 ZITS Partnership. Dist. by King Features

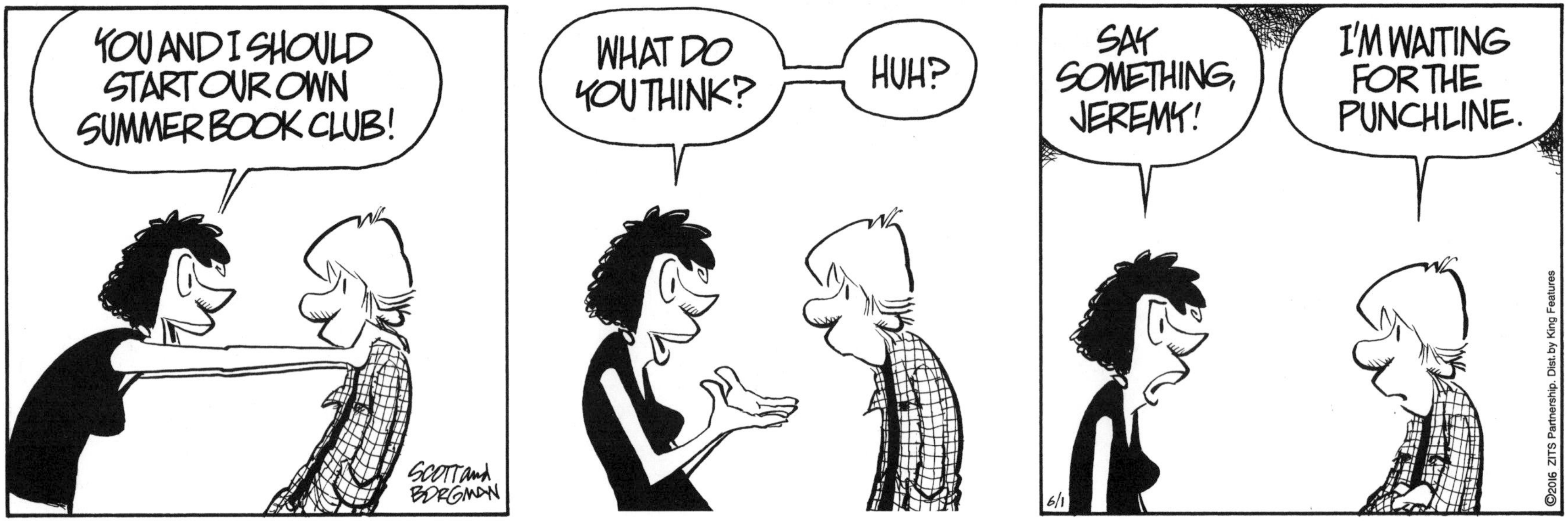
YOU AND I SHOULD START OUR OWN SUMMER BOOK CLUB!
SCOTT and BORGMAN
WHAT DO YOU THINK?
HUH?
SAY SOMETHING, JEREMY!
I'M WAITING FOR THE PUNCHLINE.
6/1
©2016 ZITS Partnership. Dist. by King Features

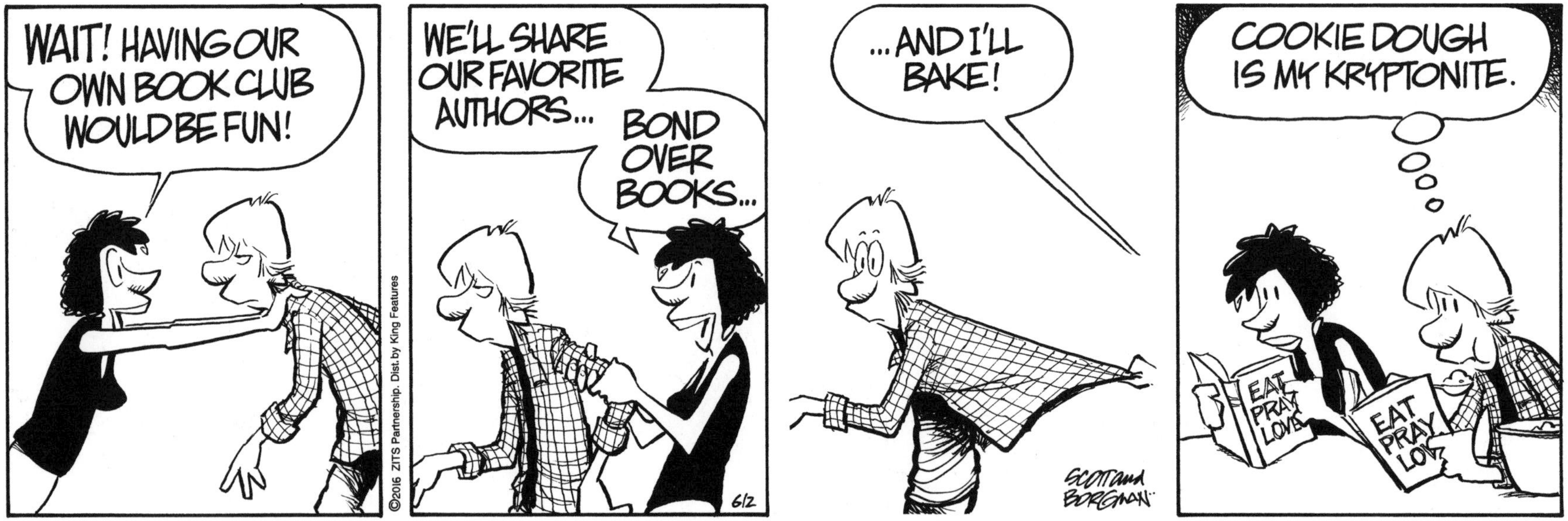
WAIT! HAVING OUR OWN BOOK CLUB WOULD BE FUN!
©2016 ZITS Partnership. Dist. by King Features
WE'LL SHARE OUR FAVORITE AUTHORS...
BOND OVER BOOKS...
6/2
...AND I'LL BAKE!
SCOTT and BORGMAN
COOKIE DOUGH IS MY KRYPTONITE.
EAT PRAY LOVE
EAT PRAY LOVE

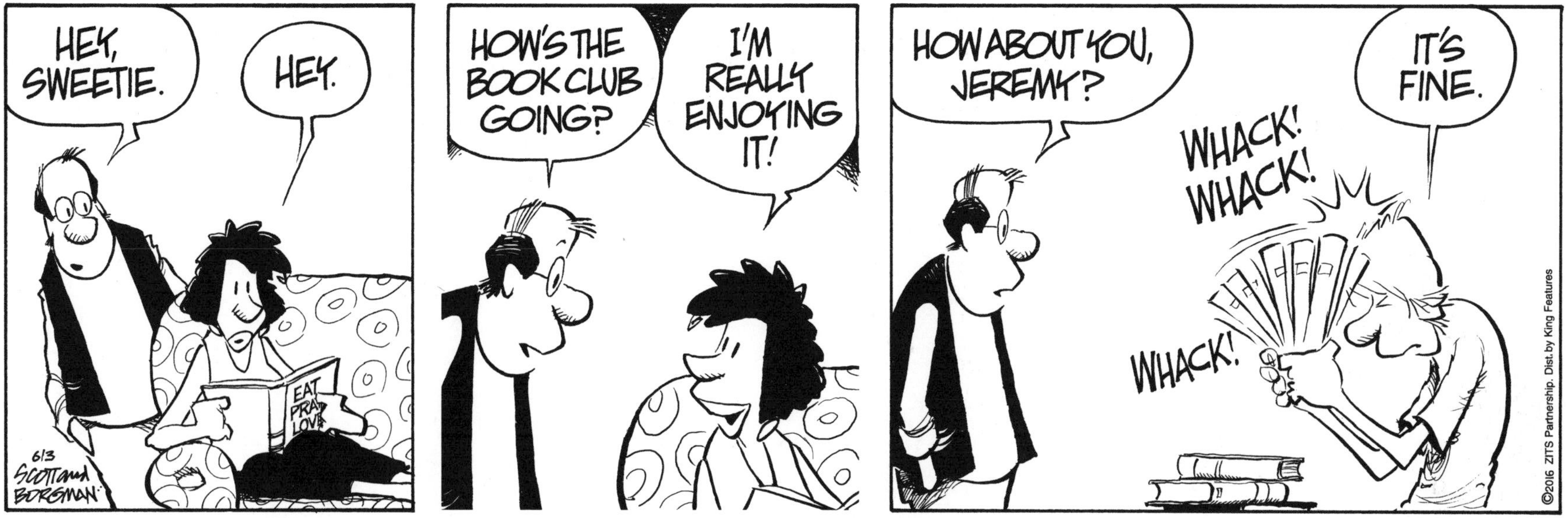
HEY, SWEETIE.
HEY.
EAT PRAY LOVE
6/13 SCOTT and BORGMAN
HOW'S THE BOOK CLUB GOING?
I'M REALLY ENJOYING IT!
HOW ABOUT YOU, JEREMY?
IT'S FINE.
WHACK! WHACK!
WHACK!
©2016 ZITS Partnership. Dist. by King Features

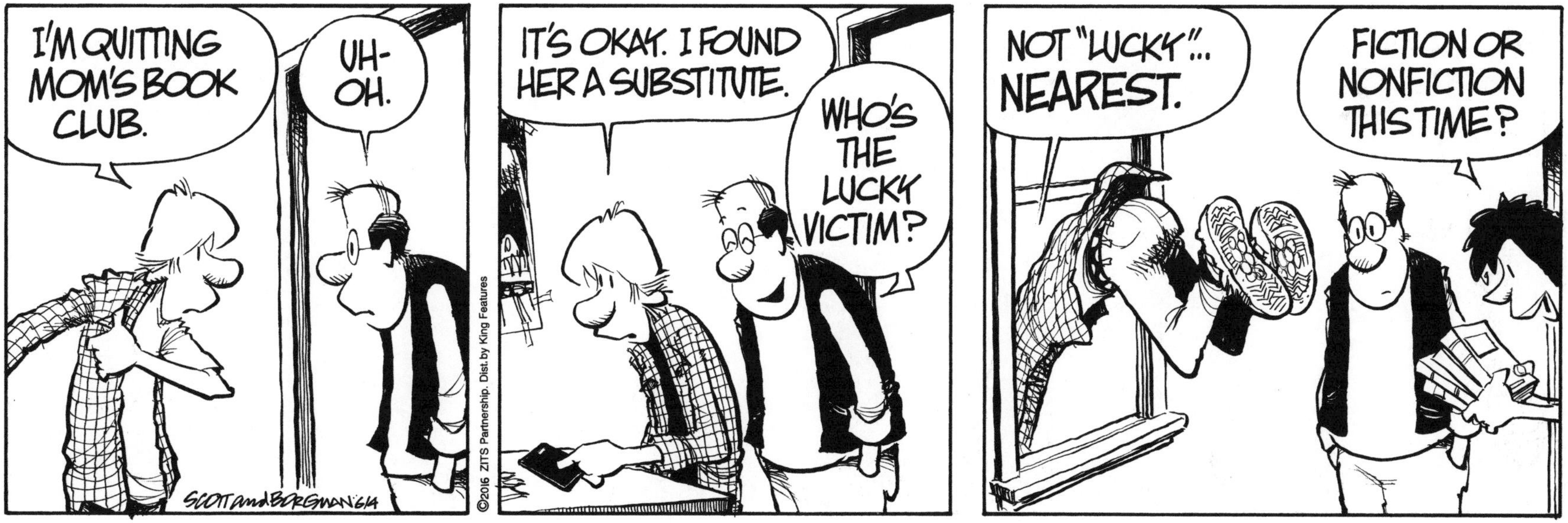
I'M QUITTING MOM'S BOOK CLUB.
UH-OH.
SCOTT and BORGMAN 6/14
IT'S OKAY. I FOUND HER A SUBSTITUTE.
WHO'S THE LUCKY VICTIM?
©2016 ZITS Partnership. Dist. by King Features
NOT "LUCKY"... NEAREST.
FICTION OR NONFICTION THIS TIME?

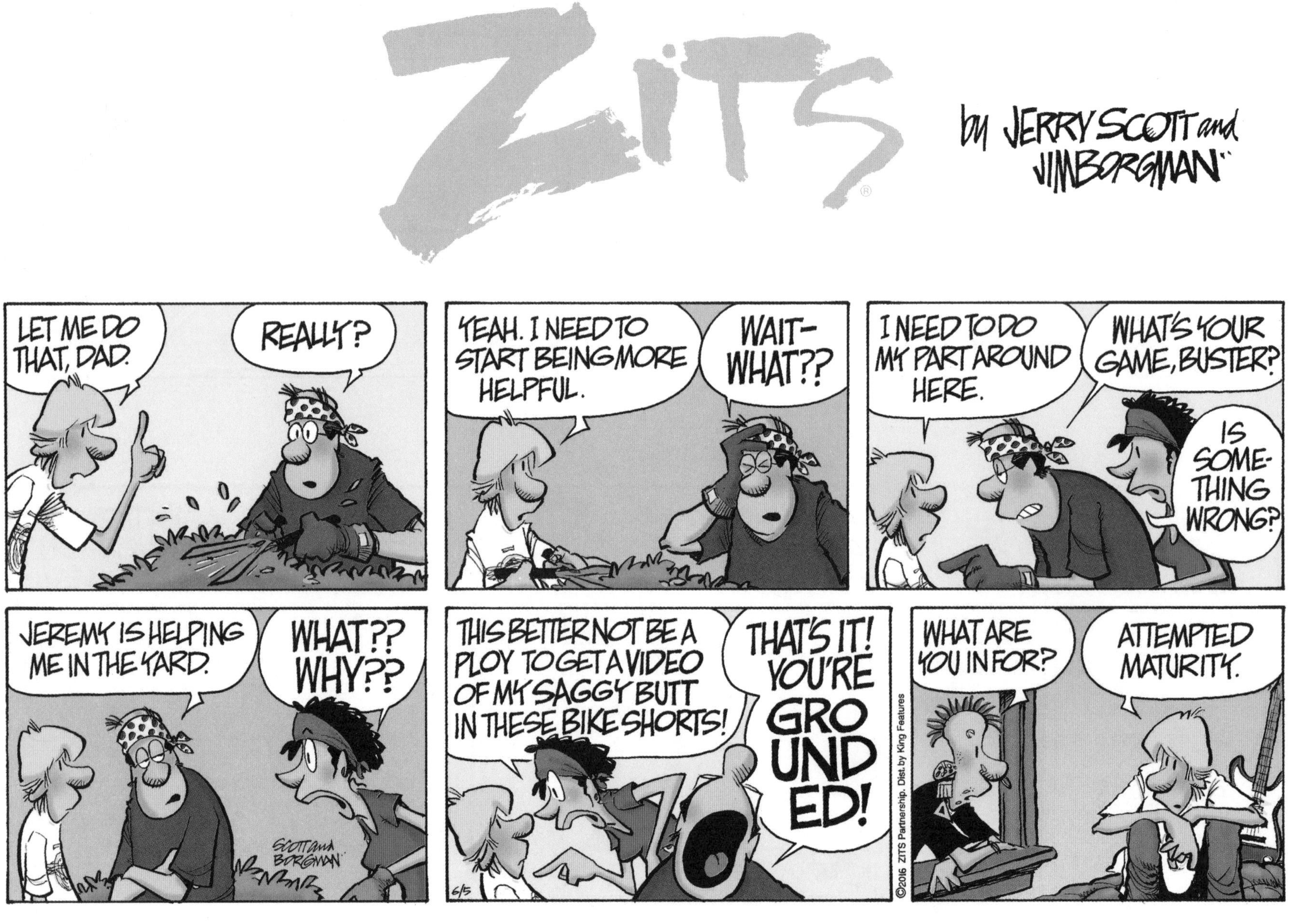
ZITS
by JERRY SCOTT and JIM BORGMAN
LET ME DO THAT, DAD.
REALLY?
YEAH. I NEED TO START BEING MORE HELPFUL.
WAIT- WHAT??
I NEED TO DO MY PART AROUND HERE.
WHAT'S YOUR GAME, BUSTER?
IS SOME-THING WRONG?
JEREMY IS HELPING ME IN THE YARD.
WHAT?? WHY??
SCOTT and BORGMAN
THIS BETTER NOT BE A PLOY TO GET A VIDEO OF MY SAGGY BUTT IN THESE BIKE SHORTS!
THAT'S IT! YOU'RE GRO UND ED!
6/5
©2016 ZITS Partnership. Dist. by King Features
WHAT ARE YOU IN FOR?
ATTEMPTED MATURITY.

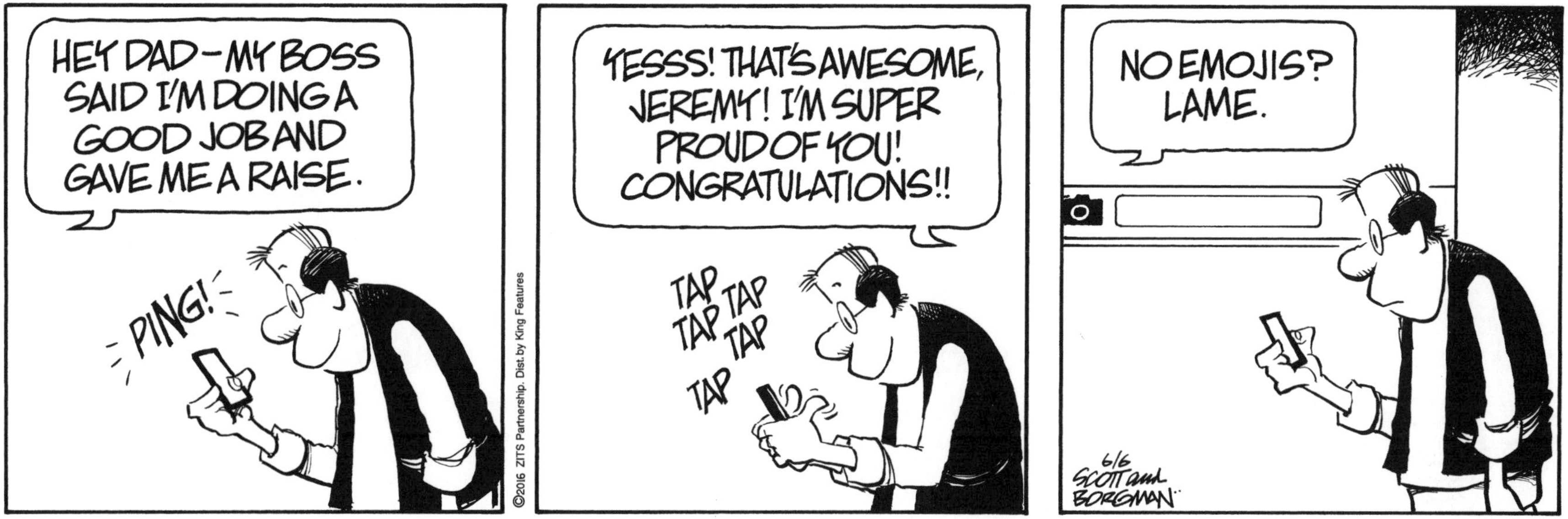
HEY DAD—MY BOSS SAID I'M DOING A GOOD JOB AND GAVE ME A RAISE.
PING!
©2016 ZITS Partnership. Dist. by King Features
YESSS! THAT'S AWESOME, JEREMY! I'M SUPER PROUD OF YOU! CONGRATULATIONS!!
TAP TAP TAP TAP TAP
NO EMOJIS? LAME.
6/6
SCOTT and BORGMAN

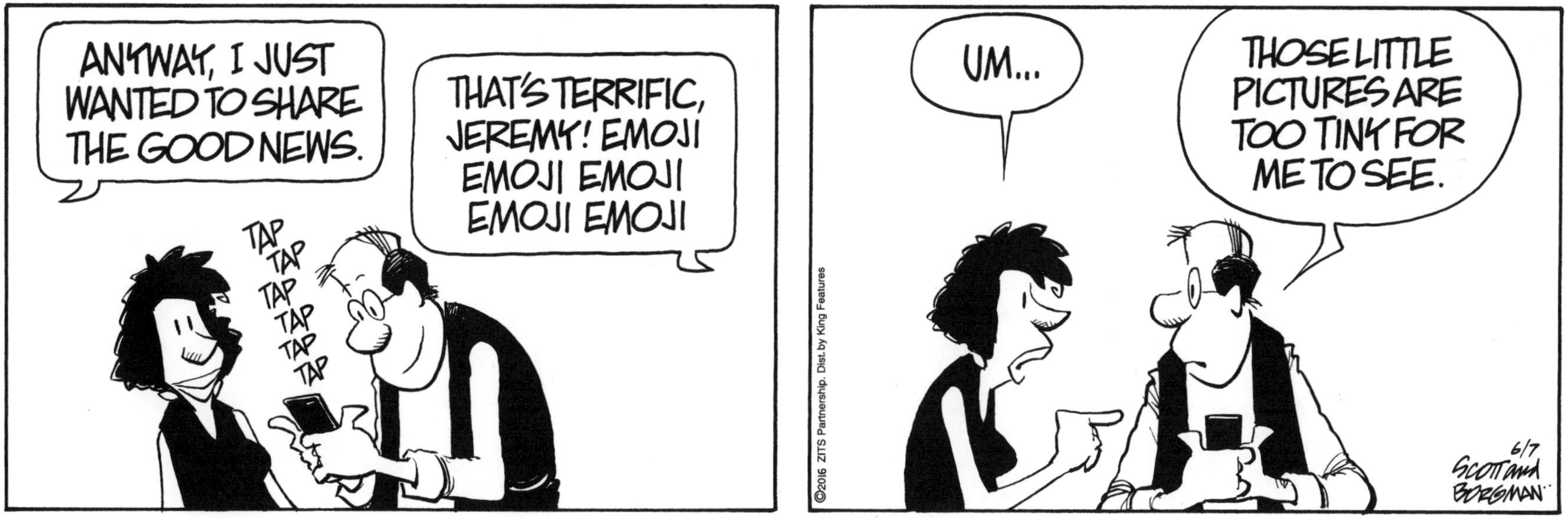
ANYWAY, I JUST WANTED TO SHARE THE GOOD NEWS.
THAT'S TERRIFIC, JEREMY! EMOJI EMOJI EMOJI EMOJI EMOJI
TAP TAP TAP TAP TAP TAP
©2016 ZITS Partnership. Dist. by King Features
UM...
THOSE LITTLE PICTURES ARE TOO TINY FOR ME TO SEE.
6/7
SCOTT and BORGMAN

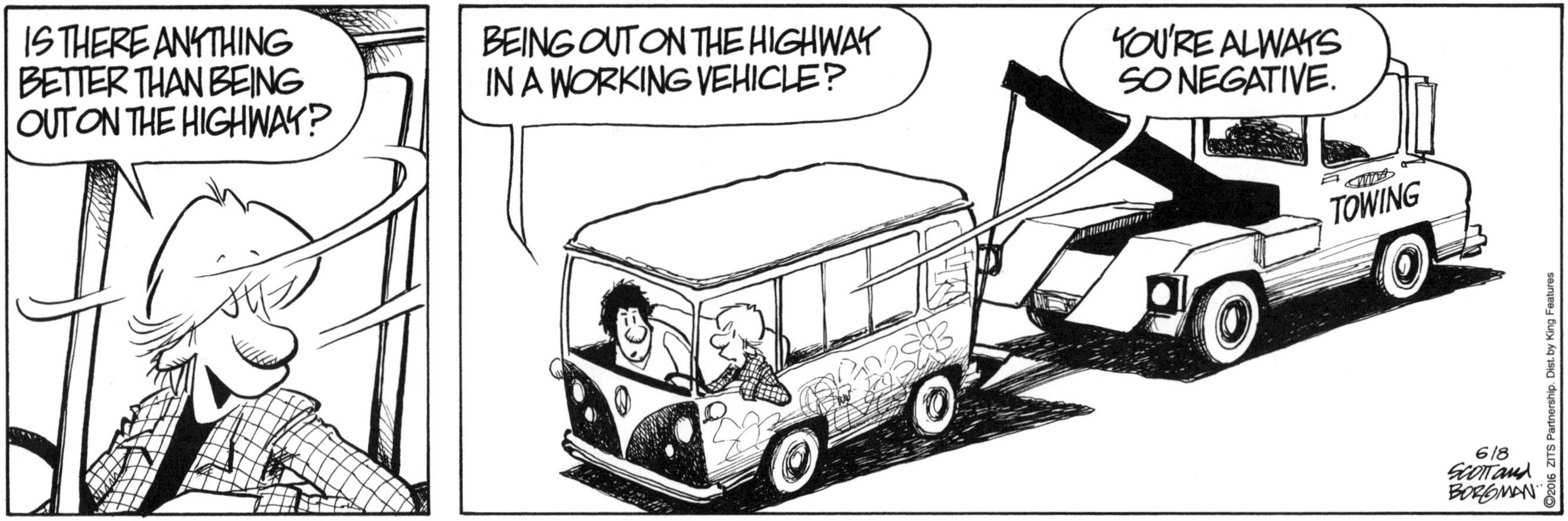
IS THERE ANYTHING BETTER THAN BEING OUT ON THE HIGHWAY?
BEING OUT ON THE HIGHWAY IN A WORKING VEHICLE?
YOU'RE ALWAYS SO NEGATIVE.
TOWING
6/8 SCOTT and BORGMAN
©2016 ZITS Partnership. Dist. by King Features

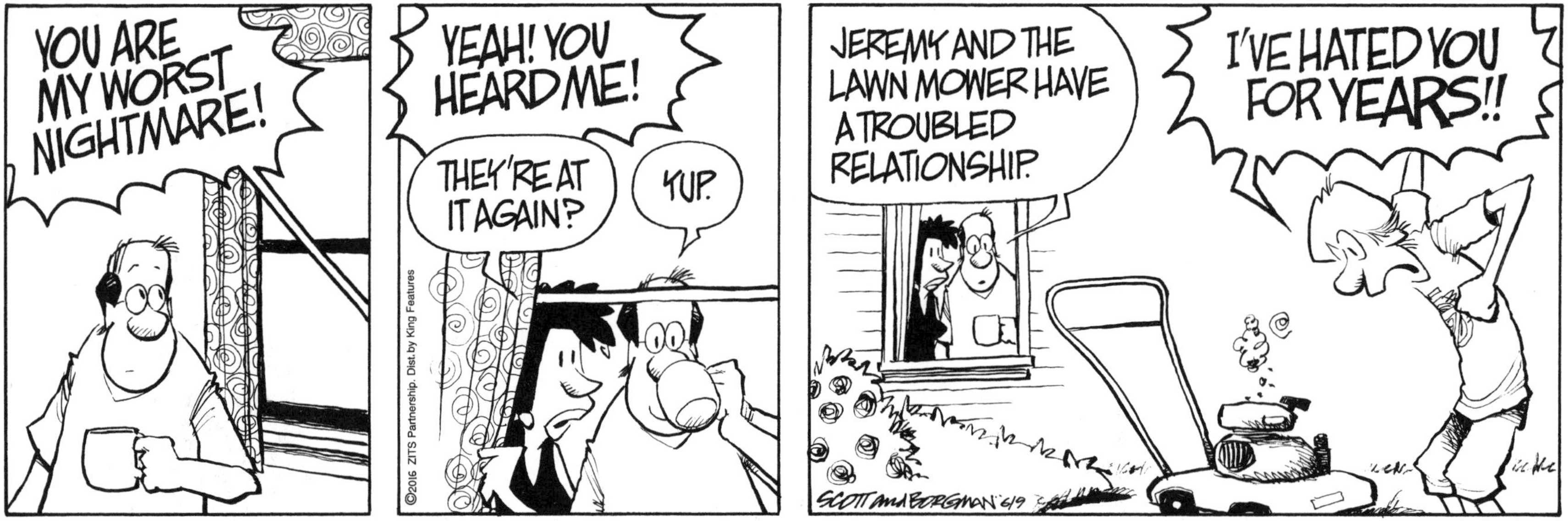
YOU ARE MY WORST NIGHTMARE!
YEAH! YOU HEARD ME!
THEY'RE AT IT AGAIN?
YUP.
©2016 ZITS Partnership. Dist. by King Features
JEREMY AND THE LAWN MOWER HAVE A TROUBLED RELATIONSHIP.
I'VE HATED YOU FOR YEARS!!
SCOTT and BORGMAN 6/9

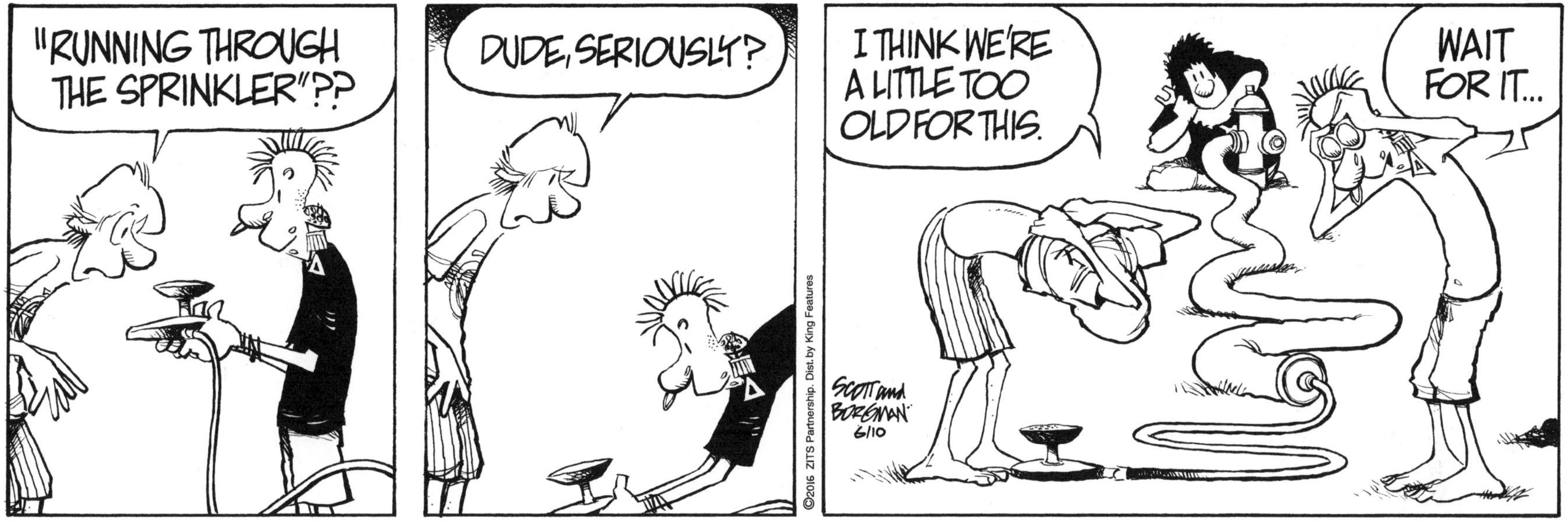
"RUNNING THROUGH THE SPRINKLER"??
DUDE, SERIOUSLY?
I THINK WE'RE A LITTLE TOO OLD FOR THIS.
WAIT FOR IT...
©2016 ZITS Partnership. Dist. by King Features
SCOTT and BORGMAN 6/10

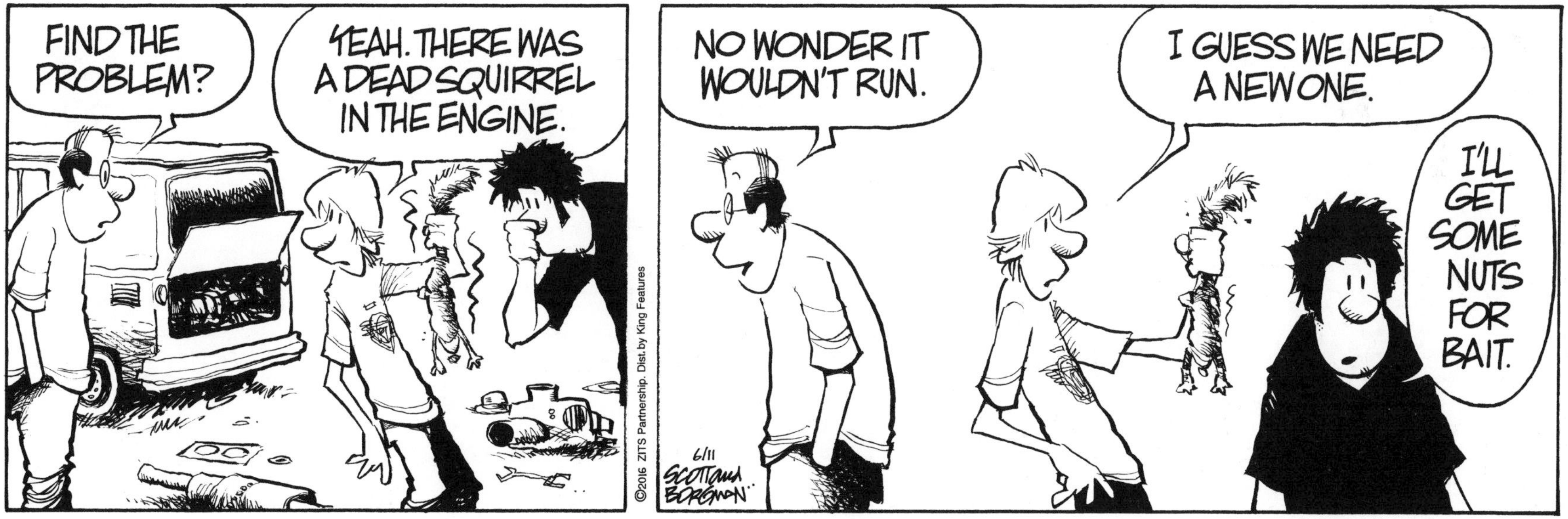
FIND THE PROBLEM?
YEAH. THERE WAS A DEAD SQUIRREL IN THE ENGINE.
©2016 ZITS Partnership. Dist. by King Features
NO WONDER IT WOULDN'T RUN.
I GUESS WE NEED A NEW ONE.
I'LL GET SOME NUTS FOR BAIT.
6/11 SCOTT and BORGMAN

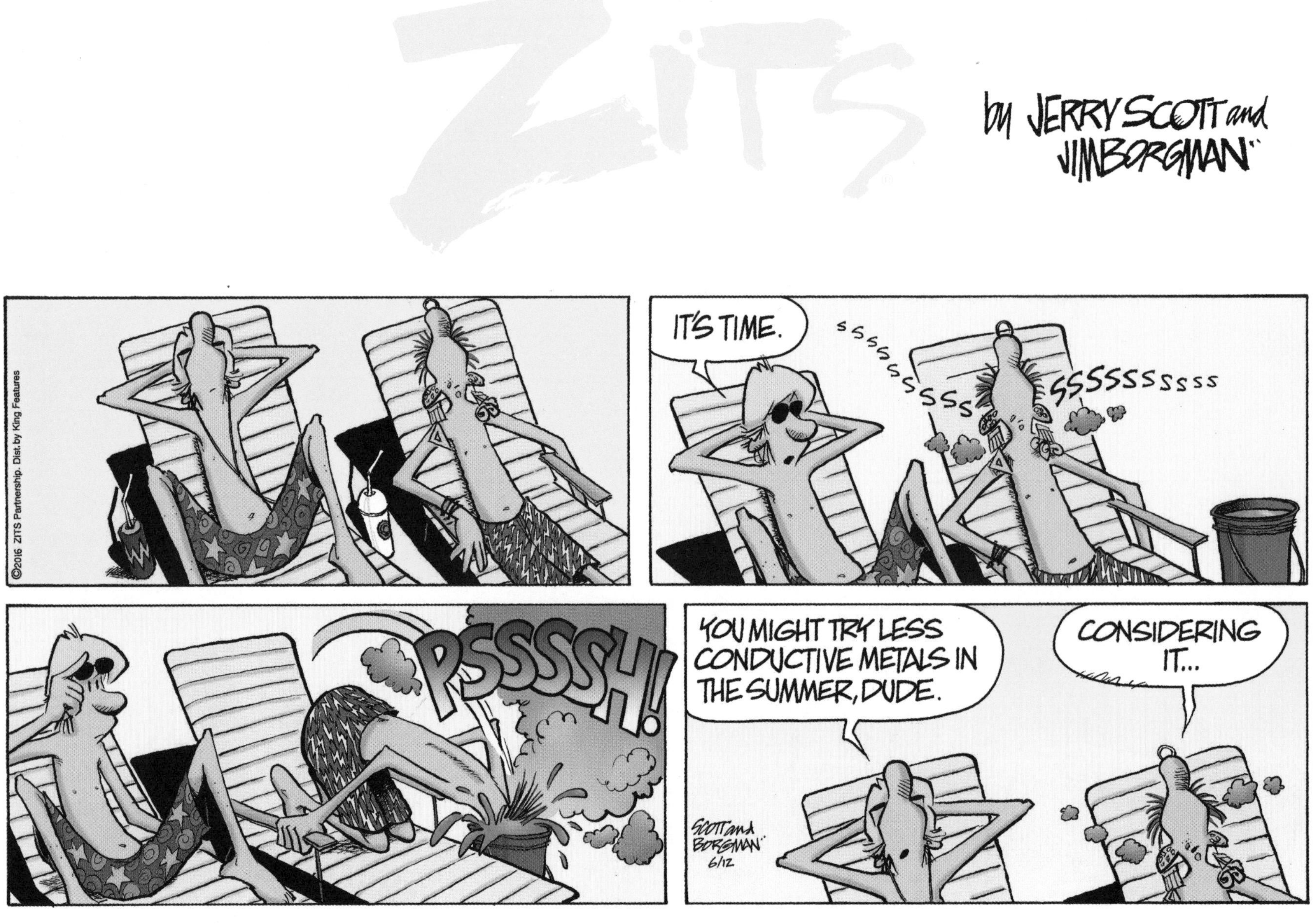
ZITS
by JERRY SCOTT and JIM BORGMAN
©2016 ZITS Partnership. Dist. by King Features
IT'S TIME.
SSSSSSSSSSS
SSSSSSSSSSS
PSSSSH!
YOU MIGHT TRY LESS CONDUCTIVE METALS IN THE SUMMER, DUDE.
CONSIDERING IT...
SCOTT and BORGMAN 6/12

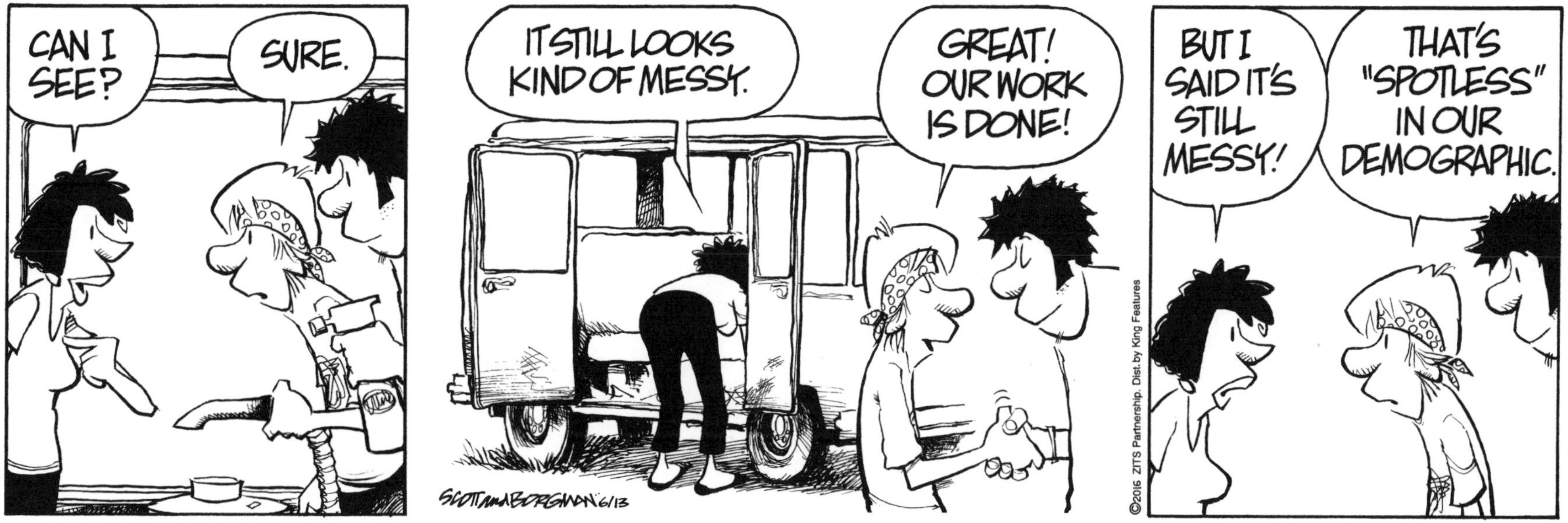
CAN I SEE?
SURE.
IT STILL LOOKS KIND OF MESSY.
GREAT! OUR WORK IS DONE!
SCOTT and BORGMAN 6/13
©2016 ZITS Partnership. Dist. by King Features
BUT I SAID IT'S STILL MESSY!
THAT'S "SPOTLESS" IN OUR DEMOGRAPHIC.

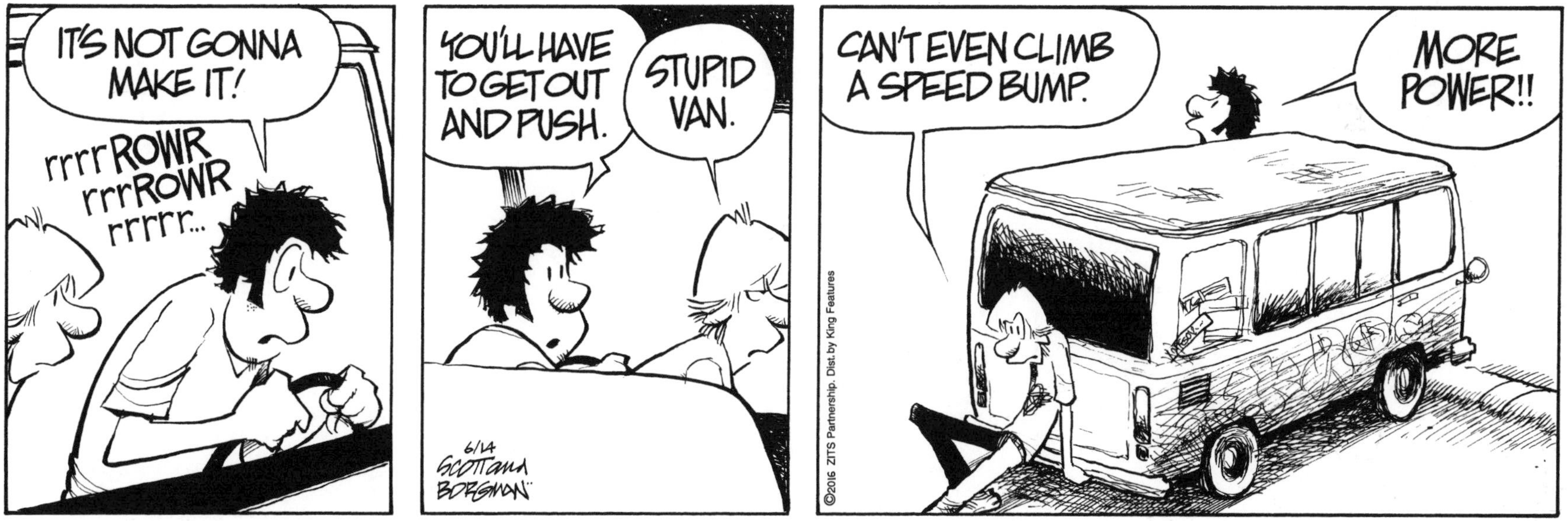
IT'S NOT GONNA MAKE IT!
rrrrROWR rrrROWR rrrrr...
YOU'LL HAVE TO GET OUT AND PUSH.
STUPID VAN.
6/14 SCOTT and BORGMAN
©2016 ZITS Partnership. Dist. by King Features
CAN'T EVEN CLIMB A SPEED BUMP.
MORE POWER!!

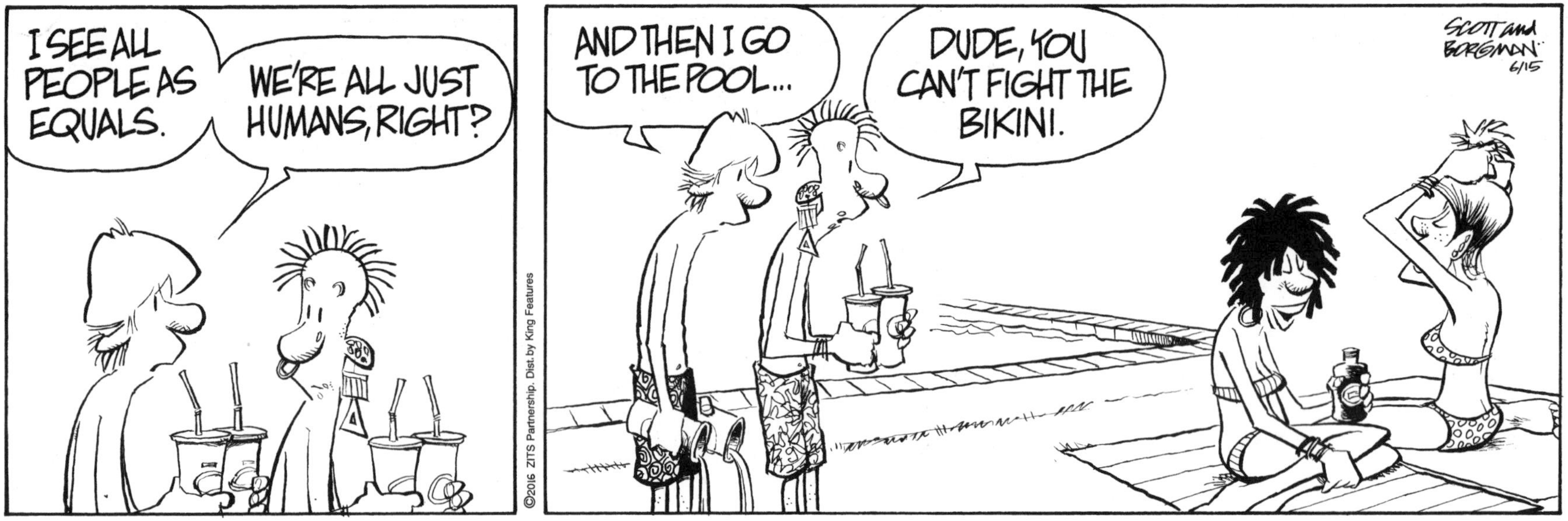
I SEE ALL PEOPLE AS EQUALS.
WE'RE ALL JUST HUMANS, RIGHT?
©2016 ZITS Partnership. Dist. by King Features
AND THEN I GO TO THE POOL...
DUDE, YOU CAN'T FIGHT THE BIKINI.
SCOTT and BORGMAN 6/15

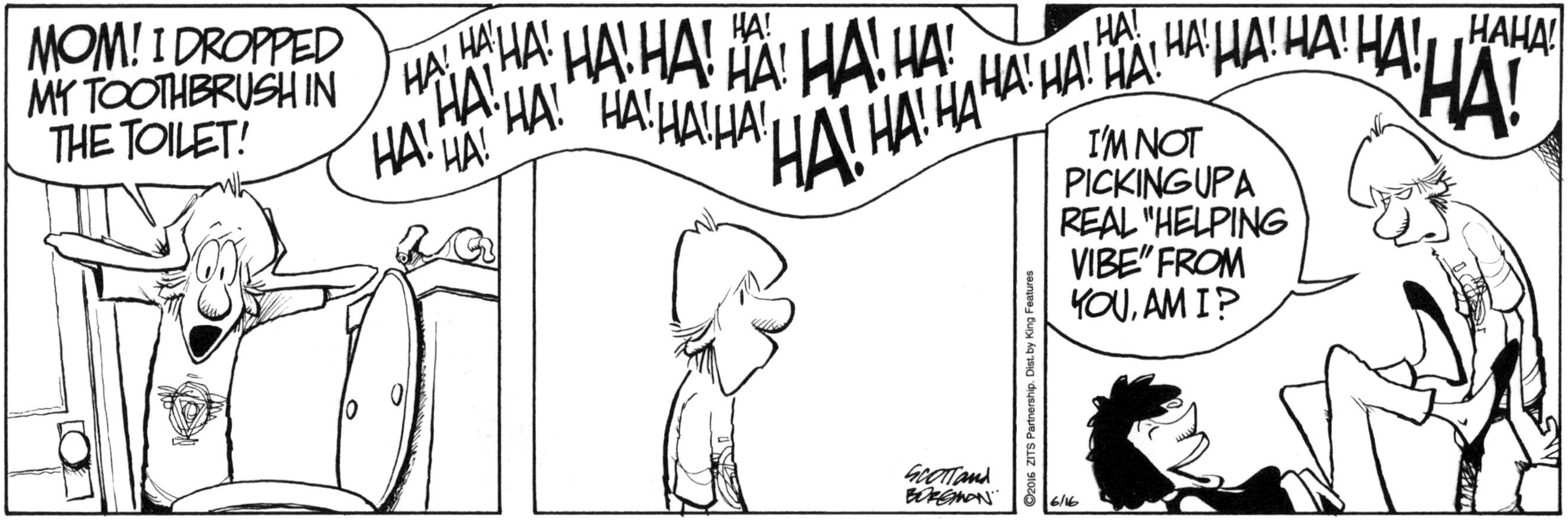
MOM! I DROPPED MY TOOTHBRUSH IN THE TOILET!
HA! HA! HA! HA! HA! HA! HA! HA! HA! HA! HA! HA! HA! HA! HA! HA! HA! HA! HA! HA! HA! HA! HA! HA! HA! HA! HA! HAHA! HA!
SCOTT and BORGMAN
©2016 ZITS Partnership. Dist. by King Features
6/16
I'M NOT PICKING UP A REAL "HELPING VIBE" FROM YOU, AM I?

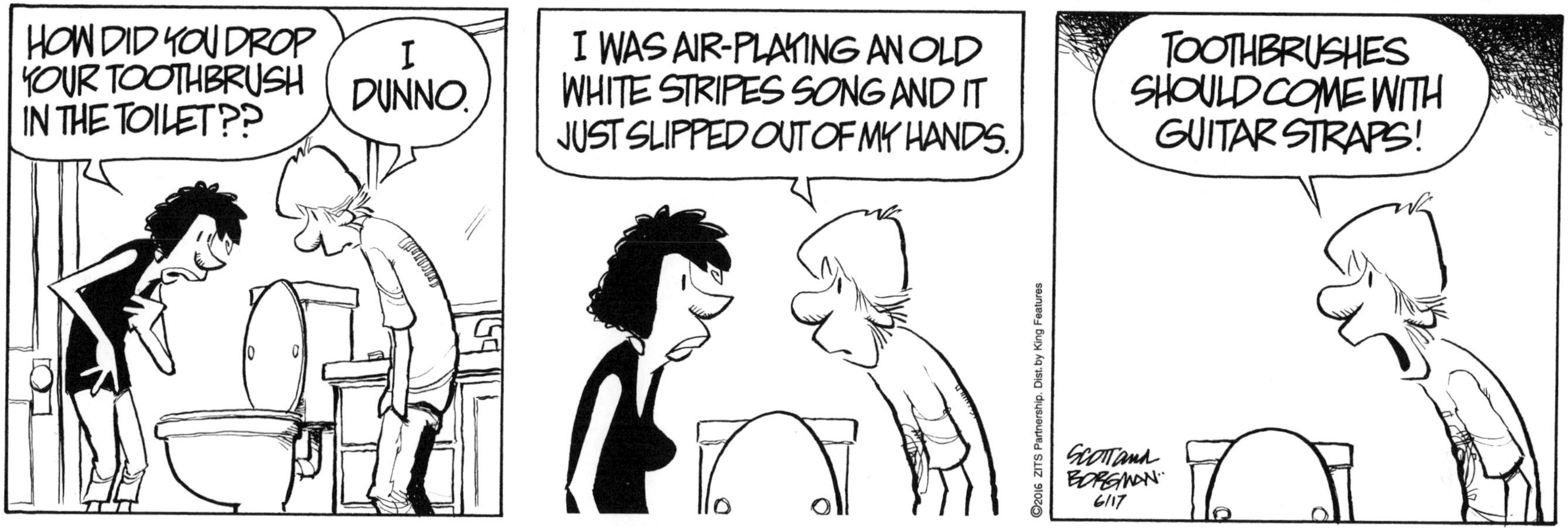

HOW DID YOU DROP YOUR TOOTHBRUSH IN THE TOILET??
I DUNNO.
I WAS AIR-PLAYING AN OLD WHITE STRIPES SONG AND IT JUST SLIPPED OUT OF MY HANDS.
TOOTHBRUSHES SHOULD COME WITH GUITAR STRAPS!
©2016 ZITS Partnership. Dist. by King Features
SCOTT and BORGMAN 6/17

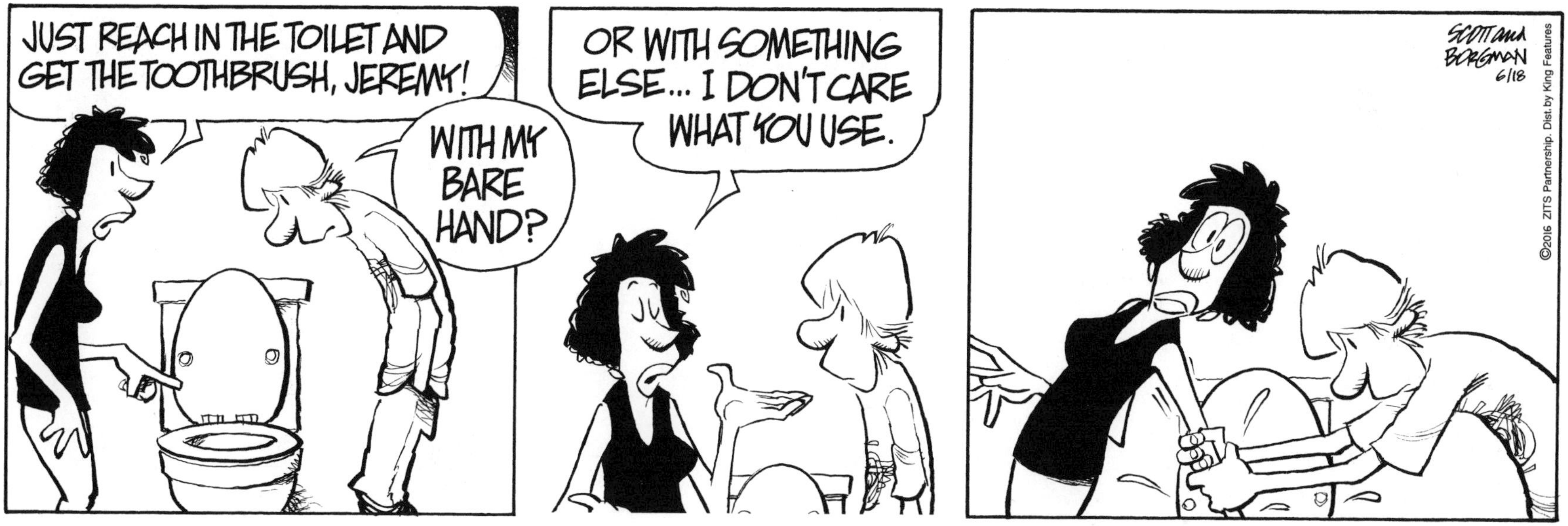

JUST REACH IN THE TOILET AND GET THE TOOTHBRUSH, JEREMY!
WITH MY BARE HAND?
OR WITH SOMETHING ELSE... I DON'T CARE WHAT YOU USE.
SCOTT and BORGMAN 6/18
©2016 ZITS Partnership. Dist. by King Features

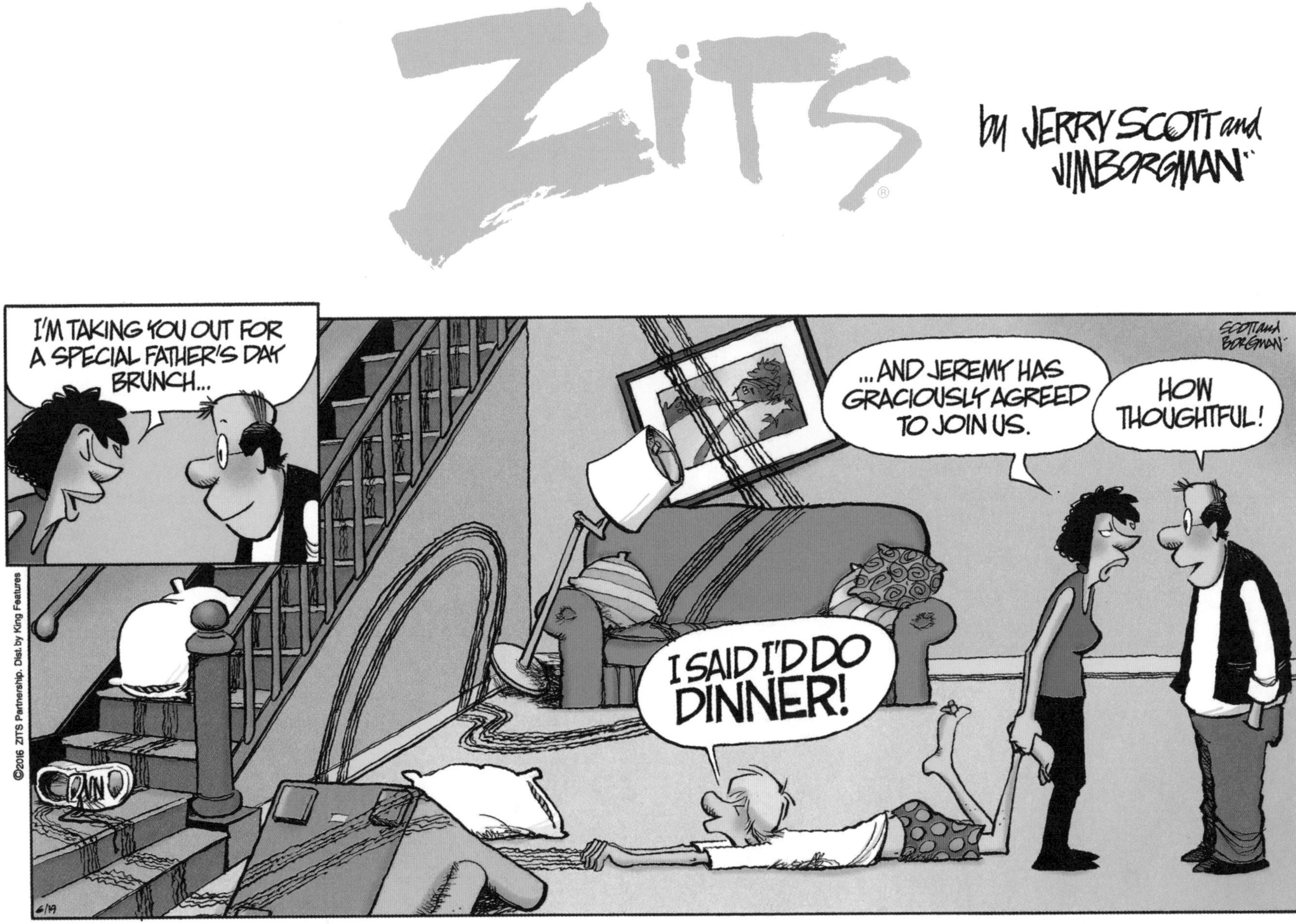
ZITS
by JERRY SCOTT and JIM BORGMAN
I'M TAKING YOU OUT FOR A SPECIAL FATHER'S DAY BRUNCH...
...AND JEREMY HAS GRACIOUSLY AGREED TO JOIN US.
HOW THOUGHTFUL!
I SAID I'D DO DINNER!
SCOTT and BORGMAN
©2016 ZITS Partnership. Dist. by King Features

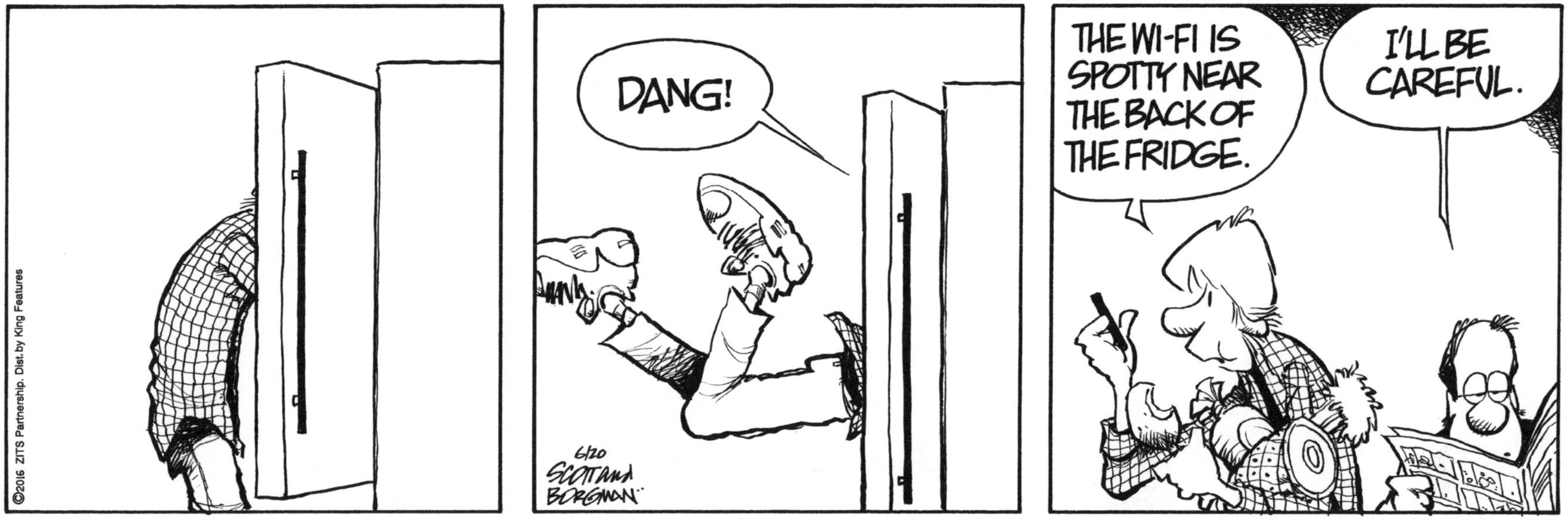
©2016 ZITS Partnership. Dist. by King Features
DANG!
6/20
SCOTT and BORGMAN
THE WI-FI IS SPOTTY NEAR THE BACK OF THE FRIDGE.
I'LL BE CAREFUL.

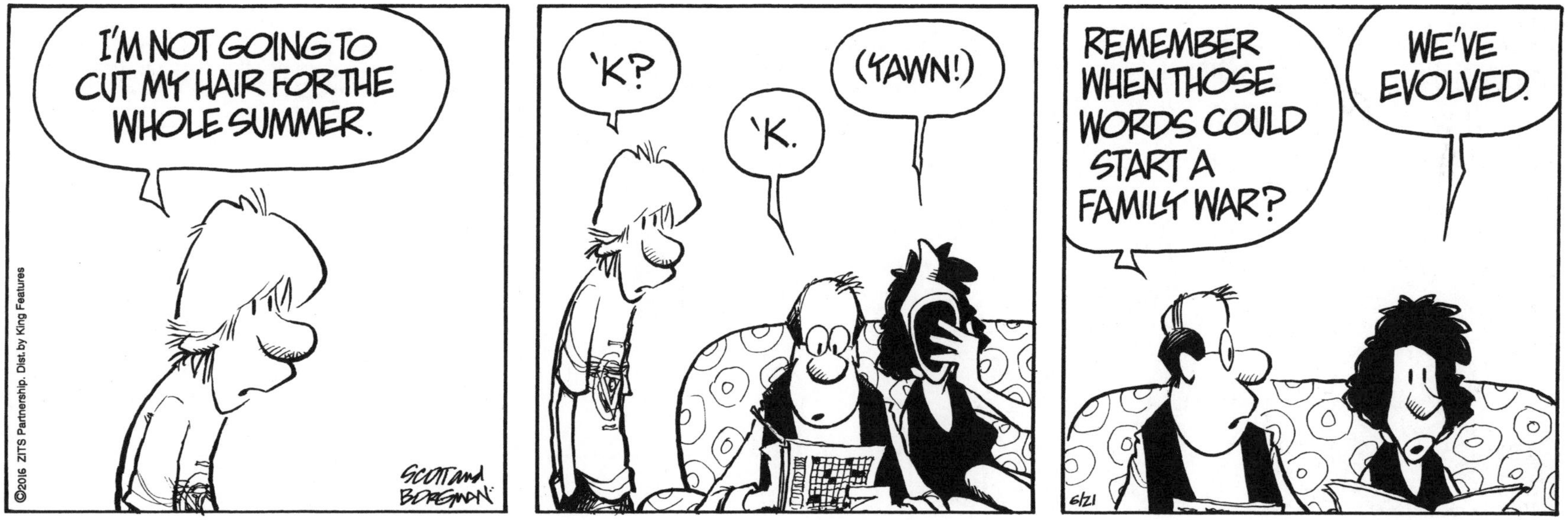
©2016 ZITS Partnership. Dist. by King Features
I'M NOT GOING TO CUT MY HAIR FOR THE WHOLE SUMMER.
SCOTT and BORGMAN
'K?
'K.
(YAWN!)
REMEMBER WHEN THOSE WORDS COULD START A FAMILY WAR?
WE'VE EVOLVED.
6/21

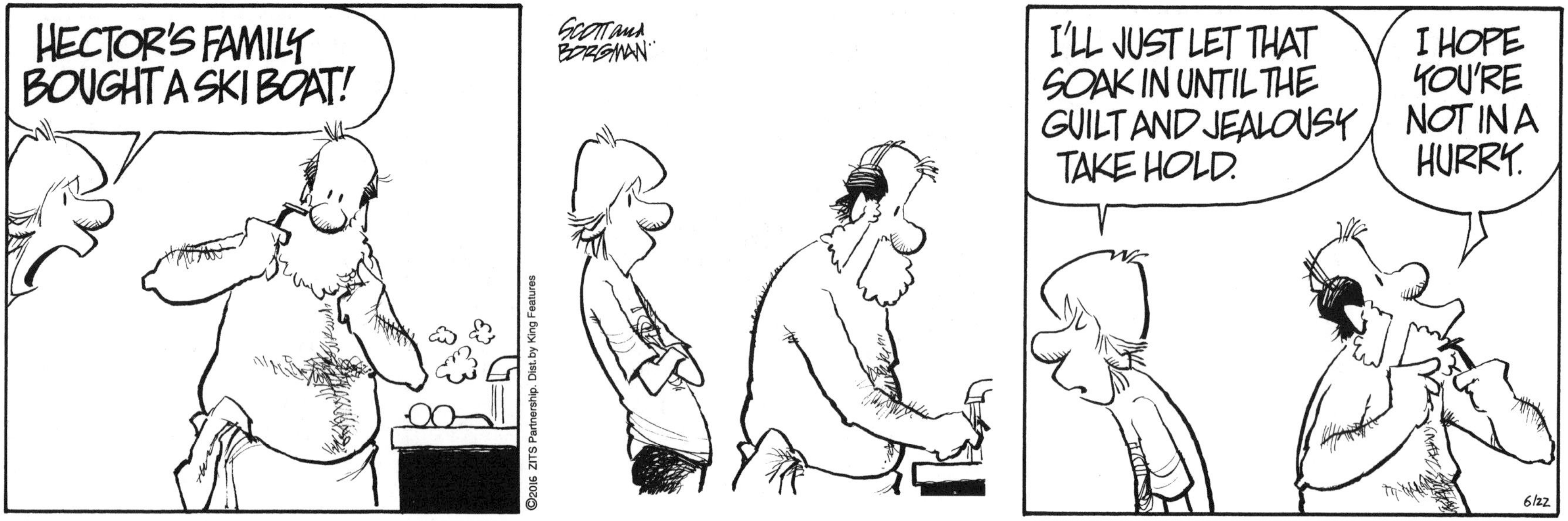
HECTOR'S FAMILY BOUGHT A SKI BOAT!
SCOTT and BORGMAN..
©2016 ZITS Partnership. Dist. by King Features
I'LL JUST LET THAT SOAK IN UNTIL THE GUILT AND JEALOUSY TAKE HOLD.
I HOPE YOU'RE NOT IN A HURRY.
6/22

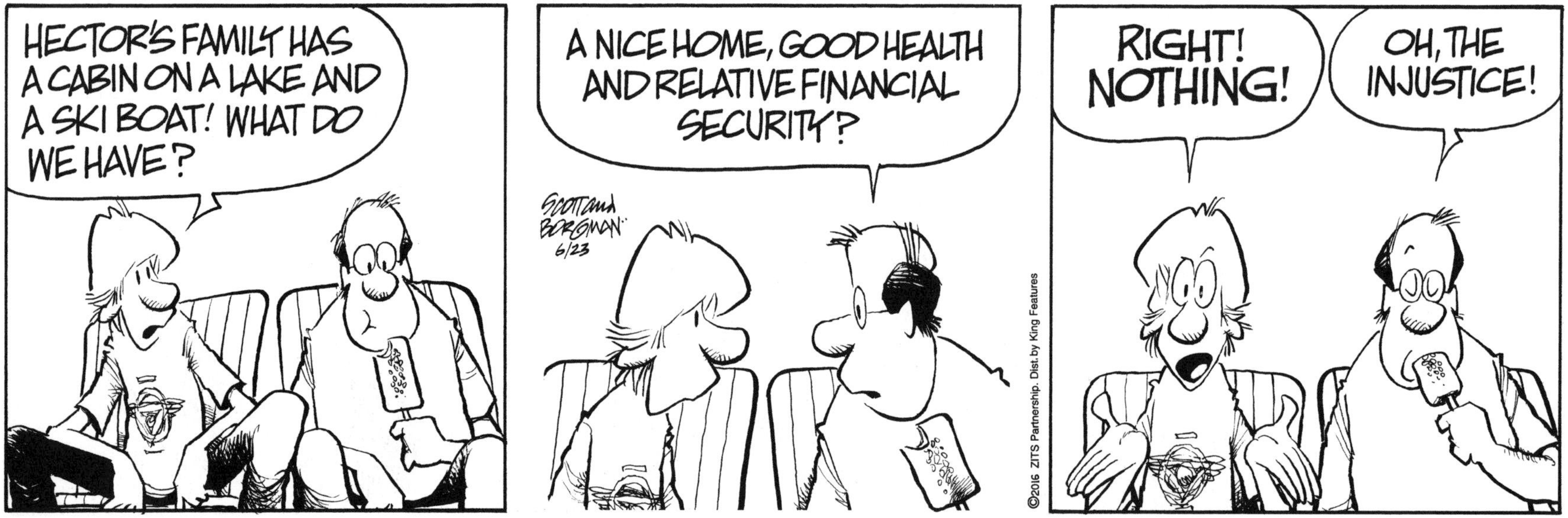
HECTOR'S FAMILY HAS A CABIN ON A LAKE AND A SKI BOAT! WHAT DO WE HAVE?
A NICE HOME, GOOD HEALTH AND RELATIVE FINANCIAL SECURITY?
SCOTT and BORGMAN.. 6/23
©2016 ZITS Partnership. Dist. by King Features
RIGHT! NOTHING!
OH, THE INJUSTICE!

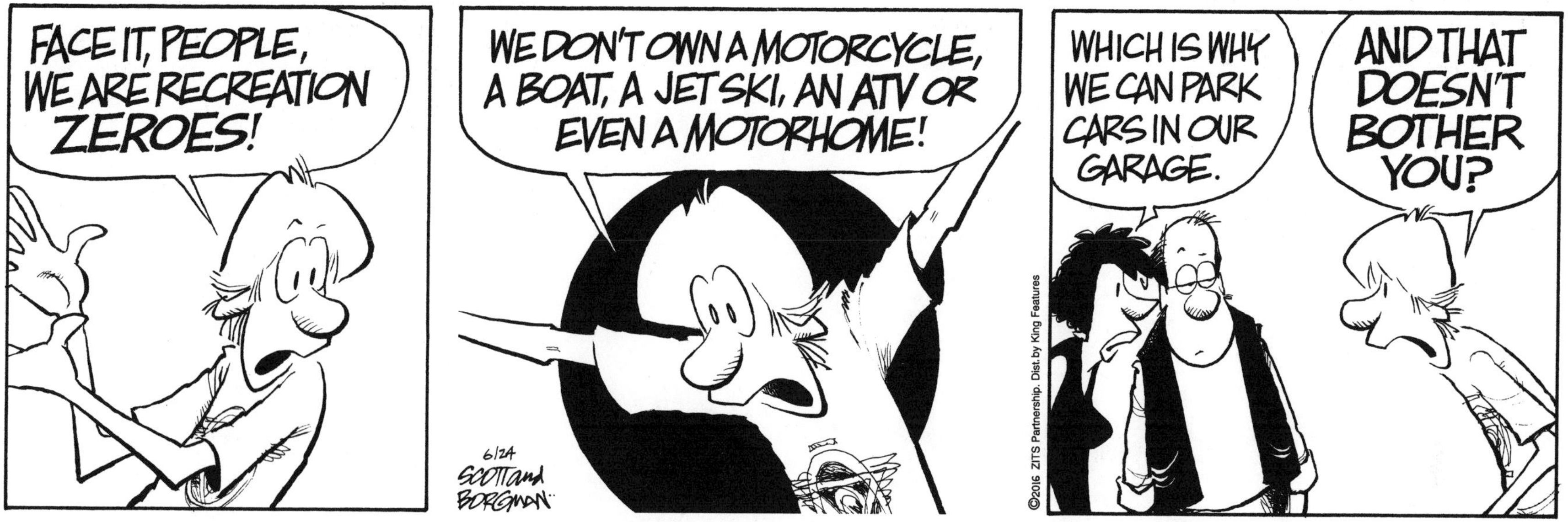
FACE IT, PEOPLE, WE ARE RECREATION ZEROES!
WE DON'T OWN A MOTORCYCLE, A BOAT, A JET SKI, AN ATV OR EVEN A MOTORHOME!
6/24
SCOTT and BORGMAN
WHICH IS WHY WE CAN PARK CARS IN OUR GARAGE.
AND THAT DOESN'T BOTHER YOU?
©2016 ZITS Partnership. Dist. by King Features

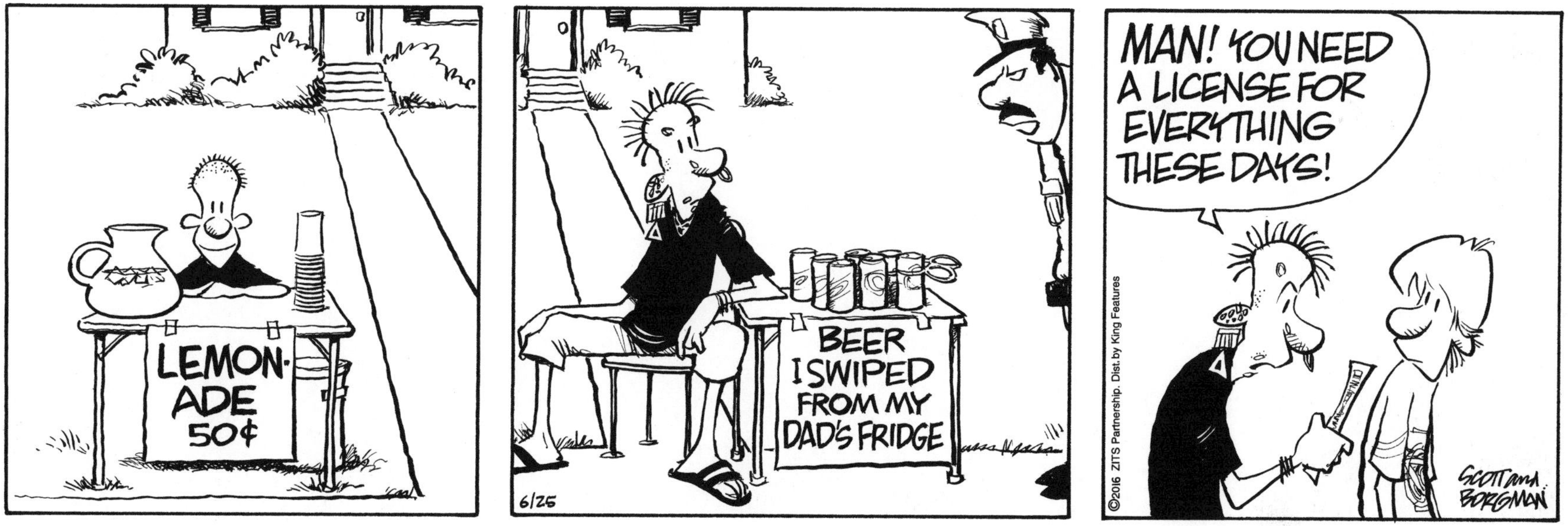
LEMON-ADE 50¢
BEER I SWIPED FROM MY DAD'S FRIDGE
6/25
MAN! YOU NEED A LICENSE FOR EVERYTHING THESE DAYS!
©2016 ZITS Partnership. Dist. by King Features
SCOTT and BORGMAN

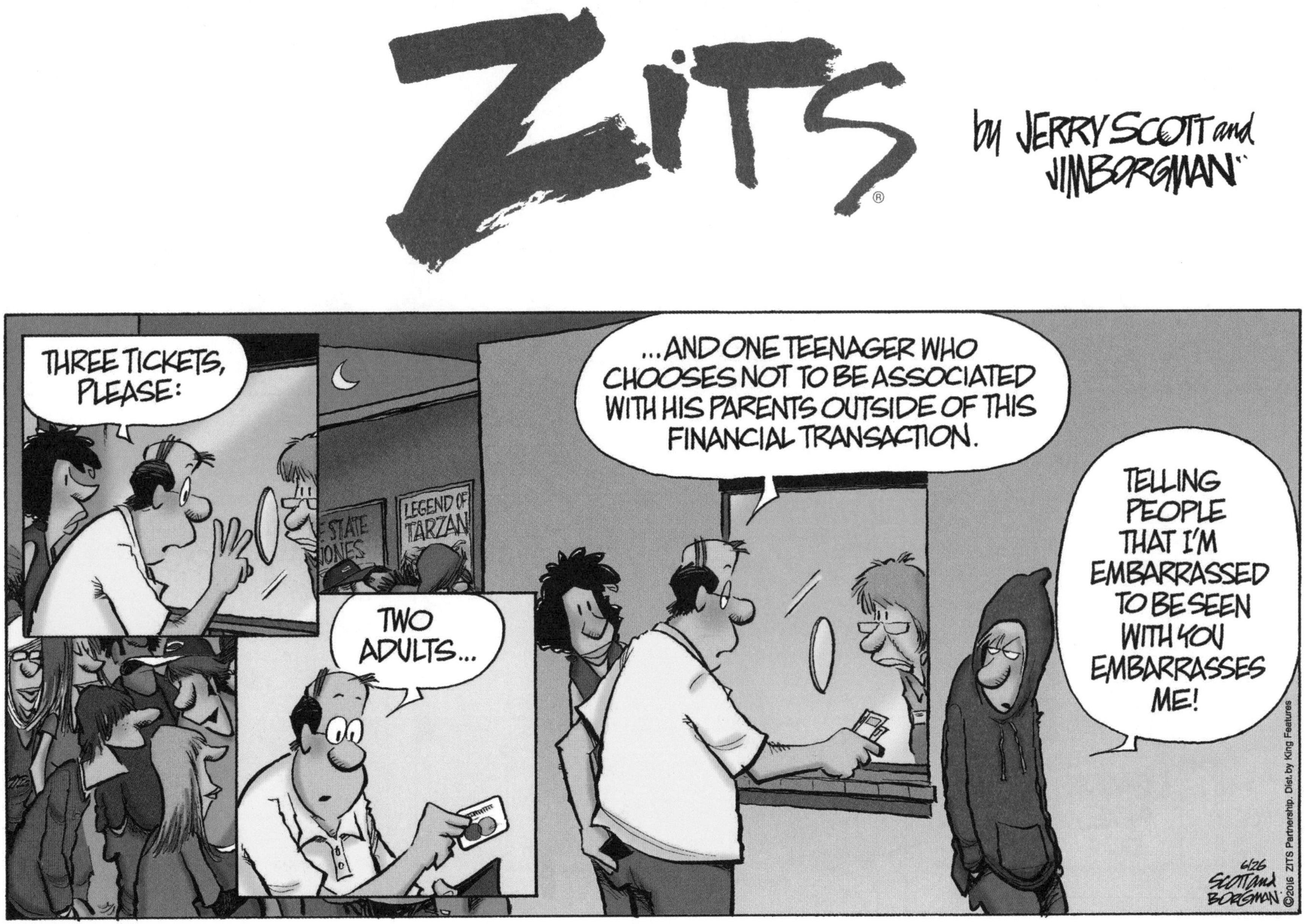
ZITS
by JERRY SCOTT and JIM BORGMAN
THREE TICKETS, PLEASE:
TWO ADULTS...
...AND ONE TEENAGER WHO CHOOSES NOT TO BE ASSOCIATED WITH HIS PARENTS OUTSIDE OF THIS FINANCIAL TRANSACTION.
TELLING PEOPLE THAT I'M EMBARRASSED TO BE SEEN WITH YOU EMBARRASSES ME!
6/26 SCOTT and BORGMAN
©2016 ZITS Partnership. Dist. by King Features

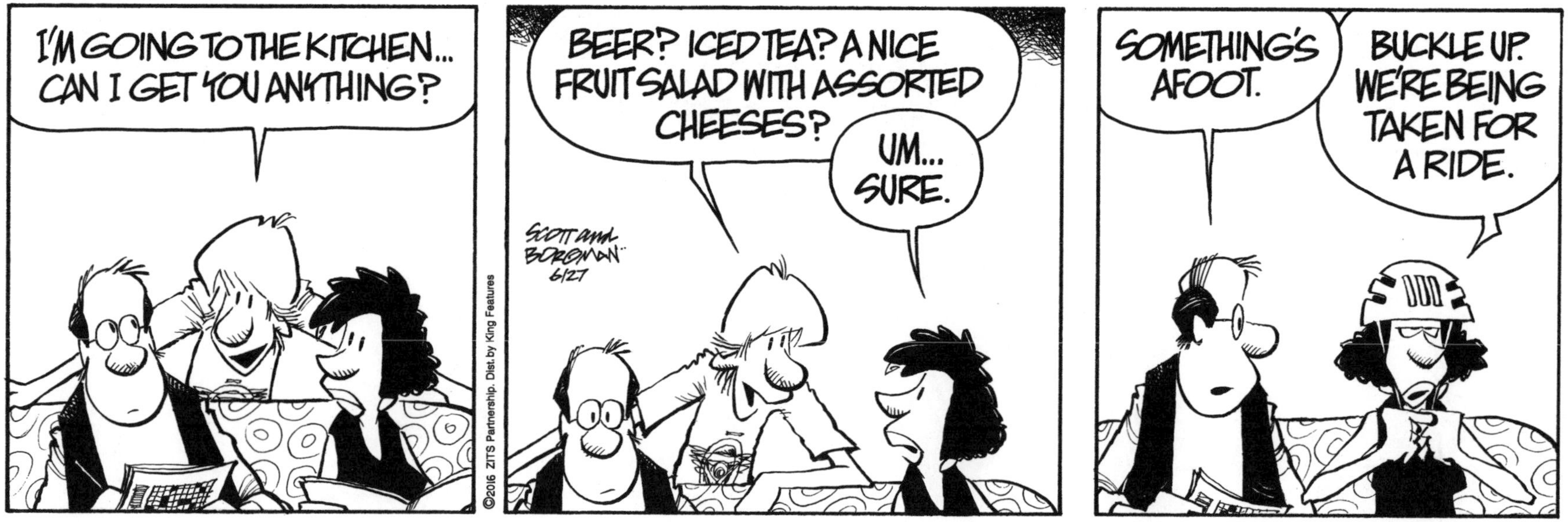
I'M GOING TO THE KITCHEN... CAN I GET YOU ANYTHING?
BEER? ICED TEA? A NICE FRUIT SALAD WITH ASSORTED CHEESES?
UM... SURE.
SCOTT and BORGMAN 6/27
©2016 ZITS Partnership. Dist. by King Features
SOMETHING'S AFOOT.
BUCKLE UP. WE'RE BEING TAKEN FOR A RIDE.

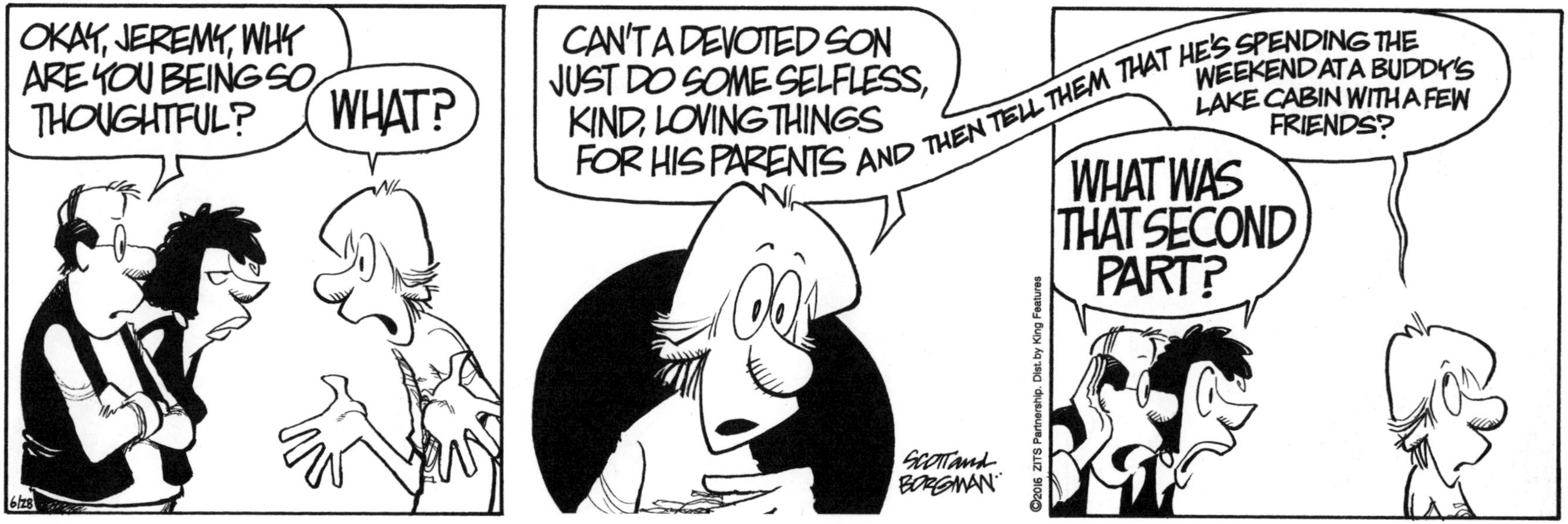
OKAY, JEREMY, WHY ARE YOU BEING SO THOUGHTFUL?
WHAT?
6/28
CAN'T A DEVOTED SON JUST DO SOME SELFLESS, KIND, LOVING THINGS FOR HIS PARENTS AND THEN TELL THEM THAT HE'S SPENDING THE WEEKEND AT A BUDDY'S LAKE CABIN WITH A FEW FRIENDS?
SCOTT and BORGMAN
©2016 ZITS Partnership. Dist. by King Features
WHAT WAS THAT SECOND PART?

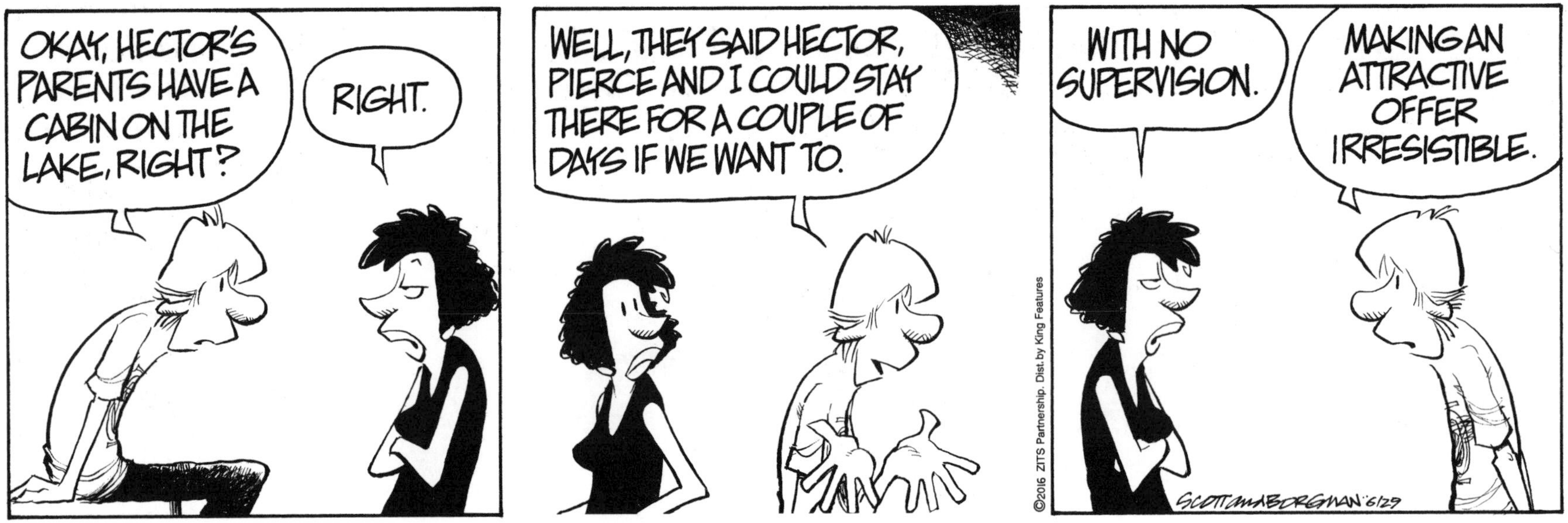
OKAY, HECTOR'S PARENTS HAVE A CABIN ON THE LAKE, RIGHT?
RIGHT.
WELL, THEY SAID HECTOR, PIERCE AND I COULD STAY THERE FOR A COUPLE OF DAYS IF WE WANT TO.
©2016 ZITS Partnership. Dist. by King Features
WITH NO SUPERVISION.
MAKING AN ATTRACTIVE OFFER IRRESISTIBLE.
SCOTT AND BORGMAN 6/29

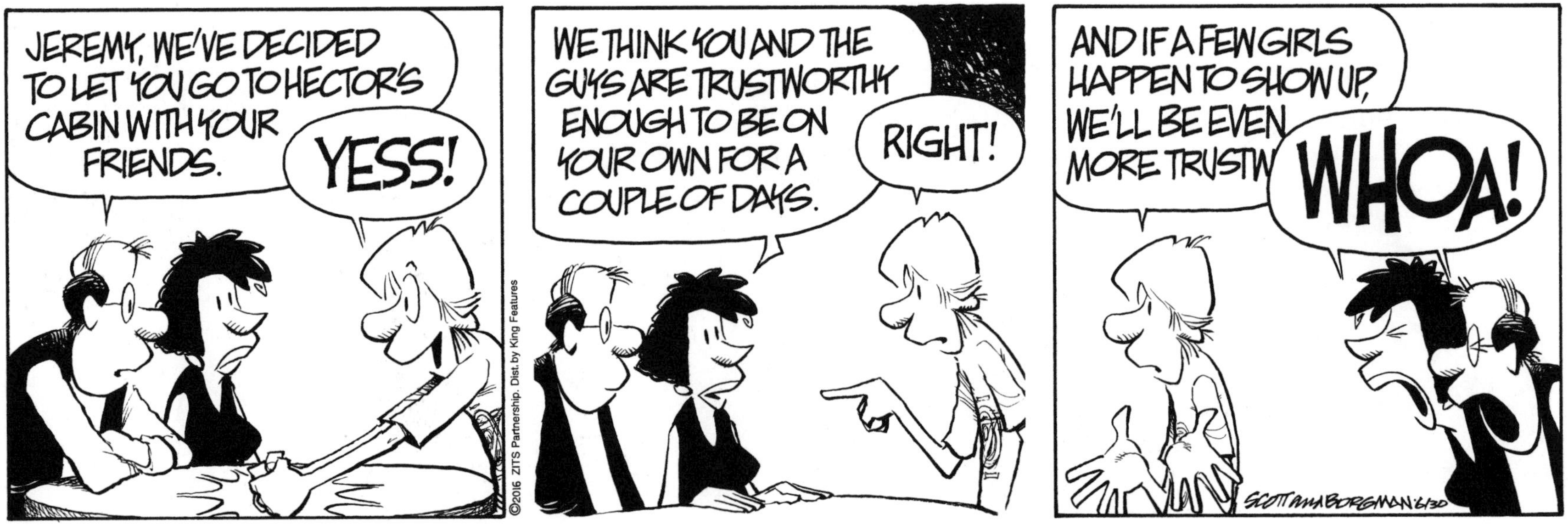
JEREMY, WE'VE DECIDED TO LET YOU GO TO HECTOR'S CABIN WITH YOUR FRIENDS.
YESS!
©2016 ZITS Partnership. Dist. by King Features
WE THINK YOU AND THE GUYS ARE TRUSTWORTHY ENOUGH TO BE ON YOUR OWN FOR A COUPLE OF DAYS.
RIGHT!
AND IF A FEW GIRLS HAPPEN TO SHOW UP, WE'LL BE EVEN MORE TRUSTW
WHOA!
SCOTT AND BORGMAN 6/30

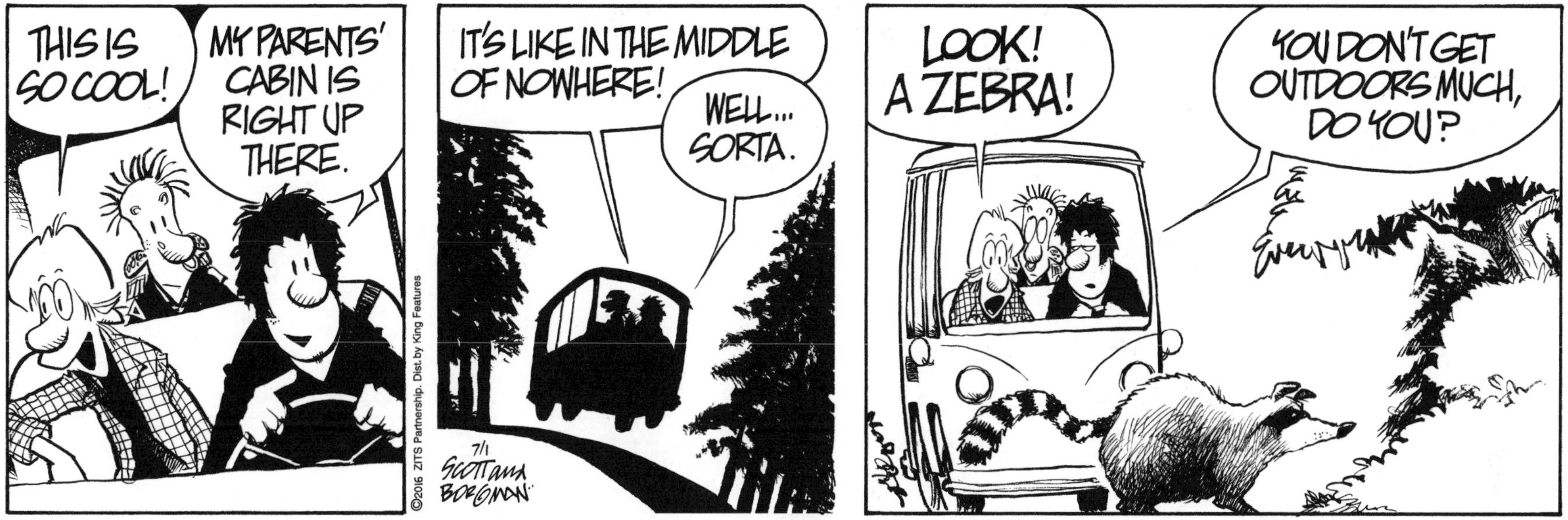
THIS IS SO COOL!
MY PARENTS' CABIN IS RIGHT UP THERE.
IT'S LIKE IN THE MIDDLE OF NOWHERE!
WELL... SORTA.
LOOK! A ZEBRA!
YOU DON'T GET OUTDOORS MUCH, DO YOU?
©2016 ZITS Partnership. Dist. by King Features
7/1 SCOTT and BORGMAN

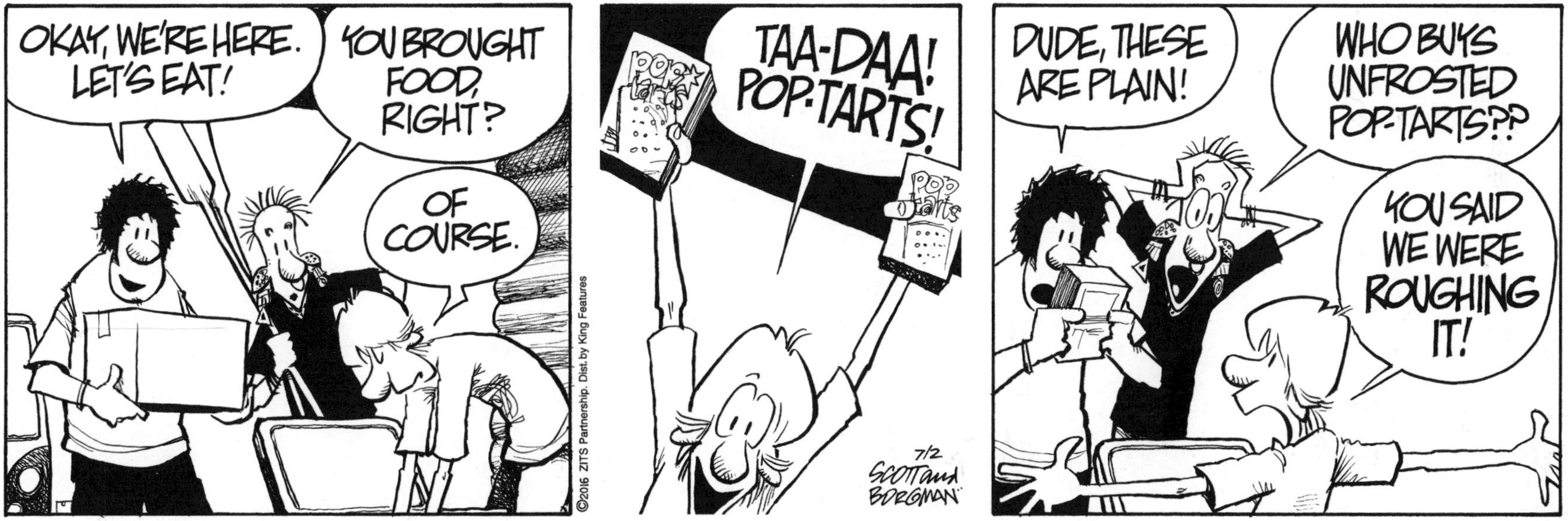
OKAY, WE'RE HERE. LET'S EAT!
YOU BROUGHT FOOD, RIGHT?
OF COURSE.
TAA-DAA! POP-TARTS!
DUDE, THESE ARE PLAIN!
WHO BUYS UNFROSTED POP-TARTS??
YOU SAID WE WERE ROUGHING IT!
©2016 ZITS Partnership. Dist. by King Features
7/2 SCOTT and BORGMAN

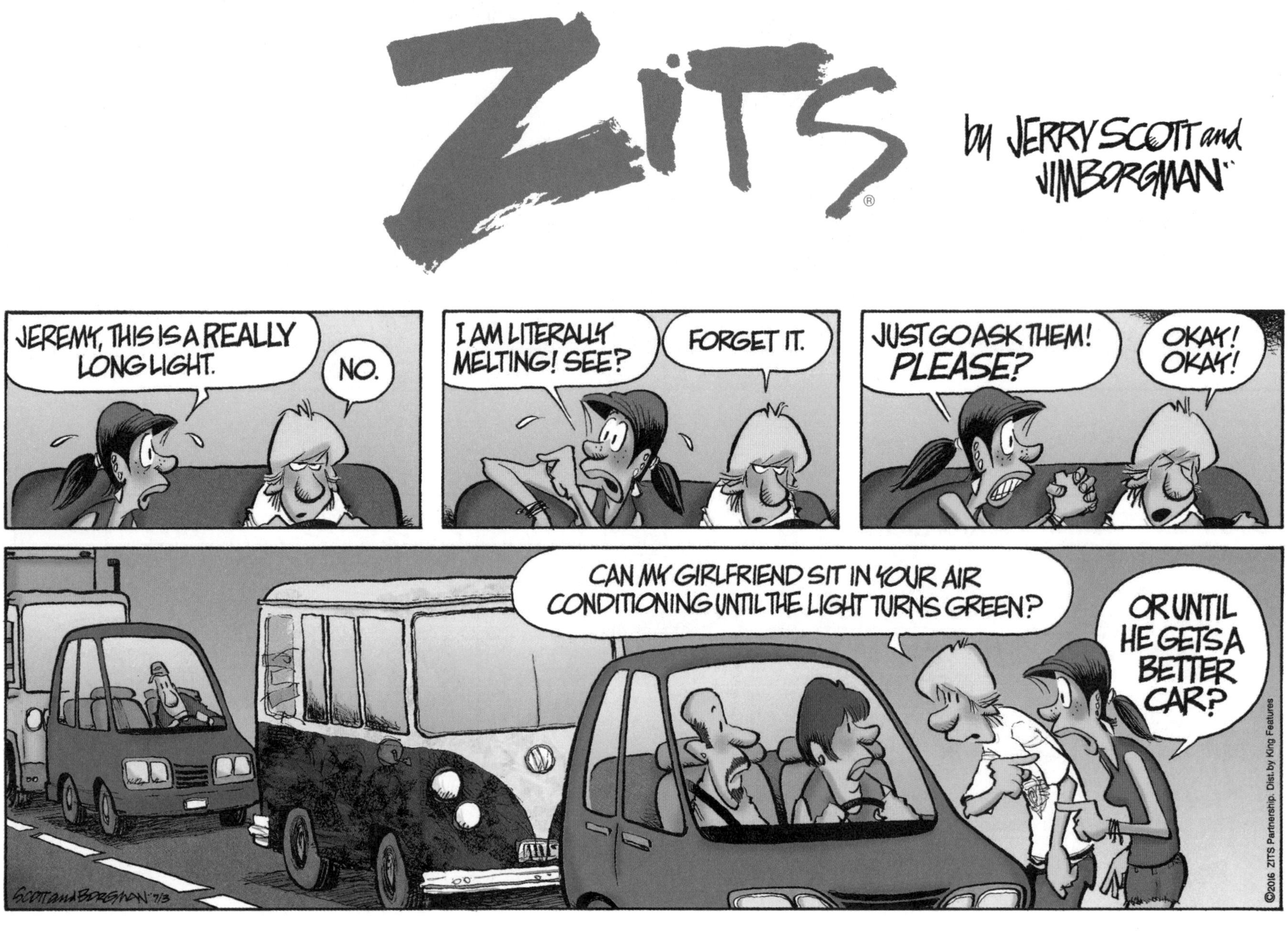
ZITS
by JERRY SCOTT and JIM BORGMAN
JEREMY, THIS IS A REALLY LONG LIGHT.
NO.
I AM LITERALLY MELTING! SEE?
FORGET IT.
JUST GO ASK THEM! PLEASE?
OKAY! OKAY!
CAN MY GIRLFRIEND SIT IN YOUR AIR CONDITIONING UNTIL THE LIGHT TURNS GREEN?
OR UNTIL HE GETS A BETTER CAR?
SCOTT and BORGMAN 7/3
©2016 ZITS Partnership. Dist. by King Features

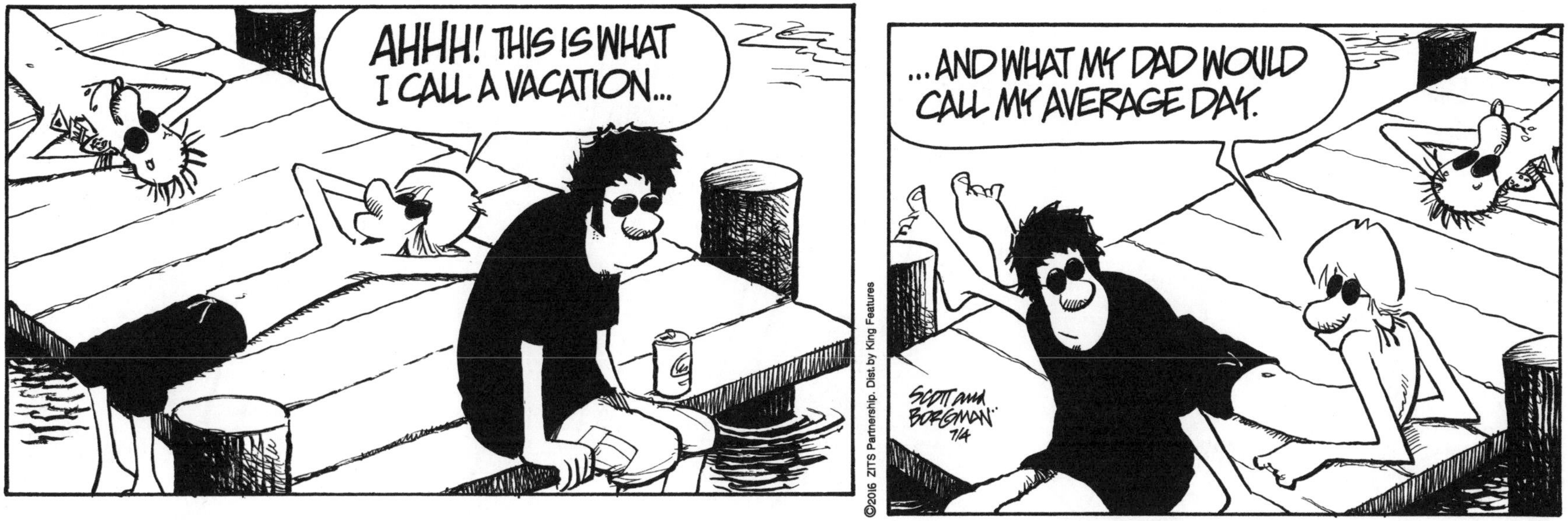
AHHH! THIS IS WHAT I CALL A VACATION...
...AND WHAT MY DAD WOULD CALL MY AVERAGE DAY.
SCOTT AND BORGMAN 7/4
©2016 ZITS Partnership. Dist. by King Features

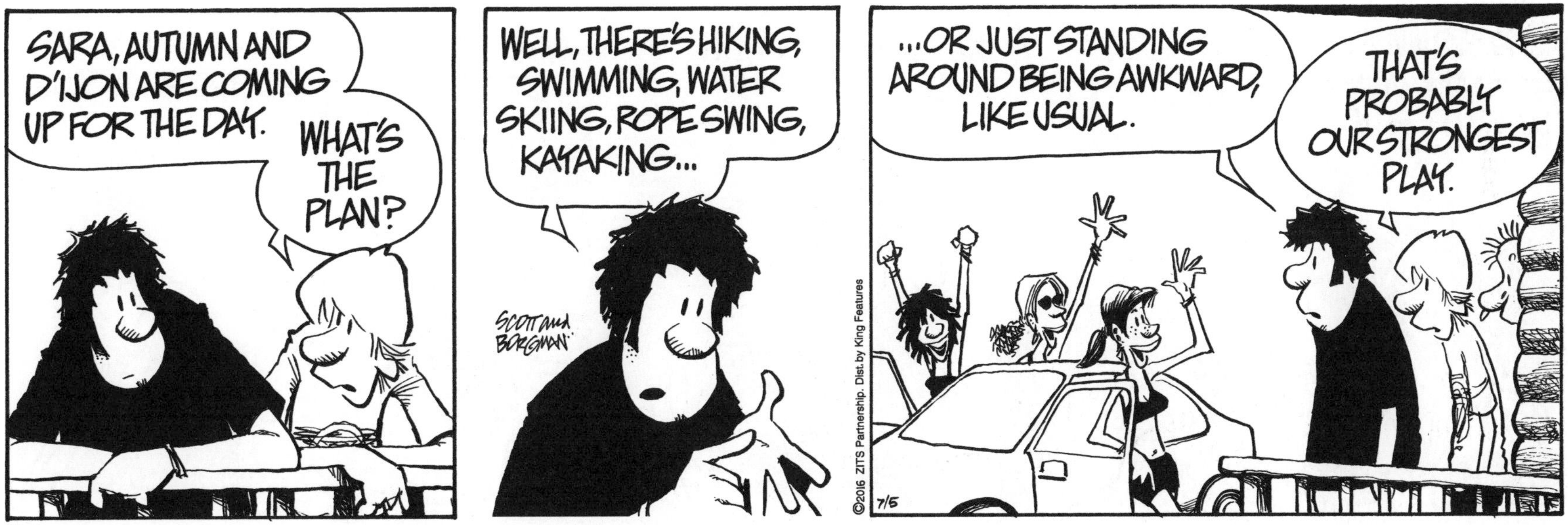
SARA, AUTUMN AND D'IJON ARE COMING UP FOR THE DAY.
WHAT'S THE PLAN?
WELL, THERE'S HIKING, SWIMMING, WATER SKIING, ROPE SWING, KAYAKING...
SCOTT AND BORGMAN
...OR JUST STANDING AROUND BEING AWKWARD, LIKE USUAL.
THAT'S PROBABLY OUR STRONGEST PLAY.
7/5
©2016 ZITS Partnership. Dist. by King Features

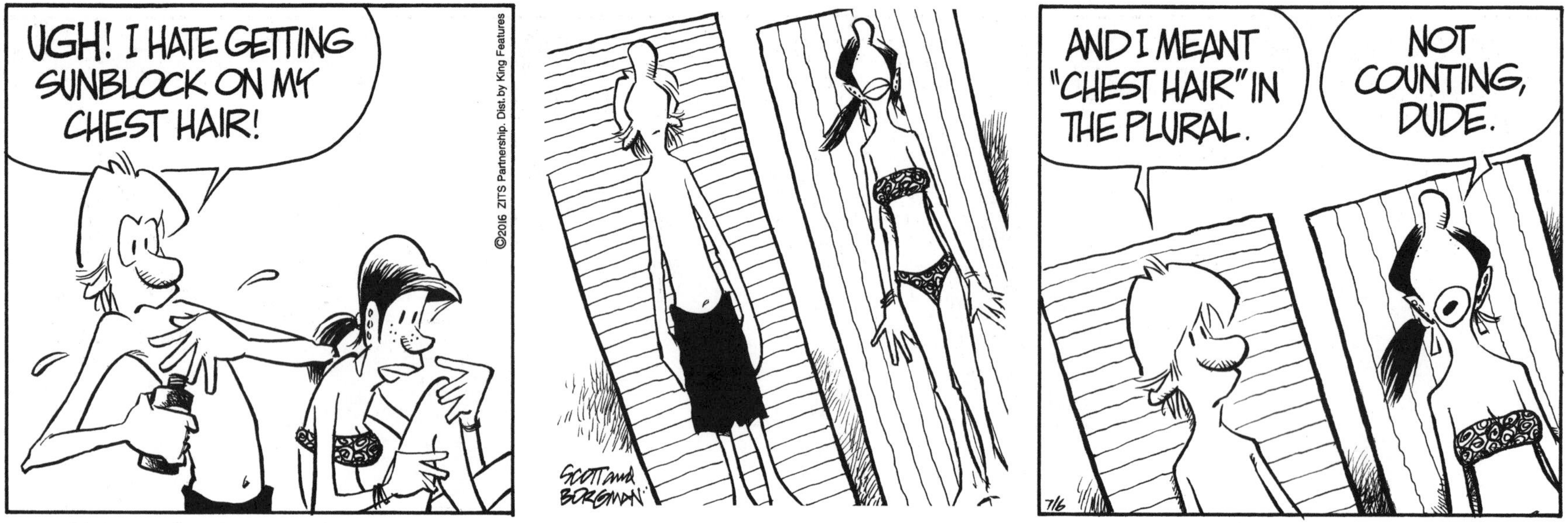
UGH! I HATE GETTING SUNBLOCK ON MY CHEST HAIR!
©2016 ZITS Partnership. Dist. by King Features
SCOTT and BORGMAN
AND I MEANT "CHEST HAIR" IN THE PLURAL.
NOT COUNTING, DUDE.
7/6

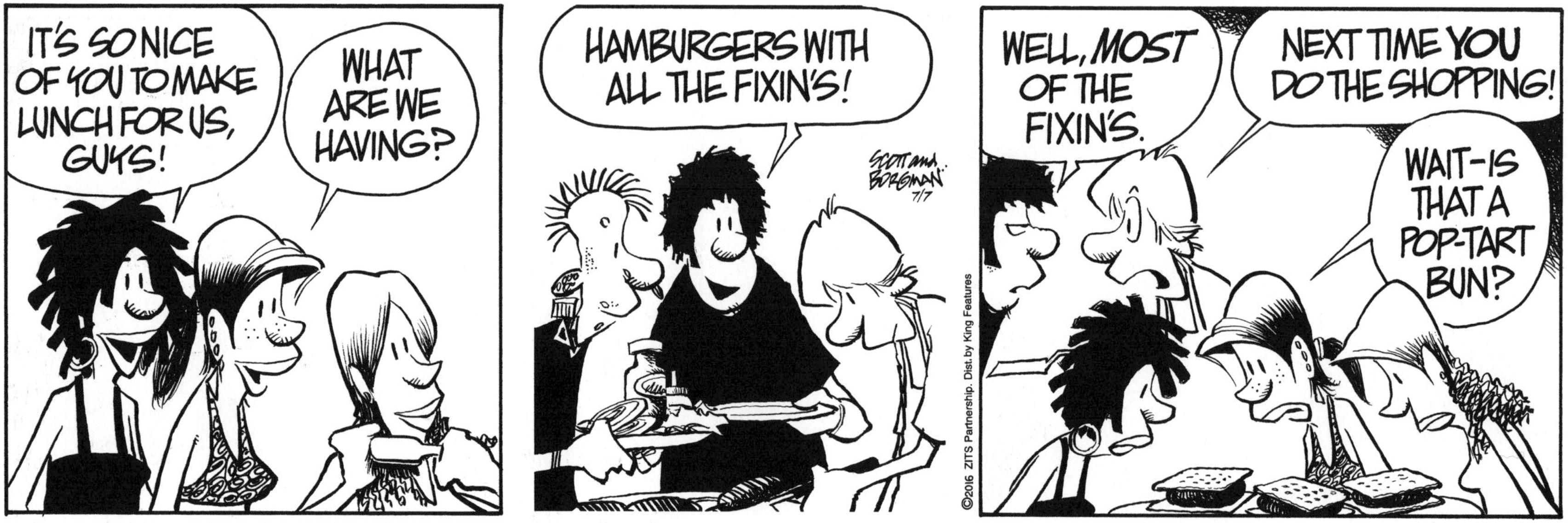
IT'S SO NICE OF YOU TO MAKE LUNCH FOR US, GUYS!
WHAT ARE WE HAVING?
HAMBURGERS WITH ALL THE FIXIN'S!
SCOTT and BORGMAN 7/7
©2016 ZITS Partnership. Dist. by King Features
WELL, *MOST* OF THE FIXIN'S.
NEXT TIME **YOU** DO THE SHOPPING!
WAIT-IS THAT A POP-TART BUN?

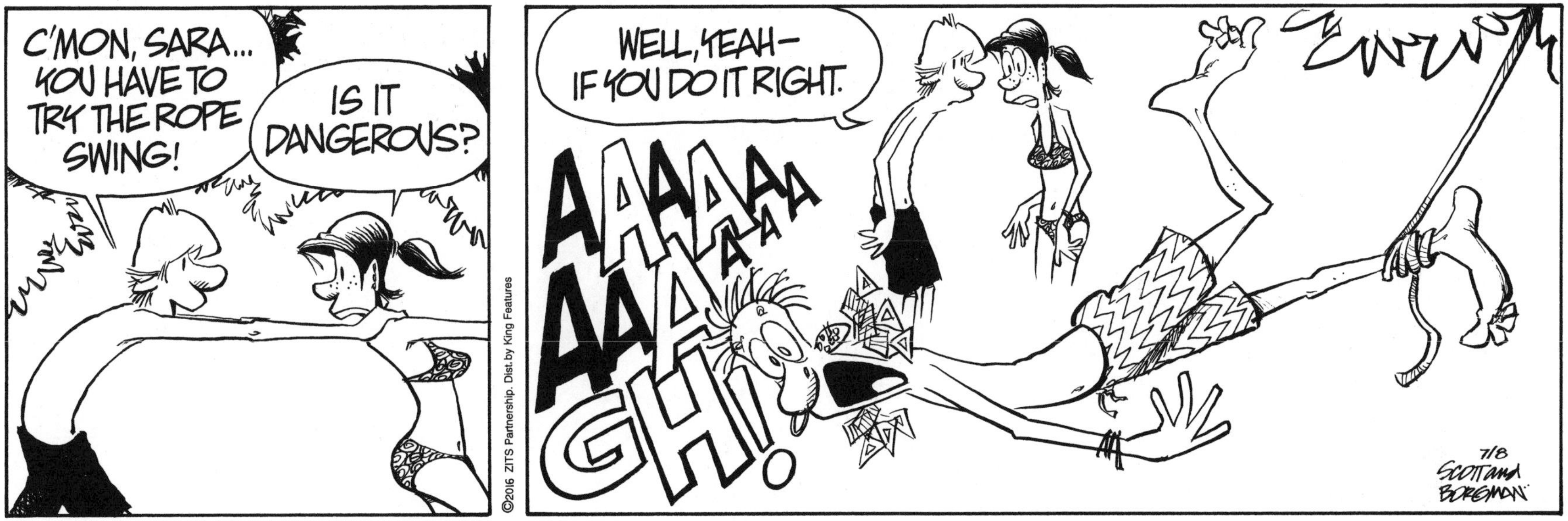
C'MON, SARA... YOU HAVE TO TRY THE ROPE SWING!
IS IT DANGEROUS?
©2016 ZITS Partnership. Dist. by King Features
WELL, YEAH– IF YOU DO IT RIGHT.
AAAAAAAAAAAGH!
7/8 SCOTT and BORGMAN

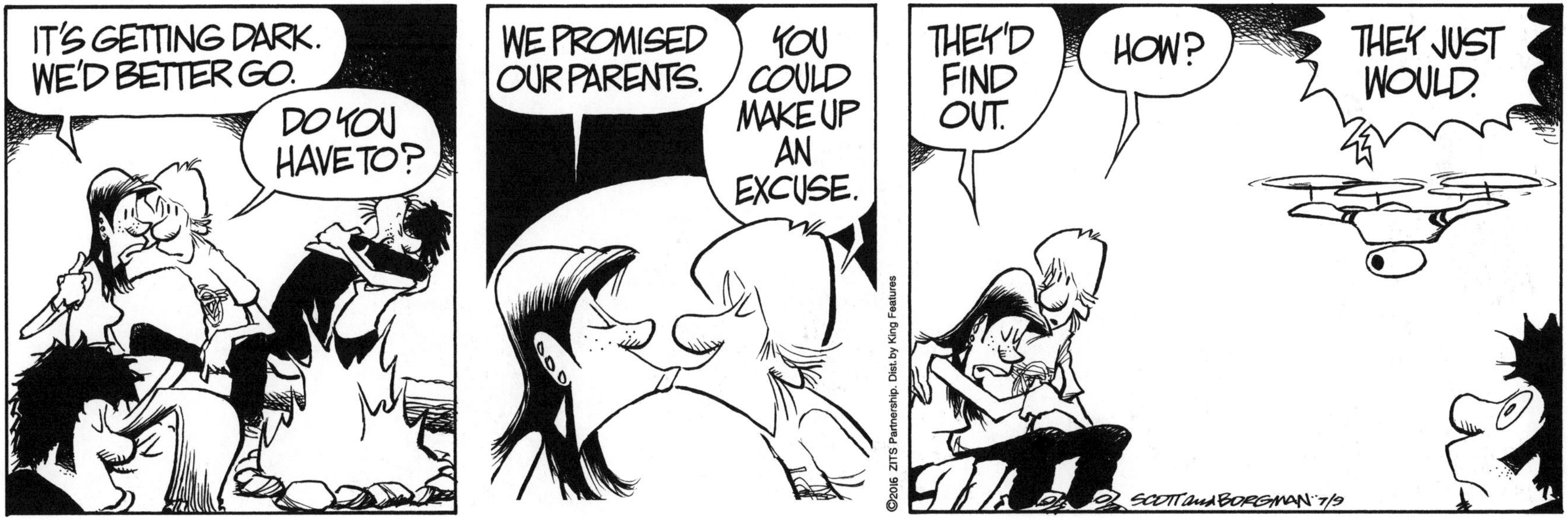
IT'S GETTING DARK. WE'D BETTER GO.
DO YOU HAVE TO?
WE PROMISED OUR PARENTS.
YOU COULD MAKE UP AN EXCUSE.
©2016 ZITS Partnership. Dist. by King Features
THEY'D FIND OUT.
HOW?
THEY JUST WOULD.
SCOTT and BORGMAN 7/9

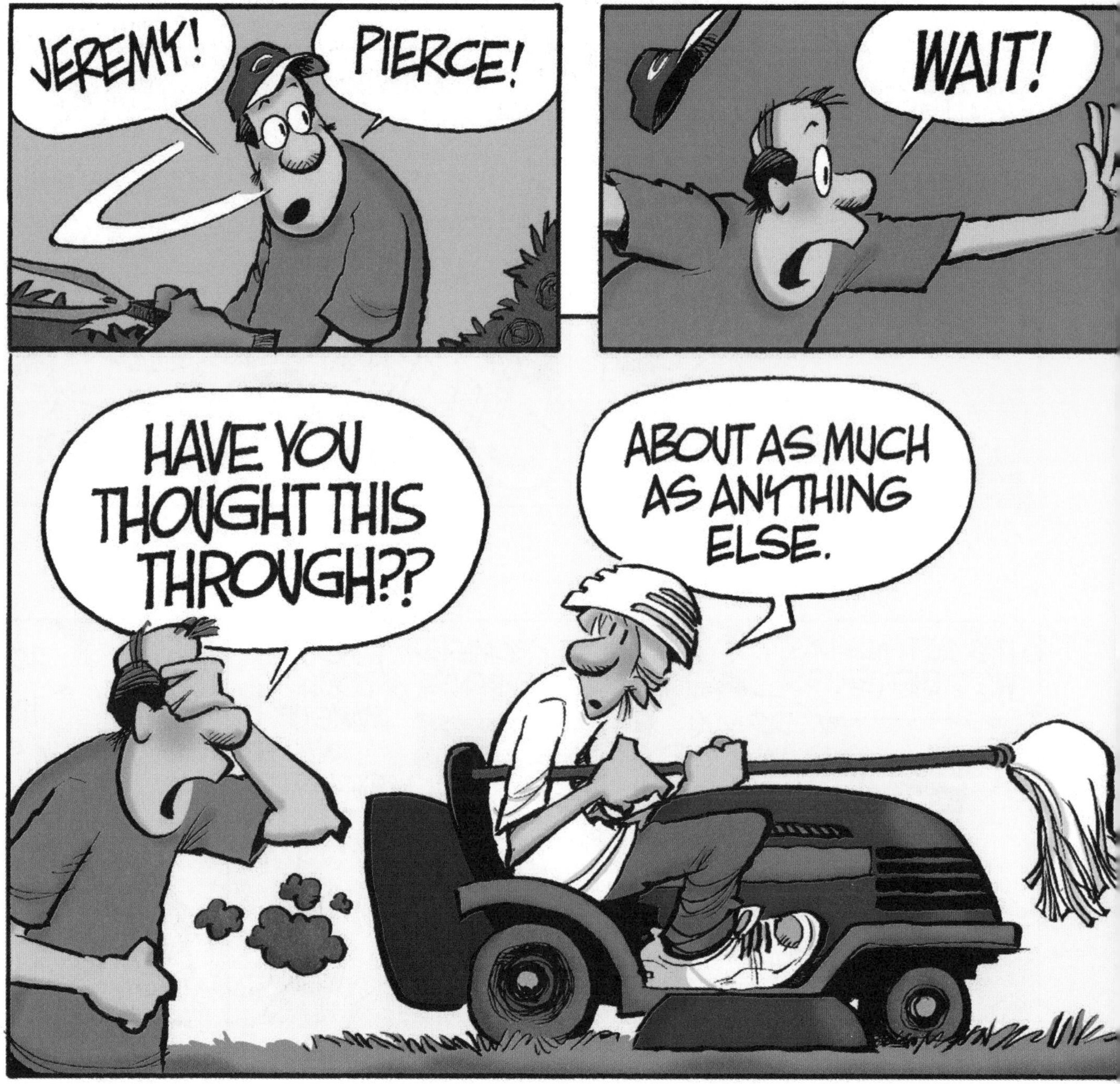
JEREMY!
PIERCE!
WAIT!
HAVE YOU THOUGHT THIS THROUGH??
ABOUT AS MUCH AS ANYTHING ELSE.

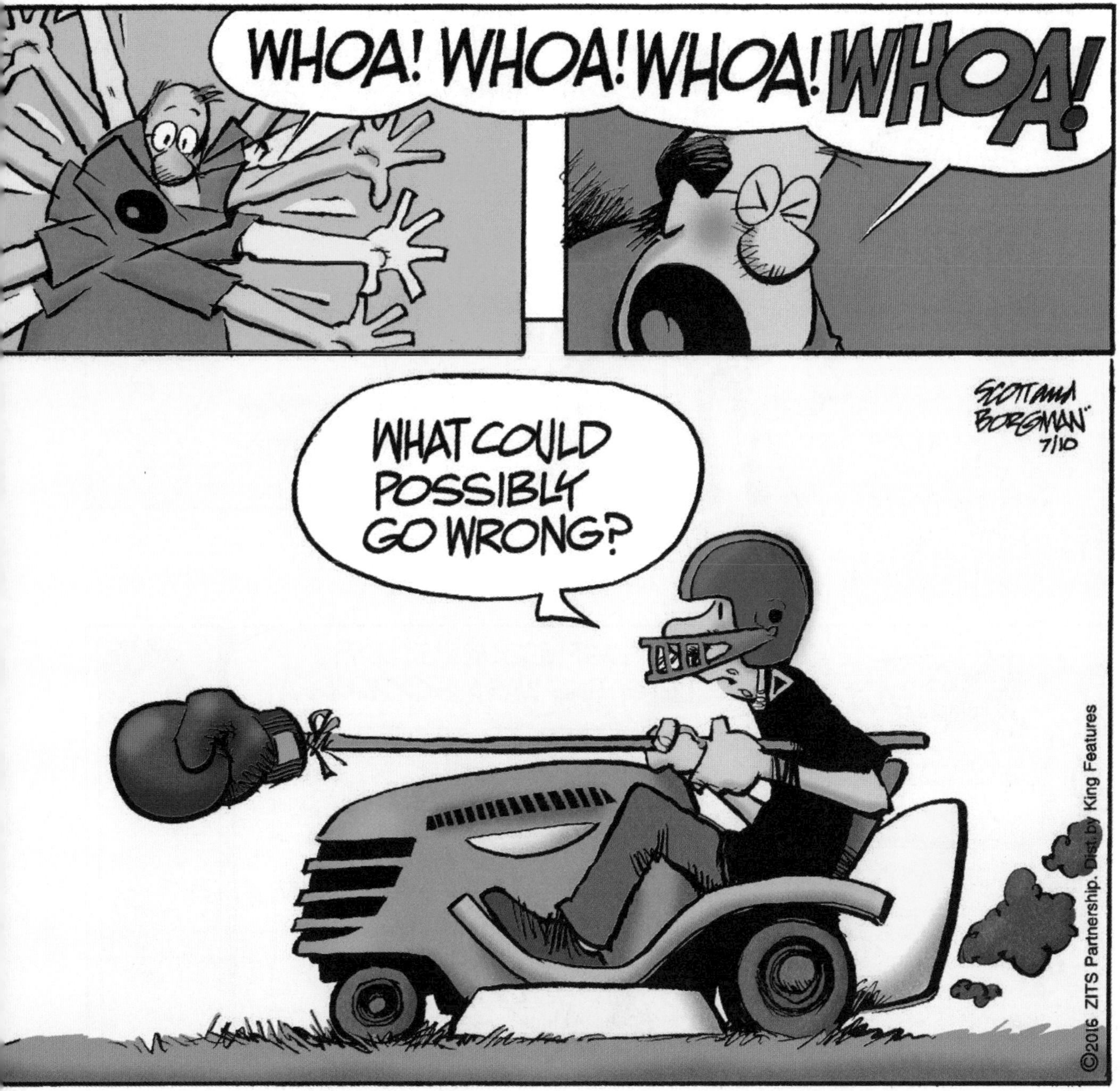
WHOA! WHOA! WHOA! WHOA!
WHAT COULD POSSIBLY GO WRONG?
SCOTT AND BORGMAN 7/10
©2016 ZITS Partnership. Dist. by King Features

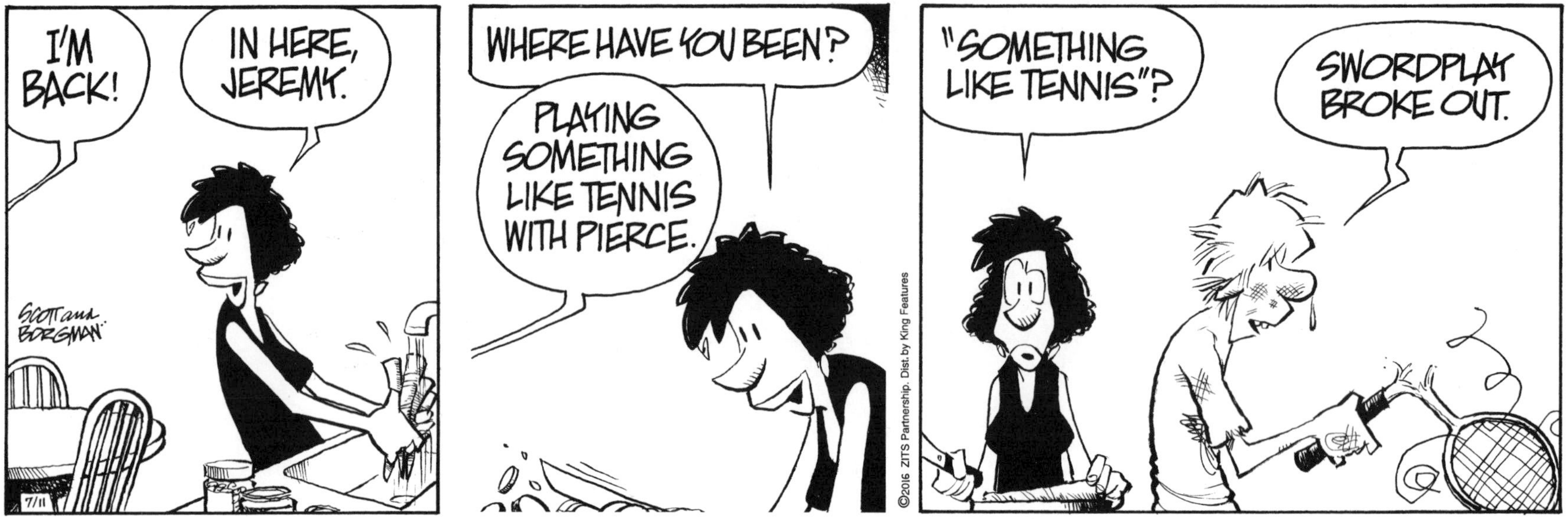
I'M BACK!
IN HERE, JEREMY.
WHERE HAVE YOU BEEN?
PLAYING SOMETHING LIKE TENNIS WITH PIERCE.
"SOMETHING LIKE TENNIS"?
SWORDPLAY BROKE OUT.
SCOTT and BORGMAN
7/11
©2016 ZITS Partnership. Dist. by King Features

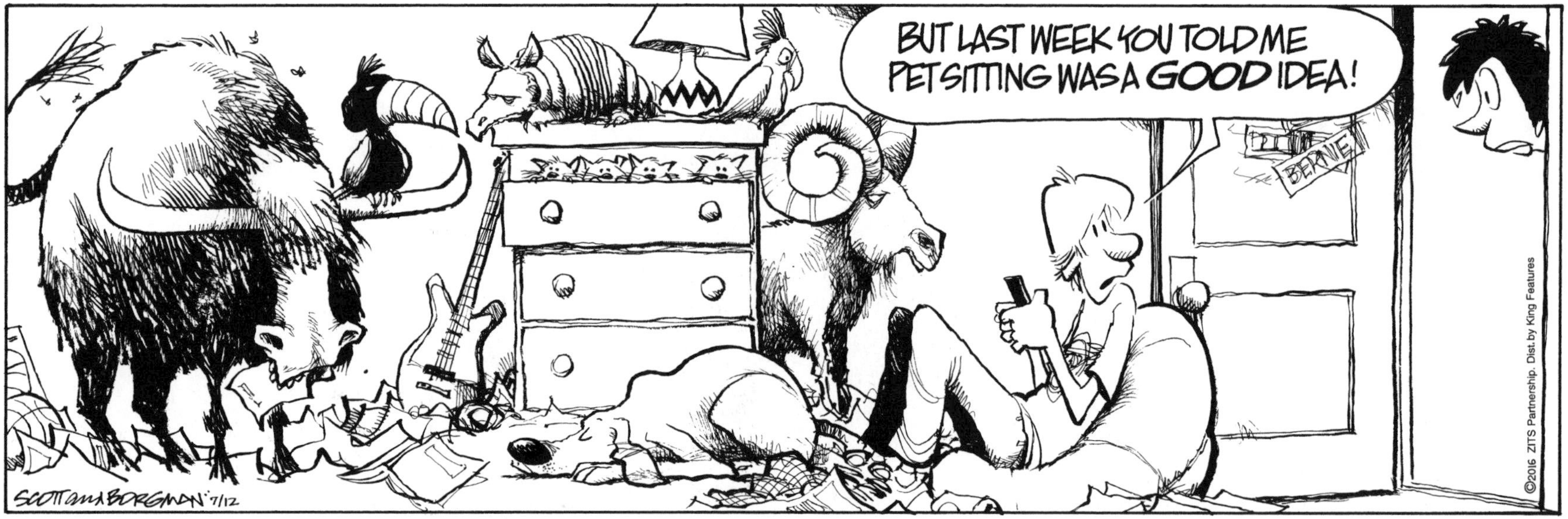
BUT LAST WEEK YOU TOLD ME PET SITTING WAS A **GOOD** IDEA!
BERNIE
SCOTT and BORGMAN 7/12
©2016 ZITS Partnership. Dist. by King Features

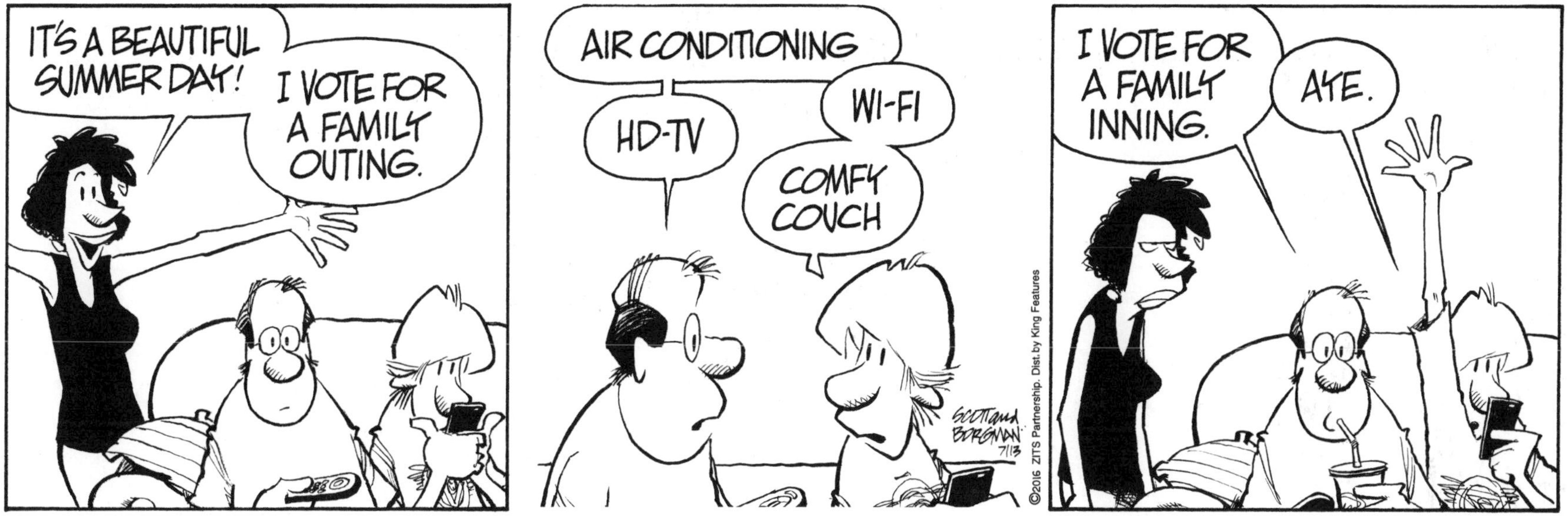
IT'S A BEAUTIFUL SUMMER DAY!
I VOTE FOR A FAMILY OUTING.
AIR CONDITIONING
HD-TV
WI-FI
COMFY COUCH
SCOTT and BORGMAN 7/13
©2016 ZITS Partnership. Dist. by King Features
I VOTE FOR A FAMILY INNING.
AYE.

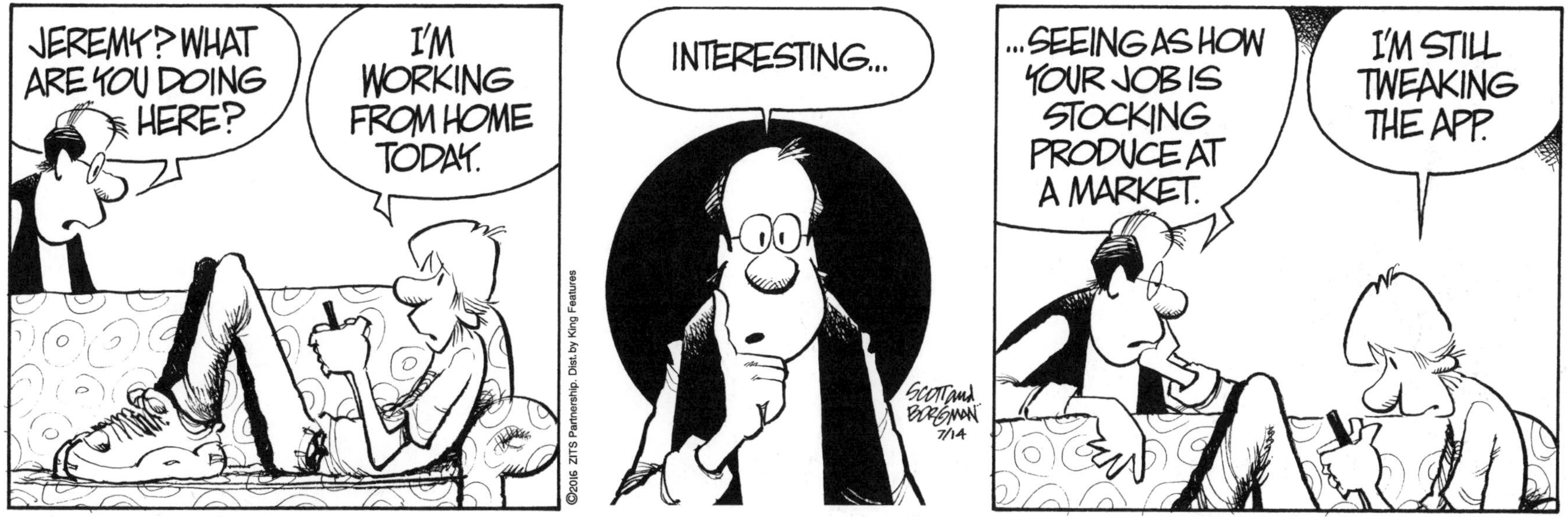
JEREMY? WHAT ARE YOU DOING HERE?
I'M WORKING FROM HOME TODAY.
©2016 ZITS Partnership. Dist. by King Features
INTERESTING...
SCOTT and BORGMAN 7/14
...SEEING AS HOW YOUR JOB IS STOCKING PRODUCE AT A MARKET.
I'M STILL TWEAKING THE APP.

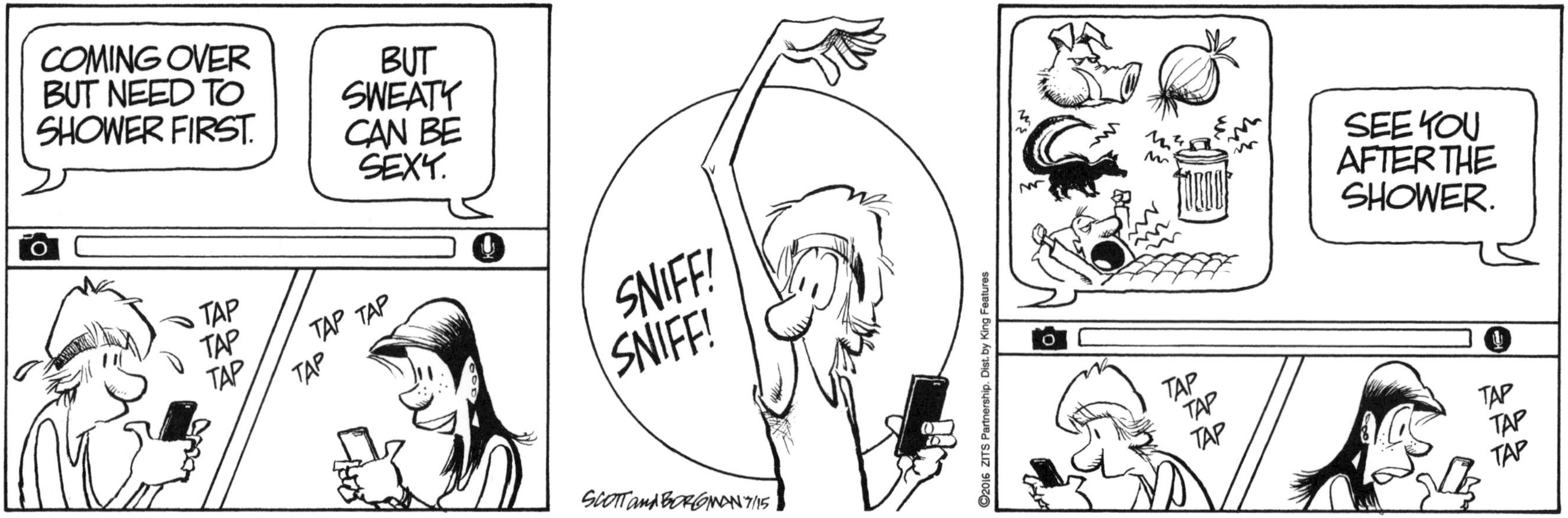
COMING OVER BUT NEED TO SHOWER FIRST.
BUT SWEATY CAN BE SEXY.
TAP TAP TAP
TAP TAP TAP
SNIFF! SNIFF!
SCOTT and BORGMAN 7/15
©2016 ZITS Partnership. Dist. by King Features
SEE YOU AFTER THE SHOWER.
TAP TAP TAP
TAP TAP TAP

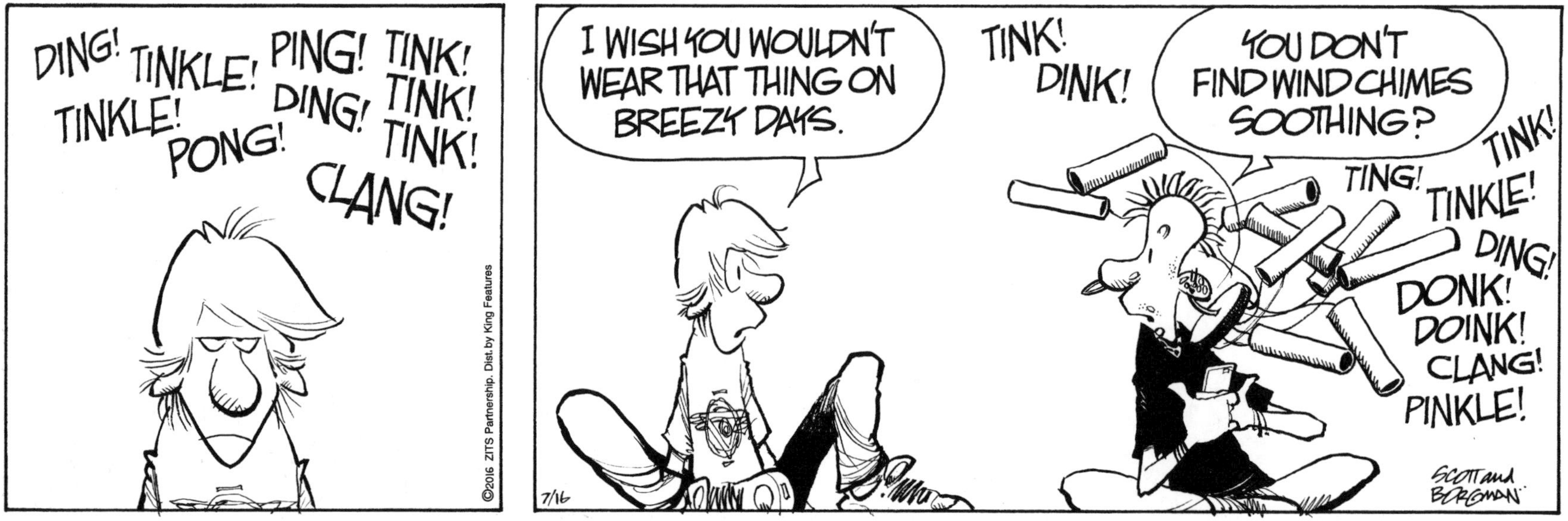
DING! TINKLE! PING! TINK! TINKLE! DING! TINK! PONG! TINK! CLANG!
©2016 ZITS Partnership. Dist. by King Features
I WISH YOU WOULDN'T WEAR THAT THING ON BREEZY DAYS.
TINK! DINK!
YOU DON'T FIND WIND CHIMES SOOTHING?
TING! TINK! TINKLE! DING! DONK! DOINK! CLANG! PINKLE!
7/16
SCOTT and BORGMAN

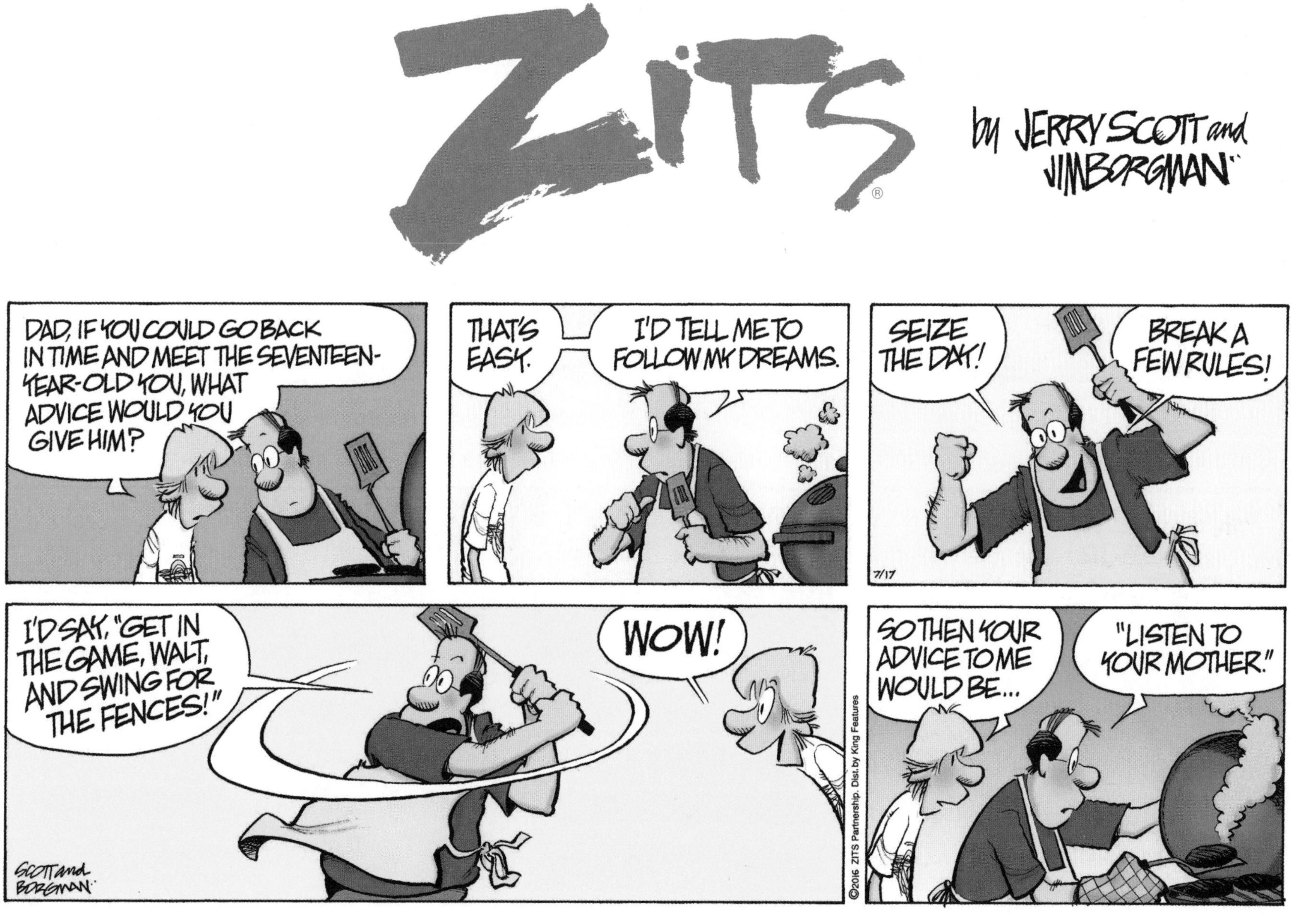
ZITS®
by JERRY SCOTT and JIM BORGMAN
DAD, IF YOU COULD GO BACK IN TIME AND MEET THE SEVENTEEN-YEAR-OLD YOU, WHAT ADVICE WOULD YOU GIVE HIM?
THAT'S EASY.
I'D TELL ME TO FOLLOW MY DREAMS.
SEIZE THE DAY!
BREAK A FEW RULES!
7/17
I'D SAY, "GET IN THE GAME, WALT, AND SWING FOR THE FENCES!"
WOW!
SCOTT and BORGMAN
©2016 ZITS Partnership. Dist. by King Features
SO THEN YOUR ADVICE TO ME WOULD BE...
"LISTEN TO YOUR MOTHER."

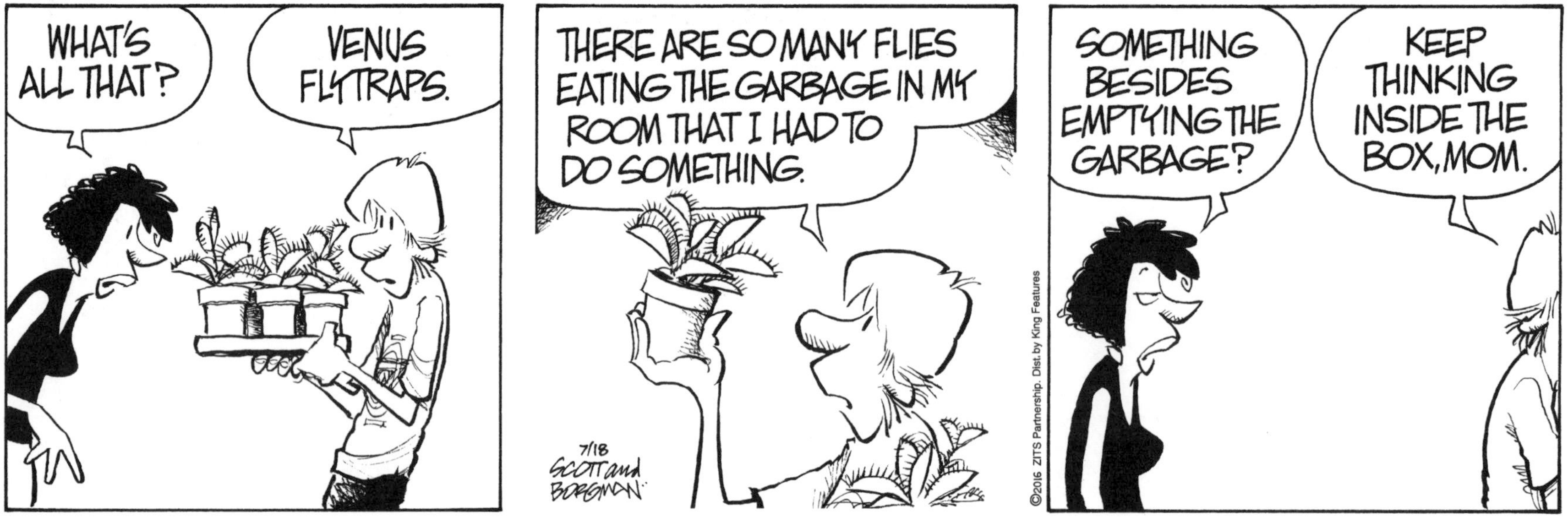
WHAT'S ALL THAT?
VENUS FLYTRAPS.
THERE ARE SO MANY FLIES EATING THE GARBAGE IN MY ROOM THAT I HAD TO DO SOMETHING.
7/18
SCOTT and BORGMAN
©2016 ZITS Partnership. Dist. by King Features
SOMETHING BESIDES EMPTYING THE GARBAGE?
KEEP THINKING INSIDE THE BOX, MOM.

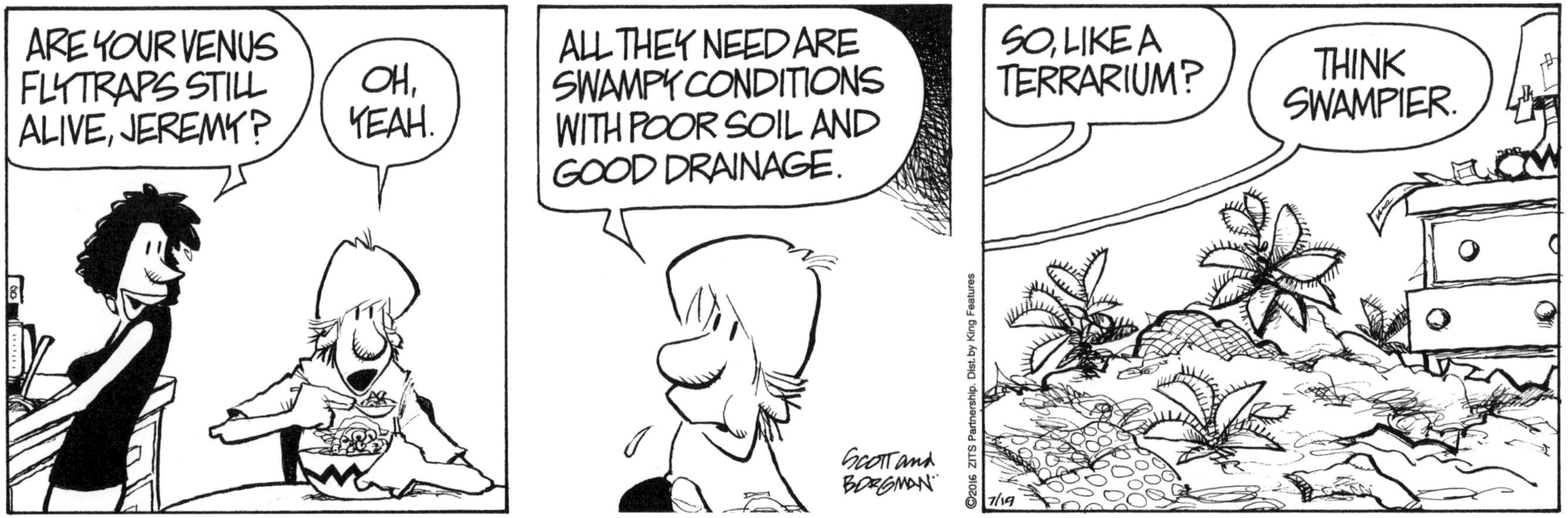
ARE YOUR VENUS FLYTRAPS STILL ALIVE, JEREMY?
OH, YEAH.
ALL THEY NEED ARE SWAMPY CONDITIONS WITH POOR SOIL AND GOOD DRAINAGE.
SCOTT and BORGMAN
©2016 ZITS Partnership. Dist. by King Features
7/19
SO, LIKE A TERRARIUM?
THINK SWAMPIER.

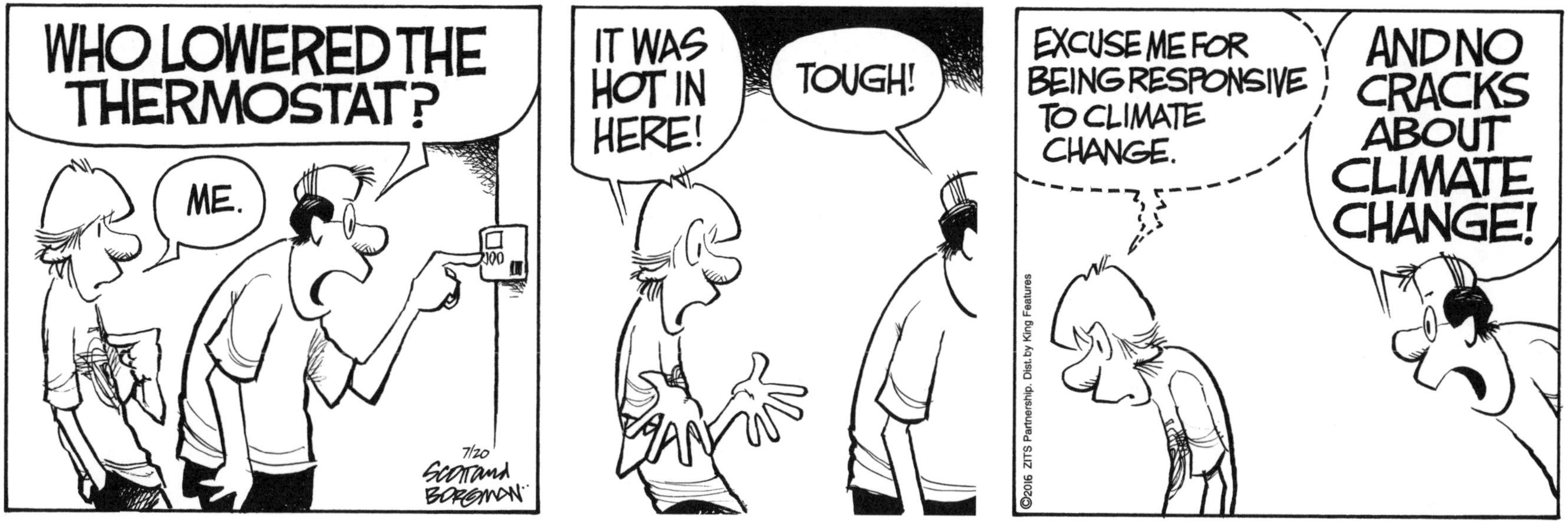
WHO LOWERED THE THERMOSTAT?
ME.
IT WAS HOT IN HERE!
TOUGH!
EXCUSE ME FOR BEING RESPONSIVE TO CLIMATE CHANGE.
AND NO CRACKS ABOUT CLIMATE CHANGE!
7/20
SCOTT AND BORGMAN
©2016 ZITS Partnership. Dist. by King Features

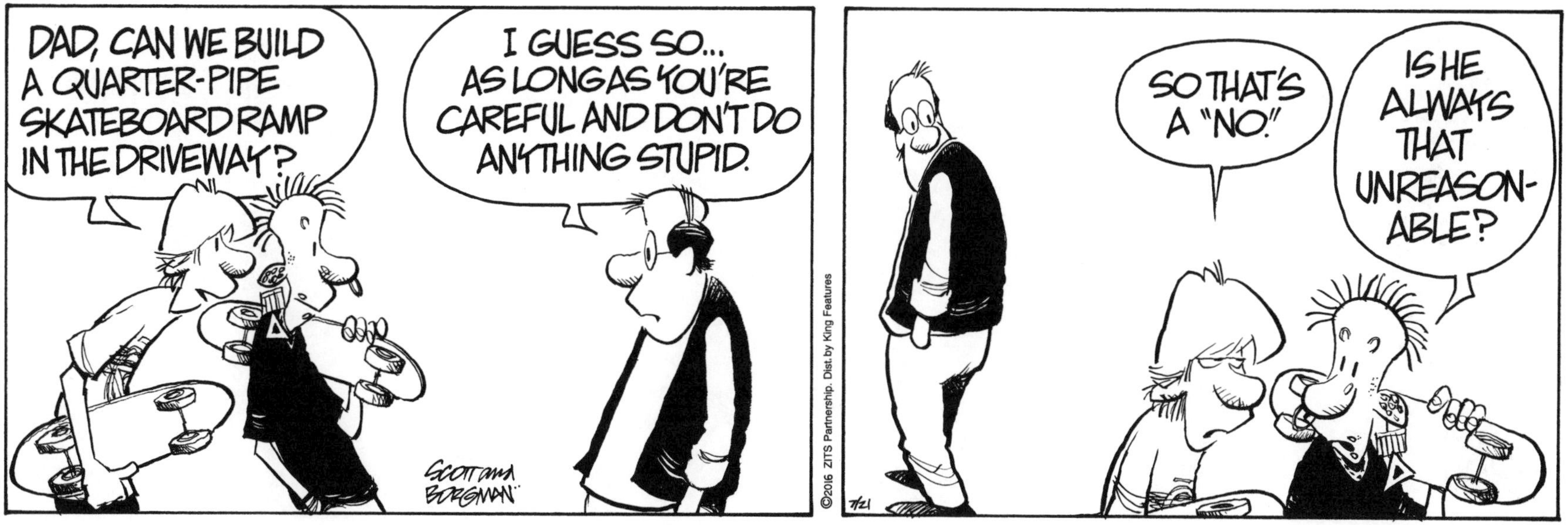
DAD, CAN WE BUILD A QUARTER-PIPE SKATEBOARD RAMP IN THE DRIVEWAY?
I GUESS SO... AS LONG AS YOU'RE CAREFUL AND DON'T DO ANYTHING STUPID.
SO THAT'S A "NO."
IS HE ALWAYS THAT UNREASON-ABLE?
SCOTT AND BORGMAN
7/21
©2016 ZITS Partnership. Dist. by King Features

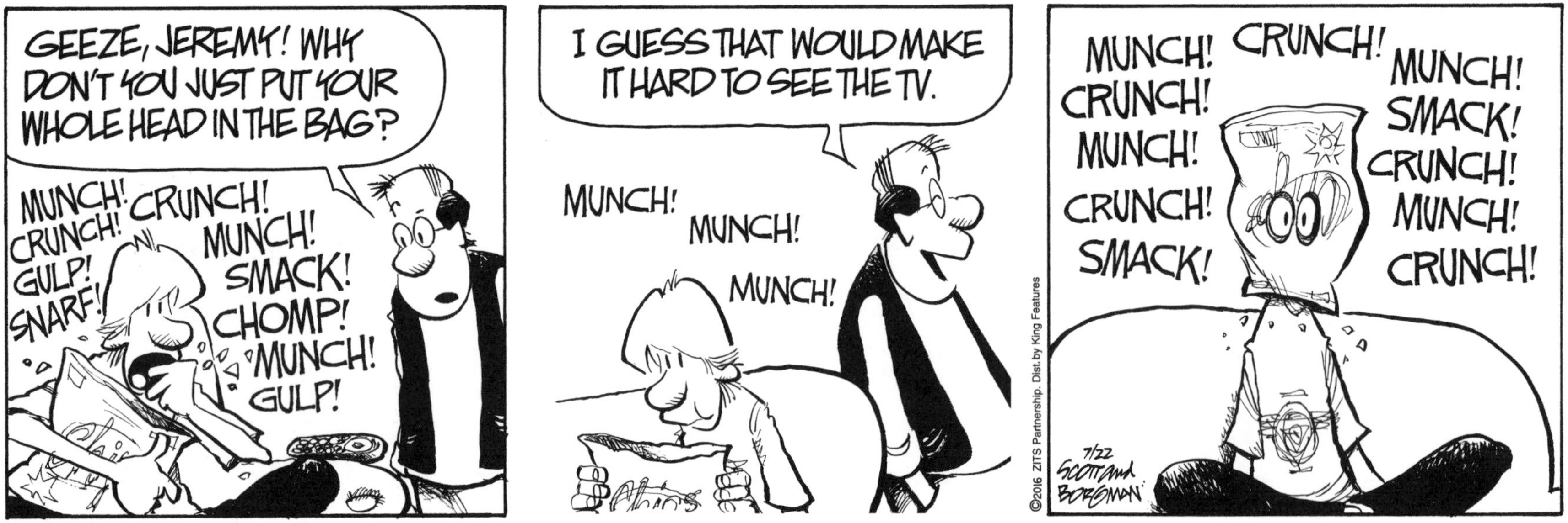
GEEZE, JEREMY! WHY DON'T YOU JUST PUT YOUR WHOLE HEAD IN THE BAG?
MUNCH! CRUNCH! GULP! SNARF! CRUNCH! MUNCH! SMACK! CHOMP! MUNCH! GULP!
I GUESS THAT WOULD MAKE IT HARD TO SEE THE TV.
MUNCH! MUNCH! MUNCH!
©2016 ZITS Partnership. Dist. by King Features
MUNCH! CRUNCH! MUNCH! CRUNCH! SMACK! CRUNCH! MUNCH! SMACK! CRUNCH! MUNCH! CRUNCH!
7/22 SCOTT and BORGMAN

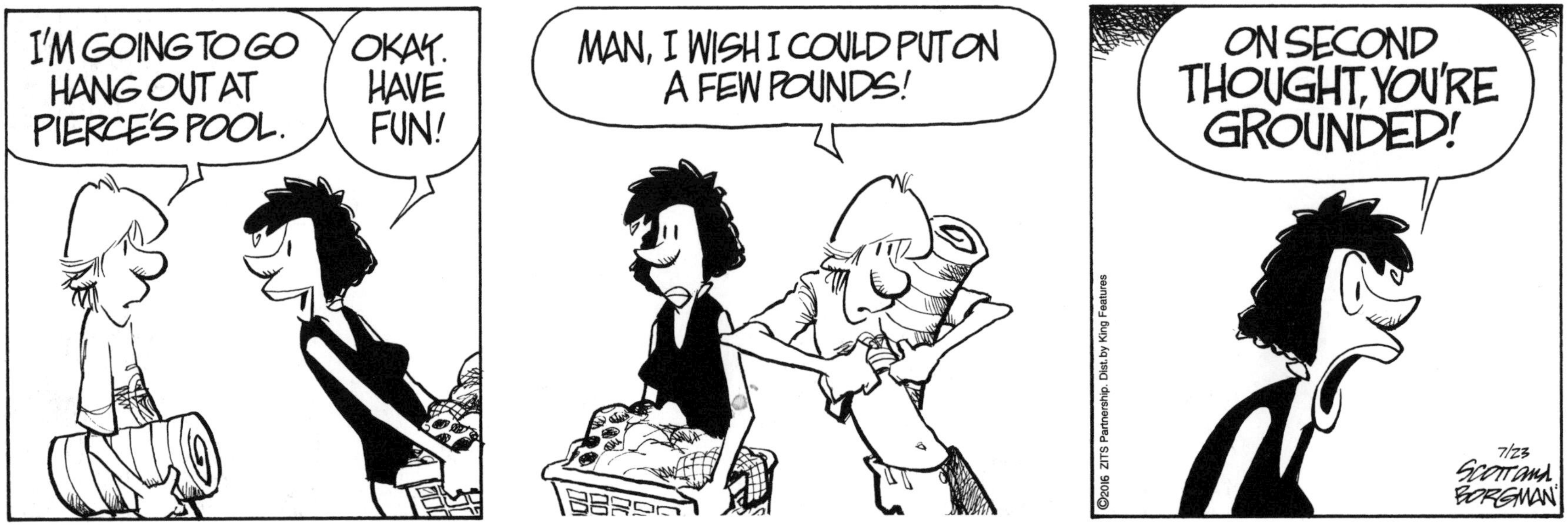
I'M GOING TO GO HANG OUT AT PIERCE'S POOL.
OKAY. HAVE FUN!
MAN, I WISH I COULD PUT ON A FEW POUNDS!
©2016 ZITS Partnership. Dist. by King Features
ON SECOND THOUGHT, YOU'RE GROUNDED!
7/23 SCOTT and BORGMAN

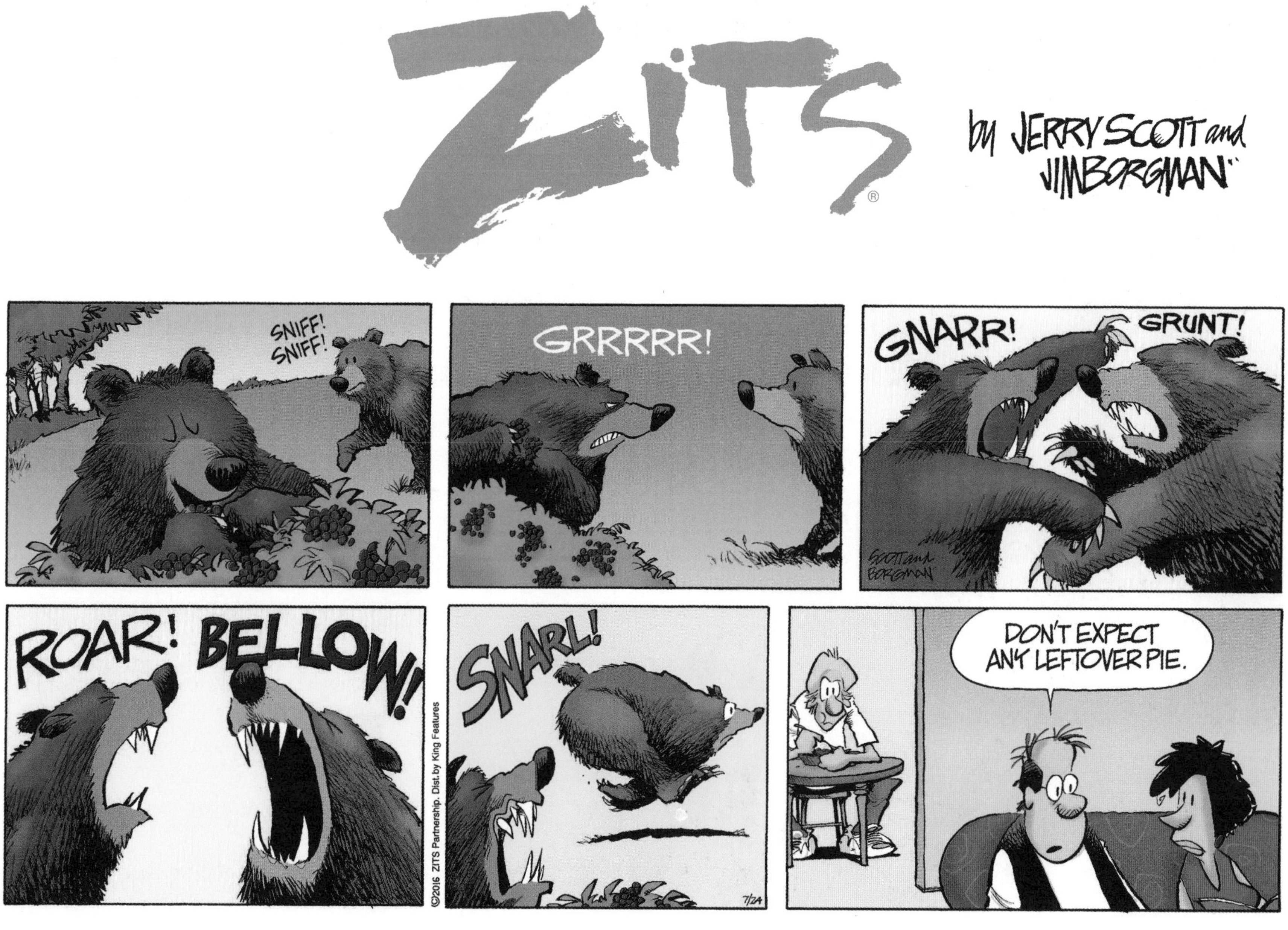
ZITS®
by JERRY SCOTT and JIM BORGMAN
SNIFF! SNIFF!
GRRRRR!
GNARR!
GRUNT!
SCOTT and BORGMAN
ROAR!
BELLOW!
©2016 ZITS Partnership. Dist. by King Features
SNARL!
7/24
DON'T EXPECT ANY LEFTOVER PIE.

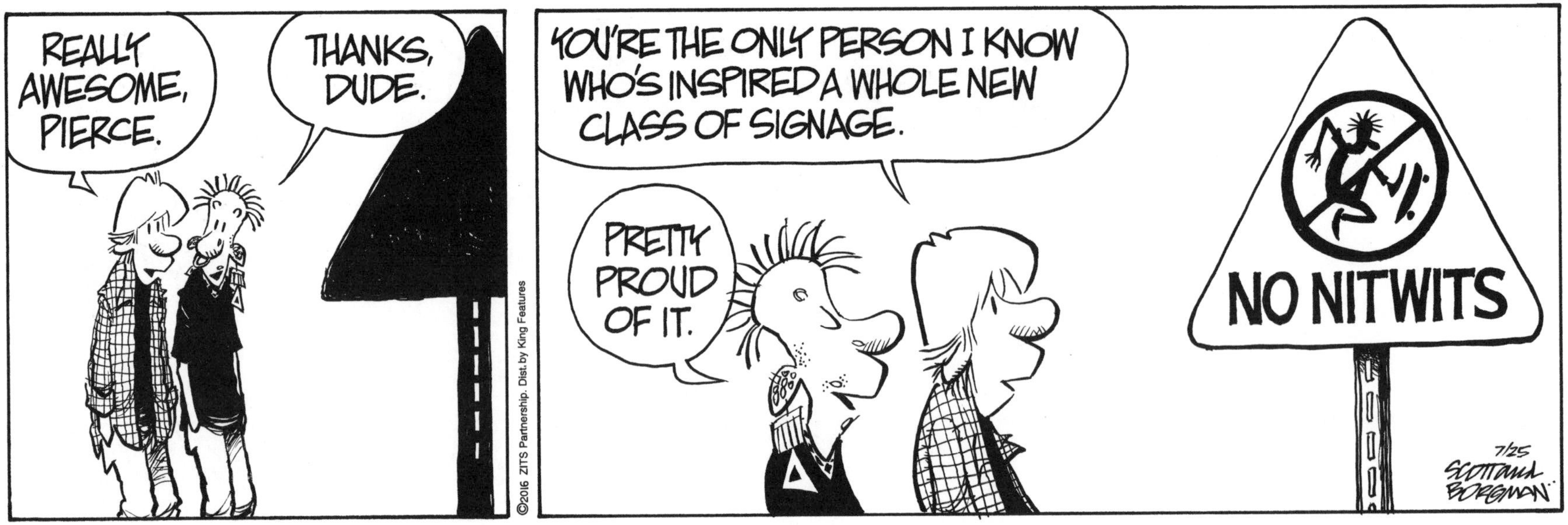
REALLY AWESOME, PIERCE.
THANKS, DUDE.
©2016 ZITS Partnership. Dist. by King Features
YOU'RE THE ONLY PERSON I KNOW WHO'S INSPIRED A WHOLE NEW CLASS OF SIGNAGE.
PRETTY PROUD OF IT.
NO NITWITS
7/25
SCOTT and BORGMAN

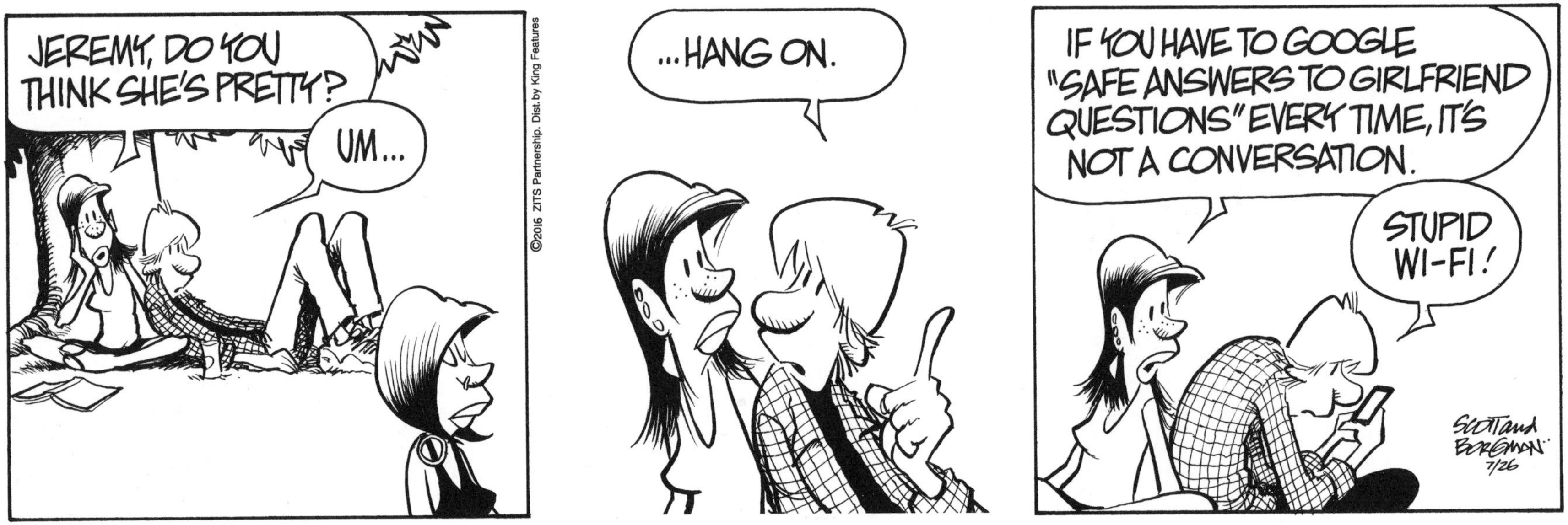
JEREMY, DO YOU THINK SHE'S PRETTY?
UM...
©2016 ZITS Partnership. Dist. by King Features
...HANG ON.
IF YOU HAVE TO GOOGLE "SAFE ANSWERS TO GIRLFRIEND QUESTIONS" EVERY TIME, IT'S NOT A CONVERSATION.
STUPID WI-FI!
SCOTT and BORGMAN
7/26

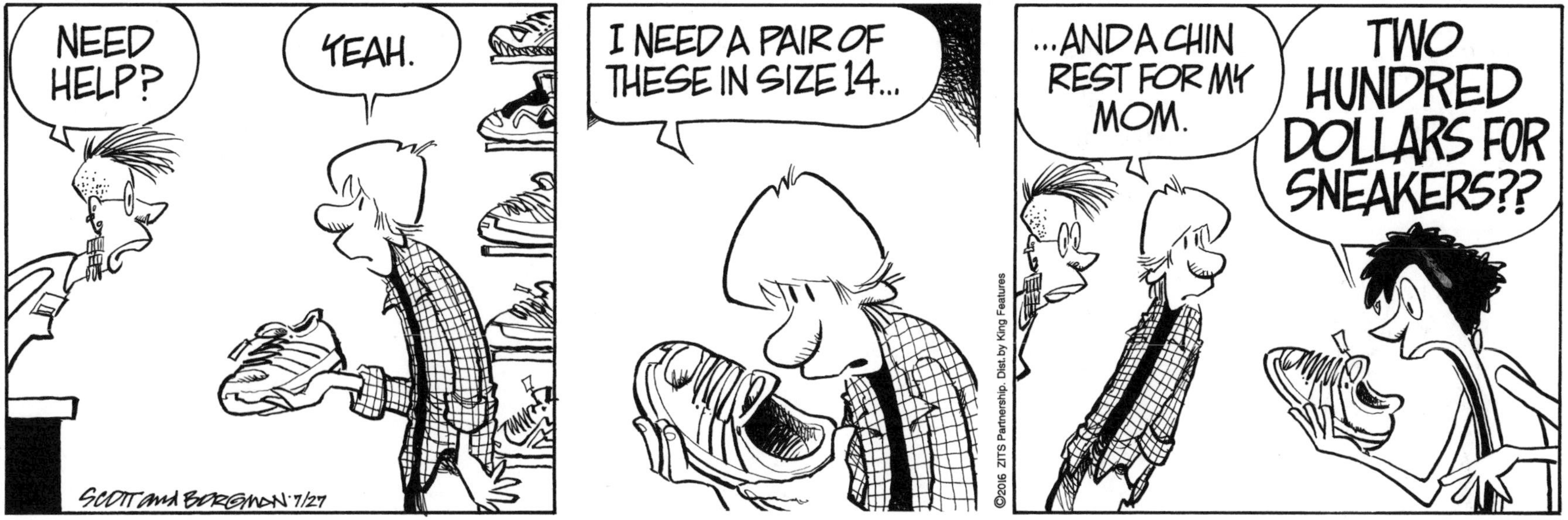
NEED HELP?
YEAH.
I NEED A PAIR OF THESE IN SIZE 14...
...AND A CHIN REST FOR MY MOM.
TWO HUNDRED DOLLARS FOR SNEAKERS??
©2016 ZITS Partnership. Dist. by King Features

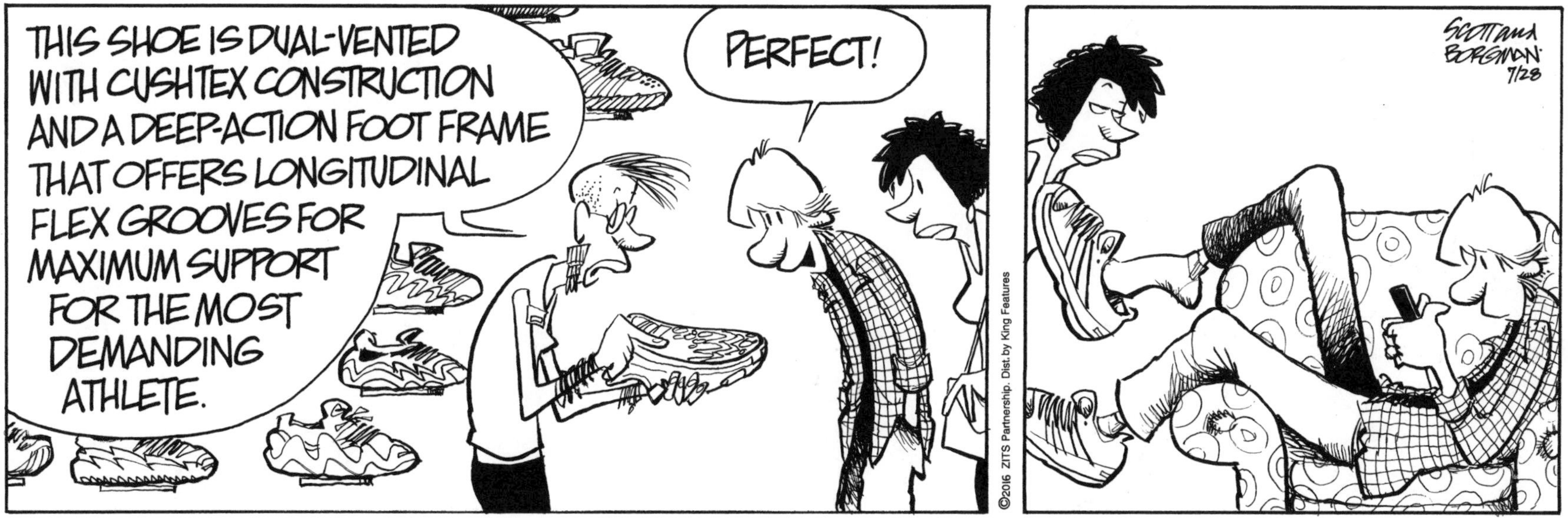
THIS SHOE IS DUAL-VENTED WITH CUSHTEX CONSTRUCTION AND A DEEP-ACTION FOOT FRAME THAT OFFERS LONGITUDINAL FLEX GROOVES FOR MAXIMUM SUPPORT FOR THE MOST DEMANDING ATHLETE.
PERFECT!
©2016 ZITS Partnership. Dist. by King Features

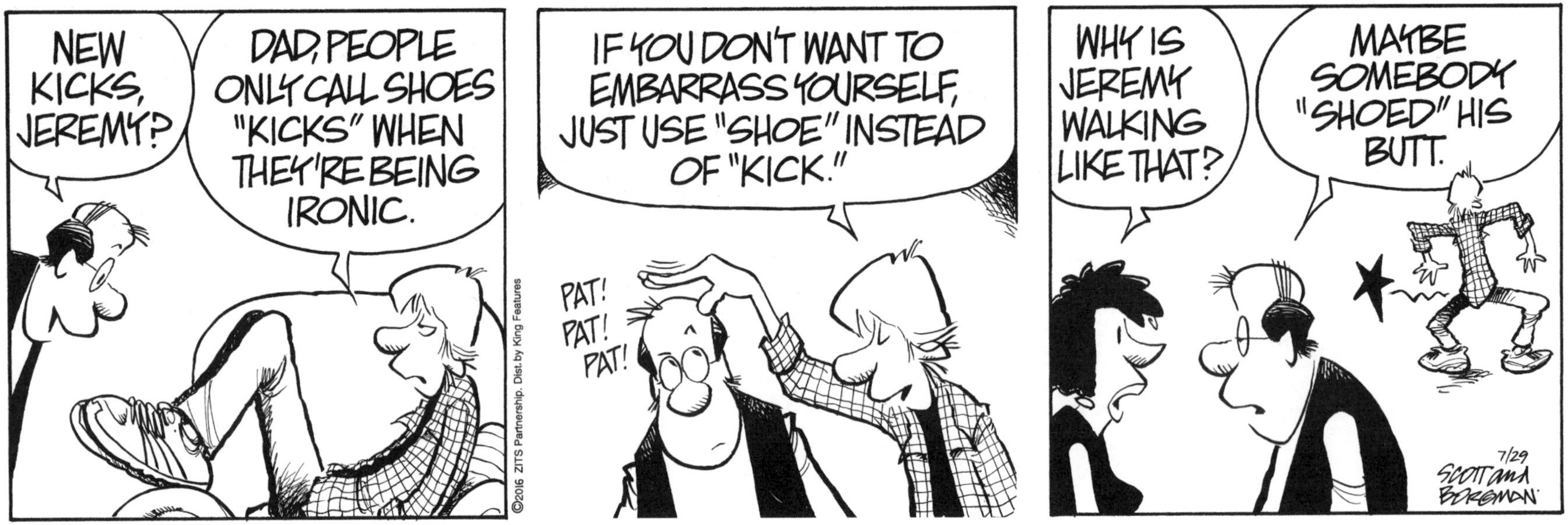
NEW KICKS, JEREMY?
DAD, PEOPLE ONLY CALL SHOES "KICKS" WHEN THEY'RE BEING IRONIC.
IF YOU DON'T WANT TO EMBARRASS YOURSELF, JUST USE "SHOE" INSTEAD OF "KICK."
PAT! PAT! PAT!
WHY IS JEREMY WALKING LIKE THAT?
MAYBE SOMEBODY "SHOED" HIS BUTT.
©2016 ZITS Partnership. Dist. by King Features
7/29 SCOTT and BORGMAN

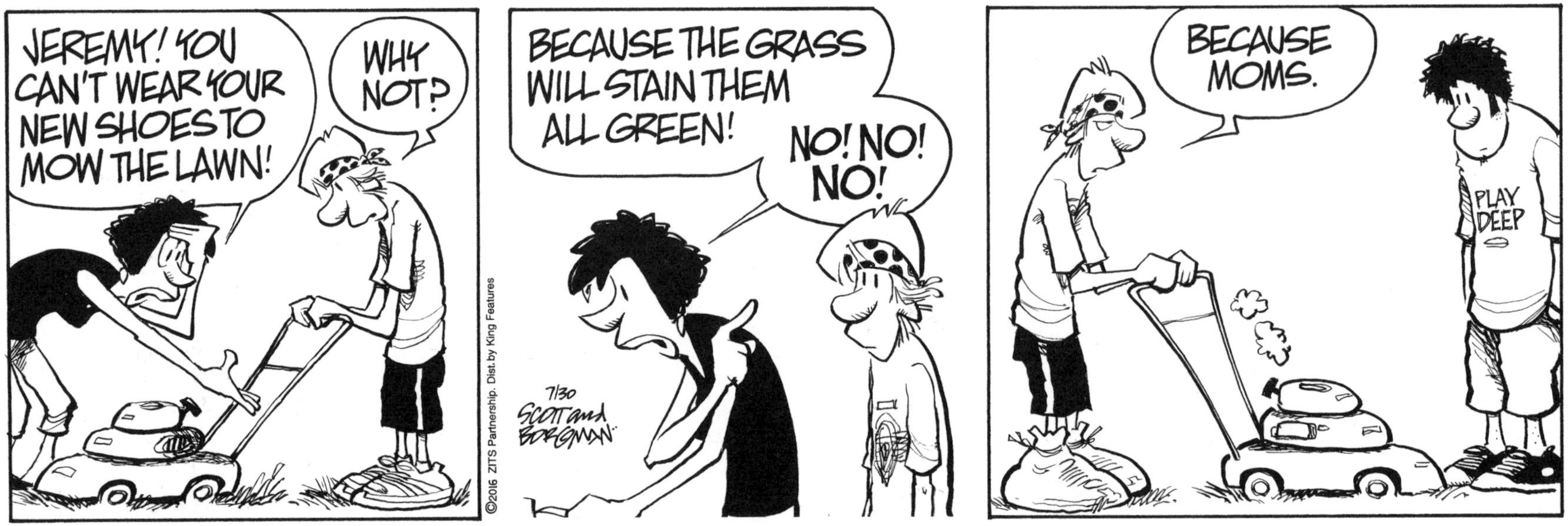
JEREMY! YOU CAN'T WEAR YOUR NEW SHOES TO MOW THE LAWN!
WHY NOT?
BECAUSE THE GRASS WILL STAIN THEM ALL GREEN!
NO! NO! NO!
BECAUSE MOMS.
PLAY DEEP
©2016 ZITS Partnership. Dist. by King Features
7/30 SCOTT and BORGMAN

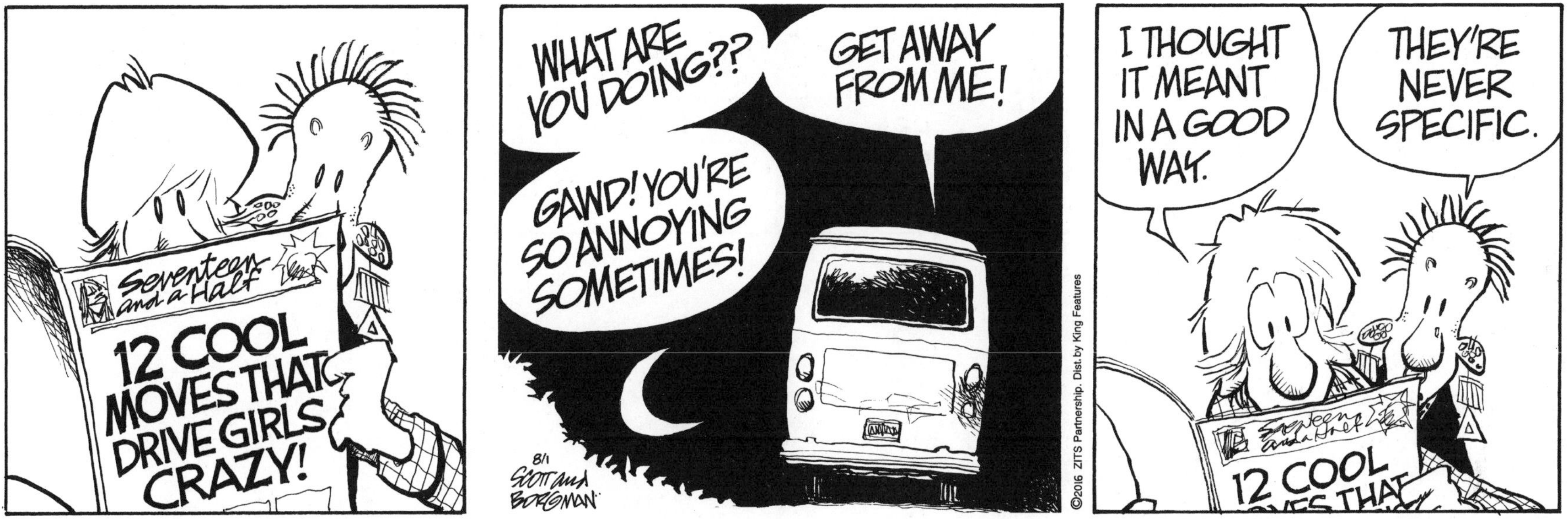
Seventeen and a Half
12 COOL MOVES THAT DRIVE GIRLS CRAZY!
WHAT ARE YOU DOING??
GET AWAY FROM ME!
GAWD! YOU'RE SO ANNOYING SOMETIMES!
8/1 SCOTT and BORGMAN
©2016 ZITS Partnership. Dist. by King Features
I THOUGHT IT MEANT IN A GOOD WAY.
THEY'RE NEVER SPECIFIC.
Seventeen and a Half
12 COOL

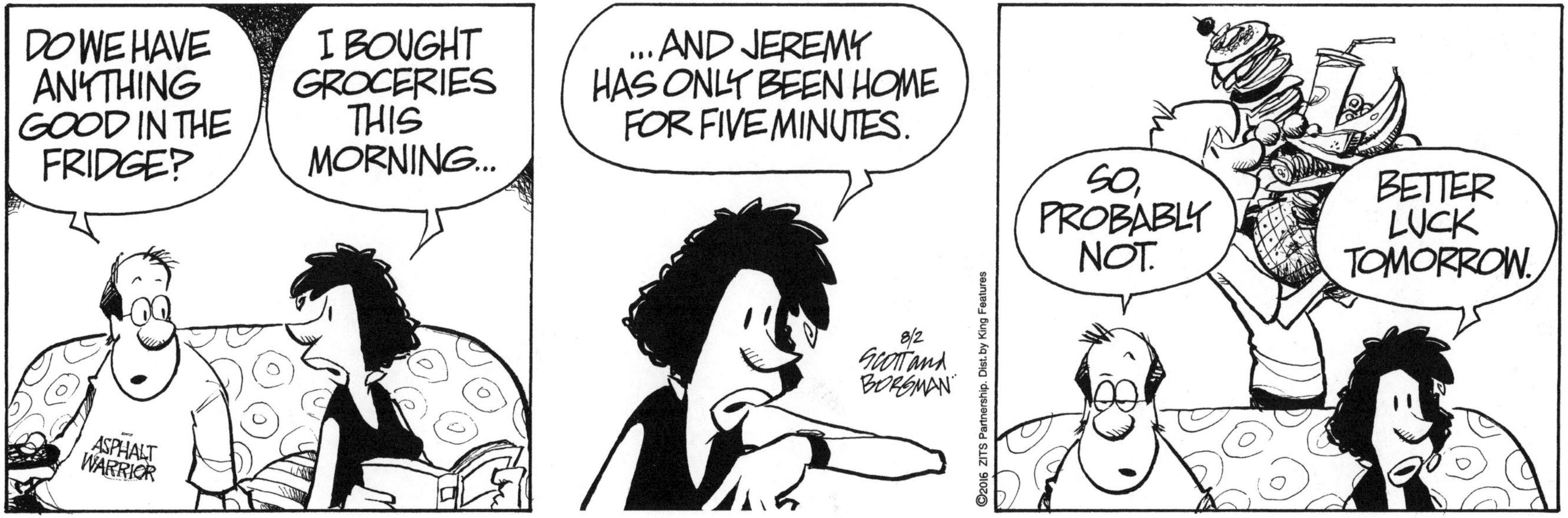
DO WE HAVE ANYTHING GOOD IN THE FRIDGE?
I BOUGHT GROCERIES THIS MORNING...
ASPHALT WARRIOR
...AND JEREMY HAS ONLY BEEN HOME FOR FIVE MINUTES.
8/2 SCOTT and BORGMAN
©2016 ZITS Partnership. Dist. by King Features
SO, PROBABLY NOT.
BETTER LUCK TOMORROW.

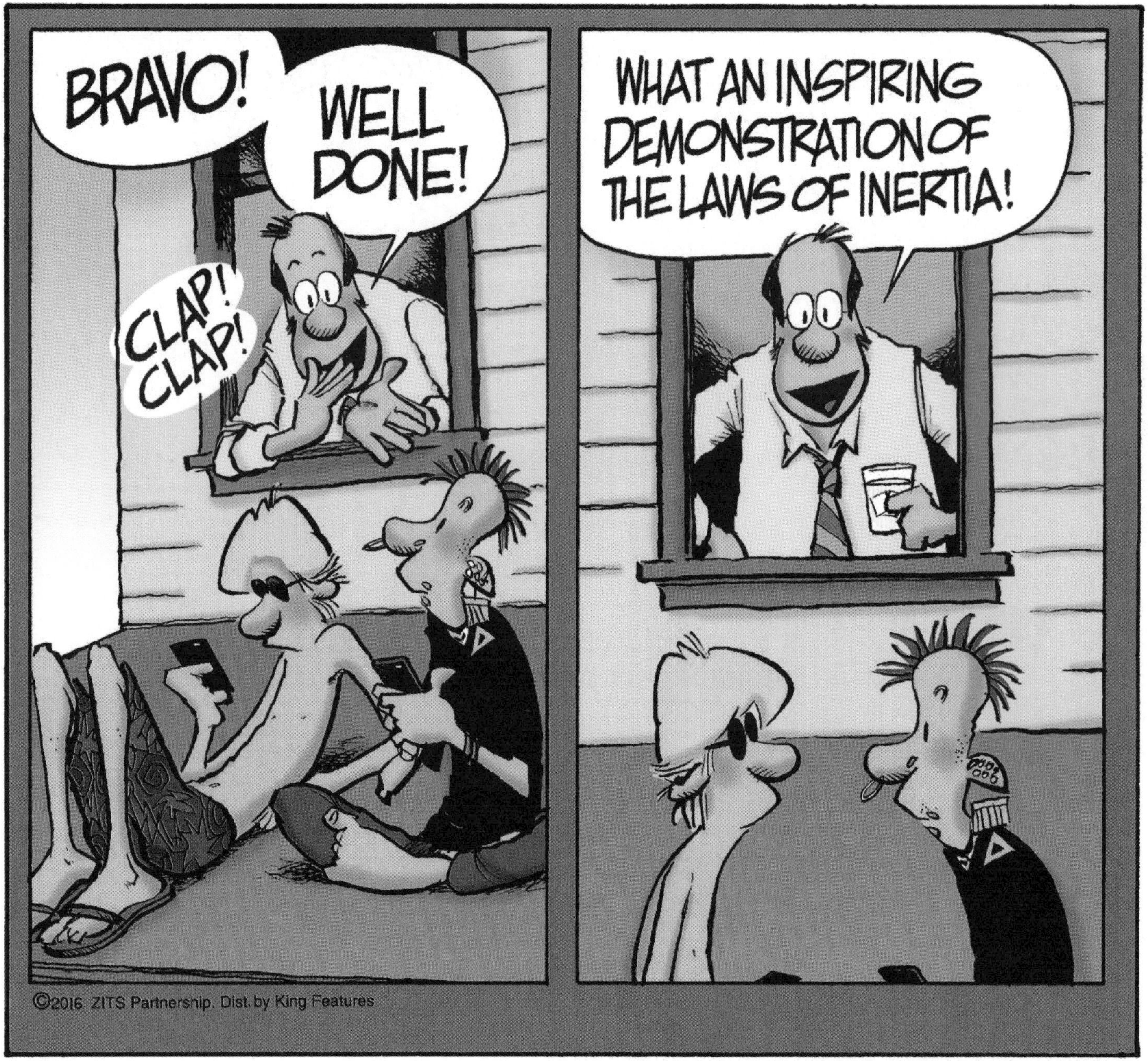
BRAVO!
WELL DONE!
CLAP! CLAP!
WHAT AN INSPIRING DEMONSTRATION OF THE LAWS OF INERTIA!
©2016 ZITS Partnership. Dist. by King Features

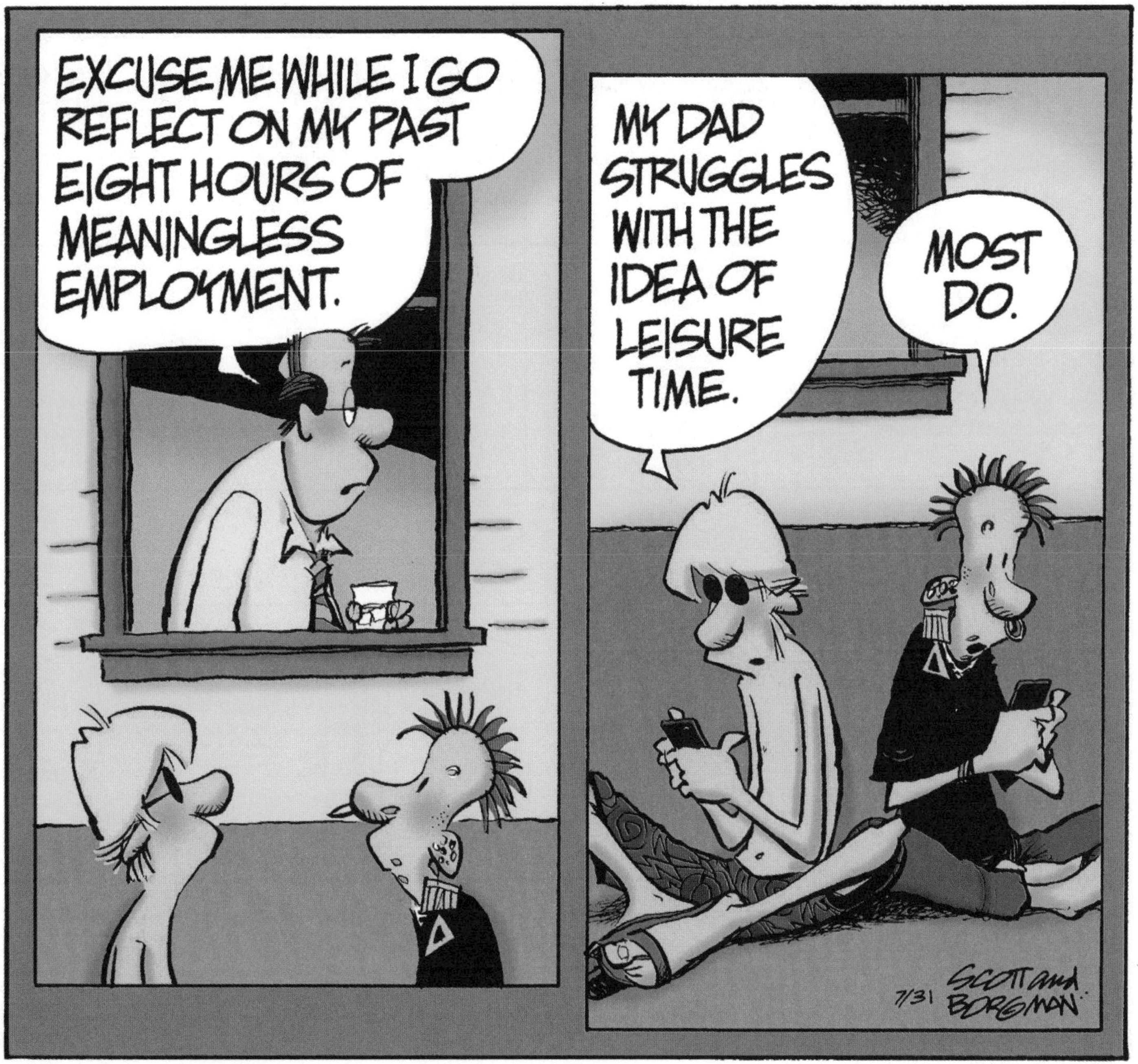
EXCUSE ME WHILE I GO REFLECT ON MY PAST EIGHT HOURS OF MEANINGLESS EMPLOYMENT.
MY DAD STRUGGLES WITH THE IDEA OF LEISURE TIME.
MOST DO.
7/31
SCOTT and BORGMAN

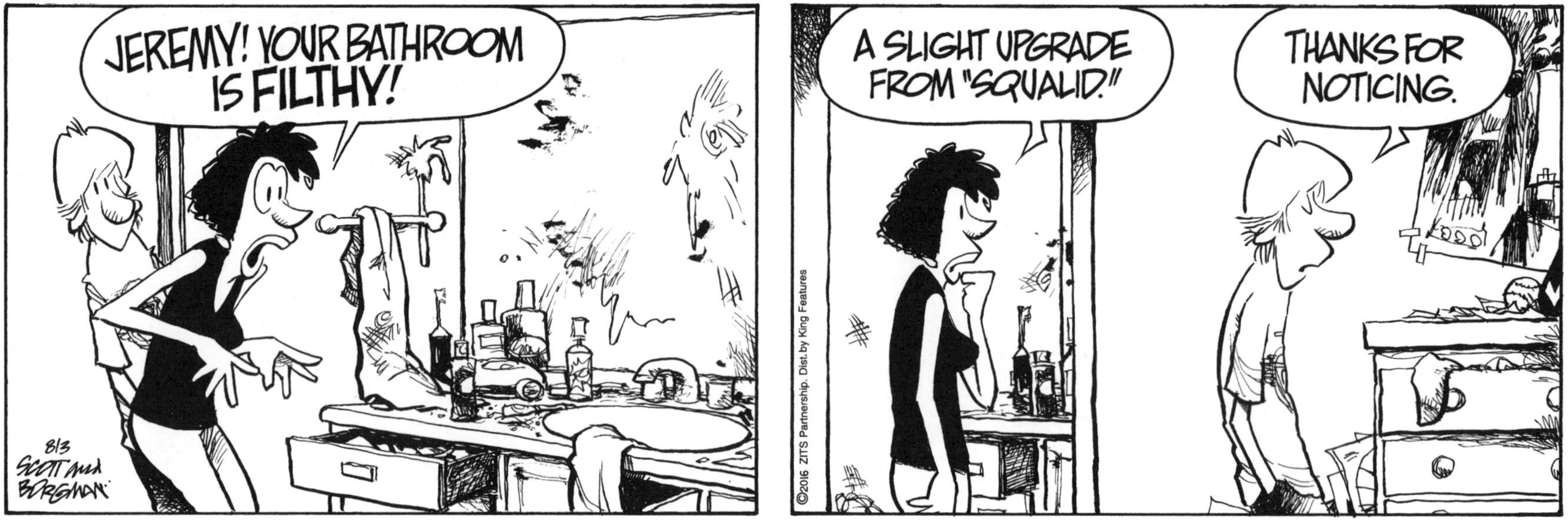
JEREMY! YOUR BATHROOM IS FILTHY!
A SLIGHT UPGRADE FROM "SQUALID."
THANKS FOR NOTICING.
©2016 ZITS Partnership. Dist. by King Features

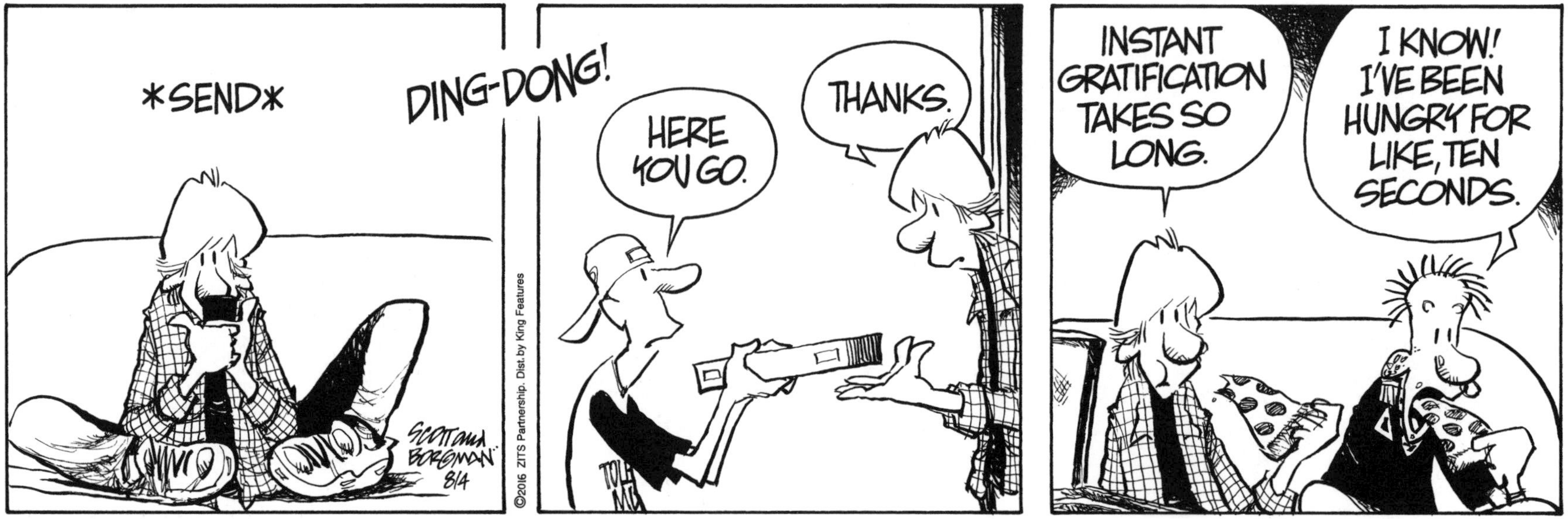
SEND
DING-DONG!
HERE YOU GO.
THANKS.
INSTANT GRATIFICATION TAKES SO LONG.
I KNOW! I'VE BEEN HUNGRY FOR LIKE, TEN SECONDS.
©2016 ZITS Partnership. Dist. by King Features

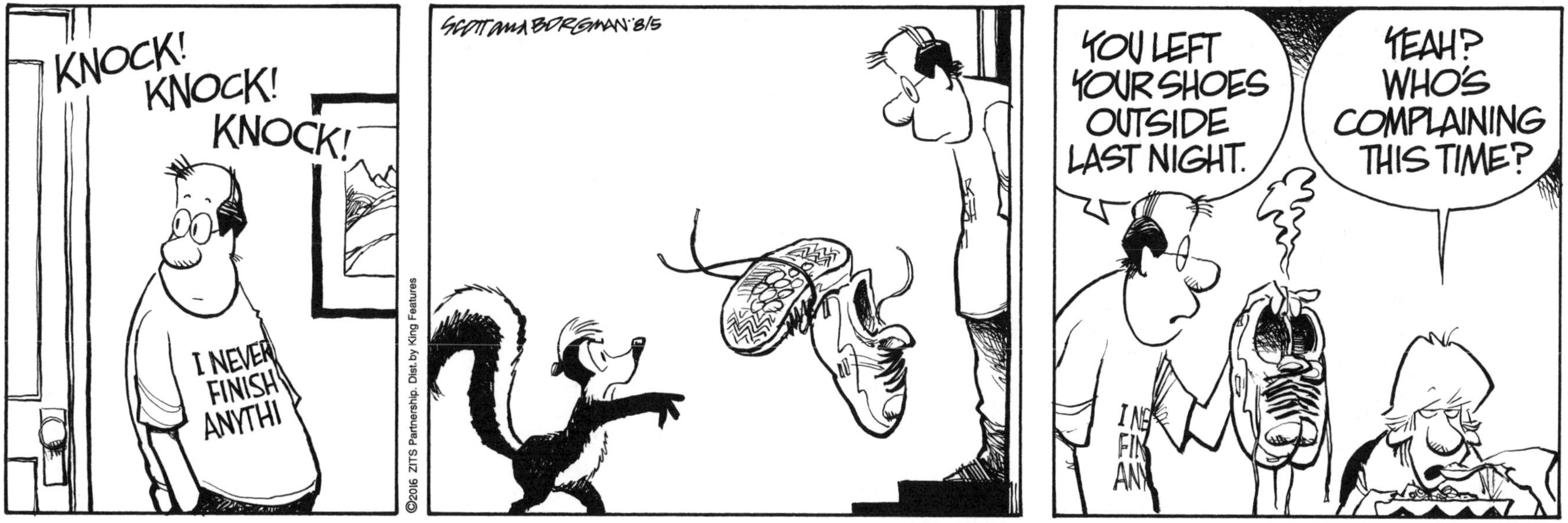
KNOCK! KNOCK! KNOCK!
I NEVER FINISH ANYTHI
SCOTT and BORGMAN 8/5
©2016 ZITS Partnership. Dist. by King Features
YOU LEFT YOUR SHOES OUTSIDE LAST NIGHT.
YEAH? WHO'S COMPLAINING THIS TIME?

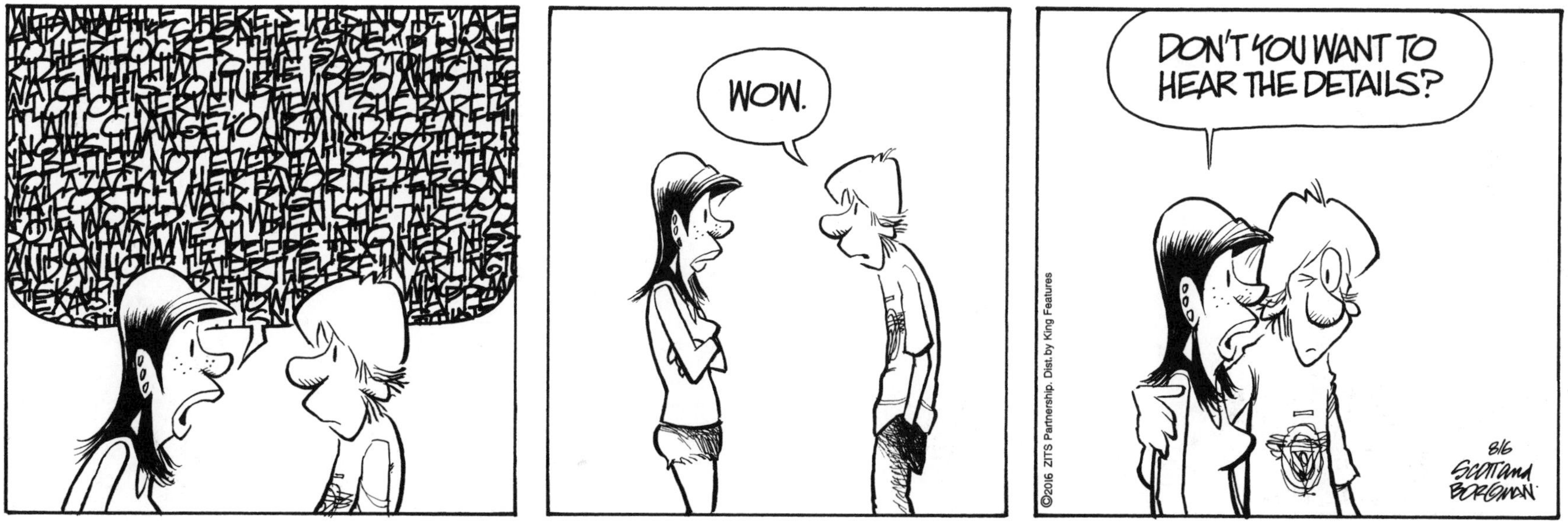
WOW.
©2016 ZITS Partnership. Dist. by King Features
DON'T YOU WANT TO HEAR THE DETAILS?
8/6 SCOTT and BORGMAN

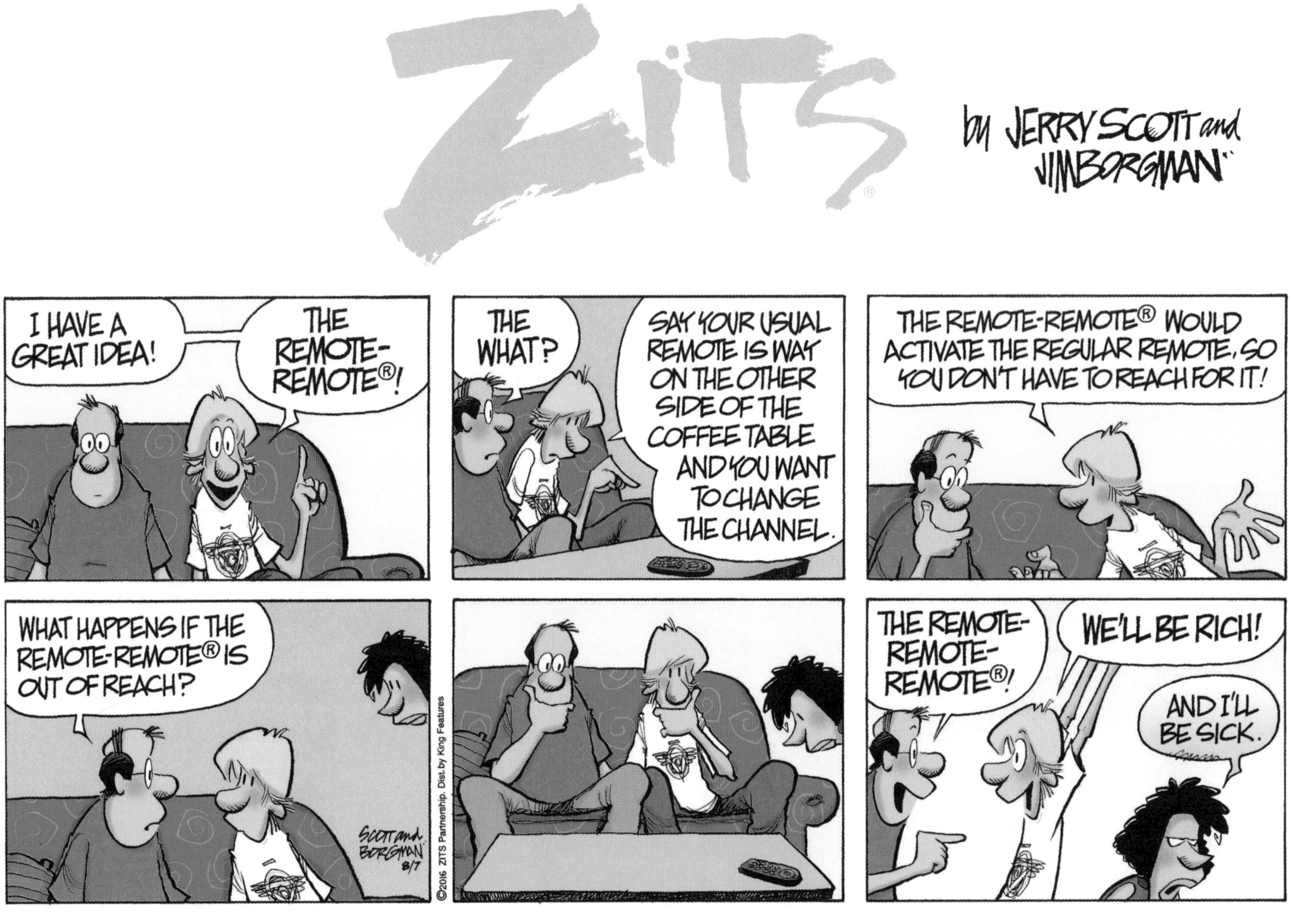
ZITS®
by JERRY SCOTT and JIM BORGMAN
I HAVE A GREAT IDEA!
THE REMOTE-REMOTE®!
THE WHAT?
SAY YOUR USUAL REMOTE IS WAY ON THE OTHER SIDE OF THE COFFEE TABLE AND YOU WANT TO CHANGE THE CHANNEL.
THE REMOTE-REMOTE® WOULD ACTIVATE THE REGULAR REMOTE, SO YOU DON'T HAVE TO REACH FOR IT!
WHAT HAPPENS IF THE REMOTE-REMOTE® IS OUT OF REACH?
SCOTT and BORGMAN 8/7
©2016 ZITS Partnership. Dist. by King Features
THE REMOTE-REMOTE-REMOTE®!
WE'LL BE RICH!
AND I'LL BE SICK.

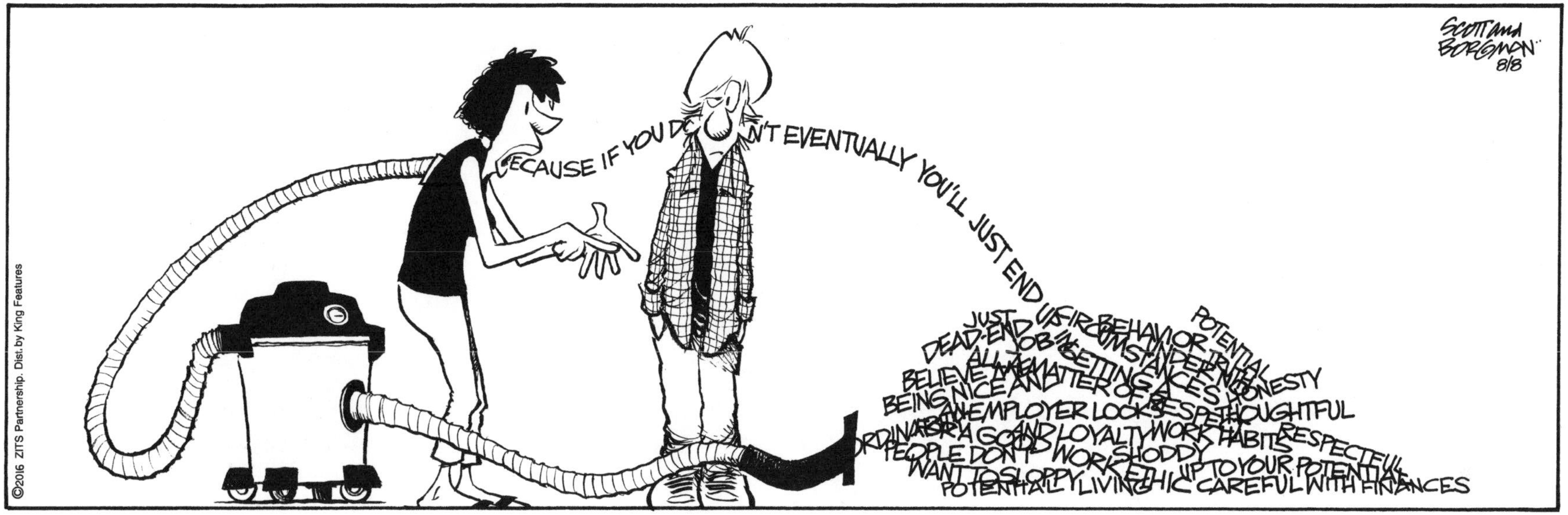
SCOTT and BORGMAN 8/8
ECAUSE IF YOU D N'T EVENTUALLY YOU'LL JUST END
JUST DEAD-END JOB
BELIEVE
BEING NICE AND
AN EMPLOYER LOOKS
THOUGHTFUL
HONESTY
POTENTIAL
RESPECTFUL
LOYALTY WORK HABITS
PEOPLE DON'T
SHODDY
WANT TO SLOPPY
UP TO YOUR POTENTIAL
POTENTIAL LIVING
CAREFUL WITH FINANCES
©2016 ZITS Partnership. Dist. by King Features

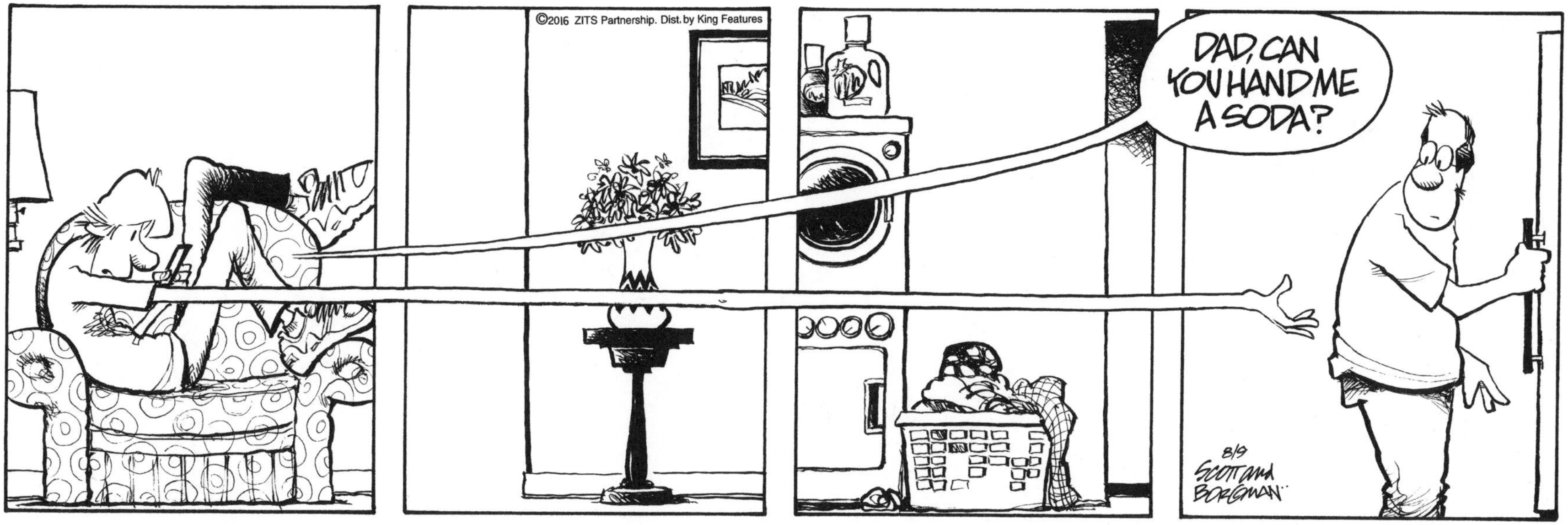
©2016 ZITS Partnership. Dist. by King Features
DAD, CAN YOU HAND ME A SODA?
8/9 SCOTT and BORGMAN

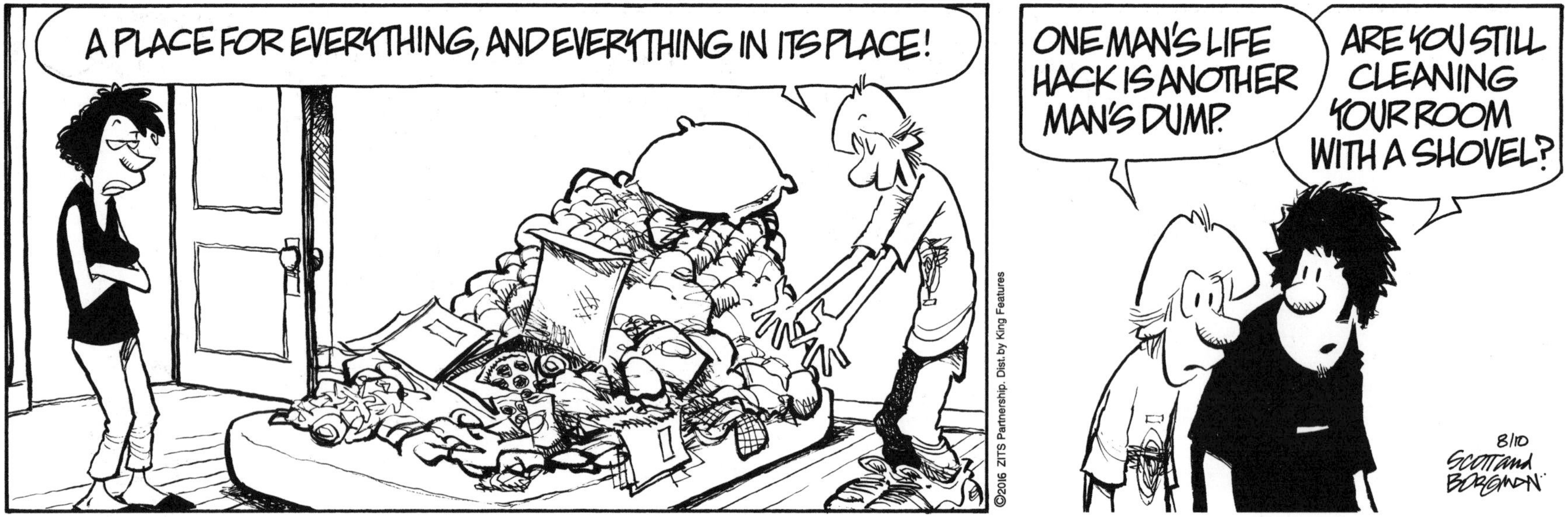
A PLACE FOR EVERYTHING, AND EVERYTHING IN ITS PLACE!
ONE MAN'S LIFE HACK IS ANOTHER MAN'S DUMP.
ARE YOU STILL CLEANING YOUR ROOM WITH A SHOVEL?
©2016 ZITS Partnership. Dist. by King Features
8/10
SCOTT and BORGMAN

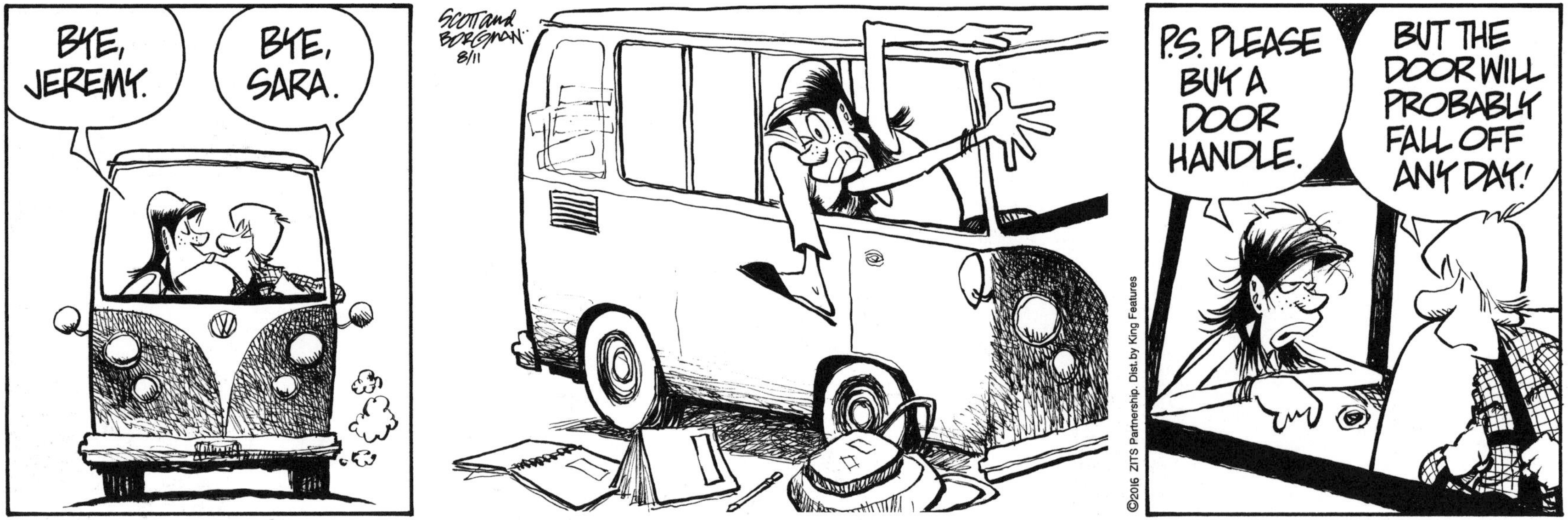
BYE, JEREMY.
BYE, SARA.
SCOTT and BORGMAN 8/11
P.S. PLEASE BUY A DOOR HANDLE.
BUT THE DOOR WILL PROBABLY FALL OFF ANY DAY!
©2016 ZITS Partnership. Dist. by King Features

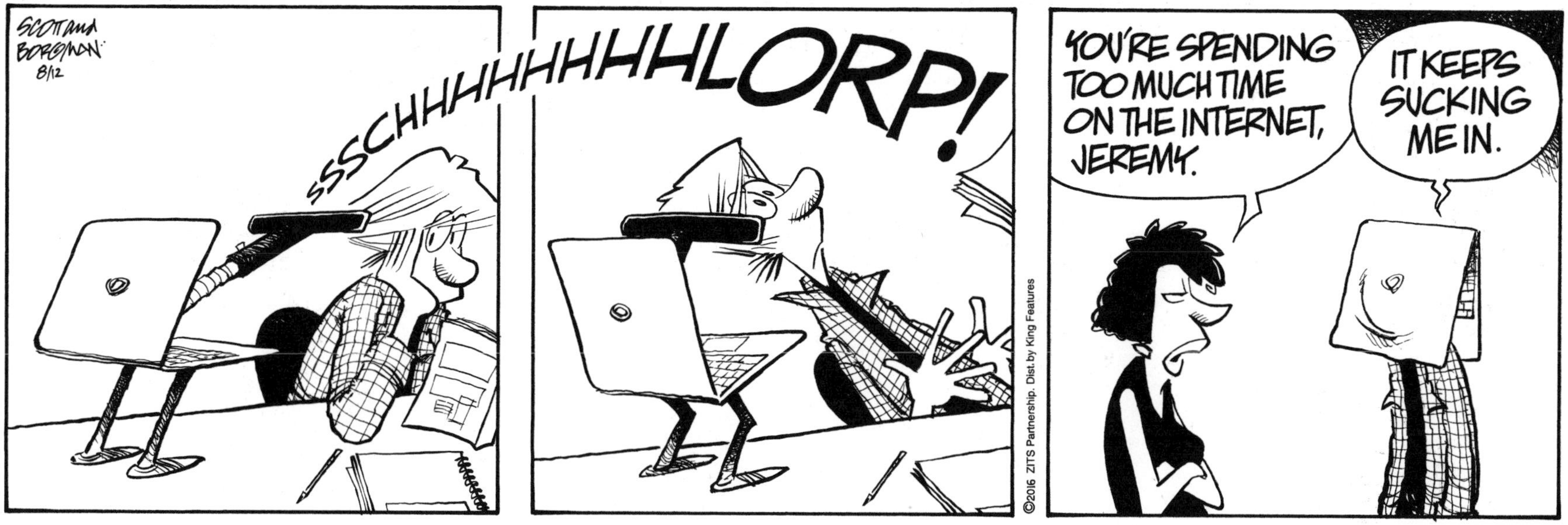
SCOTT and BORGMAN 8/12
SSSCHHHHHHHHLORP!
©2016 ZITS Partnership. Dist. by King Features
YOU'RE SPENDING TOO MUCH TIME ON THE INTERNET, JEREMY.
IT KEEPS SUCKING ME IN.

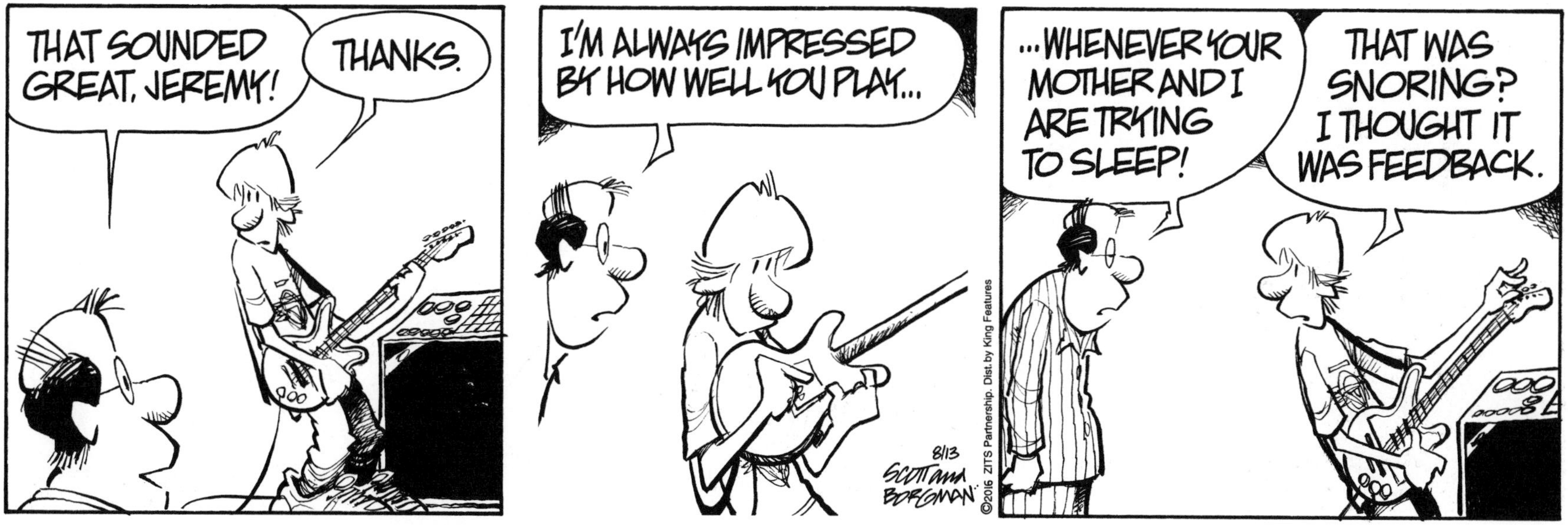
THAT SOUNDED GREAT, JEREMY!
THANKS.
I'M ALWAYS IMPRESSED BY HOW WELL YOU PLAY...
8/13 SCOTT and BORGMAN
©2016 ZITS Partnership. Dist. by King Features
...WHENEVER YOUR MOTHER AND I ARE TRYING TO SLEEP!
THAT WAS SNORING? I THOUGHT IT WAS FEEDBACK.

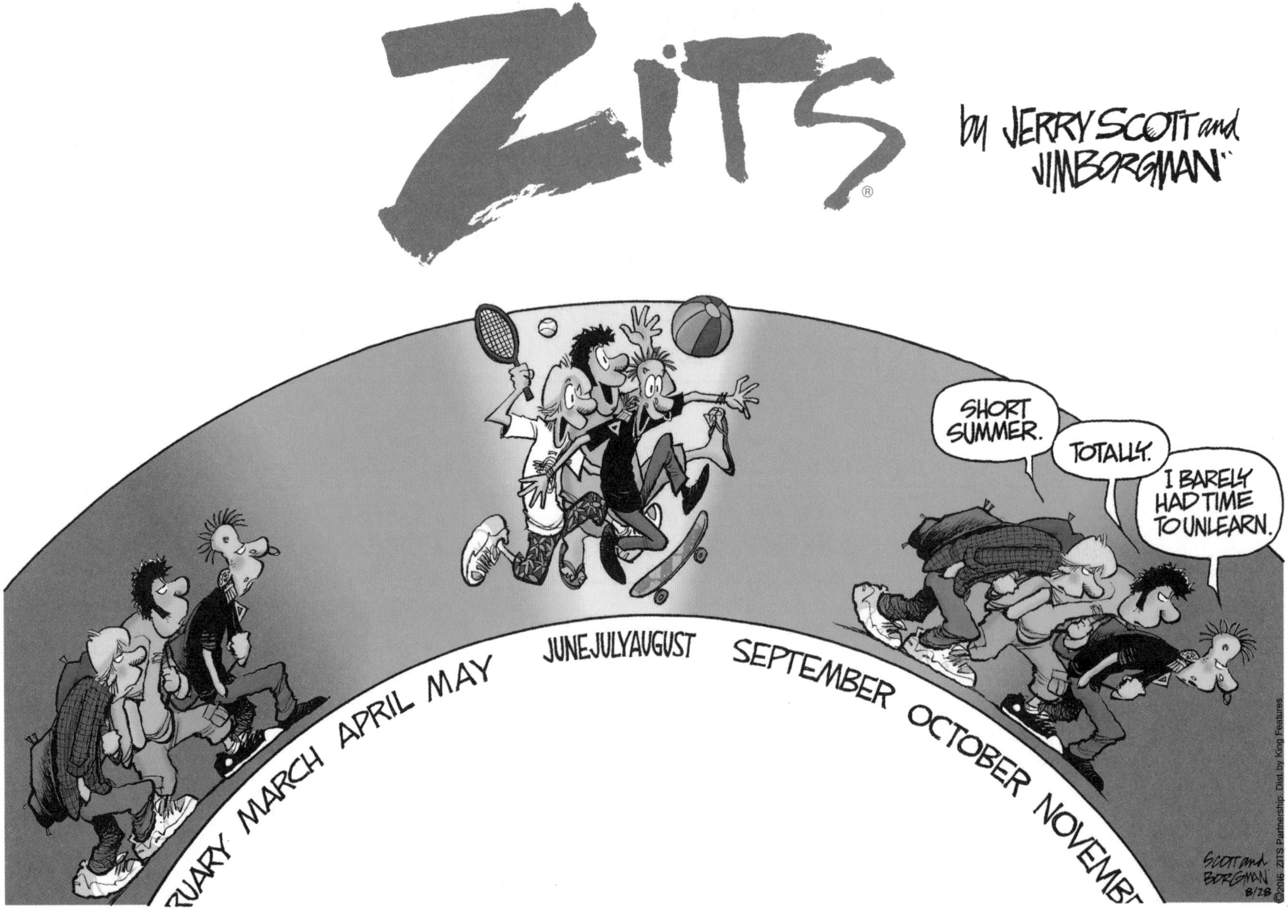
ZITS®
by JERRY SCOTT and JIM BORGMAN
...RUARY MARCH APRIL MAY
JUNEJULYAUGUST
SEPTEMBER OCTOBER NOVEMB...
SHORT SUMMER.
TOTALLY.
I BARELY HAD TIME TO UNLEARN.
SCOTT and BORGMAN 8/28
©2016 ZITS Partnership. Dist. by King Features

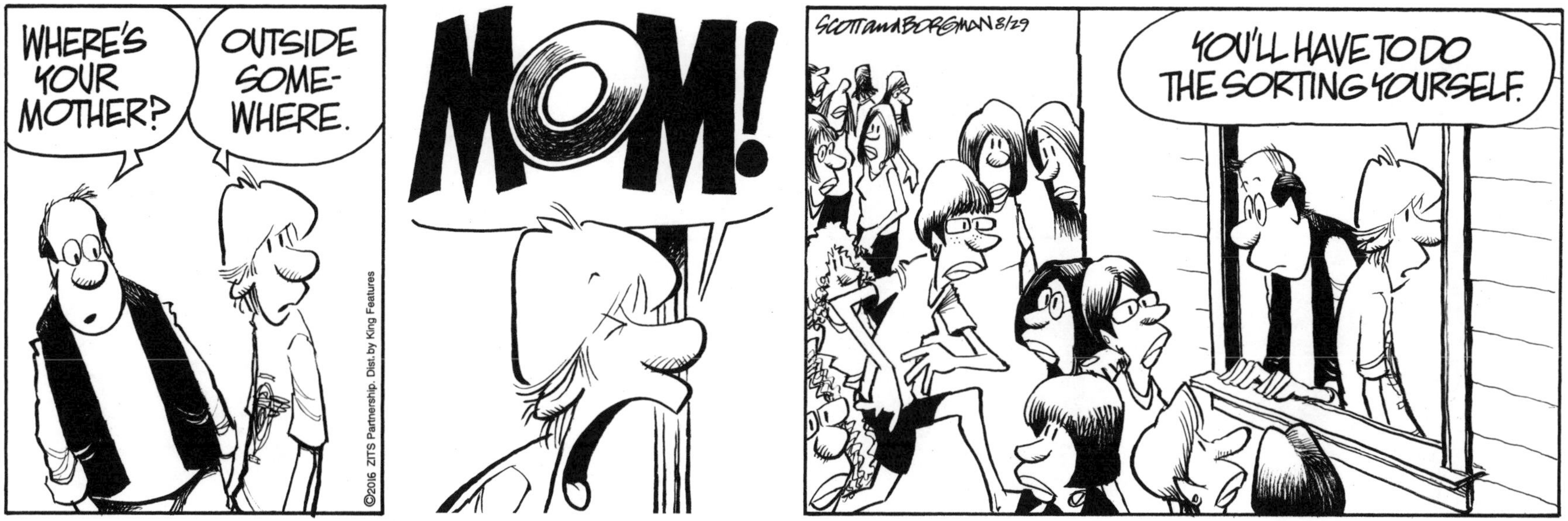
WHERE'S YOUR MOTHER?
OUTSIDE SOME-WHERE.
©2016 ZITS Partnership. Dist. by King Features
MOM!
SCOTT and BORGMAN 8/29
YOU'LL HAVE TO DO THE SORTING YOURSELF.

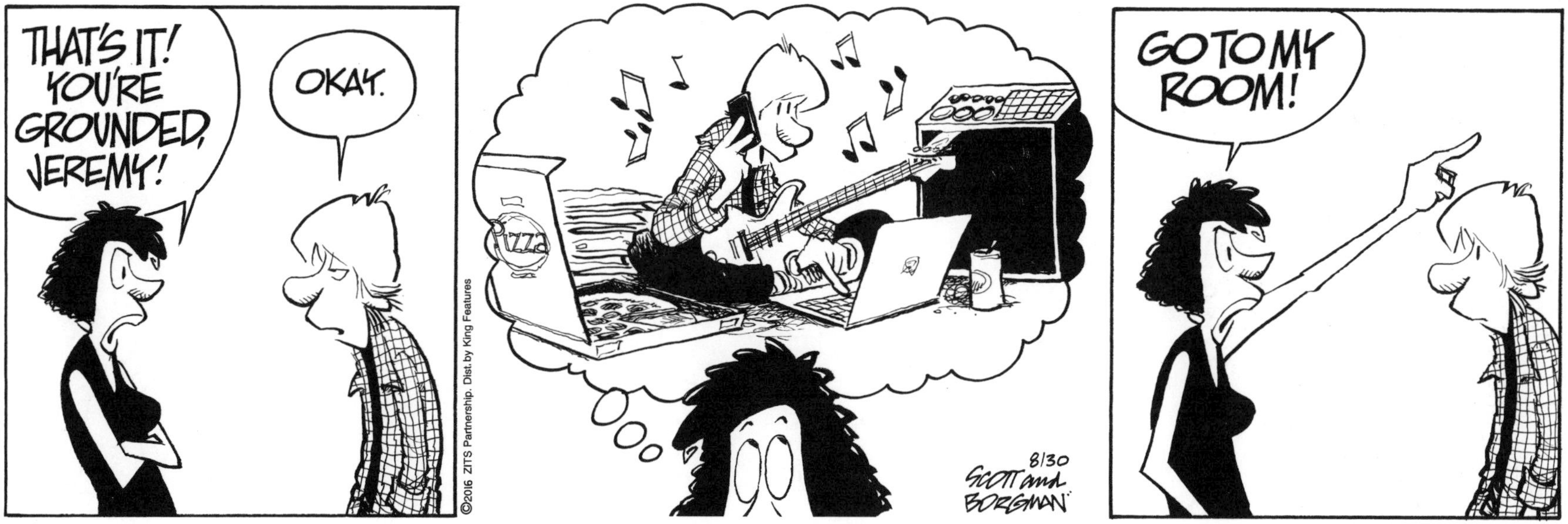
THAT'S IT! YOU'RE GROUNDED, JEREMY!
OKAY.
©2016 ZITS Partnership. Dist. by King Features
PIZZA
8/30 SCOTT and BORGMAN
GO TO MY ROOM!

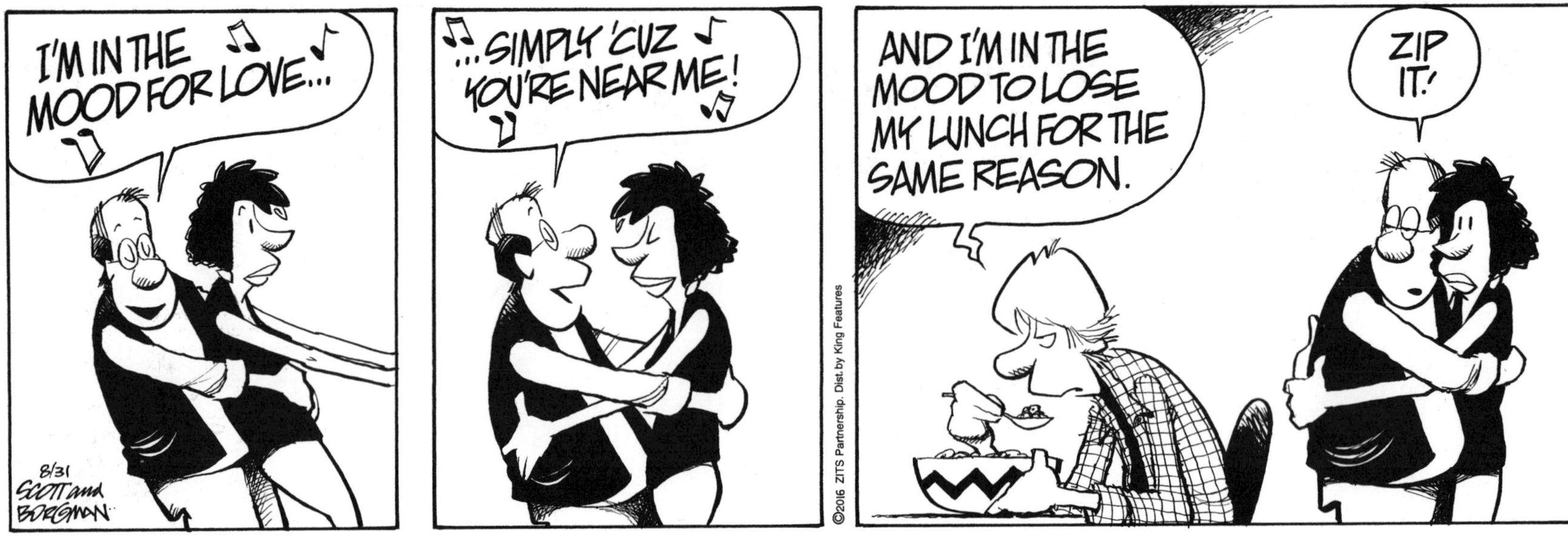
I'M IN THE MOOD FOR LOVE...
...SIMPLY 'CUZ YOU'RE NEAR ME!
AND I'M IN THE MOOD TO LOSE MY LUNCH FOR THE SAME REASON.
ZIP IT!
8/31
SCOTT and BORGMAN
©2016 ZITS Partnership. Dist. by King Features

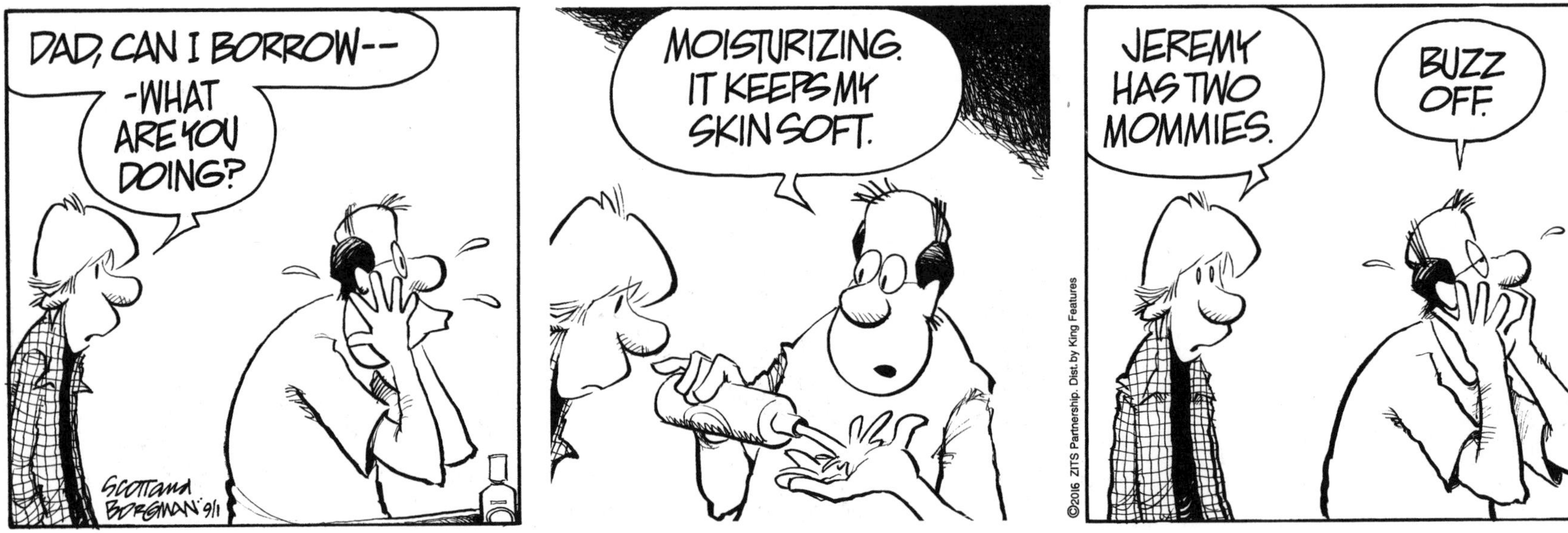
DAD, CAN I BORROW--
-WHAT ARE YOU DOING?
SCOTT and BORGMAN 9/1
MOISTURIZING. IT KEEPS MY SKIN SOFT.
©2016 ZITS Partnership. Dist. by King Features
JEREMY HAS TWO MOMMIES.
BUZZ OFF.

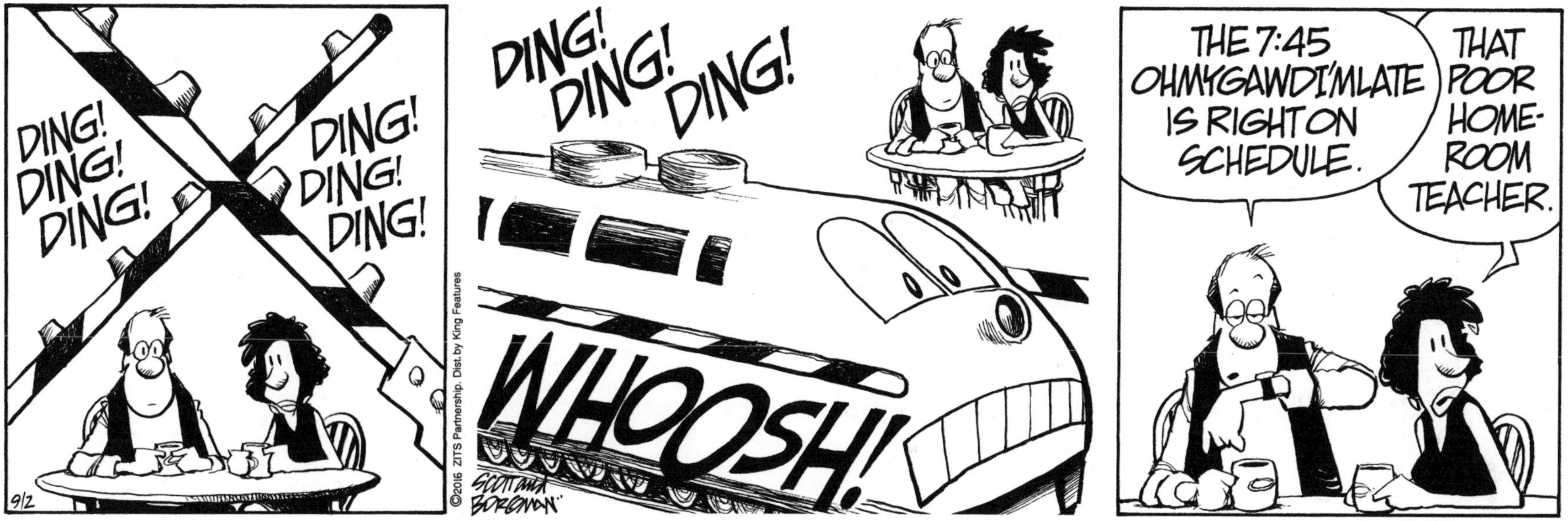
DING!
DING!
DING!
DING!
DING!
DING!
9/2
DING!
DING!
DING!
WHOOSH!
©2016 ZITS Partnership. Dist. by King Features
SCOTT AND BORGMAN
THE 7:45 OHMYGAWDI'MLATE IS RIGHT ON SCHEDULE.
THAT POOR HOME-ROOM TEACHER.

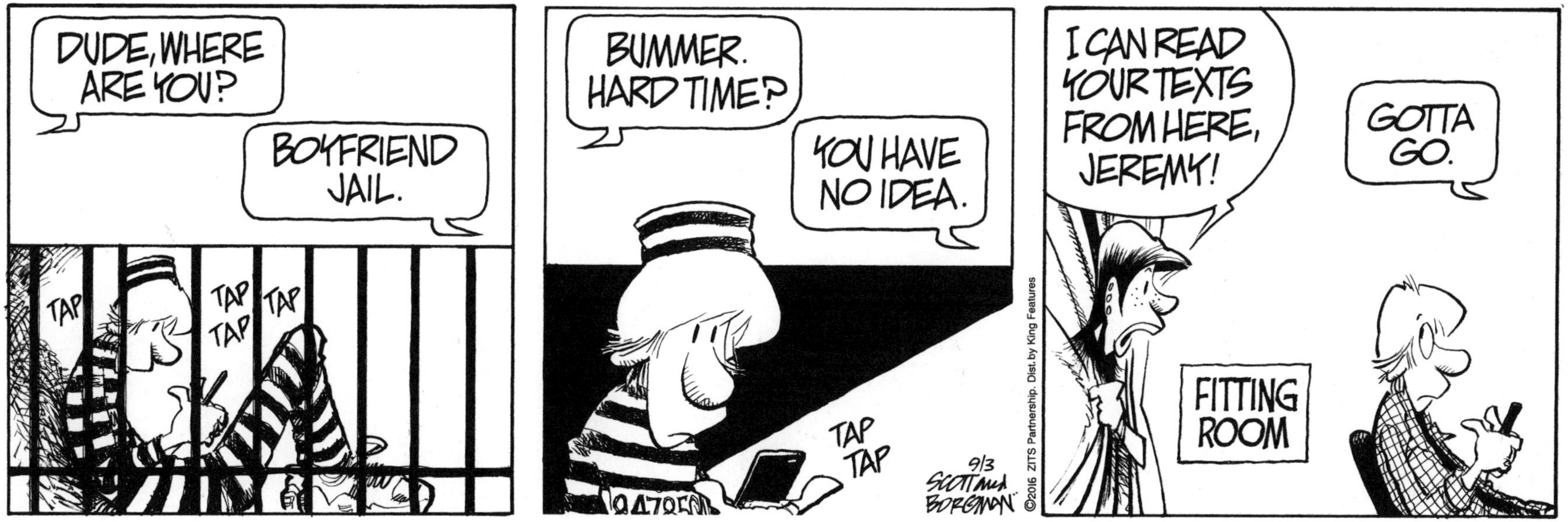
DUDE, WHERE ARE YOU?
BOYFRIEND JAIL.
TAP
TAP TAP
TAP
BUMMER. HARD TIME?
YOU HAVE NO IDEA.
TAP TAP
9/3
SCOTT AND BORGMAN
©2016 ZITS Partnership. Dist. by King Features
I CAN READ YOUR TEXTS FROM HERE, JEREMY!
GOTTA GO.
FITTING ROOM

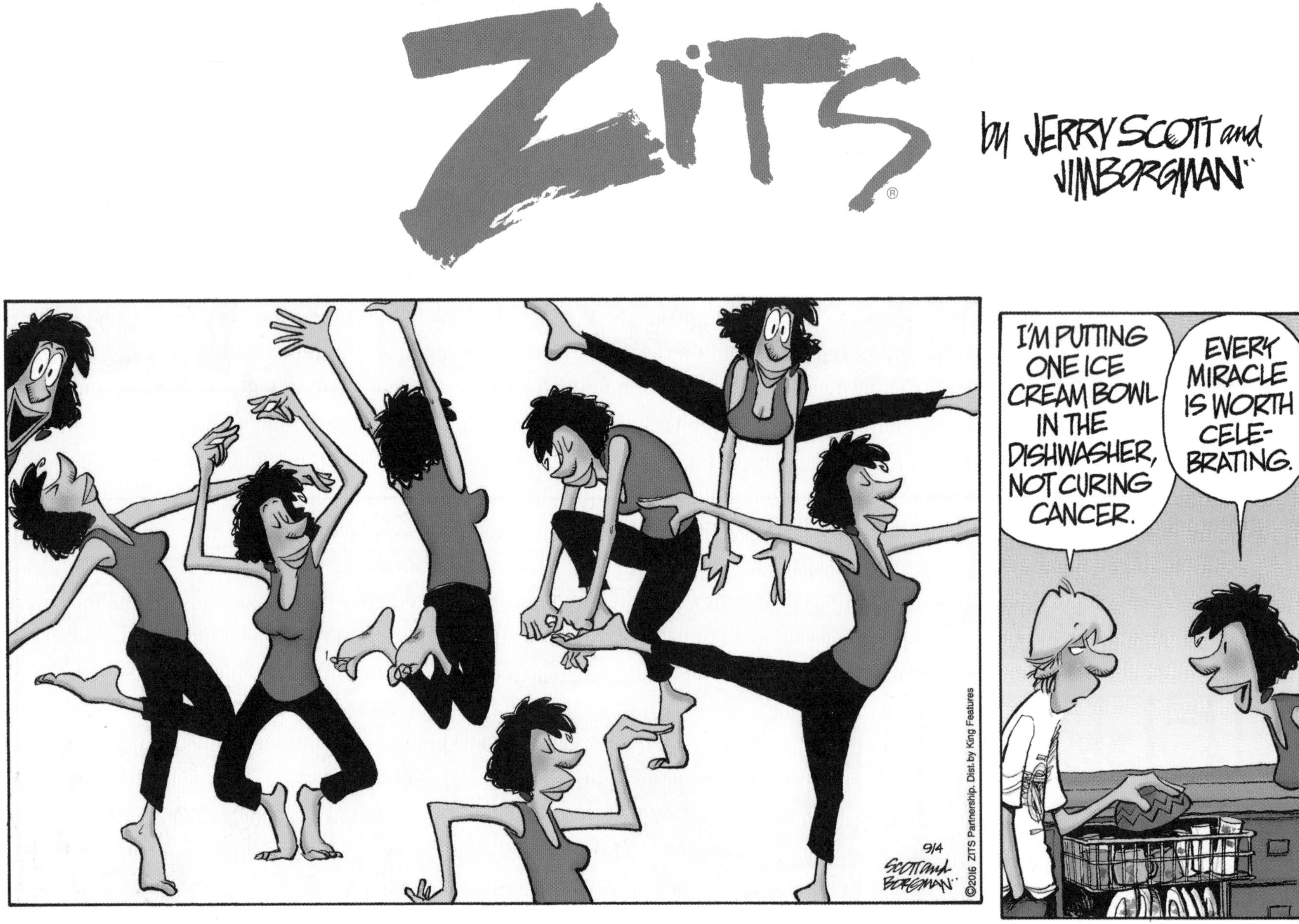
ZITS
by JERRY SCOTT and JIM BORGMAN
9/4
SCOTT and BORGMAN
©2016 ZITS Partnership. Dist. by King Features
I'M PUTTING ONE ICE CREAM BOWL IN THE DISHWASHER, NOT CURING CANCER.
EVERY MIRACLE IS WORTH CELE-BRATING.

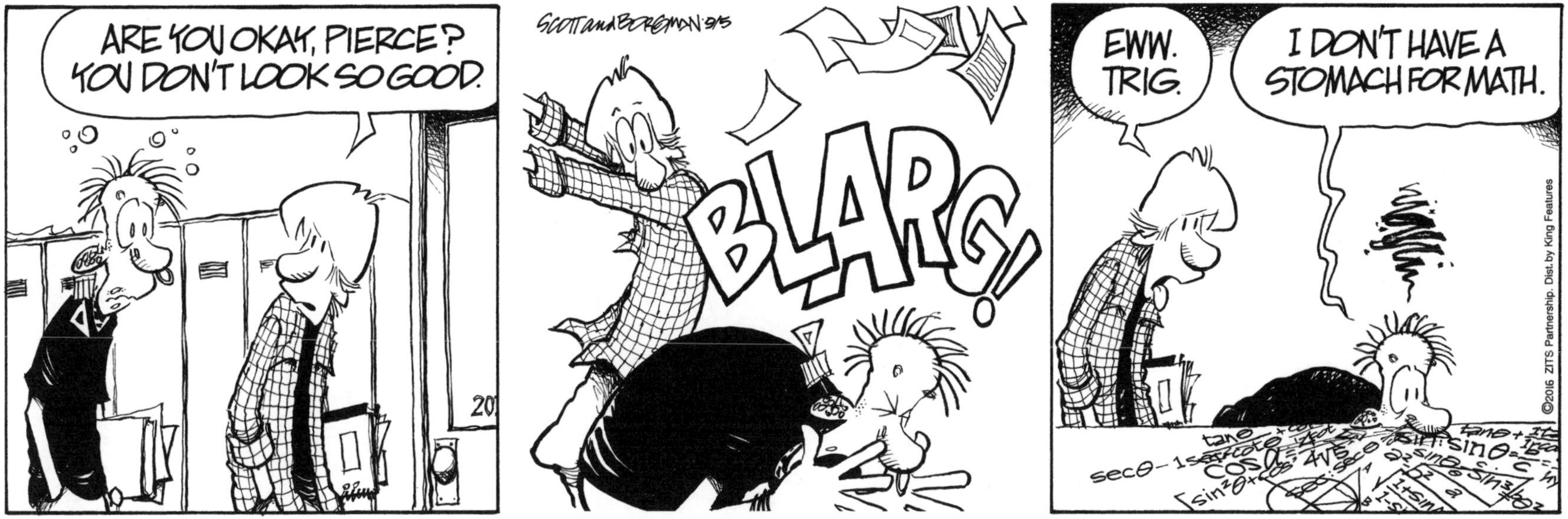

ARE YOU OKAY, PIERCE? YOU DON'T LOOK SO GOOD.
SCOTT and BORGMAN 9/15
BLARG!!
EWW. TRIG.
I DON'T HAVE A STOMACH FOR MATH.
©2016 ZITS Partnership. Dist. by King Features

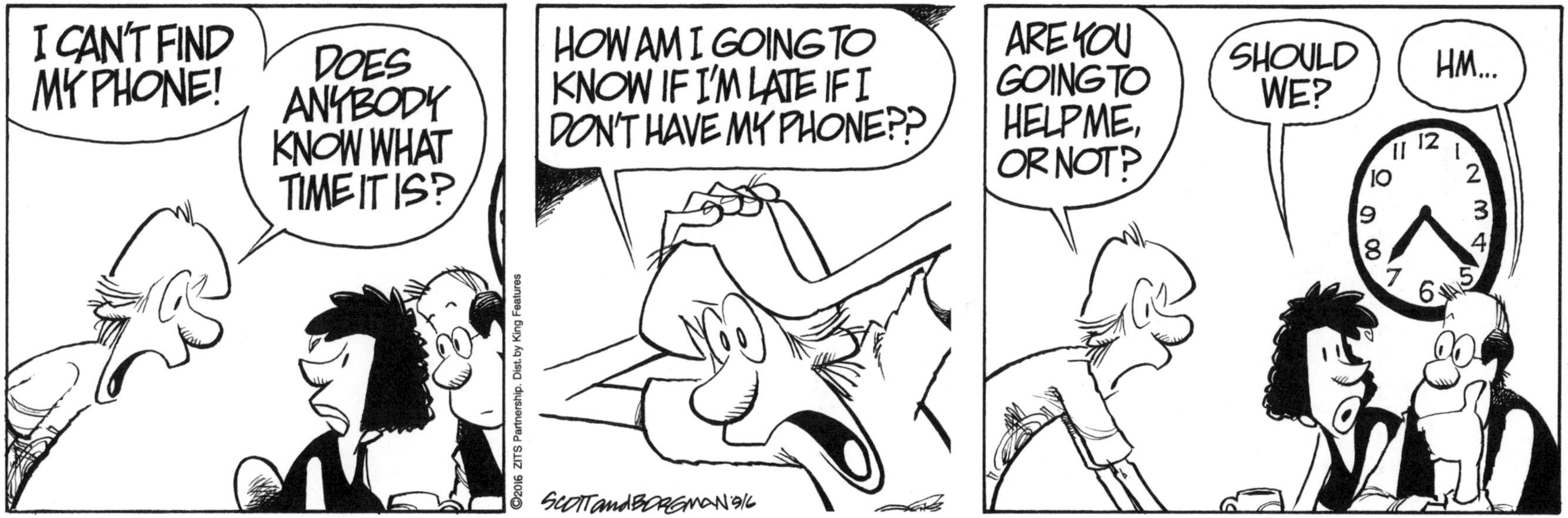

I CAN'T FIND MY PHONE!
DOES ANYBODY KNOW WHAT TIME IT IS?
©2016 ZITS Partnership. Dist. by King Features
HOW AM I GOING TO KNOW IF I'M LATE IF I DON'T HAVE MY PHONE??
SCOTT and BORGMAN 9/16
ARE YOU GOING TO HELP ME, OR NOT?
SHOULD WE?
HM...

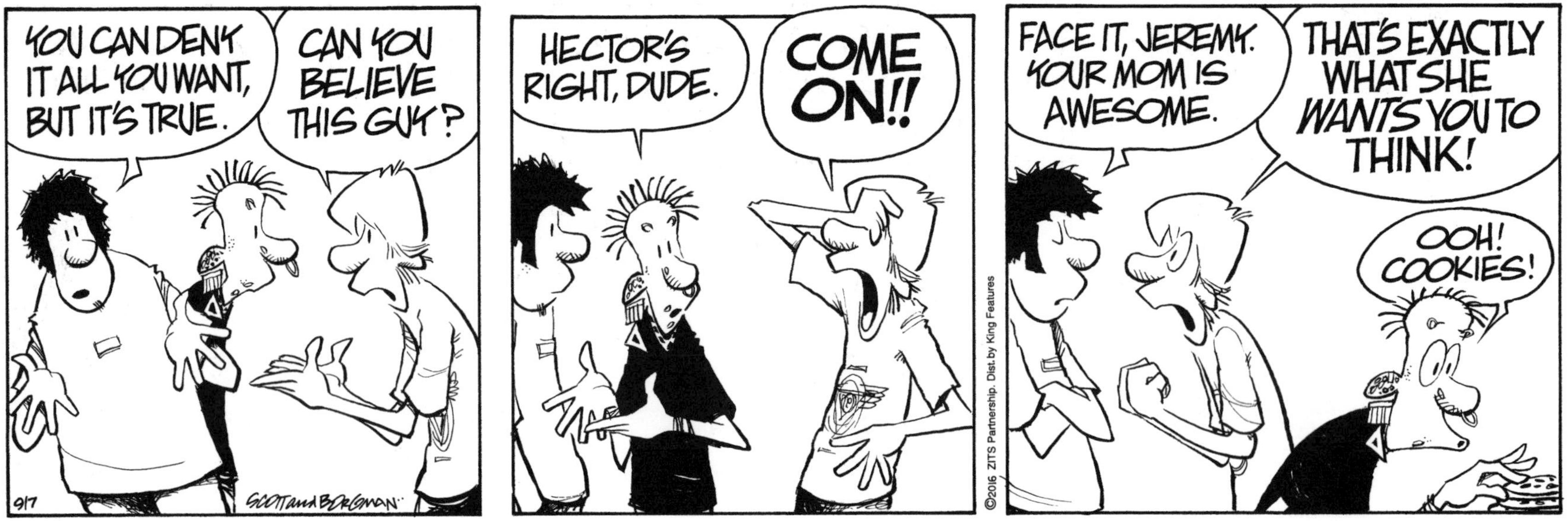
YOU CAN DENY IT ALL YOU WANT, BUT IT'S TRUE.
CAN YOU BELIEVE THIS GUY?
HECTOR'S RIGHT, DUDE.
COME ON!!
FACE IT, JEREMY. YOUR MOM IS AWESOME.
THAT'S EXACTLY WHAT SHE *WANTS* YOU TO THINK!
OOH! COOKIES!
9/7
SCOTT and BORGMAN
©2016 ZITS Partnership. Dist. by King Features

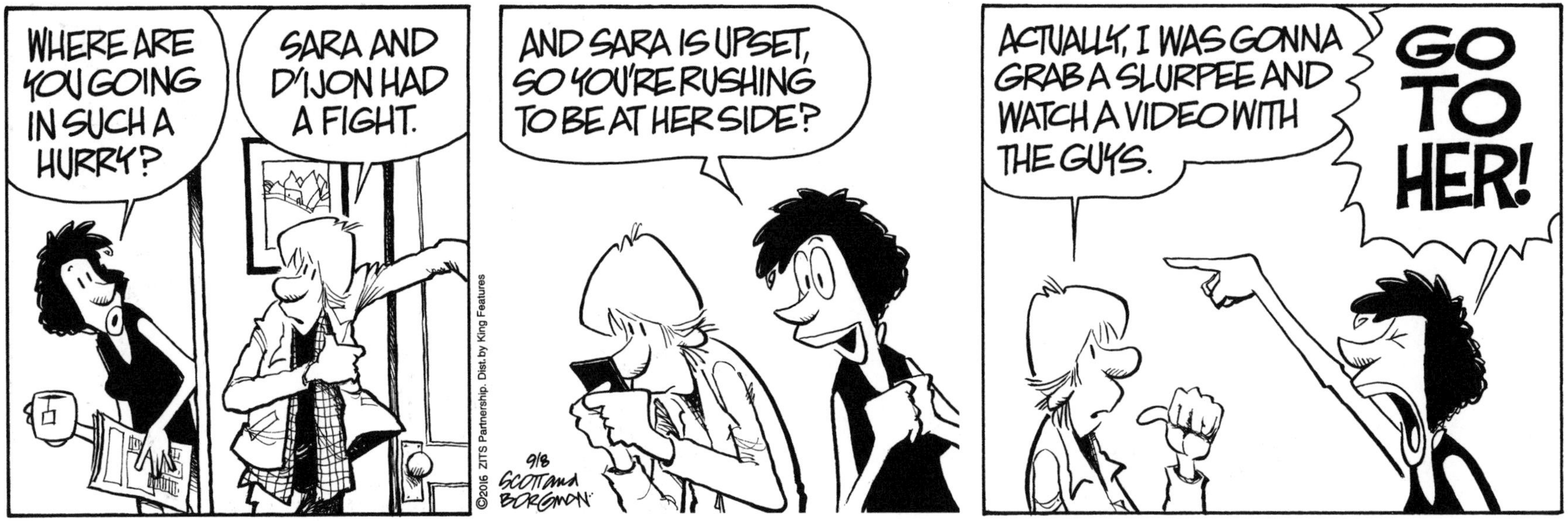
WHERE ARE YOU GOING IN SUCH A HURRY?
SARA AND D'IJON HAD A FIGHT.
AND SARA IS UPSET, SO YOU'RE RUSHING TO BE AT HER SIDE?
ACTUALLY, I WAS GONNA GRAB A SLURPEE AND WATCH A VIDEO WITH THE GUYS.
GO TO HER!
9/8
SCOTT and BORGMAN
©2016 ZITS Partnership. Dist. by King Features

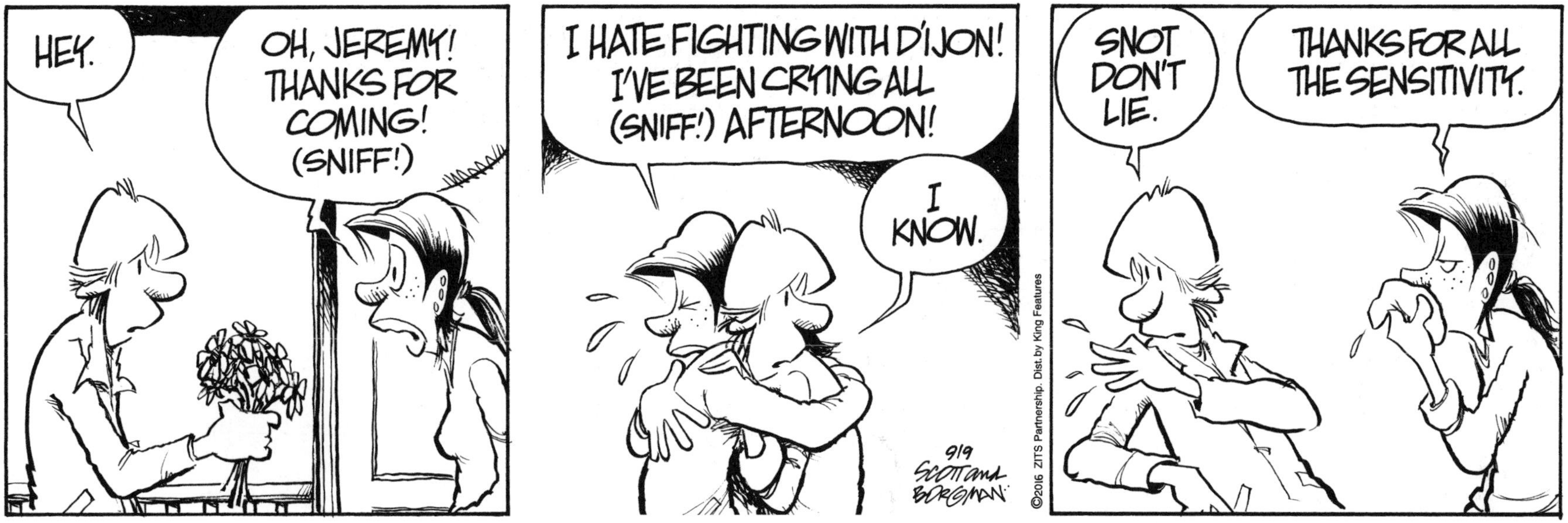
HEY.
OH, JEREMY! THANKS FOR COMING! (SNIFF!)
I HATE FIGHTING WITH D'IJON! I'VE BEEN CRYING ALL (SNIFF!) AFTERNOON!
I KNOW.
9/9
SCOTT and BORGMAN
©2016 ZITS Partnership. Dist. by King Features
SNOT DON'T LIE.
THANKS FOR ALL THE SENSITIVITY.

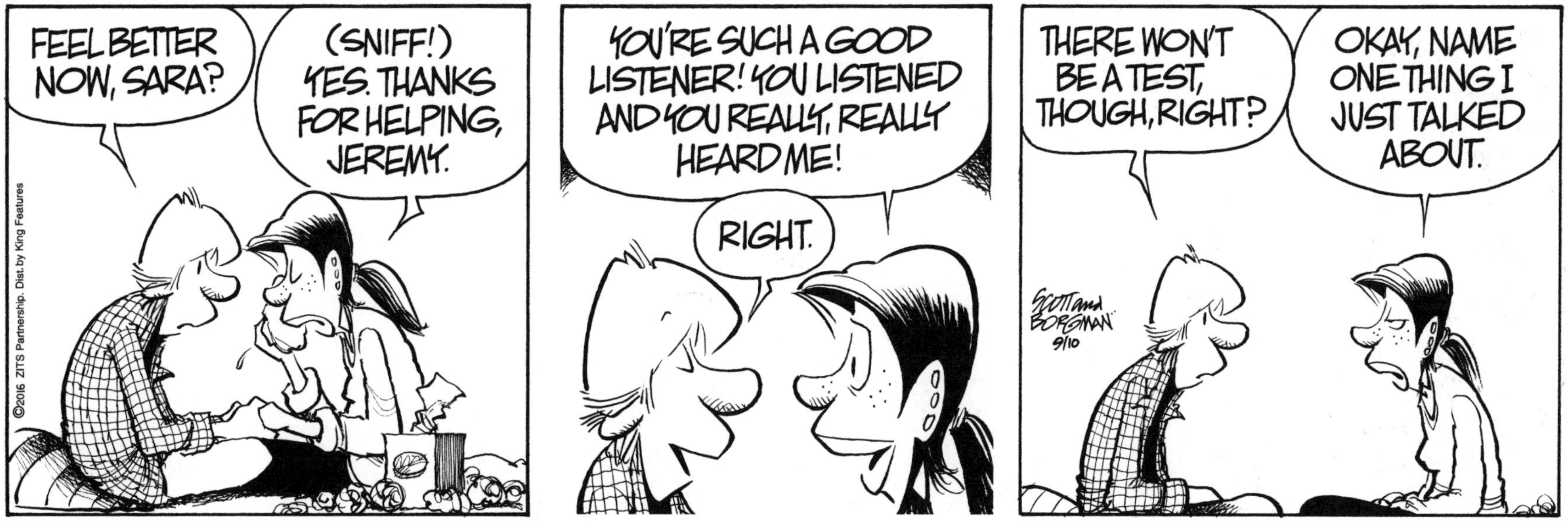
FEEL BETTER NOW, SARA?
(SNIFF!) YES. THANKS FOR HELPING, JEREMY.
©2016 ZITS Partnership. Dist. by King Features
YOU'RE SUCH A GOOD LISTENER! YOU LISTENED AND YOU REALLY, REALLY HEARD ME!
RIGHT.
THERE WON'T BE A TEST, THOUGH, RIGHT?
OKAY, NAME ONE THING I JUST TALKED ABOUT.
SCOTT and BORGMAN
9/10

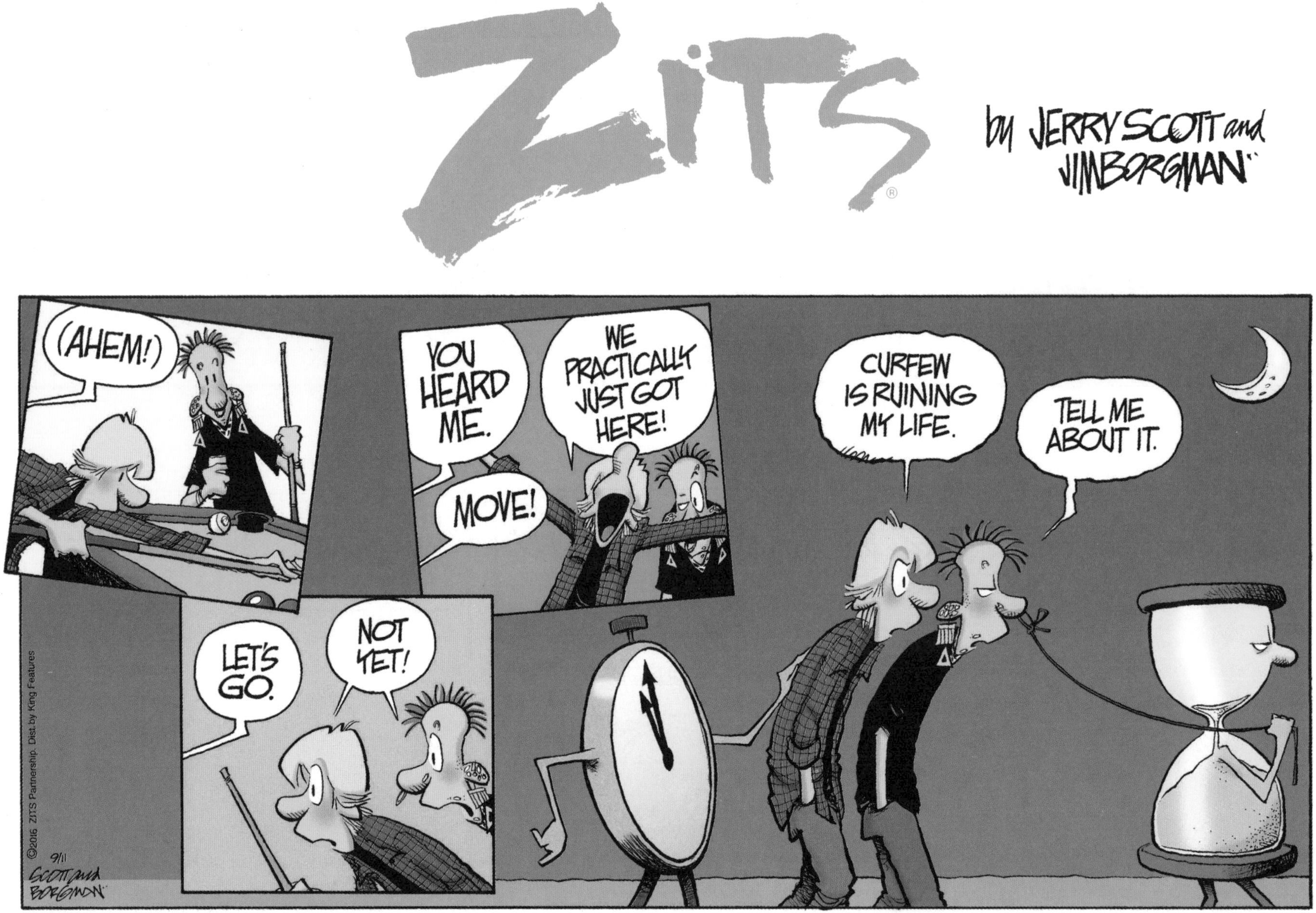
ZITS
by JERRY SCOTT and JIM BORGMAN
(AHEM!)
YOU HEARD ME.
WE PRACTICALLY JUST GOT HERE!
MOVE!
LET'S GO.
NOT YET!
CURFEW IS RUINING MY LIFE.
TELL ME ABOUT IT.
©2016 ZITS Partnership. Dist. by King Features
9/11
SCOTT and BORGMAN

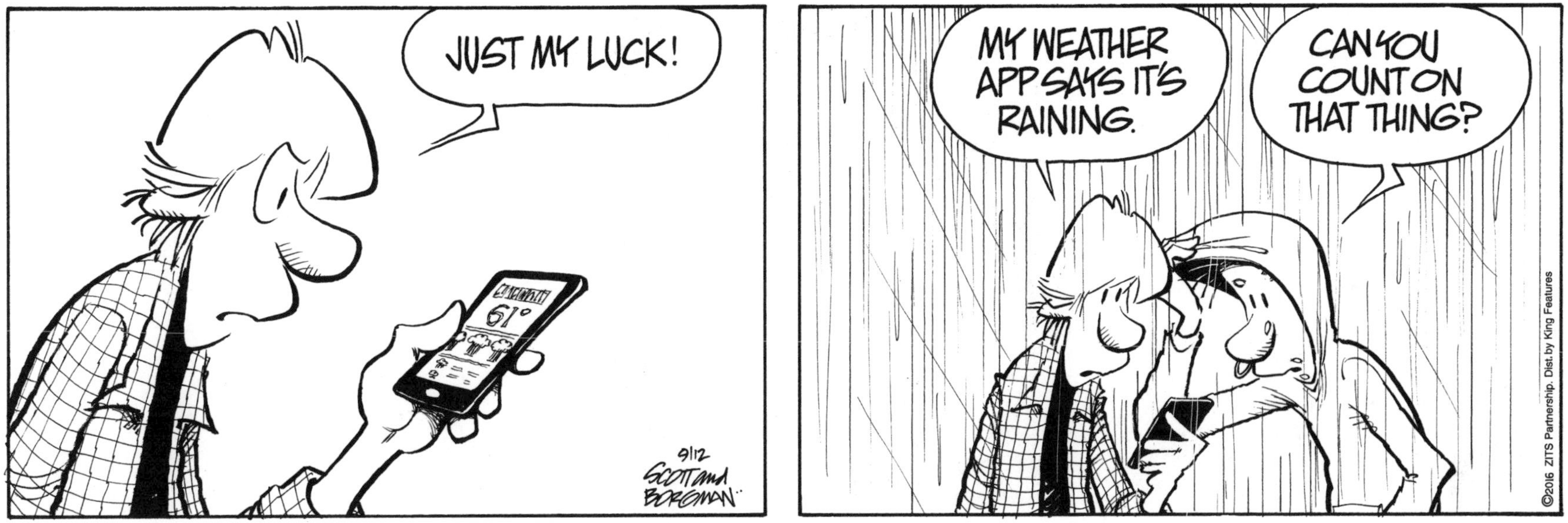
JUST MY LUCK!
61°
9/12 SCOTT and BORGMAN
MY WEATHER APP SAYS IT'S RAINING.
CAN YOU COUNT ON THAT THING?
©2016 ZITS Partnership. Dist. by King Features

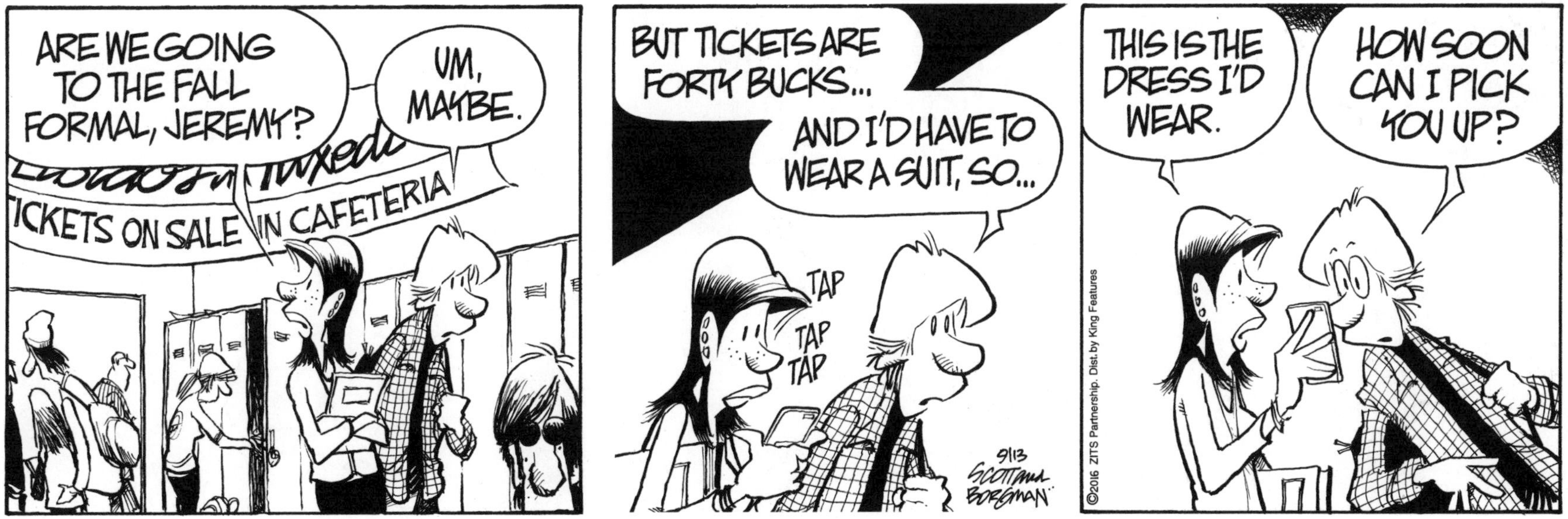
ARE WE GOING TO THE FALL FORMAL, JEREMY?
UM, MAYBE.
ICKETS ON SALE IN CAFETERIA
BUT TICKETS ARE FORTY BUCKS...
AND I'D HAVE TO WEAR A SUIT, SO...
TAP
TAP
TAP
9/13 SCOTT and BORGMAN
©2016 ZITS Partnership. Dist. by King Features
THIS IS THE DRESS I'D WEAR.
HOW SOON CAN I PICK YOU UP?

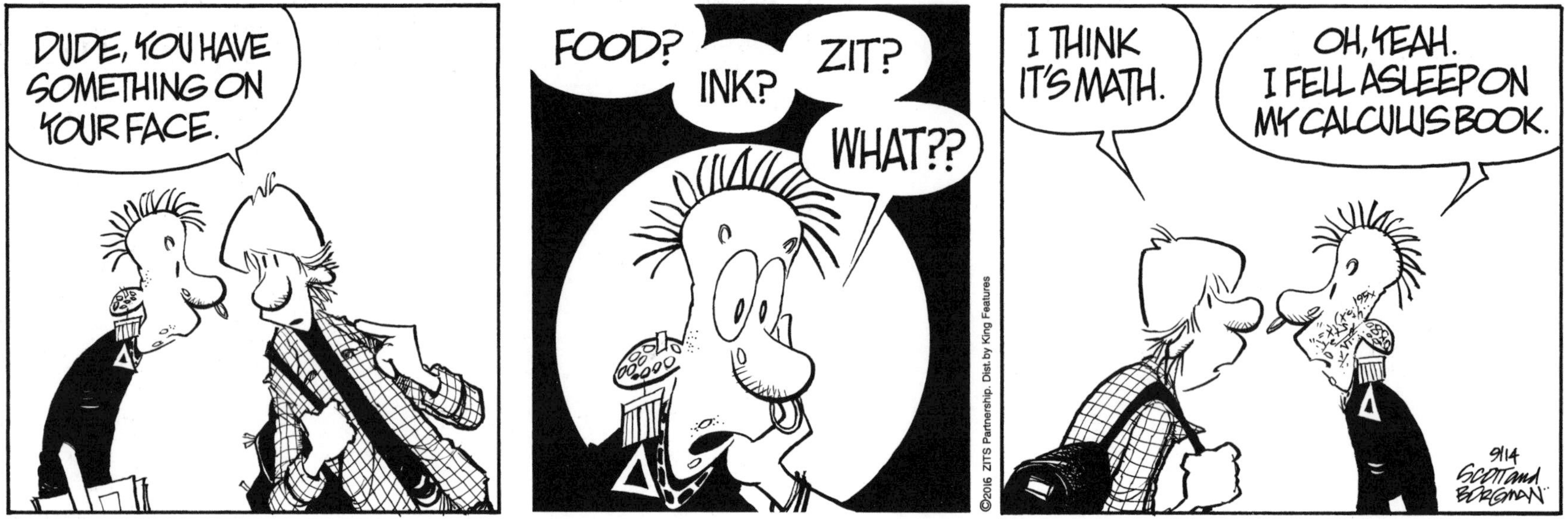
DUDE, YOU HAVE SOMETHING ON YOUR FACE.
FOOD?
INK?
ZIT?
WHAT??
I THINK IT'S MATH.
OH, YEAH. I FELL ASLEEP ON MY CALCULUS BOOK.
9/14
SCOTT and BORGMAN
©2016 ZITS Partnership. Dist. by King Features

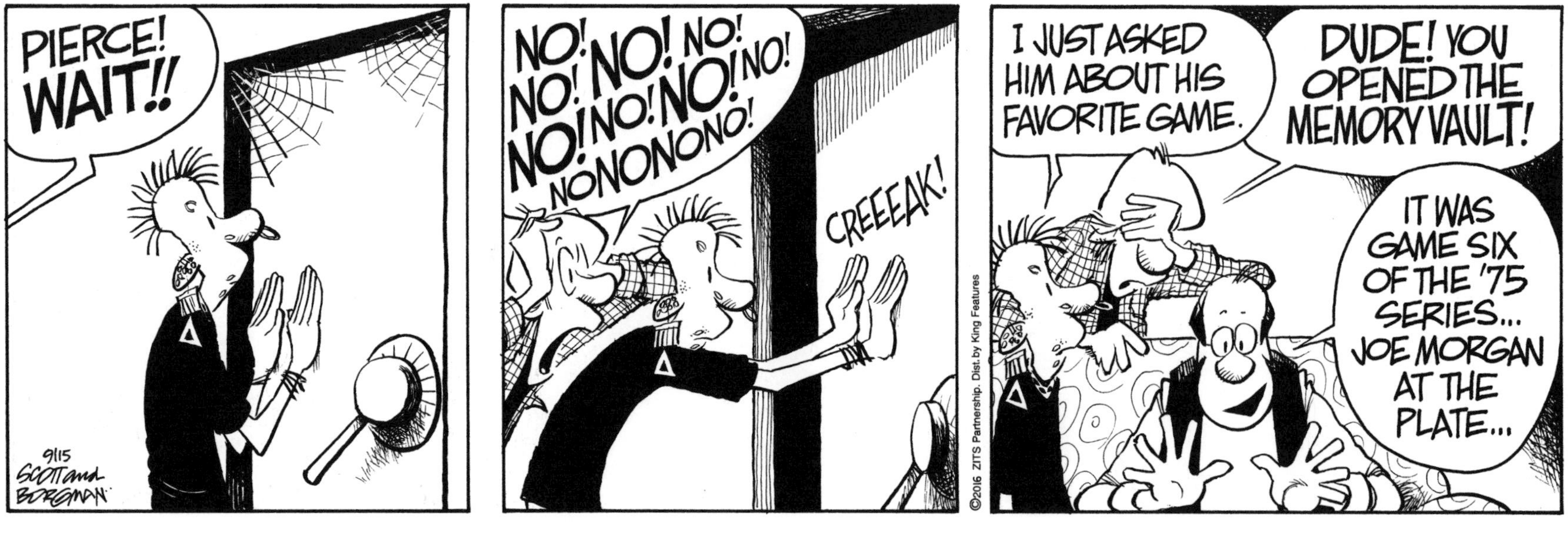
PIERCE! WAIT!!
9/15
SCOTT and BORGMAN
NO! NO! NO! NO! NO! NO! NO! NO! NO! NO! NONONONONO!
CREEEAK!
I JUST ASKED HIM ABOUT HIS FAVORITE GAME.
DUDE! YOU OPENED THE MEMORY VAULT!
IT WAS GAME SIX OF THE '75 SERIES... JOE MORGAN AT THE PLATE...
©2016 ZITS Partnership. Dist. by King Features

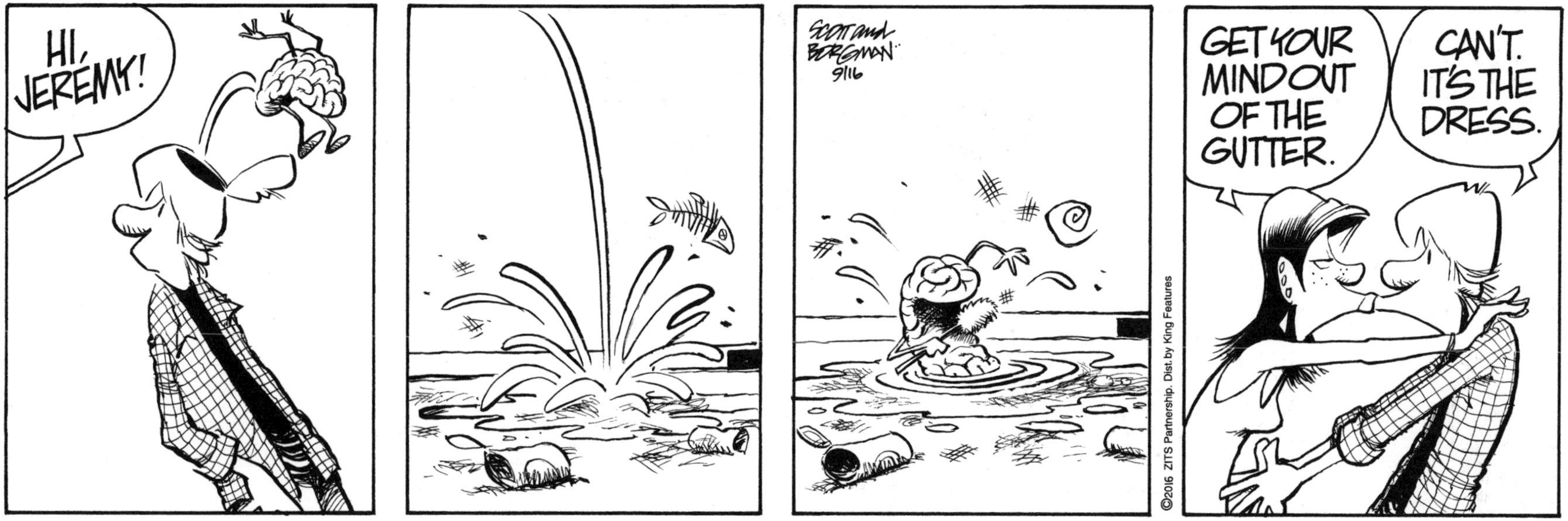
HI, JEREMY!
SCOTT and BORGMAN 9/16
GET YOUR MIND OUT OF THE GUTTER.
CAN'T. IT'S THE DRESS.
©2016 ZITS Partnership. Dist. by King Features

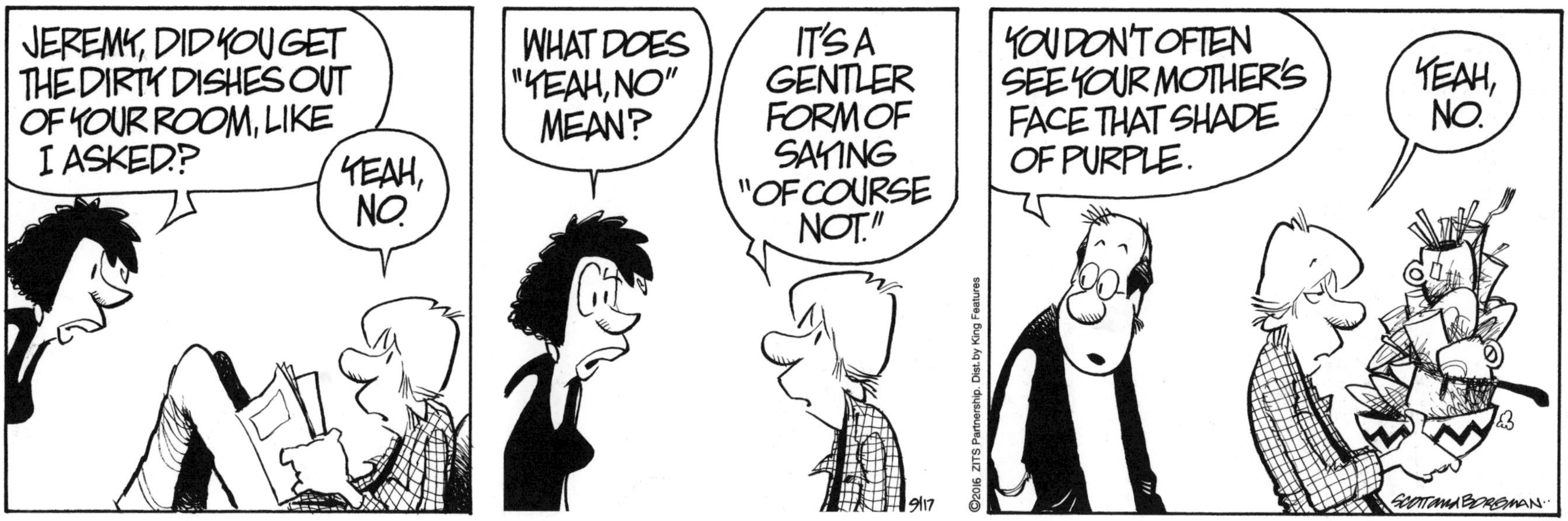
JEREMY, DID YOU GET THE DIRTY DISHES OUT OF YOUR ROOM, LIKE I ASKED?
YEAH, NO.
WHAT DOES "YEAH, NO" MEAN?
IT'S A GENTLER FORM OF SAYING "OF COURSE NOT."
9/17
©2016 ZITS Partnership. Dist. by King Features
YOU DON'T OFTEN SEE YOUR MOTHER'S FACE THAT SHADE OF PURPLE.
YEAH, NO.
SCOTT and BORGMAN

ZITS®

by JERRY SCOTT and JIM BORGMAN

WHEN THE BELL RINGS, TRY NOT TO STAND BETWEEN ME AND THE CAFETERIA.
NOTED.
9/18 SCOTT and BORGMAN
©2016 ZITS Partnership. Dist. by King Features

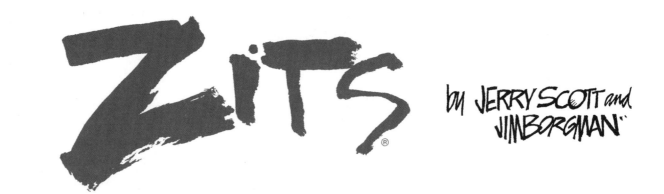

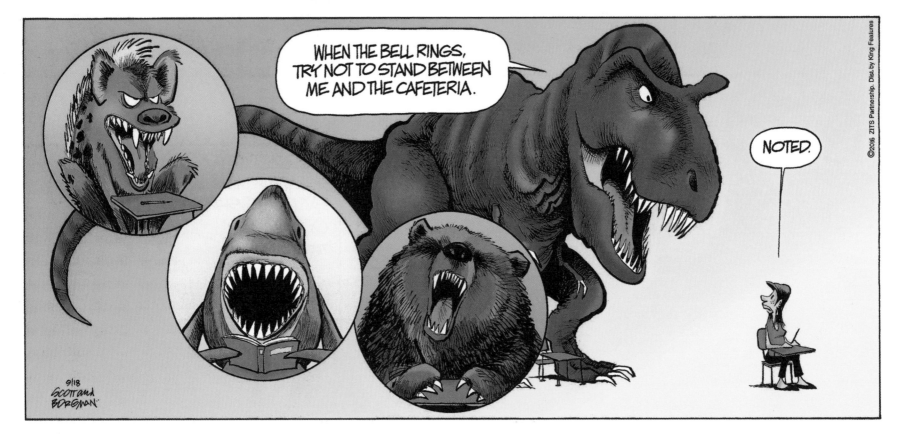

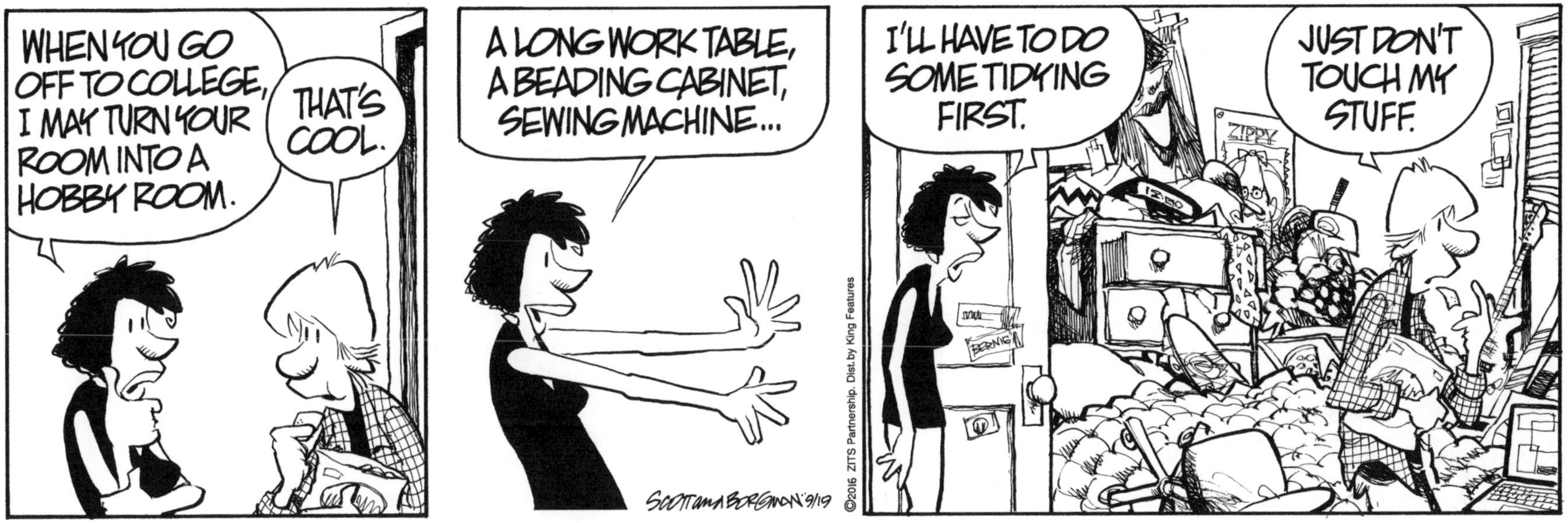
WHEN YOU GO OFF TO COLLEGE, I MAY TURN YOUR ROOM INTO A HOBBY ROOM.
THAT'S COOL.
A LONG WORK TABLE, A BEADING CABINET, SEWING MACHINE...
I'LL HAVE TO DO SOME TIDYING FIRST.
JUST DON'T TOUCH MY STUFF.
ZIPPY
©2016 ZITS Partnership. Dist. by King Features

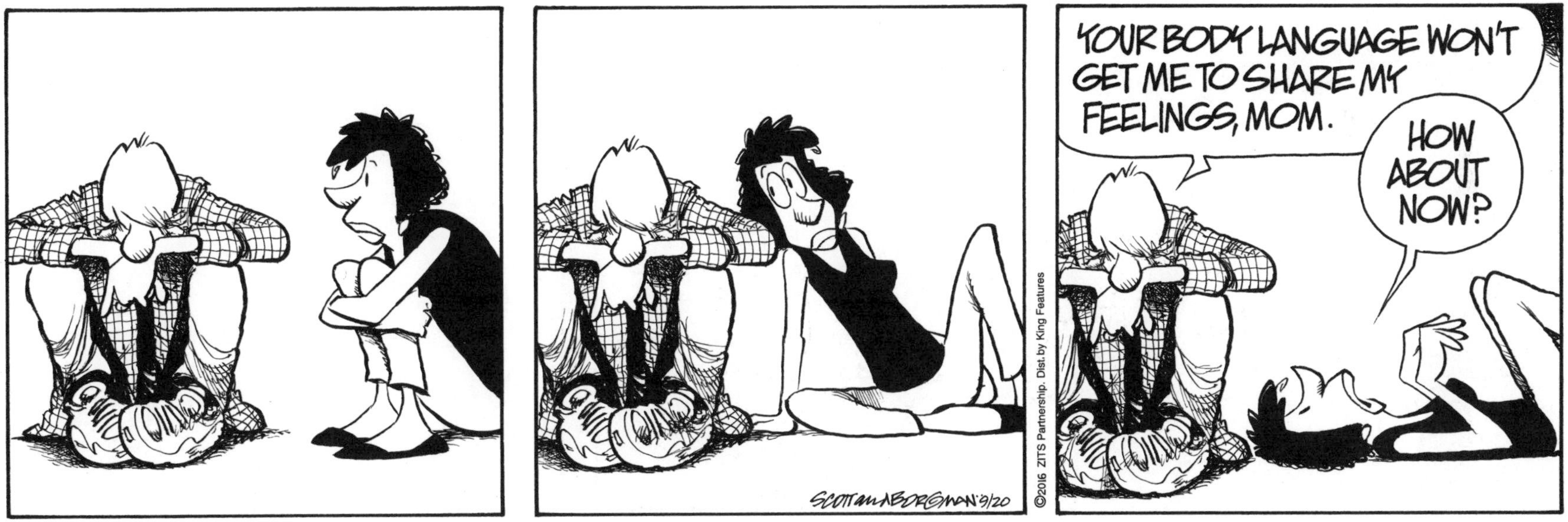
YOUR BODY LANGUAGE WON'T GET ME TO SHARE MY FEELINGS, MOM.
HOW ABOUT NOW?
©2016 ZITS Partnership. Dist. by King Features

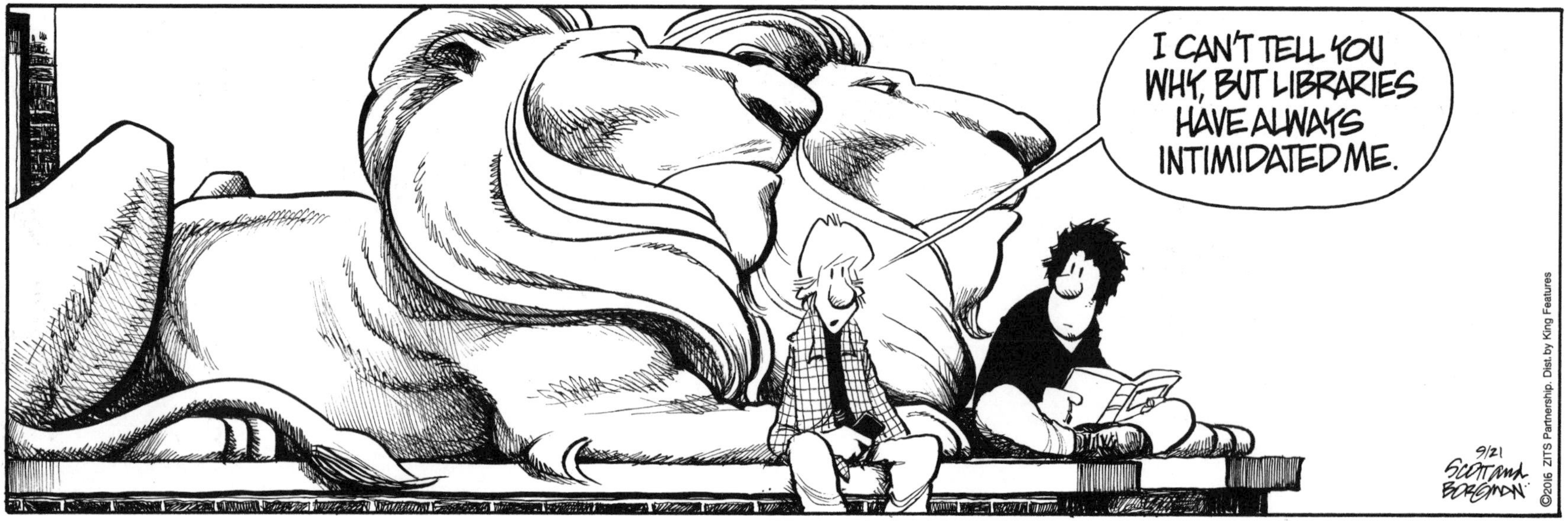
I CAN'T TELL YOU WHY, BUT LIBRARIES HAVE ALWAYS INTIMIDATED ME.
9/21 SCOTT and BORGMAN
©2016 ZITS Partnership. Dist. by King Features

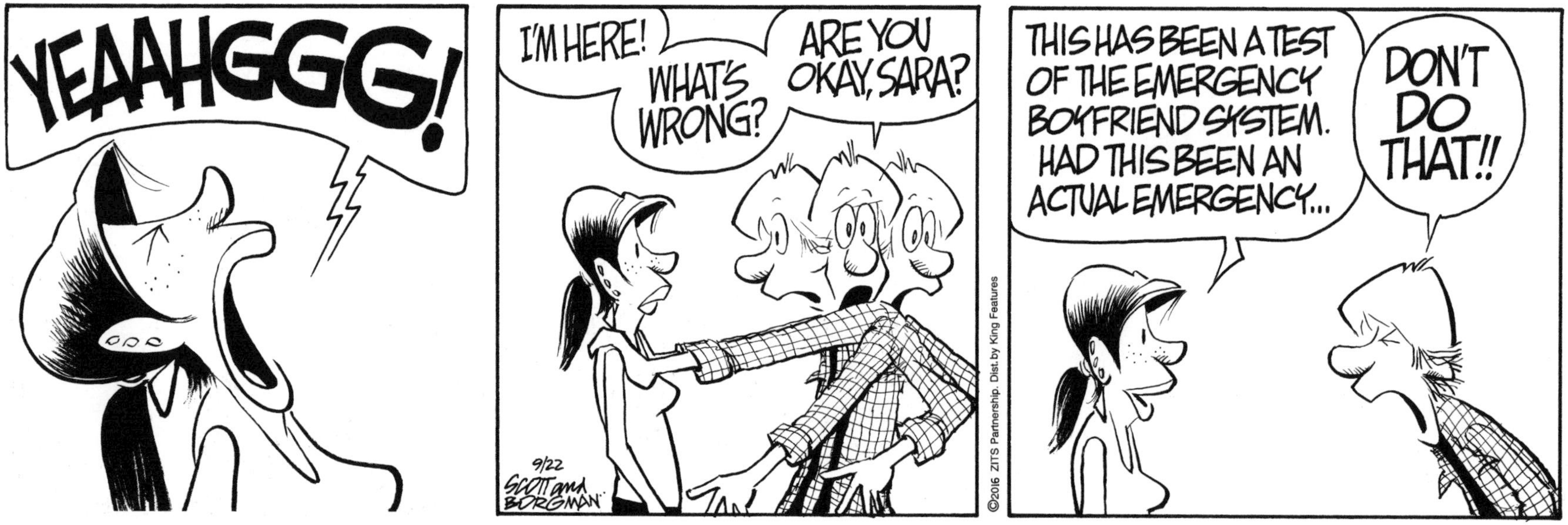
YEAAHGGG!
I'M HERE!
WHAT'S WRONG?
ARE YOU OKAY, SARA?
9/22 SCOTT and BORGMAN
©2016 ZITS Partnership. Dist. by King Features
THIS HAS BEEN A TEST OF THE EMERGENCY BOYFRIEND SYSTEM. HAD THIS BEEN AN ACTUAL EMERGENCY...
DON'T DO THAT!!

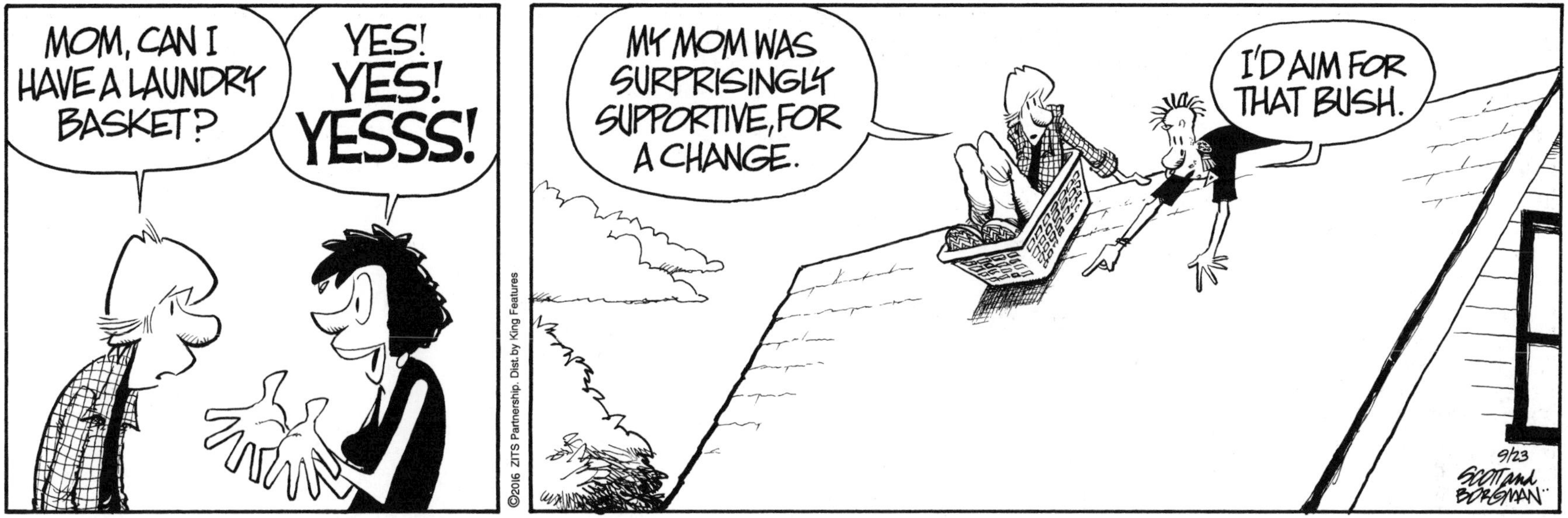
MOM, CAN I HAVE A LAUNDRY BASKET?
YES! YES! YESSS!
MY MOM WAS SURPRISINGLY SUPPORTIVE, FOR A CHANGE.
I'D AIM FOR THAT BUSH.
©2016 ZITS Partnership. Dist. by King Features
9/23
SCOTT and BORGMAN

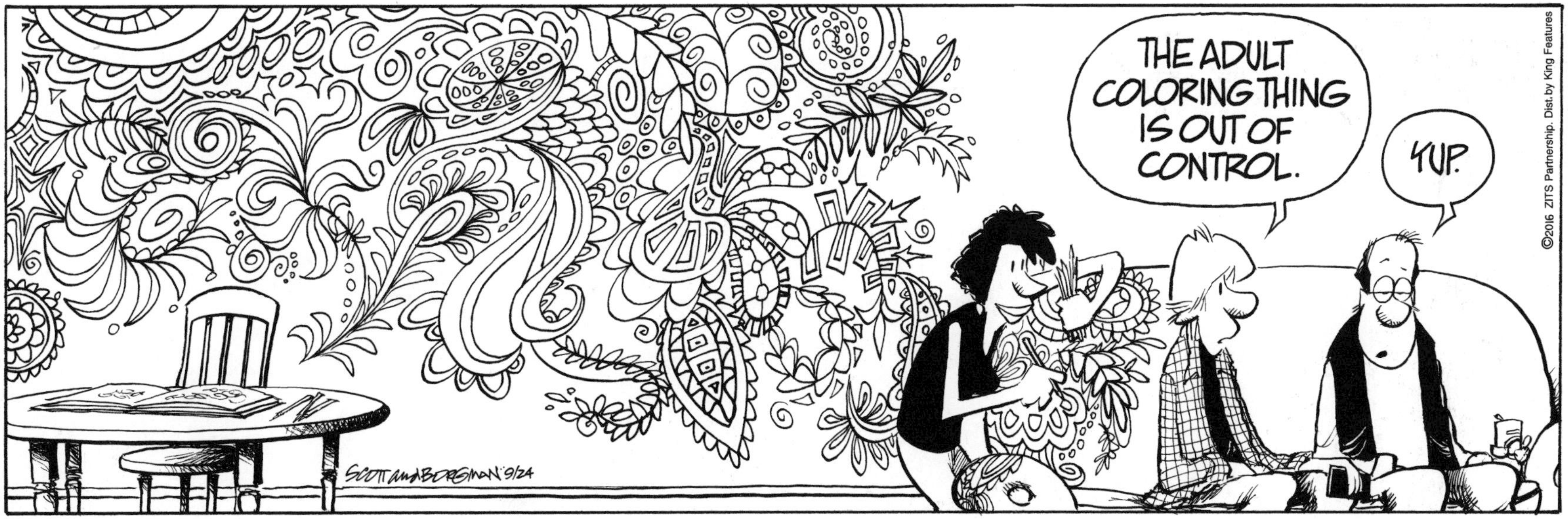
THE ADULT COLORING THING IS OUT OF CONTROL.
YUP.
©2016 ZITS Partnership. Dist. by King Features
SCOTT and BORGMAN 9/24

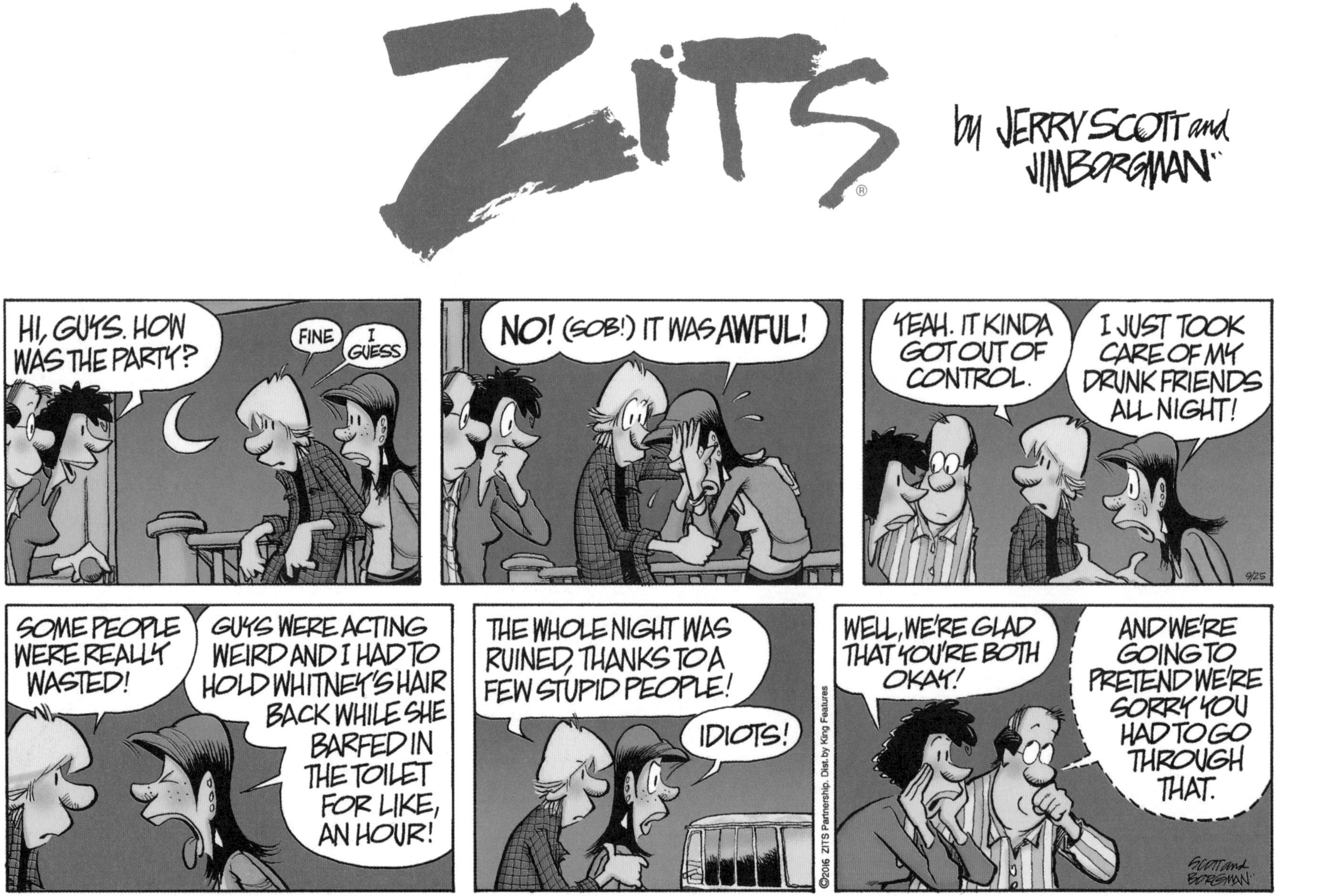
ZITS®
by JERRY SCOTT and JIM BORGMAN
HI, GUYS. HOW WAS THE PARTY?
FINE
I GUESS
NO! (SOB!) IT WAS AWFUL!
YEAH. IT KINDA GOT OUT OF CONTROL.
I JUST TOOK CARE OF MY DRUNK FRIENDS ALL NIGHT!
9/25
SOME PEOPLE WERE REALLY WASTED!
GUYS WERE ACTING WEIRD AND I HAD TO HOLD WHITNEY'S HAIR BACK WHILE SHE BARFED IN THE TOILET FOR LIKE, AN HOUR!
THE WHOLE NIGHT WAS RUINED, THANKS TO A FEW STUPID PEOPLE!
IDIOTS!
©2016 ZITS Partnership. Dist. by King Features
WELL, WE'RE GLAD THAT YOU'RE BOTH OKAY!
AND WE'RE GOING TO PRETEND WE'RE SORRY YOU HAD TO GO THROUGH THAT.
SCOTT and BORGMAN

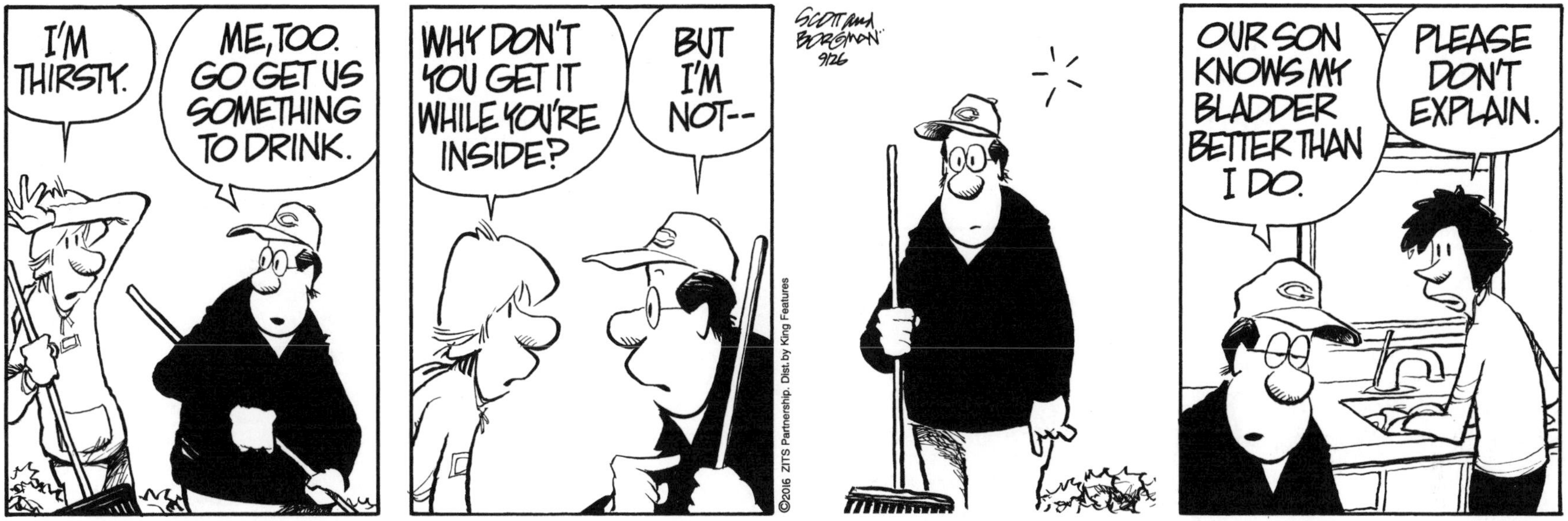
I'M THIRSTY.
ME, TOO. GO GET US SOMETHING TO DRINK.
WHY DON'T YOU GET IT WHILE YOU'RE INSIDE?
BUT I'M NOT--
SCOTT and BORGMAN 9/26
©2016 ZITS Partnership. Dist. by King Features
OUR SON KNOWS MY BLADDER BETTER THAN I DO.
PLEASE DON'T EXPLAIN.

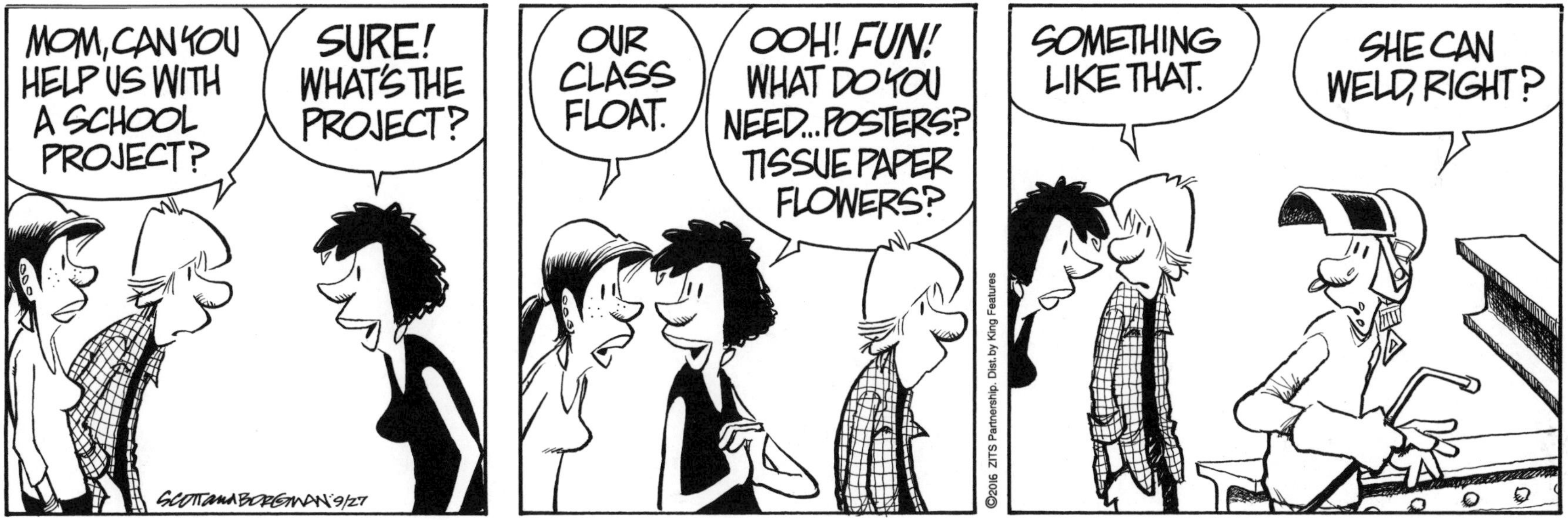
MOM, CAN YOU HELP US WITH A SCHOOL PROJECT?
SURE! WHAT'S THE PROJECT?
SCOTT and BORGMAN 9/27
OUR CLASS FLOAT.
OOH! FUN! WHAT DO YOU NEED...POSTERS? TISSUE PAPER FLOWERS?
©2016 ZITS Partnership. Dist. by King Features
SOMETHING LIKE THAT.
SHE CAN WELD, RIGHT?

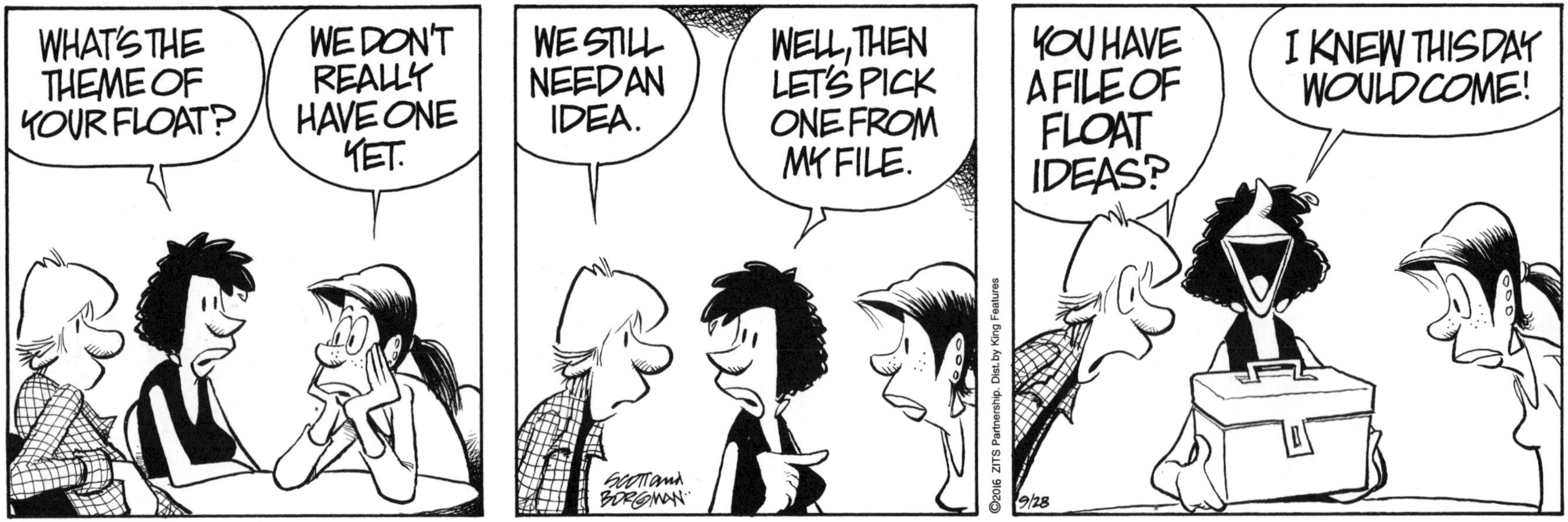
WHAT'S THE THEME OF YOUR FLOAT?
WE DON'T REALLY HAVE ONE YET.
WE STILL NEED AN IDEA.
WELL, THEN LET'S PICK ONE FROM MY FILE.
YOU HAVE A FILE OF FLOAT IDEAS?
I KNEW THIS DAY WOULD COME!
SCOTT and BORGMAN
©2016 ZITS Partnership. Dist. by King Features
9/28

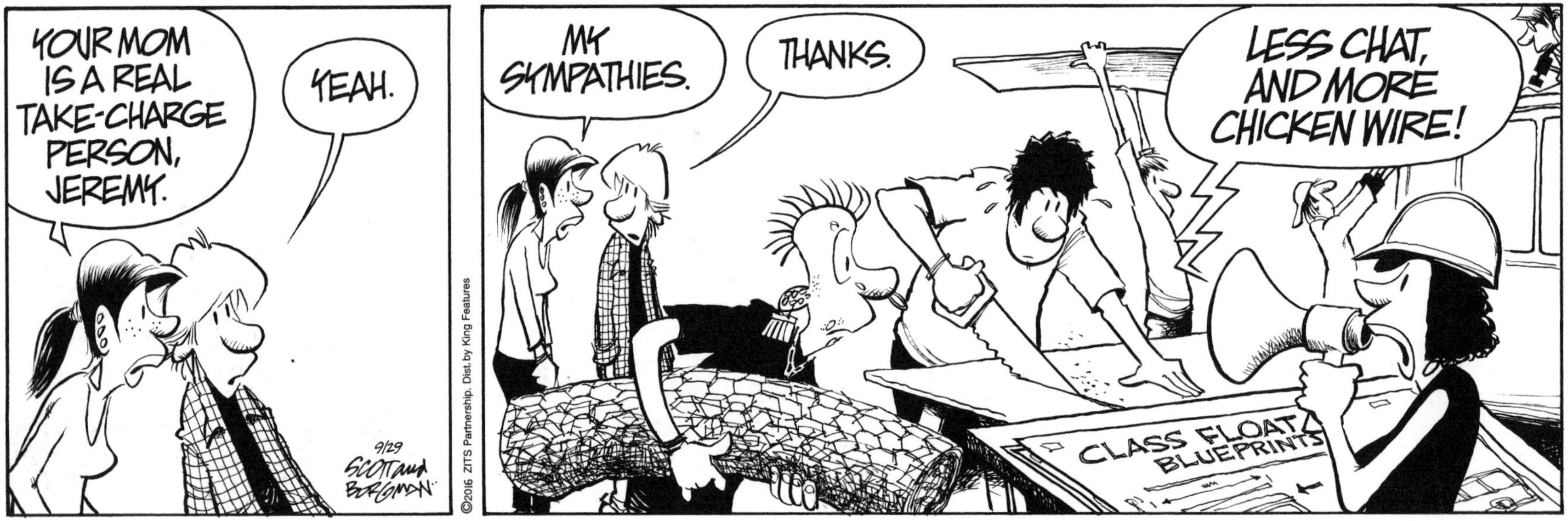
YOUR MOM IS A REAL TAKE-CHARGE PERSON, JEREMY.
YEAH.
9/29
SCOTT and BORGMAN
©2016 ZITS Partnership. Dist. by King Features
MY SYMPATHIES.
THANKS.
LESS CHAT, AND MORE CHICKEN WIRE!
CLASS FLOAT BLUEPRINTS

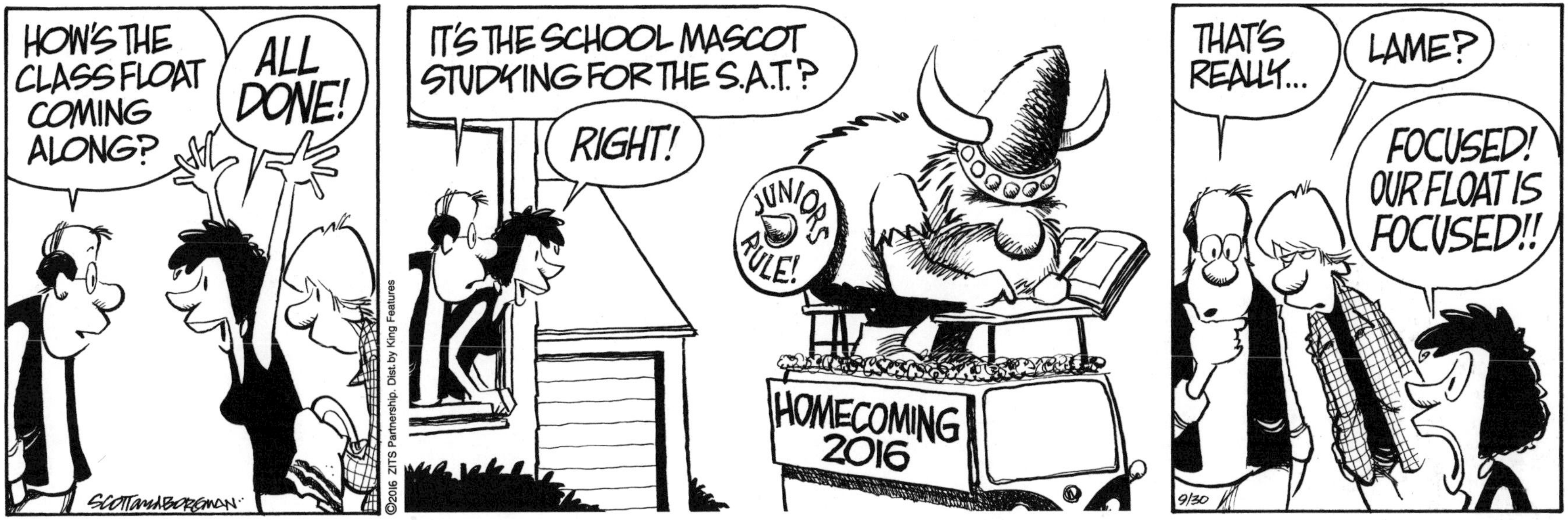
HOW'S THE CLASS FLOAT COMING ALONG?
ALL DONE!
IT'S THE SCHOOL MASCOT STUDYING FOR THE S.A.T.?
RIGHT!
JUNIORS RULE!
HOMECOMING 2016
THAT'S REALLY...
LAME?
FOCUSED! OUR FLOAT IS FOCUSED!!
SCOTT and BORGMAN
©2016 ZITS Partnership. Dist. by King Features
9/30

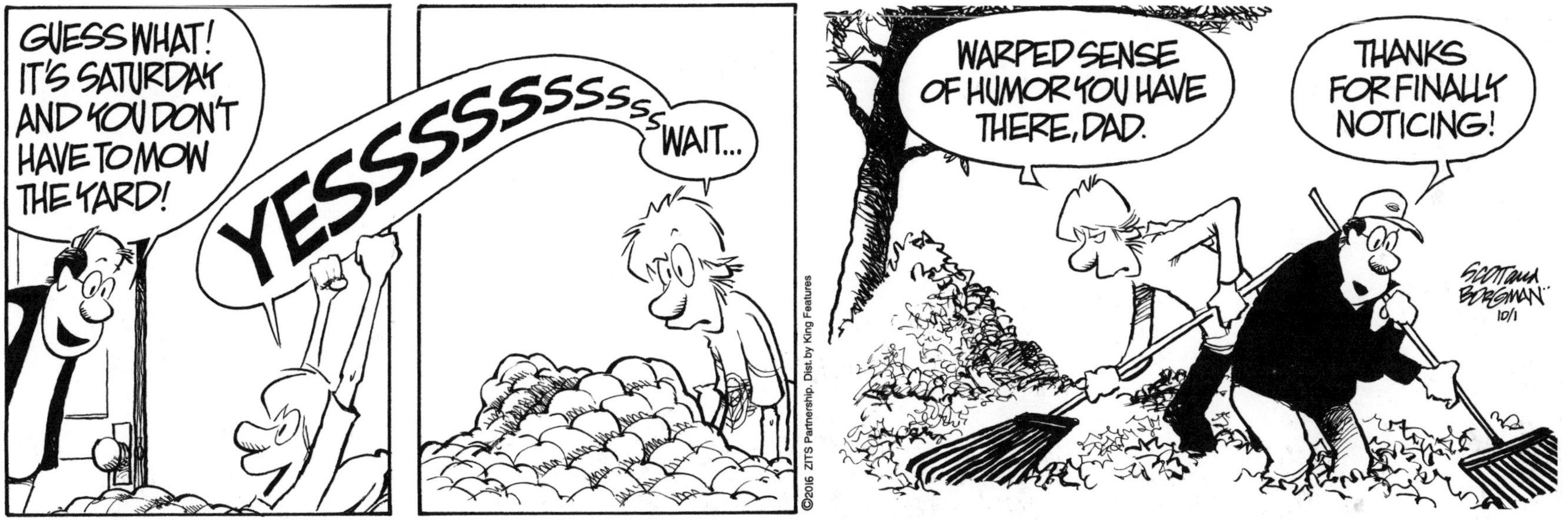
GUESS WHAT! IT'S SATURDAY AND YOU DON'T HAVE TO MOW THE YARD!
YESSSSSSSSsss
WAIT...
WARPED SENSE OF HUMOR YOU HAVE THERE, DAD.
THANKS FOR FINALLY NOTICING!
SCOTT and BORGMAN
10/1
©2016 ZITS Partnership. Dist. by King Features

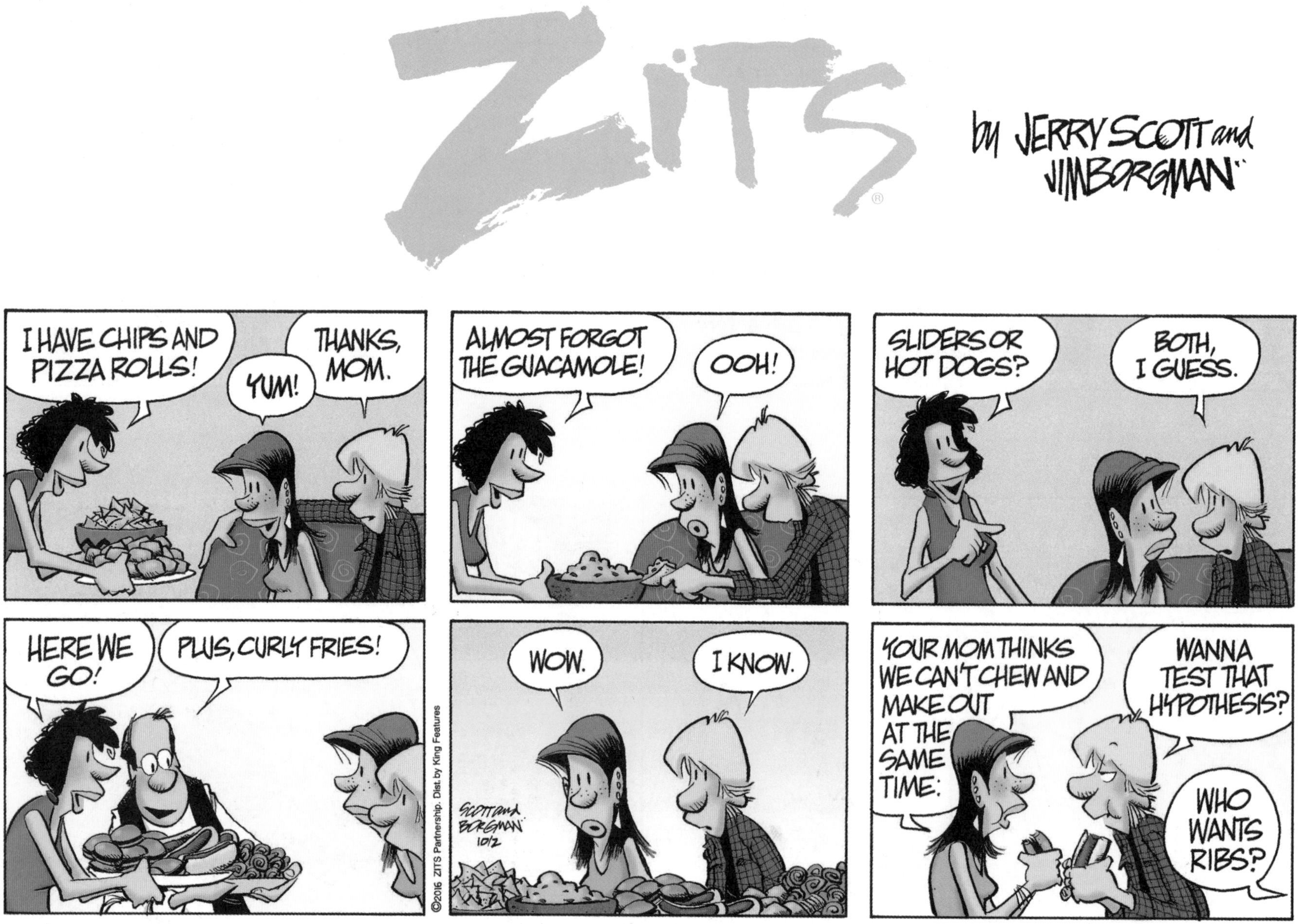
ZITS
by JERRY SCOTT and JIM BORGMAN
I HAVE CHIPS AND PIZZA ROLLS!
YUM!
THANKS, MOM.
ALMOST FORGOT THE GUACAMOLE!
OOH!
SLIDERS OR HOT DOGS?
BOTH, I GUESS.
HERE WE GO!
PLUS, CURLY FRIES!
©2016 ZITS Partnership. Dist. by King Features
SCOTT and BORGMAN 10/2
WOW.
I KNOW.
YOUR MOM THINKS WE CAN'T CHEW AND MAKE OUT AT THE SAME TIME.
WANNA TEST THAT HYPOTHESIS?
WHO WANTS RIBS?

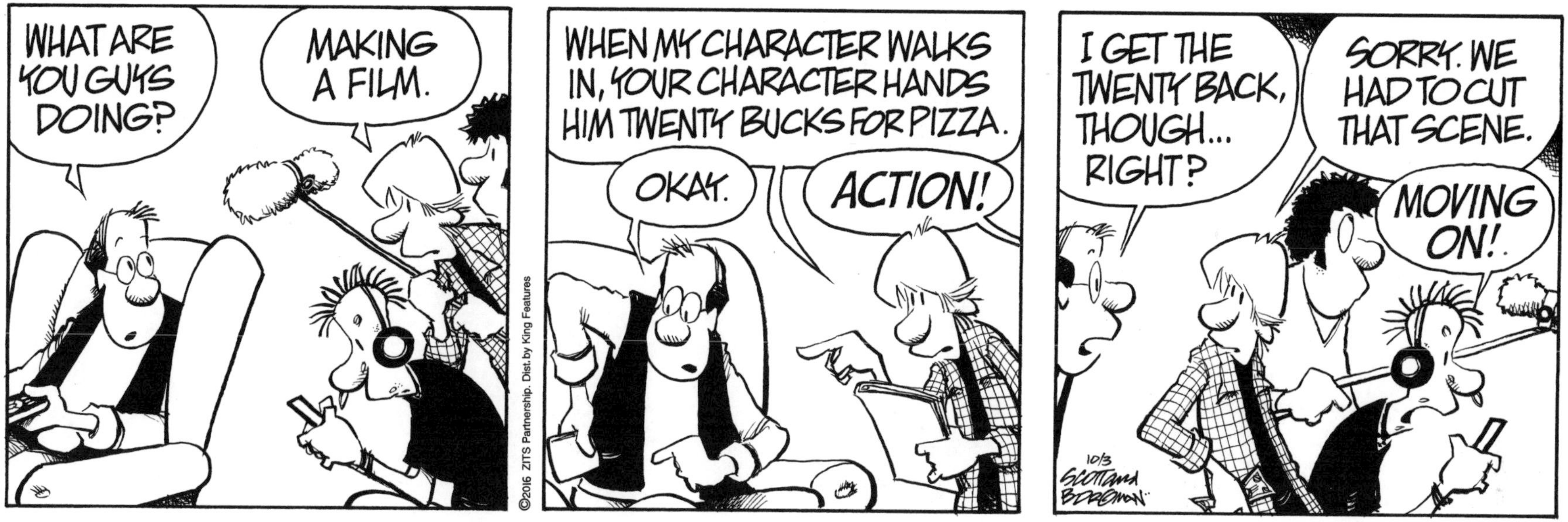
WHAT ARE YOU GUYS DOING?
MAKING A FILM.
WHEN MY CHARACTER WALKS IN, YOUR CHARACTER HANDS HIM TWENTY BUCKS FOR PIZZA.
OKAY.
ACTION!
I GET THE TWENTY BACK, THOUGH... RIGHT?
SORRY. WE HAD TO CUT THAT SCENE.
MOVING ON!
©2016 ZITS Partnership. Dist. by King Features
10/3
SCOTT AND BORGMAN

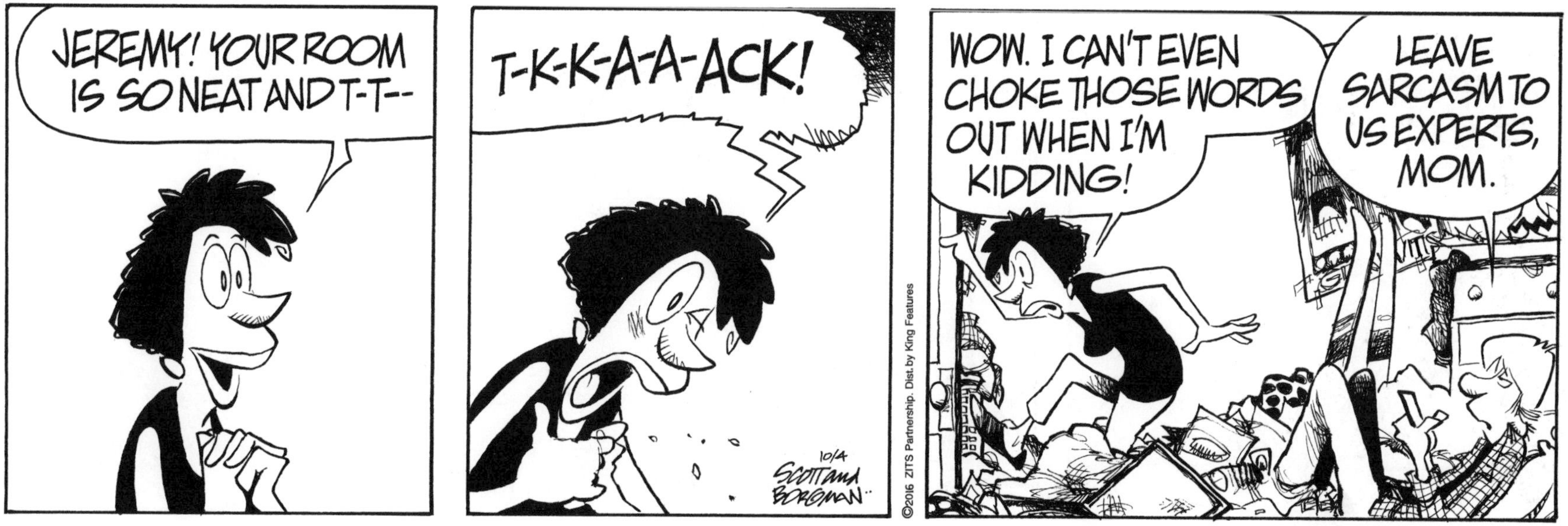
JEREMY! YOUR ROOM IS SO NEAT AND T-T--
T-K-K-A-A-ACK!
WOW. I CAN'T EVEN CHOKE THOSE WORDS OUT WHEN I'M KIDDING!
LEAVE SARCASM TO US EXPERTS, MOM.
©2016 ZITS Partnership. Dist. by King Features
10/4
SCOTT AND BORGMAN

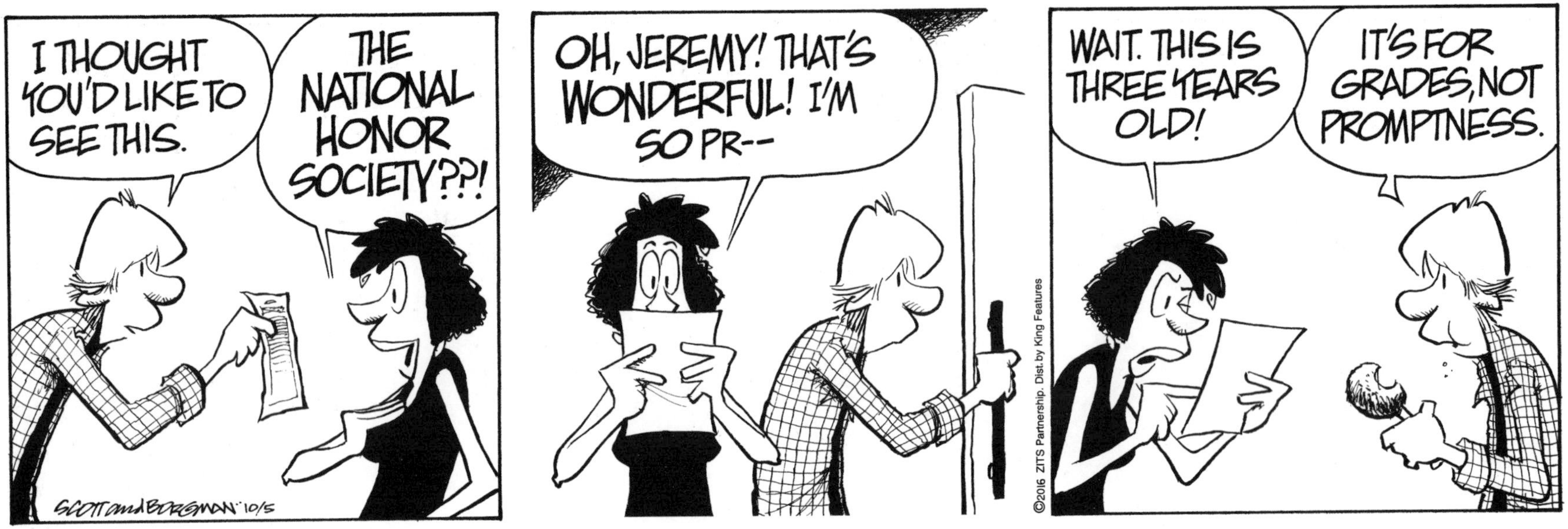
I THOUGHT YOU'D LIKE TO SEE THIS.
THE NATIONAL HONOR SOCIETY??!
OH, JEREMY! THAT'S WONDERFUL! I'M SO PR--
WAIT. THIS IS THREE YEARS OLD!
IT'S FOR GRADES, NOT PROMPTNESS.
SCOTT and BORGMAN 10/5
©2016 ZITS Partnership. Dist. by King Features

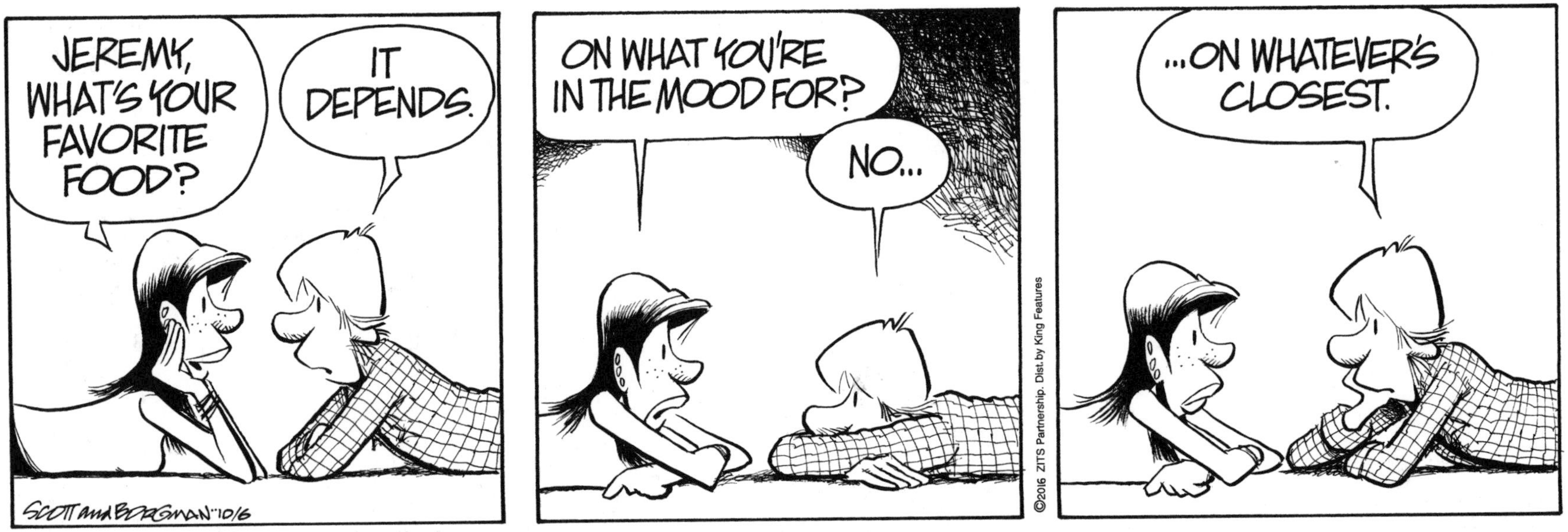
JEREMY, WHAT'S YOUR FAVORITE FOOD?
IT DEPENDS.
ON WHAT YOU'RE IN THE MOOD FOR?
NO...
...ON WHATEVER'S CLOSEST.
SCOTT and BORGMAN 10/6
©2016 ZITS Partnership. Dist. by King Features

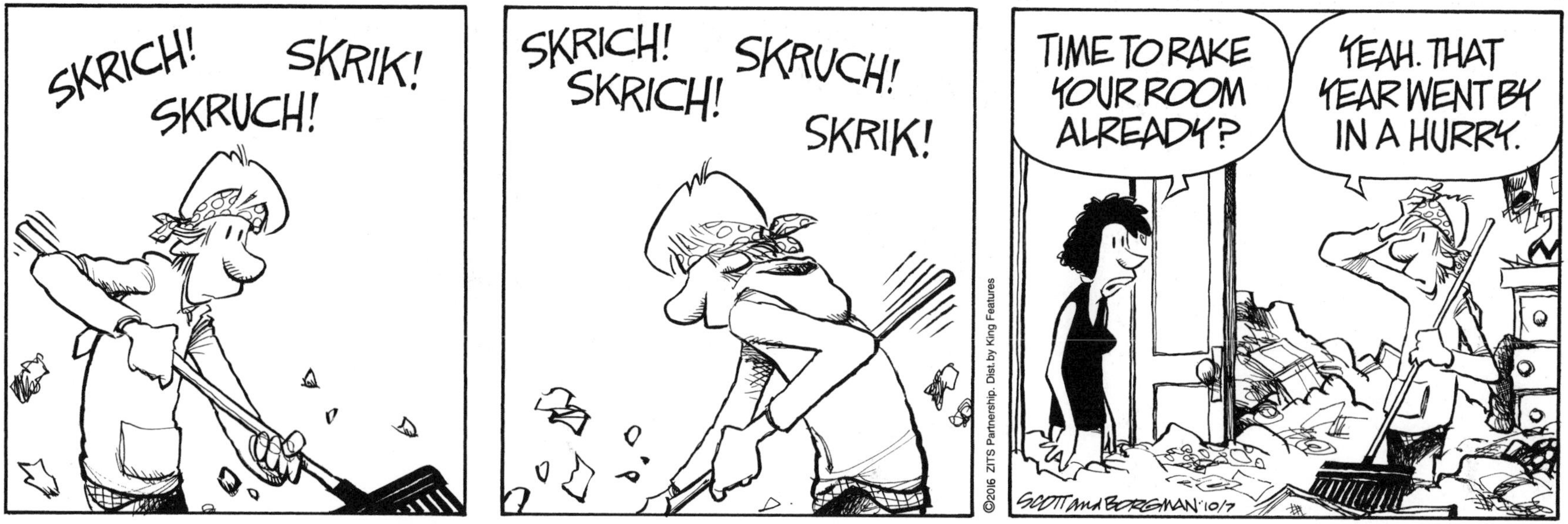
SKRICH!
SKRIK!
SKRUCH!
SKRICH!
SKRICH!
SKRUCH!
SKRIK!
TIME TO RAKE YOUR ROOM ALREADY?
YEAH. THAT YEAR WENT BY IN A HURRY.
SCOTT and BORGMAN 10/7
©2016 ZITS Partnership. Dist. by King Features

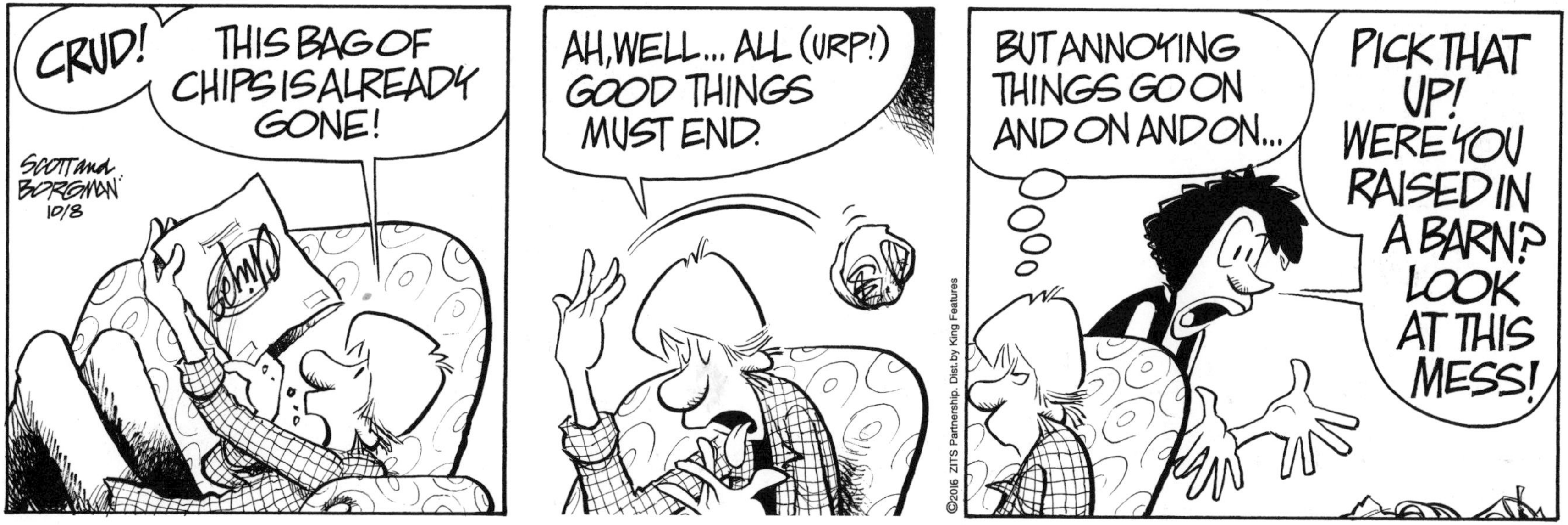
CRUD!
THIS BAG OF CHIPS IS ALREADY GONE!
SCOTT and BORGMAN 10/8
AH, WELL... ALL (URP!) GOOD THINGS MUST END.
©2016 ZITS Partnership. Dist. by King Features
BUT ANNOYING THINGS GO ON AND ON AND ON...
PICK THAT UP! WERE YOU RAISED IN A BARN? LOOK AT THIS MESS!

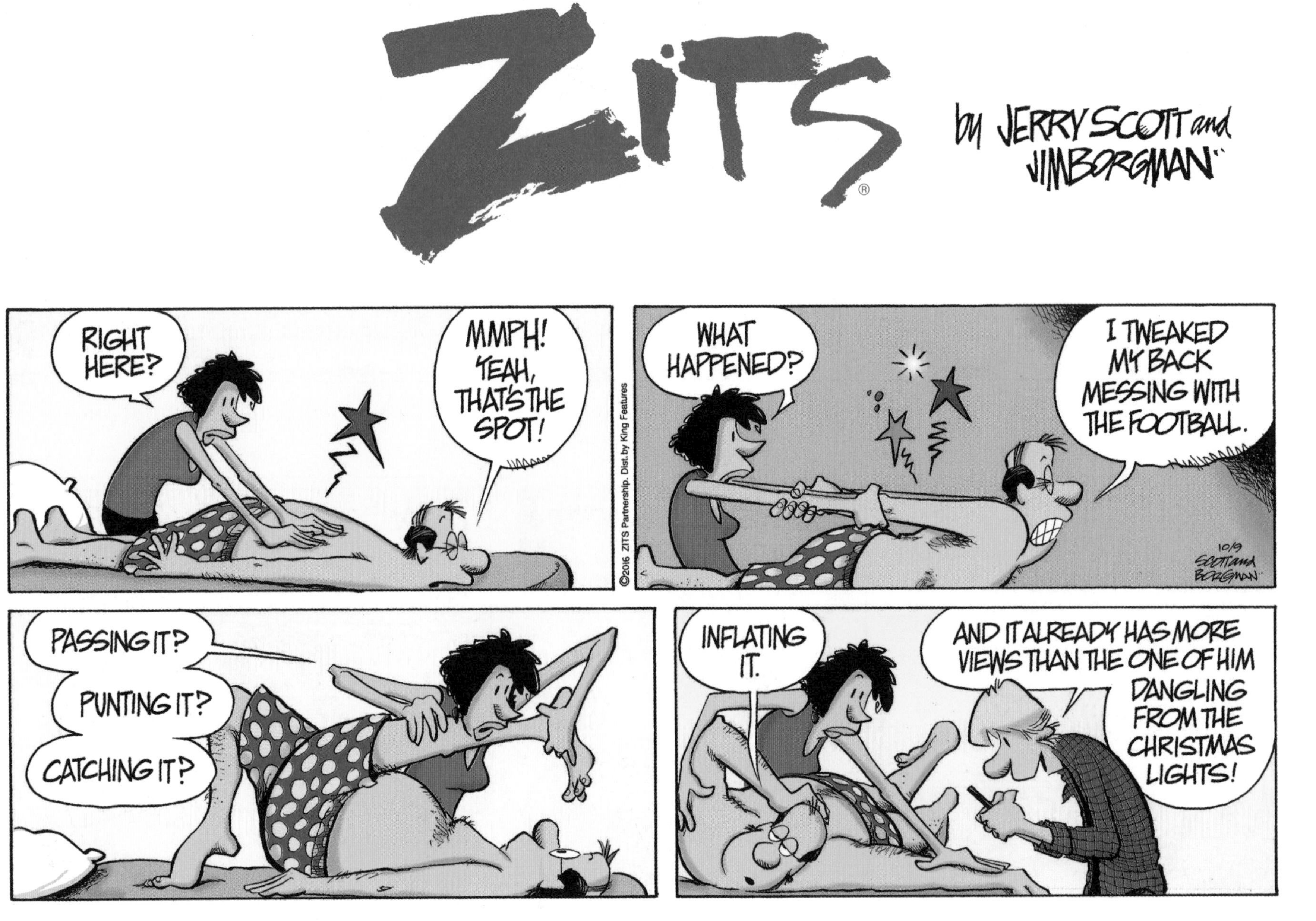
ZITS®
by JERRY SCOTT and JIM BORGMAN
RIGHT HERE?
MMPH! YEAH, THAT'S THE SPOT!
©2016 ZITS Partnership. Dist. by King Features
WHAT HAPPENED?
I TWEAKED MY BACK MESSING WITH THE FOOTBALL.
10/9 SCOTT and BORGMAN
PASSING IT?
PUNTING IT?
CATCHING IT?
INFLATING IT.
AND IT ALREADY HAS MORE VIEWS THAN THE ONE OF HIM DANGLING FROM THE CHRISTMAS LIGHTS!

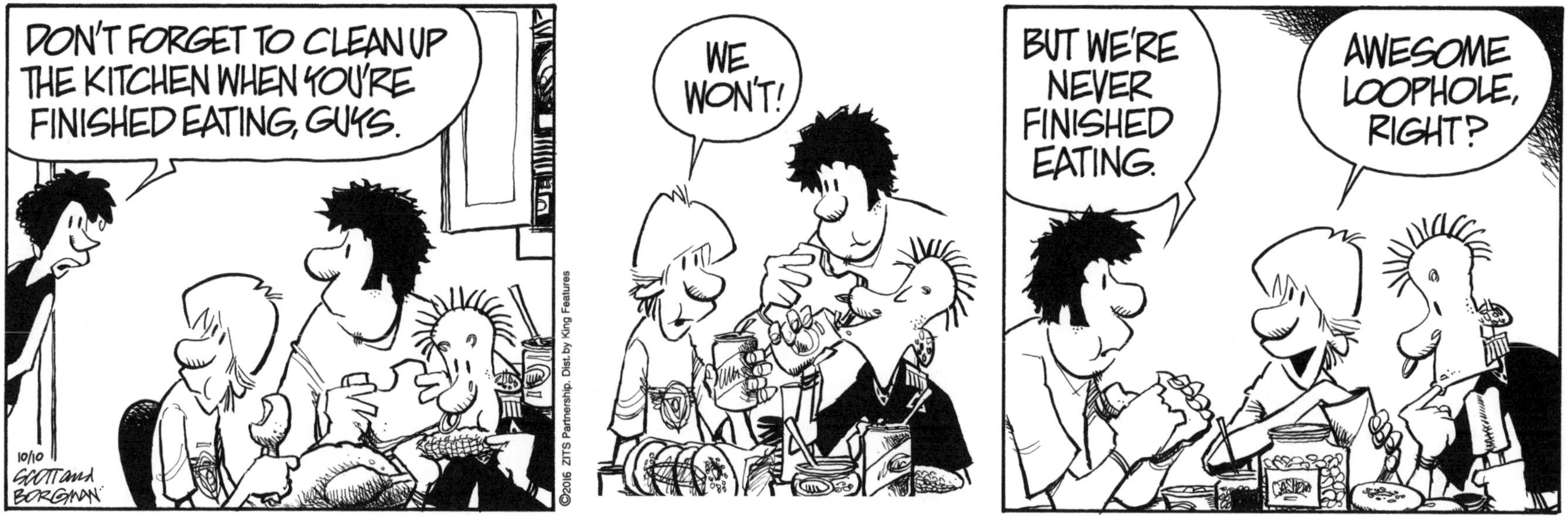
DON'T FORGET TO CLEAN UP THE KITCHEN WHEN YOU'RE FINISHED EATING, GUYS.
10/10
SCOTT and BORGMAN
WE WON'T!
©2016 ZITS Partnership. Dist. by King Features
BUT WE'RE NEVER FINISHED EATING.
AWESOME LOOPHOLE, RIGHT?

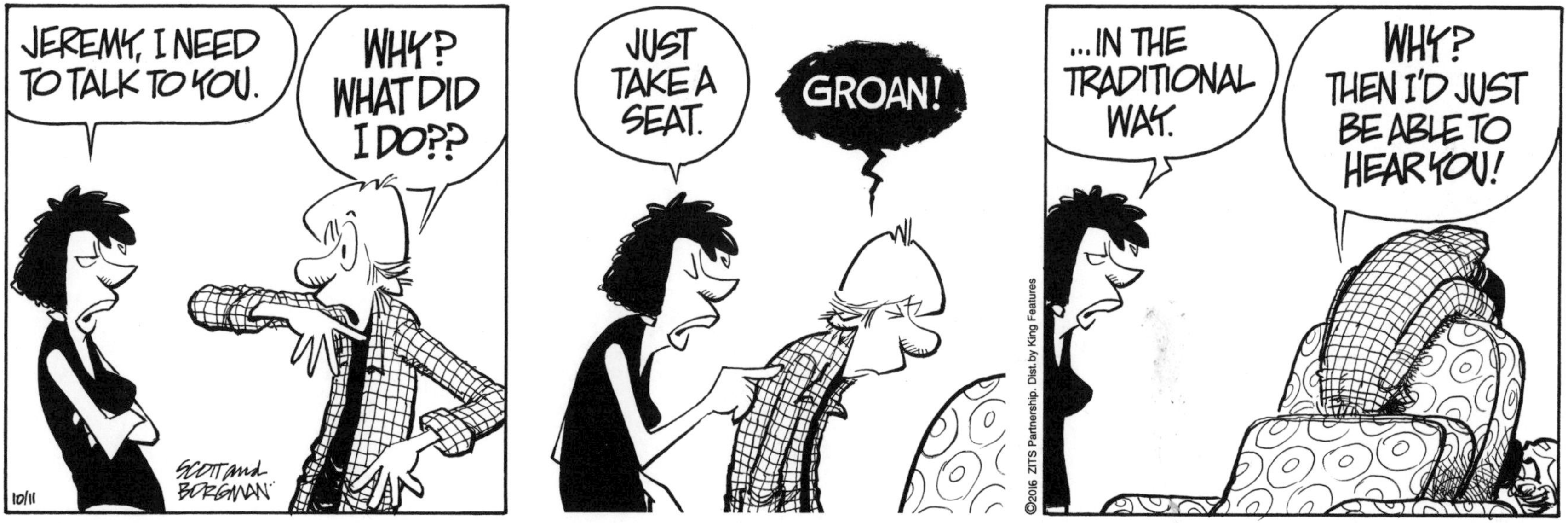
JEREMY, I NEED TO TALK TO YOU.
WHY? WHAT DID I DO??
SCOTT and BORGMAN
10/11
JUST TAKE A SEAT.
GROAN!
©2016 ZITS Partnership. Dist. by King Features
...IN THE TRADITIONAL WAY.
WHY? THEN I'D JUST BE ABLE TO HEAR YOU!

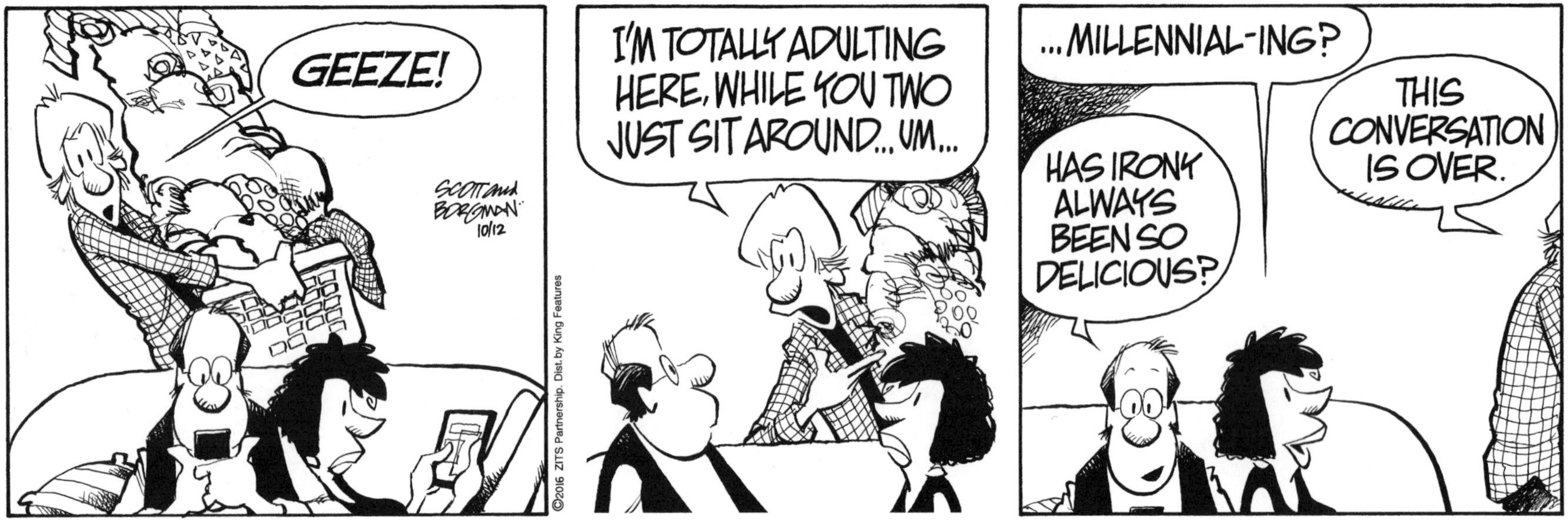
GEEZE!
SCOTT and BORGMAN 10/12
I'M TOTALLY ADULTING HERE, WHILE YOU TWO JUST SIT AROUND... UM...
©2016 ZITS Partnership. Dist. by King Features
...MILLENNIAL-ING?
HAS IRONY ALWAYS BEEN SO DELICIOUS?
THIS CONVERSATION IS OVER.

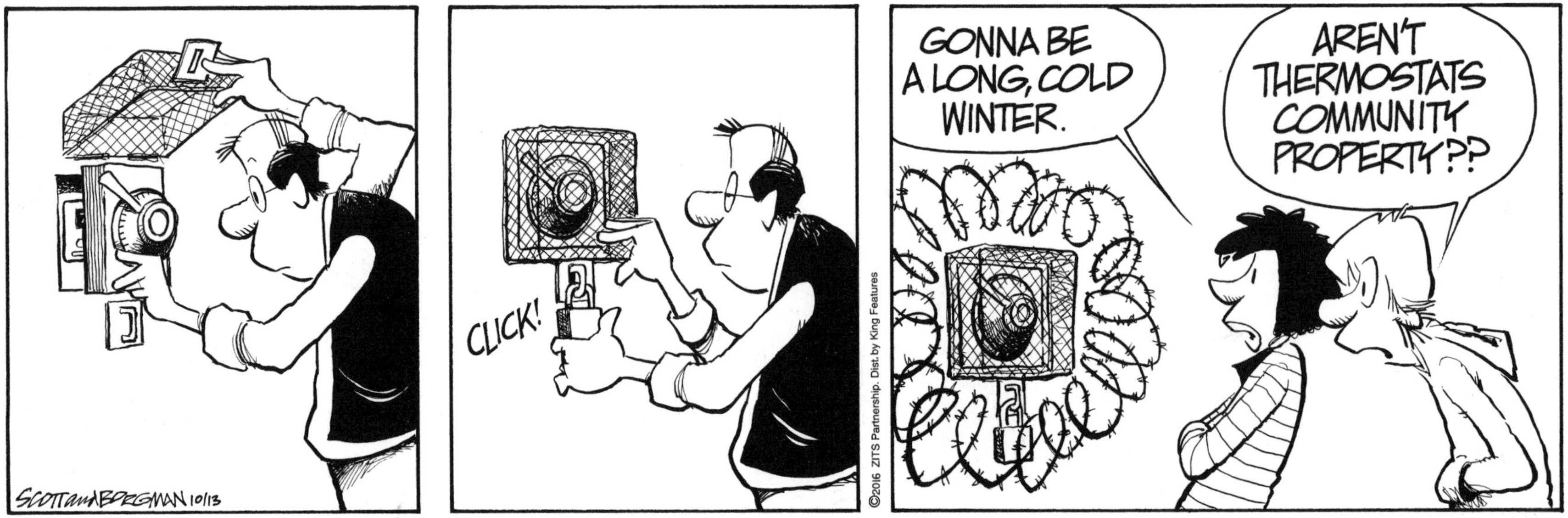
SCOTT and BORGMAN 10/13
CLICK!
©2016 ZITS Partnership. Dist. by King Features
GONNA BE A LONG, COLD WINTER.
AREN'T THERMOSTATS COMMUNITY PROPERTY??

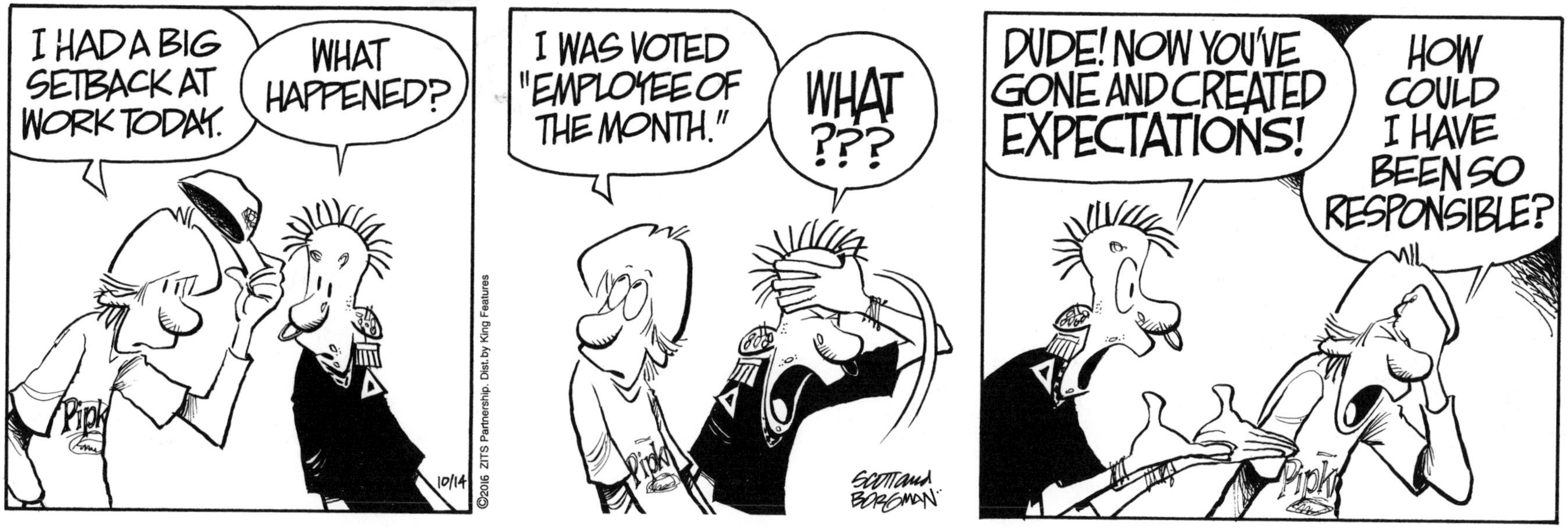
I HAD A BIG SETBACK AT WORK TODAY.
WHAT HAPPENED?
I WAS VOTED "EMPLOYEE OF THE MONTH."
WHAT ???
DUDE! NOW YOU'VE GONE AND CREATED EXPECTATIONS!
HOW COULD I HAVE BEEN SO RESPONSIBLE?
10/14
SCOTT and BORGMAN
©2016 ZITS Partnership. Dist. by King Features

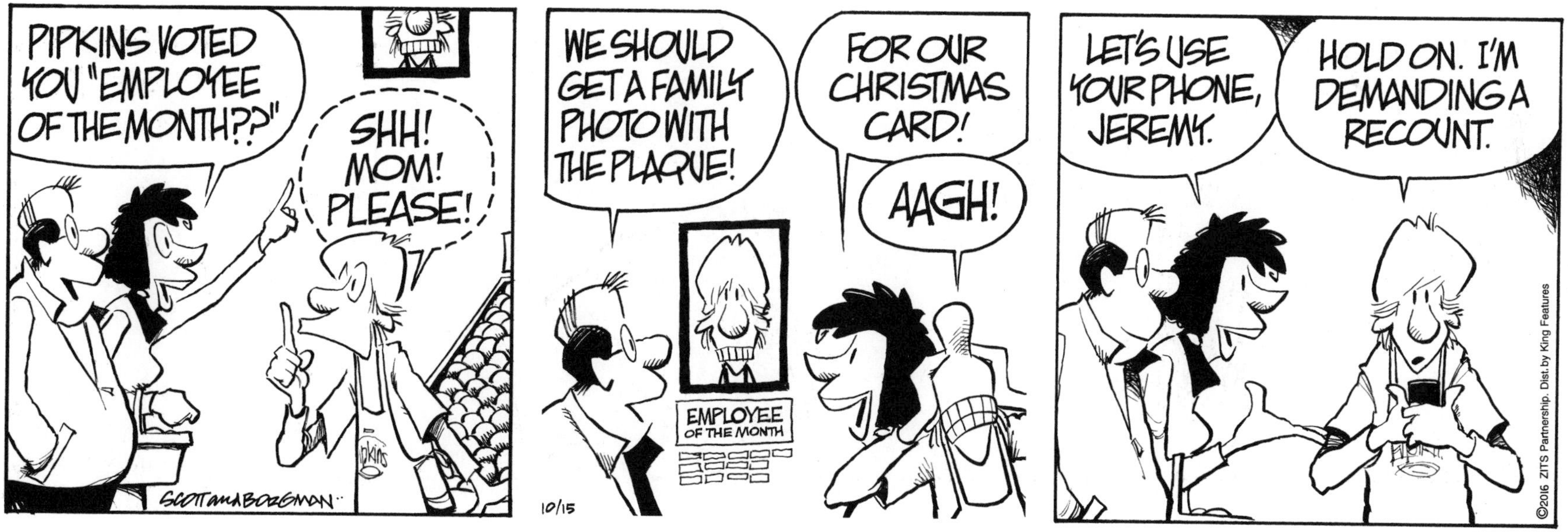
PIPKINS VOTED YOU "EMPLOYEE OF THE MONTH??"
SHH! MOM! PLEASE!
SCOTT and BORGMAN
WE SHOULD GET A FAMILY PHOTO WITH THE PLAQUE!
FOR OUR CHRISTMAS CARD!
AAGH!
EMPLOYEE OF THE MONTH
10/15
LET'S USE YOUR PHONE, JEREMY.
HOLD ON. I'M DEMANDING A RECOUNT.
©2016 ZITS Partnership. Dist. by King Features

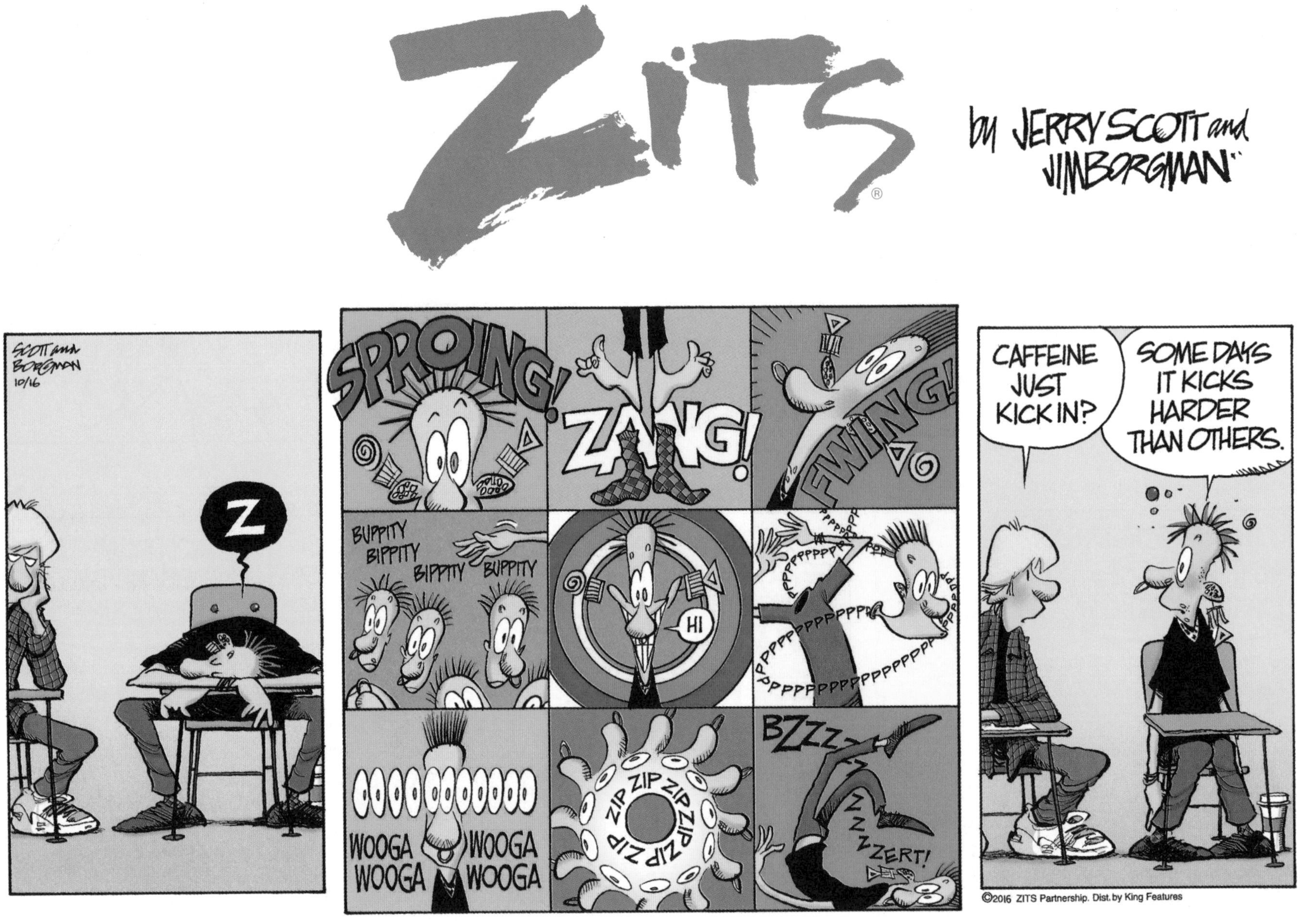
ZITS
by JERRY SCOTT and JIM BORGMAN
SCOTT and BORGMAN 10/16
Z
SPROING!
ZANG!
FWING!
BUPPITY BIPPITY BIPPITY BUPPITY
HI
WOOGA WOOGA
WOOGA WOOGA
ZIP ZIP ZIP ZIP ZIP ZIP ZIP
BZZZ
ZZZERT!
CAFFEINE JUST KICK IN?
SOME DAYS IT KICKS HARDER THAN OTHERS.
©2016 ZITS Partnership. Dist. by King Features

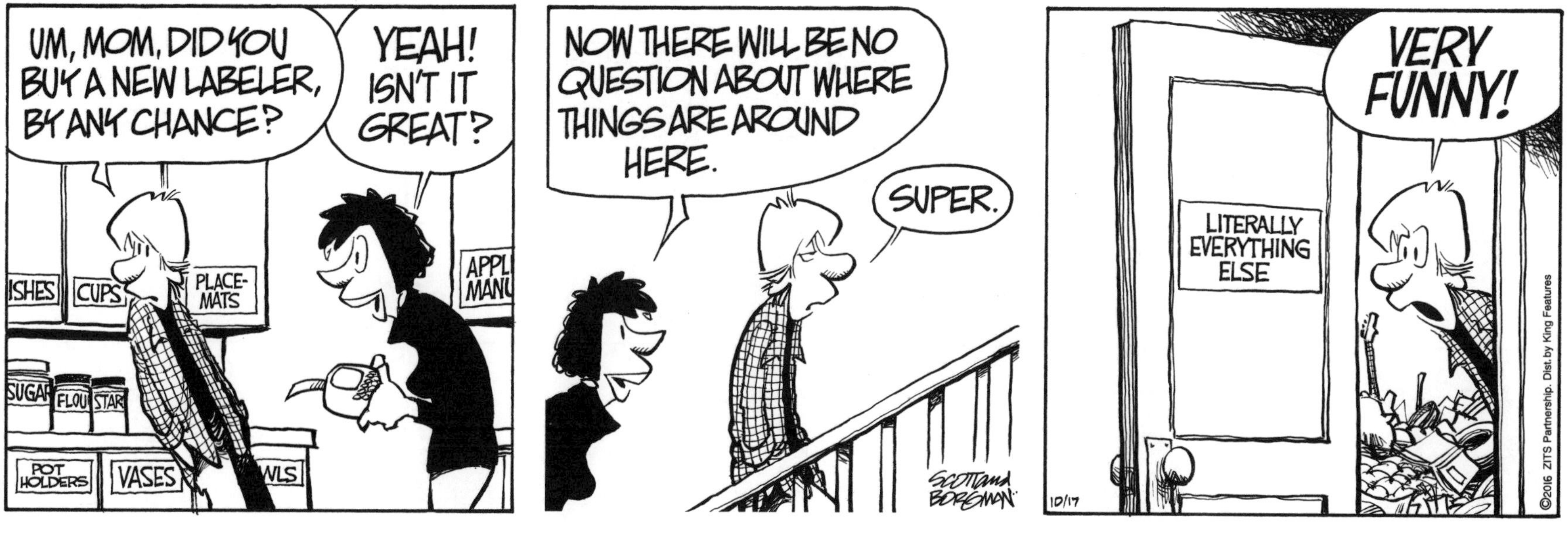
UM, MOM, DID YOU BUY A NEW LABELER, BY ANY CHANCE?
YEAH! ISN'T IT GREAT?
ISHES
CUPS
PLACE-MATS
APPL MANU
SUGAR
FLOU
STAR
POT HOLDERS
VASES
WLS
NOW THERE WILL BE NO QUESTION ABOUT WHERE THINGS ARE AROUND HERE.
SUPER.
SCOTT and BORGMAN
10/17
LITERALLY EVERYTHING ELSE
VERY FUNNY!
©2016 ZITS Partnership. Dist. by King Features

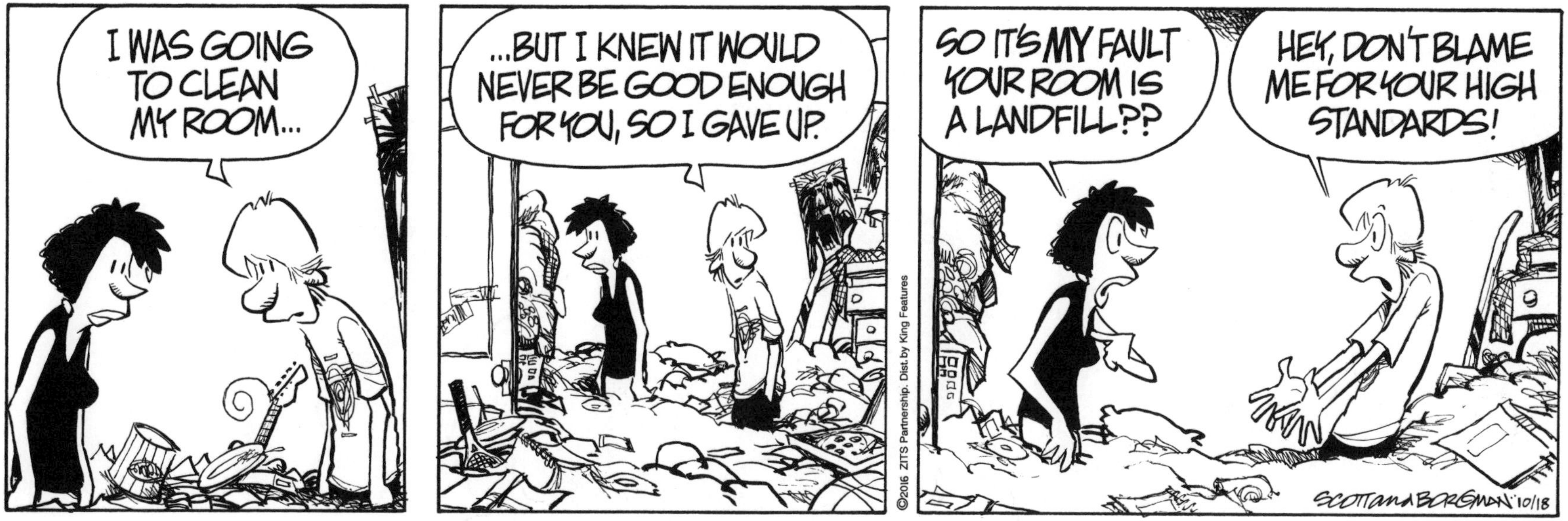
I WAS GOING TO CLEAN MY ROOM...
...BUT I KNEW IT WOULD NEVER BE GOOD ENOUGH FOR YOU, SO I GAVE UP.
©2016 ZITS Partnership. Dist. by King Features
SO IT'S MY FAULT YOUR ROOM IS A LANDFILL??
HEY, DON'T BLAME ME FOR YOUR HIGH STANDARDS!
SCOTT and BORGMAN 10/18

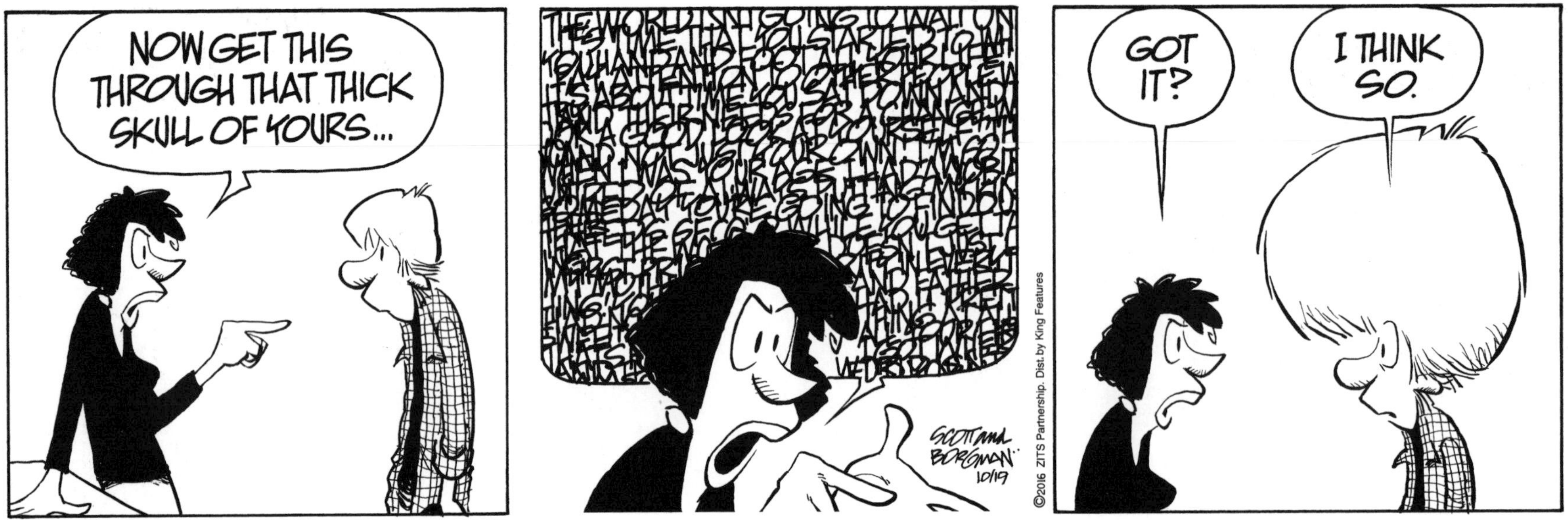
NOW GET THIS THROUGH THAT THICK SKULL OF YOURS...
SCOTT and BORGMAN 10/19
©2016 ZITS Partnership. Dist. by King Features
GOT IT?
I THINK SO.

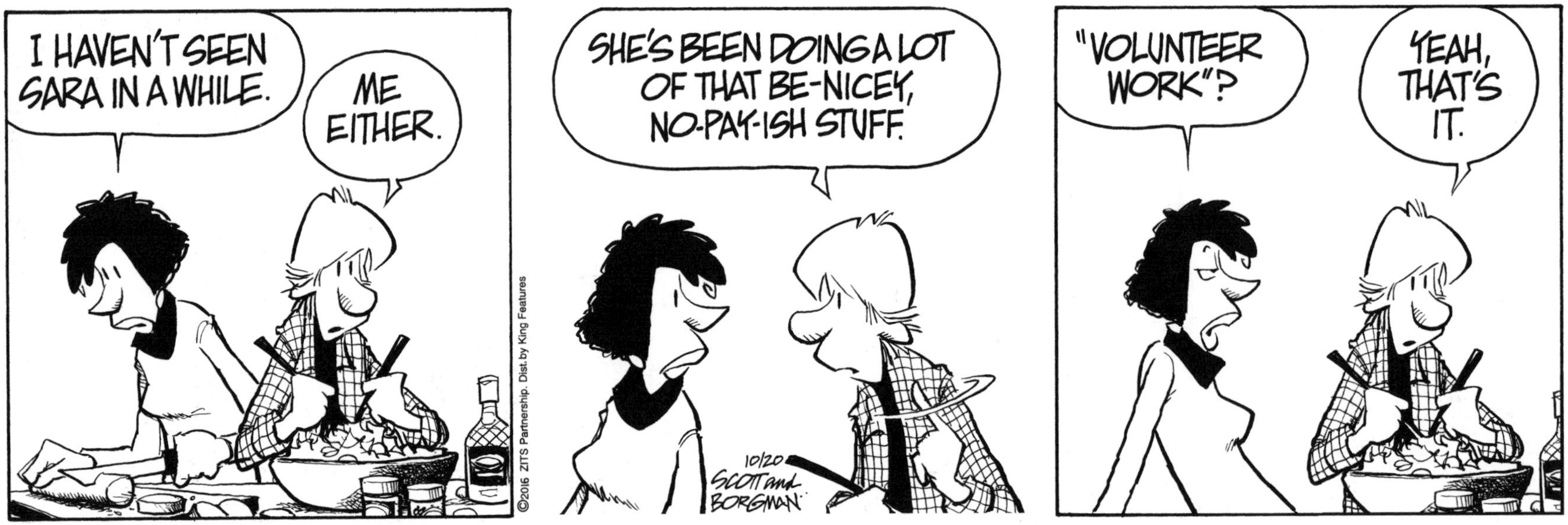
I HAVEN'T SEEN SARA IN A WHILE.
ME EITHER.
©2016 ZITS Partnership. Dist. by King Features
SHE'S BEEN DOING A LOT OF THAT BE-NICEY, NO-PAY-ISH STUFF.
10/20 SCOTT and BORGMAN
"VOLUNTEER WORK"?
YEAH, THAT'S IT.

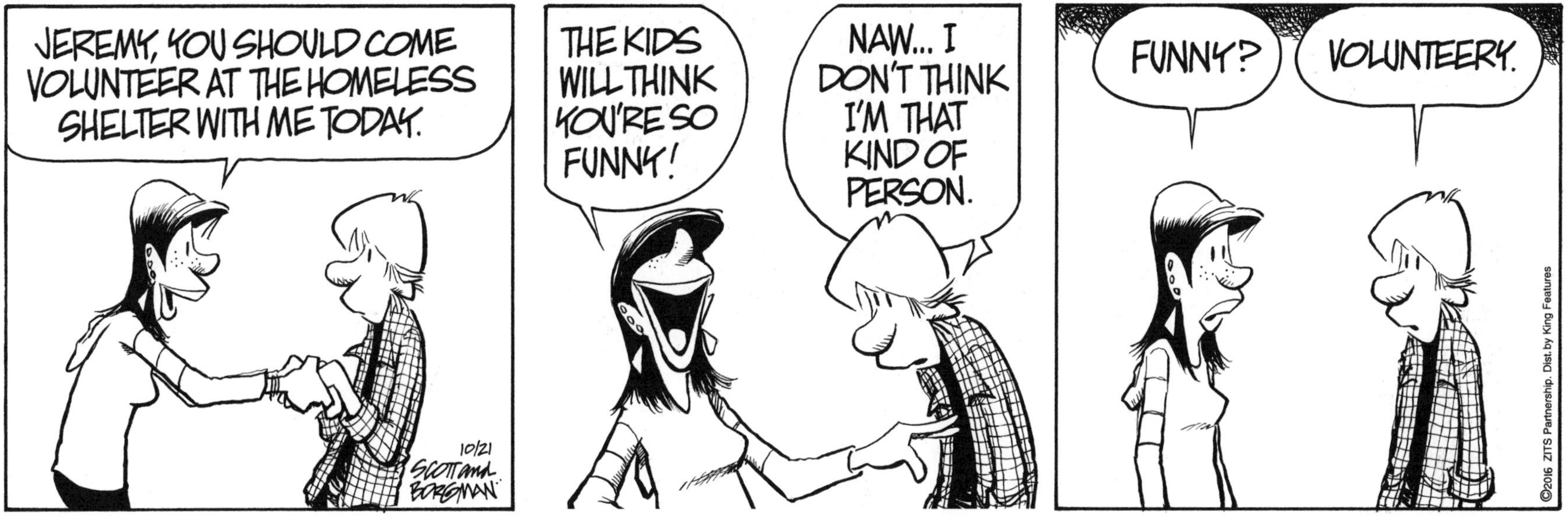
JEREMY, YOU SHOULD COME VOLUNTEER AT THE HOMELESS SHELTER WITH ME TODAY.
10/21
SCOTT and BORGMAN
THE KIDS WILL THINK YOU'RE SO FUNNY!
NAW... I DON'T THINK I'M THAT KIND OF PERSON.
FUNNY?
VOLUNTEERY.
©2016 ZITS Partnership. Dist. by King Features

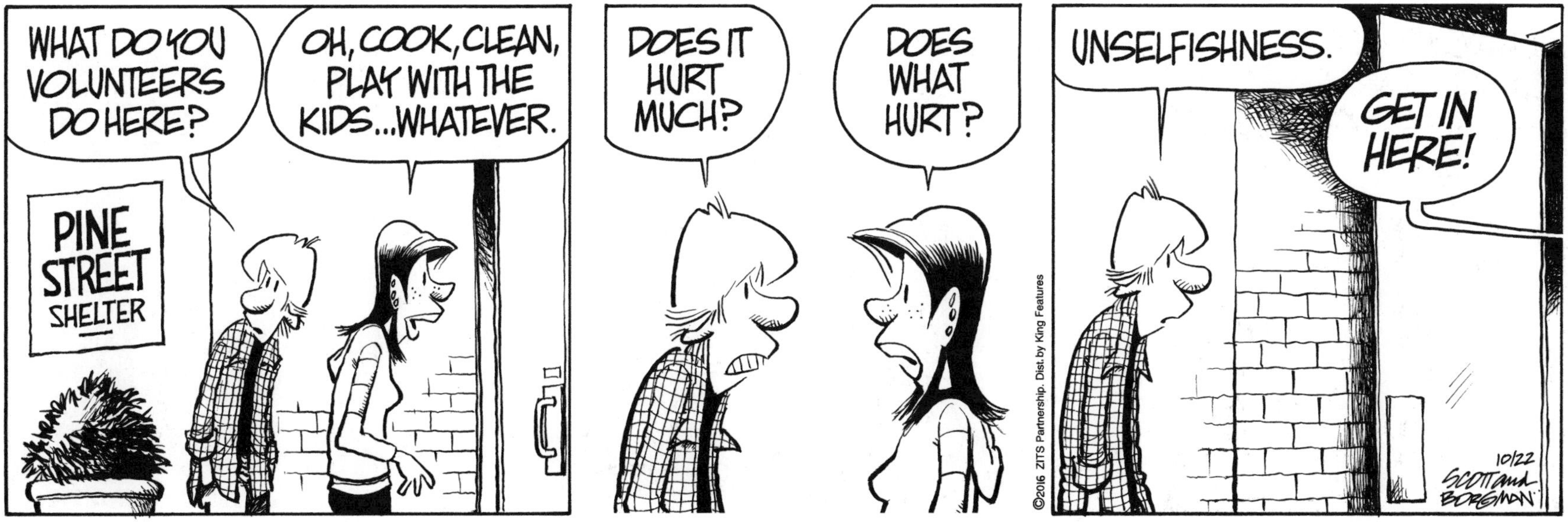
WHAT DO YOU VOLUNTEERS DO HERE?
OH, COOK, CLEAN, PLAY WITH THE KIDS...WHATEVER.
PINE STREET SHELTER
DOES IT HURT MUCH?
DOES WHAT HURT?
©2016 ZITS Partnership. Dist. by King Features
UNSELFISHNESS.
GET IN HERE!
10/22
SCOTT and BORGMAN

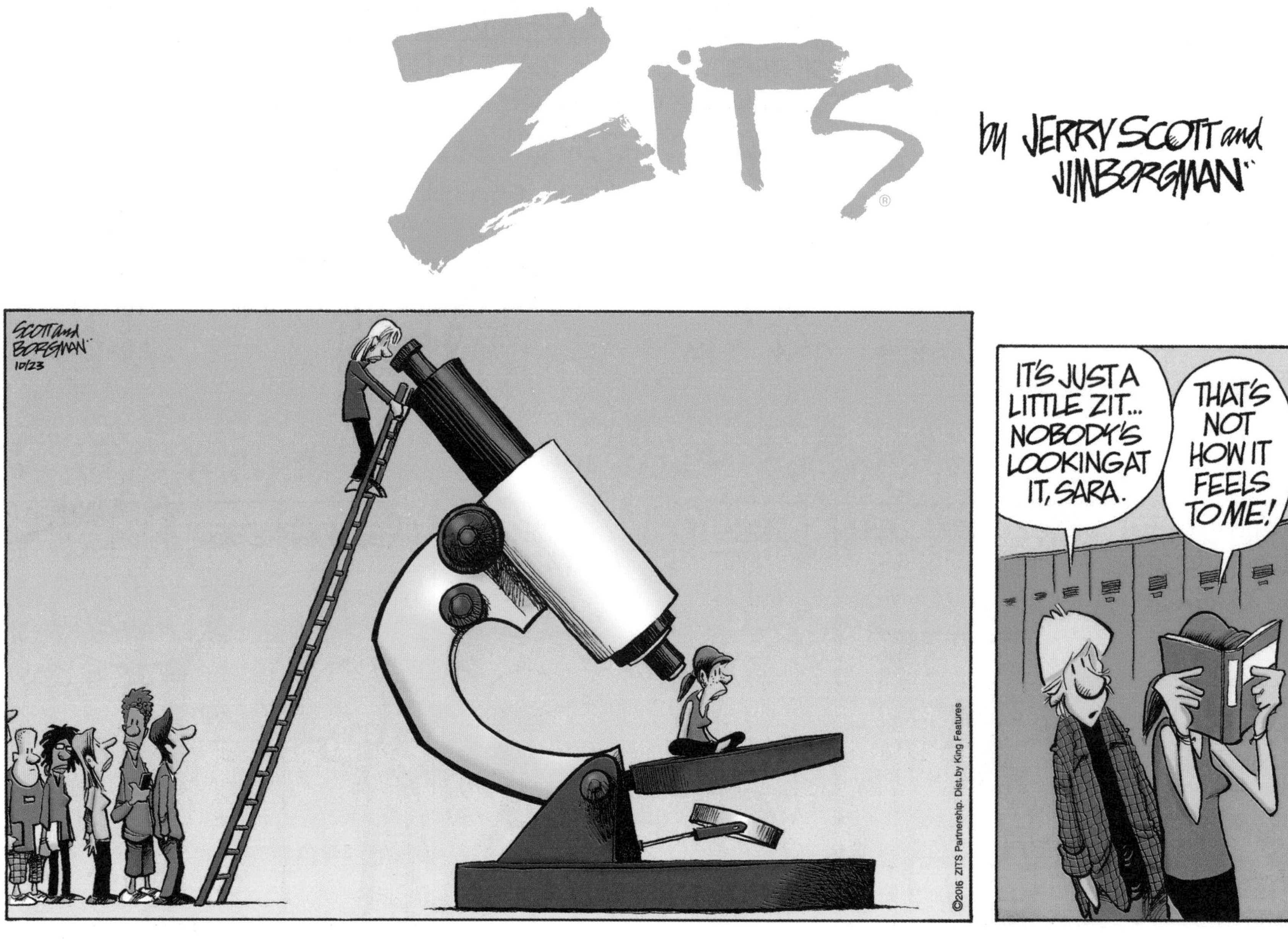
ZITS
by JERRY SCOTT and JIM BORGMAN
SCOTT and BORGMAN 10/23
©2016 ZITS Partnership. Dist.by King Features
IT'S JUST A LITTLE ZIT... NOBODY'S LOOKING AT IT, SARA.
THAT'S NOT HOW IT FEELS TO ME!

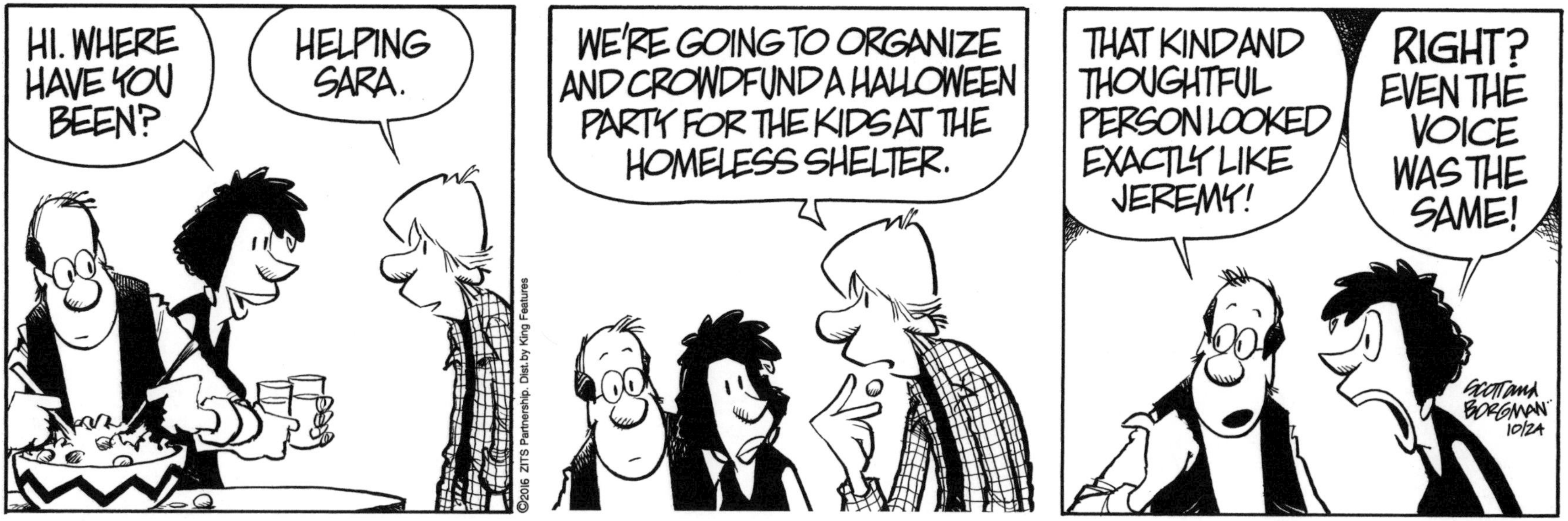
HI. WHERE HAVE YOU BEEN?
HELPING SARA.
©2016 ZITS Partnership. Dist. by King Features
WE'RE GOING TO ORGANIZE AND CROWDFUND A HALLOWEEN PARTY FOR THE KIDS AT THE HOMELESS SHELTER.
THAT KIND AND THOUGHTFUL PERSON LOOKED EXACTLY LIKE JEREMY!
RIGHT? EVEN THE VOICE WAS THE SAME!
SCOTT and BORGMAN 10/24

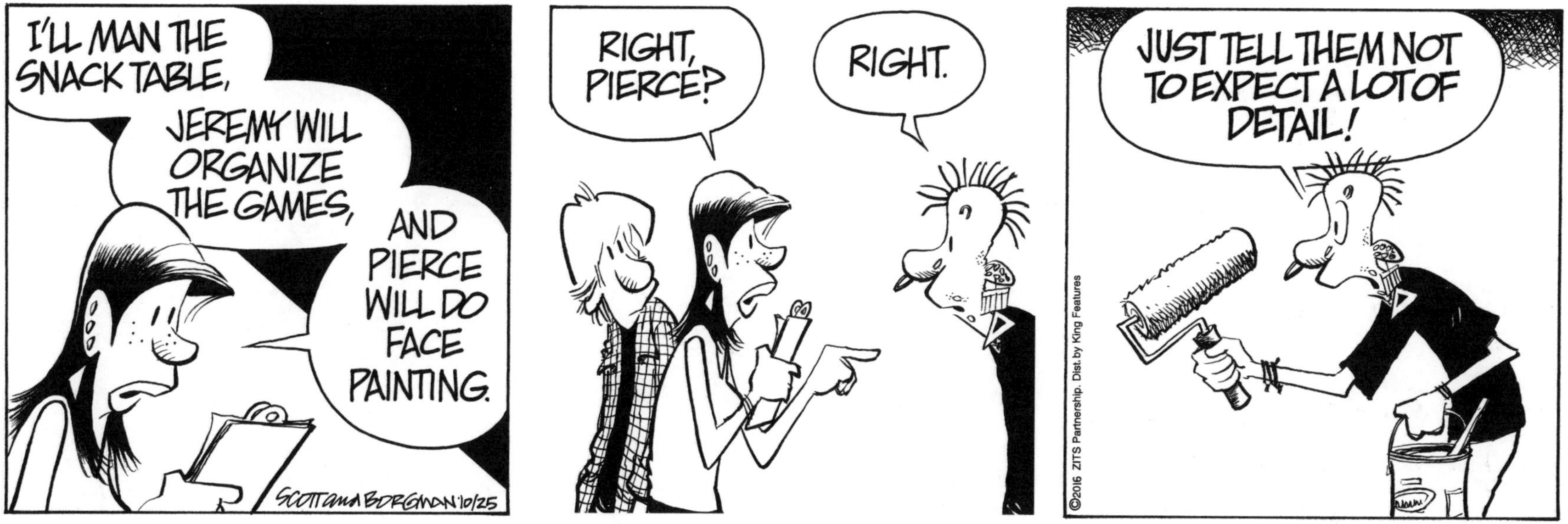
I'LL MAN THE SNACK TABLE,
JEREMY WILL ORGANIZE THE GAMES,
AND PIERCE WILL DO FACE PAINTING.
SCOTT and BORGMAN 10/25
RIGHT, PIERCE?
RIGHT.
©2016 ZITS Partnership. Dist. by King Features
JUST TELL THEM NOT TO EXPECT A LOT OF DETAIL!

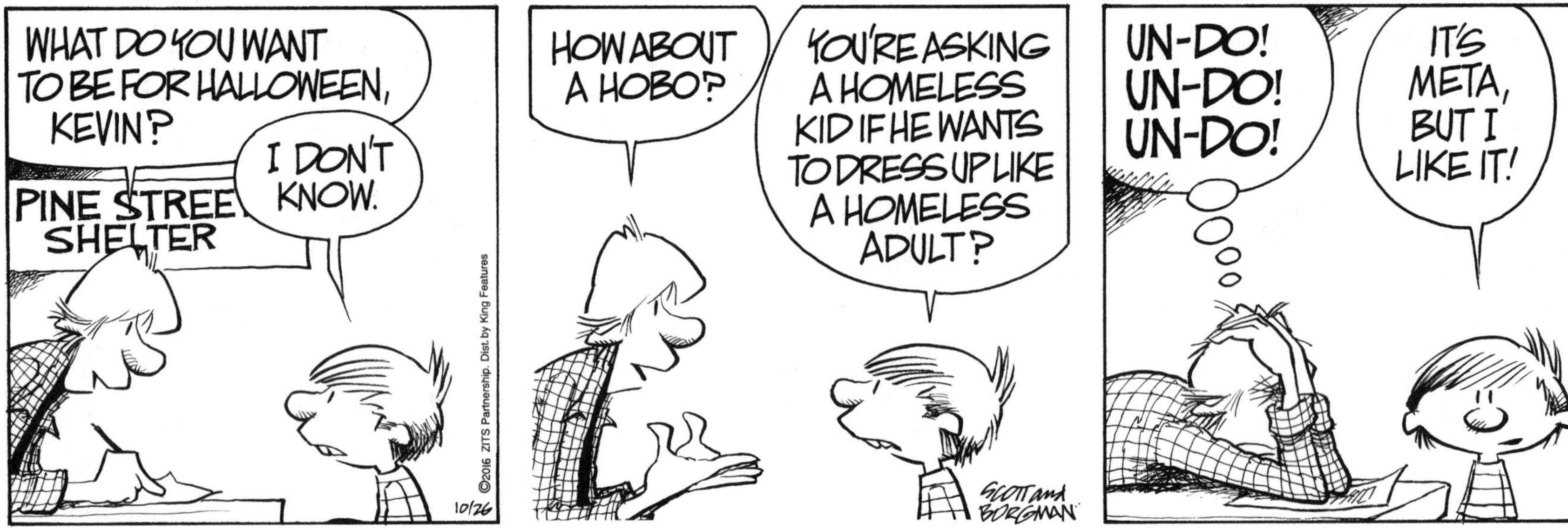
WHAT DO YOU WANT TO BE FOR HALLOWEEN, KEVIN?
PINE STREE SHELTER
I DON'T KNOW.
©2016 ZITS Partnership. Dist. by King Features
10/26
HOW ABOUT A HOBO?
YOU'RE ASKING A HOMELESS KID IF HE WANTS TO DRESS UP LIKE A HOMELESS ADULT?
SCOTT AND BORGMAN
UN-DO! UN-DO! UN-DO!
IT'S META, BUT I LIKE IT!

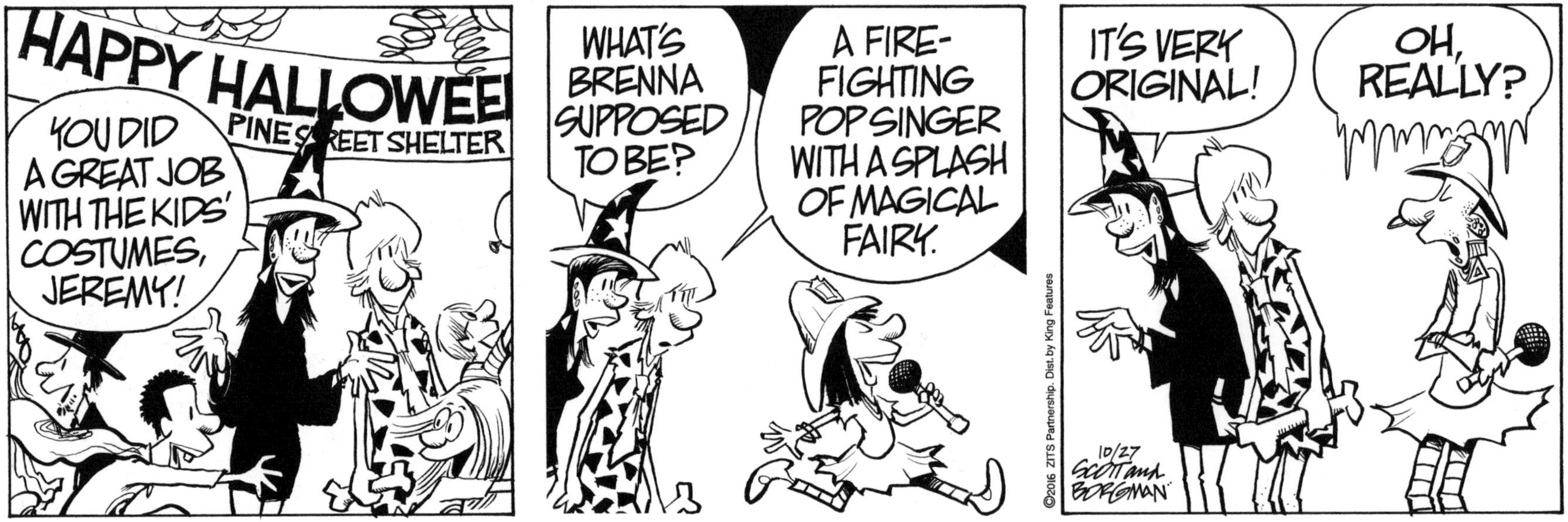
HAPPY HALLOWEE
PINE S REET SHELTER
YOU DID A GREAT JOB WITH THE KIDS' COSTUMES, JEREMY!
WHAT'S BRENNA SUPPOSED TO BE?
A FIRE-FIGHTING POP SINGER WITH A SPLASH OF MAGICAL FAIRY.
©2016 ZITS Partnership. Dist. by King Features
10/27
SCOTT AND BORGMAN
IT'S VERY ORIGINAL!
OH, REALLY?

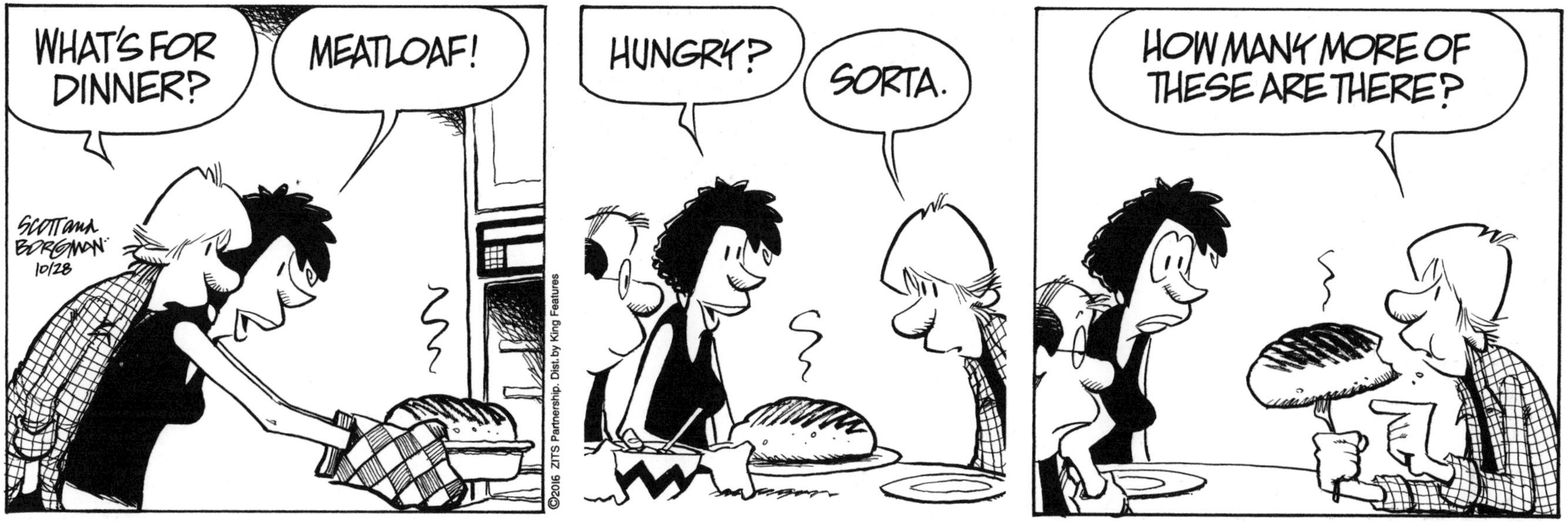
WHAT'S FOR DINNER?
MEATLOAF!
SCOTT and BORGMAN 10/28
©2016 ZITS Partnership. Dist. by King Features
HUNGRY?
SORTA.
HOW MANY MORE OF THESE ARE THERE?

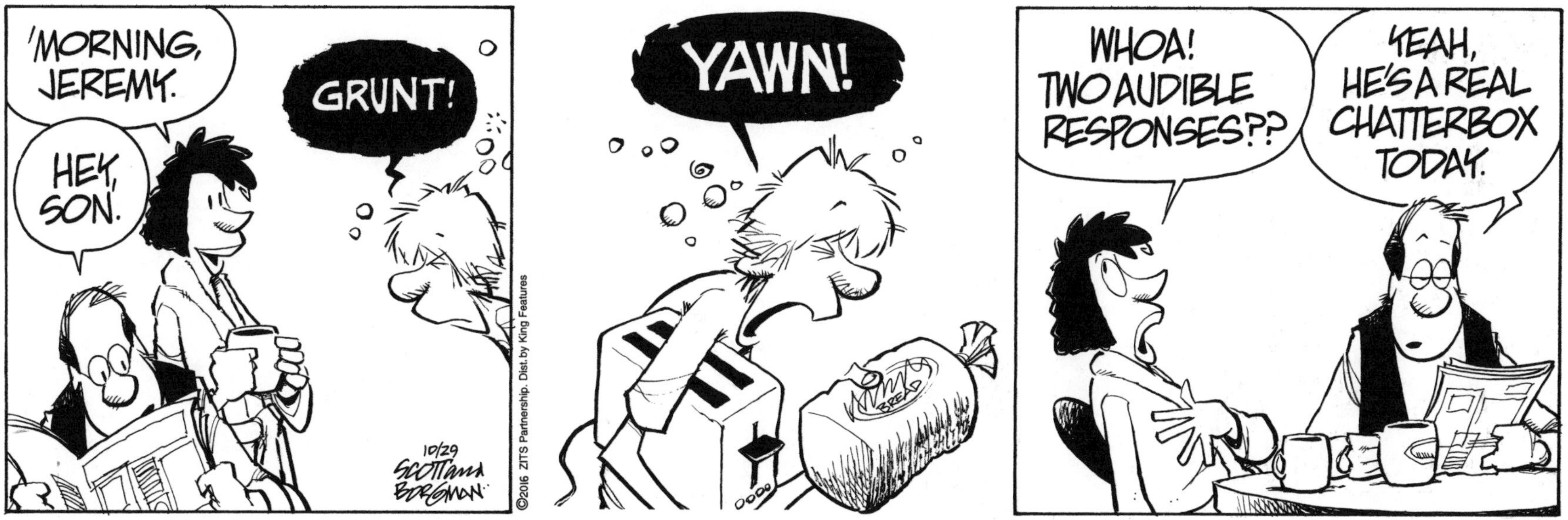
'MORNING, JEREMY.
HEY, SON.
GRUNT!
10/29 SCOTT and BORGMAN
©2016 ZITS Partnership. Dist. by King Features
YAWN!
WHOA! TWO AUDIBLE RESPONSES??
YEAH, HE'S A REAL CHATTERBOX TODAY.

ZITS®

by JERRY SCOTT and JIM BORGMAN

Z
Z
SCOTT and BORGMAN 10/30
OUR SCHOOL DAY REALLY NEEDS TO START LATER.
Y'THINK?
©2016 ZITS Partnership. Dist. by King Features

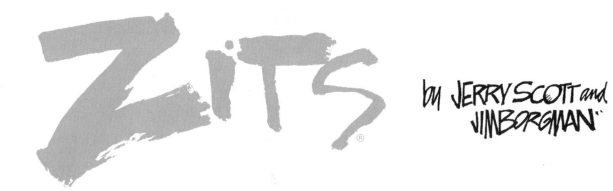

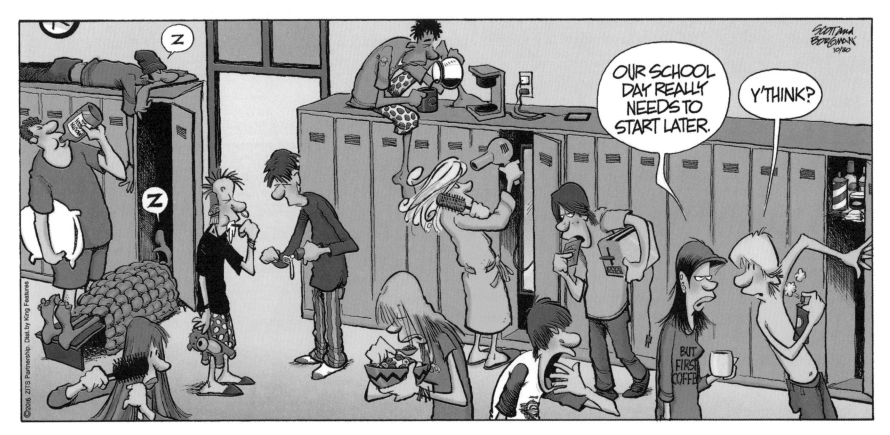

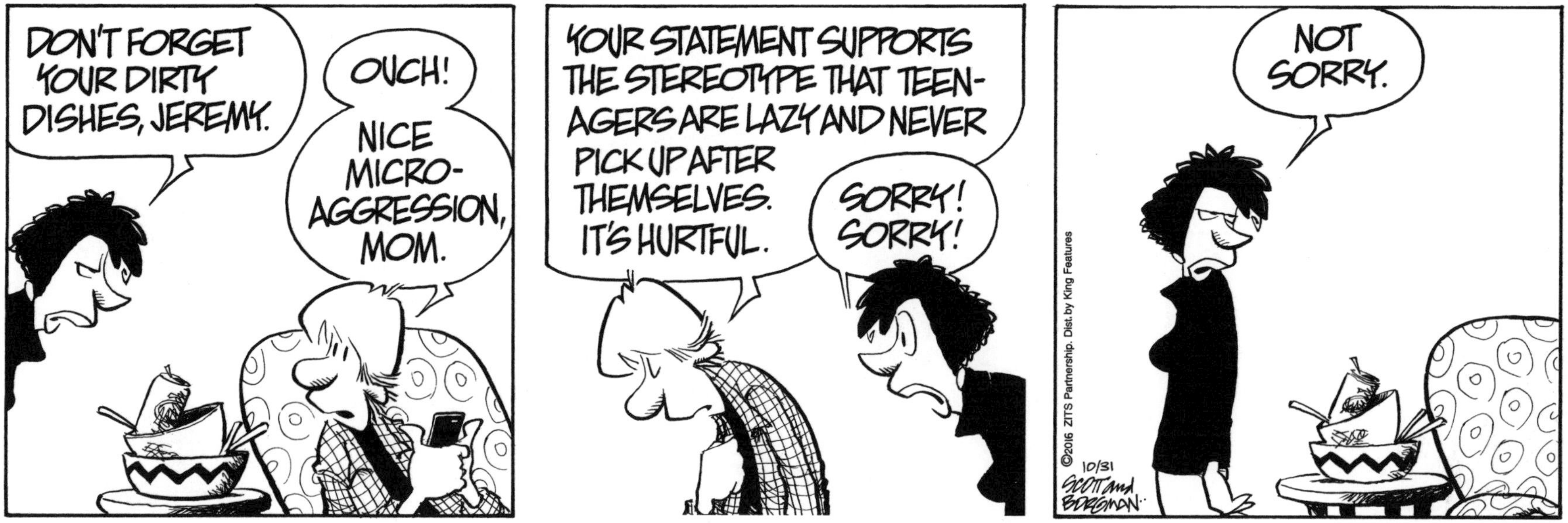
DON'T FORGET YOUR DIRTY DISHES, JEREMY.
OUCH!
NICE MICRO-AGGRESSION, MOM.
YOUR STATEMENT SUPPORTS THE STEREOTYPE THAT TEEN-AGERS ARE LAZY AND NEVER PICK UP AFTER THEMSELVES. IT'S HURTFUL.
SORRY! SORRY!
NOT SORRY.
©2016 ZITS Partnership. Dist. by King Features
10/31 SCOTT and BORGMAN

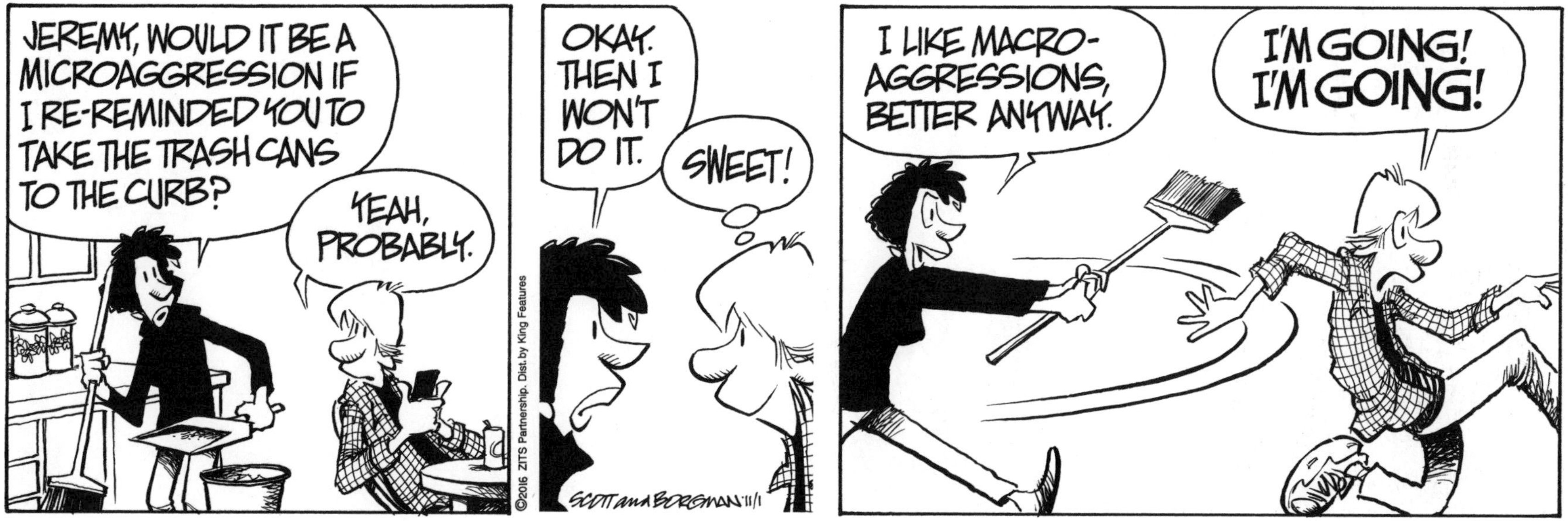
JEREMY, WOULD IT BE A MICROAGGRESSION IF I RE-REMINDED YOU TO TAKE THE TRASH CANS TO THE CURB?
YEAH, PROBABLY.
©2016 ZITS Partnership. Dist. by King Features
OKAY. THEN I WON'T DO IT.
SWEET!
SCOTT and BORGMAN 11/1
I LIKE MACRO-AGGRESSIONS, BETTER ANYWAY.
I'M GOING! I'M GOING!

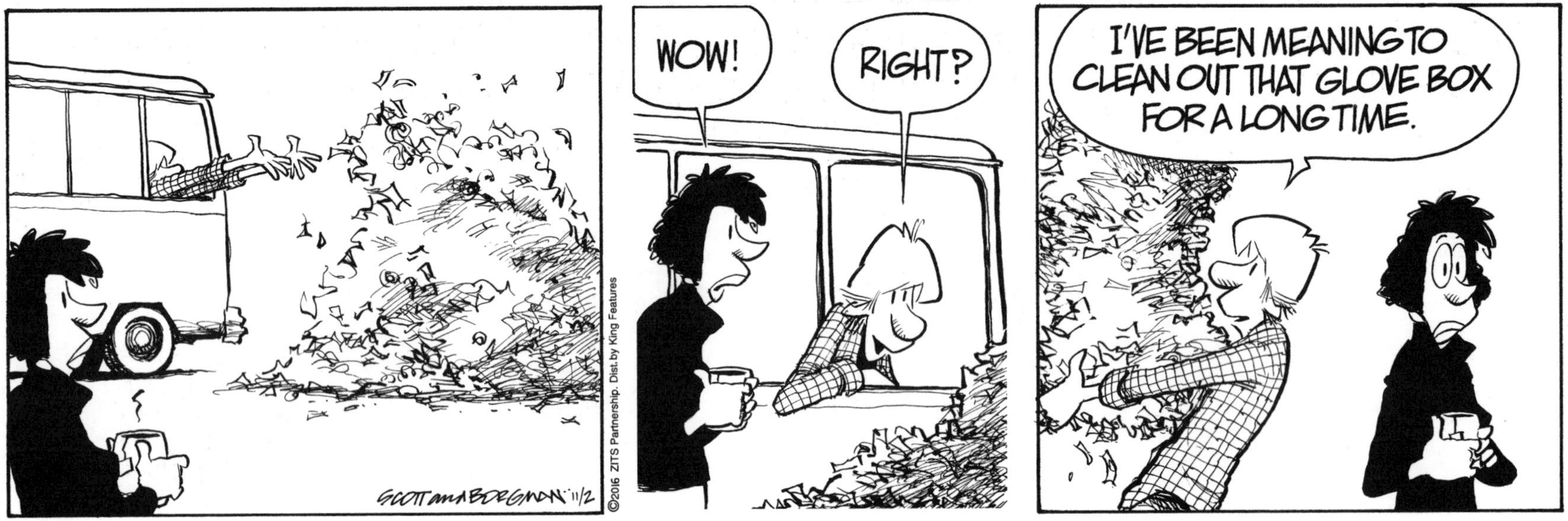
SCOTT and BORGMAN 11/2
©2016 ZITS Partnership. Dist. by King Features
WOW!
RIGHT?
I'VE BEEN MEANING TO CLEAN OUT THAT GLOVE BOX FOR A LONG TIME.

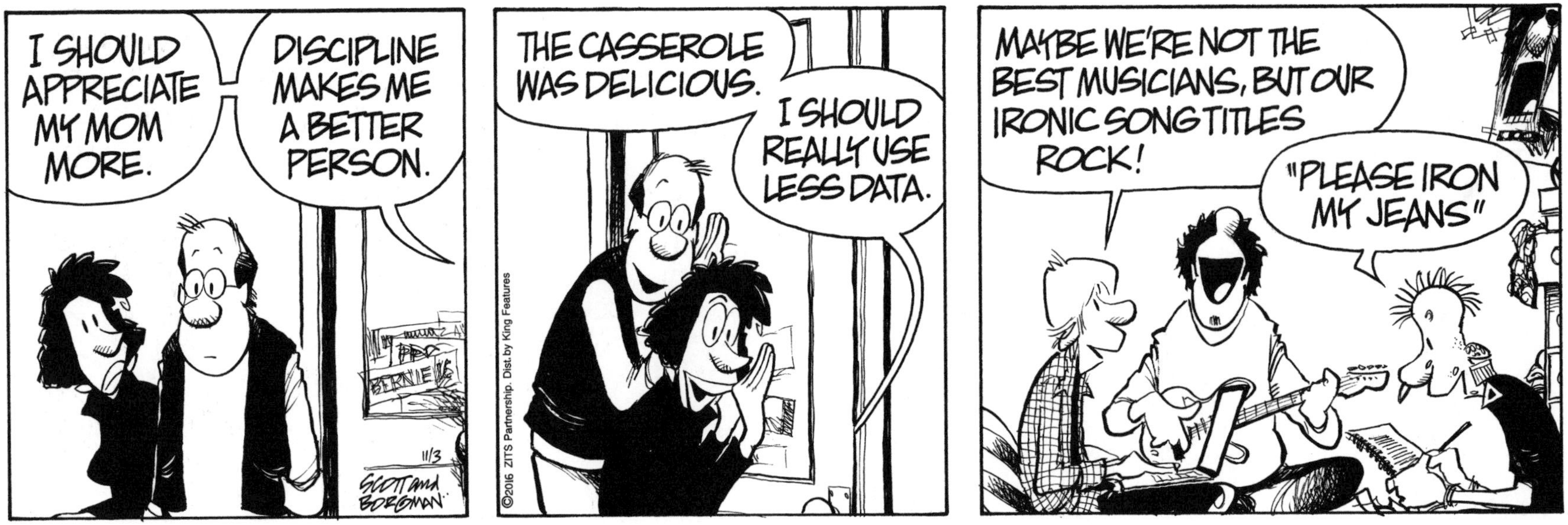
I SHOULD APPRECIATE MY MOM MORE.
DISCIPLINE MAKES ME A BETTER PERSON.
11/3
SCOTT and BORGMAN
©2016 ZITS Partnership. Dist. by King Features
THE CASSEROLE WAS DELICIOUS.
I SHOULD REALLY USE LESS DATA.
MAYBE WE'RE NOT THE BEST MUSICIANS, BUT OUR IRONIC SONG TITLES ROCK!
"PLEASE IRON MY JEANS"

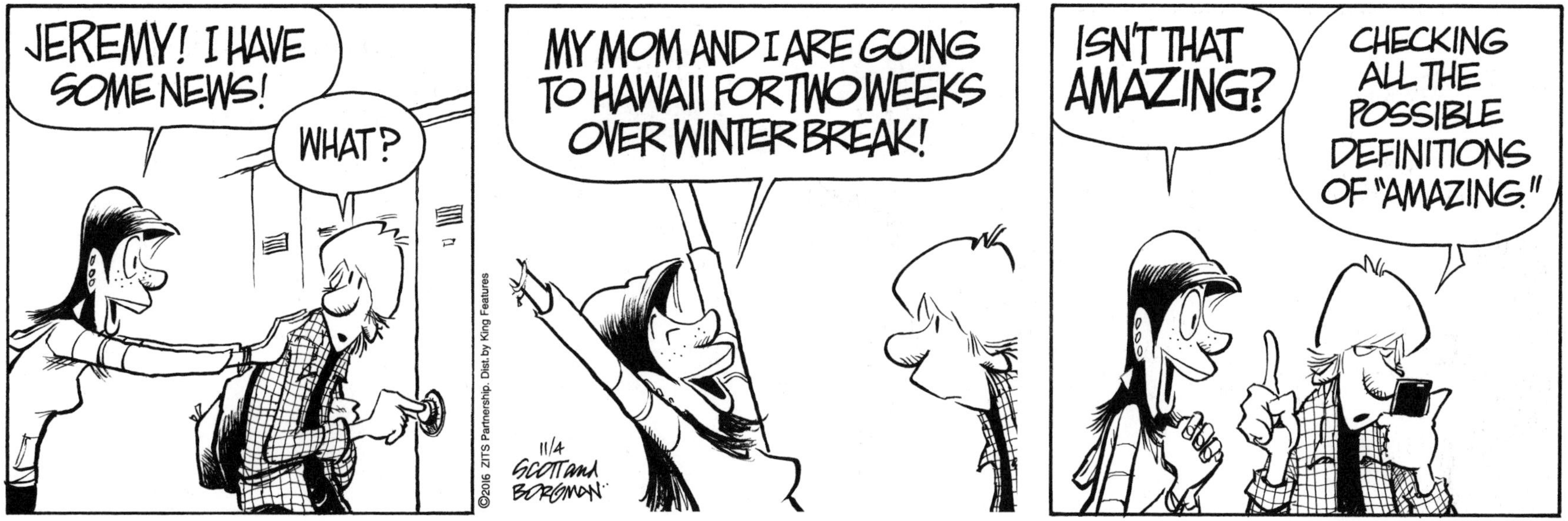
JEREMY! I HAVE SOME NEWS!
WHAT?
©2016 ZITS Partnership. Dist. by King Features
MY MOM AND I ARE GOING TO HAWAII FOR TWO WEEKS OVER WINTER BREAK!
11/4
SCOTT and BORGMAN
ISN'T THAT AMAZING?
CHECKING ALL THE POSSIBLE DEFINITIONS OF "AMAZING."

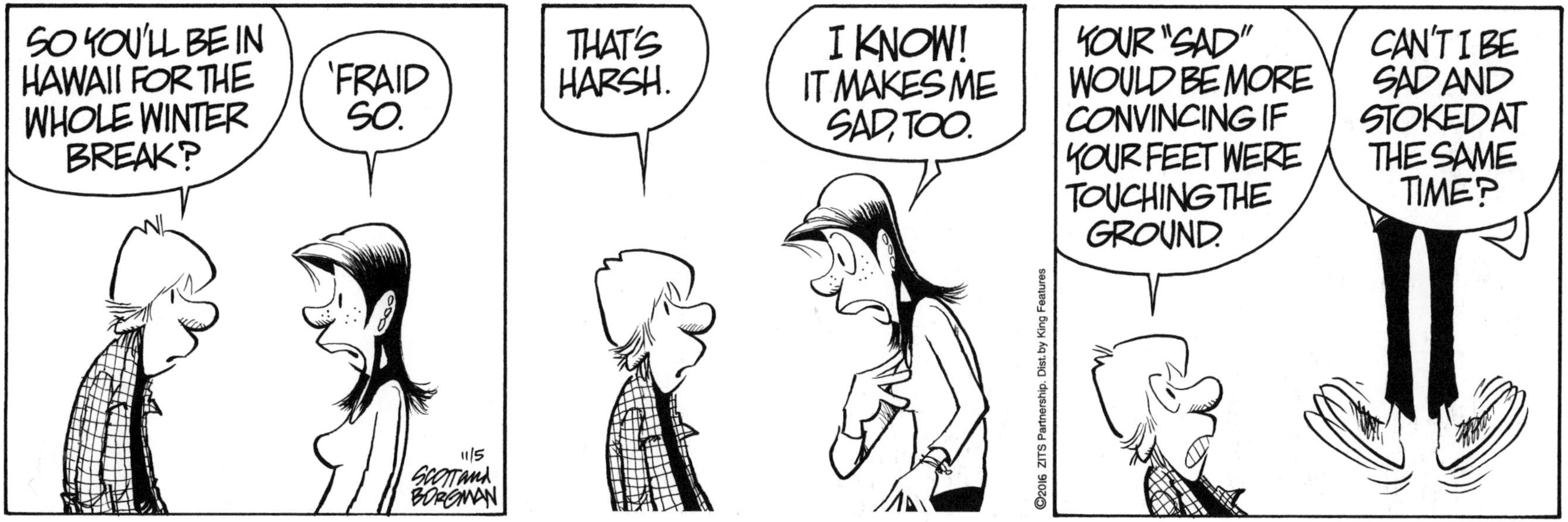
SO YOU'LL BE IN HAWAII FOR THE WHOLE WINTER BREAK?
'FRAID SO.
11/5
SCOTT and BORGMAN
THAT'S HARSH.
I KNOW! IT MAKES ME SAD, TOO.
©2016 ZITS Partnership. Dist. by King Features
YOUR "SAD" WOULD BE MORE CONVINCING IF YOUR FEET WERE TOUCHING THE GROUND.
CAN'T I BE SAD AND STOKED AT THE SAME TIME?

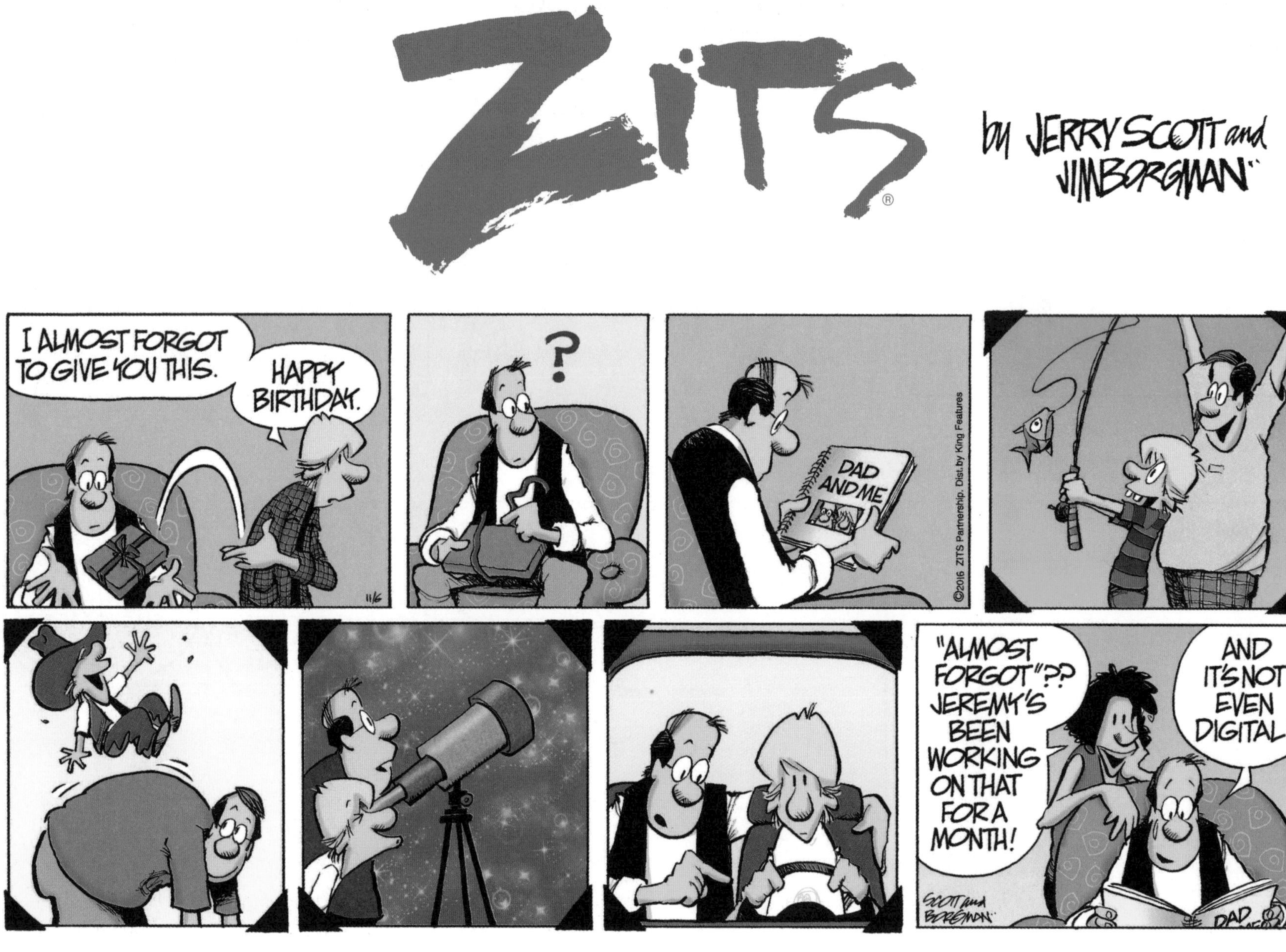
ZITS®
by JERRY SCOTT and JIM BORGMAN
I ALMOST FORGOT TO GIVE YOU THIS.
HAPPY BIRTHDAY.
11/6
?
DAD AND ME
©2016 ZITS Partnership. Dist. by King Features
"ALMOST FORGOT"?? JEREMY'S BEEN WORKING ON THAT FOR A MONTH!
AND IT'S NOT EVEN DIGITAL!
SCOTT and BORGMAN
DAD

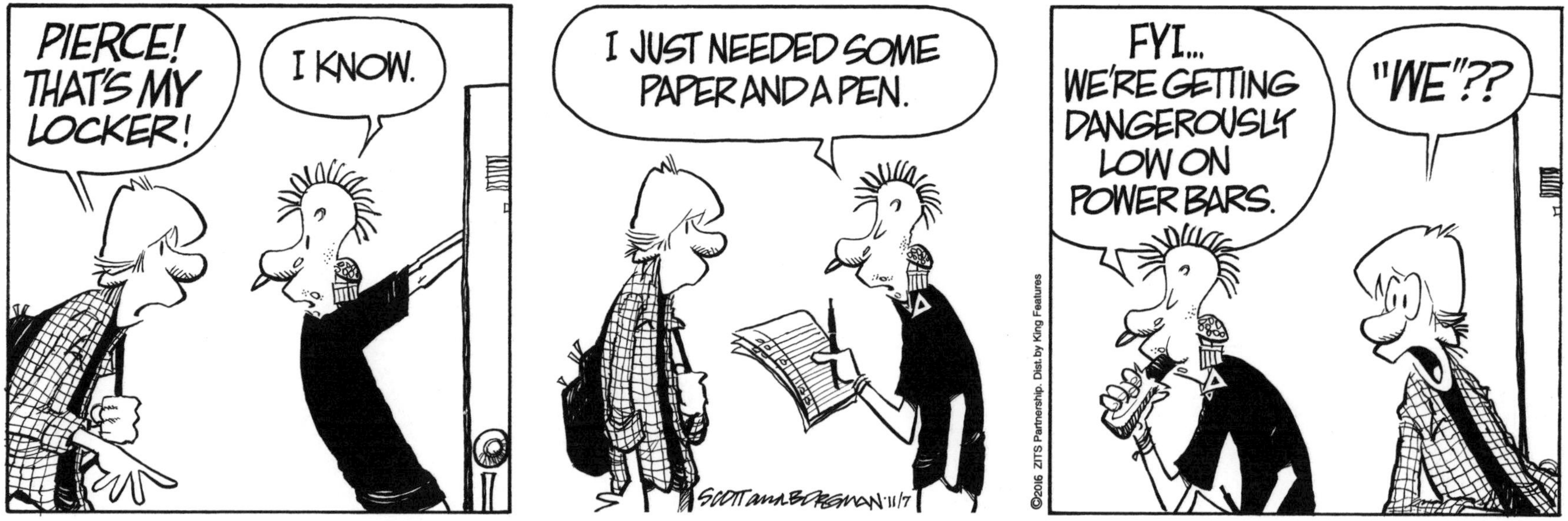
PIERCE! THAT'S MY LOCKER!
I KNOW.
I JUST NEEDED SOME PAPER AND A PEN.
SCOTT and BORGMAN 11/7
FYI... WE'RE GETTING DANGEROUSLY LOW ON POWER BARS.
"WE"??
©2016 ZITS Partnership. Dist. by King Features

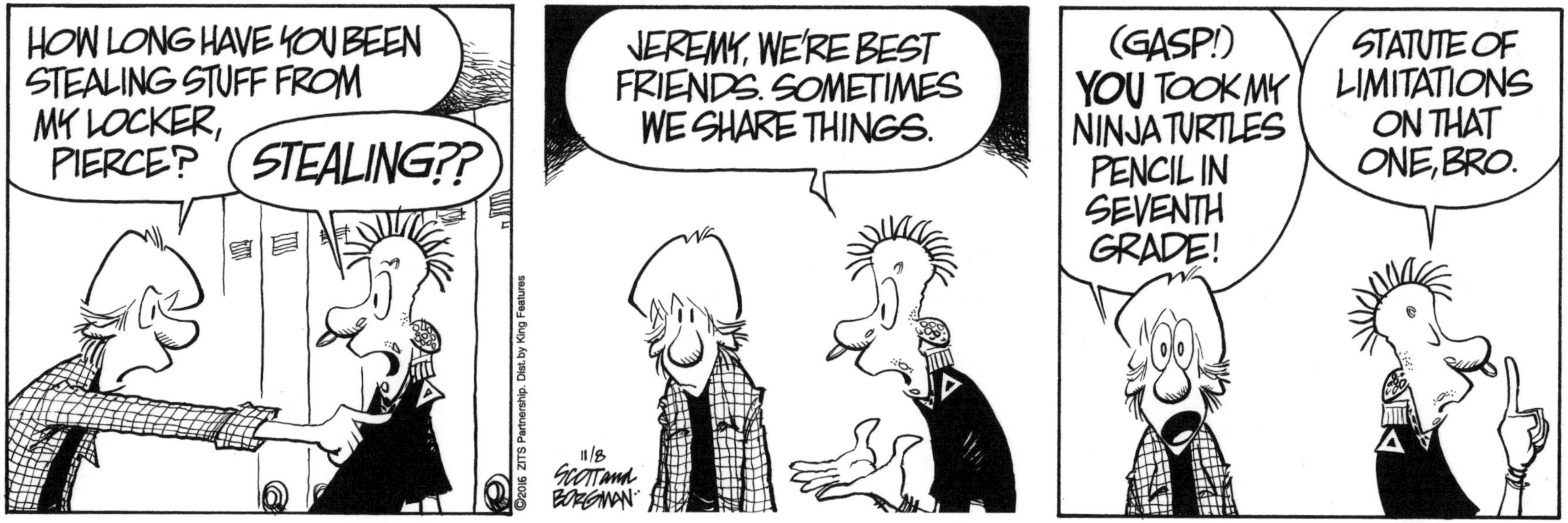
HOW LONG HAVE YOU BEEN STEALING STUFF FROM MY LOCKER, PIERCE?
STEALING??
©2016 ZITS Partnership. Dist. by King Features
JEREMY, WE'RE BEST FRIENDS. SOMETIMES WE SHARE THINGS.
11/8 SCOTT and BORGMAN
(GASP!) YOU TOOK MY NINJA TURTLES PENCIL IN SEVENTH GRADE!
STATUTE OF LIMITATIONS ON THAT ONE, BRO.

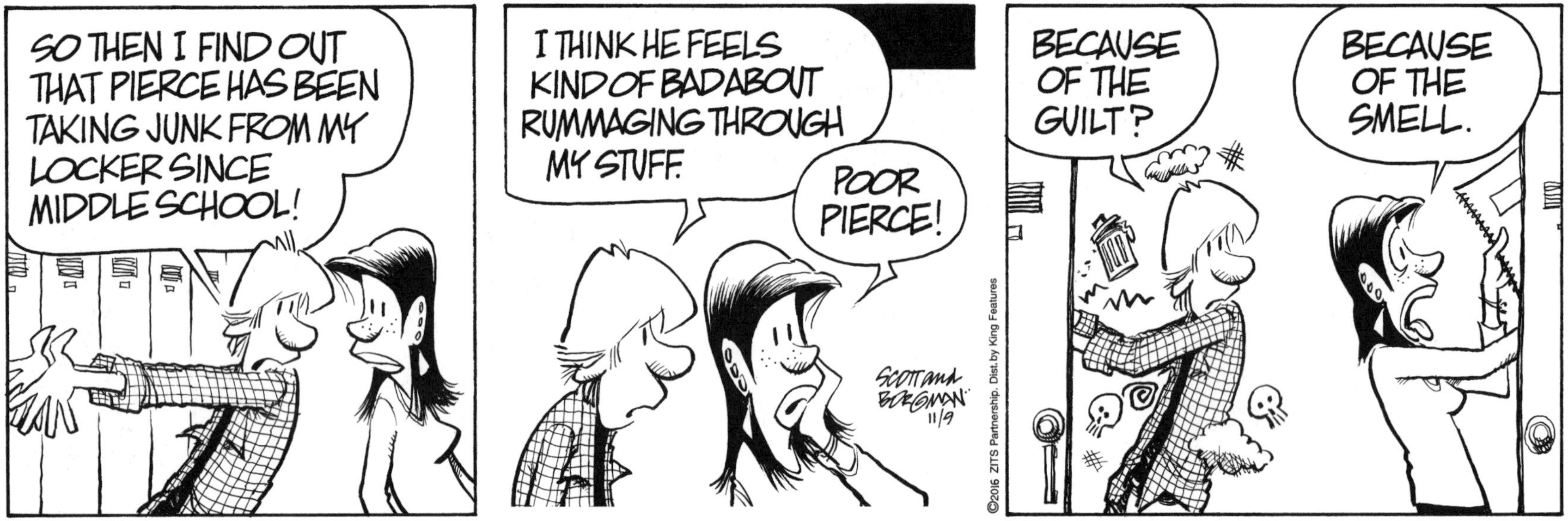
SO THEN I FIND OUT THAT PIERCE HAS BEEN TAKING JUNK FROM MY LOCKER SINCE MIDDLE SCHOOL!
I THINK HE FEELS KIND OF BAD ABOUT RUMMAGING THROUGH MY STUFF.
POOR PIERCE!
SCOTT and BORGMAN 11/9
BECAUSE OF THE GUILT?
BECAUSE OF THE SMELL.
©2016 ZITS Partnership. Dist. by King Features

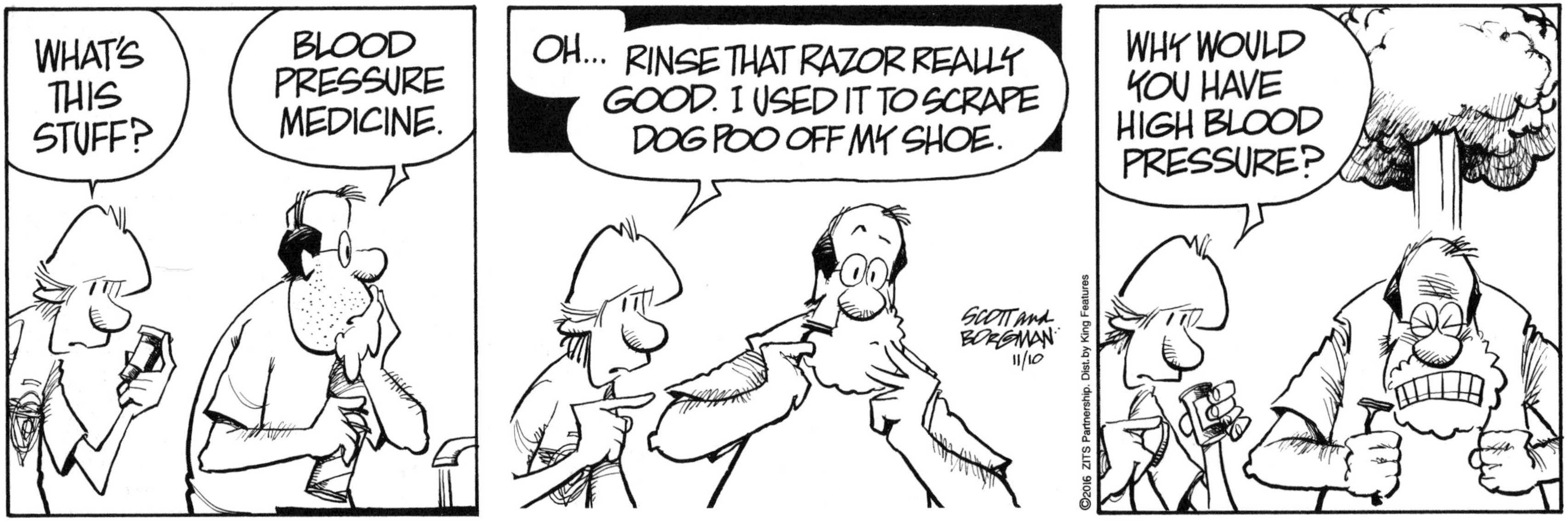
WHAT'S THIS STUFF?
BLOOD PRESSURE MEDICINE.
OH... RINSE THAT RAZOR REALLY GOOD. I USED IT TO SCRAPE DOG POO OFF MY SHOE.
SCOTT and BORGMAN 11/10
WHY WOULD YOU HAVE HIGH BLOOD PRESSURE?
©2016 ZITS Partnership. Dist. by King Features

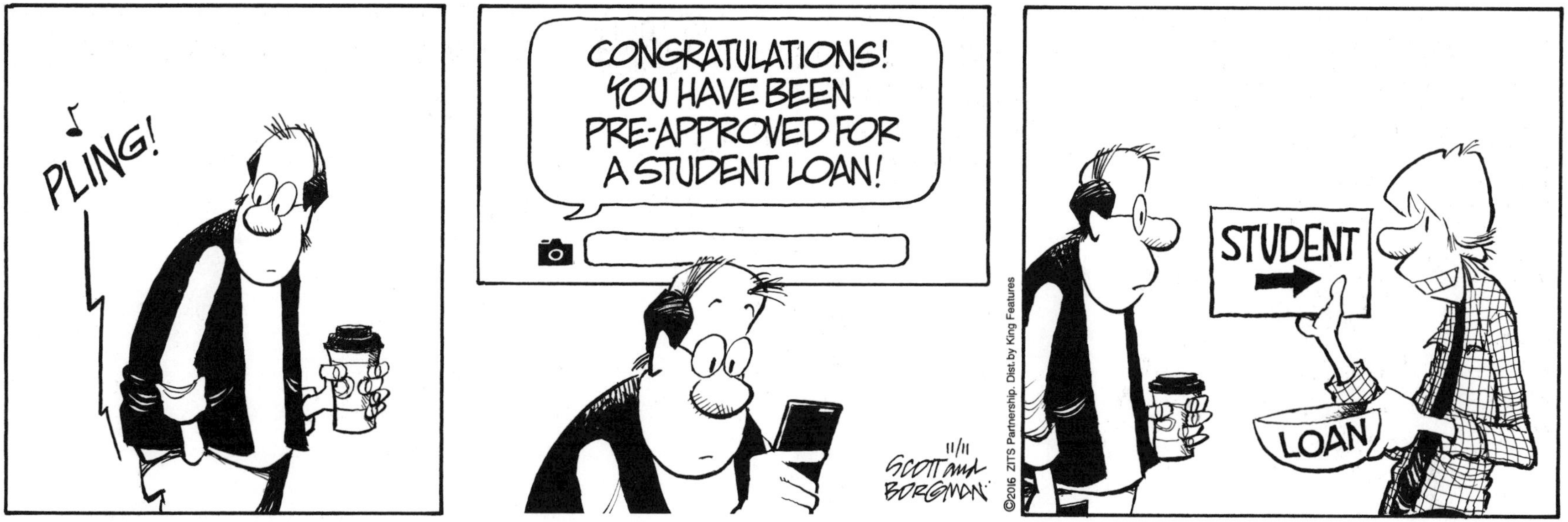
PLING!
CONGRATULATIONS! YOU HAVE BEEN PRE-APPROVED FOR A STUDENT LOAN!
11/11 SCOTT and BORGMAN
©2016 ZITS Partnership. Dist. by King Features
STUDENT
LOAN

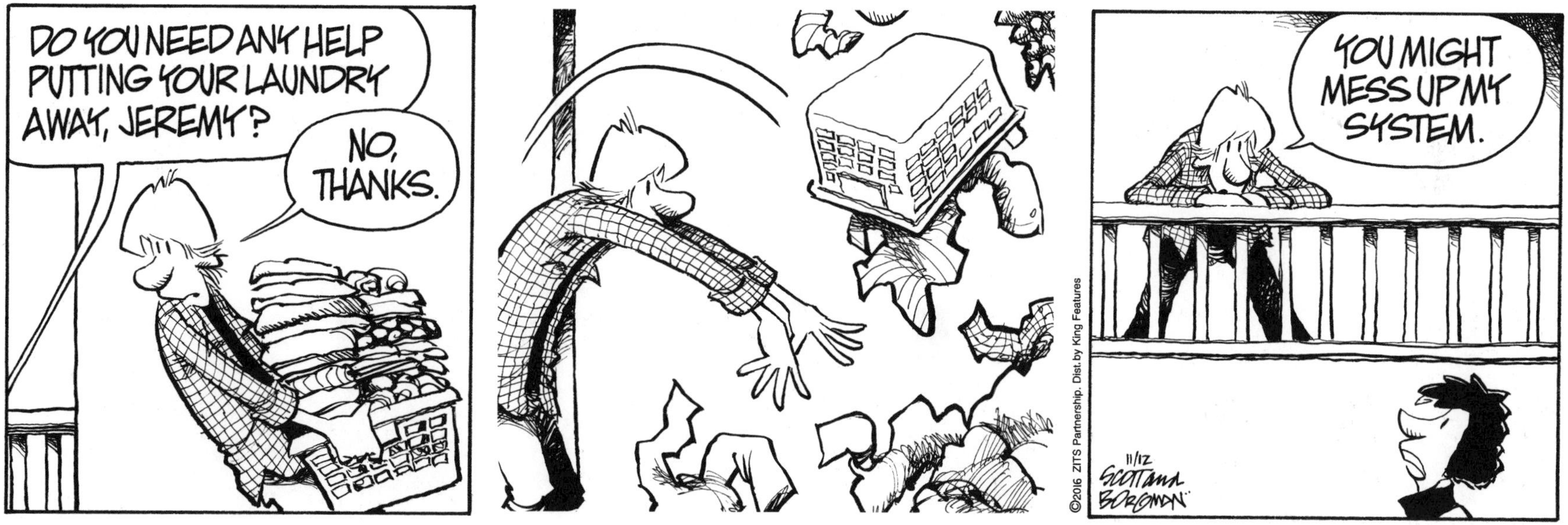
DO YOU NEED ANY HELP PUTTING YOUR LAUNDRY AWAY, JEREMY?
NO, THANKS.
©2016 ZITS Partnership. Dist. by King Features
YOU MIGHT MESS UP MY SYSTEM.
11/12 SCOTT and BORGMAN

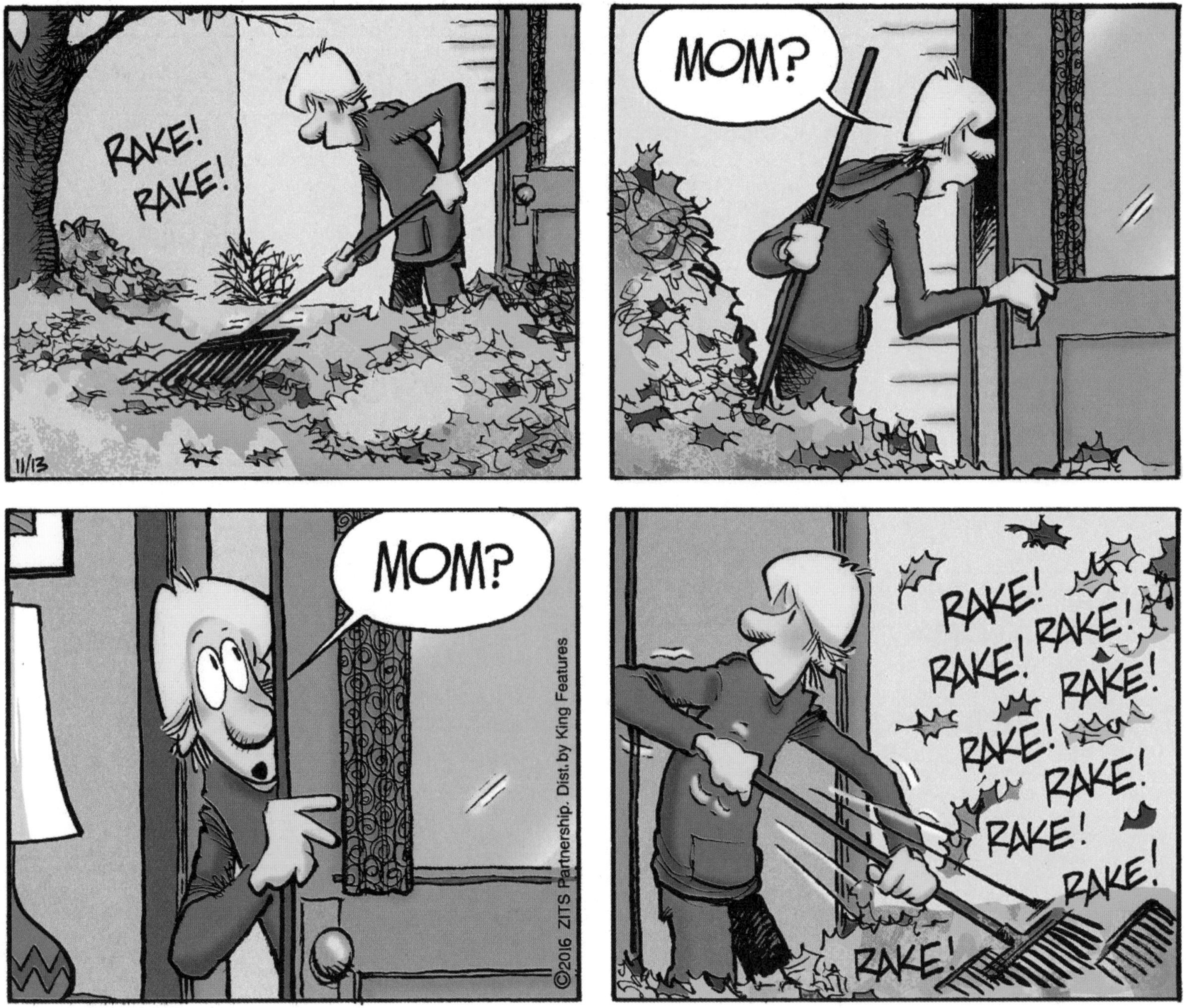
RAKE! RAKE!
11/13
MOM?
MOM?
©2016 ZITS Partnership. Dist. by King Features
RAKE! RAKE! RAKE! RAKE! RAKE! RAKE! RAKE! RAKE! RAKE! RAKE!

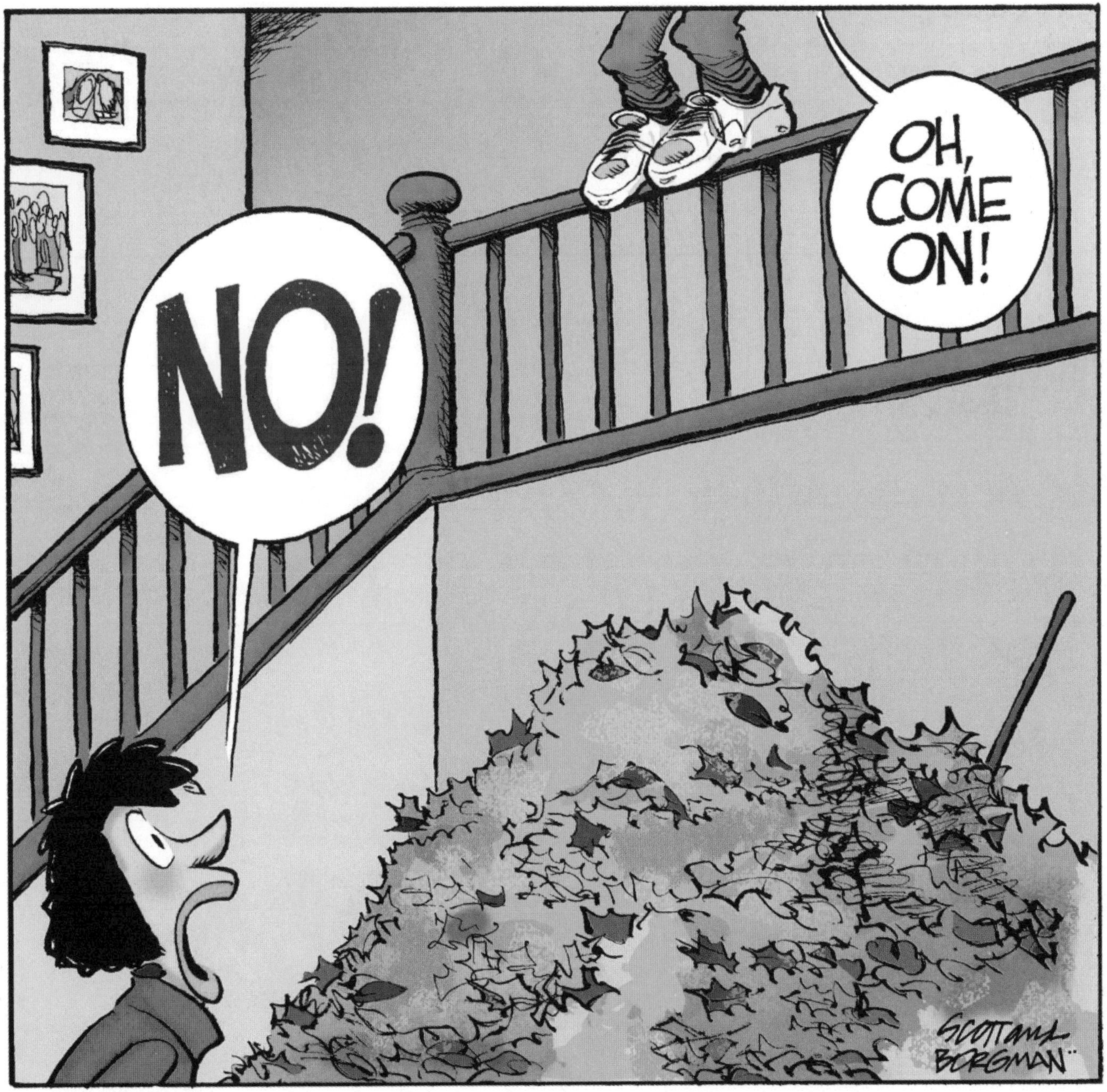
NO!
OH, COME ON!
SCOTTANDBORGMAN

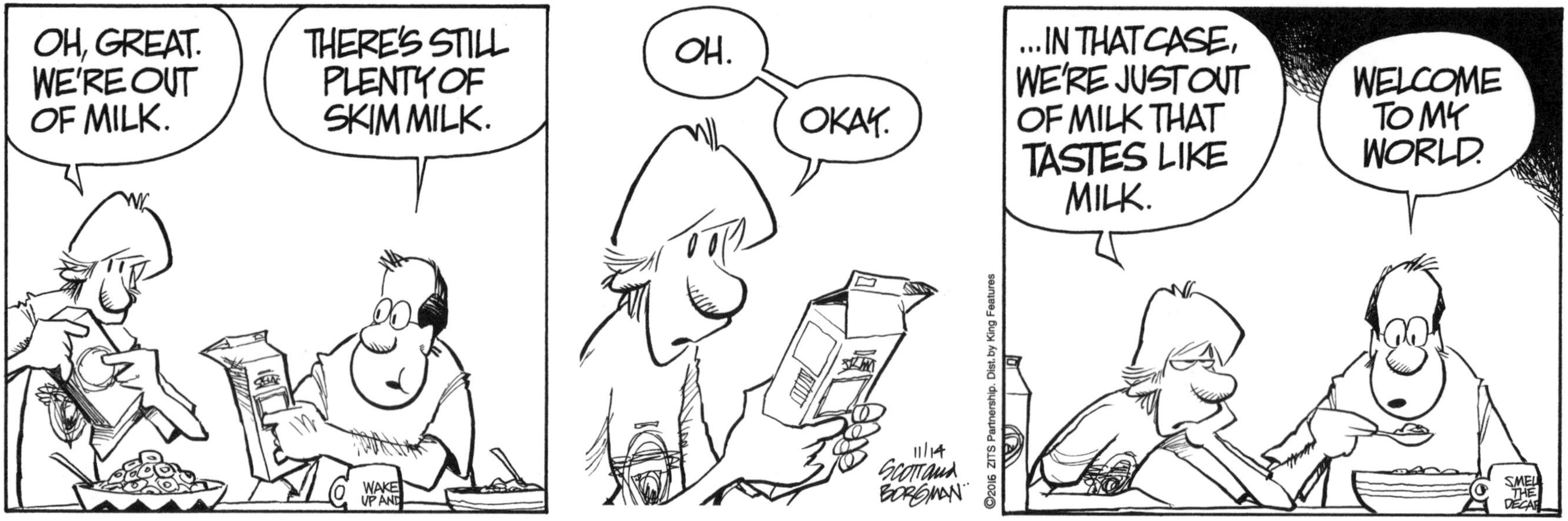
OH, GREAT. WE'RE OUT OF MILK.
THERE'S STILL PLENTY OF SKIM MILK.
OH.
OKAY.
...IN THAT CASE, WE'RE JUST OUT OF MILK THAT TASTES LIKE MILK.
WELCOME TO MY WORLD.
WAKE UP AND
SMELL THE DECAF
11/14
SCOTT and BORGMAN
©2016 ZITS Partnership. Dist. by King Features

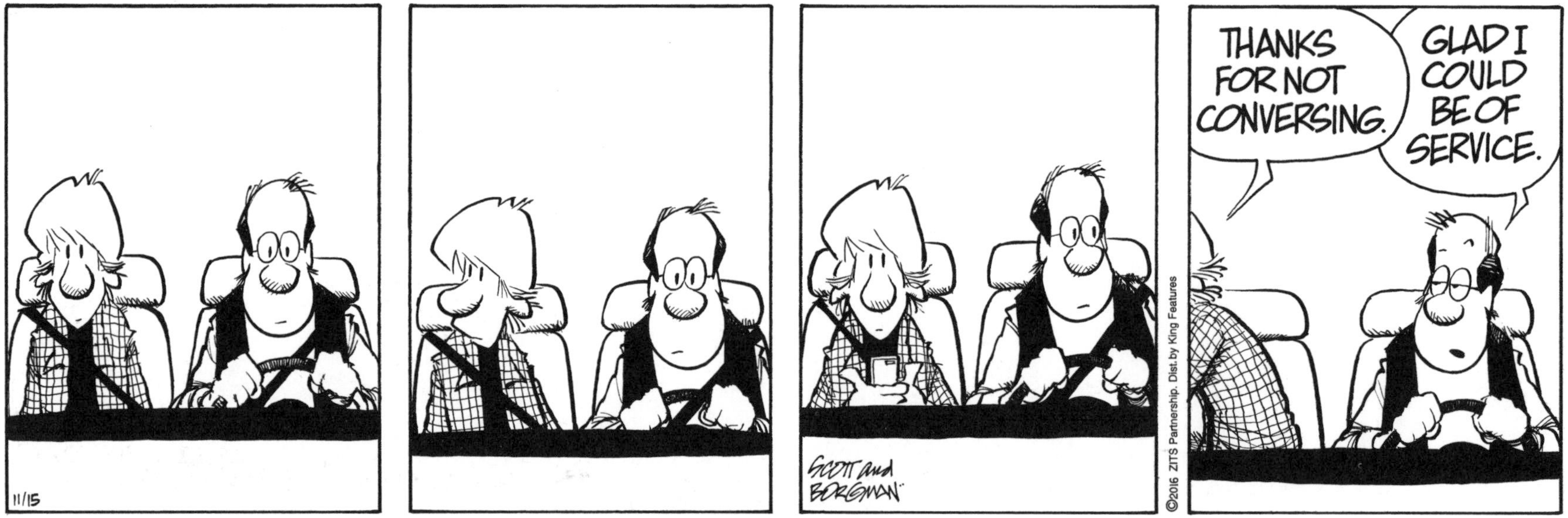
11/15
SCOTT and BORGMAN
©2016 ZITS Partnership. Dist. by King Features
THANKS FOR NOT CONVERSING.
GLAD I COULD BE OF SERVICE.

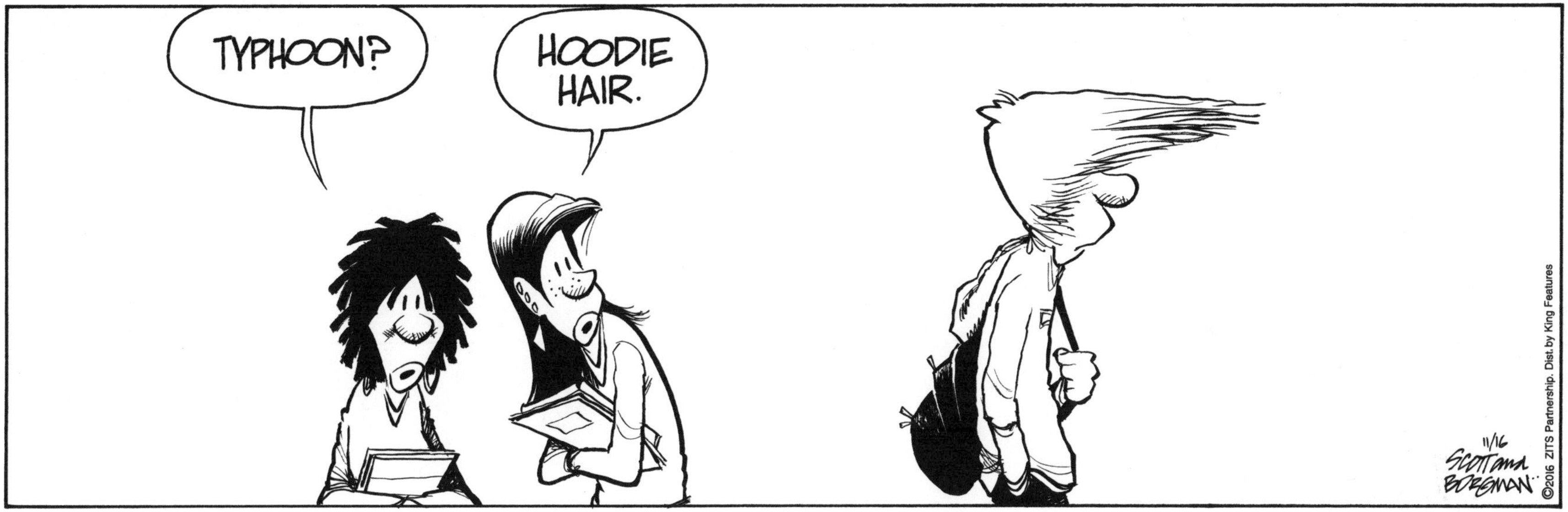
TYPHOON?
HOODIE HAIR.
11/16 SCOTT and BORGMAN
©2016 ZITS Partnership. Dist. by King Features

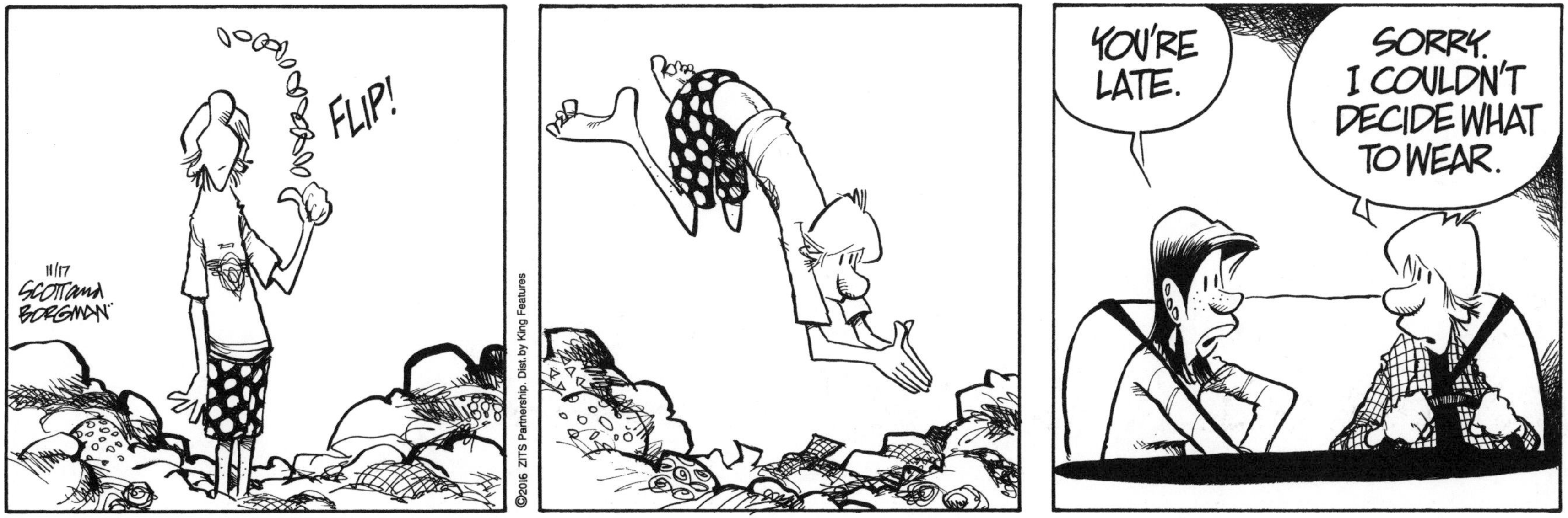
FLIP!
11/17 SCOTT and BORGMAN
©2016 ZITS Partnership. Dist. by King Features
YOU'RE LATE.
SORRY. I COULDN'T DECIDE WHAT TO WEAR.

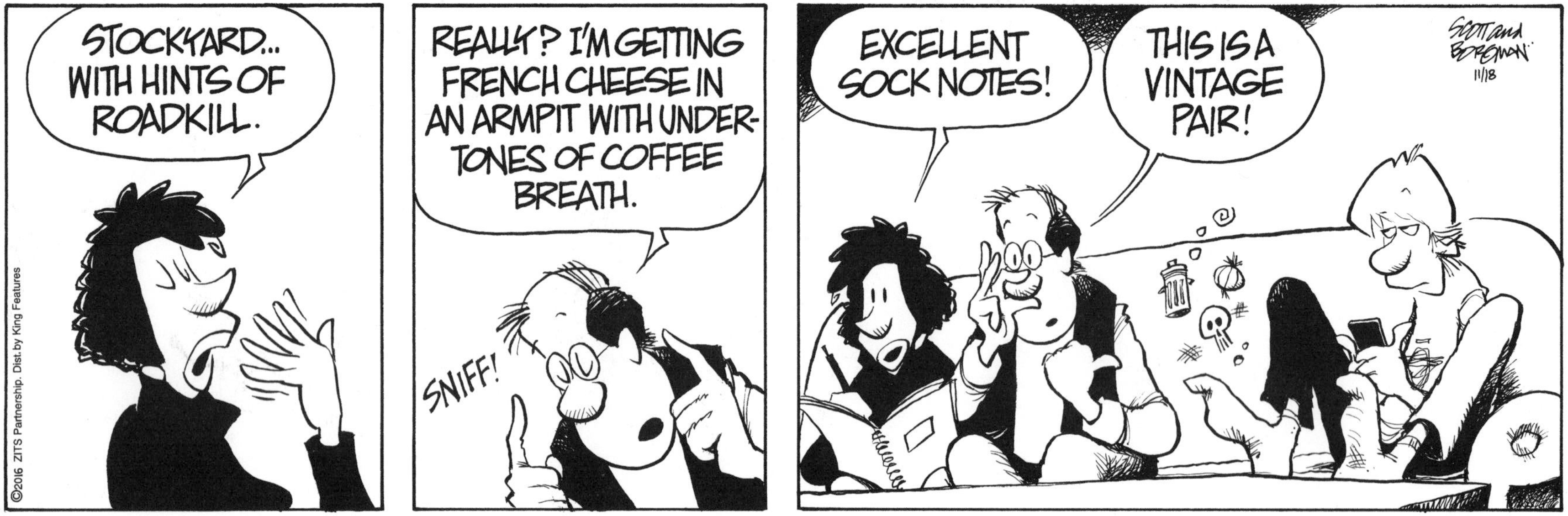
STOCKYARD... WITH HINTS OF ROADKILL.
REALLY? I'M GETTING FRENCH CHEESE IN AN ARMPIT WITH UNDER-TONES OF COFFEE BREATH.
SNIFF!
EXCELLENT SOCK NOTES!
THIS IS A VINTAGE PAIR!
SCOTT and BORGMAN 11/18
©2016 ZITS Partnership. Dist. by King Features

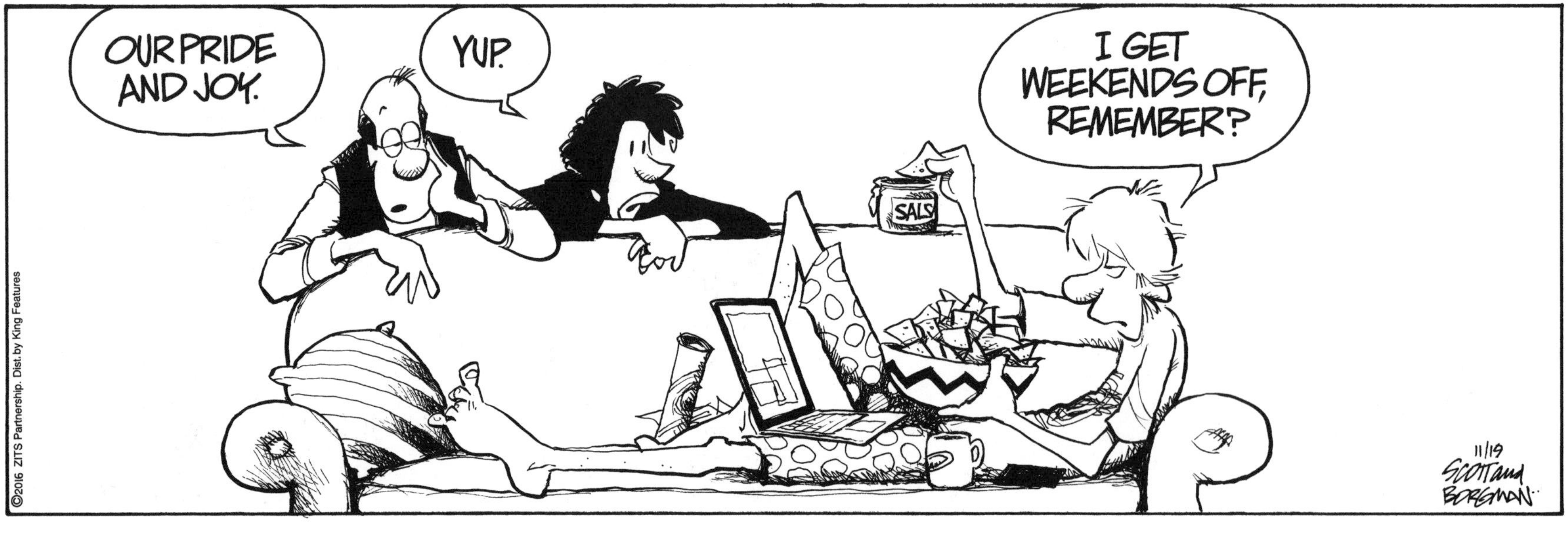
OUR PRIDE AND JOY.
YUP.
I GET WEEKENDS OFF, REMEMBER?
SALS
11/19 SCOTT and BORGMAN
©2016 ZITS Partnership. Dist. by King Features

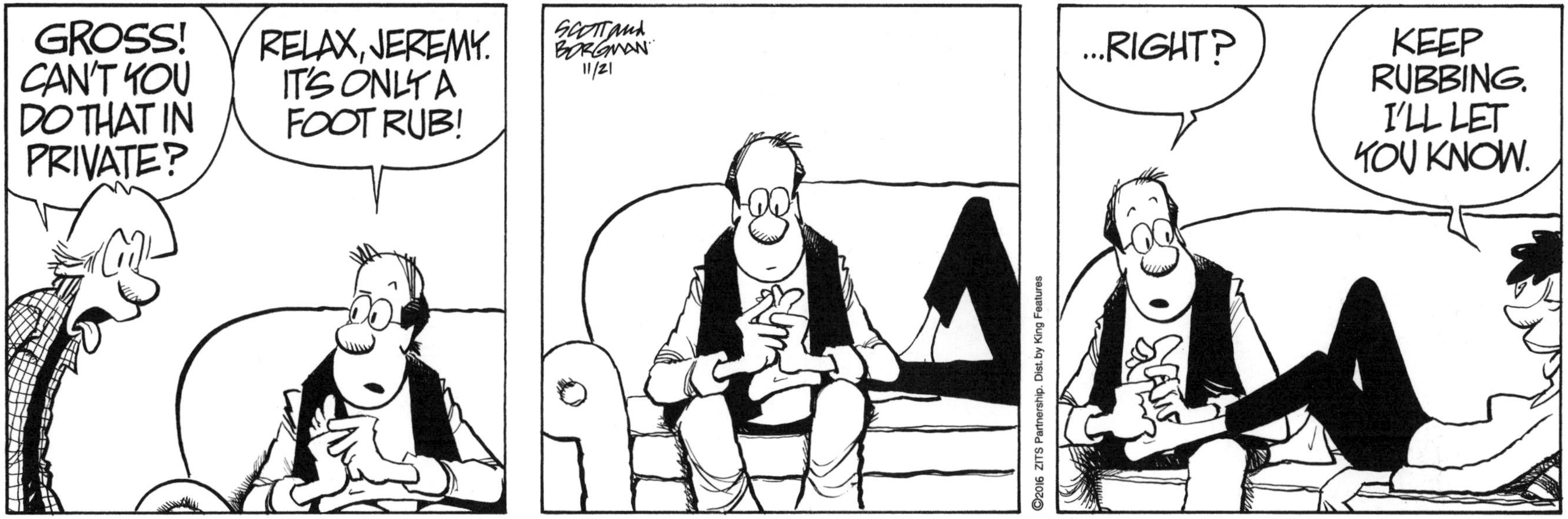
GROSS! CAN'T YOU DO THAT IN PRIVATE?
RELAX, JEREMY. IT'S ONLY A FOOT RUB!
SCOTT and BORGMAN 11/21
...RIGHT?
KEEP RUBBING. I'LL LET YOU KNOW.
©2016 ZITS Partnership. Dist. by King Features

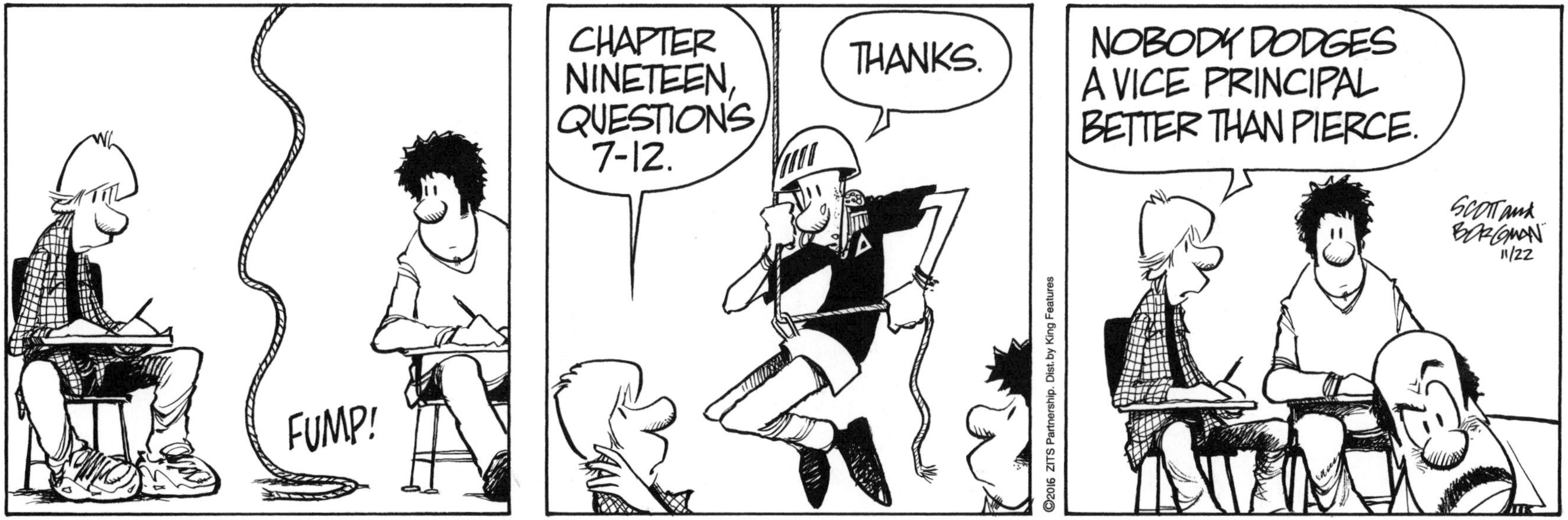
FUMP!
CHAPTER NINETEEN, QUESTIONS 7-12.
THANKS.
NOBODY DODGES A VICE PRINCIPAL BETTER THAN PIERCE.
SCOTT and BORGMAN 11/22
©2016 ZITS Partnership. Dist. by King Features

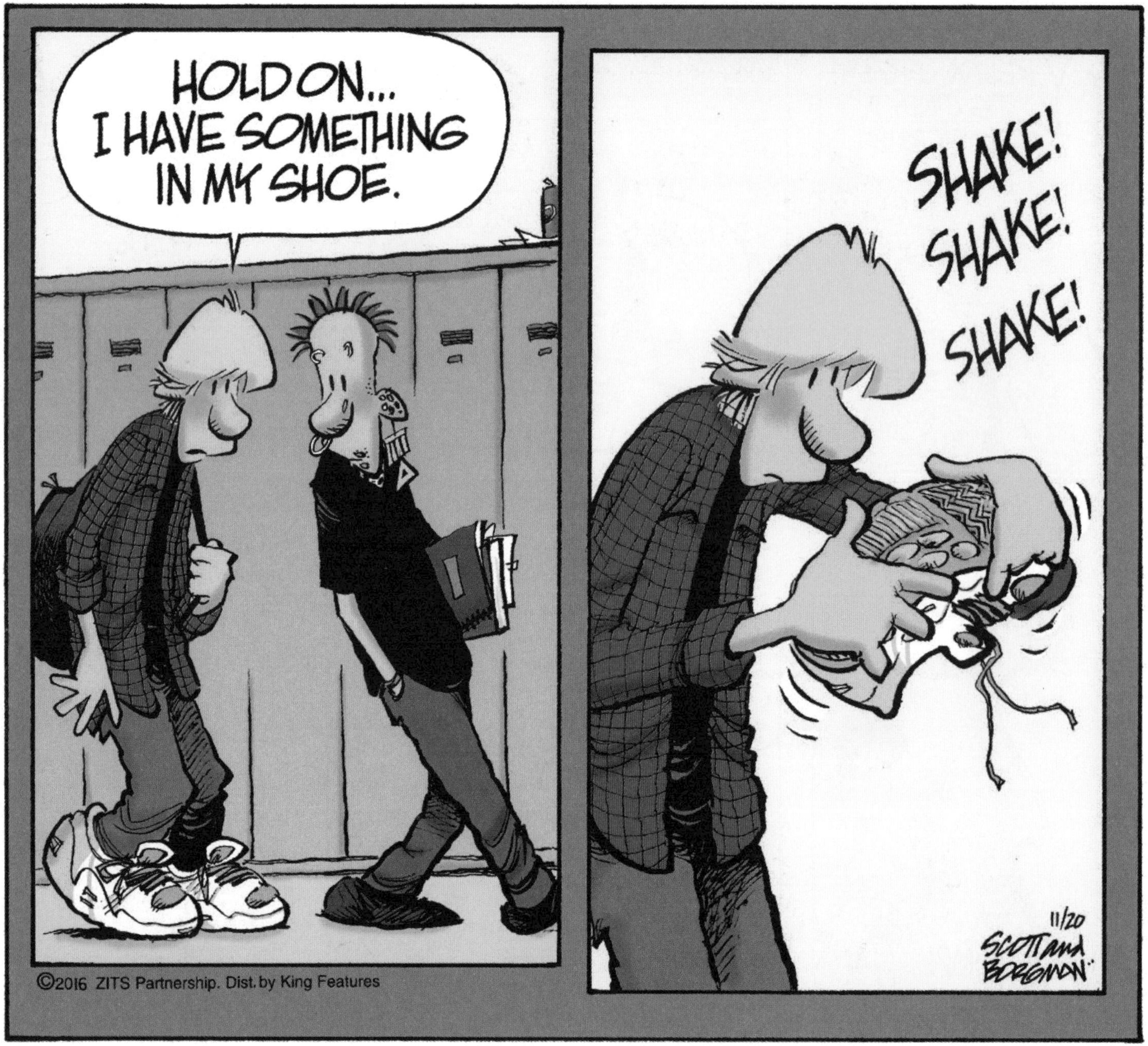
HOLD ON... I HAVE SOMETHING IN MY SHOE.
SHAKE! SHAKE! SHAKE!
11/20
SCOTT AND BORGMAN
©2016 ZITS Partnership. Dist. by King Features

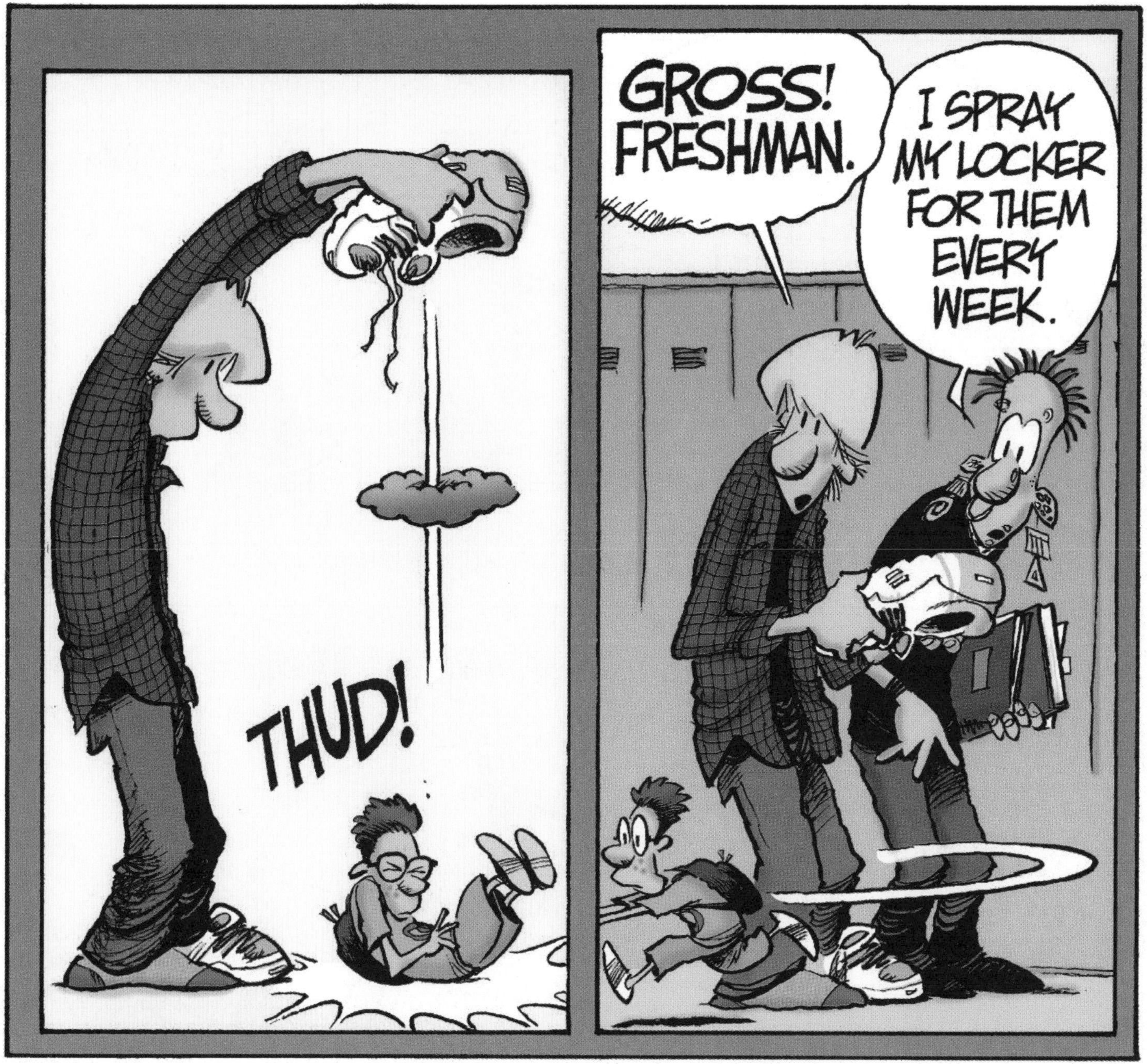
THUD!
GROSS! FRESHMAN.
I SPRAY MY LOCKER FOR THEM EVERY WEEK.

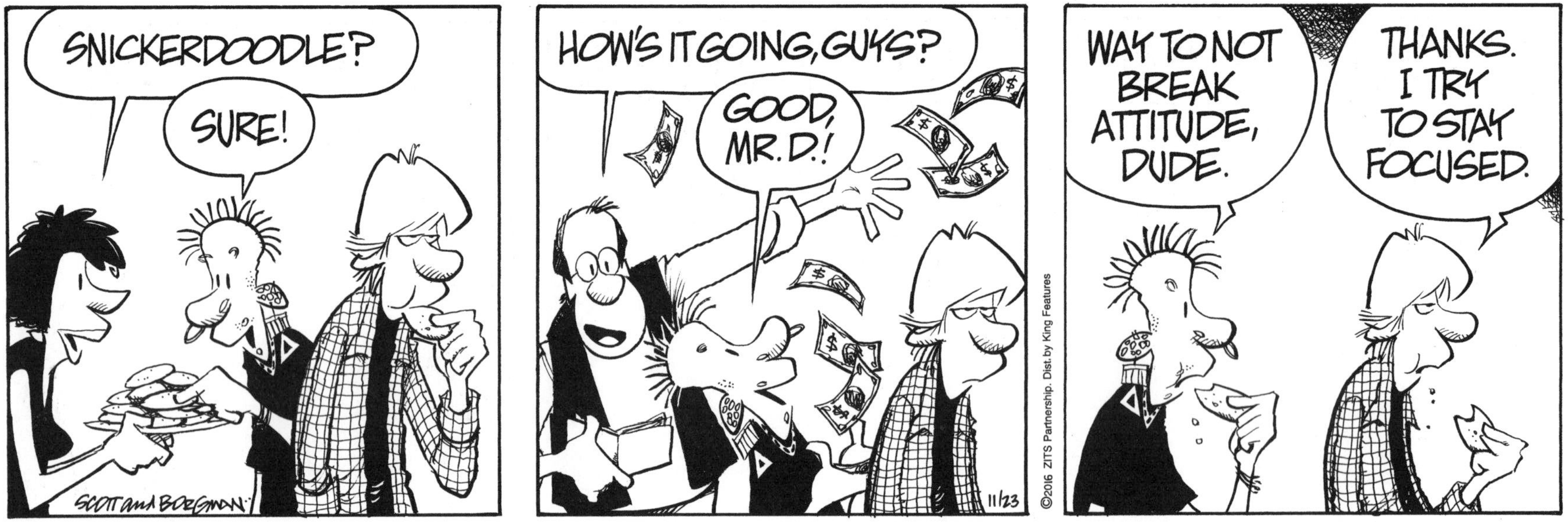
SNICKERDOODLE?
SURE!
SCOTT and BORGMAN
HOW'S IT GOING, GUYS?
GOOD, MR. D.!
11/23
©2016 ZITS Partnership. Dist. by King Features
WAY TO NOT BREAK ATTITUDE, DUDE.
THANKS. I TRY TO STAY FOCUSED.

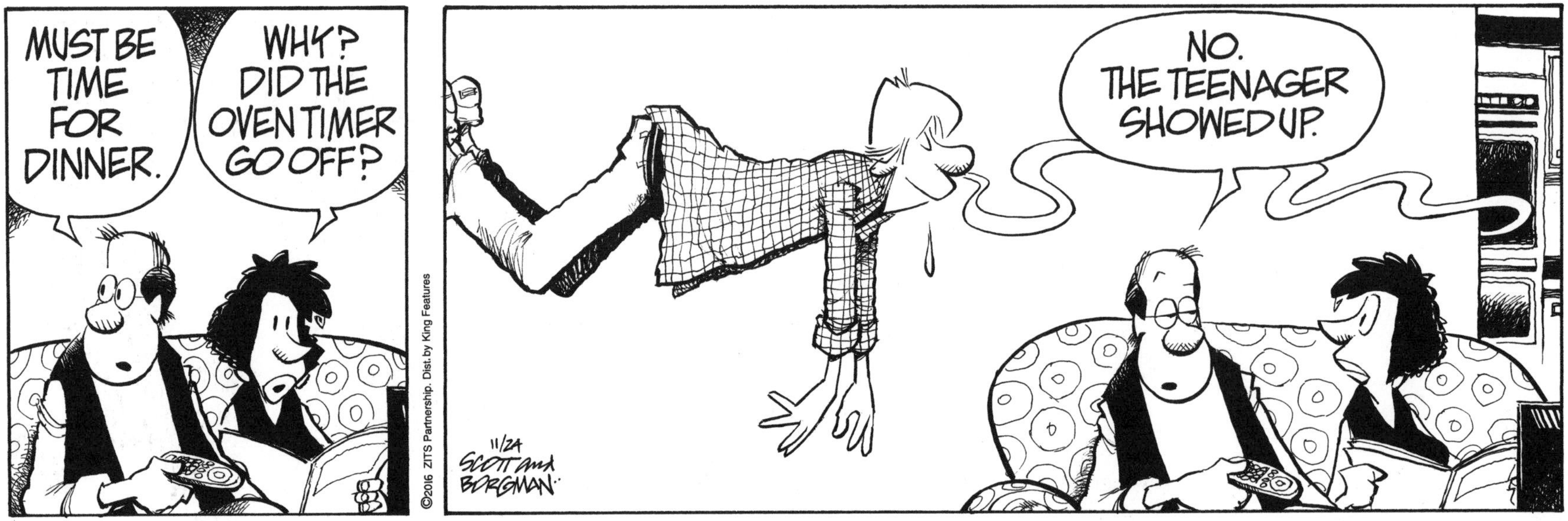
MUST BE TIME FOR DINNER.
WHY? DID THE OVEN TIMER GO OFF?
©2016 ZITS Partnership. Dist. by King Features
11/24
SCOTT and BORGMAN
NO. THE TEENAGER SHOWED UP.

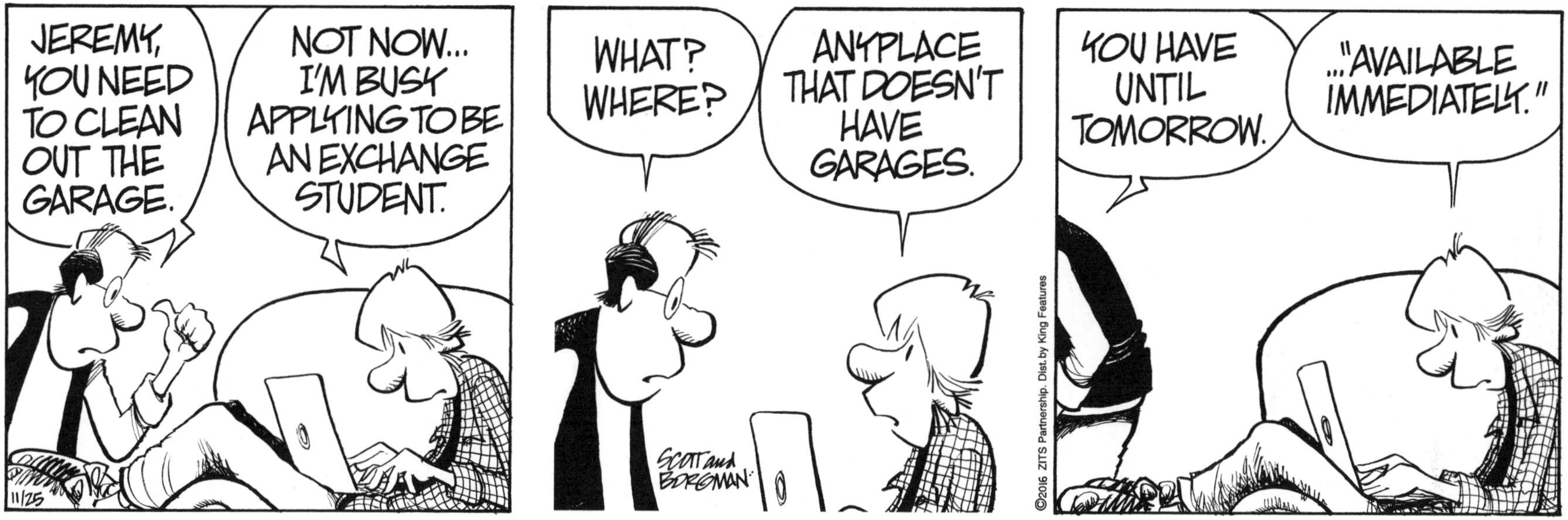
JEREMY, YOU NEED TO CLEAN OUT THE GARAGE.
NOT NOW... I'M BUSY APPLYING TO BE AN EXCHANGE STUDENT.
WHAT? WHERE?
ANYPLACE THAT DOESN'T HAVE GARAGES.
YOU HAVE UNTIL TOMORROW.
..."AVAILABLE IMMEDIATELY."
SCOTT and BORGMAN
11/25
©2016 ZITS Partnership. Dist. by King Features

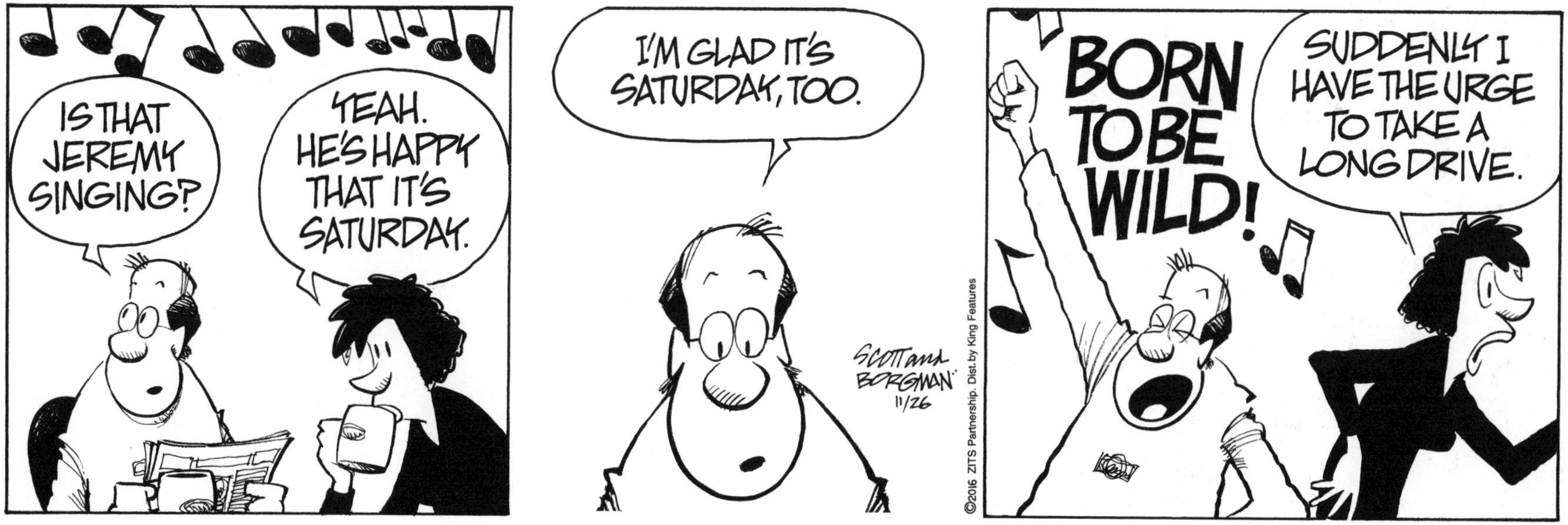
IS THAT JEREMY SINGING?
YEAH. HE'S HAPPY THAT IT'S SATURDAY.
I'M GLAD IT'S SATURDAY, TOO.
BORN TO BE WILD!
SUDDENLY I HAVE THE URGE TO TAKE A LONG DRIVE.
SCOTT and BORGMAN
11/26
©2016 ZITS Partnership. Dist. by King Features

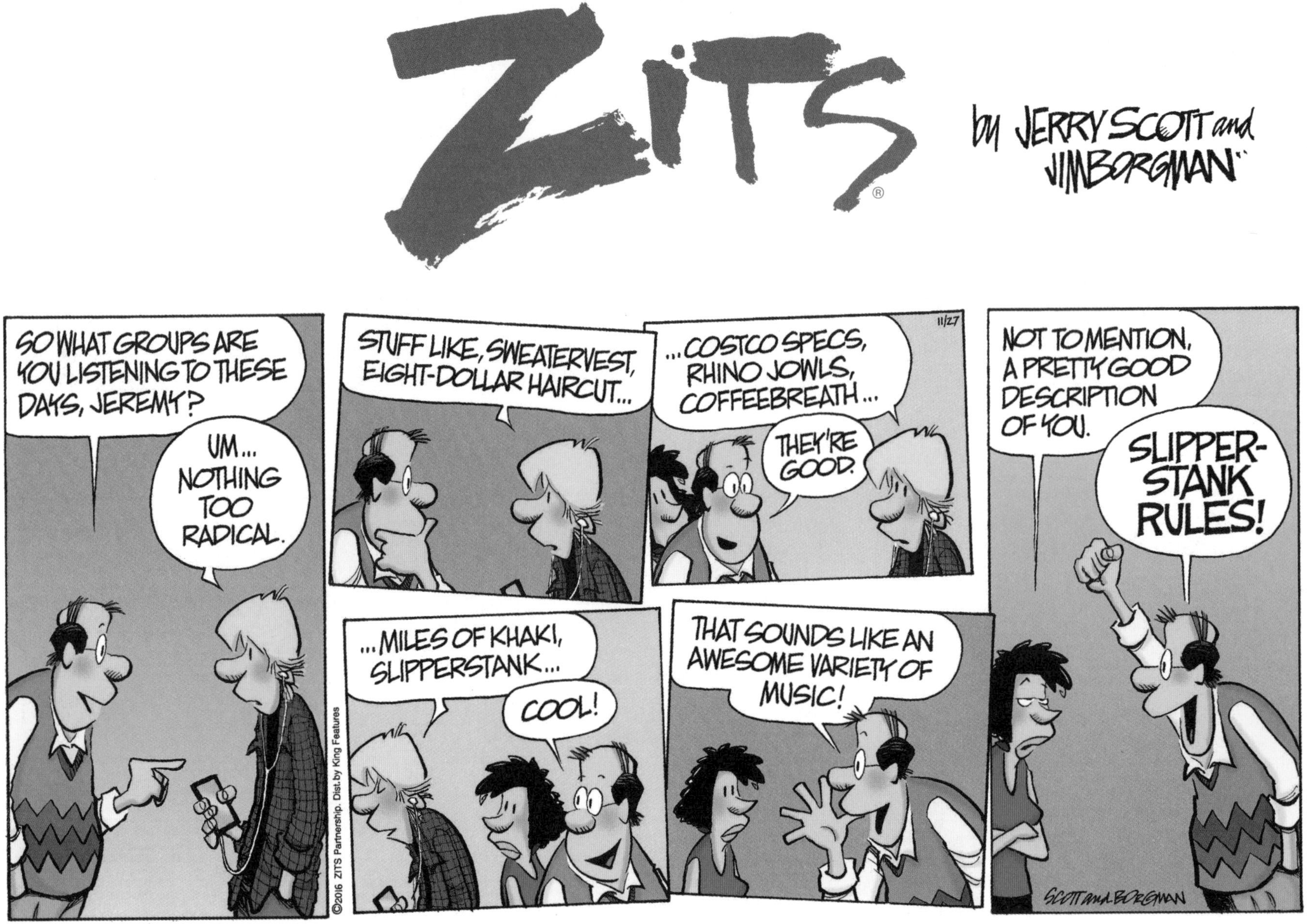
ZITS
by JERRY SCOTT and JIM BORGMAN
SO WHAT GROUPS ARE YOU LISTENING TO THESE DAYS, JEREMY?
UM... NOTHING TOO RADICAL.
STUFF LIKE, SWEATERVEST, EIGHT-DOLLAR HAIRCUT...
...COSTCO SPECS, RHINO JOWLS, COFFEEBREATH...
THEY'RE GOOD.
...MILES OF KHAKI, SLIPPERSTANK...
COOL!
THAT SOUNDS LIKE AN AWESOME VARIETY OF MUSIC!
NOT TO MENTION, A PRETTY GOOD DESCRIPTION OF YOU.
SLIPPER-STANK RULES!
©2016 ZITS Partnership. Dist. by King Features
SCOTT and BORGMAN

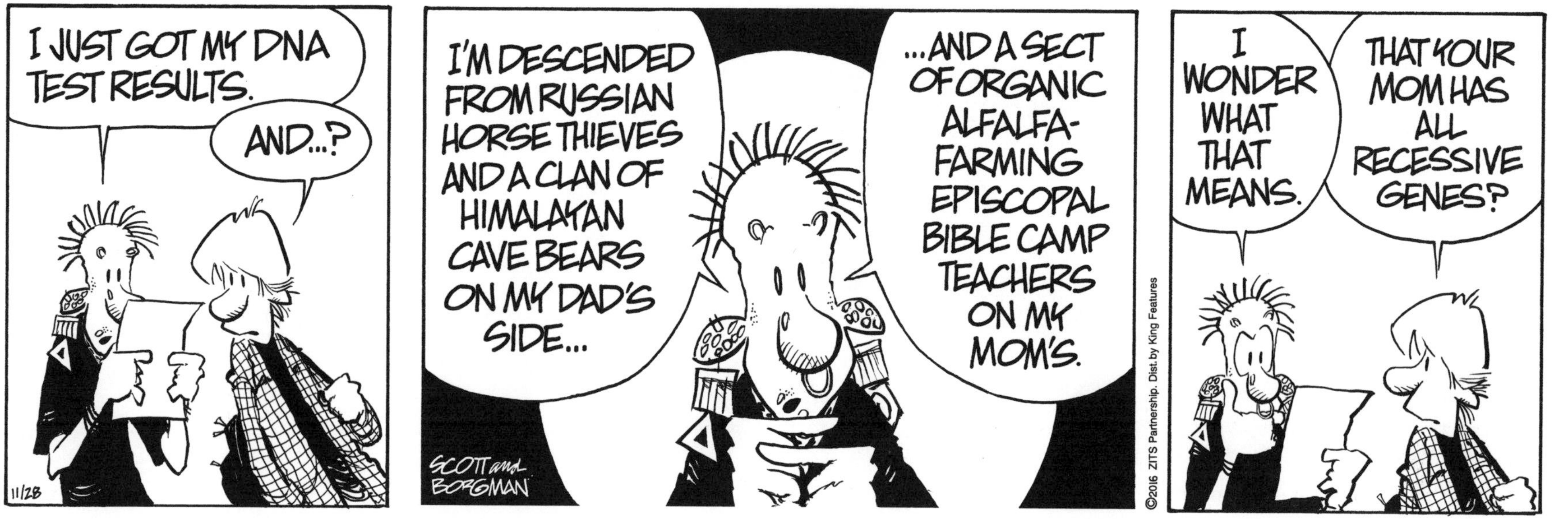
I JUST GOT MY DNA TEST RESULTS.
AND...?
I'M DESCENDED FROM RUSSIAN HORSE THIEVES AND A CLAN OF HIMALAYAN CAVE BEARS ON MY DAD'S SIDE...
...AND A SECT OF ORGANIC ALFALFA-FARMING EPISCOPAL BIBLE CAMP TEACHERS ON MY MOM'S.
I WONDER WHAT THAT MEANS.
THAT YOUR MOM HAS ALL RECESSIVE GENES?
SCOTT and BORGMAN
11/28
©2016 ZITS Partnership. Dist. by King Features

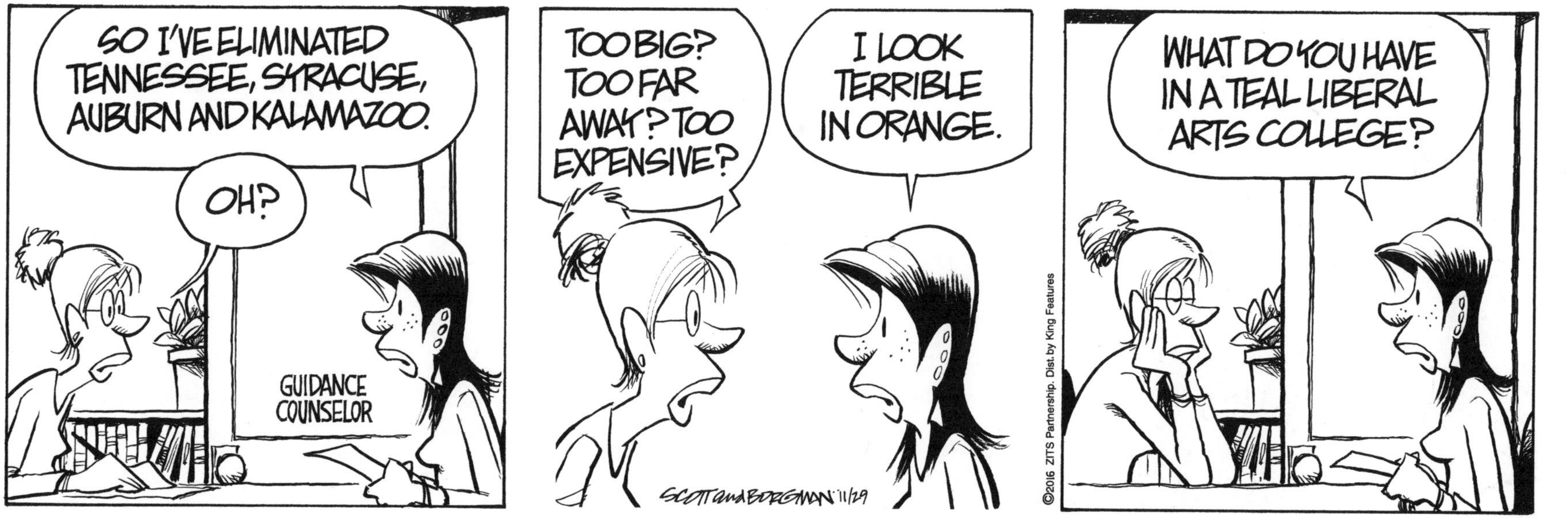
SO I'VE ELIMINATED TENNESSEE, SYRACUSE, AUBURN AND KALAMAZOO.
OH?
GUIDANCE COUNSELOR
TOO BIG? TOO FAR AWAY? TOO EXPENSIVE?
I LOOK TERRIBLE IN ORANGE.
WHAT DO YOU HAVE IN A TEAL LIBERAL ARTS COLLEGE?
SCOTT and BORGMAN 11/29
©2016 ZITS Partnership. Dist. by King Features

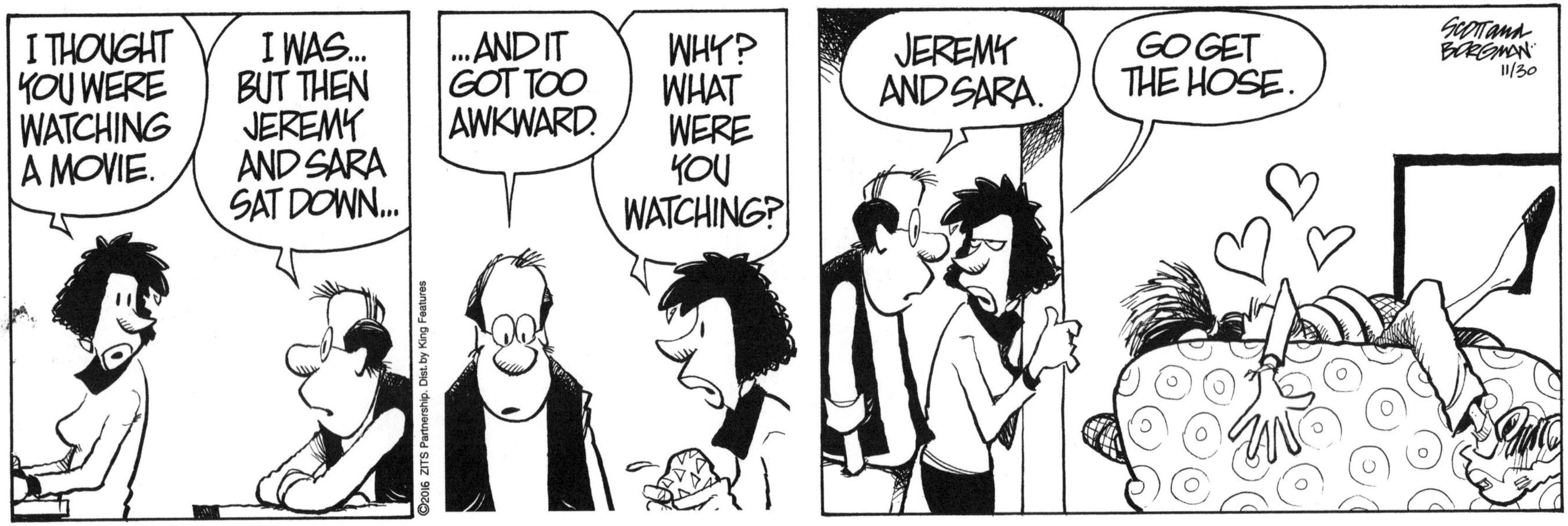
I THOUGHT YOU WERE WATCHING A MOVIE.
I WAS... BUT THEN JEREMY AND SARA SAT DOWN...
©2016 ZITS Partnership. Dist. by King Features
...AND IT GOT TOO AWKWARD.
WHY? WHAT WERE YOU WATCHING?
JEREMY AND SARA.
GO GET THE HOSE.
SCOTT and BORGMAN
11/30

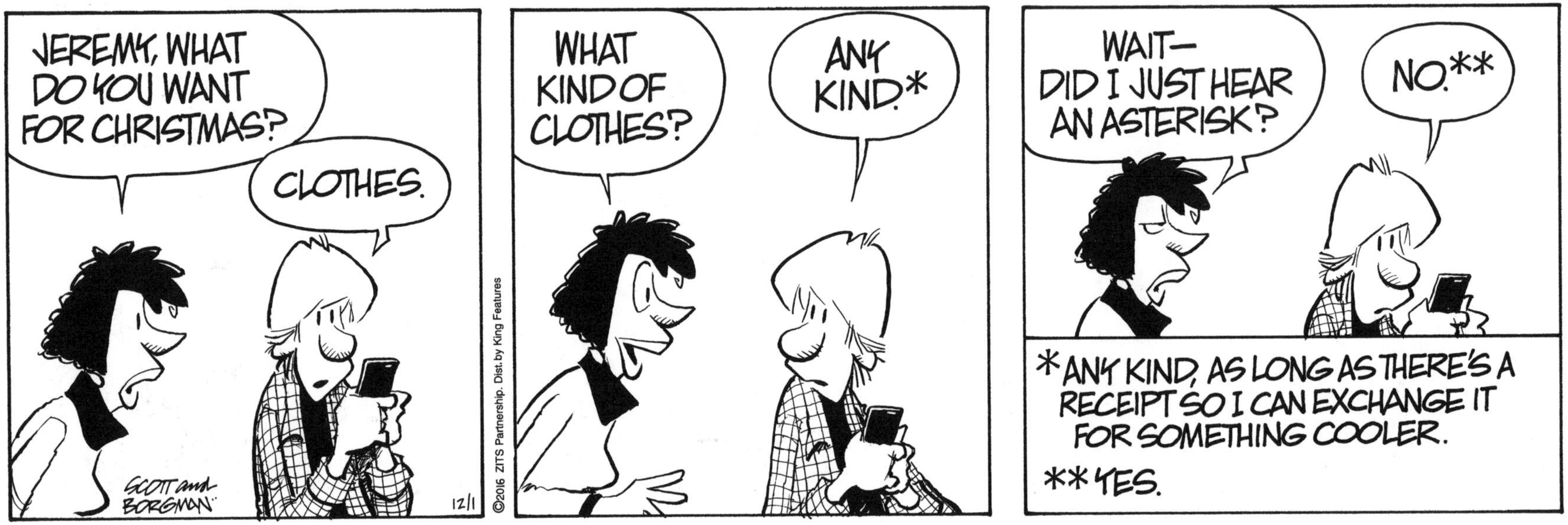
JEREMY, WHAT DO YOU WANT FOR CHRISTMAS?
CLOTHES.
SCOTT and BORGMAN
12/1
©2016 ZITS Partnership. Dist. by King Features
WHAT KIND OF CLOTHES?
ANY KIND.*
WAIT— DID I JUST HEAR AN ASTERISK?
NO.**
*ANY KIND, AS LONG AS THERE'S A RECEIPT SO I CAN EXCHANGE IT FOR SOMETHING COOLER.
**YES.

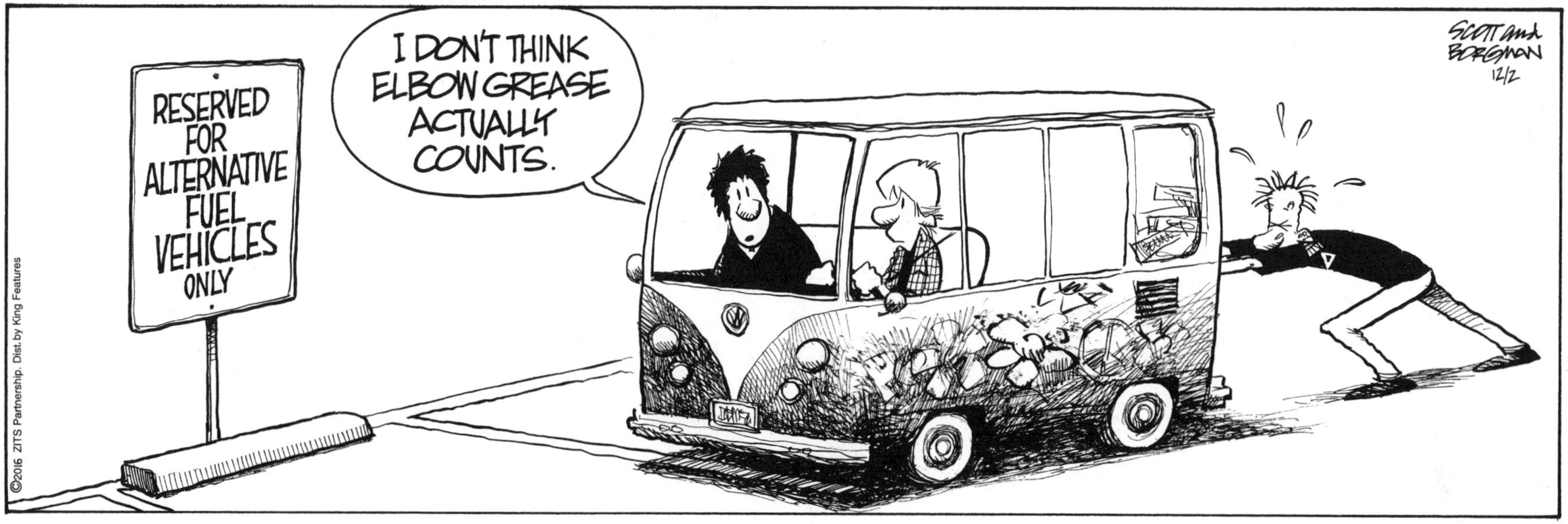
RESERVED FOR ALTERNATIVE FUEL VEHICLES ONLY
I DON'T THINK ELBOW GREASE ACTUALLY COUNTS.
SCOTT and BORGMAN 12/2
©2016 ZITS Partnership. Dist. by King Features

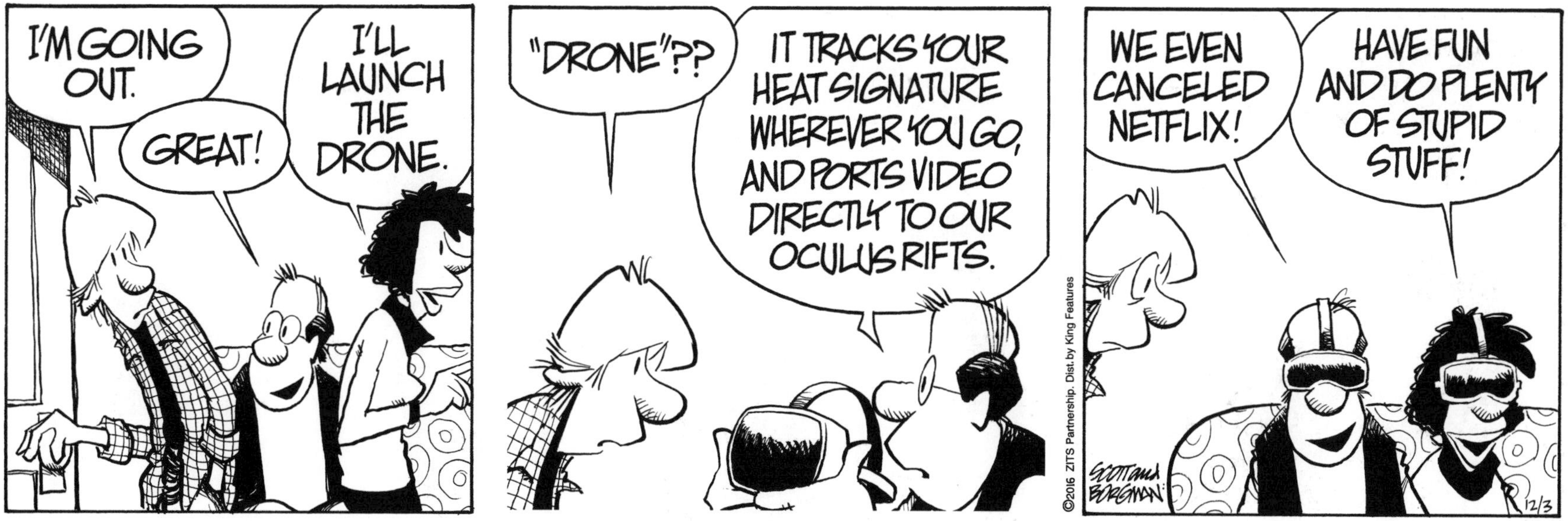
I'M GOING OUT.
GREAT!
I'LL LAUNCH THE DRONE.
"DRONE"??
IT TRACKS YOUR HEAT SIGNATURE WHEREVER YOU GO, AND PORTS VIDEO DIRECTLY TO OUR OCULUS RIFTS.
©2016 ZITS Partnership. Dist. by King Features
WE EVEN CANCELED NETFLIX!
HAVE FUN AND DO PLENTY OF STUPID STUFF!
SCOTT and BORGMAN 12/3

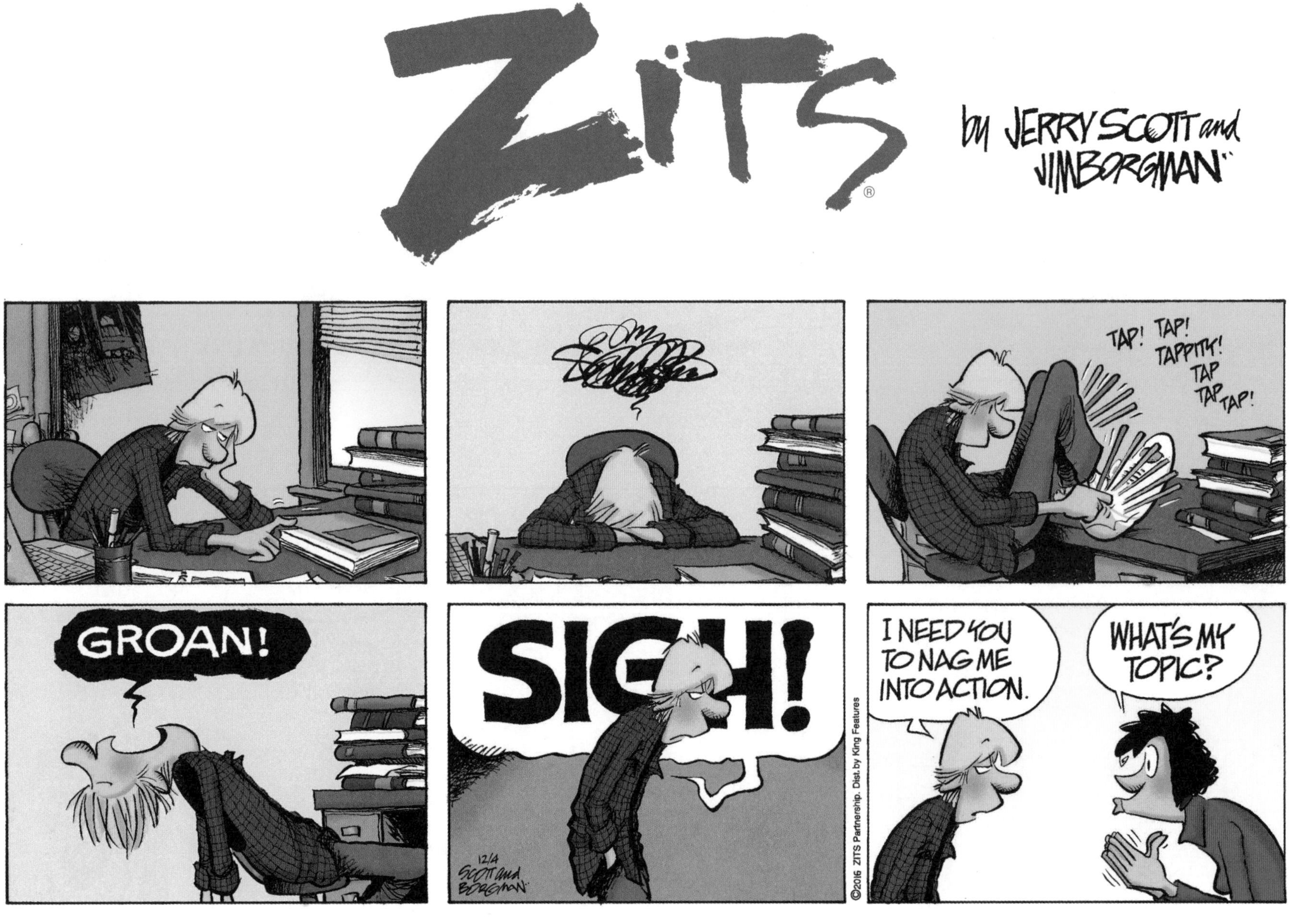
ZITS
by JERRY SCOTT and JIM BORGMAN
TAP! TAP! TAPPITY! TAP TAP TAP!
GROAN!
SIGH!
12/4 SCOTT and BORGMAN
©2016 ZITS Partnership. Dist. by King Features
I NEED YOU TO NAG ME INTO ACTION.
WHAT'S MY TOPIC?

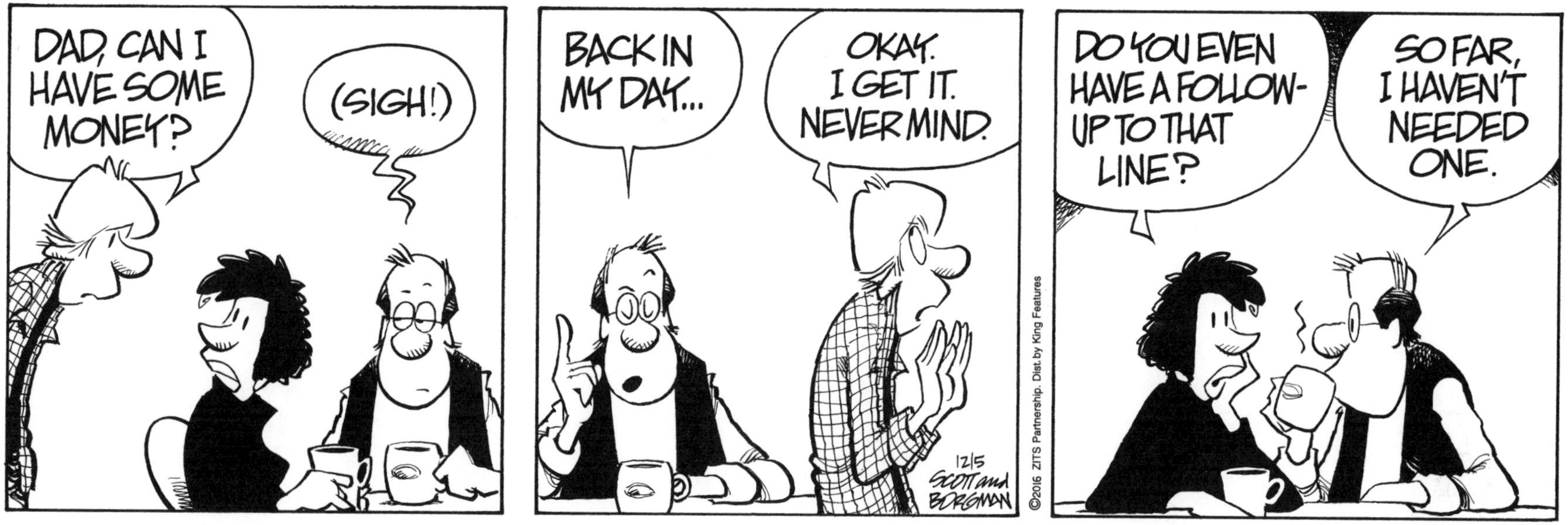
DAD, CAN I HAVE SOME MONEY?
(SIGH!)
BACK IN MY DAY...
OKAY. I GET IT. NEVER MIND.
12/5 SCOTT and BORGMAN
©2016 ZITS Partnership. Dist. by King Features
DO YOU EVEN HAVE A FOLLOW-UP TO THAT LINE?
SO FAR, I HAVEN'T NEEDED ONE.

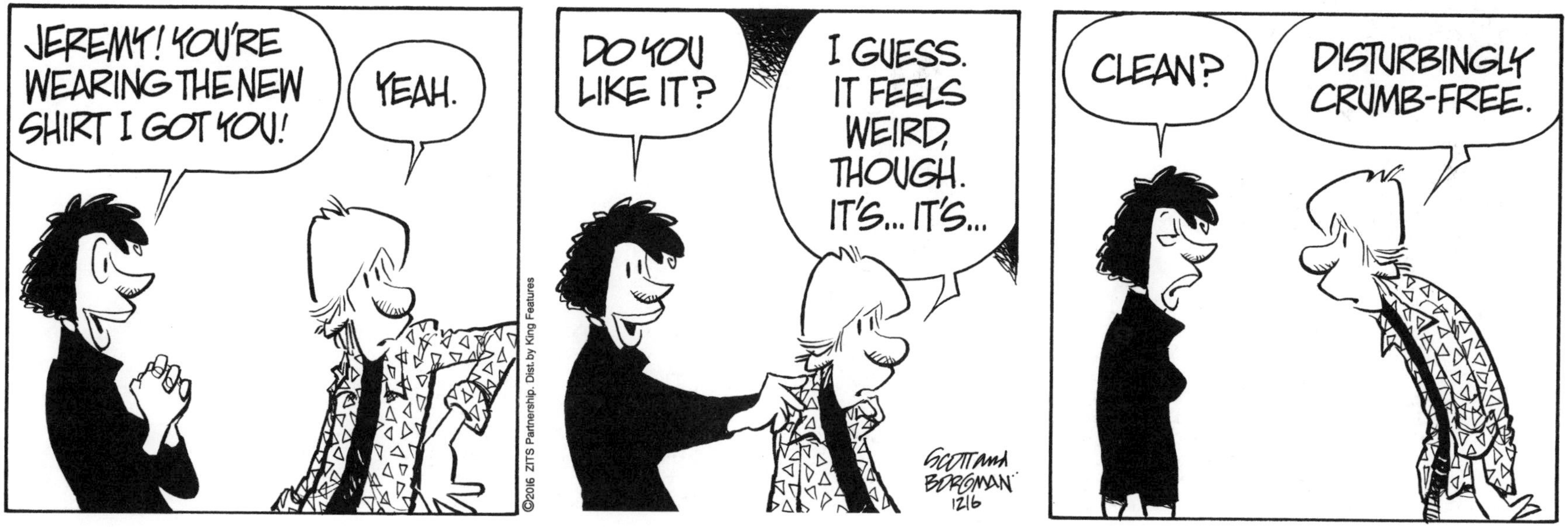
JEREMY! YOU'RE WEARING THE NEW SHIRT I GOT YOU!
YEAH.
©2016 ZITS Partnership. Dist. by King Features
DO YOU LIKE IT?
I GUESS. IT FEELS WEIRD, THOUGH. IT'S... IT'S...
SCOTT and BORGMAN 12/6
CLEAN?
DISTURBINGLY CRUMB-FREE.

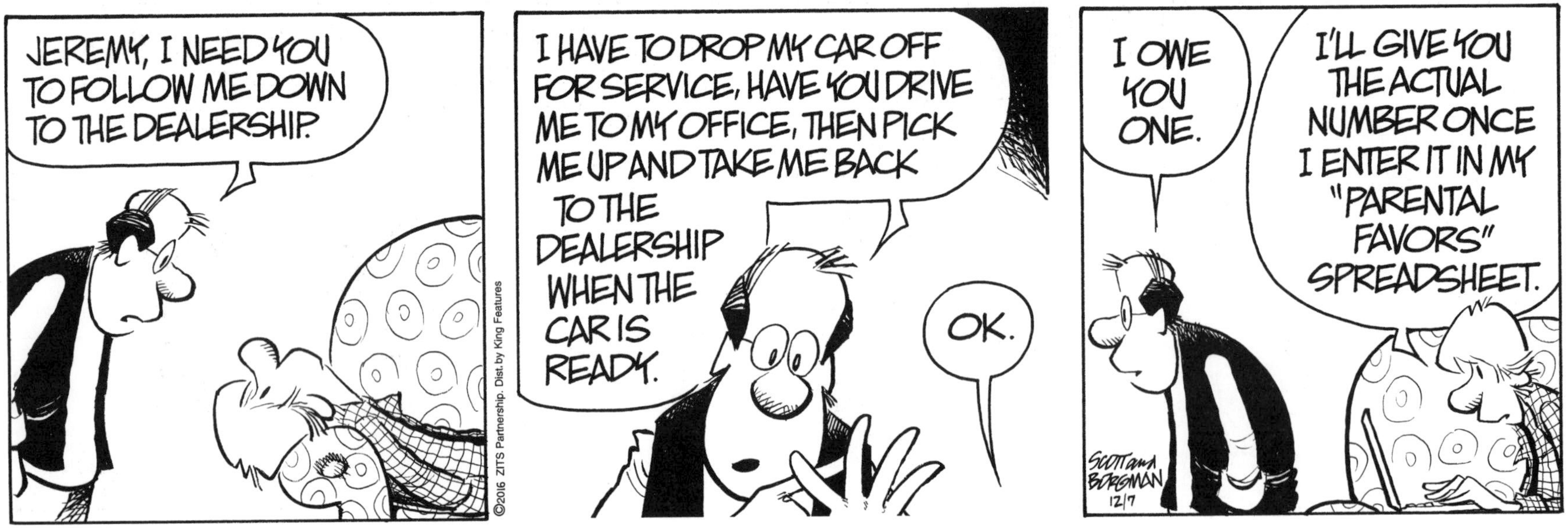
JEREMY, I NEED YOU TO FOLLOW ME DOWN TO THE DEALERSHIP.
I HAVE TO DROP MY CAR OFF FOR SERVICE, HAVE YOU DRIVE ME TO MY OFFICE, THEN PICK ME UP AND TAKE ME BACK TO THE DEALERSHIP WHEN THE CAR IS READY.
OK.
I OWE YOU ONE.
I'LL GIVE YOU THE ACTUAL NUMBER ONCE I ENTER IT IN MY "PARENTAL FAVORS" SPREADSHEET.
©2016 ZITS Partnership. Dist. by King Features
SCOTT and BORGMAN 12/7

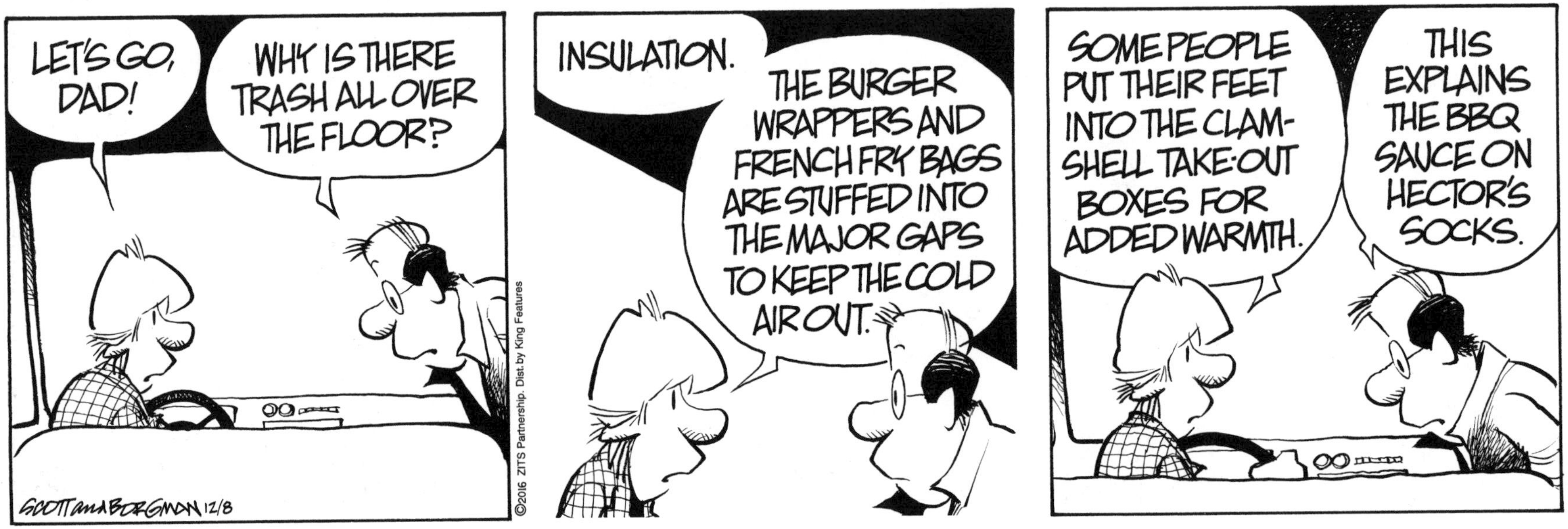
LET'S GO, DAD!
WHY IS THERE TRASH ALL OVER THE FLOOR?
INSULATION.
THE BURGER WRAPPERS AND FRENCH FRY BAGS ARE STUFFED INTO THE MAJOR GAPS TO KEEP THE COLD AIR OUT.
SOME PEOPLE PUT THEIR FEET INTO THE CLAM-SHELL TAKE-OUT BOXES FOR ADDED WARMTH.
THIS EXPLAINS THE BBQ SAUCE ON HECTOR'S SOCKS.
©2016 ZITS Partnership. Dist. by King Features
SCOTT and BORGMAN 12/8

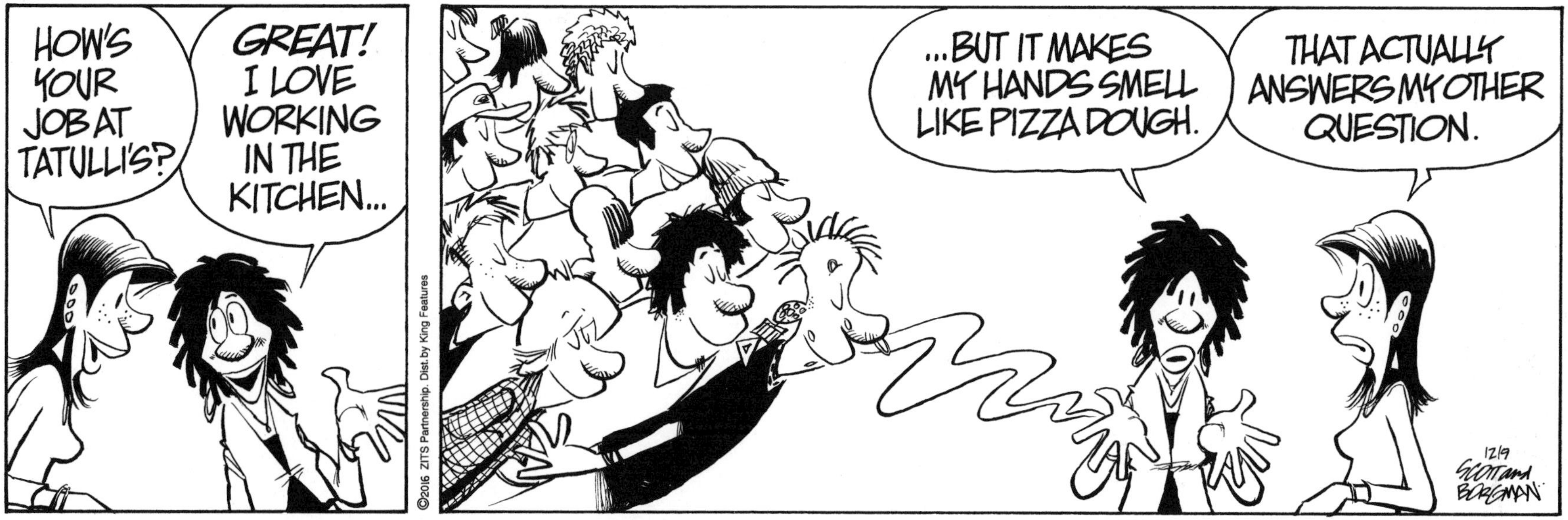
HOW'S YOUR JOB AT TATULLI'S?
GREAT! I LOVE WORKING IN THE KITCHEN...
©2016 ZITS Partnership. Dist. by King Features
...BUT IT MAKES MY HANDS SMELL LIKE PIZZA DOUGH.
THAT ACTUALLY ANSWERS MY OTHER QUESTION.
12/9 SCOTT and BORGMAN

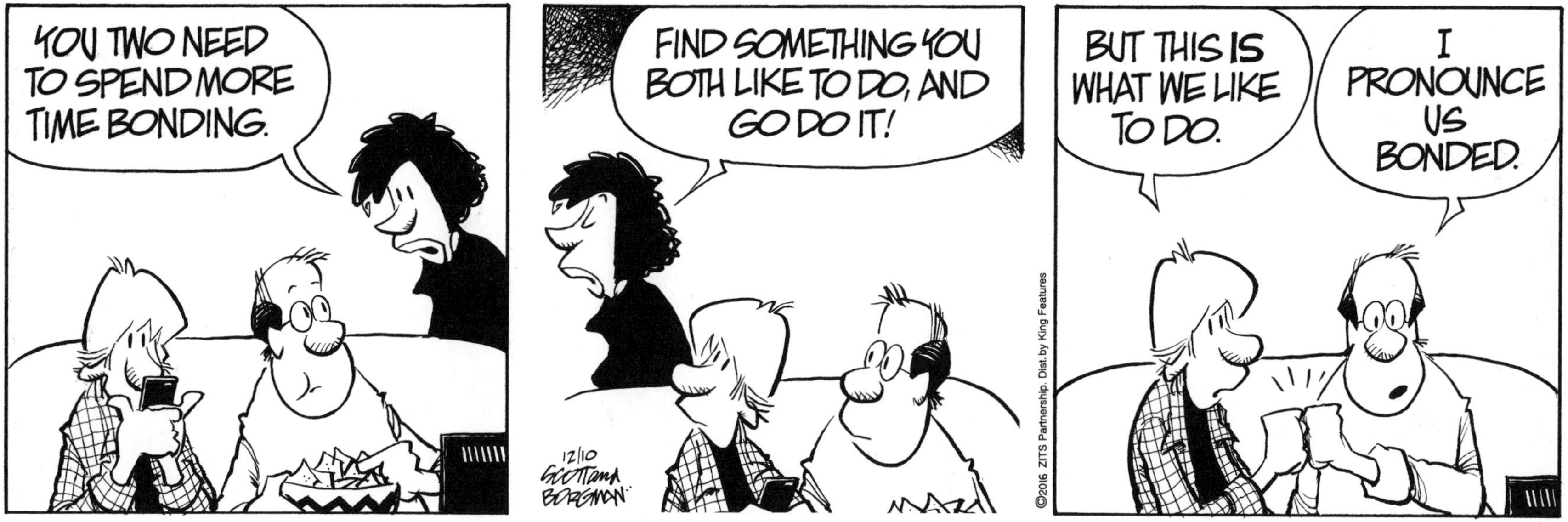
YOU TWO NEED TO SPEND MORE TIME BONDING.
FIND SOMETHING YOU BOTH LIKE TO DO, AND GO DO IT!
12/10 SCOTT and BORGMAN
©2016 ZITS Partnership. Dist. by King Features
BUT THIS IS WHAT WE LIKE TO DO.
I PRONOUNCE US BONDED.

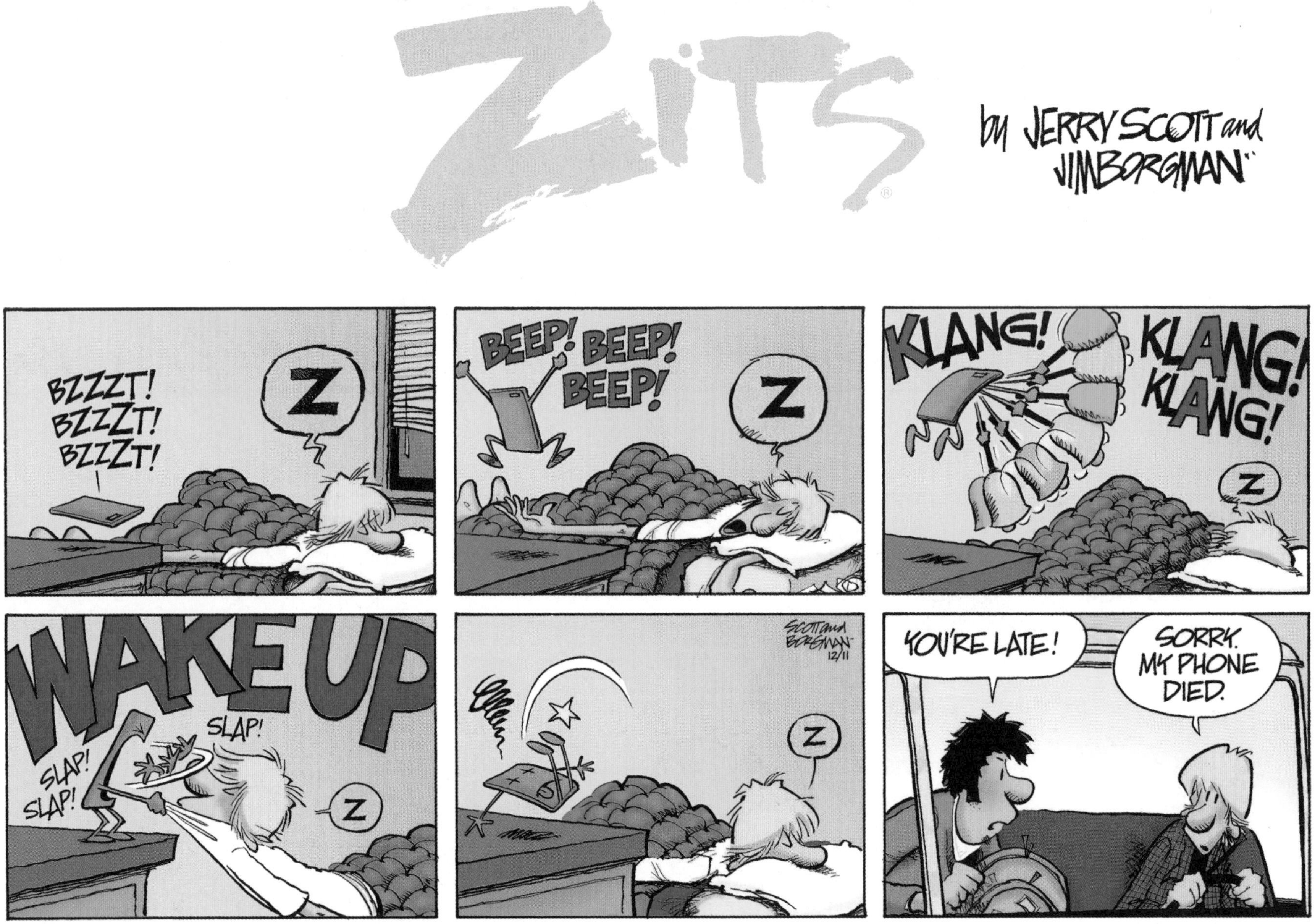
ZITS
by JERRY SCOTT and JIM BORGMAN
BZZZT! BZZZT! BZZZT!
Z
BEEP! BEEP! BEEP!
Z
KLANG! KLANG! KLANG!
Z
WAKE UP
SLAP! SLAP! SLAP!
Z
SCOTT and BORGMAN 12/11
Z
YOU'RE LATE!
SORRY. MY PHONE DIED.

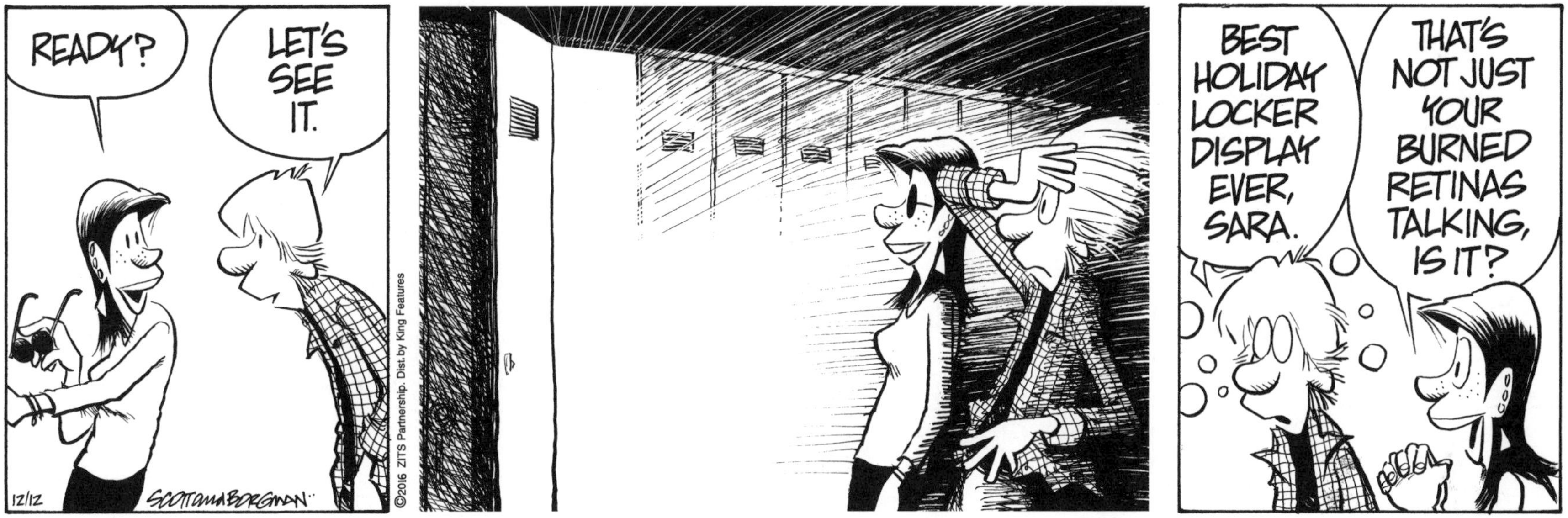
READY?
LET'S SEE IT.
12/12
SCOTT and BORGMAN
©2016 ZITS Partnership. Dist. by King Features
BEST HOLIDAY LOCKER DISPLAY EVER, SARA.
THAT'S NOT JUST YOUR BURNED RETINAS TALKING, IS IT?

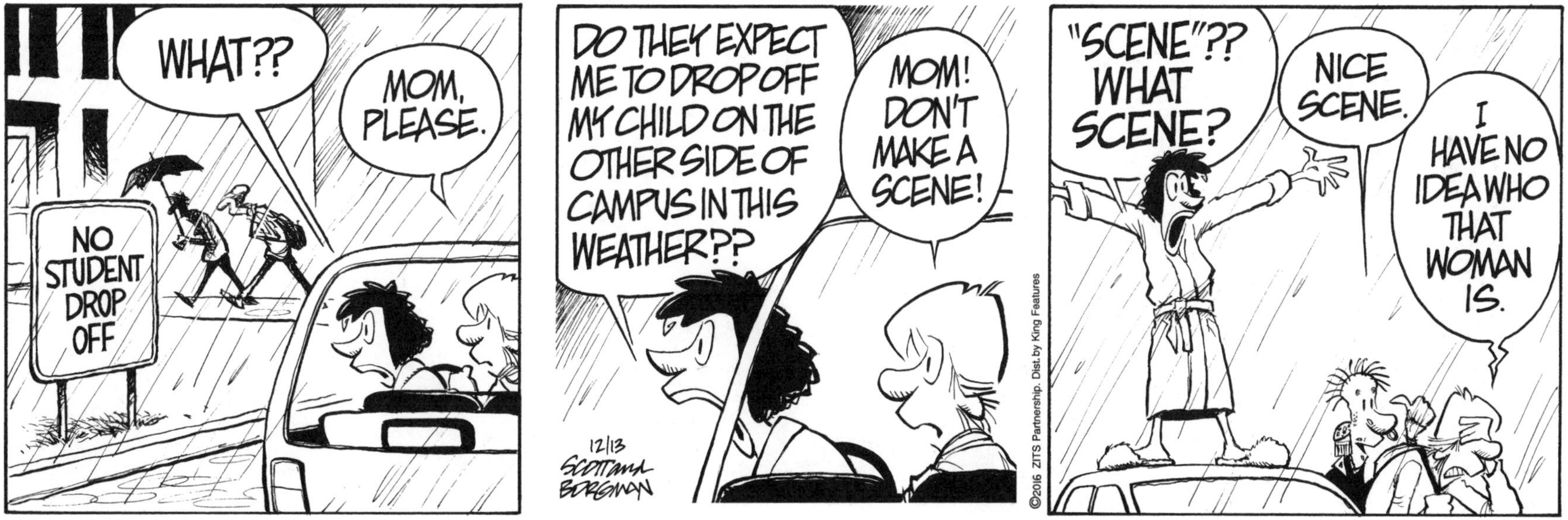
NO STUDENT DROP OFF
WHAT??
MOM, PLEASE.
DO THEY EXPECT ME TO DROP OFF MY CHILD ON THE OTHER SIDE OF CAMPUS IN THIS WEATHER??
MOM! DON'T MAKE A SCENE!
12/13
SCOTT and BORGMAN
©2016 ZITS Partnership. Dist. by King Features
"SCENE"?? WHAT SCENE?
NICE SCENE.
I HAVE NO IDEA WHO THAT WOMAN IS.

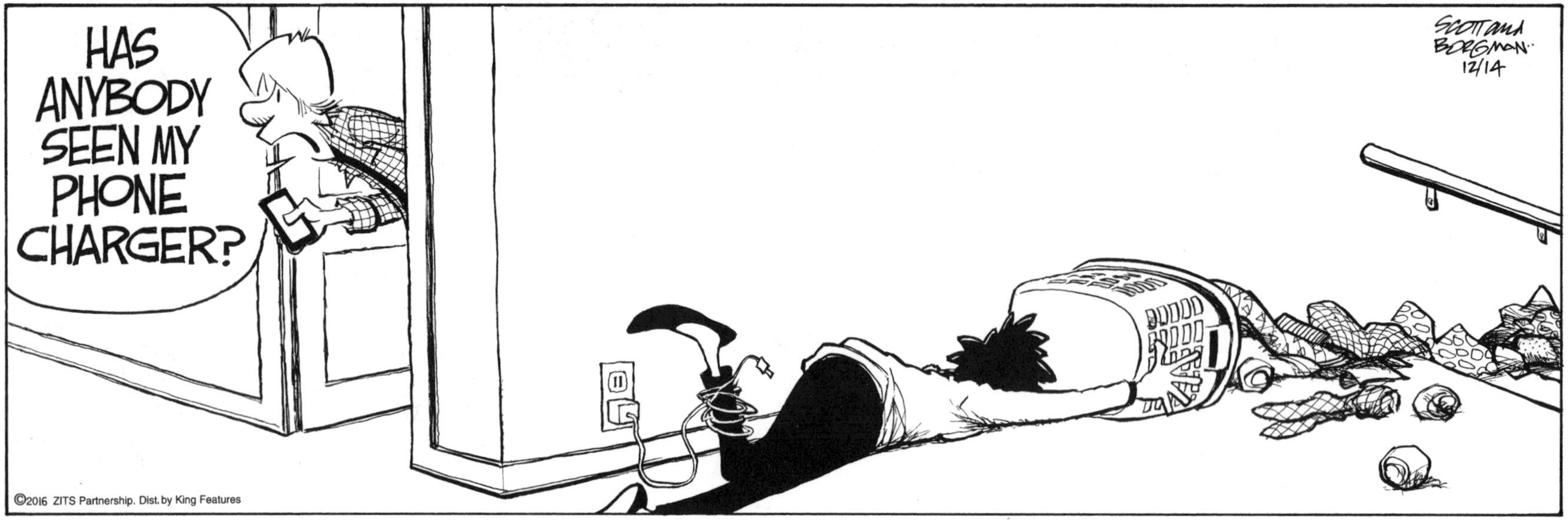
HAS ANYBODY SEEN MY PHONE CHARGER?
SCOTT AND BORGMAN.. 12/14
©2016 ZITS Partnership. Dist. by King Features

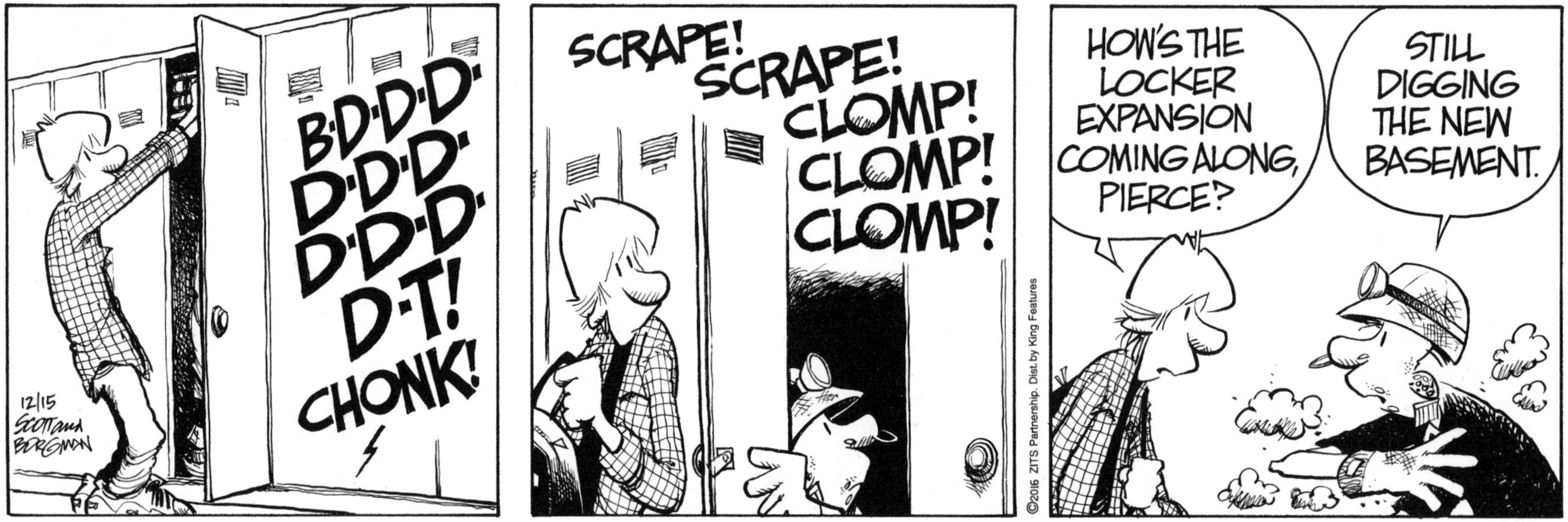
12/15 SCOTT AND BORGMAN
B·D·D·D· D·D·D· D·D·D· D·T!
CHONK!
SCRAPE! SCRAPE!
CLOMP! CLOMP! CLOMP!
©2016 ZITS Partnership. Dist. by King Features
HOW'S THE LOCKER EXPANSION COMING ALONG, PIERCE?
STILL DIGGING THE NEW BASEMENT.

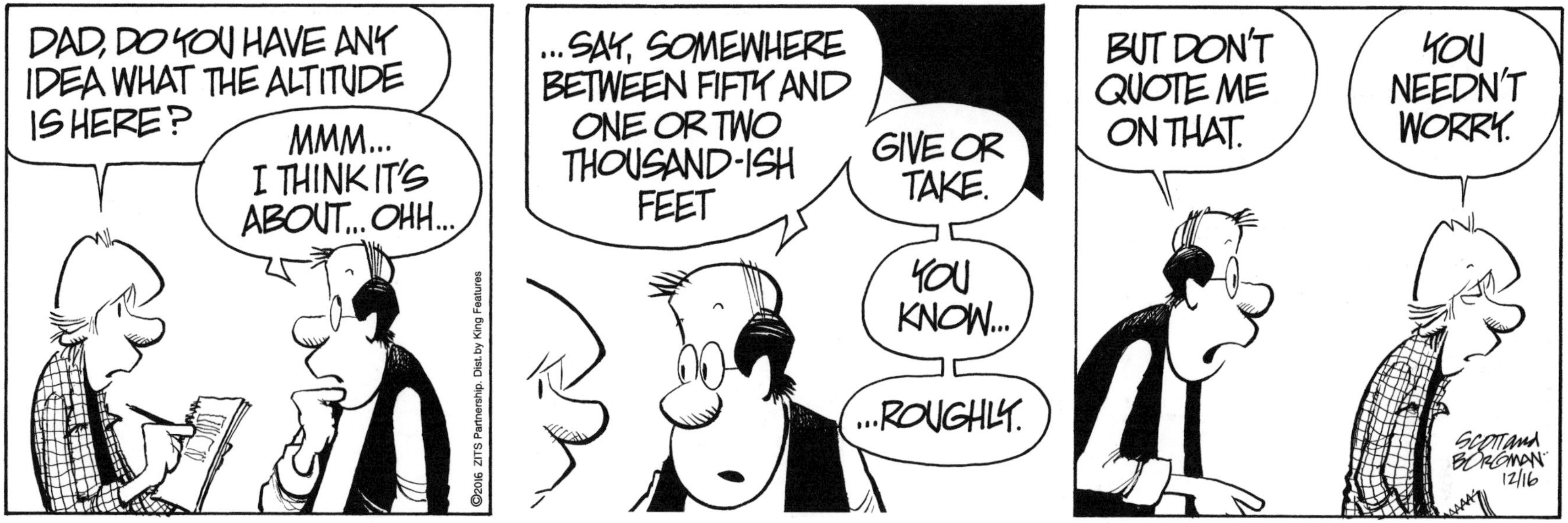
DAD, DO YOU HAVE ANY IDEA WHAT THE ALTITUDE IS HERE?
MMM... I THINK IT'S ABOUT... OHH...
©2016 ZITS Partnership. Dist. by King Features
...SAY, SOMEWHERE BETWEEN FIFTY AND ONE OR TWO THOUSAND-ISH FEET
GIVE OR TAKE.
YOU KNOW...
...ROUGHLY.
BUT DON'T QUOTE ME ON THAT.
YOU NEEDN'T WORRY.
SCOTT and BORGMAN 12/16

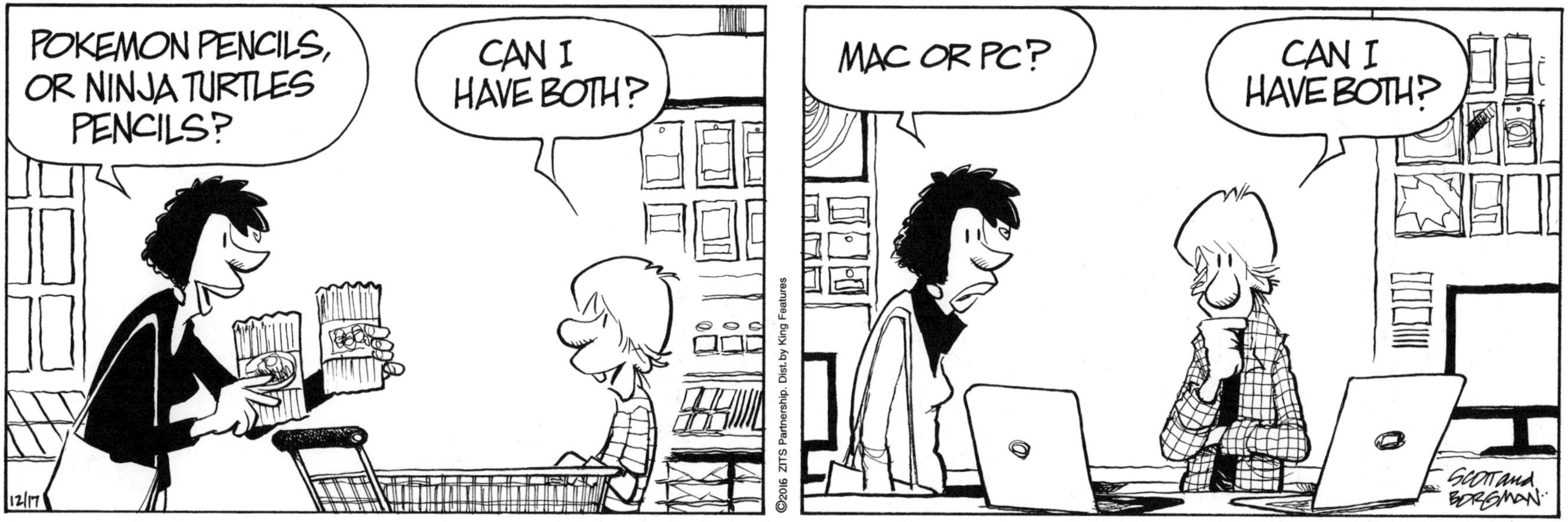
POKEMON PENCILS, OR NINJA TURTLES PENCILS?
CAN I HAVE BOTH?
12/17
©2016 ZITS Partnership. Dist. by King Features
MAC OR PC?
CAN I HAVE BOTH?
SCOTT and BORGMAN

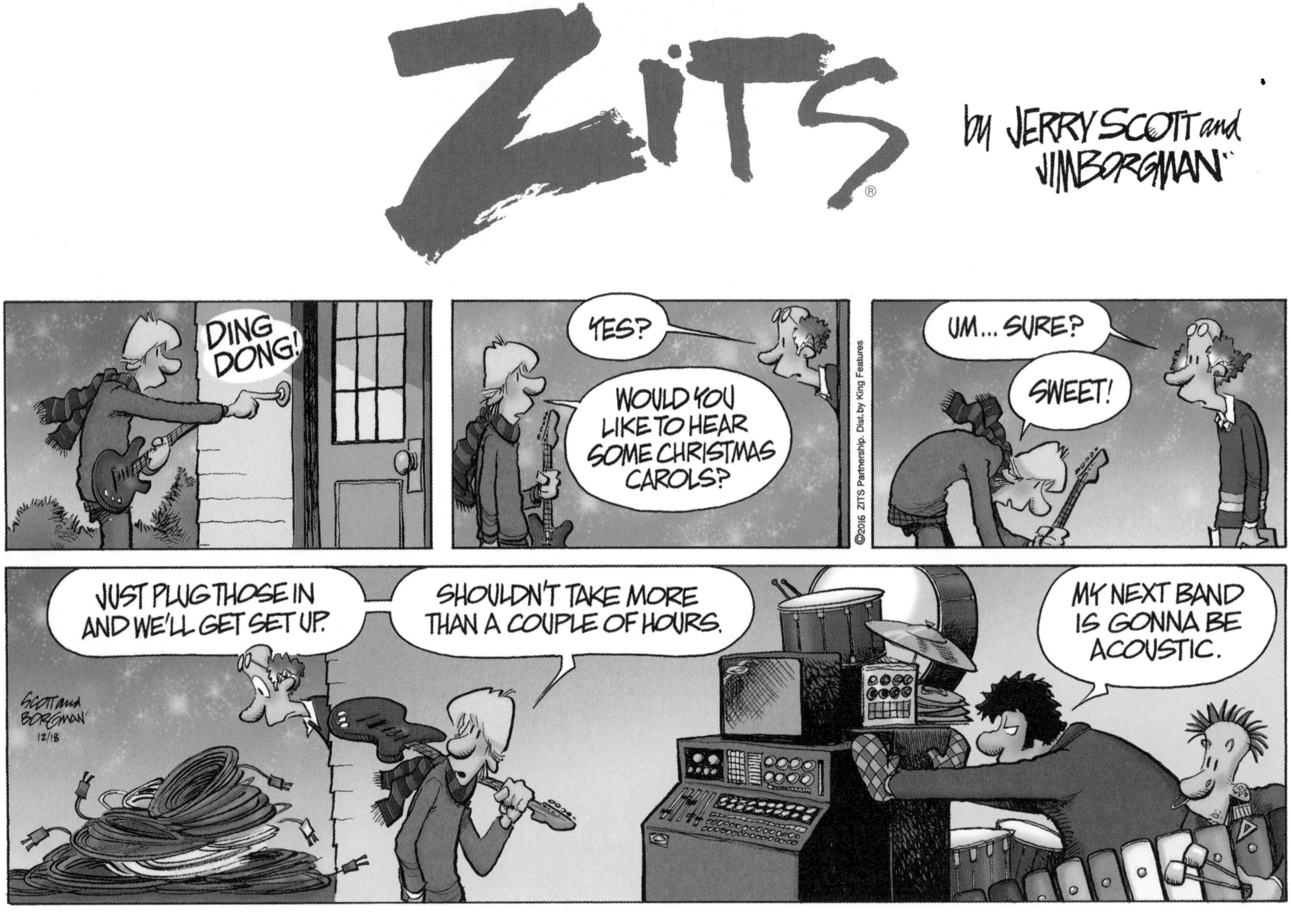
ZITS®
by JERRY SCOTT and JIM BORGMAN
DING DONG!
YES?
WOULD YOU LIKE TO HEAR SOME CHRISTMAS CAROLS?
©2016 ZITS Partnership. Dist. by King Features
UM... SURE?
SWEET!
JUST PLUG THOSE IN AND WE'LL GET SET UP.
SHOULDN'T TAKE MORE THAN A COUPLE OF HOURS.
MY NEXT BAND IS GONNA BE ACOUSTIC.
SCOTT and BORGMAN 12/18

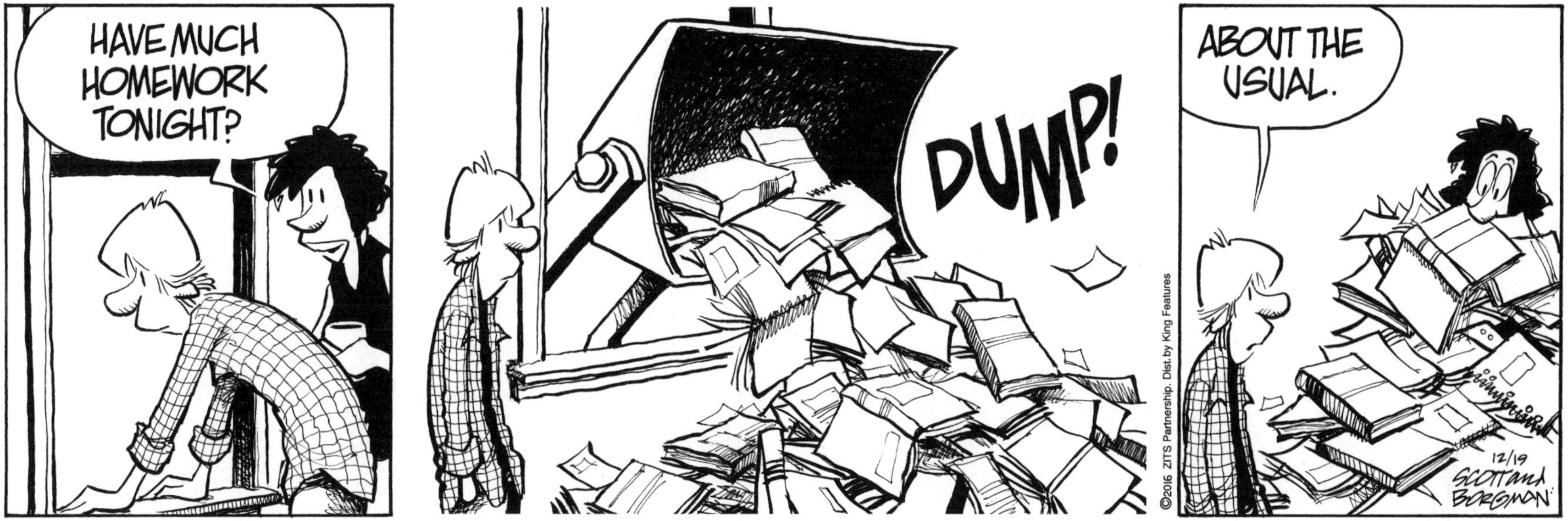
HAVE MUCH HOMEWORK TONIGHT?
DUMP!
ABOUT THE USUAL.
©2016 ZITS Partnership. Dist. by King Features
12/19
SCOTT and BORGMAN

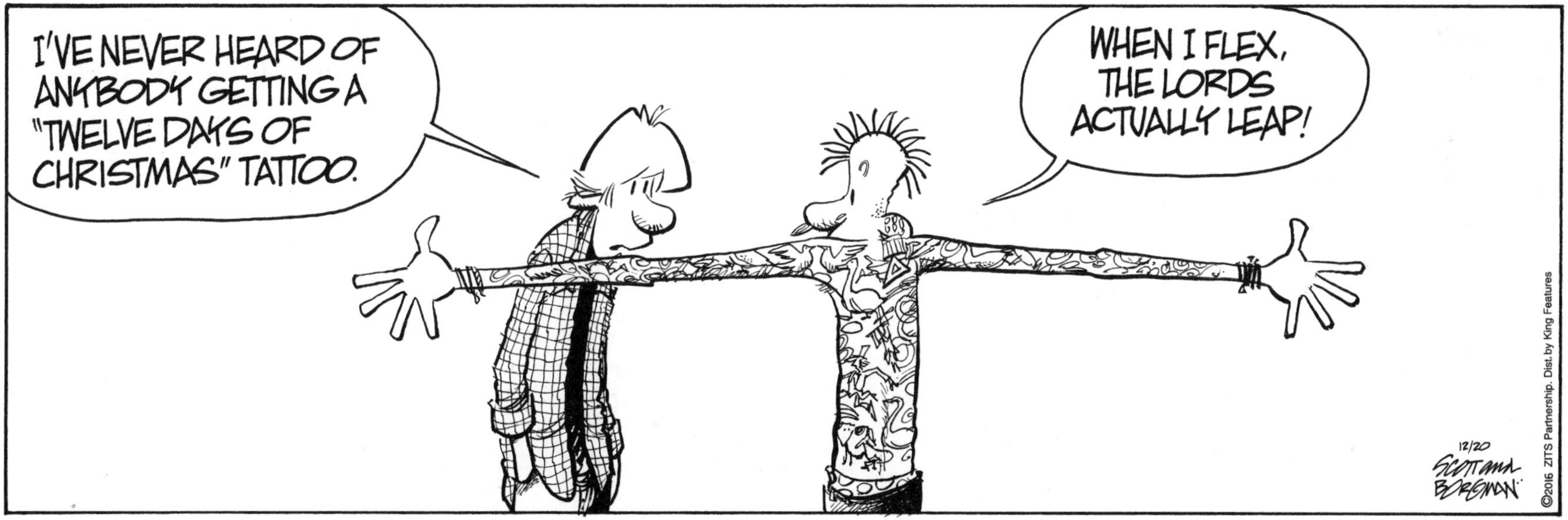
I'VE NEVER HEARD OF ANYBODY GETTING A "TWELVE DAYS OF CHRISTMAS" TATTOO.
WHEN I FLEX, THE LORDS ACTUALLY LEAP!
©2016 ZITS Partnership. Dist. by King Features
12/20
SCOTT and BORGMAN

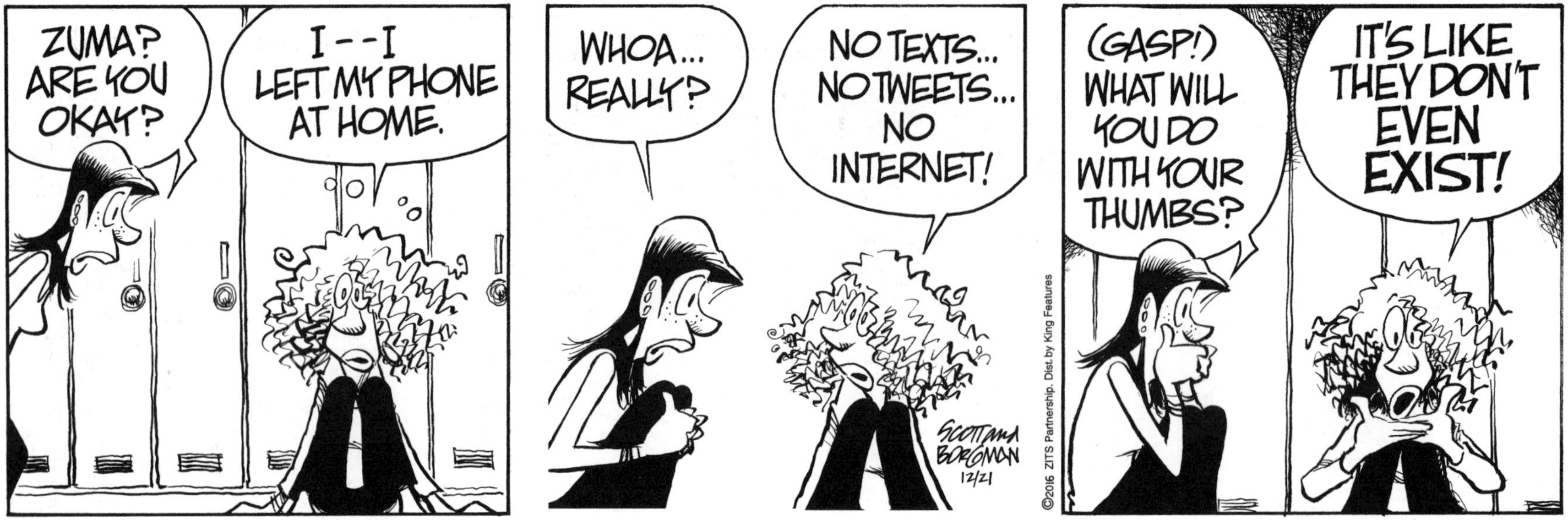
ZUMA? ARE YOU OKAY?
I--I LEFT MY PHONE AT HOME.
WHOA... REALLY?
NO TEXTS... NO TWEETS... NO INTERNET!
(GASP!) WHAT WILL YOU DO WITH YOUR THUMBS?
IT'S LIKE THEY DON'T EVEN EXIST!
SCOTT AND BORGMAN 12/21
©2016 ZITS Partnership. Dist. by King Features

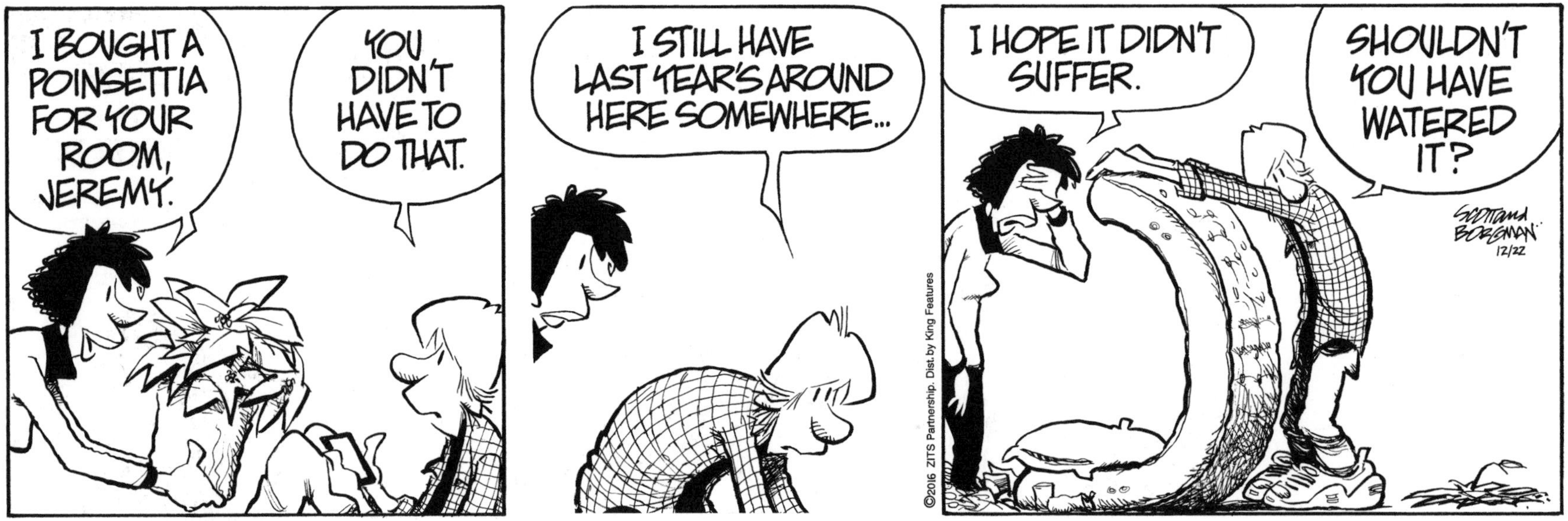
I BOUGHT A POINSETTIA FOR YOUR ROOM, JEREMY.
YOU DIDN'T HAVE TO DO THAT.
I STILL HAVE LAST YEAR'S AROUND HERE SOMEWHERE...
I HOPE IT DIDN'T SUFFER.
SHOULDN'T YOU HAVE WATERED IT?
SCOTT AND BORGMAN 12/22
©2016 ZITS Partnership. Dist. by King Features

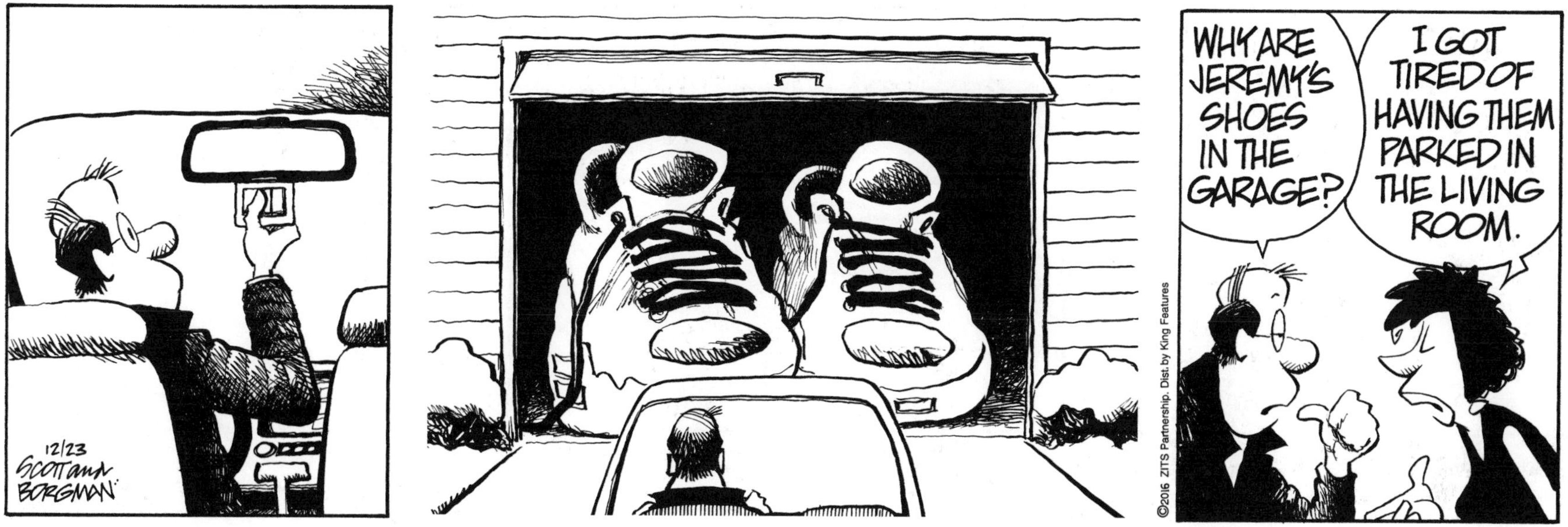
12/23 SCOTT and BORGMAN
WHY ARE JEREMY'S SHOES IN THE GARAGE?
I GOT TIRED OF HAVING THEM PARKED IN THE LIVING ROOM.
©2016 ZITS Partnership. Dist. by King Features

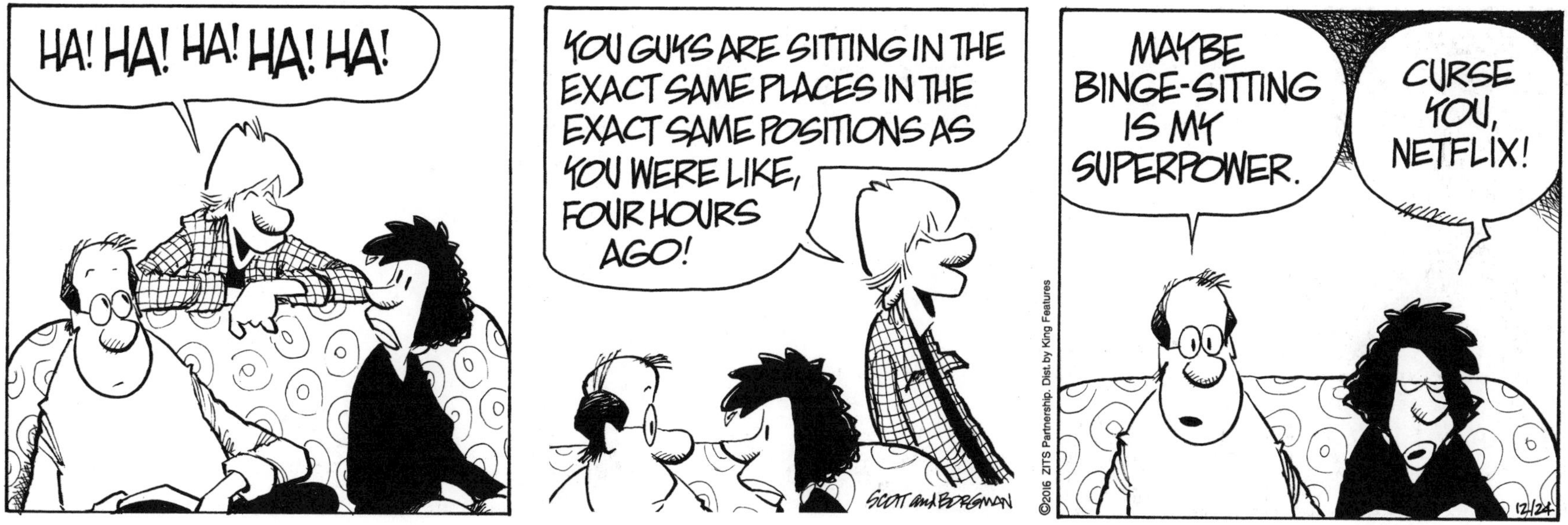
HA! HA! HA! HA! HA!
YOU GUYS ARE SITTING IN THE EXACT SAME PLACES IN THE EXACT SAME POSITIONS AS YOU WERE LIKE, FOUR HOURS AGO!
SCOTT and BORGMAN
©2016 ZITS Partnership. Dist. by King Features
MAYBE BINGE-SITTING IS MY SUPERPOWER.
CURSE YOU, NETFLIX!
12/24

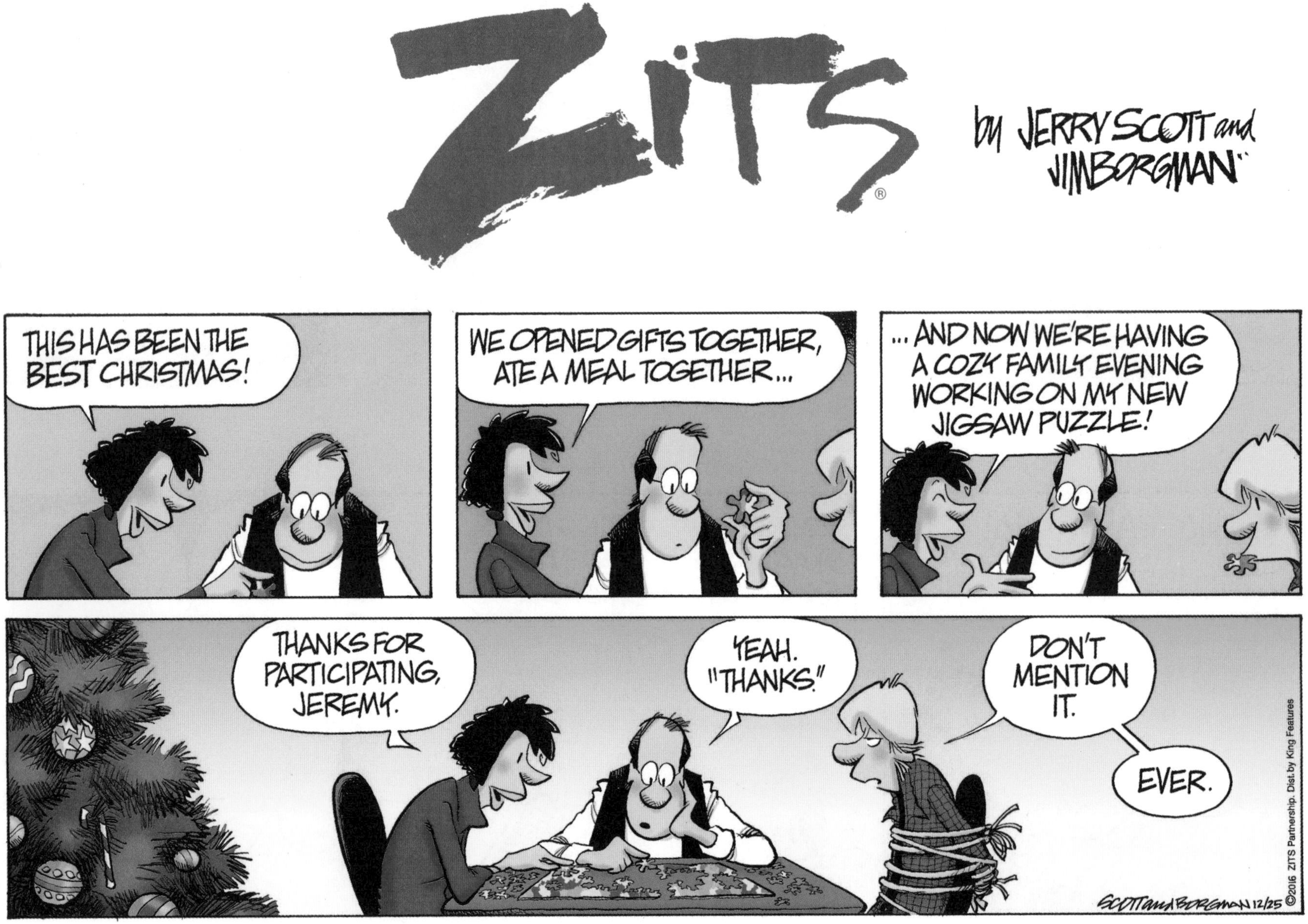
ZITS
by JERRY SCOTT and JIM BORGMAN
THIS HAS BEEN THE BEST CHRISTMAS!
WE OPENED GIFTS TOGETHER, ATE A MEAL TOGETHER...
...AND NOW WE'RE HAVING A COZY FAMILY EVENING WORKING ON MY NEW JIGSAW PUZZLE!
THANKS FOR PARTICIPATING, JEREMY.
YEAH. "THANKS."
DON'T MENTION IT.
EVER.
SCOTT and BORGMAN 12/25
©2016 ZITS Partnership. Dist. by King Features

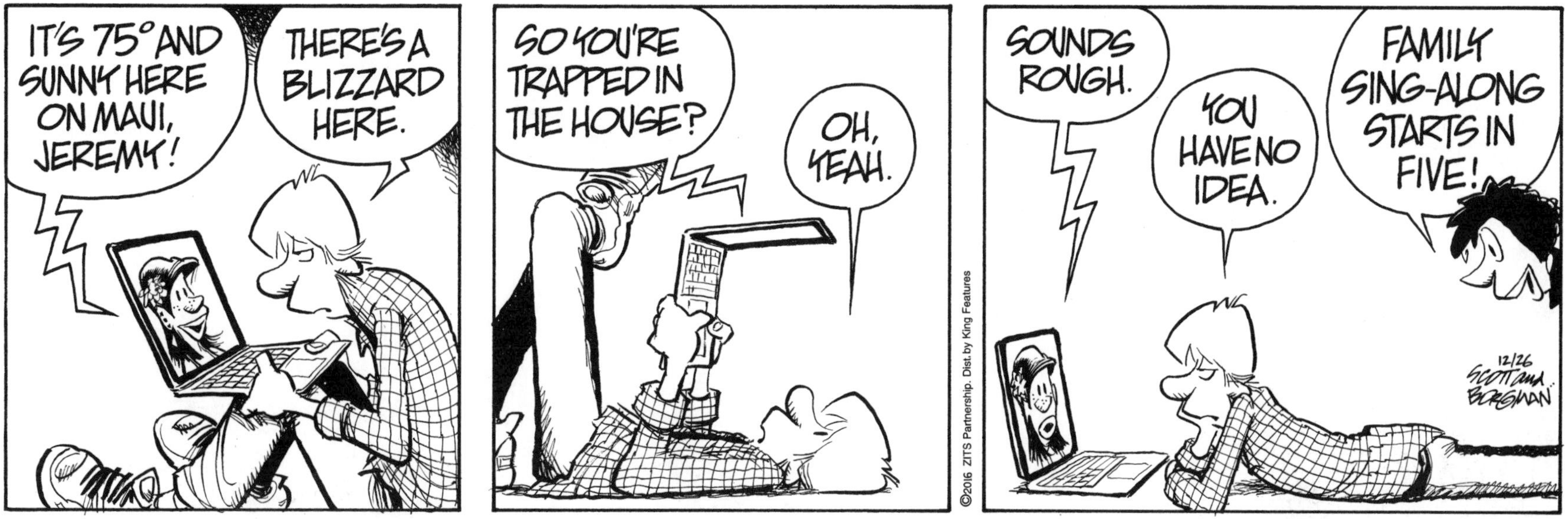
IT'S 75° AND SUNNY HERE ON MAUI, JEREMY!
THERE'S A BLIZZARD HERE.
SO YOU'RE TRAPPED IN THE HOUSE?
OH, YEAH.
SOUNDS ROUGH.
YOU HAVE NO IDEA.
FAMILY SING-ALONG STARTS IN FIVE!
12/26 SCOTT and BORGMAN
©2016 ZITS Partnership. Dist. by King Features

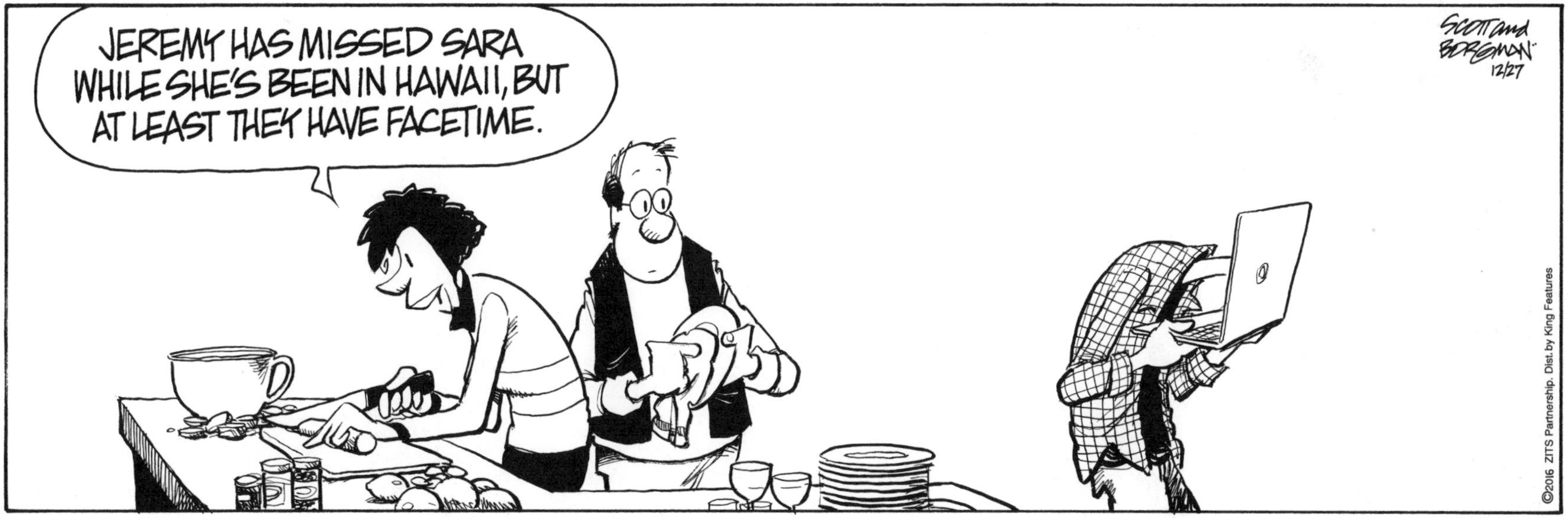
JEREMY HAS MISSED SARA WHILE SHE'S BEEN IN HAWAII, BUT AT LEAST THEY HAVE FACETIME.
SCOTT and BORGMAN 12/27
©2016 ZITS Partnership. Dist. by King Features

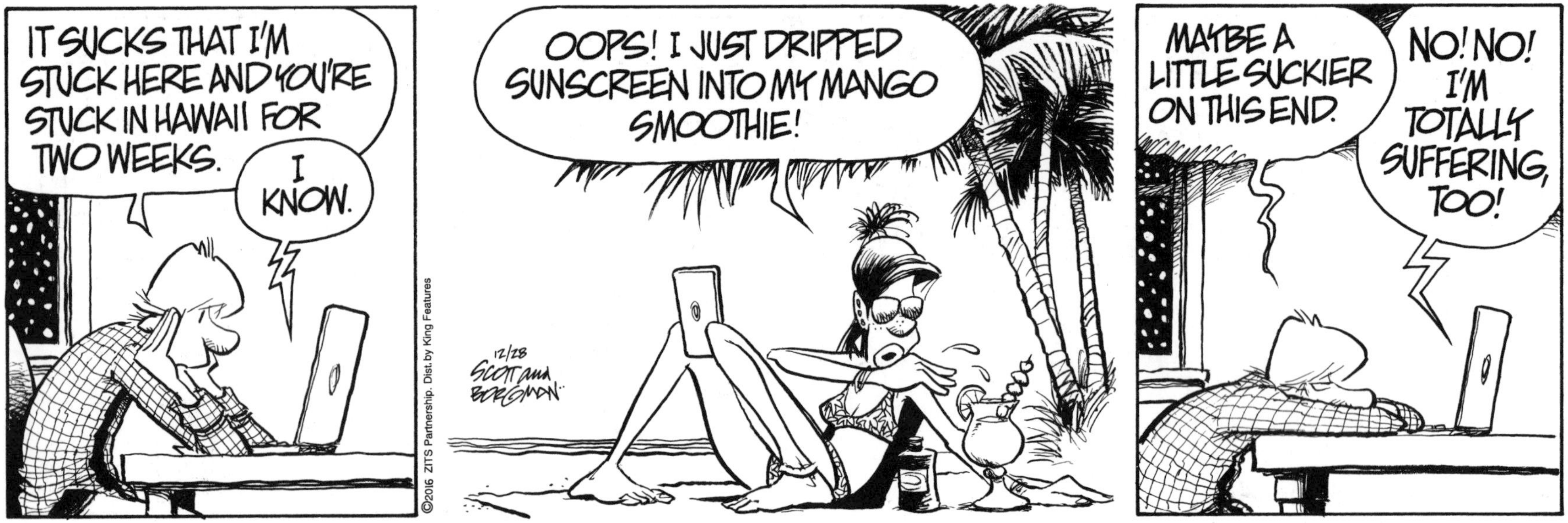
IT SUCKS THAT I'M STUCK HERE AND YOU'RE STUCK IN HAWAII FOR TWO WEEKS.
I KNOW.
©2016 ZITS Partnership. Dist. by King Features
12/28 SCOTT and BORGMAN
OOPS! I JUST DRIPPED SUNSCREEN INTO MY MANGO SMOOTHIE!
MAYBE A LITTLE SUCKIER ON THIS END.
NO! NO! I'M TOTALLY SUFFERING, TOO!

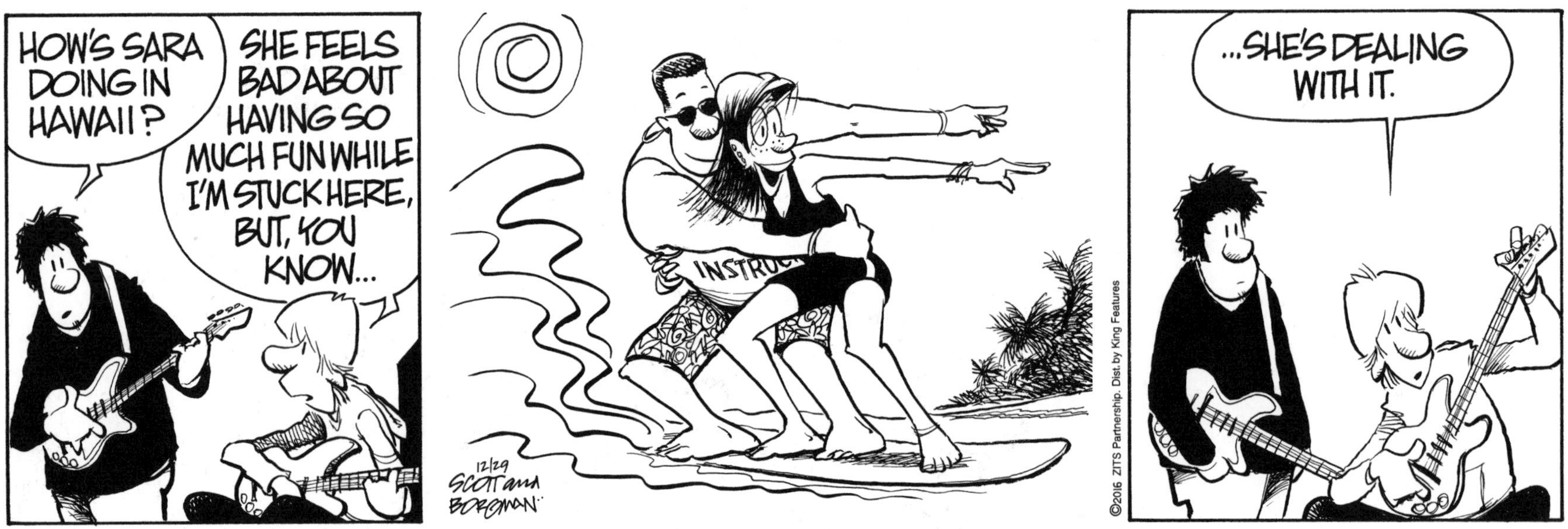
HOW'S SARA DOING IN HAWAII?
SHE FEELS BAD ABOUT HAVING SO MUCH FUN WHILE I'M STUCK HERE, BUT, YOU KNOW...
INSTRUC
12/29 SCOTT and BORGMAN
©2016 ZITS Partnership. Dist. by King Features
...SHE'S DEALING WITH IT.

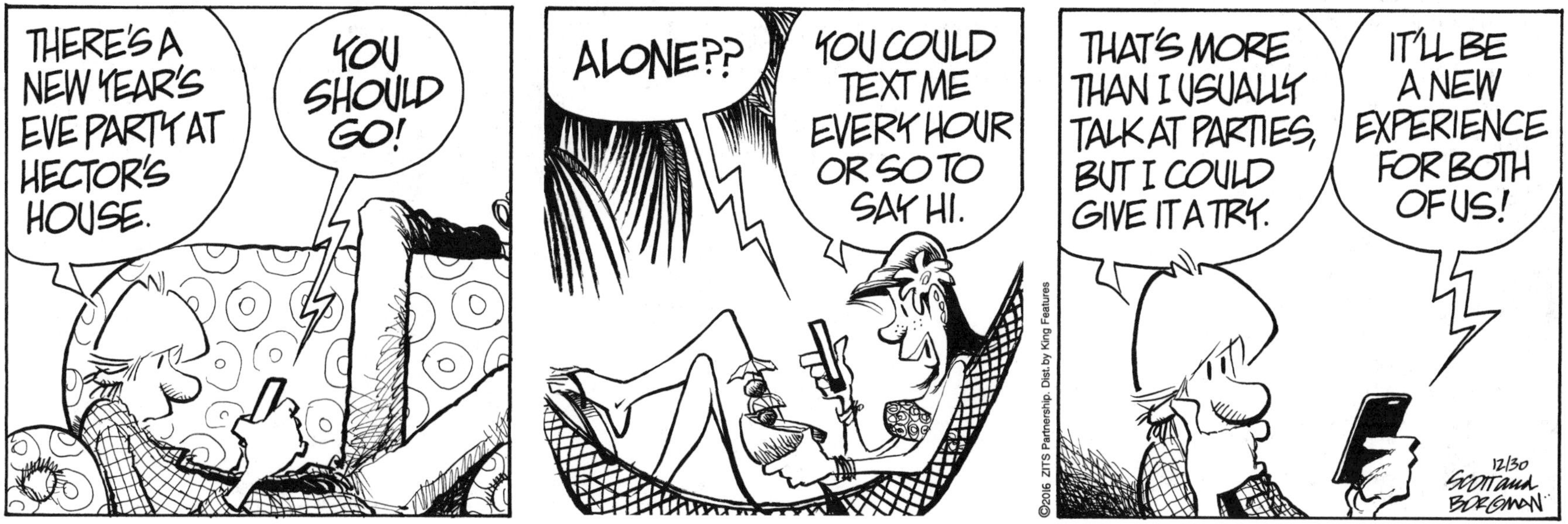
THERE'S A NEW YEAR'S EVE PARTY AT HECTOR'S HOUSE.
YOU SHOULD GO!
ALONE??
YOU COULD TEXT ME EVERY HOUR OR SO TO SAY HI.
THAT'S MORE THAN I USUALLY TALK AT PARTIES, BUT I COULD GIVE IT A TRY.
IT'LL BE A NEW EXPERIENCE FOR BOTH OF US!
©2016 ZITS Partnership. Dist. by King Features
12/30
SCOTT and BORGMAN

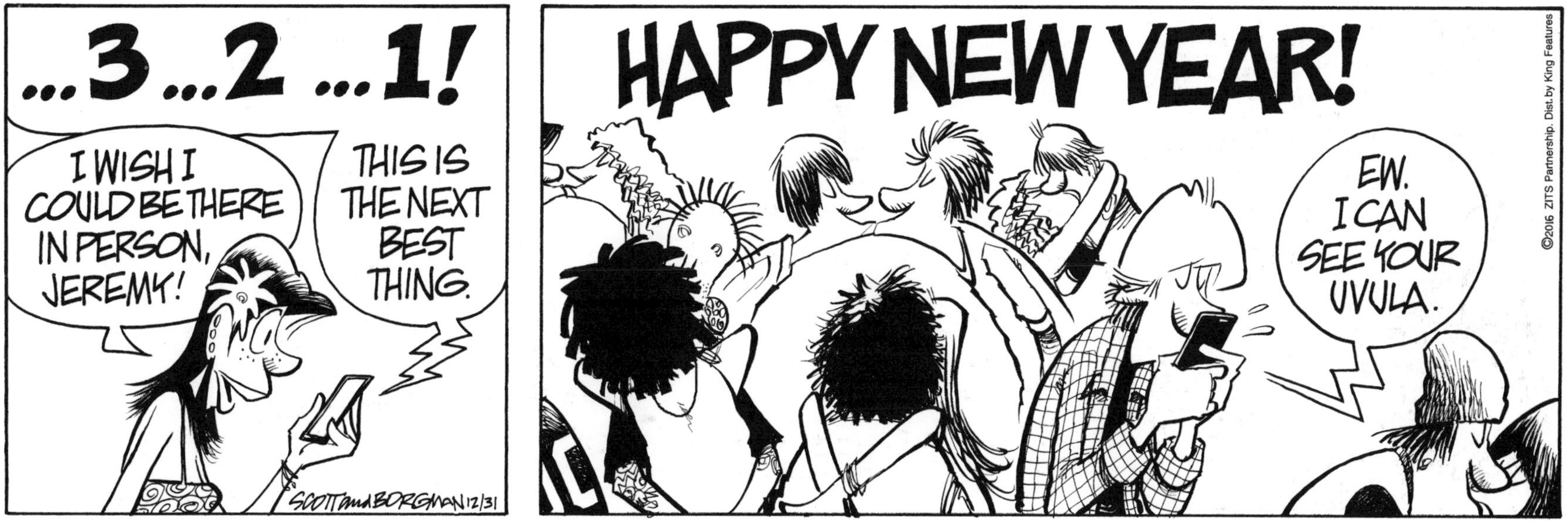
...3 ...2 ...1!
I WISH I COULD BE THERE IN PERSON, JEREMY!
THIS IS THE NEXT BEST THING.
SCOTT and BORGMAN 12/31
HAPPY NEW YEAR!
EW. I CAN SEE YOUR UVULA.
©2016 ZITS Partnership. Dist. by King Features